职业教育双语教材
Bilingual Textbooks of Vocational Education

汽车发动机
电控系统故障诊断与修复

Fault Diagnosis and Repair of
Automobile Engine Electronic Control System

英汉双语教材

刘新宇 主编
Edited by Xinyu Liu

化学工业出版社
Chemical Industry Press

· 北京 ·
BeiJing

内 容 简 介

本书对汽车发动机电控系统的结构、工作原理及检修内容进行详细介绍，同时对电控发动机上的传感器、执行器对电控系统工作的影响也做了详细说明。具体内容包括汽油发动机电控系统整体认知、汽油发动机电控燃油喷射系统检修、汽油发动机电控点火系统检修、汽油发动机怠速控制系统检修、汽油发动机辅助控制系统检修、汽油发动机电控系统典型故障检修。

本书可作为高职高专院校、中等职业学校相关专业的教材，并可作为培训用书，也可供相关技术人员参考。

图书在版编目（CIP）数据

汽车发动机电控系统故障诊断与修复：英、汉/刘新宇主编. —北京：化学工业出版社，2021.8
ISBN 978-7-122-39837-6

Ⅰ.①汽… Ⅱ.①刘… Ⅲ.①汽车-发动机-电子系统-控制系统-故障诊断-双语教学-高等职业教育-教材-英、汉②汽车-发动机-电子系统-控制系统-车辆修理-双语教学-高等职业教育-教材-英、汉 Ⅳ.①U472.43

中国版本图书馆 CIP 数据核字（2021）第 175091 号

责任编辑：韩庆利　　　　　　　　　　　　文字编辑：宋　旋　陈小滔
责任校对：宋　玮　　　　　　　　　　　　装帧设计：刘丽华

出版发行：化学工业出版社（北京市东城区青年湖南街 13 号　邮政编码 100011）
印　　装：大厂聚鑫印刷有限责任公司
787mm×1092mm　1/16　印张 21¾　字数 536 千字　2021 年 8 月北京第 1 版第 1 次印刷

购书咨询：010-64518888　　　　　　　　　　售后服务：010-64518899
网　　址：http://www.cip.com.cn
凡购买本书，如有缺损质量问题，本社销售中心负责调换。

定　　价：68.00 元　　　　　　　　　　　　　　　　　　　　　版权所有　违者必究

前言

"汽车发动机电控系统故障诊断与修复"课程是高职院校汽车检测与维修技术专业的一门核心专业课程，主要介绍汽车电控发动机系统的结构原理及检修内容。学生学习该课程能够为进入该行业顶岗实习以及工作奠定一个很好的基础。

在本书的编写过程中，编者始终贯彻以大众轿车构造为主体，结合实际车辆和诊断设备，通过六个项目对现代轿车发动机电控系统的结构、工作原理及检修内容进行详细介绍，同时对电控发动机上的传感器、执行器对电控系统工作的影响也做了详细说明。在项目实施内容中，通过对实操及注意事项的学习达到提高学生思考能力的目的。为了让读者能够在较短的时间内掌握本书的内容，及时检查自己的学习效果，巩固和加深对所学知识的理解，每个项目后还附有习题及思考题。

本书编者都来自教学第一线，有着丰富的教学经验和扎实的专业理论知识及专业实践技能。在本书的编写过程中，以典型工作项目来进行教材的编写，为教师与学生分别理清了教学与学习的思路，同时突出了对学生实际操作能力的培养，满足了职业教育学生的人才培养要求。

本书由天津交通职业学院刘新宇主编，曹向红、李嘉泽副主编，张瑞静参编。其中，天津交通职业学院张瑞静编写项目一，天津交通职业学院刘新宇编写项目二，天津交通职业学院曹向红编写项目三、项目四、项目五，天津交通职业学院李嘉泽编写项目六。

由于编者水平有限，书中存在不妥之处在所难免，衷心希望广大读者批评指正。

编 者

目录

项目一　汽油发动机电控系统整体认知　001

一、项目情境引入　001
二、项目相关知识　001
　（一）概述　001
　（二）发动机电控单元 ECU 的组成及功能　007
　（三）发动机电控系统故障自诊断系统测试　011
三、项目实施　012
　（一）实施要求　012
　（二）实施步骤　012
　（三）注意事项　013
小结　014
习题及思考　014

项目二　汽油发动机电控燃油喷射系统检修　015

一、项目情境引入　015
二、项目相关知识　015
　（一）燃油喷射系统的分类　015
　（二）燃油喷射系统的组成　017
　（三）发动机燃油喷射系统传感器的结构原理　019
　（四）发动机燃油喷射系统执行器的结构原理　037
　（五）发动机断油控制过程　042
　（六）发动机燃油喷射的控制过程　044
　（七）喷油脉冲宽度的控制　047
三、项目实施　050
　（一）实施要求　050
　（二）实施步骤　050
　（三）注意事项　059
四、知识与技能拓展　059
　（一）ECU 控制的燃油泵控制电路　059
　（二）燃油泵开关控制的燃油泵控制电路　060
　（三）燃油泵继电器控制的燃油泵控制电路　060
小结　061
习题及思考　061

项目三 汽油发动机电控点火系统检修 ········ 062

一、项目情境引入 ········ 062
二、项目相关知识 ········ 062
（一）汽油机点火系统的作用 ········ 062
（二）汽油机点火系统分类 ········ 062
（三）对点火系统的基本要求 ········ 063
（四）微机控制点火系统的结构组成 ········ 064
（五）微机控制点火系统的控制过程 ········ 068
（六）微机控制点火系统高压电的分配方式 ········ 072
（七）爆震控制 ········ 076
三、项目实施 ········ 078
（一）实施要求 ········ 078
（二）实施步骤 ········ 078
（三）注意事项 ········ 080
四、知识与技能拓展 ········ 081
（一）点火系统波形分析 ········ 081
（二）故障案例 ········ 084
小结 ········ 085
习题及思考 ········ 085

项目四 汽油发动机怠速控制系统检修 ········ 086

一、项目情境引入 ········ 086
二、项目相关知识 ········ 086
（一）怠速控制阀的分类 ········ 086
（二）怠速控制阀的原理 ········ 087
（三）发动机怠速控制过程 ········ 090
三、项目实施 ········ 093
（一）实施要求 ········ 093
（二）实施步骤 ········ 093
（三）注意事项 ········ 097
四、知识与技能拓展 ········ 098
（一）电子节气门怠速控制执行机构 ········ 098
（二）直动式节气门的基本设定 ········ 099
小结 ········ 099
习题及思考 ········ 100

项目五 汽油发动机辅助控制系统检修 ········ 101

一、项目情境引入 ········ 101

二、项目相关知识 ·· 101
　（一）汽车排放对环境影响 ·· 101
　（二）排放控制系统的分类 ·· 101
　（三）各种排放控制系统的原理 ··· 102
三、项目实施 ·· 117
　（一）实施的要求 ·· 117
　（二）实施步骤 ··· 117
　（三）注意事项 ··· 125
四、知识与技能拓展 ·· 125
　（一）可变配气相位与气门升程电子控制系统 ···································· 125
　（二）VTEC 系统工作原理 ·· 126
小结 ·· 127
习题及思考 ·· 127

项目六　汽油发动机电控系统典型故障检修 ·································· 128

一、项目情境引入 ·· 128
二、项目相关知识 ·· 128
　（一）发动机电子控制系统故障诊断原则 ··· 128
　（二）电子控制系统的故障诊断的基本方法 ······································· 129
　（三）电子控制系统的故障诊断的流程 ·· 130
　（四）电子控制系统的故障诊断的排除程序 ······································· 133
　（五）电控发动机常见故障诊断的排除程序 ······································· 135
三、项目实施 ·· 137
　（一）实施要求 ··· 137
　（二）实施步骤 ··· 137
　（三）注意事项 ··· 139
四、知识与技能拓展 ·· 139
　（一）启动困难 ··· 139
　（二）急速过高 ··· 140
　（三）混合气过稀 ·· 140
　（四）混合气过浓 ·· 140
　（五）启动失速 ··· 140
小结 ·· 145
习题及思考 ·· 145

参考文献 ·· 146

项目一

汽油发动机电控系统整体认知

一、项目情境引入

为了能够对电控系统的故障进行诊断排除，必须熟悉汽车发动机电控系统的结构原理，所以在本项目的学习中必须掌握电控系统各传感器、汽车电脑及执行器的应用，了解电控系统的控制方式及优点，同时要熟悉掌握自诊断系统的功能，通过对诊断仪使用的学习，使学生掌握诊断仪读取数据流的正确方法及使用的注意事项，认识到诊断仪读取数据流的重要性。

二、项目相关知识

（一）概述

1. 汽车电控技术的应用

20 世纪 80 年代以来，提高汽车性能以及汽车的节能环保，主要取决于电子控制技术。汽车电子控制技术已经广泛应用于汽油机控制、柴油机控制、汽车底盘控制、汽车车身控制和汽车故障诊断等技术领域。

当今世界衡量汽车先进水平和档次高低的标志主要是汽车品牌、汽车外观和汽车电子化程度的高低。汽车制造商普遍认为：增加汽车电子装置的数量，促进汽车电子化是夺取未来汽车市场的有效手段。汽车设计人员普遍认为：电子技术在汽车上的应用，已经成为汽车设计研究部门考虑汽车结构革新的重要手段。汽油机应用电子控制喷油技术能够精确控制空燃比和实现闭环控制，如果再加装三元催化转换器，就可使汽油发动机的有害排放物降低 95% 以上；柴油机应用高压共轨式电子控制喷油技术，能够精确控制喷油量和高达 160～200MPa 的喷油压力，不仅能够降低油耗和减少排放，而且还能提高动力性；汽车防抱死制动系统、电子制动力分配系统、电子车身稳定系统的技术应用大大提高了汽车制动时的稳定性，尤其是可使汽车在湿滑或冰雪路面上的事故发生率降低 24%～28%。

21 世纪以来，发动机电子控制喷油技术、汽油机电子控制点火技术、防抱死制动技术和安全气囊等技术在国内外轿车上都已经普遍采用。

2. 汽车电控技术的发展

（1）汽车电子控制技术是汽车技术与电子技术结合的产物

汽车电子控制技术飞速发展的根本动力和原因包括两个方面：一方面是全球能源紧缺、环境保护和交通安全问题，促使汽车油耗法规、排放法规和安全法规的要求不断提高；另一方面是电子技术水平不断提高。汽车油耗法规促进了汽车底盘和车身电子控制技术的发展。随着汽车油耗法规、排放法规、安全法规要求的不断提高，汽车发动机燃油喷射电子控制系统、防抱死制动和安全气囊系统已经成为国内外轿车的标准配置。

(2) 汽车电子控制技术发展历程

汽车电子技术发展始于20世纪60年代，分为四个阶段。

第一阶段，从20世纪60年代中期到70年代中期，主要是为了改善部分性能而对汽车产品进行的技术改造，如在汽车上装用了第一个电子装置——晶体管收音机。

第二阶段，从20世纪70年代末期到90年代中期，为解决安全、污染和节能三大问题，研制出电控燃油喷射系统、电子控制防滑（防抱死）制动装置和集成电路（IC）点火装置。

第三阶段，从20世纪90年代中期以后，电子技术在汽车上的应用已逐步扩展到车用汽油发动机以外的底盘、车身和车用柴油发动机等多个领域。

第四阶段，20世纪90年代后期以来，CAN-BUS技术（控制器局域网络）普遍应用，CAN-BUS是应用在现场、微机化测量设备之间实现双向串行多节点的数字通信系统，是一种开放式、数字化、多点通信的底层控制网络。目前，CAN-BUS总线在汽车上的应用越来越普及。

3. 发动机电控系统的优点

汽油机电控技术的应用使汽油机的综合性能得到了全面的提高，其主要的优点如下：

(1) 改善了各缸混合气的均匀性

采用电控多点喷射，燃油喷射在各缸进气门附近，使各缸混合气的浓度基本一致。这样不但有利于提高发动机的经济性，而且也有利于降低一氧化碳（CO）和碳氢化合物（HC）的排放量。

(2) 提高发动机的动力性和经济性

由于电控燃油喷射系统的进气管中不存在化油器中的喉管，进气系统的进气阻力和进气压力损失较小，充气效率较高，因此，发动机具有较好的动力性和经济性。另外，电控燃油喷射系统不对进气进行预热，这样提高了进气的密度，对提高发动机动力性有利。

(3) 减少排放污染

电控燃油喷射系统采用氧传感器反馈控制时，能够精确地控制空燃比 $A/F \approx 14.7$，使三元催化转换器具有最高的转换效率，从而大大减少 CO、HC 和 NO_x 等有害气体的排放量。另外，现代汽油机电控系统还包括废气再循环、二次空气喷射系统、最佳点火提前角等控制功能，从而可使汽油机有害物的排放量进一步减少。

(4) 工况过渡圆滑

当发动机运行工况发生变化时，由于电控燃油喷射系统能根据传感器输入信号迅速调整喷油量或喷射正时，提供与该种工况相适应的最佳空燃比，提高了燃油机对加、减速工况的响应速度及工况过渡的平稳性。另外，采用电控燃油喷射方式，汽油的雾化质量好，蒸发速度快，在各种工况下混合气都具有良好的品质，这也有利于提高汽油机非稳定工况的性能。

(5) 改善了汽油机对地理及气候环境的适应性

当汽车在不同地理环境或不同气候条件的地区行驶时，对于采用体积流量方式测量进气量的电控燃油喷射系统，电控系统能根据大气压力、环境温度及时对空燃比进行修正，从而使汽车在各种地理环境及气候条件下运行时，无需调整都能保证良好的综合性能。

(6) 提高了汽油机高、低温启动性能和暖机性能

发动机在高温或低温条件下启动时，电控燃油喷射系统能根据启动时发动机冷却水的温度，提供与启动条件相适应的喷油量，使汽油机在高温和低温条件下都能顺利启动。低温启动后，电控燃油喷射系统又能根据发动机冷却水温度自动调整喷油量和空气供给量，加快汽油机暖机过程，使发动机很快就能进入正常运行状态。

4. 应用在发动机上的电控系统

汽车电控技术得益于电子技术、计算机技术和信息技术的迅猛发展，而推动汽车电控技术发展的动力因素是改善汽车的性能，解决降低能耗、减少污染、提高安全性和舒适性等问题。进入21世纪，电控技术不仅渗透到汽车的各个系统和总成，而且通过信息技术实现了各系统与总成的协调和集中控制。目前，发动机上常用的电控系统有电控燃油喷射系统、电控点火系统、怠速控制系统、排放控制系统、进气控制系统、增压控制系统、巡航控制系统、警告提示系统、自诊断与报警系统、失效保护系统等。

（1）电控燃油喷射系统

电控单元（Electrical Control Unit，ECU）主要根据进气量确定基本的喷油量，再根据其他传感器（如冷却液温度传感器、节气门位置传感器）信号对喷油量进行修正，使发动机在各种运行工况下均能获得最佳浓度的混合气；同时还包括喷油正时控制、断油控制和燃油泵控制。

（2）电控点火系统

电控点火系统的功能是点火提前角控制。根据各相关传感器信号，判断发动机的运行工况和运行条件，选择最理想的点火提前角点燃混合气，从而改善发动机的燃烧过程。

（3）怠速控制系统

发动机在汽车运转、空调压缩机工作、发动机负荷加大等不同怠速运转工况下，由ECU控制怠速控制阀，使发动机怠速始终处于最佳转速。

（4）排放控制系统

排放控制系统是对发动机排放控制装置实行电子控制。排放控制的项目主要有废气再循环（EGR）控制、活性炭罐电磁阀控制、氧传感器和空燃比闭环控制、二次空气喷射控制、曲轴箱通风控制等。

（5）进气控制系统

电控系统根据发动机工况的变化，控制进气量和气流，提高充气效率和改善雾化条件，从而提高发动机的动力性。

（6）增压控制系统

对于装备涡轮增压器的发动机，电控系统通过控制增压强度，使进气管的压力适合发动机各种工况。

（7）巡航控制系统

在巡航操作模式下，电控系统自动调整节气门开度，使车辆维持设定的车速运行，从而提高了驾驶的舒适性。

（8）警告提示系统

ECU控制各种指示和警告装置，显示有关控制系统的工作状况，当控制系统出现故障时，能及时发出警告信号。如氧传感器失效、催化器过热、油箱温度过高等。

（9）自诊断与报警系统

当控制系统出现故障时，ECU将会点亮仪表板上的"检查发动机"（Check Engine）灯，提醒驾驶员注意，发动机已经出现故障，并将故障信息储存到ECU中，通过一定的程序，可以将故障码调出，供修理人员参考。

（10）失效保护系统

在发动机电控系统中，当某传感器失效或线路断路时，电控系统会按预定的程序设定一个参考信号以使发动机继续运转，维持车辆行驶，同时通过报警系统提示驾驶员及时维修。

5. 发动机电控系统组成及功能

电控系统主要由传感器、ECU、执行器三个部分组成。

传感器作为输入部分，是用于测量物理信号（温度、压力等），按一定规律转换成便于传输和处理的另一种物理量（一般为电量）的装置。

传感器相当于人的眼、耳、鼻、舌等器官。在汽车电子控制系统中，传感器的功用是将汽车各部件运行的状态参数（各种非电量信号）转换成电量信号并输送到各种电控单元。

车用传感器安装在汽车上的不同部位。汽车型号和档次不同，装备传感器的多少也不相同。有的汽车只有几只传感器（如发动机控制系统只有6～8只），有的汽车装备的传感器很多。一般来说，汽车装备传感器越多，汽车的档次就越高。

按检测项目不同，汽车电子控制系统采用的传感器可分为以下几种类型。

① 流量传感器。如发动机燃油喷射系统采用的翼片式、量芯式、涡流式、热丝式与热膜式空气流量传感器。

② 位置传感器。如发动机燃油喷射和微机控制点火系统采用的曲轴位置传感器（又称为发动机转速曲轴位置传感器）、凸轮轴位置传感器、节气门位置传感器；电子调节悬架系统采用的车身位置（又称为车身高度）传感器；信息显示系统和液面监控系统采用的各种液面位置（或高度）传感器；自动变速器系统采用的选挡操纵手柄传感器；巡航控制系统采用的节气门位置传感器；电子控制动力转向系统采用的方向盘转角传感器等。

③ 压力传感器。如发动机控制系统采用的进气歧管压力传感器、大气压力传感器、排气压力传感器、汽缸压力传感器；自动变速器系统采用的燃油压力传感器；发动机爆震控制系统采用的爆震传感器等。

④ 温度传感器。如发动机冷却液温度传感器、进气温度传感器、排气温度传感器、燃油温度传感器；自动变速器系统采用的自动传动液温度传感器；空调控制系统采用的车内温度传感器等。

⑤ 浓度传感器。如发动机控制系统采用的氧传感器；安全控制系统采用的酒精浓度传感器等。

⑥ 速度传感器。如防抱死制动系统采用的车轮速度传感器、车身纵向和横向加（减）速度传感器；发动机控制系统采用的转速传感器；发动机、自动变速器以及巡航控制系统采用的车速传感器；变速器输入轴转速传感器以及输出轴转速传感器等。

电控单元：汽车电子控制单元（ECU），又称为汽车电子控制器或汽车电子控制组件，俗称"汽车电脑"。电控单元是以单片微型计算机（即单片机）为核心所组成的电子控制装置，具有强大的数学运算、逻辑判断、数据处理与数据管理等功能。电控单元是汽车电子控制系统的控制中心，其主要功用是分析处理传感器采集的各种信息，并向受控装置（即执行器或执行元件）发出控制指令。

执行器又称执行元件，是电子控制系统的执行机构。执行器的功用是接收电控单元（ECU）发出的指令，完成具体的执行动作。汽车电子控制系统不同，采用执行器的数量和种类也不相同。发动机燃油喷射系统的执行器有电动燃油泵和电磁喷油器；发动机怠速控制系统的执行器是怠速控制阀；燃油蒸气回收系统的执行器是活性炭罐电磁阀；位置控制点火系统的执行器有点火控制器和点火线圈；防抱死制动系统的执行器有两位两通电磁阀或三位三通电磁阀、制动液回液泵电动机；安全气囊系统的执行器是气囊点火器；座椅安全带收紧系统的执行器是收紧器点火器；自动变速系统的执行器有自动传动液液压油泵、换挡电磁阀和锁止电磁阀；汽车巡航控制系统的执行器有巡航控制电动机或巡航控制电磁阀等。

汽车发动机电子控制系统的主要功能是提高汽车的动力性、经济性和排放性能。随着汽车电子控制技术的发展与进步，世界各大汽车公司或电子技术公司开发研制的发动机电子控制系统千差万别。控制系统的功能、控制参数和控制精度不同，采用控制部件（传感器、电控单元和执行器）的类型或数量也不尽相同。通过对各种控制部件进行不同的组合，便可组成若干个子控制系统。桑塔纳2000GSi型轿车AJR型发动机电子控制系统的结构示意图如图1-1所示。

其组件在车上的布置如图1-2所示，AJR型发动机电子控制系统的组成如图1-3所示。

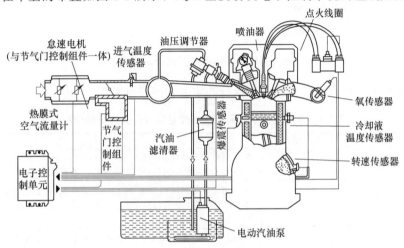

图 1-1 AJR型发动机电子控制系统结构示意图

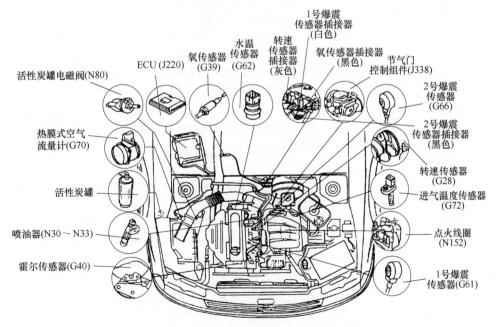

图 1-2 汽油喷射系统和点火系统位置布置图

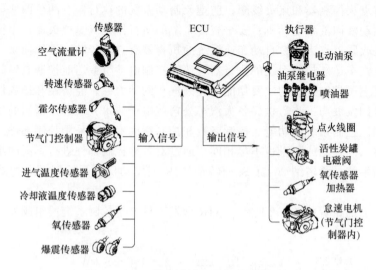

图 1-3 AJR 型发动机电子控制系统的组成

汽车发动机电子控制系统传感器、执行的主要功能详见表 1-1、表 1-2。

表 1-1 发动机电子控制系统各传感器与开关信号的作用

序号	类型	英文缩写	主要功能
1	空气流量计	MAFS	在 L 型电控燃油喷射系统中,由空气流量计测量发动机的进气量,并将信号输入 ECU,作为燃油喷射和点火控制的主控制信号
2	进气管绝对压力传感器	MAPS	在 D 型电控燃油喷射系统中,由进气管绝对压力传感器测量进气管内气体的绝对压力,并将该信号输入 ECU,作为燃油喷射和点火控制的主控制信号
3	节气门位置传感器	TPS	检测节气门的开度及开度变化,如全关(怠速)、全开及节气门开闭的速率(单位时间内开闭的角度)信号,此信号输入 ECU,用于燃油喷射控制及其他辅助控制
4	凸轮轴位置传感器	CPS	给 ECU 提供曲轴转角基准位置信号(G 信号),作为喷油正时控制和点火正时控制的主控制信号
5	曲轴位置传感器(转速传感器)	CPS	用来检测曲轴转角位移,给 ECU 提供发动机转速信号和曲轴转角信号,作为喷油正时控制和点火工时控制的主控制信号
6	冷却液温度传感器	ECTS	给 ECU 提供发动机冷却液温度信号,作为燃油喷射控制和点火控制的修正信号。冷却液温度传感器信号也是其他控制系统(如怠速控制和废气再循环控制等)的控制信号
7	进气温度传感器	IATS	给 ECU 提供进气温度信号,作为燃油喷射控制和点火控制的修正信号
8	爆震传感器	KS	检测汽油机是否爆震及爆震强度,将此信号输入 ECU,作为点火正时控制的修正(反馈)信号
9	氧传感器	O_2S	检测排气中的氧含量,向 ECU 输送空燃比的反馈信号,进行喷油量的闭环控制
10	启动开关	STA	给 ECU 提供一个启动信号,作为燃油喷射和点火控制的修正信号
11	蓄电池电压	U_{BAT}	向 ECU 提供电压信号,作为燃油喷射控制的修正信号

表 1-2 发动机电子控制系统执行器的主要功能

序号	类型	英文缩写	主要功能
1	喷油器	INJ	根据 ECU 的喷油脉冲信号,精确计算燃油喷射量
2	点火器	ICM	根据 ECU 脉冲信号,控制点火
3	怠速控制阀	ISCV	控制发动机的怠速转速

续表

序号	类型	英文缩写	主要功能
4	节气门控制电动机	TC	根据 ECU 控制节气门的开度
5	电动燃油泵	FP	供给燃油喷射系统规定压力的燃油
6	废气再循环阀	EGRV	根据 ECU 控制废气再循环量
7	进气控制阀	IACV	根据 ECU 控制进气系统工作
8	活性炭罐电磁阀	ACCV	根据电控单元的控制指令信号,回收发动机内部的燃油蒸气,以便减少污染
9	真空电磁阀	VSV	根据 ECU 控制真空管路通断
10	二次空气喷射阀	SAIV	根据 ECU 脉冲信号控制二次空气喷射量
11	巡航控制电磁阀	CCSV	根据 ECU 控制巡航系统
12	空调控制真空电磁阀	ACU	根据 ECU 控制空调工作

汽车发动机电子控制系统是一个综合控制系统,并具有多种控制功能。将发动机电子控制系统的传感器和执行器进行不同的组合,就可组成燃油喷射系统、微机控制点火系统、空燃比反馈控制系统、发动机爆震控制系统、超速断油控制系统、减速断油控制系统、清除溢流控制系统、怠速控制系统、燃油蒸气回收系统和故障自诊断系统等。此外,某一控制系统也可能同时具有多种控制功能。例如,电子控制燃油喷射系统能够精确控制喷油量,且喷射的燃油雾化良好、燃烧完全。因此,不仅能够提高汽车的动力性,而且还能提高汽车的经济性和排放性。

在汽车电子控制系统中,发动机电子控制系统的控制部件最多、控制参数最多、控制功能最强、控制过程最复杂。因此,只要熟悉发动机电子控制系统的结构原理与控制过程,掌握该系统的故障诊断与检修方法,学习其他电子控制系统就能迎刃而解。

6. 电控系统的控制方式

电控系统的控制方式分为开环控制和闭环控制两种方式。开环控制是指 ECU 根据传感器的信号对执行器进行控制,而控制的结果是否达到预期目标对其控制过程没有影响。开环控制示意图如图 1-4 所示。闭环控制也叫反馈控制,在开环的基础上,它对控制结果进行检测,并反馈给 ECU,进行原先的控制修正。闭环控制示意图如图 1-5 所示。

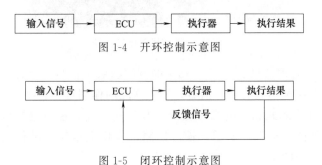

图 1-4 开环控制示意图

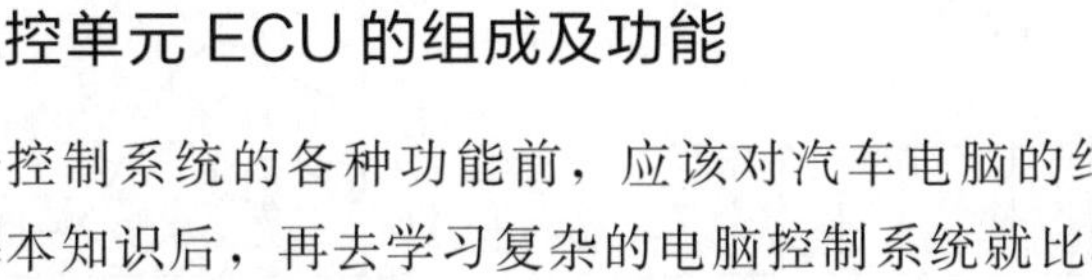

图 1-5 闭环控制示意图

(二)发动机电控单元 ECU 的组成及功能

在学习发动机电子控制系统的各种功能前,应该对汽车电脑的结构和工作原理有所了解,有了汽车电脑的基本知识后,再去学习复杂的电脑控制系统就比较容易了。此外,对汽车而言,发动机电脑(ECU)是最为重要的部件之一,了解它的工作原理及其内部参数的设计思路,将对汽车维修人员在实际工作中进行故障诊断和车辆检测提供极大的帮助。

(1) 发动机电脑（ECU）

发动机电脑是发动机的"大脑"，各种传感器则是发动机的"眼睛和耳朵"，执行器就是发动机的"手和脚"。发动机电脑采集各传感器的信号并进行处理和运算后，控制执行器动作，最终控制发动机机械系统的运转。

图1-6所示为发动机电脑的基本构成示意图，主要由输入回路、A/D（模拟/数字）转换器、微处理器和输出回路组成。图1-7为发动机电脑外形图。

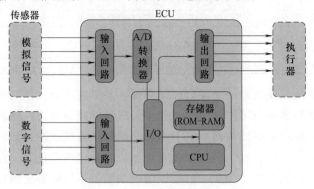

图1-6　发动机电脑的基本构成

图1-7　发动机电脑外形图

① 输入回路。微处理器只能识别0～5V的方波状数字信号，但传感器输送给发动机电脑的信号有两种，对应于不同的输入信号，输入回路的作用也不相同。

a．数字信号：如霍尔式和光电式传感器、卡门式空气流量传感器以及各种开关的输入信号。其输入特性如图1-8（a）所示，输入回路的作用就是对其进行削峰后转换成0～5V的方波状数字信号，如图1-9所示。

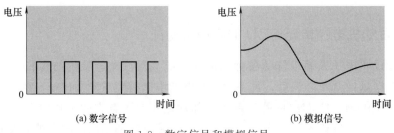

图1-8　数字信号和模拟信号

b. 模拟信号：如冷却液温度传感器、电位计式节气门位置传感器以及热丝式空气流量传感器的输入信号。其输入特征如图 1-8（b）所示，输入回路的作用就是将信号波形的杂波过滤掉，并削峰后输入到 A/D 转换器将模拟信号转换成数字信号，如图 1-9 所示。

② A/D（模拟/数字）转换器。微处理器不能直接处理模拟信号，A/D 转换器的作用就是将模拟信号转换成数字信号，如图 1-10 所示，然后输入微处理器进行处理。

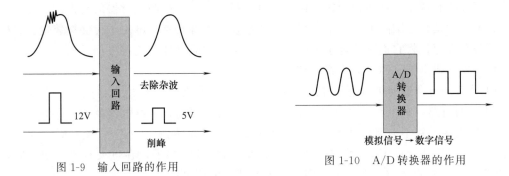

图 1-9　输入回路的作用　　　　　图 1-10　A/D 转换器的作用

③ 微处理器。微处理器主要由以下三部分组成：中央处理器（CPU）；存储器（RAM，ROM）；输入/输出（I/O）接口。

a. 中央处理器（CPU）。中央处理器（CPU）是整个控制系统的核心，所有的数据都要在 CPU 内进行运算，它由进行算术、逻辑运算的运算器、暂时存储数据的寄存器、按照程序执行各装置之间信号传送及控制任务的控制器等组成。当接收到各传感器的信号后，中央处理器根据达到预先设计的要求进行算术运算和逻辑运算，并控制燃油喷射、点火、怠速以及排放等系统。

b. 存储器（RAM，ROM）。存储器主要用来储存信息资料。存储器一般分为两种，一种是能读出也能写入的存储器，叫随机存储器 RAM（Random Access Memory）；另外一种是只能读出的存储器，叫只读存储器 ROM（Read-Only Memory）。

（a）随机存储器（RAM）。RAM 主要用来存储计算机操作时的可变数据，如用来存储计算机输入、输出数据和计算过程中产生的中间数据等，根据需要，存储的数据可随时调出或更新。RAM 在计算机中起暂时存储信息的作用，当电源切断时，所有存入 RAM 的数据会完全丢失。在发动机运行过程中，为了长期保存 RAM 的某些数据，如故障代码、空燃比学习修正值等，防止点火开关关闭时这些数据的丢失，RAM 一般都通过专用的电源后备电路与蓄电池直接连接，使它不受点火开关的控制。但如果专用电源后备电路断开或蓄电池上的电源线拔掉时，存入 RAM 的数据也会丢失。

（b）只读存储器（ROM）。ROM 用来存储固定数据，即存放各种永久性的程序和永久性、半永久性的数据，如电子控制燃油喷射发动机系统中的一系列控制程序软件、喷油特性脉谱、点火控制特性脉谱以及其他特性数据等。这些信息资料一般都是在制造时由厂家一次性存入，运用中无法改变其中的内容，即计算机工作时，新的数据不能存入，需要时能读出存入的原始数据资料。当电源切断时，存入 ROM 的信息不会丢失，通电后又可以立即使用。

（c）输入/输出（I/O）接口。输入/输出接口是 CPU 与输入装置（传感器）、输出装置（执行器）间进行信息交流的控制电路，输入/输出装置一般都通过 I/O 接口才能与电脑连接。根据 CPU 的命令，I/O 接口以所需要的频率接收输入信号，并按发出控制信号的形式和要求，以最佳的速度将输出信号送出（或送入中间存储器）。此外，输入/输出接口还起着数据缓冲、电瓶匹配、时序匹配等多个作用。

④ 输出回路。电脑输出的是电压很低的数字信号，用这种信号一般不能直接驱动执行器工作。输出回路的作用就是将这种低电压的数字信号转换成可以驱动执行器工作的控制信号。输出回路一般采用大功率的电子元件（如三极管、场效应管等），由微处理器输出的信号控制其导通和截止，从而控制执行器的供电或搭铁回路来控制执行器的动作。

目前的发动机电脑除上述基本装置外，还增设了电源装置、电磁干扰保护装置、自检装置、后备系统等，将它们紧凑地组装在一起，既节省空间又使其工作更加可靠。

(2) 发动机电脑（ECU）电源电路

ECU必须有合适的供电电压才能控制发动机管理系统。ECU电源电路就是由蓄电池向ECU供电的电路，它主要是由蓄电池、EFI（电子燃油喷射）主继电器及点火开关灯组成。

ECU电源电路不但要保证ECU在点火开关接通（即转到"ON"位置）时立即获得电源电压，而且还要保证ECU特定的端子（比如"BATT"端子）在点火开关关闭（即转到"OFF"位置）时也要与电源连通（即获得不间断的电源电压）。

当点火开关接通时，ECU经过一个保险丝获得电源电压，并将蓄电池电压（一般为12～14V）调节到5V或12V后供给内部和外部的元件使用。

在点火开关关闭时，ECU也需要供电，以保存相应的车辆参数和诊断故障代码等信息。因此，还有一个电路通过一个独立的保险丝不间断地为ECU提供蓄电池电压，若此电路断路，将使ECU中存储的怠速学习参数、燃油修正参数、故障码等信息全部丢失。

① EFI主继电器。EFI主继电器的作用是接通ECU和其电源间的连线，其功能是防止ECU电路的电压下降。当点火开关接通（ON）时，电流流过继电器线圈，各触点接通，电流经保险丝流入ECU。

对于未装步进电机式怠速空气控制阀的ECU电源电路，EFI主继电器由点火开关控制。

对于装有步进电机式怠速空气控制阀的ECU电源电路，EFI主继电器由发动机电脑直接控制。

② ECU电源电路

a. 未装步进电机式怠速空气控制阀的ECU电源电路。这种电源电路如图1-11所示，图中EFI主继电器由点火开关控制。当接通点火开关后，主继电器吸合，电流通过继电器流向电脑的两个"+B"端子。当断开点火开关后，继电器马上断开，流向发动机电脑的两个"+B"端子的电流被切断。

b. 装有步进电机式怠速空气控制阀的ECU电源电路。装有步进电机式怠速空气控制阀的ECU电源电路如图1-12所示，点火开关接通，ECU的"BATT"端子供电，ECU通过内部的主继电器控制电路，控制继电器电源端子通电，将EFI主继电器吸合，蓄电池电压加到ECU的两个"+B"端子上。当断开点火开关后，ECU通过主继电器控制电路继续供电让EFI主继电器延时断电，以便步进电机能有时间退回到初始位置，使旁通气道开度达到最大，为下一次启动做准备。

由电路图可见，上述两种电源电路都有一条导线通过EFI保险丝直接从蓄电池连接到发动机控制模块的"+BATT"端子，其作用是不管点火开关在"ON"位置还是"OFF"位置，蓄电池都向发动机电脑的随机存储器（RAM）持续供电，以保证发动机电脑能随时存储故障码、空燃比修正值等数据。所以有些车型可以用拔下EFI保险一定时间（如丰田

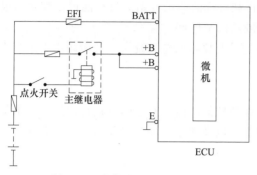
图 1-11 未装步进电机式怠速
空气控制阀的 ECU 电源电路

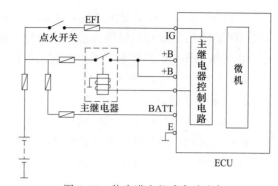
图 1-12 装步进电机式怠速空气
控制阀的 ECU 电源电路

车 10s 以上)的方法来清除 RAM 中存储的故障代码,其原因就是切断了持续供电电流。

(三)发动机电控系统故障自诊断系统测试

汽车电子控制系统的电子控制单元内部一般都有一个故障自诊断电路系统(OBD),它能在运行过程中不断监测电子控制系统各部分的工作情况,并能检测出电子控制系统中大部分故障,将故障以代码的形式存储在电子控制单元的存储器内。只要不拆下蓄电池,这些故障代码将一直保存在电子控制单元内。维修人员可按照特定的方法将故障代码读出,为检测与诊断发动机电子控制系统提供依据。

1. OBD-Ⅱ简介

在汽车技术发展的历程中,由于世界各大汽车制造公司的技术特点各不相同,缺乏统一的标准,导致各种汽车自诊断系统的故障诊断座形式和位置、读取与清除故障码的方法各异,这给汽车用户和维修人员带来了很大不便。为此,20 世纪 70 年代,汽车电控系统中开始采用了第一代随车诊断系统(OBD-Ⅰ);1994 年以后,美国、日本和欧洲的主要汽车制造厂家生产的电控汽车逐步开始采用第二代随车诊断系统(OBD-Ⅱ)。

OBD 是"ON-BOARD DIAGNOSTICS"的英文缩写,即随车诊断系统。OBD-Ⅱ则是指第二代随车诊断系统。OBD-Ⅱ是由美国汽车工程学会(SAE)提出,经环保机构(EPA)和加利福尼亚州空气资源委员会(CARB)认证通过。OBD-Ⅱ的主要特点如下:

① 汽车按标准装用统一的 16 端子诊断座,如图 1-13 所示,并将诊断座统一安装在驾驶室仪表盘下方。

② OBD-Ⅱ具有数据传输功能,并规定了两个传输线标准:欧洲统一标准(ISO-Ⅱ)规定数据传输用"7"号和"15"号端子,美国统一标准(SAE-J1850)规定数据传输用"2"号和"10"号端子。

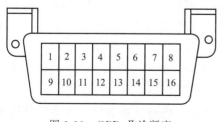
图 1-13 OBD-Ⅱ诊断座

图 1-14 OBD-Ⅱ故障码形式

③ OBD-Ⅱ具有行车记录功能，能记录车辆行驶过程的有关数据资料；能记忆和重新显示故障码的功能，可利用仪器方便、快速地调取或清除故障码。

④ 装用 OBD-Ⅱ的汽车，采用相同的故障码代号及故障码意义统一。故障码由1个英文字母和4个数字组成，如图 1-14 所示。

2. 诊断仪的使用

通过电控系统自诊断系统的功能，以及车用诊断仪的功能，对诊断仪进行使用，要求能够掌握正确运用诊断仪读取汽车故障码的方法和步骤以及注意事项，以及能够对读取的故障码查找出故障原因，并能够运用诊断仪对故障码进行清除。

三、项目实施

（一）实施要求

丰田 5A、AJR 发动机台架；汽车。

（二）实施步骤

目前，发动机电脑技术已经相当成熟，在正常使用情况下发动机电脑本身不太容易出现故障。但在实际维修中很多维修人员不按照维修手册规定的程序诊断故障，他们在几次尝试仍未能解决发动机故障时，往往将故障归咎于发动机电脑，从而造成故障诊断的不准确，同时也增加了车主的经济负担。

（1）发动机电脑的故障及产生原因

发动机电脑的故障主要是：焊点松脱、电容元件失效、集成电路损坏、电控单元固定脚螺栓松动、电子元件损坏等。发动机电脑一旦出现故障，会造成发动机不能启动或难于启动、无高速、耗油量大等现象。出现这些故障，除使用时间过长、自然磨损老化外，一般由以下原因引起。

① 环境因素。水是最主要的原因。如果发动机电脑中进水，将造成短路和不可恢复的腐蚀、接头损坏等。其次是过热和振动，这可能会在线路板中引起微小的裂纹。

② 电压或电流超载。通常是由电磁阀或执行器电路内的短路引起的。如果短路的电磁阀或执行器未被发现或修复就更换发动机电脑，所造成的超载电压还可能损坏新的发动机电脑。因此，在更换新电脑之前，一定要彻底查清原电脑损坏的原因。

③ 不规范的操作。如在拆卸过程中未采取静电防护措施，安装发动机电脑之前未断开蓄电池，用内阻较小的电阻表测量其端子等。

（2）发动机电脑的维修

工作正常的发动机电脑，需要所有传感器输入正确的信号、蓄电池电压正确、接地良好。因此，在怀疑发动机电脑本身有故障之前，应当先检查并确认这几个方面没有问题。

一般发动机电脑不可修复，一旦确认有故障，则必须更换，更换新的发动机控制模块时必须注意以下几点。

① 准确识别。发动机电脑种类繁多，准确地识别是正确更换的前提。许多发动机电脑表面上看去完全一样，但其内部的电路和标定却可能不完全一样。对于更换发动机电脑而

言,十分接近是不够的,必须完全符合所修车辆的需要。正确地识别发动机电脑不仅需要车辆的年、厂、型和发动机排量,还要知道发动机电脑上写的 OEM 零件号。大多数供货商都有这两种分类表。因此,如果不能确定,可以找出 ECU 上的 OEM 零件号,然后通过这个零件号在供货商的交叉索引中查找所需的 ECU。

② 更换的技巧。更换发动机电脑实际上就是换一个盒子。对于有些车型,发动机电脑可能不容易更换,因为它通常被埋在仪表板、杂物箱或控制台中其他零部件的下面或后面。无论发动机在哪个位置,在拆卸旧发动机电脑和安装新发动机电脑之前都应断开蓄电池。在装好发动机电脑并重新连接好后,再重新接上蓄电池。此时,工作并没有结束。许多发动机电脑在安装后或断开电源后必须要经过"再学习"过程。对于某些车型,可能要经过特定程序才能建立基本怠速。而有些车型可能需要经过短时间的驾驶让电脑调整自己。

(3) 电源电路检修的注意事项

一般汽车的 ECU 电源电路向发动机控制模块提供的电压为 12～14V,如果提供的电压过大,将可能烧毁 ECU;而如果提供的电压过小(如小于 10V),又会影响发动机控制模块的正常工作甚至不工作。此外,如果 EFI 主继电器失灵,也会造成发动机控制模块不工作或工作不正常。所以当怀疑发动机控制模块有故障时,首先要检查 ECU 电源电路是否正常。

对电源电路进行诊断维修时,必须首先弄清楚电路中:

哪几条线是接蓄电池正极(+BATT);

哪几条线是接点火开关控制的电源(+B,+B);

哪些是由 ECU 提供的电源(+5V);

哪条是接地线(E1、E2)。

然后再利用万用表等仪器根据电路图进行检查。

(4) 利用万用表检测汽车电控单元

电控单元及其控制线路的故障可用专用的检测仪,或通用的电控单元诊断仪来检测。这些仪器可准确地查出故障的所在之处。如果没有这些仪器,则可利用万用表来测量电控单元一侧插座上各引脚的电压或工作电阻,据此判断电控单元及其控制线路有无故障。这时必须以被检车型的详细维修技术资料作为依据,包括:电控单元一侧插座上各引脚分别与哪些装置相连接;各引脚在发动机不同工作状态下的标准电压值等。检测时如发现异常,则表明有故障。与执行器连接部分异常,则表明电控单元有故障;与传感器连接部分异常,则可能传感器或线路有故障。测量电阻时,应拆下线束插头。将测量结果分别与标准值进行比较,即可判断出故障所在之处。

(三)注意事项

① 汽车电脑要轻拿轻放,避免汽车电脑掉到地上摔坏。

② 上实验台测试电压信号时,注意操作流程和相对应的测试端口。

③ 在实物台架上,测试端口与电控单元直接相连,不要将任何电压加在发动机实验台的测试端口上,以免损坏电控单元。

④ 遵守实验室规章制度,未经许可,不得移动和拆卸仪器与设备。

⑤ 注意人身安全和教具完好。

⑥ 严禁未经许可,擅自扳动教具、设备的电器开关、点火开关和启动开关。

小 结

本项目讲授了汽车电控单元的基本结构和工作原理。通过本项目的学习,学生应能够认识到发动机电控系统工作的优点,掌握电控系统各个传感器、执行器在工作中的作用。同时讲授了诊断仪的使用方法,在使用诊断仪时提前应做什么准备,并且有些故障在不同的工况下显示是不同的,或不显示。所以还要利用诊断仪读取发动机动态数据流的方法,对发动机进行动态数据的分析,并能够判断故障原因。

习题及思考

1. 汽车电控单元的结构和工作原理。
2. 对汽车电控单元电源电路检修的注意事项是什么?
3. 汽车电控单元电源电路由哪三部分组成?
4. 诊断仪有哪些功用?
5. 使用诊断仪的注意事项有哪些?
6. 利用诊断仪读取数据流有何好处?

项目二

汽油发动机电控燃油喷射系统检修

一、项目情境引入

燃油供给系统是发动机电控系统的重要部分，在熟悉燃油供给系统主要组成部件的布置和结构基础上，掌握电动燃油泵、燃油压力调节器、燃油滤清器等部件的作用及类型、结构及原理、维护与检修方法；同时要掌握燃油控制系统主要传感器（如空气流量计、进气压力传感器、节气门位置传感器、冷却液温度传感器、曲轴与凸轮轴位置传感器等）、电控单元、执行器（喷油器）等部件的作用及类型、结构及原理、维护与检修方法，只有这样才能更深入地掌握电控燃油喷射系统的工作原理，才能够根据电控系统故障现象分析原因所在。

二、项目相关知识

（一）燃油喷射系统的分类

发动机电子控制燃油喷射系统是随着机械式控制系统、机电结合式控制系统和电子控制技术的发展而逐步发展形成的。为了便于全面了解发动机燃油喷射控制系统的总体情况，有必要向读者介绍发动机燃油喷射系统的分类情况。

1. 按喷油器与汽缸的数量关系分类

（1）单点燃油喷射系统

单点燃油喷射系统是在节气门体上安装一个或两个喷油器，向进气歧管中喷射燃油从而形成可燃混合气。如图 2-1 所示，这种喷射系统因喷油器安装在节气门体上集中进行燃油喷射，所以又称为节气门体燃油喷射系统或集中燃油喷射系统。这种喷射系统用节气门的开启角度和发动机转速来控制空燃比，省去了空气流量传感器，结构和控制方式更加简单，又兼顾了发动机性能和成本，对发动机结构的影响也较小。但这种节气门体的燃油喷射系统对混合气的控制精度比较低，各个汽缸混合气的均匀性也比较差。

（2）多点燃油喷射系统

多点燃油喷射系统根据喷油器的安装位置又可分

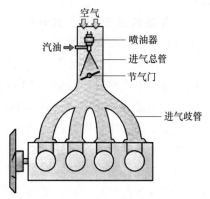

图 2-1 单点燃油喷射系统

为进气道喷射和缸内喷射两种。

① 进气道喷射。进气道喷射是指在每一个汽缸的进气门前安装一个喷油器，如图2-2所示。喷油器喷射出燃油后，在进气门附近与空气混合形成可燃混合气，这种喷射系统能较好地保证各缸混合气总量和浓度的均匀性。目前大多数车型都采用这种多点燃油喷射系统。

② 缸内喷射。缸内喷射是指将高压燃油直接喷射到汽缸内，如图2-3所示。这种喷射技术使用特殊的喷油器，燃油喷雾效果更好，并可在缸内产生浓度渐变的分层混合气（从火花塞往外逐渐变稀）。因此可以用超稀的混合气工作，油耗和排放也远远低于普通汽油发动机。此外，这种喷射方式使混合气体积和温度降低，爆震燃烧的倾向减少，发动机的压缩比可比进气道喷射时大大提高。

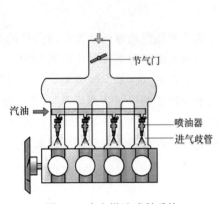

图2-2 多点燃油喷射系统

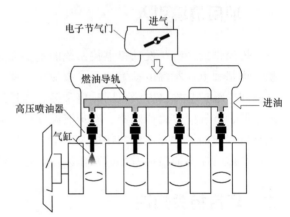

图2-3 缸内直接喷射系统

与单点燃油喷射系统相比较，多点燃油喷射系统对混合气的控制更为有效，主要因为这种控制系统是在每个汽缸口或每个汽缸内均安装一个喷油器，保证了发动机每个汽缸内混合气浓度的均匀性。同时这种系统是将燃油喷射在进气门处或直接喷到汽缸内，燃油和空气混合得更充分，而且无需预热进气歧管来帮助燃油雾化，反之可以冷却进气来提高进气量，增大功率，节气门响应更快。燃油与空气混合进入汽缸燃烧后，氧传感器将排气中氧含量的检测结果输送给发动机控制模块（ECU），发动机控制模块能及时进行混合气浓度的反馈修正；此外，将燃油喷射在进气门附近或汽缸内，避免了进气管的形状和表面质量对混合气的影响。

2. 按喷油器的喷射方式分类

（1）连续性燃油喷射系统

连续性燃油喷射系统大多应用于机械式或机电混合式的燃油喷射系统中，这种燃油喷射系统是在每个汽缸口均安装一个喷油器，只要系统给它提供一定的压力，喷油器就会持续不断的喷射出燃油，其喷油量的大小不是取决于喷油器，而是取决于燃油分配器中燃油计量槽孔的开度及计量槽孔内外两端的压差。

（2）间歇性燃油喷射系统

间歇性燃油喷射系统是在发动机运转期间间歇性地向进气歧管中喷油，其喷油量的大小取决于喷油器的开启时间，即发动机控制模块（ECU）发出的喷油脉冲宽度。这种燃油喷射方式广泛地应用于现代电控燃油喷射系统中。

这两种系统相比较而言，因为连续性燃油喷射系统控制喷油量的大多是机械元件，所以对混合气的相对控制精度比较差，而间歇性的电控燃油喷射系统则可以很好地解决这方面的技术问题。

3. 按喷油器的控制方式分类

（1）同时喷射系统

同时喷射是指在发动机运转期间，由电控单元 ECU 的同一个指令控制所有的喷油器同时开启或同时关闭，如图 2-4 所示，如丰田海艾斯 HIACE 小客车用 2RZ-E 型就采用了同时喷射系统。此外，当采用分组喷射或顺序喷射的燃油喷射系统发生故障、控制系统处于应急状态运行时，一般都采用同时喷射方式喷油。其目的是供给充足的燃油维持发动机运转，以便将汽车行驶到维修厂修理。

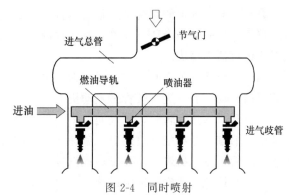

图 2-4　同时喷射

（2）分组喷射系统

分组喷射是指将喷油器分组，由电控单元 ECU 分别发出喷油指令控制各组喷油器喷射燃油，如图 2-5 所示，同一组喷油器同时喷油。大部分中、低档轿车采用了分组喷射方式喷油。

（3）顺序喷射系统

顺序喷射是指在发动机运转期间，由电控单元 ECU 控制喷油器按进气冲程的顺序轮流喷射燃油，顺序喷射又称为次序喷射，如图 2-6 所示。

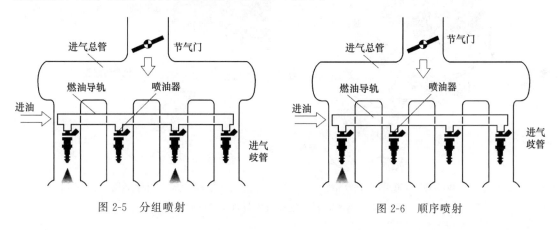

图 2-5　分组喷射　　　　　　　　　　图 2-6　顺序喷射

喷油正时由 ECU 根据凸轮轴位置传感器信号判定第一缸活塞位置，在第一缸活塞到达排气冲程上止点前一定角度时，发出喷油脉冲信号控制第一缸喷油器喷射燃油。第一缸喷油器喷油之后，ECU 将根据汽缸点火顺序，轮流控制其他汽缸的喷油器在其活塞到达排气冲程上止点前一定角度时喷射燃油，从而实现顺序喷射。

（二）燃油喷射系统的组成

汽车发动机燃油喷射系统是由空气供给系统、燃油供给系统和燃油喷射电子控制系统三个子系统组成。

1. 空气供给系统

功用:为发动机可燃混合气的形成提供必要的空气,并测量和控制空气量。

根据燃油喷射式发动机怠速进气量的控制方式不同,供气系统分为旁通空气道式和直接供气式两种。如丰田 5A 发动机采用的是旁通空气道式空气进给系统,桑塔纳 AGR 发动机采用的是直接供气式空气进给系统。

(1) 旁通空气道式空气供给系统

设有旁通空气道的空气供给系统结构如图 2-7(a)所示。主要由空气滤清器、空气流量传感器、进气软管、旁通空气道、怠速控制阀、进气歧管、动力腔、节气门位置传感器、进气温度传感器等组成。

当发动机正常工作时,空气通道为:进气口—空气滤清器—空气流量传感器—进软气管—节气门—动力腔—进气歧管—发动机进气门—发动机汽缸。

当发动机怠速运转时,空气通道为:进气口—空气滤清器—空气流量传感器—进软气管—节气门前端的旁通空气道入口—怠速转速控制阀—节气门后端的旁通空气道出口—动力腔—进气歧管—发动机进气门—发动机汽缸。

(2) 直接供气式空气进给系统

怠速转速采用节气门直接控制的发动机控制系统没有设置旁通空气道,其供气系统的结构如图 2-7(b)所示。主要由空气滤清器、空气流量传感器、进气软管、进气歧管、动力腔、节气门位置传感器、进气温度传感器等组成。

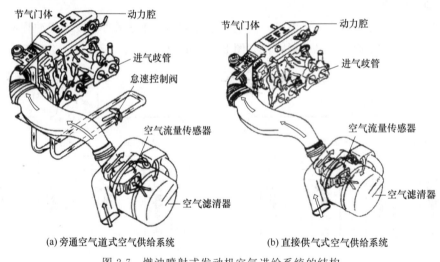

(a) 旁通空气道式空气供给系统　　　(b) 直接供气式空气供给系统

图 2-7　燃油喷射式发动机空气进给系统的结构

发动机正常工作和怠速运转时的空气通道完全相同,其空气通道为:进气口—空气滤清器—空气流量传感器—进气软管—节流阀体—动力腔—进气歧管—发动机进气门—发动机汽缸。

空气经滤清器过滤后,经节流阀体流入动力腔,再分配给各缸进气歧管。进入发动机汽缸的空气量多少,由电控单元(ECU)根据安装在进气道上的空气流量传感器检测的进气量信号求得。

2. 燃油供给系统

燃油供给系统简称供油系统,其功用是向发动机提供混合气燃烧所需的燃油。燃油喷射式发动机供油系统的结构如图2-8所示,主要由燃油箱、电动燃油泵、输油管、燃油滤清器、油压调节器、燃油分配管、喷油器和回油管等组成。燃油分配管又称为供油总管或油架。

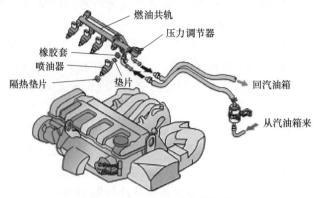

图2-8 燃油供给系统的结构

发动机工作时,电动汽油泵将汽油从油箱里泵出,先经汽油滤清器过滤,再经油压调节器调节油压,使油路中的油压高于进气歧管压力300kPa左右,最后经燃油分配管分配到各缸喷油器。当喷油器接收到电控单元ECU发出的喷油指令时,再将汽油喷射在进气门附近,并与供气系统提供的空气混合形成雾化良好的可燃混合气。当进气门打开时,混合气被吸入汽缸燃烧做功。

进入发动机汽缸的燃油流过的路径为汽油箱—汽油泵—输油管—汽油滤清器—燃油分配管—喷油器。喷油器将燃油喷射在进气门附近(缸内喷射系统则直接喷入汽缸)。

当汽油泵泵入供油系统的燃油增多、油路中的油压升高时,油压调节器将自动调节燃油压力,保证供给喷油器的油压基本不变。供油系统过剩的燃油由回油管流回油箱,回油路径为:汽油箱—汽油泵—输油管—汽油滤清器—燃油分配管—油压调节器—回油管—油箱。但部分现代新型汽油喷射发动机,压力调节器装在汽油箱内的电动汽油泵总成上,所以无回油管。

3. 燃油喷射电子控制系统

电子控制系统主要由传感器、电控单元和执行器三部分组成。

① 传感器:把各种反映发动机工况和汽车运行状况的参数(非电量参数)转变为电信号(电压或电流)提供给电控单元,使电控单元正确地控制发动机运转或汽车运行。

② 电控单元:接收来自各个传感器传来的信号,并完成对这些信息的处理和发出指令控制执行器的动作。

③ 执行器:用来完成电控单元发出的各种指令,是电控单元指令的执行者。

(三)发动机燃油喷射系统传感器的结构原理

1. 空气流量传感器

空气流量传感器(AFS)又称为空气流量计,是进气歧管空气流量传感器的简称,其功用是检测发动机进气量的大小,并将空气流量信号转换成电信号输入电控单元ECU,以供ECU计算确定喷油时间(即喷油量)和点火时间。空气流量信号是发动机电控单元ECU计算喷油时间和点火时间的主要依据。

根据检测进气量的方式不同,空气流量传感器分为"D"型(即压力型)和"L"型(即流量型)两种类型。

"D"型空气流量传感器是利用压力传感器检测进气歧管内绝对压力的传感器。测量进气量的方法属于间接测量方法。装备"D"型空气流量传感器的喷射系统称为"D"型燃油喷射系统,电控单元利用该绝对压力和发动机转速来计算吸入汽缸的空气量,故又称为速度-密度型燃油喷射控制系统。由于空气在进气歧管内流动时会产生压力波动,发动机怠速(节气门关闭)时的进气量与汽车加速(节气门全开)时的进气量之差可达40倍以上,进气气流的最大流速可达80m/s,因此"D"型燃油喷射系统的测量精度不高,但控制系统的成本比较低。

"L"型空气流量传感器是利用流量传感器直接测量吸入进气管空气流量的传感器。"L"型空气流量传感器安装在空气滤清器至节气门之间的进气通道上。因为采用直接测量方法,所以进气量的测量精度较高,控制效果优于"D"型燃油喷射系统。"L"型空气流量传感器又分为体积流量型和质量流量型两种类型。汽车发动机燃油喷射系统采用的体积流量型传感器有翼片式、卡门涡流式和热式空气流量传感器三种,质量流量型传感器有热丝式和热膜式空气流量传感器两种。

在"L"型空气流量传感器中,由于质量流量型传感器内部没有移动部件,且气流流动阻力很小,因此具有工作性能稳定、测量精度高的优点,但是其制作成本较高。在质量流量型传感器中,热膜式空气流量传感器的使用寿命远远长于热丝式流量传感器。

由于目前翼片式、卡门涡流式空气流量传感器已经被淘汰,所以在这里只介绍热式空气流量传感器,热式空气流量传感器分为热丝式和热膜式两种。

热丝式与热膜式空气流量传感器都是直接检测发动机吸入空气的质量流量的传感器。两种传感器的检测原理完全相同,热丝式空气流量传感器的检测元件是铂金属丝,热膜式空气流量传感器的检测元件是铂金属膜。铂金属元件的响应速度很快,能在几毫秒内反映出空气流量的变化,因此测量精度不受进气气流脉动的影响(气流脉动在发动机大负荷、低转速运转时最为明显)。此外它们还具有进气阻力小、无磨损部件等优点。目前大多数中高档轿车都采用了这种传感器。

(1) 传感器的结构特点

热丝式与热模式空气流量传感器主要由发热元件(热丝或热膜)、温度补偿电阻(冷丝或冷膜)、信号取样电阻和控制电路等组成。

① 热丝式空气流量传感器的结构特点:热丝式空气流量传感器的结构如图2-9所示,传感器壳体两端设置有与进气道相连接的圆形连接接头,空气入口和出口都设有防止传感器受到机械损伤的防护网。传感器入口与空气滤清器一端的进气管连接。出口与节流阀体一端的进气管连接。

传感器内部套装有一个取样管,取样管中设有一根直径很小(约70μm)的铂金属丝作为发热元件,因此称为热丝,并制作成"Ⅱ"形张紧在取样管内。

因为进气温度变化会使热丝的温度发生变化而影响进气量的测量精度,所以在热丝附近的气流上游设有一只温度补偿电阻。该温度补偿电阻相当于一只进气温度传感器,其电阻值随进气温度的变化而变化。当进气温度降低(或升高)使发热元件的阻值减小(或增大)时,温度补偿电阻的阻值也会减小(或增大)。这样温度补偿电阻的温度起到一个参考基准的作用,控制电路提供的电流将使温度补偿电阻的温度始终低于发热元件温度120℃,使进气温度的变化不至于影响发热元件（热丝）测量进气量的精度。

早期制作的空气流量传感器采用铂金属丝制作温度补偿电阻，该电阻丝靠近进气口一侧，称之为冷丝。由于电阻丝在使用中容易折断而导致传感器报废，因此目前普遍采用在氧化铝陶瓷基片上印刷制作铂膜电阻的方法来制作温度补偿电阻。

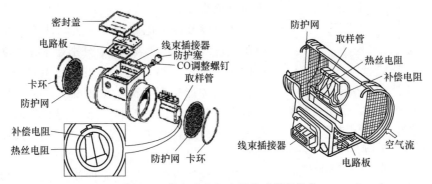

图 2-9　热丝式空气流量传感器结构

② 热膜式空气流量传感器的结构特点：热膜式空气流量传感器是热丝式传感器的改进产品，其发热元件采用平面形铂金属薄膜（厚度约 200nm）电阻器，故称为热膜电阻。热膜电阻的制作方法是：首先在氧化铝陶瓷基片上采用蒸发工艺淀积铂金属薄膜，然后通过光刻工艺制作成梳状图形电阻，将电阻值调节到设计要求的阻值后，在其表面覆盖一层绝缘保护膜，再引出电极引线而制成。

在传感器内部的进气通道上设有一个矩形护套（相当于取样管），热膜电阻设在护套内。为了防止污物沉积到热膜电阻上影响测量精度，在护套的空气入口一侧设有空气过滤层，用以过滤空气中的污物。为了防止进气温度变化使测量精度受到影响，在热膜电阻附近的气流上游设有铂金属式温度补偿电阻。如图 2-10 所示，温度补偿电阻和热膜电阻与传感器内部控制电路连接，控制电路与线束连接器插座连接，线束插座设在传感器壳体中部。

热膜式空气流量传感器与热丝式相比，因为热膜电阻的阻值较大，所以消耗电流较小，使用寿命较长。但是，由于其发热元件表面制作有一层绝缘保护膜，存在辐射热传导作用，因此相应特性略低于热丝式空气流量传感器。

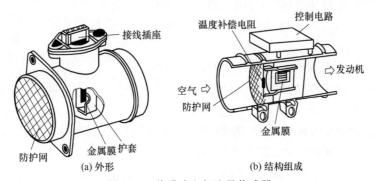

图 2-10　热膜式空气流量传感器

（2）传感器的工作原理

利用热丝或热膜作为发热元件的空气流量传感器，其测量原理完全相同，并与日常生活中使用的电吹风机的工作原理相似。为了叙述方便，下面将热丝与热膜统称为发热元件。

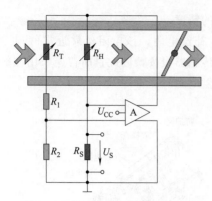

图 2-11 热丝式与热膜式空气流量
传感器 AFS 原理电路

R_T—温度补偿电阻（进气温度传感器）；

R_H—发热元件电阻（热丝或热膜）；

R_S—信号取样电阻；R_1，R_2—精密
电阻；A—控制电路

理论和实验证明：在强制气流的冷却作用下，发热元件在单位时间内的散热量跟发热元件的温度与气流温度之差成正比。为此在热丝式与热膜式空气流量传感器中，采用了图 2-11 所示的恒温差控制电路来实现流量检测。

在恒温差控制电路中，发热元件 R_H 和温度补偿电阻（进气温度传感器）R_T 分别连接在惠斯通电桥电路的两个臂上。当发热元件的温度高于进气温度时，电桥电压才能达到平衡。加热电流（50～120mA）由具有电流放大作用的控制电路 A 进行控制，其目的是使发热元件的温度 T_H 与温度补偿电阻的温度 T_T 之差保持恒定，即 $\Delta T = T_H - T_T = 120℃$。

当空气气流流经发热元件使其受到冷却时，发热元件温度降低，阻值减小，电桥电压失去平衡，控制电路将增大供给发热元件的电流，使其温度高于温度补偿电阻的 120℃。电流增量的大小，取决于发热元件受到冷却的程度，即取决于流过传感器的空气量。

当电桥电流增大时，取样电阻 R_S 上的电压就会升高，从而将空气流量的变化转换为电压信号 U_S 的变化。输出电压与空气流量之间近似于 4 次方根的关系，特性曲线如图 2-12 所示，信号电压输入 ECU 后，ECU 便可根据信号电压的高低计算出空气质量流量 Q_M 的大小。

当发动机怠速或空气为热空气（如夏季行车）时，因为怠速时节气门全闭或接近全闭，所以空气量很小；又因空气温度越高，空气密度越小，所以在体积相同的情况下，热空气的质量小，因此，发热元件受到冷却的程度小，阻值减小的幅度小，保持电桥平衡需要的加热电流小，故取样电阻上的信号电压低。电控单元 ECU 根据信号电压即可计算出空气量，捷达 AT、GTX 型轿车怠速时的空气流量标准值为 2.0～5.0g/s。

当发动机负荷增大或空气为冷空气时，因为节气门开度增大空气流速加快使空气流量增大；而冷空气密度大，在体积相同的情况下冷空气质量大，

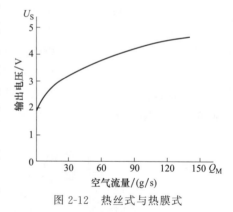

图 2-12 热丝式与热膜式
AFS 输出特性曲线

所以发热元件受到冷却的程度增大，阻值减小的幅度增大，保持电桥平衡需要的加热电流增大，因此当发动机负荷增大时，信号电压升高。

热丝式空气流量传感器在使用一段时间后，由于热丝表面受空气尘埃影响，其热辐射能力降低会影响传感器的测量精度，因此控制电路中设计有"自洁电路"来实现自洁功能。每当 ECU 接收到发动机熄火的信号时，ECU 将控制自洁电路接通，将热丝加热到 1000℃并持续 1s 左右，使黏附在热丝上的尘埃烧掉。另一种防止热丝沾污的方法是提高热丝的保持温度，一般将保持温度设定在 200℃以上，以便烧掉黏附的污物。热膜式传感器铂金属膜的

面积比热丝的表面积大得多，且覆盖有一层绝缘保护膜，因此不会沾污而影响测量精度。

2. 进气压力传感器

在发动机燃油喷射系统中，如果安装了歧管压力传感器，就无须安装空气流量传感器；反之，如果安装了空气流量传感器，那么就无须安装歧管压力传感器。丰田 5A 电控发动机安装的就是进气压力传感器。歧管压力传感器的安装位置比较灵活，只要能将进气歧管内的进气压力引入传感器的真空管内，传感器就可安放在任何位置。轿车将传感器通过连接软管安装在进气稳压箱上，如图 2-13 所示为丰田 5A 发动机进气压力传感器的安装位置。

图 2-13　进气压力传感器的安装位置

（1）歧管压力传感器的结构特点

各型汽车用歧管压力传感器的结构大同小异。如图 2-14（a）所示，主要由硅膜片、真空室、混合集成电路、真空管和线束插接器等组成。

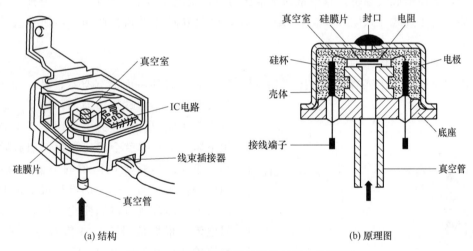

图 2-14　压敏电阻式进气管绝对压力传感器

传感器壳体被硅膜片分割成两个互不相通的腔室。一腔室预置真空，另一腔室导入进气压力。

硅膜片是压力转换元件，用单晶硅制成。硅膜片的长和宽约为 3mm、厚度约为 160μm，在硅膜片的中央部位采用腐蚀方法制作有一个直径为 2mm、厚度约为 50μm 的薄膜片；在薄膜片的表面上，采用集成电路加工技术与台面扩散技术制作四只梳状阻值相等的半导体力敏电阻，通常称为固态压阻器件或固态电阻，如图 2-15（a）所示，并利用低阻扩散层（P 型扩散层）将四只电阻连接成惠斯通电桥电路，如图 2-15（b）所示，然后再与传感器内部的信号放大电路和温度补偿电路等混合集成电路连接。

在硅膜片上，根据力敏电阻扩散制作的方向不同分为径向电阻和切向电阻，扩散电阻的长边与膜片半径垂直的电阻称为切向电阻 R_t（图中电阻 R_4、R_2 所示），扩散电阻的长边与

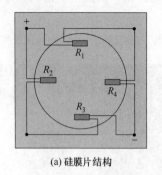
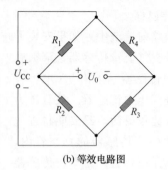

(a) 硅膜片结构　　　　　　(b) 等效电路图

图 2-15　硅膜片及应变电阻

膜片半径平行的电阻称为径向电阻 R_r（图中电阻 R_1、R_3 所示）。

硅杯一般用线胀系数接近于单晶硅（线胀系数为 $32\times10^{-7}/\text{℃}$）的铁镍锆合金（线胀系数为 $47\times10^{-7}/\text{℃}$）制成，设置在硅膜片与传感器底座之间，用于吸收底座材质与硅膜片热胀系数不同而加到硅膜片上的热应力，从而提高传感器的测量精度。硅杯与壳体以及底座之间形成的腔室制作成为真空室。壳体底部设有排气孔，利用排气孔将该腔室抽真空后，再用锡焊密封，从而形成真空室。真空室为基准压力室，基准压力室一般为零。在导压管入口设有滤清器，用于过滤导入空气中的尘埃或杂质，以免硅膜片受到腐蚀和脏污而导致传感器失效。

（2）传感器的工作原理

压阻效应式压力传感器结构如图 2-14（b）所示，硅膜片一面通真空室，另一面导入进气歧管压力。在歧管压力的作用下，硅膜片就会产生应力，在应力的作用下，半导体力敏电阻的电阻率就会发生变化而引起阻值变化，惠斯通电桥上电阻值的平衡就被打破。当电桥输入端输入一定的电压或电流时，在电桥的输出端就可得到变化的信号电压或信号电流。根据信号电压或信号电流的大小，就可检测出歧管压力的高低。

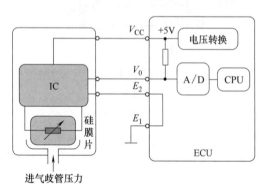

图 2-16　传感器原理电路

传感器的原理电路如图 2-16 所示。

当发动机工作时，进气歧管压力随进气流量的变化而变化。当节气门开度增大（即进气流量增大）时，空气流通截面增大，气流速度降低，进气歧管压力升高，硅膜片应力增大，力敏电阻的阻值变化量增大，电桥输出的电压升高，经混合集成电路放大和处理后，传感器输入电控单元（ECU）的信号电压升高。反之，当节气门开度由大变小（即进气流量减少）时，进气流通截面减小，气流速度升高，进气歧管压力降低，硅膜片应力减小，力敏电阻的阻值变化量减小，电桥输出电压降低，输入 ECU 的信号电压降低。

进气压力传感器的压力变化与输出电压的关系如图 2-17 所示。

3. 节气门位置传感器的检测

节气门位置传感器（Throttle Position Sensor，TPS），安装在节气门体轴上，传统方式是由驾驶员操纵油门踏板上的拉索来控制进气量。当油门踏板踩下时，节气门开度增大，进气量也随之增大。与此同时，空气流量计控制的空气量也随之增大，喷油量也相应增多，混合气总量变大。

节气门位置传感器一方面用来确定节气门的开度位置，反映发动机所处工况；另一方面反映节气门开闭的速度，在急加速或急减速时，空气流量计由于惯性或灵敏度影响使其反应没有那么快，这样会影响汽车的动力性能和燃油经济性能。空气流量计这个缺陷可由节气门位置传感器弥补，故节气门位置传感器信号也是喷油量

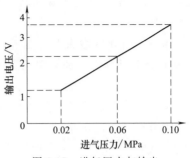

图 2-17　进气压力与输出信号电压之间的关系

控制的一个重要信号。在自动变速器车上，节气门位置传感器信号同时输入给变速器电脑，来控制变速器换挡时机和变矩器锁止时机。根据结构和原理不同，可分为可变电阻式、触点式和组合式三种。

(1) 触点式 TPS 结构与原理

① 触点式节气门位置传感器的结构特点。触点式节气门位置传感器 TPS 的结构如图 2-18 所示，主要由导向凸轮、节气门轴、控制杆、活动触点、急速触点、功率触点、导向槽、接线端子组成，凸轮随节气门轴转动，节气门轴随油门开度大小的变化而变化。

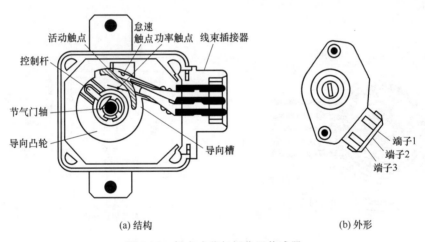

(a) 结构　　(b) 外形

图 2-18　触点式节气门位置传感器

② 触点式 TPS 的输出特性。触点式节气门位置传感器的输出特性如图 2-19 所示。当节气门关闭时，急速触点 IDL 闭合、功率触点 PSW 断开，急速触点 IDL 输出端子输出的信号为低电平 0，功率触点 PSW 输出的信号为高电平。ECU 接收到 TPS 输入的这两个信号时，如果车速传感器输入 ECU 的信号表示车速为零，那么 ECU 将判定发动机处于急速状态，并控制喷油器增加喷油量，保证发动机急速转速稳定而不致熄火。如果车速传感器输入 ECU 的信号表示车速不为零，那么

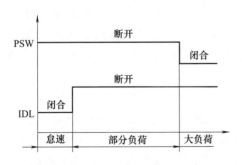

图 2-19　触点式节气门位置传感器输出特性

ECU将判定发动机处于减速状态运行,并控制喷油器停止喷油,以降低排放和提高燃油的经济性。

当节气门开度增大时,凸轮随节气门轴转动并将怠速触点IDL顶开,如果功率触点PSW保持断开状态,那么IDL端子和PSW端子都将输出高电平1。ECU接收到这两个高电平信号时,将判定发动机处于部分负荷状态,此时ECU将根据空气流量传感器信号和曲轴转速信号计算喷油量,保证发动机的经济性和排放性能。

当节气门接近全部开启(80%以上负荷)时,凸轮转动使功率触点PSW闭合,PSW端子输出低电平0,IDL端子保持断开而输出高电平1。ECU接收到这两个信号时,将判定发动机处于大负荷状态运行,并控制喷油器增加喷油量,保证发动机输出足够的功率,故大负荷触点称为功率触点。在此状态下,控制系统将进入开环控制模式,ECU不采用氧传感器信号。如果此时空调系统仍在工作,那么ECU将中断空调主继电器信号约15s,以便切断空调电磁离合器线圈电流,使空调压缩机停止工作,增大发动机的输出功率,提高汽车的动力性。

(2)组合式节气门位置传感器

① 组合式TPS的结构特点。丰田轿车用组合式节气门位置传感器的基本结构与原理电路如图2-20所示,主要由可变电阻、活动触点、节气门轴、怠速触点和壳体组成。可变电阻为镀膜电阻,制作在传感器底板上,可变电阻的滑臂随节气门轴一同转动,滑臂与输入端子V_{TA}连接。

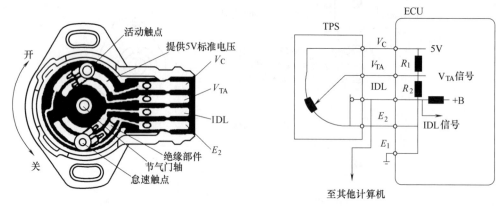

图2-20 组合式节气门位置传感器

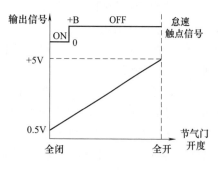

图2-21 组合式节气门位置
传感器输出特性

② 组合式TPS的输出特性。组合式TPS的输出特性如图2-21所示。当节气门关闭或开度很小时,怠速触点闭合,其输入端IDL输出低电平(0V),当节气门开度开到一定程度时,怠速触点断开,输出端IDL输出高电平(5V)。

随着节气门开度变化增大,可变电阻的滑臂便随节气门轴转动,滑臂上的触点便在镀膜电阻上滑动,传感器输出端子"V_{TA}"与"E_2"之间的信号电压随之发生变化,节气门开度越大,输出电压越高。传感器输出的线性信号经过A/D转换器转换成数字信号后再输入 ECU。

4. 曲轴与凸轮轴位置传感器

在发动机电控单元 ECU 控制喷油器喷油和控制火花塞跳火时,首先需要知道究竟是哪一个汽缸的活塞即将到达排气冲程上止点和压缩冲程上止点,然后才能根据曲轴转角信号控制喷油提前角与点火提前角。

(1) 曲轴与凸轮轴位置传感器的功用

曲轴位置传感器有时称为发动机转速传感器,用来检测曲轴转角和发动机转速信号,输送给 ECU,以便确定燃油喷射时刻和点火控制时刻。曲轴位置传感器是发动机控制系统中最主要的传感器之一,是确认曲轴转角位置和发动机转速不可缺少的信号之一,发动机控制模块用此信号控制燃油喷射量、喷油正时、点火时刻、点火线圈充电闭合角、怠速转速和电动汽油泵的运行。

凸轮轴位置传感器用来检测凸轮轴位置信号,输送给 ECU,以使 ECU 确定第一缸压缩上止点,从而进行顺序喷油控制和点火时刻控制;同时,还用于发动机启动时识别第一次点火时刻;因此也称为判缸传感器。

(2) 曲轴与凸轮轴位置传感器的分类

曲轴位置传感器和凸轮轴位置传感器通常安装在一起,只是各车型安装位置不同,如曲轴、凸轮轴、飞轮或分电器等处。根据结构和工作原理不同,可分为电磁式、霍尔式和光电式三种类型。

① 光电式 CPS

a. 传感器的结构特点。日产公司生产的光电式曲轴与凸轮轴位置传感器是由分电器改进而成,结构如图 2-22 所示,主要由信号发生器、信号盘(即信号转子)、配电器、传感器壳体和线束插头等组成。

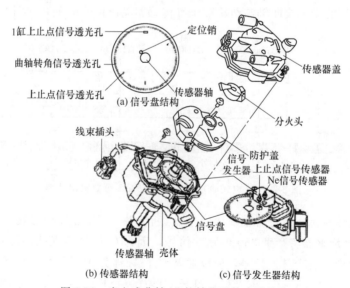

图 2-22 光电式曲轴/凸轮轴位置传感器结构

信号盘是传感器的信号转子,压装在传感器轴上,结构如图 2-22 (a) 所示,在靠近信号盘的边缘位置制作有间隔弧度均匀的内、外两圈透光孔。其中,外圈制作有 360 个长方形透光孔(缝隙),间隔弧度为 1°(透光孔占 0.5°,遮光部分占 0.5°),用于产生曲轴转角与转速信号；内圈制作有 6 个透光孔（长方形孔），间隔弧度为 60°，用于产生各个汽缸的上止点位置信号，其中有 1 个长方形宽边稍长的透光孔，用于产生第一缸上止点位置信号。

信号发生器固定在传感器壳体上，由 Ne 信号（曲轴位置信号）发生器、G 信号（凸轮轴位置信号）发生器以及信号处理电路组成，如图 2-22（b）所示，Ne 信号与 G 信号发生器均由一只发光二极管和一只光敏晶体管（三极管）组成，两只 LED 分别对着两只光敏三极管。

b. 曲轴转速、转角信号和汽缸识别信号的产生原理。光电式传感器工作原理如图 2-23 所示，因为传感器轴上的斜齿轮与发动机配气机构凸轮轴上的斜齿轮啮合，所以当发动机带动传感器轴转动时，信号盘上的透光孔便从信号发生器的发光二极管 LED 与光敏三极管之间转过。

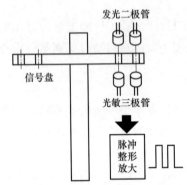

图 2-23 光电式传感器工作原理

当信号盘上的透光孔旋转到 LED 与光敏晶体管之间时，LED 发出的光线就会照射到光敏晶体管上，此时光敏晶体管导通，其集电极输出低电平（0.1～0.3V）；当信号盘上的遮光部分旋转到 LED 与光敏晶体管之间时，LED 发出的光线就不能照射到光敏晶体管上，此时光敏晶体管截止，其集电极输出高电平（4.8～5.2V）。如果信号盘连续旋转，透光孔和遮光部分就会交替地输出高电平和低电平。

当传感器轴随曲轴和配气凸轮轴转动时，信号盘上的透光孔和遮光部分便从 LED 与光敏晶体管之间转过，LED 发出的光线受信号盘透光和遮光作用就会交替照射到信号发生器的光敏晶体管上，信号传感器中就会产生与曲轴位置和凸轮轴位置对应的脉冲信号。日产公司采用的光电式曲轴与凸轮轴位置传感器输出信号的关系如图 2-24 所示。

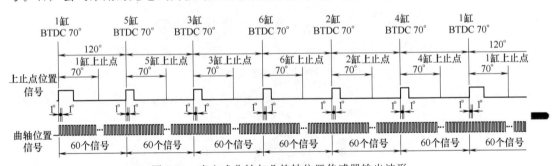

图 2-24 光电式曲轴与凸轮轴位置传感器输出波形

由于曲轴旋转两转，传感器轴带动信号盘旋转一圈，因此 G 信号传感器将产生 6 个脉冲信号，Ne 信号传感器将产生 360 个脉冲信号，因为 G 信号透光孔间隔弧度为 60°，曲轴每旋转 120°就会产生一个脉冲信号，所以通常 G 信号称为 120°信号。设计安装保证 120°信号在上止点前 70°（BTDC70°）时产生，且长方形宽边稍长的透光孔产生的信号对应于发动机第一缸活塞上止点前 70°，以便 ECU 控制喷油提前角与点火提前角。因为 Ne 信号透光孔间隔弧度为 1°（透光孔占 0.5°，遮光部分占 0.5°），所以在每一个脉冲周期中，高、低电平各占 1°曲轴转角，360 个信号表示曲轴旋转 720°。

由图 2-24 可见，当 ECU 接收到 G 信号发生器输入的宽脉冲信号时，便可确定第一缸活塞处于压缩上止点前70°位置；ECU接收到下一个G信号时，则判定第五缸活塞处于压缩上止点前70°位置。ECU接收到上止点位置信号（G信号）后，再根据曲轴转角信号（Ne信号）便可将喷油提前角和点火提前角的控制精度控制在1°（曲轴转角）范围内。

② 磁电式曲轴位置传感器。威驰轿车丰田5A发动机凸轮轴位置传感器，发动机转速曲轴位置传感器，桑塔纳轿车AJR发动机所应用的曲轴位置传感器采用的都是这种类型的。

磁感应式传感器主要由信号转子、传感线圈、永久磁铁和导磁磁轭组成，工作原理如图2-25所示。永久磁铁的磁力线经转子、线圈、托架构成封闭回路，转子旋转时，由于转子凸起与托架间的磁隙不断发生变化，通过线圈的磁通也不断变化，线圈中便产生感应电压，并以交流形式输出。在实用结构中，常将发动机转速和曲轴位置传感器一同装于分电器上，使用复合转子与耦合线圈。

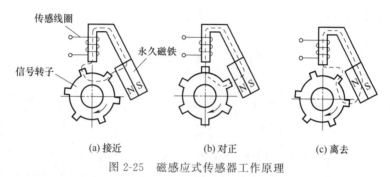

图 2-25 磁感应式传感器工作原理

磁力线穿过的路径为：永久磁铁N极—定子与转子间的气隙—转子凸齿—信号转子—转子凸齿与定子磁头间的气隙—磁头—导磁板（磁轭）—永久磁铁S极。当信号转子旋转时，磁路中的气隙就会周期性地发生变化，磁路的磁阻和穿过信号线圈磁头的磁通量随之发生周期性的变化。根据电磁感应原理，传感线圈中就会感应产生交变电动势。

当信号转子按顺时针方向旋转、转子凸齿接近磁头时，凸齿与磁头间的气隙减小，磁路磁阻减小，磁通量Φ增多，磁通变化率增大$\left(\dfrac{d\Phi}{dT}>0\right)$，感应电动势$E$为正（$E>0$），如图2-26中曲线$abc$所示。当转子凸齿接近磁头边缘时，磁通量$\Phi$急剧增多，磁通变化率最大$\left[\dfrac{d\Phi}{dT}=\left(\dfrac{d\Phi}{dT}\right)\max\right]$，感应电动势$E$最高（$E=E_{\max}$），如图2-26中曲线$b$点所示。转子转过$b$点位置后，虽然磁通量$\Phi$仍在增多，但磁通变化率减小，因此，感应电动势$E$降低。

当转子旋转到凸齿的中心线与磁头的中心线对齐时，如图2-25（b）所示，虽然转子凸齿与磁头间的气隙最小，磁路的磁阻最小，磁通量Φ最大。但是，由于磁通量不可能继续增加，磁通变化率为零，因此感应电动势E为零，如图2-26中曲线c点所示。

当转子沿顺时针方向继续旋转，凸齿离开磁头时，如图2-25（c）所示，凸齿与磁头间的气隙增大，磁路磁阻增大，磁通量Φ减少$\left(\dfrac{d\Phi}{dT}<0\right)$，所以感应电动势$E$为负值，如图2-26中曲线$cda$所示。当凸齿转到将要离开磁头边缘时，磁通量$\Phi$急剧较少，磁通变化率达到负向最大值$\left[\dfrac{d\Phi}{dT}=-\left(\dfrac{d\Phi}{dT}\right)\max\right]$，感应电动势$E$也达到负向最大值（$E=-E_{\max}$），如图2-26中曲线上的$d$点所示。

由此可见，信号转子每转过一个凸齿，传感线圈中就会产生一个周期的交变电动势，即电动势出现一次最大值和一次最小值,传感线圈也就相应地输出一个交变电压信号。

磁感应式传感器的突出优点是不需要外加电源,永久磁铁起着将机械能变换为电能的作用,其磁能不会损失。当发动机转速变化时,转子凸齿转动的速度将发生变化,铁芯中的磁通变化率也将随之发生变化。转速越高,磁通变化率就越大,传感线圈中的感应电动势也就越高。转速不同时,磁通和感应电动势的变化情况如图 2-26(b)所示。

由于转子凸齿与磁头间的气隙直接影响磁路的磁阻和传感线圈输出电压的高低,因此,转子凸齿与磁头间的气隙在使用中不能随意变动。气隙如有变化,必须按规定进行调整,气隙大小一般设计为 0.2~0.4mm。

③ 霍尔式曲轴与凸轮轴位置传感器

a. 霍尔传感器工作原理。各种类型的霍尔式和差动霍尔式传感器都是根据霍尔效应制成。霍尔效应是美国约翰·霍普金斯大学物理学家霍尔博士首先发现的。

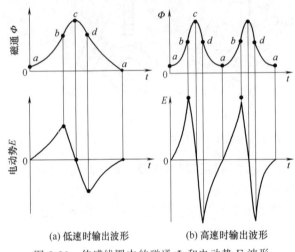

(a)低速时输出波形　　(b)高速时输出波形

图 2-26　传感线圈中的磁通 Φ 和电动势 E 波形

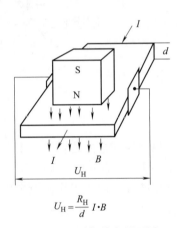

图 2-27　霍尔效应原理图

(a) 霍尔效应。霍尔博士于 1879 年发现:把一个通有电流 I 的长方形白金导体垂直于磁力线放入磁感应强度为 B 的磁场中时,如图 2-27 所示,在白金导体的两个横向侧面上就会产生一个垂直于电流方向和磁场方向的电压 U_H,当取消磁场时电压立即消失。该电压称为霍尔电压,U_H 与通过白金导体的电流 I 和磁感应强度 B 成正比,即

$$U_H = \frac{R_H}{d} I \cdot B \tag{2-1}$$

式中,R_H 为霍尔系数;d 为白金导体的厚度。

利用霍尔效应制成的元件称为霍尔元件,利用霍尔元件制成的传感器称为霍尔效应式传感器,简称霍尔式传感器或霍尔传感器。霍尔效应在自动控制技术领域直到 1947 年发现半导体器件之后才得以应用,从 20 世纪 70 年代开始在汽车技术领域得到了广泛应用。

实验证明,半导体材料也存在霍尔效应,且霍尔系数远远大于金属材料的霍尔系数。因此,一般都用半导体材料制作霍尔元件。利用霍尔效应不仅可以通过接通和切断磁场来检测电压,而且可以检测导线中流过的电流,因为导线周围的磁场强度与流过导线的电流成正比关系。20 世纪 80 年代以来,汽车上应用的霍尔式传感器与日俱增,主要原因在于霍尔式传感器有两个突出优点:一是输出电压信号近似于方波信号;二是输出电压高低与被测物体的转速无关。霍尔效应式传感器与磁感应式传感器不同的是需外加电源。

(b) 霍尔式传感器的结构原理。霍尔式传感器的基本结构如图 2-28 所示,主要由转子、永久磁铁、霍尔晶体管和放大器等组成。转子安装在转子轴上。霍尔集成电路由霍尔元件、放大电路、稳压电路、温度补偿电路、信号变换电路和输出电路等组成。

当转子随转子轴一同转动时,转子上的叶片便在霍尔集成电路与永久磁铁之间转动,霍尔集成电路中的磁场就会发生变化,霍尔元件中就会产生霍尔电压,经过信号处理电路处理后,就可输出方波信号。

当传感器轴转动时,转子上的叶片便从霍尔集成电路与永久磁铁之间的气隙中转过。当叶片进入气隙

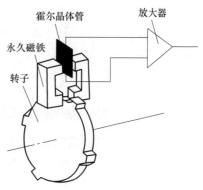

图 2-28 霍尔式传感器的基本结构

时,霍尔集成电路中的磁场被叶片旁路,霍尔电压 U_H 为零,集成电路输出级的三极管截止,传感器输出的信号电压 U_0 为高电平(实测表明:当电源电压 $U_{cc}=14.4V$ 时,信号电压 $U_0=9.8V$;当电源电压 $U_{cc}=5V$ 时,信号电压 $U_0=4.8V$)。

当叶片离开气隙时,永久磁铁的磁通便经霍尔集成电路和导磁钢片构成回路,此时霍尔元件产生电压($U_H=1.9\sim2.0V$),霍尔集成电路输出级的三极管导通,传感器输出的信号电压 U_0 为低电平(实测表明:当电源电压 $U_{cc}=14.4V$ 或 $U_{cc}=5V$ 时,信号电压 $U_0=0.1\sim0.3V$)。

b. 捷达与桑塔纳轿车用霍尔式凸轮轴位置传感器

(a) 传感器的结构特点。捷达 AT、GTX、桑塔纳 2000GSi、3000 型轿车采用的霍尔式凸轮轴位置传感器安装在发动机配气凸轮轴的一端,如图 2-29 所示,主要由霍尔信号发生器和信号转子组成。

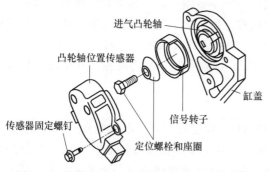

图 2-29 桑塔纳 2000GSi 型霍尔式 CPS 的结构

信号转子又称为触发叶轮,安装在配气凸轮轴的一端,用定位螺栓和座圈定位固定。信号转子的隔板又称为叶片,在隔板上制有一个窗口,窗口对应产生的信号为低电平信号,隔板(叶片)对应产生的信号为高电平信号。霍尔式信号发生器主要由霍尔集成电路、永久磁铁和导磁钢片等组成。霍尔集成电路由霍尔元件、放大电路、稳压电路、温度补偿电路、信号变换电路和输出电路等组成。霍尔元件用硅半导体材料制成,与永久磁铁之间留有 $0.2\sim0.4mm$ 的间隙。当信号转子随配气凸轮轴一同转动时,隔板和窗口便从霍尔集成电路与永久磁铁之间的气隙中转过。

(b) 传感器的工作原理。由霍尔式传感器的工作原理可知,当隔板(叶片)进入气隙(即在气隙内)时,霍尔元件不产生电压,传感器输出高电平(5V)信号;当隔板(叶片)离开气隙(即窗口进入气隙)时,霍尔元件产生电压,传感器输出低电平信号(0.1V)。

凸轮轴位置传感器输出的信号与曲轴位置传感器输出的信号之间的关系如图 2-30 所示。发动机曲轴每转两转,霍尔传感器信号转子就转一圈,对应产生一个低电平信号和一个

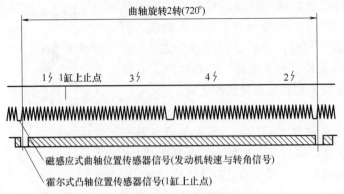

图 2-30 桑塔纳 2000GSi 曲轴/凸轮轴位置传感器输出波形的对应关系

高电平信号,其中低电平信号对应于 1 缸压缩上止点前一定角度。

发动机工作时,磁感应式曲轴位置传感器 CPS 和霍尔式凸轮轴位置传感器 CIS 产生的信号电压不断输入电控单元 ECU。当 ECU 同时接收到曲轴位置传感器大齿缺对应的低电平信号和凸轮轴位置传感器窗口对应的低电平信号时,便可判定第一缸活塞处于压缩冲程、第四缸活塞处于排气冲程,再根据曲轴位置传感器小齿缺对应输出的信号即可控制点火提前角和喷油提前角。

5 氧传感器(带加热器)

氧传感器是排气氧传感器(EGO)的简称,又称为氧量传感器 O_2S。氧传感器安装在排气管上,在使用三元催化转换器降低排放污染的发动机上,氧传感器是必不可少的。三元催化转换器安装在排气管的中段,它能净化排气中 CO、HC 和 NO_x 三种主要的有害成分,但只在混合气的空燃比处于接近理论空燃比的一个窄小范围内,三元催化转换器才能有效地起到净化作用。故在排气管中插入氧传感器,借检测废气中的氧浓度测定空燃比。并将其转换成电压信号或电阻信号,反馈给 ECU。ECU 控制空燃比收敛于理论值。

目前使用的氧传感器有氧化锆(ZrO_2)式和氧化钛(TiO_2)式两种,其中应用最多的是氧化锆式氧传感器。

(1)氧化锆式氧传感器

氧化锆式氧传感器的基本元件是氧化锆(ZrO_2)陶瓷管(固体电解质),亦称锆管(如图 2-31 所示)。锆管固定在带有安装螺纹的固定套中,内外表面均覆盖着一层多孔性的铂膜,其内表面与大气接触,外表面与废气接触。氧传感器的接线端有一个金属护套,其上开有一个用于锆管内腔与大气相通的孔,电线将锆管内表面的铂极经绝缘套从此接线端引出。

氧化锆在温度超过 300℃后,才能进行正常工作。早期使用的氧传感器靠排气加热,这种传感器必须在发动机启动运转数分钟后才能开始工作,它只有一根接线与 ECU 相连[如图 2-32(a)所示]。现在,大部分汽车使用带加热器的氧传感器[如图 2-32(b)所示],这种传感器内有一个电加热元件,可在发动机启动后的 20~30s 内迅速将氧传感器加热至工作温度。它有三根接线,一根接 ECU,另外两根分别接地和电源。

锆管的陶瓷体是多孔的,渗入其中的氧气,在温度较高时发生电离。由于锆管内、外侧氧含量不一致,存在浓差,因而氧离子从大气侧向排气一侧扩散,从而使锆管成为一个微电池,在两铂极间产生电压(如图 2-33 所示)。当混合气的实际空燃比小于理论空燃比,即发动机以较浓的混合气运转时,排气中氧含量少,但 CO、HC、H_2 等较多。这些气体在锆管

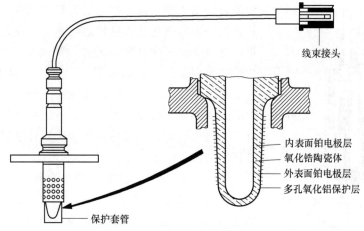

图 2-31 氧化锆式氧传感器

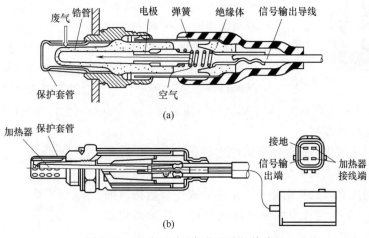

图 2-32 两种不同的氧化锆式氧传感器

外表面的铂催化作用下与氧发生反应,将耗尽排气中残余的氧,使锆管外表面氧气浓度变为零,这就使得锆管内、外侧氧浓度差加大,两铂极间电压陡增。因此,传感器产生的电压将在理论空燃比时发生突变:稀混合气时,输出电压几乎为零;浓混合气时,输出电压接近1V。

要准确地保持混合气浓度为理论空燃比是不可能的。实际上的反馈控制只能使混合气在理论空燃比附近一个较小的范围内波动,故氧传感器的输出电压在0.1~0.8V之间不断变化(通常每10s内变化8次以上)。如果氧传感器输出电压变化过缓(每10s少于8次)或电压保持不变(不论保持在高电位或低电位),则表明氧传感器有故障,需检修。

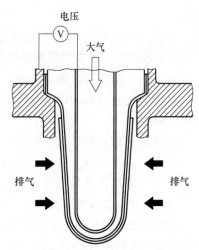

图 2-33 氧传感器的工作原理

(2) 氧化钛式氧传感器

氧化钛式氧传感器是利用二氧化钛(TiO_2)材料的电阻值随排气中氧含量的变化而变

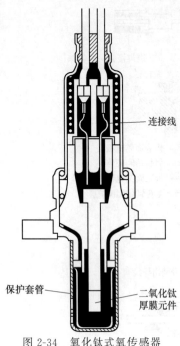

图 2-34 氧化钛式氧传感器

化的特性制成的,故又称电阻型氧传感器。氧化钛式氧传感器的外形和氧化锆式氧传感器相似。在传感器前端的护罩内是一个二氧化钛厚膜元件(如图 2-34 所示)。纯二氧化钛在常温下是一种高电阻的半导体,但表面一旦缺氧,其晶格便出现缺陷,电阻随之减小。由于二氧化钛的电阻也随温度不同而变化,因此,在氧化钛式氧传感器内部也有一个电加热器,以保持氧化钛式氧传感器在发动机工作过程中的温度恒定不变。

如图 2-35 所示,ECU 2 号端子将一个恒定的 1V 电压加在氧化钛式氧传感器的一端上,传感器的另一端子与 ECU 4 号端子相接。当排出的废气中氧浓度随发动机混合气浓度变化而变化时,氧传感器的电阻随之改变,ECU 4 号端子上的电压降也随着变化,当 4 号端子上的电压高于参考电压时,ECU 判定混合气过浓,当 4 号端子上的电压低于参考电压时,ECU 判定混合气过稀。通过 ECU 的反馈控制,可保持混合气的浓度在理论空燃比附近。在实际的反馈控制过程中,氧化钛式氧传感器与 ECU 连接的 4 号端子上的电压也是在 0.1~0.9 V 之间不断变化,这一点与氧化锆式氧传感器是相似的。

(3) 空燃比反馈控制

为了获得三元催化转换器所要求的空燃比,必须十分精确地控制喷油量。但在如下情况下,仅凭空气流量计测得进气量信号达不到这么高的控制精度,都会造成燃烧后排出的 CO、HC、NO_x 在排气管中的混合比例不对,三元催化转换效率下降,造成排放污染严重。

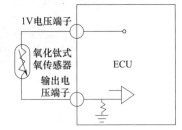

图 2-35 氧化钛式氧传感器工作原理

① 如喷油器漏油或堵塞时会造成实际混合气过浓或过稀;

② 点火系统缺火或火花能量不足会造成没有燃烧完的混合气直接进入三元催化转换器燃烧,造成动力性、经济性和排放性下降;

③ 气门正时不对,混合气也会直接进入三元催化转换器燃烧;

④ 空气流量计后的进气歧管漏气会造成生成的 NO_x 过多或空气流量计有故障后的输出曲线有偏差;

⑤ 水温传感器输出曲线有偏差;

⑥ 燃油系统喷油压力调节装置失效,使系统压力不正确;

⑦ 进气温度传感器信号输出曲线有偏差等。

因此必须借助安装在排气管中的氧传感器送来的反馈信号,对理论空燃比进行反馈控制。电脑根据氧传感器的输入信号,对混合气空燃比进行控制的方法称为闭环控制。它是一个简单而实用的闭环控制系统。这个控制系统需要经过一定时间间隔,控制过程才能响应,即从进气管内形成混合气开始,至氧传感器检测排气中的含氧浓度,需要经过一定时间。这一过程的时间包括混合气吸入汽缸、排气流过氧传感器以及氧传感器的响应时间等。由于存在滞后时间,要完全准确地使空燃比保持在理论空燃比 14.7 是不可能的,因此实际控制的混合气的空燃比总是保持在理论空燃比14.7附近的一个狭窄范围内。

（4）反馈控制的实施条件

采用氧传感器进行反馈控制即闭环控制期间，原则上供给的混合气是在理论空燃比附近。但在有些条件下是不适宜的，如发动机启动时以及刚启动未暖机时，由于发动机冷却水温度低，这时需要较浓的混合气，如按反馈控制供给的混合气在理论空燃比附近，发动机可能会熄火。又如发动机在大负荷、高转速运转时（实际在高速公路、车速超过130km/h，风阻很大，要保证高车速必须大油门才能维持发动机高转速高扭矩，发动机转速高，车速才能高）也需要较浓的混合气，如按反馈控制供给的混合气也在理论空燃比附近，则发动机会运转不良。所以在有些情况下必须停止反馈控制，即进入开环控制状态。一般遇到以下情况反馈控制作用解除：

① 发动机启动时；

② 冷启动后暖机过程；

③ 汽车大负荷或超速行驶时；

④ 燃油中断停供时；

⑤ 从氧传感器送来的空燃比过稀信号持续时间大于规定值（如10s以上）时；

⑥ 从氧传感器送来的空燃比过浓信号持续时间大于规定值（如4s以上）时。

此外，由于氧传感器的温度在300℃以下不会产生电压信号，当然反馈控制也不会发生作用。

6. 温度传感器

（1）温度传感器的功用

温度是反映发动机热负荷状态的重要参数，为了保证电控单元能够精确地控制发动机正常运行，必须随时监测发动机的进气温度，以便修正控制参数，准确计算吸入汽缸空气的质量流量以及进行排气净化处理等。空气质量大小与进气温度（密度）和大气（进气）压力高低密切相关。当进气温度低时空气密度大，相同体积气体的质量增大；反之，当进气温度升高时，相同体积气体的质量将减小。在采用各种歧管压力式或空气流量式传感器的燃油喷射系统中，都需要加装进气温度传感器，有些还需要加装大气压力传感器，以便随时监测周围环境温度和大气压力的变化，修正喷油量，使电控单元自动适应外部环境寒冷或高温温度以及不同海拔高度大气压力的变化情况。

进气温度传感器（Intake Air Temperature Sensor，IATS）的功能是检测进气温度，并将温度信号转换为电信号输入发动机电控单元。进气温度信号是多种控制功能的修正信号，包括燃油脉宽、点火正时、怠速控制和尾气排放等，若进气温度传感器信号中断，将导致发动机热启动困难，燃油脉宽增加，尾气排放恶化。

冷却液温度传感器（Coolant Temperature Sensor，CTS）通常又称为水温传感器，属负温度系数型热敏电阻式温度传感器，安装在发动机冷却液出水管上，其功能是检测发动机冷却液的温度，并将温度信号转换为电信号传送给发动机电控单元，电控单元根据该信号修正喷油时间和点火时间，使发动机工况处于最佳运行状态。冷却液温度传感器信号是许多控制功能的修正信号，如喷油量修正、点火提前角修正、活性炭罐电磁阀控制等。冷却液温度信号也是汽车上其它电控系统的重要参考信号，如电控自动变速器系统、自动空调系统。在一些车型的电控自动变速器系统中，若检测到发动机冷却液温度低于60℃，为保护行驶装置，自动变速器控制单元将进入"安全运行模式"，不会允许车辆升入超速挡，汽车只能在

90km/h 以下速度行驶。如果冷却液温度传感器故障或信号中断,发动机电控单元将启动备用模式,把水温值设定在 80℃ 左右,同时记录故障代码。此时车辆虽然能够正常行驶,但会出现发动机冷、热车均启动困难、油耗增加、怠速稳定性降低、废气排放量升高等等。

(2) 温度传感器的分类

① 按检测对象分类。如进气温度传感器、冷却液温度传感器、排气温度传感器和润滑油温度传感器等。这种分类方法简单实用,使用者根据测量对象即可方便地选择使用所需的传感器。

② 按结构与物理性能分类。温度传感器的种类很多,常用的有热敏电阻式、金属热电阻式、线绕电阻式、半导体晶体管式等。现代汽车广泛采用热敏电阻式温度传感器。

(3) 热敏电阻式温度传感器

① 热敏电阻式温度传感器的结构特点。热敏电阻又可分为正温度系数(PTC)型热敏电阻、负温度系数(NTC)型热敏电阻、临界温度型热敏电阻和线性热敏电阻。汽车上常用的是负温度系数型热敏电阻式温度传感器,如热敏电阻是利用陶瓷半导体材料的电阻随温度变化而变化的特性制成的,其突出优点是灵敏度高、响应及时、结构简单、制造方便、成本低廉。其结构主要由热敏电阻、金属或塑料壳体、接线插座与连接导线组成。温度传感器的结构如图 2-36 所示,分为单端子式和两端子式。

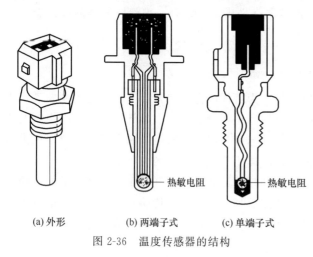

(a) 外形　　(b) 两端子式　　(c) 单端子式

图 2-36　温度传感器的结构

热敏电阻是温度传感器的主要部件,汽车用热敏电阻是在陶瓷半导体材料中掺入适量金属氧化物,并在 1000℃ 以上的高温条件下烧结而成,控制掺入氧化物的比例和烧结温度,即可得到不同特性的热敏电阻,从而满足使用要求。例如,如果测量发动机冷却液温度,则热敏电阻的工作温度为 -30～+130℃。如果测量发动机的排气温度,热敏电阻的工作温度则为 600～1000℃。

热敏电阻的外形制作成珍珠形、圆盘形、垫圈形、梳状芯片形、厚膜形等,放置在传感器的金属管壳内。在热敏电阻的两个端面各引出一个电极并连接到传感器插座上。

传感器壳体上制作有螺纹,以便安装与拆卸。接线插座分为单端子和两端子式两种,中高档轿车燃油喷射系统一般采用两端子式温度传感器,低档轿车燃油喷射系统以及汽车仪表一般采用单端子式温度传感器。如传感器插座上只有一个接线端子,则壳体为传感器的一个电极。

② 车用温度传感器的特性与电路。汽车电子控制系统普遍采用了负温度系数(NTC)型热敏电阻式温度传感器,其阻值与温度的关系曲线如图 2-37 所示。NTC 型热敏电阻具有温度升高阻值减小,温度降低阻值增大的特性,而且成明显的非线性关系。温度传感器的工作电路如图 2-38 所示。

传感器的两个电极用导线与 ECU 插座连接。ECU 内部串联一只分压电阻,ECU 向热敏电阻和分压电阻组成的分压电路提供一个稳定的电压(5V),传感器输入 ECU 的信号电压等于热敏电阻上的分压值。

当被测对象的温度升高时，传感器阻值减小，热敏电阻上的分压值降低；反之，当被测对象的温度降低时，传感器阻值增大，热敏电阻上的分压值升高。ECU 根据接收到的信号电压值，便可计算求得对应的温度值，从而进行实时控制。

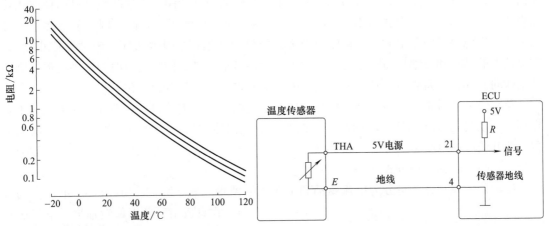

图 2-37　温度传感器的阻值与温度的关系曲线　　图 2-38　冷却液温度传感器的工作电路

（四）发动机燃油喷射系统执行器的结构原理

1. 喷油器

喷油器是电控燃油供给系统中应用的执行器。喷油器是电控燃油喷射系统中的重要执行器，它接收来自发动机控制模块的信号，精确地喷射燃油。

电控燃油喷射系统全部采用电磁式喷油器，单点喷射系统的喷油器安装在节气门体空气入口处，多点喷射系统的喷油器安装在各缸进气歧管或汽缸盖上的各缸进气道处。

（1）喷油器结构及工作原理

按喷油口的结构不同，喷油器可分为轴针式和孔式两种，如图 2-39 所示。

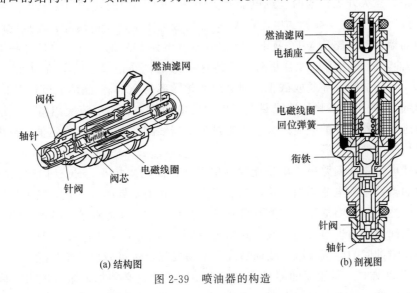

(a) 结构图　　(b) 剖视图

图 2-39　喷油器的构造

喷油器主要由滤网、线束连接器、电磁线圈、回位弹簧、衔铁和针阀等组成，针阀与衔铁制成一体。轴针式喷油器的针阀下部有轴针伸入喷口。

喷油器不喷油时，回位弹簧通过衔铁使针阀紧压在阀座上，防止滴油。当电磁线圈通电时，产生电磁吸力，将衔铁吸起并带动针阀离开阀座，同时回位弹簧被压缩。阀体使弹簧压缩而上升，上升行程很小，一般为0.1～0.2mm。燃油经过针阀并由轴针与喷口的环隙或喷孔中喷出。喷出燃油的形状为小于30°的圆锥雾状。由于燃油压力较高，因此喷出燃油为雾状燃油。当电磁线圈断电时，电磁吸力消失。回位弹簧迅速使针阀关闭，喷油器停止喷油。在喷油器的结构和喷油压力一定时，喷油器的喷油量取决于针阀的开启时间，即电磁线圈的通电时间。回位弹簧弹力对针阀密封性和喷油器断油的干脆程度会产生影响。

单点燃油喷射系统的喷油器一般都采用下部进油式，即进油口设在喷油器侧面，而不是在顶部，主要是可降低喷油器的高度，以便在节气门体内安装。此外，各车型装用的喷油器，按其线圈的电阻值可分为高阻（电阻为13～16Ω）和低阻（电阻为2～3Ω）两种类型。

（2）喷油器的驱动方式

喷油器的驱动方式可分为电流驱动和电压驱动两种方式，如图2-40所示。电流驱动方式只适用于低阻值喷油器，电压驱动方式对高阻值和低阻值喷油器均可使用。

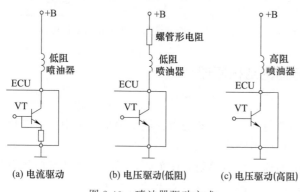

图2-40 喷油器驱动方式

① 电流驱动方式。在采用电流驱动方式的喷油器控制电路中，不需附加电阻，低阻喷油器直接与蓄电池连接，通过ECU中的晶体三极管对流过喷油器线圈的电流进行控制。

蓄电池通过点火开关和主继电器（或熔丝）直接给喷油器和ECU供电，ECU控制喷油器和主继电器线圈的搭铁回路。点火开关接通时，继电器触点闭合，ECU中的喷油器驱动电路使晶体三极管VT_1导通，流过喷油器线圈的电流在VT_1发射极电阻上产生电压降；A点的电压达到设定值时，喷油器驱动电路使VT_1截止。当蓄电池电压为14V时，流过喷油器线圈的峰值电流为8A，喷油器针阀达到最大升程后，保持这一稳定、静止状态的电流为2A；在此过程中，VT_1以20Hz的频率导通或截止，即电压变化频率为20Hz。晶体三极管VT_2的作用是吸收VT_1导通和截止时在喷油器线圈中产生的反电动势，防止电流突然减小。继电器的作用是防止流过喷油器线圈的电流过大，若流过喷油器线圈的电流超过设定值，继电器触点自动断开，以切断喷油器电源。

在喷油器电流驱动回路中，由于无附加电阻，回路的阻抗小，ECU向喷油器发出指令时，流过喷油器线圈的电流增加迅速，电磁线圈产生磁力使针阀开启快，喷油器喷油迟滞时间缩短，响应性更好。喷油器针阀的开启时刻总是比ECU向喷油器发出指令的时刻晚，此时间即称为喷油器喷油迟滞时间（或无效喷油时间）。此外，采用电流驱动方式，保持针阀开启使喷油器喷油时的电流较小，喷油器线圈不易发热，也可减少功率损耗。

② 电压驱动方式。低阻喷油器采用电压驱动方式时，必须加入附加电阻。因为低阻喷油器线圈的匝数较少，加入附加电阻，可减小工作时流过线圈的电流，以防止线圈发热而损

坏。附加电阻与喷油器的连接方式有三种，如图 2-41 所示。

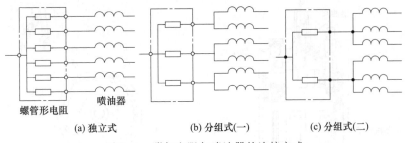

图 2-41 附加电阻与喷油器的连接方式

电压驱动方式中的喷油器驱动电路较简单，但因其回路中的阻抗大，喷油器的喷油滞后时间长。其中，电压驱动高阻喷油器的喷油滞后时间最长，电压驱动低阻喷油器次之，电流驱动的喷油器最短。

2. 电动燃油泵

电动燃油泵是电控发动机燃油供给系统组成的最重要的部件，它为燃油供给系统提供所需要的燃油压力动力源。对于燃油供给系统的正常工作起着至关重要的作用。

（1）电动燃油泵的功用及分类

① 电动燃油泵功用。电动燃油泵是电控燃油喷射发动机的基本部件之一。它一般由小型直流电动机驱动，工作时把燃油从油箱中吸出，加压后输送到管路中，和燃油压力调节器配合建立合适的系统压力。电动燃油泵的电动机和燃油泵连成一体，密封在同一壳体内。

电动燃油泵向喷油器提供油压高于进气歧管压力 250~300kPa，因为燃油是从油箱内泵出，经压缩或动量转换将油压提高后，通过输油管送到喷油器，所以油泵的最高油压需要 450~600kPa，其供油量比发动机最大耗油量大得多，多余的汽油将从回油管返回油箱。

② 电动燃油泵分类

a. 电动燃油泵按安装位置不同，可分为内置式和外置式两种。

内置式电动燃油泵安装在油箱中，具有噪声小、不易产生气阻、不易泄漏、安装管路较简单等优点，应用更为广泛。有些车型在油箱内还设有一个小油箱，并将燃油泵置于小油箱中，这样可防止在油箱燃油不足时，因汽车转弯或倾斜引起燃油泵周围燃油的移动，使燃油泵吸入空气而产生气阻。

外置式电动燃油泵串接在油箱外部的输油管路中，优点是容易布置，安装自由度大，但噪声大，且燃油供给系统易产生气阻，所以只有少数车型上应用。

b. 目前各车型装用的电动燃油泵按其结构不同，有涡轮式、滚柱式、转子式和侧槽式。内置式电动燃油泵多采用涡轮式，外置式电动燃油泵则多数为滚柱式。

经常用的有滚柱式、叶片式和齿轮式三种油泵。桑塔纳 GLi、2000GLi 型轿车采用的有德国博世公司生产的由低压叶片泵和高压齿轮泵组成的 EKP10 型双级电动燃油泵；红旗 CA7200E 型轿车采用的齿轮式电动燃油泵。

（2）电动燃油泵的组成及原理

① 涡轮式电动燃油泵。如图 2-42 所示，涡轮式电动燃油泵主要由燃油泵电动机、涡轮泵、出油阀、卸压阀等组成。油箱内循燃油进入燃油泵内的进油室前，首先经过滤网初步过滤。

涡轮泵主要由叶轮、叶片、泵壳体和泵盖组成，叶轮安装在燃油泵电动机的转子轴上。油泵电动机通电时，燃油泵电动机驱动涡轮泵叶轮旋转，由于离心力的作用，使叶轮周围小

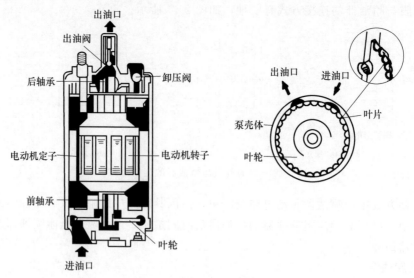

图 2-42 涡轮式电动燃油泵

槽内的叶片贴紧泵壳,并将燃油从进油室带往出油室。由于进油室燃油不断被带走,所以形成一定的真空度,将油箱内的燃油经进油口吸入;而出油室燃油不断增多,燃油压力升高,当油压达到一定值时,则顶开出油阀经出油口输出。出油阀还可在燃油泵不工作时,阻止燃油倒流回油箱,这样可保持油路中有一定的残余压力,便于下次启动。

燃油泵工作中,燃油流经燃油泵内腔,对燃油泵电动机起到冷却和润滑的作用。燃油泵不工作时,出油阀关闭,使油管内保持一定的残余压力,以便于发动机启动和防止气阻产生。卸压阀安装在进油室和出油室之间,当燃油泵输出油压达到 0.4MPa 时,卸压阀开启,使油泵内的进、出油室连通,燃油泵工作只能使燃油在其内部循环,以防止输油压力过高。

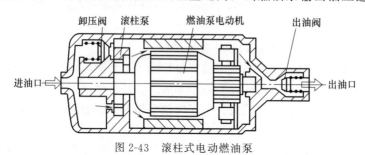

图 2-43 滚柱式电动燃油泵

涡轮式电动燃油泵具有泵油量大、泵油压力较高(可达 600kPa 以上)、供油压力稳定、运转噪声小、使用寿命长等优点,所以应用最为广泛。

② 滚柱式电动燃油泵。如图 2-43 所示,滚柱式电动燃油泵主要由燃油泵电动机、滚柱式燃油泵、出油阀、卸压阀等组成。滚柱式电动燃油泵的输油压力波动较大,在出油端必须安装阻尼减振器,这使燃油泵的体积增大,所以一般都安装在油箱外面,即属外置式。

阻尼减振器主要由膜片和弹簧组成,它可吸收燃油压力波的能量,降低压力波动,以便提高喷油控制精度。

滚柱泵的工作原理如图 2-44 所示。装有滚柱的转子呈偏心状,置于泵壳内,由直流电动

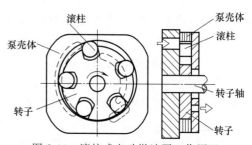

图 2-44 滚柱式电动燃油泵工作原理

机驱动，当转子旋转时，位于转子槽内的滚柱在离心力的作用下，紧压在泵体内表面上，对周围起密封作用，在相邻两个滚柱之间形成了工作腔。在燃油泵运转过程中，工作腔转过出油口后，其容积不断增大，形成一定的真空度。当转到与进油口连通时将燃油吸入；而吸满燃油的工作腔转过进油口后，其容积又不断减小，使燃油压力提高，受压燃油流过电动机，从出油口输出。出油阀和卸压阀的作用与涡轮式电动燃油泵相同。

3. 燃油压力调节器

（1）燃油压力调节器的作用和类型

① 作用。燃油压力调节器的作用就是保持输油管内燃油压力与进气管内气体压力的差值恒定，即根据进气管内压力的变化来调节燃油压力。

② 类型。根据安装位置分为两种，一种与油轨（也称燃油分配管）相连，特点是带回油管；另一种在油箱中，特点是无回油管。

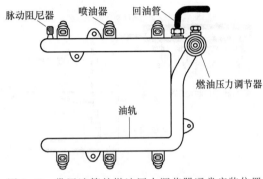

图 2-45 带回油管的燃油压力调节器通常安装位置

（2）燃油压力调节器结构与原理

① 带回油管的燃油压力调节器，其安装位置如图 2-45 所示。

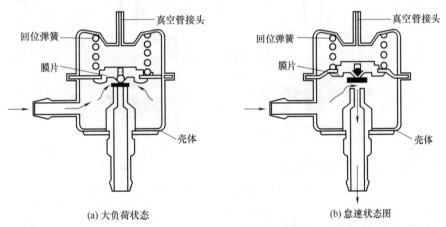

图 2-46 燃油压力调节器工作原理

工作原理如图 2-46 所示，供油系统的燃油从油压调节器进油口进入调节器油腔，燃油压力作用到与阀体相连的金属膜片上。当燃油压力升高使油压作用到膜片上的压力与真空管作用到膜片上的吸力之和超过调节器弹簧时的弹力时，油压推动膜片向上拱曲，调节器阀门打开，部分燃油从回油口油管流回油箱，使燃油压力降低。如图 2-46（b）所示，当燃油压力降低到调节器控制的系统油压时，球阀关闭，使系统油压保持一定压力值不变。当燃油油压作用到膜片上的压力与真空管作用到膜片上的吸力之和低于调节器弹簧时的弹力时，调节器阀门关闭，不回油。所

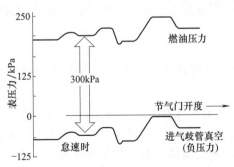

图 2-47 进气歧管内压力、燃油分配管内压力与节气门开度的变化关系

以燃油压力调节器的作用是保持系统油压与大气压差恒定的作用。如图 2-47 所示为进气歧管内压力、燃油分配管内压力与节气门开度的变化关系。

② 无回油管的燃油压力调节器。无回油管的燃油压力调节器安装位置与结构总成如图 2-48 所示，它与油泵总成安装在一起，结构与工作原理如图 2-49 所示，直接将系统多余的油压泄回到油箱，这种无回油管的燃油压力调节器一般在燃油总管上装设一个燃油脉动阻尼器来进一步调节系统油压。

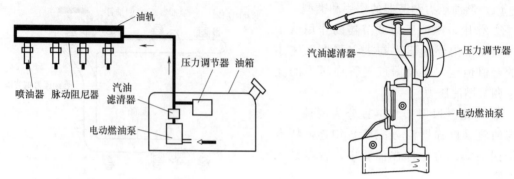

图 2-48 无回油管的燃油压力调节器总成

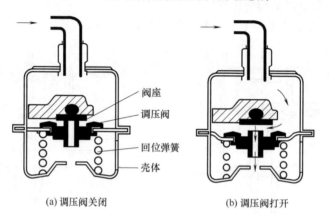

图 2-49 无回油管的燃油压力调节器结构与工作原理

（五）发动机断油控制过程

断油控制是指在某些特殊工况下，燃油喷射系统暂时中断喷油器喷油，以满足发动机运行的特殊要求。断油控制包括发动机减速断油控制、限速断油控制、清除溢流、断油控制和升挡断油控制，控制过程如图 2-50 所示。

1. 减速断油控制

减速断油控制是指当发动机在高转速运转过程中突然减速时，ECU 自动控制喷油器中断燃油喷射。

当高速行驶的汽车突然松开油门踏板减速时，发动机将在汽车惯性力的作用下高速旋转，由于节气门已经关闭，进入汽缸的空气很少，因此，如不停止喷油，混合气将会很浓而导致燃烧不完全，有害气体的排放量将急剧增加。减速断油的目的就是节约燃油，并减少有害气体的排放量。

减速断油控制的过程如图 2-50 所示，ECU 根据节气门位置、发动机转速和冷却液温度

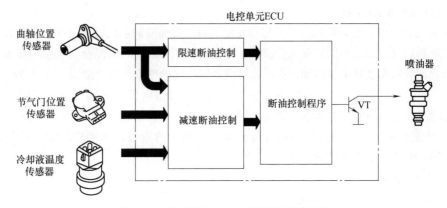

图 2-50 限速断油与减速断油控制示意图

等传感器信号,判断是否满足以下三个减速断油控制条件:
① 节气门位置传感器的怠速触点闭合;
② 冷却液温度已经达到正常温度;
③ 发动机转速高于某一转速。

当三个条件全部满足时,ECU 立即发出停止喷油指令,控制喷油器停止喷油。当喷油停止、发动机转速降低到燃油复供转速或节气门开启(怠速触点断开)时,ECU 再发出指令控制喷油器恢复喷油,控制曲线如图 2-51 所示。

燃油停供转速和复供转速与冷却液温度和发动机负荷有关,由 ECU 根据发动机温度、负荷等参数确定。冷却液温度越低,发动机负荷越大(如空调接通),燃油停供转速和复供转速就越高。

2. 限速断油控制

限速断油控制是指当发动机转速超过允许的极限转速时,ECU 立即控制喷油器中断燃油喷射。燃油喷射式发动机采用限速断油控制的目的是防止发动机超过限速运转而损坏机件。

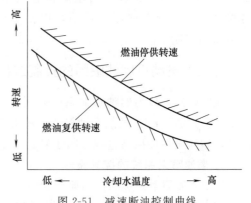

图 2-51 减速断油控制曲线

发动机工作时,转速越高,曲柄连杆机构的离心力就越大。当离心力过大时,发动机就有"飞车"而损坏的危险。因此,每台发动机都有一个极限转速值,一般为 6000~7000r/min。桑塔纳 2000GLi、2000GSi、3000 型轿车为 6400r/min,捷达 AT、GTX 型轿车为 6800r/min。

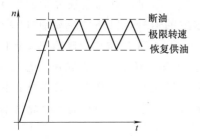

图 2-52 限速断油控制曲线

在发动机运转过程中,ECU 随时都将曲轴位置传感器测得的发动机实际转速与存储器中存储的极限转速进行比较。当实际转速达到或超过安全转速 80~100r/min 时,ECU 就发出停止喷油指令,控制喷油器停止喷油,限制发动机转速进一步升高。控制曲线如图 2-52 所示。

喷油器停止喷油后,发动机转速将降低。当发动机转速下降至低于安全转速 80~100r/min 时,ECU 将控制喷油器恢复喷油。

3. 清除溢流断油控制

在装备燃油喷射式发动机的汽车上启动发动机时，燃油喷射系统将向发动机供给较浓的混合气，以便顺利启动。如果多次启动未能成功，那么淤积在汽缸内的浓混合气就会浸湿火花塞，使其不能跳火而导致发动机不能启动。火花塞被混合气浸湿的现象称为"溢流"或"淹缸"。

当出现溢流现象时，发动机将不能正常启动。这时可将发动机油门踏板踩到底，接通启动开关启动发动机，ECU 自动控制喷油器停止喷油，以便排除汽缸内的燃油蒸气，使火花塞干燥，并能跳火，这种控制称为清除溢流断油控制。清除溢流断油控制的条件是：

① 点火开关处于启动位置；
② 节气门全开；
③ 发动机转速低于 500r/min。

只有在三个条件同时满足时，断油控制系统才能进入清除溢流状态工作。

由此可见，在启动燃油喷射式发动机时，不必踩下加速踏板，直接接通启动开关即可。否则，断油控制系统可能进入清除溢流状态而使发动机无法启动。

当接通启动开关启动机运转而发动机不能启动时，可利用断油控制系统清除溢流的功能先将溢流清除，然后再进行启动。

4. 升挡断油控制

在电控自动变速器汽车上，在行驶过程中，如果变速器需自动升挡时，变速器 ECU 会向发动机 ECU 发出扭矩传感器信号，发动机 ECU 接收到这个信号后，立即发出指令，使个别汽缸停止喷油，以便降低发动机转速，减轻换挡冲击，这种控制称为升挡断油控制。

（六）发动机燃油喷射的控制过程

众所周知，D 型燃油喷射系统采用歧管压力式传感器 MAP；L 型燃油喷射系统采用空气流量传感器 AFS。虽然发动机燃油喷射系统采用传感器和执行器的数量与形式各不相同，但是，燃油喷射的控制过程大同小异。

1. 燃油喷射系统的控制原理

L 型燃油喷射系统的控制原理如图 2-53 所示。

在发动机工作过程中，凸轮轴位置传感器 CIS 向 ECU 提供反映活塞上止点位置的信号，以便计算确定喷油提前角（提前时间）；曲轴位置传感器 CPS 向 ECU 提供反映发动机曲轴转速和转角的信号，空气流量传感器 AFS（或进气歧管绝对压力传感器 MAP）向 ECU 提供反映进气量多少的信号，ECU 根据这两个信号计算喷油量（喷油时间）；节气门位置传感器 TPS 向 ECU 提供反映发动机负荷大小的信号，ECU 根据 TPS 信号确定增加或减少喷油量；水温传感器 CTS 向 ECU 提供发动机冷却液温度信号，以便计算确定喷油量的修正值；氧传感器 EGO 向 ECU 提供反映发动机可燃混合气浓度的信号，以便增减喷油量的大小，实现空燃比反馈控制，降低废气排放量；车速传感器 VSS 向 ECU 提供反映汽车车速的信号，以便判断发动机运行在怠速状态（节气门关闭、车速为零）还是运行在减速状态（节气门关闭、车速不为零），从而确定是否停止供油；点火启动开关信号包括点火开关接通信号 IGN 和启动开关接通信号 STA，用于 ECU 判断发动机工作状态（启动状态或正常工作状态）并运行相应的控制程序。

例如，当点火开关接通时，ECU 的 IGN 端子将从点火开关接收到一个高电平信号，此

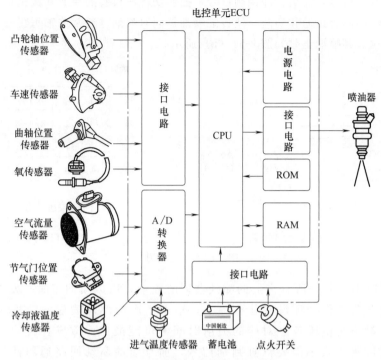

图 2-53 L 型燃油喷射系统的控制原理

时 ECU 将自动接通电动燃油泵电路使油泵工作 1~2s，以便发动机启动时油路中具有足够的燃油；当点火开关接通启动挡时，ECU 的 STA 端子将从点火开关接收到一个高电平信号，此时 ECU 将控制运行启动程序，增大喷油量，以便启动发动机。

蓄电池电压信号 U_{BAT} 就是汽车电源电压信号，蓄电池正极柱经导线直接与 ECU 的电源电压端子连接，不受点火开关和其他开关控制。当电源电压变化时，ECU 将改变喷油脉冲宽度，修正喷油器的喷油持续时间；当发动机停止工作时，蓄电池将向 ECU 和存储器等提供 5~20mA 电流，以便存储器保存故障代码等信息而不致丢失；在点火开关断开时，对于采用步进电机的控制系统，ECU 还将控制燃油喷射主继电器继续接通 2s，使步进电机回到初始位置。各种传感器的信号输入 ECU 后，ECU 根据数学计算和逻辑判断结果，发出脉冲信号指令控制喷油器喷油。

2. 喷射正时控制

喷油正时就是指喷油器在什么时刻（相对于发动机曲轴转角位置）开始喷油。

对于采用多点间歇性燃油喷射方式的发动机来说，按照喷油时刻与曲轴转角的关系可分为同步喷射和异步喷射两类。

同步喷射是指发动机各缸工作循环，在既定的曲轴位置进行喷油，同步喷油有规律性。

异步喷射是指喷油与发动机的工作不同步，无规律性，是在同步喷油的基础上，为改善发动机的性能额外增加的喷油。如发动机冷启动和急加速时的临时性喷油。

在同步喷射发动机中，又分为同时喷射、分组喷射和顺序喷射三种基本类型。

（1）同时喷射正时控制

采用同时喷射方式的喷油器的控制电路和控制程序都比较简单，其控制电路如图 2-54（a）所示，从图中可以看出，所有的喷油器是并联的。发动机电脑（ECU）根据曲轴位置传感器产生的基准信号，发出脉冲控制信号，控制功率三极管的导通和截止，从而控制各喷油器电磁线圈电路同时接通和切断，使各缸喷油器同时喷油。通常曲轴每转一转，各缸喷油器同时喷射一次。其喷油正时如图2-54（b）所示。

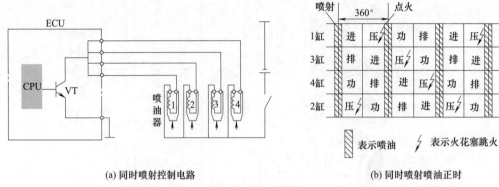

图 2-54 同时喷射

由于这种喷射方式是所有汽缸的喷油器同时喷油，所以喷油正时与发动机进气、压缩、做功、排气等工作循环没有什么关系，早期生产的燃油喷射发动机大多采用同时喷射方式。其缺点是由于各缸对应的喷射时间不可能最佳，造成各缸的混合气形成不均匀。但这种喷射方式不需要汽缸判别信号，而且喷油驱动回路通用性好，其电路结构与软件都较简单。

（2）分组喷射正时控制

分组喷射一般是把所有汽缸喷油器分成2~4组。发动机电脑控制各组喷油器轮流交替进行燃油喷射。四缸发动机一般将喷油器分为两组，其控制电路如图2-55（a）所示，每一工作循环中，各喷油器均喷射一次或两次。图2-55（b）为分组喷射的正时图。

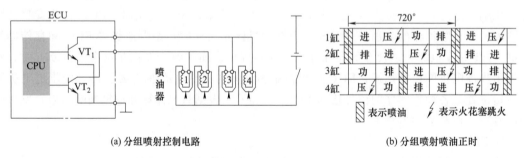

图 2-55 分组喷射

相对于同时喷射的发动机而言，采用分组喷射的发动机在性能方面有所提高，主要体现在能有更多的汽缸在合适的时候喷射燃油，改善了混合气的均匀性。

（3）顺序喷射正时控制

顺序燃油喷射也叫独立燃油喷射。曲轴每转两圈，各缸的喷油器按照发动机的点火顺序，依次在最合适的曲轴转角位置进行燃油喷射。顺序燃油喷射系统的控制电路如图2-56（a）所示。各缸喷油器分别由发动机电脑的一个功率放大电路控制。功率放大器回路的数量与喷油器的数目相等。

采用顺序燃油喷射方式的发动机电脑需要"知道"在哪一时刻该向哪一缸喷射燃油，因

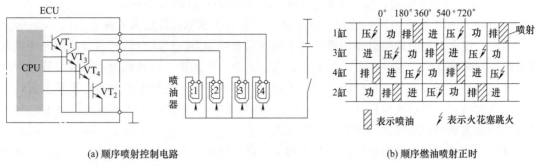

(a) 顺序喷射控制电路　　　　　　　　(b) 顺序燃油喷射正时

图 2-56　顺序喷射

此必须具备汽缸识别信号，通常叫作判缸信号，该信号多来自曲轴位置传感器和凸轮轴位置传感器。采用顺序燃油喷射控制时，应具有正时和缸序两个控制功能。发动机电脑工作时，通过曲轴位置传感器输入的信号就可以知道活塞在上止点前的具体位置，再与凸轮轴位置传感器的判缸信号相配合，可以确定是哪一缸在上止点，同时还可以判定是处于压缩行程还是排气行程。因此当发动机电脑根据判缸信号、曲轴位置信号，确定该缸处于排气行程且活塞运动至上止点前某一位置时，便输出喷油控制指令，接通喷油器电磁线圈的搭铁电路，该缸喷油器即开始进行燃油喷射。图 2-56（b）为顺序燃油喷射正时图。

（七）喷油脉冲宽度的控制

喷油脉冲宽度控制的目的是控制喷油量使发动机燃烧时混合气的浓度符合发动机运行工况的需求。喷油脉冲宽度的控制实际上是由发动机电脑根据发动机运转工况及各种影响因素进行计算、最后输出喷油脉冲控制信号的过程。

喷油脉冲宽度的控制大致可分为两大类：

发动机启动过程中的控制。它不是根据吸入发动机的空气质量计算得出喷油脉冲宽度，而是一种很粗放的控制；

发动机启动后正常运行时的控制。它是根据发动机吸入的空气质量计算得出喷油脉冲宽度，这种控制方式比较精确，形成的混合气浓度比较理想。

1. 启动时喷油脉冲宽度的控制

发动机启动时，发动机电脑（ECU）主要根据启动信号状态或发动机的转速（如 400r/min 以下），判定发动机是否处于启动工况。

冷车启动时，由于发动机冷却液的温度、发动机的转速都很低，喷入的燃油不易雾化，所以会引起混合气变稀。为了能够产生足够浓度的可燃混合气，使发动机顺利启动，在启动时应该延长喷射脉冲宽度，即增大燃油喷射量。

启动时一般不根据吸入的空气质量来计算喷油脉冲宽度，而是根据当时发动机冷却液的温度、自启动开始累积的转数以及启动时间等来确定喷油脉冲宽度，一般情况下，启动时喷油脉冲宽度可由下式确定，即

启动喷油脉冲宽度（ms）＝由发动机冷却液温度决定的启动喷油脉冲宽度（ms）＋无效喷射时间（ms）

发动机冷却液温度越低，燃油越不易雾化，喷油脉冲宽度就应该越长。在发动机冷启动中，常采用以下两种方式来增加喷油脉冲宽度。

① 通过冷启动喷油器，往进气歧管中喷入一部分附加燃油来实现。
② 由发动机电脑（ECU）直接控制喷油器延长其喷油脉冲宽度来实现。

当前，很多电控燃油喷射发动机已经不设冷启动喷油器，启动时的燃油增量由发动机电脑直接控制喷油器来实现。在启动工况时，为了对混合气加浓，同时也为了在进气管与汽缸内形成均匀的可燃混合气，尽可能避免燃油对火花塞的浸润，就要求喷油器在发动机每转一转进行多次喷射（异步喷射）。因为对喷油器的控制是通过发动机电脑内部的控制电路与软件的功能来实现的，所以这种控制系统更复杂一些。

这种燃油喷射系统主要根据发动机冷却液温度、转速以及自启动开始累积的转数、时间等参数控制喷油器的持续喷油时间。

2. 启动后喷油器喷油脉冲宽度的确定

（1）启动后喷油器的喷油脉冲宽度

发动机启动后正常运转时，喷油器的喷油脉冲宽度是以一个进气行程中吸入汽缸的空气质量为基准计算出来的。发动机电脑根据空气流量传感器或进气压力传感器、冷却液温度传感器、进气温度传感器、大气压力传感器和发动机转速传感器等输入的信号，计算出一个进气行程中吸入汽缸的空气质量和基本的喷射脉冲宽度，再综合考虑发动机的动力性、经济性、排放性等因素，对基本喷油脉冲宽度进行修正，即按照发动机电脑内存储的针对各种工况的最理想目标空燃比来决定喷油脉冲宽度。目标空燃比、进气质量和所需燃油量的关系如下：

$$目标空燃比(A/F) = \frac{每个进气行程中进入汽缸的空气质量(g)}{每次燃烧所需要的燃油量(g)}$$

依据上式，根据每一进气行程中吸入汽缸的空气质量（g）与目标空燃比（A/F），就可以计算出每次燃烧所需要的燃油质量（g），即

$$每次燃烧所需要的燃油质量(g) = \frac{每个进气行程中进入汽缸的空气质量(g)}{目标空燃比(A/F)}$$

喷油器的每次喷油量仅与喷油器的开启时间成正比，所以在发动机的实际控制过程中，每次燃烧所需要的燃油量，是通过控制喷油器的开启时间，即喷油脉冲宽度来实现的。

由目标空燃比决定的喷油脉冲宽度可用下式计算，即

喷油脉冲宽度(ms) = 基本喷油脉冲宽度(ms) × 基本喷油脉冲宽度修正系数 + 喷油器无效喷油时间（ms）

不同燃烧喷射系统的软件设计不同，计算方式可能也有所不同。

（2）基本喷油脉冲宽度的确定

基本喷油脉冲宽度是为了实现目标空燃比，利用空气流量传感器（或进气压力传感器）、发动机转速传感器的输入信号计算出喷油脉冲宽度。根据所采用的空气流量传感器（或进气压力传感器）类型的不同，确定基本燃油喷射脉冲宽度的过程也有所差异。

采用翼片式空气流量传感器、卡门涡旋式空气流量传感器和进气压力传感器的电控燃油喷射系统，其基本喷油脉冲宽度是发动机电脑根据空气流量传感器和发动机转速传感器的信号以及设定的目标空燃比（A/F），再辅以进气温度传感器及大气压力传感器的修正信号来确定的。上述传感器在发动机每一个工作循环内检测的进气量越大，喷油器的喷油脉冲宽度也就越大。

（3）喷油修正量的确定

① 与进气温度有关的修正。因为冷空气的密度比热空气的密度大，因此，在其他因素相同时，吸入发动机的空气质量随空气温度的升高而减少，为了避免混合气随温度升高而逐

渐加浓，发动机电脑将根据进气温度对基本喷油脉冲宽度进行修正，即进气温度越高，喷油器的基本喷油脉冲宽度就越小。

② 与大气压力有关的修正。因为大气压力和密度随着海拔高度的增加而降低，所以汽车在高原地区行驶时传感器检测到同样的控制流量时，实际进入发动机的空气质量流量降低。为了避免混合气过浓与油耗过高，应根据大气压力传感器输入的信号，对基本喷油脉冲宽度进行修正。对采用翼片式、卡门涡旋式空气流量传感器和进气压力传感器的大气压力传感器检测到的大气压力越低，喷油器的基本喷油脉冲宽度越小。

一般将汽车从平原开到高原后，如果出现油耗增大，尾气排放有害物增大甚至冒黑烟的现象时，就应该检查是否是大气压力修正系统有问题，导致混合气过浓引起上述故障。

采用热丝式或热膜式空气流量传感器检测进气量时，由于传感器本身是质量流量传感器，因而不需要进行温度及大气压力的修正，其基本喷油脉冲宽度就是发动机电脑根据空气流量传感器和发动机转速传感器的信号以及设定的目标空燃比来确定的。发动机每一个工作循环内空气流量传感器检测的进气量越大，则喷油器的基本喷油脉冲宽度也就越大。

③ 与发动机温度相关的喷油脉冲宽度的修正。如图 2-57 所示为发动机 ECU 根据冷却液温度传感器等相应传感器给来的信号确定对喷油量的修正，从图中可以看出，随着发动机温度的升高，喷油量的修正在减小。下面分三种情况介绍与发动机温度相关的燃油修正。

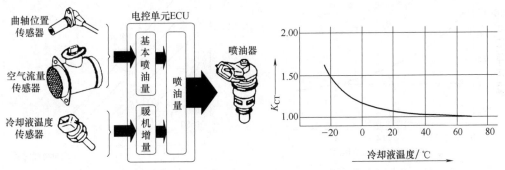

图 2-57 ECU 根据冷却液温度信号修正

a. 刚启动后喷油脉冲宽度的修正。在发动机冷启动后的数十秒内，由于空气流动速度低，发动机温度低，所以燃油的雾化能力很差，此时应对喷油脉冲宽度进行修正。发动机温度越冷，燃油增量越大，需修正的时间也越长。发动机冷启动后的增量修正，实际是对此时燃油供给不足的一种补偿措施。

b. 暖机时喷油脉冲宽度的修正。发动机启动后，为了尽快使发动机、三元催化转换器和氧传感器达到正常工作温度，使控制系统进入闭环工作状态，需要对暖机时的喷油脉冲宽度进行修正，即增加燃油喷射量，这也是对发动机冷态时燃油供给不足的一种补偿措施。在进行启动后燃油增量修正的同时，也进行暖机燃油增量修正。一直要持续到冷却液温度达到规定值才会停止。

c. 高温时喷油脉冲宽度的修正。一般汽车在高速行驶时，由于行驶中风冷作用且燃油一直在流动，所以燃油温度不会太高，在 50℃ 左右。但如果此时发动机熄火，燃油停止流动，此时发动机就会成为热源，使燃油温度升高，一旦达到 80～100℃，油箱和油管内的燃油就会出现沸腾，产生燃油蒸气。这样在喷油器喷射的燃油中，因还有蒸气而使喷油量减少造成混合气变稀。为了解决燃油蒸气引起的混合气稀化问题，应采取高温启动时燃油喷射脉冲宽度修正的措施。一般是当冷却液温度上升到设定值（如100℃）以上时，进行高温燃油增量修正。

④ 蓄电池电压的修正。喷油器的电磁线圈为感应性负载，其电流按指数规律变化，因此当喷油脉冲到来时，喷油器阀门开启和关闭都将滞后一定时间，蓄电池电压的高低对喷油器开启滞后的时间影响较大，电压越低，开启滞后时间越长，在开启和关闭过程中的喷射为无效喷射期，所以要考虑蓄电池电压变化对无效喷油时间的影响，对喷油时间进行加以修正，即当蓄电池电压降低时，增加喷油脉冲宽度；当蓄电池电压升高时，减小喷油脉冲宽度，如图2-58所示。

⑤ 加速时喷油增量的修正。当汽车加速时，为了保证发动机能够输出足够的转矩，改善加速性能，必须增大喷油量。在发动机运转过程中，ECU将根据节气门位置传感器信号和进气量传感器信号的变化速率，判定发动机是否处于加速工况。汽车加速时，节气门突然开大，节气门位置传感器信号的变化速率增大，与此同时，空气流量突然增大，歧管压力突然增大，进气量传感器信号突然升高，ECU接收到这些信号后，立即发出增大喷油量的控制指令，使混合气加浓。燃油增量比例大小与加浓时间取决于加速时发动机冷却液的温度，如图2-59所示。冷却液温度越低，燃油增量比例越大，加浓持续时间越长。

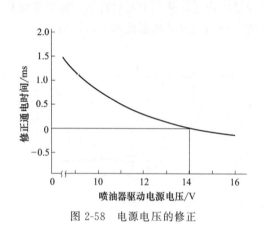

图2-58 电源电压的修正

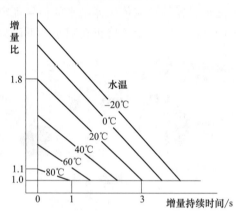

图2-59 喷油修正量与冷却液温度的关系

三、项目实施

（一）实施要求

丰田5A、AJR发动机台架；汽车；汽车万用表、诊断仪。

（二）实施步骤

1. 发动机燃油喷射系统传感器的检修

（1）空气流量传感器的检测

空气流量传感器既是一种精密部件，也是供气系统最重要的部件。当其出现故障时，ECU就接收不到正确的进气量信号来控制喷油量，混合气就会过浓或过稀，从而导致发动机运转失常。检修或拆卸空气流量传感器时，应细心操作、切忌碰撞，以免损伤其零件。

对于现代的轿车而言，大部分都采用了热丝或热膜式空气流量传感器，故这里只向大家介绍该种传感器的检测知识。

各型热丝式与热膜式空气流量传感器的检修方法基本相同，现在以桑塔纳轿车用热膜式空气流量传感器为例，说明其检修方法。

桑塔纳2000GSi轿车AJR发动机结构及电路图如图2-60所示。

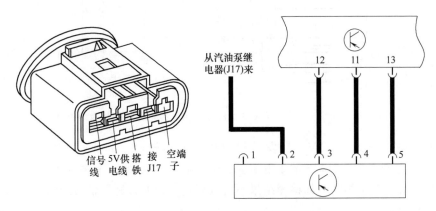

图 2-60　桑塔纳 2000AJR 空气流量计

① 检测电源电压。检测电源电压时，拔下传感器线束插头，接通点火开关，用万用表直流电压挡检测传感器插头上电源端子与搭铁端子之间的电压。

检测桑塔纳轿车空气流量传感器的电源电压时，拔下传感器上的5端子线束插头（编者注：代号为1的端子为备用端子，没有连接导线），如图2-60所示，然后接通点火开关，检测线束插头上端子2与发动机缸体之间的电压；规定值应不低于11.5V。如果电压为零，说明燃油泵继电器触点未闭合或电源线路断路，需要检修燃油泵继电器或电源线路。

② 检测传感器的信号电压。检查信号电压时，拔下传感器线束插头，将蓄电池正负极分别与传感器插座上的电源端子和搭铁端子连接，用万用表直流电压挡测量信号输出端的电压；当向传感器空气入口吹气时，信号电压应随之升高。

③ 就车检查热丝式流量传感器的自洁功能。先将空气流量传感器的线束插头与插座插好，然后启动发动机并将转速升高到2500r/min以上，再使发动机怠速运转。拆下空气流量传感器空气入口一端的进气管，断开点火开关，与此同时从传感器空气入口处观察热丝能否在发动机熄火5s后红热并持续1s时间（编者注：热膜式以及保持温度高于200℃热丝式流量传感器无此功能）。

(2) 歧管压力传感器的检修

各型汽车歧管压力传感器的检修方法大同小异，下面以威驰轿车用歧管压力传感器的检修方法为例说明。该歧管压力传感器的安装位置及电路连接如图2-61所示。

① 检查真空软管连接情况。仔细检查MAP的真空软管与节气门体的连接情况，如连接不良或漏气，就会影响传感器性能并直接影响发动机工作，可视情修理或更换真空软管。

② 检测传感器电源电压。当点火开关接通时，检测传感器1端子上的电压应为4.5～5.5V。如电压为零，再检测ECU线束插头9端子上的电压，如电压为4.5～5.5V，说明传感器电源线断路或插头松动。

③ 检测传感器信号电压。传感器输出的信号电压可用高阻抗数字式万用表直流电压挡进行检测。传感器插座上有1、2、3三个端子，当点火开关接通，发动机未启动时，检测输

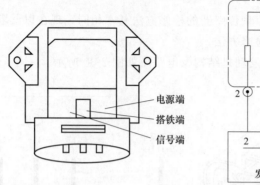

图 2-61 威驰轿车丰田 5A 发动机进气压力传感器的结构及电路图

出端子 3 上的电压应为 4~5V；当发动机热机怠速运转时，3 端子电压应下降到 1.5~2.1V；当节气门开度增大时，3 端子电压应逐渐升高。如检测 ECU 线束插头 1 端子上的电压，则应与 3 端子电压相同。如检测结果不符合规定，说明传感器信号线断路、插头松动或传感器内部有故障。

④ 检测传感器负极导线连接情况。用万用表电阻挡检测传感器 2 端子与发动机缸体之间的电阻值应当小于 0.5Ω，如阻值过大，说明传感器负极导线断路或 ECU 插头连接不良。

(3) 节气门位置传感器的检修

用于电控汽车上的节气门位置传感器承担"电子加速泵"的作用。如果拆除节气门位置传感器或其发生故障，发动机仍正常工作，但是会出现加速迟缓的现象。

① 触点式节气门位置传感器的检修。检修触点开关式 TPS 时，可用万用表测量传感器信号输出端子的输出电压和触点接触电阻进行判断。

检测输出电压时，将传感器正常连接，接通点火开关，输出电压应为高电平或低电平，且当节气门轴转动时，输出电压应当交替变化（由低电平"0"变为高电平"1"或由高电平"1"变为低电平"0"）。

检测触点状态时，拔下传感器线束插头，测量触点接触电阻应小于 0.5Ω，如果阻值过大，说明触点烧蚀而接触不良，应予修磨或更换传感器。

② 可变电阻式节气门位置传感器检测。检修可变电阻式 TPS，可用万用表检测传感器的电阻值和电压值进行判断。

a. 带怠速触点可变电阻式节气门位置传感器的检测。如图 2-20 所示，检测节气门位置传感器的电阻。首先拔下传感器的线束插头，然后，用万用表检测 IDL 与 E 端子之间的电阻值，在节气门全闭时电阻值应<0.5Ω；当节气门打开后，测量 IDL 与 E 端子之间的电阻值应为 ∞；用万用表检测信号输出端 V_{AT} 与搭铁端子 E 之间的阻值，应随着节气门开度的加大阻值增加，且在数值变化的过程中不能存在∞的现象。如果在节气门开度变化的过程中，V_{AT} 与搭铁端子 E 之间的阻值出现了阻值为∞的现象，说明滑背与镀膜电阻接触不良，需要更换传感器。

检测传感器的电源端 V_c 与搭铁端 E 之间的阻值，阻值应为 1000~10000Ω，如果阻值为∞，说明镀膜电阻断路。需要更换传感器。

检测传感器线束。用万用表电阻挡检测线束电阻时，断开点火开关，拔下电控单元和传感器线束插头，检测两插头上相应端子之间的导线电阻值应当小于 0.5Ω。如果阻值过大或为无穷大,说明线束与端子接触不良或断路,应予以修理。

检测电源电压与信号电压。检测时,接通点火开关,用万用表直流电压挡检测传感器的电源电压应为5.0V。当节气门关闭时,检测传感器的信号电压应为0.5~1.0V;当节气门开度逐渐增大时,信号电压应随之升高;当节气门全开时,信号电压应为4.0~4.8V。如果检测结果与此不符,则需更换传感器。

b. 不带怠速触点的可变电阻式节气门位置传感器的检测。丰田5A发动机采用了不带怠速触点的可变电阻式节气门位置传感器,其检测的方法项目与带怠速触点可变电阻式节气门位置传感器的检测相比较,只是少了触点的检测,其它检测内容都一样,这里不再叙述。

(4) 磁感应式曲轴与凸轮轴位置传感器的检修

① 曲轴位置传感器的检测。各型磁感应式传感器的检测方法基本相同,以桑塔纳2000GSi、威驰轿车丰田5A发动机所用磁感应式曲轴位置传感器检测为例介绍。

a. 检测传感线圈电阻值。如图2-62所示分别为桑塔纳轿车AJR发动机与丰田5A发动机曲轴位置传感器电路图,拔下传感器线束插头,对于AJR发动机检测传感器的2端子与3端子之间的电阻,对于丰田5A发动机检测传感器的1端子与2端子之间的电阻,正常情况下,都应该有一定的数值,只是车型不同,线圈的阻值有所不同,同时在测量的过程中,当检测状态(热态、冷态)不同时,同一车型传感器线圈的阻值也会不同,但是所测得的结果不可能为0或∞,否则说明传感器线圈短路或断路。对于桑塔纳AJR发动机还要检测1端子与3端子、1端子与2端子之间的电阻值,电阻值应为∞,检测1端子与搭铁之间的电阻值应不超过1.5Ω,检测2端子与63端子之间的电阻以及3端子与56端子之间的电阻,电阻值均不能超过1.5Ω。对于丰田5A发动机还要检测1端子与5端子、2端子与13端子之间的电阻值,电阻值均不能超过1.5Ω。

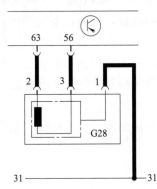
(a) 桑塔纳AJR发动机曲轴位置传感器

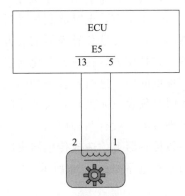
(b) 威驰丰田5A发动机

图2-62 曲轴位置传感器电路图

b. 检测传感器磁路气隙。用非导磁厚薄规测量信号转子与传感线圈磁头之间的气隙,气隙大小应为0.2~0.4mm,气隙不符合规定则需要更换传感器总成。

c. 磁电式曲轴位置传感器信号电压输出的检测。关闭点火开关,断开曲轴位置传感器与汽车电控单元的连接插头,用万用表的交流电压挡的两个表笔分别抵触在传感器的两个端子上,此时启动发动机,万用表应显示交流电压的变化,否则传感器有故障,应予以更换。

② 凸轮轴位置传感器的检测。下面主要介绍桑塔纳轿车AJR发动机所应用的霍尔式凸轮轴位置传感器的检测内容,威驰丰田5A发动机所采用的凸轮轴位置传感器应用的是磁电式

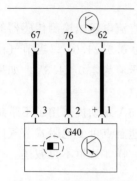

图 2-63 桑塔纳霍尔式凸轮轴位置传感器

的，检测内容与上述磁电式曲轴位置传感器一样，这里不再叙述。

如图 2-63 所示，为桑塔纳霍尔式凸轮轴位置传感器电路图。

接通点火开关，用万用表的电压挡测试 1 端子与 3 端子之间的电压值，电压应为 5V，如果电压过低或为零伏，说明线束存在断路、短路或控制单元 ECU 有故障；若高于 5V 传感器损坏。

当断开点火开关后，用万用表的电阻挡检查传感器 1 端子与 ECU 的 62 端子、传感器的 2 端子与 ECU 的 76 端子、传感器的 3 端子与 ECU 的 67 端子的电阻值，各导线间电阻值应不大于 1.5Ω。如果电阻过大或为无穷大，说明线束接触不良或导线断路，应进行维修或更换线束。

再用万用表电阻挡继续检查传感器连接器端子 1 与 2 和 3 端子间的电阻，或检查 ECU 的 62 端子与 76 和 67 端子间电阻，测得的电阻均应为无穷大。如果阻值不是无穷大，说明导线存在短路，应进行更换。

(5) 氧传感器的使用与检测

① 氧传感器的使用。氧传感器有多种形式，除结构上有差异外，在外形上也有所不同，其接线有一根、二根或者三根、四根。后两种是装有加热元件的加热式氧传感器。检测时需要使用数字式万用表或示波器来检测输出电压信号随混合气浓度变化的情况，以及 ECU 对电压信号的响应。发动机在正常工作温度时，氧传感器如不能随混合气浓度输出相应的电压，则证明失效，需要进行更换。氧传感器失效会导致混合气过浓或过稀，产生怠速不稳、油耗过大、排放过高等故障，此时发动机自诊断系统将点亮汽车仪表板上的发动机报警灯，提示要立即检修。

当混合气浓时，氧传感器输出电压大于 0.45V 时，电脑收到信号后减少喷油量；混合气稀时输出电压小于 0.45V，电脑收到信号后增加喷油量，从而控制空燃比，在有些高档车上配有两个传感器，在三元催化转换器前后方各装一个，在三元催化转换器后方装的传感器称为副氧传感器，它是作为装在三元催化转换器前端的主氧传感器的补充。电脑能够根据这两个氧传感器的提供的信号进行比较来判断三元催化转换器的好坏。当电脑探测到三元催化转换器中的故障时，仪表三元催化转换器故障灯会提示驾驶员。

氧传感器出现故障一般有两种原因：一是已到使用期限；二是碳烟、铅化物、硅胶、机油等物质沉积在氧传感器上，造成传感器失效。

氧传感器的基本电路如图 2-64 所示。

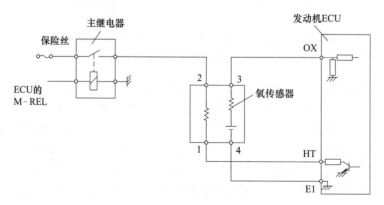

图 2-64 氧传感器的电路

② 氧传感器加热器电阻的检测。点火开关置于"OFF",拔下氧传感器的导线连接器,用万用表欧姆挡测量氧传感器接线端中加热器端子与搭铁端子(如图 2-65 所示的端子 1 和 2)间的电阻,其电阻值应符合标准值(一般为 4~40Ω;具体数值参见具体车型说明书)。如不符合标准,应更换氧传感器。测量后,接好氧传感器线束连接器,以便做进一步的检测。

③ 氧传感器反馈电压的检测。测量氧传感器反馈电压时,应先拔下氧传感器线束连接器插头,对照被测车型的电路图,从氧传感器反馈电压输出端引出一条细导线,然后插好连接器,在发动机运转时从引出线上测量反馈电压。

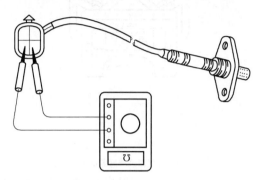

图 2-65　测量氧传感器加热器电阻

有些车型也可以从故障诊断插座内测得氧传感器的反馈电压,如丰田汽车公司生产的小轿车,可从故障诊断插座内的 OX_1 或 OX_2 插孔内直接测得氧传感器反馈电压(丰田 V 型六缸发动机两侧排气管上各有一个氧传感器,分别和故障检测插座内的 OX_1 和 OX_2 插孔连接)。

在对氧传感器的反馈电压进行检测时,最好使用指针型的电压表,以便直观地反映出反馈电压的变化情况。此外,电压表应是低量程(通常为 2V)和高阻抗(阻抗太低会损坏氧传感器)的。

④ 氧传感器外观颜色的检查。从排气管上拆下氧传感器,检查传感器外壳上的通气孔有无堵塞,陶瓷芯有无破损。如有破损,则应更换氧传感器。

通过观察氧传感器顶尖部位的颜色也可以判断故障:

淡灰色顶尖:这是氧传感器的正常颜色;

白色顶尖:由硅污染造成,此时必须更换氧传感器;

棕色顶尖:由铅污染造成,如果严重,也必须更换氧传感器;

黑色顶尖:由积炭造成,在排除发动机积炭故障后,一般可以自动清除氧传感器上的积炭。

(6) 温度传感器的测试

① 进气温度传感器的检测

a. 电阻检测。如图 2-66 所示为桑塔纳 2000GSi 型轿车 AJR 发动机的进气温度传感器端子图与线路图,进气温度传感器 G72 安装在进气歧管上。传感器插座上有两个接线端子,信号输出端子与电控单元端插座上的端子 54 连接,传感器负极与电控单元插座上的传感器搭铁端子 67 连接,如图 2-66(b)所示,利用负温度系数热敏电阻的特性,可以对进气温度传感器进行电阻测试、电压测试以确定进气温度系统工作是否正常。进气温度传感器的阻值可直接用万用表电阻挡进行测试。检测时,断开点火开关,拔下进气歧管压力传感器插头,检测传感器插座上端子"1"与"2"间的电阻值,应当符合规定值。如表 2-1 所示。如阻值过大、过小或为无穷大,说明传感器失效,应予更换新品。

b. 电压检测。检修温度传感器时,可用万用表就车检测传感器的电源电压和信号输出电压,拔下歧管压力传感器插头,接通点火开关,检测传感器 ECU 一侧插头上端子"2"与"1"间的电压应为 5V 左右。插上进气压力传感器插头,接通点火开关,检测传感器 ECU

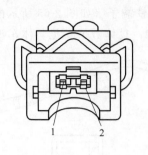 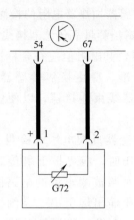

(a) 进气温度传感器端子　　　　　　　　　(b) 进气温度传感器接线

图 2-66　桑塔纳 2000 AJR 型发动机进气温度传感器

表 2-1　桑塔纳 2000GSi 型轿车进气温度传感器的阻值与温度的关系

温度/℃	阻值/Ω	温度/℃	阻值/Ω
-20	14000~20000	50	720~1000
0	5000~6500	60	530~650
10	3300~4200	70	380~480
20	2200~2700	80	280~350
30	1400~1900	90	210~280
40	1000~1400	100	170~200

一侧端子"2"与"1"间的信号电压应为 0.5~3.0V。如电压值不符合规定，说明传感器失效，应予更换。

② 冷却液温度传感器的检测。冷却液温度传感器信号用于喷油量修正、点火提前角修正、活性炭罐电磁阀控制等。如果冷却液温度传感器信号中断，就会导致发动机冷启动困难、油耗增加、怠速稳定性降低、废气排放量增大等。虽然各车型汽车采用的温度传感器阻值各不相同，但是其检修方法基本相同。如图 2-67 所示为桑塔纳 2000GSi 型轿车 AJR 发动机的冷却液温度传感器端子图与线路图。

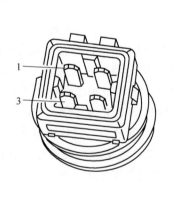 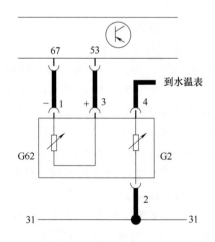

(a) 冷却液温度传感器端子　　　　　　　　(b) 冷却液传感器接线

图 2-67　桑塔纳 2000 AJR 型发动机冷却液传感器

a. 检测电源电压与信号电压。检修冷却液温度传感器时，可用万用表就车检测传感器的电源电压和信号电压。拔下冷却液温度传感器插头，接通点火开关，检测传感器 ECU 一侧插头上两个端子之间的电压应为 5V 左右。插上传感器插头，接通点火开关，检测传感器插头上两个端子间的信号电压应为 0.5~3.0V，具体阻值与温度有关。如电压值不符合规定，说明传感器失效，应予更换。

b. 检测电阻。冷却液温度传感器的阻值可用万用表电阻挡进行检测。检测时，断开点火开关，拔下温度传感器插头，拆下温度传感器，将传感器和温度表放入烧杯或加热容器中。在不同温度下，检测传感器两端子间的电阻值，应当符合规定。如图 2-68 所示，阻值偏差过大、过小或为无穷大，说明传感器失效，应予更换。检测条件与标准值如表 2-2 所示。

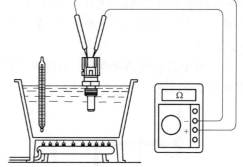

图 2-68　测量冷却液温度传感器的电阻

表 2-2　检测条件与标准参数

水温/℃	电阻值/Ω	水温/℃	电阻值/Ω	水温/℃	电阻值/Ω
50	740~900	70	390~480	90	210~270
60	540~650	80	290~360	100	160~200

虽然各型汽车采用的温度传感器的阻值各不相同，但是其检修方法基本相同。

2. 发动机燃油喷射系统及执行器的检修

（1）释放燃油系统的油压

释放燃油系统油压的目的是为了防止在拆卸时，系统内的压力油喷出，造成人身伤害和火灾。

释放方法和步骤如下：

① 接通点火开关，使发动机怠速运转；

② 拔下油泵继电器或电动燃油泵线束插头，使发动机自行熄火；

③ 再使发动机启动 2~3 次，即可完全释放燃油系统压力；

④ 关闭点火开关，插上油泵继电器或电动燃油泵线束插头。

（2）喷油器检测

以桑塔纳 2000GSi 轿车 AJR 发动机为例，当喷油器发生堵塞、发卡、滴漏时，ECU 不能检测到，必须人工检查和排除。如果有一个喷油器不工作，发动机可能会产生启动困难、怠速不稳或加速不良、动力差等现象。当喷油器控制电路开路或断路时，ECU 能检测到，可用故障诊断仪的"执行元件诊断"功能可对喷油器进行测试。

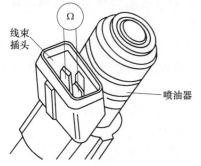

图 2-69　测量喷油器电阻

① 就车诊断喷油器工作情况。接通点火开关，使发动机怠速运转；用螺丝刀或听诊器测试各缸喷油器工作声音，若各缸喷油器工作声音清脆均匀，说明各缸喷油器工作正常；若听不到某缸喷油器工作声音，则应测量该喷油器的电磁线圈电阻及检查喷油器控制线路。

② 检测喷油器的电阻值。拔下喷油器线束插头，用万用表测量喷油器两端子之间的电阻，如图 2-69 所示，

低阻值喷油器应为 2～3Ω，高阻值喷油器应为 13～16Ω，否则应更换喷油器。

③ 喷油器控制电路检查。拆开喷油器线束连接器，接通点火开关，但不启动发动机，用万用表测量其电源端子与搭铁间电压应为 12V 电源电压（即插头端子 1 与发动机搭铁之间的电压）。否则应检查供电线路、点火开关、继电器或保险丝是否有故障。测量各喷油器插头负极端子与发动机 ECU 喷油器端子之间的阻值应小于 1Ω，如图 2-70 所示，如测量桑塔纳 2000 型喷油器端子 2 与 ECU 端子 73、80、58、65 之间的阻值应小于 1Ω，否则线路有断路。

④ 喷油器的喷油量检查。应检查单缸喷油器单位时间内的喷油量和雾化效果以及各缸喷油量的均匀性，如图 2-71 所示。

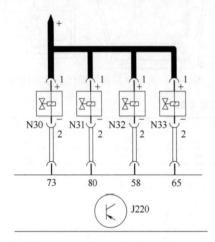

图 2-70　桑塔纳 2000 型喷油器控制电路

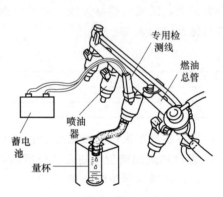

图 2-71　喷油器喷油量的测试

⑤ 喷油器密封性检查。喷油器密封性可在专用设备上进行，在检测喷油量之前，直接给燃油泵通电工作，油压达到正常时，观察喷油器有无滴漏现象。也可将喷油器和输油管从安装位置上拆下，再与燃油系统悬空连接好，打开点火开关，让燃油泵通电工作，观察喷油器有无滴漏现象。一般要求 2min 内喷油器滴油不超过 1 滴，说明喷油器密封性良好，否则应更换喷油器。

注意：低阻喷油器不能直接与蓄电池连接，必须串联一个 8～10Ω 的附加电阻。

(3) 测试燃油系统的油压

通过测试燃油系统压力，可诊断燃油系统是否有故障，进而根据测试结果确定故障性质和部位。测试时需要使用专用油压表和管接头，测试方法如下：

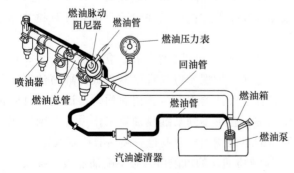

图 2-72　燃油供给系统油压的测试

① 检查油箱内燃油应足够，释放燃油系统压力。

② 检查蓄电池电压应在 12V（电压高低直接影响燃油泵的供油压力），拆下负极电缆。

③ 将专用压力表接在燃油供给系统中，如图 2-72 所示。

④ 接上负极电缆，启动发动机使其维持怠速运转。

⑤ 拆下燃油压力调节器上真空软管，用手堵住进气管一侧，检查油压表指示的压力，多点喷射系统应为 0.25～0.35MPa，单点喷射系统为 0.07～0.10MPa。

若燃油系统压力过低，可夹住回油软管以切断回油管路，再检查油压表指示压力，若压力恢复正常，说明燃油压力调节器有故障，应更换；若仍压力过低，应检查燃油系统有无泄漏，燃油泵滤网、燃油滤清器和油管路是否堵塞，若无泄漏和堵塞故障，应更换燃油泵。

若油压表指示压力过高，应检查回油管路是否堵塞；若回油管路正常，说明燃油压力调节器有故障应更换。

⑥ 如果测试燃油系统压力符合标准，使发动机运转至正常工作温度后，重新接上燃油压力调节器的真空软管，检查燃油压力表的指示应有所下降（约为 0.05MPa），否则应检查真空管路是否堵塞或漏气；若真空管路正常，说明燃油压力调节器有故障，应更换。

⑦ 将发动机熄火，等待 10min 后观察压力表的压力，多点喷射系统不低于 0.20MPa，单点喷射系统不低于 0.05MPa。若压力过低，应检查燃油系统是否有泄漏，若无泄漏，说明燃油泵出油阀、燃油压力调节器回油阀或喷油器密封不良。

⑧ 检查完毕后，应释放系统压力拆下油压表，装复燃油系统。然后，预置燃油系统压力，并启动发动机检查有无泄漏。

（三）注意事项

① 传感器是精密电子器件，要轻拿轻放，避免空气流量计掉在地上摔坏内部电路和元件。
② 对检测设备对传感器进行测试时，注意操作流程和相对应的测试端口。
③ 对燃油供给系统部件进行拆下检测时，必须进行系统油压的释放。

四、知识与技能拓展

不同车型采用的燃油泵控制电路也不同，但主要分为以下三种类型。

（一）ECU 控制的燃油泵控制电路

此种控制电路主要应用在装用 D 型 EFI 和装用热式或卡门旋涡式空气流量计的 L 型 EFI 系统中，如图 2-73 所示为日本丰田皇冠 3.0 轿车燃油泵控制电路。

蓄电池电源经主易熔线、20A 熔丝、主继电器进入 ECU 的 +B 端子，燃油泵控制 ECU 通过 FP 端子向燃油泵供电。燃油泵控制 ECU 根据发动机 ECU 端子 FPC 和 DI 的信号，控制 +B 端子与 FP 端子的连通回路，以改变输送给燃油泵的电压，从而实现对燃油泵转速的控制。当发动机高速、大负荷工作时，发动机 ECU 的 FPC 端子向燃油

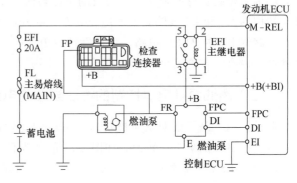

图 2-73 ECU 控制的燃油泵控制电路

泵控制 ECU 发出指令，使 FP 端子向燃油泵提供 12V 的蓄电池电压，燃油泵以高速运转。当发动机低速、小负荷工作时，发动机 ECU 的 DI 端子向燃油泵控制 ECU 发出指令，使

FP 端子向燃油泵提供较低的电压（一般为 9V），燃油泵以低速运转。

ECU 的电源端子＋B 和燃油泵控制端子 FP，分别由导线与诊断座上的相应端子相连，以便于对燃油泵进行检查。

（二）燃油泵开关控制的燃油泵控制电路

此种控制电路用于装用叶片式空气流量计的 L 型 EFI 系统，如图 2-74 所示为日本丰田凌志 ES300 轿车燃油泵控制电路。

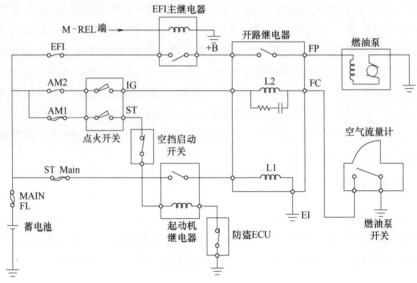

图 2-74 油泵开关控制的燃油泵控制电路

发动机启动时，点火开关 ST 端子与电源接通，起动机继电器线圈通电使其触点闭合，蓄电池经起动机继电器向开路继电器中的线圈 L1 供电使其触点闭合，从而通过主继电器、开路继电器向燃油泵供电，燃油泵工作。发动机启动后正常运转时，点火开关处于点火位置，点火开关 IG 端子与电源接通，同时空气流量计内的测量板转动使燃油泵开关闭合，开路继电器内的线圈 L2 通电，仍可保持开路继电器触点闭合，燃油泵继续工作。发动机运转中，燃油泵始终保持工作状态；但发动机停转时，空气流量计内的燃油泵开关便断开，开路继电器内的 L1 和 L2 线圈均不通电，其开关断开燃油泵电路，燃油泵停止工作。

开路继电器中的 RC 电路，可使发动机熄火时，延长电动燃油泵工作 2～3s，以便保持燃油系统内有一定的残余压力。

（三）燃油泵继电器控制的燃油泵控制电路

此种控制电路可根据发动机转速和负荷的变化，通过燃油泵继电器改变燃油泵供电线路，从而控制燃油泵工作转速。如图 2-75 所示为日本丰田凌志 LS400 轿车燃油泵控制电路。

与凌志 ES300 基本相同，点火开关接通后即通过主继电器将开路继电器的＋B 端子与电源接通，启动时开路继电器中的 L1 线圈通电，发动机正常运转时，ECU 中的晶体管 VT1 导通，开路继电器中的 L2 线圈通电，均使开路继电器触点闭合，油泵继电器 FP 端子与电源接通，燃油泵工作。发动机熄火后，ECU 中的晶体管 VT1 截止，开路继电器内的 L1 和 L2 线圈均不通电，其开关断开燃油泵电路，燃油泵停止工作。

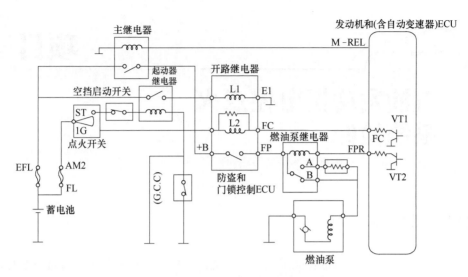

图 2-75 燃油泵继电器控制的燃油泵控制电路

发动机 ECU 控制油泵继电器。发动机低速、中小负荷工作时，ECU 中的晶体管 VT2 导通，燃油泵继电器线圈通电，使触点 A 闭合，由于将电阻串联到燃油泵电路中，所以燃油泵两端电压低于蓄电池电压，燃油泵低速运转。发动机高速、大负荷工作时，ECU 中的晶体管截止，燃油泵继电器触点 B 闭合，直接给燃油泵输送蓄电池电压，燃油泵高速运转。

小 结

本项目主要讲授了电控系统各个传感器的作用、分类及工作原理，以及电控系统中主要执行器（如电磁喷油器、电动燃油泵）的结构和工作原理，及其所有元件的检测方法，学生应掌握所有元件的检测方法、步骤及注意事项，并能够正确判断故障所在，同时对电控系统燃油控制的原理，应能够熟悉所有传感器、执行器对电控燃油供给正常工作的影响。

习题及思考

1. 汽车电控单元的结构和工作原理。
2. 对汽车电控单元电源电路检修的注意事项是什么？
3. 汽车电控单元电源电路由哪三部分组成？
4. 简述电控燃油喷射系统控制系统的控制原理。
5. 电动燃油泵的作用是什么？
6. 电动燃油泵按安装位置不同可分为几种安装方式，有什么优缺点？
7. 汽车用电动燃油泵构造分可分为几种？
8. 如何检测电动燃油泵？
9. 喷油器按阻值分，可分为几种？其电阻值常为多少？
10. 喷油器的驱动方式是什么？
11. 发动机启动困难、怠速不稳或加速不良、动力性能不良等现象与喷油器有关吗？为什么？
12. 如何检测喷油器？
13. 什么叫开环控制系统？什么叫闭环控制系统？
14. 热膜式空气流量传感器的工作原理是什么？
15. 爆震传感器的检测内容都包括哪些？

项目三

汽油发动机电控点火系统检修

一、项目情境引入

在汽油发动机中，发动机的性能不仅取决于燃油的控制，同时点火控制同等重要，在汽油机各系统中点火系统对发动机的性能影响最大，统计数字表明将近一半的故障是电气系统工作不良引起的，因此发动机性能检测往往从点火系统开始。首先使用先进电子技术的当属点火系统，而形式结构和工作原理更新最快的也非点火系统莫属。现用点火系统其结构原理不同，在检测时的接线有所不同，应区别对待。

二、项目相关知识

（一）汽油机点火系统的作用

汽车发动机的工作循环由进气、压缩、做功与排气四个行程组成，虽然在压缩终了时，汽缸内的混合气温度很高，但由于汽油的燃点较高，还不能像柴油机那样产生自燃，所以必须采用明火进行点燃。汽油机的点火方式就是采用高压电火花点燃混合气的。

为了在汽缸中定时地产生高压电火花，汽油发动机设置了专门的点火装置，称为发动机点火系统。点火系统的基本功用就是使火花塞产生火花，在汽缸内点燃燃油混合气。要点燃压缩过的燃油混合气，火花塞的瞬间点火电压必须高达2000V以上，但汽车所用的蓄电池电压一般只有12~14V，所以点火系统必须将12~14V的初级电压转换为2000V以上的次级高电压（一些新型的点火系统甚至能够产生高达10万伏的次级电压），并将这种高电压按照汽缸的点火顺序分配到各个汽缸的火花塞上，使其点火。

（二）汽油机点火系统分类

发动机点火系统，按照其组成和产生高压电方式的不同可分为传统点火系统、电子点火系统、微机控制点火系统和磁电动机点火系统。

传统点火系统以蓄电池和发电机为电源，借助点火线圈和断电器的作用，将电源提供的6V、12V或24V的低压直流电转变为高压电，再通过分电器分配到各缸火花塞，使火花塞两电极之间产生电火花，点燃可燃混合气体。传统蓄电池点火系统由于存在产生的高压电比较低、高速时工作不可靠、使用过程中须经常检查和维护等缺点，目前，已被电子点火系统和微机控制点火系统所取代。

电子点火系统以蓄电池和发电机为电源，借助点火线圈和由半导体器件（晶体三极管）组成的点火控制器将电源提供的低压电转变为高压电，再通过分电器分配到各缸火花塞，使火花塞两电极之间产生电火花，点燃可燃混合气。与传统点火系统相比具有点火可靠、使用方便等优点，但随着发动机电控技术的发展，除少部分在用车使用外，近几年已经被微机控制点火系统取代。

微机控制点火系统与上述两种点火系统相同，也是以蓄电池和发电机为电源，借点火线圈将电源的低压电转变为高压电，再由分电器将高压电分配到各缸火花塞，并由微机控制系统根据各种传感器提供的发动机工况的信息，发出点火控制信号，控制点火时刻，点燃可燃混合气。它还可以取消分电器，由微机控制系统直接将高压电分配给各缸。微机控制点火系统是目前最新型的点火系统，已被广泛应用于各种汽车中。

磁电动机点火系统由磁电动机本身直接产生高压，不需另设低压电源。它主要用于在高速满负荷工作下的赛车发动机。

微机控制点火系统的英文缩写为 MCI。汽油发动机采用微机控制点火系统能将点火提前角控制在最佳值，使可燃混合气燃烧后产生的温度和压力达到最大值，从而提高发动机的动力性，同时还能提高燃油经济性和减少有害气体的排放量。

（三）对点火系统的基本要求

点火系统应在发动机各种工况和使用条件下都能保证可靠而准确地点火。为此点火系统应满足以下基本要求。

1. 能产生足以击穿火花塞两电极间隙的电压

使火花塞两电极之间的间隙击穿并产生电火花所需要的电压，称为火花塞的击穿电压。火花塞击穿电压的大小与中心电极和侧电极之间的距离（火花塞间隙）、汽缸内的压力和温度、电极的温度、发动机的工作状况等因素有关。火花塞电极示意图如图 3-1 所示。

电极间隙越大，电极周围气体中的电子和离子距离越大，受电场力的作用减小，越不易发生碰撞电离，因此要求有更高的击穿电压方能点火。

汽缸内的压力越大或者温度越低，则汽缸内可燃混合气的密度越大，单位体积中气体分子的数量越多，离子自由运动的距离越小，越不易发生碰撞电离。只有提高加在电极上的电压，增大作用于离子上的电场力，使离子的运动加速才能发生离子间的碰撞电离，使火花塞电极间隙击穿。因此汽缸内的压力越大或者温度越低，所要求的火花塞击穿电压越高。

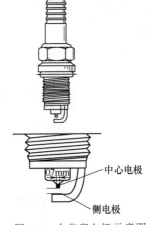

图 3-1 火花塞电极示意图

电极的温度对火花塞击穿电压也有影响。电极的温度越高，包围在电极周围的气体的密度越小，越容易发生碰撞电离，所需的火花塞击穿电压越小。实践证明，当火花塞的电极温度超过混合气的温度时，击穿电压可降低 30%～50%。

发动机工况不同时，火花塞的击穿电压将随发动机的转速、负荷、压缩比、点火提前角以及混合气的浓度的变化而变化。

启动时的击穿电压最高，因为汽缸壁、活塞及火花塞的电极都处于冷态，吸入的混合气温度低、雾化不良。压缩时混合气的温度升高不大，加之火花塞电极间可能积有汽油或机油，因此所需击穿电压最高，此外，汽车加速时，由于大量冷的混合气被突然吸入汽缸内，也需要较高的电压。

试验表明，发动机正常运行时，火花塞的击穿电压为 7~8kV，发动机冷启动时达 19kV。为了使发动机在各种不同的工况下均能可靠地点火，要求火花塞击穿电压应在 15~20kV。

2. 电火花应具有足够的点火能量

为了使混合气可靠点燃，火花塞产生的火花应具备一定的能量。发动机正常工作时，由于混合气压缩时的温度接近自燃温度，因此所需的火花能量较小，火花能量为 15~50mJ，足以点燃混合气。但在启动、怠速以及突然加速时需要较高的点火能量。为保证可靠点火，一般应保证 50~80mJ 的点火能量，启动时应能产生大于 100mJ 的点火能量。

3. 点火时刻应与发动机的工作状况相适应

首先发动机的点火时刻应满足发动机工作循环的要求；其次可燃混合气在汽缸内从开始点火到完全燃烧需要一定的时间（千分之几秒），所以要使发动机产生最大的功率，就不应在压缩行程终了（上止点）点火，而应适当地提前一个角度。这样当活塞到达上止点时，混合气已经接近充分燃烧，发动机才能发出最大功率。

4. 极其持久耐用

点火火系统工作必须非常可靠，才能经受发动机产生的振动、高温以及自身的高电压。

（四）微机控制点火系统的结构组成

微机控制点火系统主要由凸轮轴位置传感器 CIS、曲轴位置传感器 CPS、空气流量传感器 AFS、节气门位置传感器 TPS、冷却液温度传感器 CTS、进气温度传感器 IATS、车速传感器 VSS、爆震传感器 EDS、各种控制开关、电控单元 ECU、点火控制模块、点火线圈以及火花塞等组成。桑塔纳 2000GSi、3000 型轿车微机控制直接点火系统的组成如图 3-2 所示。

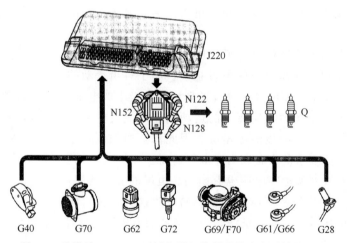

图 3-2 桑塔纳 2000GSi 型轿车微机控制直接点火系统的组成

1. 传感器与开关信号

传感器用来检测与点火有关的发动机工作和状况信息，并将检测结果输入 ECU，作为计算和控制点火时刻的依据。虽然各型汽车采用的传感器的类型、数量、结构及安装位置不尽相同，但是其作用都大同小异，而且这些传感器大多与燃油喷射系统、怠速控制系统等共用。

凸轮轴位置传感器是确定曲轴基准位置和点火基准的传感器。该传感器在曲轴旋转至某一特定的位置（如第一缸压缩上止点前某一确定的角度）时，输出一个脉冲信号，ECU将这一脉冲信号作为计算曲轴位置的基准信号，再利用曲轴转角信号计算出曲轴任一时刻所处的具体位置。

曲轴位置传感器将发动机曲轴转过的角度变换为电信号输入ECU，曲轴每转过一定角度就发出一个脉冲信号，ECU通过不断地检测脉冲个数，即可计算出曲轴转过的角度。与此同时，ECU根据单位时间内接收到的脉冲个数，即可计算出发动机的转速。在微机控制电子点火系统中，发动机曲轴转角信号用来计算具体的点火时刻，转速信号用来计算和读取基本点火提前角。凸轮轴位置和曲轴位置信号是保证ECU控制电子点火系统正常工作最基本的信号。

空气流量传感器是确定进气量大小的传感器。在L型（流量型）电控燃油喷射系统中，采用的是流量型传感器直接检测空气流量，在D型（压力型）电控燃油喷射系统中，采用的是进气歧管压力传感器通过检测节气门后进气歧管内的负压（真空度）来间接检测空气流量。空气流量信号输入ECU后，除了用于计算基本喷油时间之外，还用作负荷信号来计算和确定基本点火提前角。

进气温度传感器信号反映发动机吸入空气的温度。在微机控制电子点火系统中，ECU利用该信号对基本点火提前角进行修正。

冷却液温度传感器信号反映发动机工作温度的高低。在微机控制点火系统中，ECU除了利用该信号对基本点火提前角进行修正之外，还要利用该信号控制启动和发动机暖机期间的点火提前角。

节气门位置传感器将节气门开启角度转换为电信号输入ECU，ECU利用该信号和车速传感器信号来综合判断发动机所处的工况（怠速、中等负荷、大负荷、减速），并对点火提前角进行修正。

各种开关信号用于修正点火提前角。启动开关信号用于启动时修正点火提前角；空调开关信号用于怠速工况下使用空调时修正点火提前角；空挡安全开关仅在采用自动变速器的汽车上使用，ECU利用该开关信号来判断发动机是处于空挡停车状态还是行驶状态，然后对点火提前角进行必要的修正。

上述传感器和开关信号的结构原理与检修方法在发动机燃油喷射系统中已经介绍，下面主要介绍爆震传感器的有关知识。

2. 发动机爆震传感器应用

检测发动机爆震的方法有三种：一是检测发动机燃烧室的压力变化；二是检测发动机缸体的振动频率；三是检测混合气燃烧的噪声。通过直接检测燃烧室压力变化来检测发动机振动的测量精度高，但传感器安装复杂且耐久性差，一般用于测量仪器。测量混合气燃烧噪声的方法为非接触式检测，其耐久性好但测量精度与灵敏度较低，实际应用很少。实际应用的压力检测传感器均为间接测量式，通过检测发动机缸体振动频率来检测爆震，优点是测量灵敏度高、传感器安装方便且输出电压变化大，因此现代汽车工业广泛采用该种检测方法。

利用震动法检测爆震的传感器有磁致伸缩型和半导体压电型两种类型，其中压电型又有共振型和非共振型之分。

(1) 磁致伸缩式爆震传感器

这种爆震传感器安装在发动机上,将发动机振动频率转换成电压信号,然后输送给ECU,以检测发动机爆震的强度。当发动机的爆震强度与设定值相同时,爆震传感器输出最大的电压信号,以表示发动机由于爆震而产生使机体异常的振动频率。如图3-3、图3-4所示为应用较早的磁致伸缩式爆震传感器的外形与结构图,其内部有永久磁铁、靠永久磁铁励磁的强磁性铁芯以及铁芯周围的线圈。其工作原理是:当发动机的汽缸体出现振动时,该传感器在7kHz左右处与发动机产生共振,强磁性材料铁芯的导磁率发生变化,致使永久磁铁穿过铁芯的磁通密度也变化,从而在铁芯周围的绕组中产生感应电动势,并将这一电信号输入ECU。

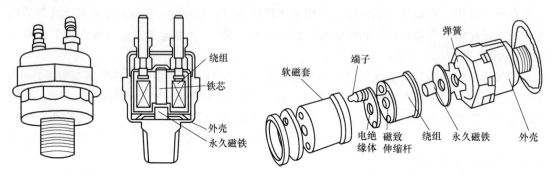

图3-3 磁致伸缩式爆震传感器的外形与结构   图3-4 磁致伸缩式爆震传感器的组成

(2) 非共振型压电式爆震传感器

非共振型压电式爆震传感器以接收加速度信号的形式,来判别爆震是否产生。传感器结构如图3-5所示。

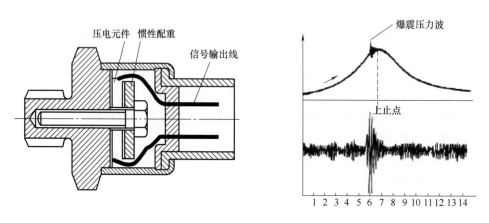

图3-5 压电非共振型爆震传感器

它由两个压电元件同极性相向对接,使用的配重用一根螺丝固定在壳体上,它将加速度变换成作用于压电元件上的压力,输出电压由两个压电元件的中央取出。这种传感器构造简单,制造时不需调整。

发动机振动时,安装在发动机缸体上的爆震传感器内部配重因受振动的影响,而产生加速度,因此,在压电元件上就会受到加速时惯性力的作用而产生电压信号。此种传感器不像

磁致伸缩式爆震传感器那样在爆震频率附近产生一个较高的输出电压,用以判断爆震的产生,而是具有平的输出特性,如图3-6 所示为非共振型压电式爆震传感器输出电压与频率的关系。因此,必须将反应发动机振动频率的输出电压信号送至识别爆震的滤波器中,判别是否有爆震信号产生。这种传感器的感测频率范围设计成由零至数十千赫兹,可检测具有很宽频带的发动机的振动频率。

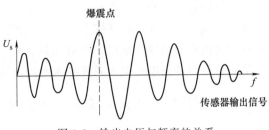

图 3-6 输出电压与频率的关系

（3）共振型压电式爆震传感器

此种形式的爆震传感器利用产生爆震时的发动机振动频率,与传感器本身的固有频率相符合,而产生共振现象,用以检测爆震是否发生。该传感器在爆震时的输出电压比无爆震时的输出电压高得多,因此无需使用滤波器,即可判别有无爆震产生。如图 3-7 所示为共振型压电式爆震传感器的结构,压电元件紧密地贴合在振荡片上。振荡片则固定在传感器的基座上。振荡片随发动机振动而振荡,波及压电元件,使其变形而产生电压信号。当发动机爆震时的振动频率与振荡片的固有频率相符合时,振荡片产生共振,此时压电元件将产生最大的电压信号。

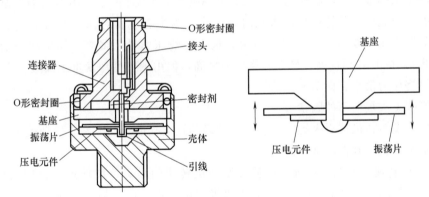

图 3-7 压电共振型爆震传感器

3. **电控单元 ECU**

现代汽车发动机大多数都采用集中控制系统,微机控制点火系统是其子系统,ECU 不仅是燃油喷射控制系统的控制核心,也是点火控制系统的控制核心。在 ECU 的只读存储器 ROM 中,除存储有监控和自检等程序之外,还存储有由台架试验测定的该型发动机在各种工况下的最佳点火提前角。随机存储器 RAM 用来存储微机工作时暂时需要存储的数据,如输入/输出数据、单片机运算得出的结果、故障代码、点火提前角修正数据等。这些数据根据需要可随时调用或被新的数据改写。CPU 不断接收上述各种传感器发送来的信号,并按预先编制的程序进行计算和判断,向点火控制器发出接通与切断点火线圈初级电路的控制信号。

4. **点火控制器**

点火控制器又称为点火电子组件或点火器,是微机控制点火系统的功率输出级,它接收 ECU 输出的点火控制信号并进行功率放大,以便驱动点火线圈工作。

点火控制器的电路、功能与结构依车型而异，有的与ECU制作在同一块电路板上，有的为独立总成，并用线束和连接器与ECU相连接，有的点火控制器与点火线圈安装在一起并配有较大面积的散热器散热。微机控制点火系统采用的点火线圈、火花塞以及配电器等部件的结构原理与普通电子点火系统基本相同。

（五）微机控制点火系统的控制过程

1. 点火提前角及其影响因素

（1）点火提前角定义及其影响

点火提前角是指从火花塞点火到活塞到达压缩上止点曲轴所转过的角度。

点火过早（点火提前角太大）会造成爆震、进气歧管回火；

点火过晚（点火提前角过小）又会使发动机性能下降、排气管放炮；

最理想的点火时机应该是将点火正时控制在爆震即将发生而还未发生的时刻。

（2）最佳点火提前角

使发动机产生最大输出功率的点火提前角称为最佳点火提前角，最佳点火提前角可以大大提高发动机的动力性、燃油经济性和排放性。

实验表明：混合气在汽缸内燃烧，当最高燃烧压力出现在上止点后4°～12°曲轴转角时，发动机的输出功率最大。汽缸压力与点火时刻的关系如图3-8所示。图中A是汽缸内混合气不燃烧时的压力波形，其特点是点火正时以上止点为中心左右对称。B、C、D分别是改变点火时刻的燃烧压力波形。在C时刻点火，最大燃烧压力做功最多、输出功率最大（阴影部分的面积）。在B时刻点火，最大燃烧压力最高，但由图可见却发生了爆震。在D时刻点火，最大燃烧压力最小、做功最少。

（3）影响点火提前角的因素

点火应该发生在最佳点火提前角时。影响最佳点火提前角的因素有发动机转速、发动机负荷、燃油辛烷值、其他因素等。

① 发动机转速。如图3-9所示，随着发动机转速的增高，最佳点火提前角应该增大，一般轿车发动机怠速为800r/min左右，点火提前角为6°～12°，而转速为4000r/min时，提前角能够达到30°。这是因为发动机转速升高时，在同一时间内，曲轴转过的角度增大，如果混合气燃烧速率不变，则最佳点火提前角应按线性规律增长。但当转速继续升高时，由于混合气压力和温度的提高及扰流增强，会使燃烧速度也随着加快，因此当转速升高到一定程度时，最佳点火提前角虽随着发动机转速的升高而增大，但增加速度减慢，因此不是线性关系。

② 发动机负荷（进气歧管绝对压力）。如图3-10所示，点火提前角随着发动机负荷（进气歧管绝对压力）的增大而减小。这是因为进气歧管绝对压力越高（真空度小、负荷大），混合气的质量越好，燃烧的速度越大，要求点火提前角就越小；反之，则要求点火提前角大。

由图3-10可见，在传统触点式点火系统中，因采用的是机械离心式调节器（随转速调节点火提前）和真空提前调节器（随负荷调节点火提前），所以实际点火提前角与理想点火提前角相差较大。而在微机控制点火系统中，实际点火提前角与理想点火提前角已经很接近了。

2. 微机控制点火系统的原理

微机控制点火系统的控制原理如图 3-8 所示，曲轴位置传感器 CPS 向 ECU 提供发动机转速、曲轴转角信号，转速信号用于计算确定点火提前角，转角信号用于控制点火时刻（点火提前角）。空气流量传感器 AFS 和节气门位置传感器 TPS 向 ECU 提供发动机负荷信号，用于计算确定点火提前角。冷却液温度信号 CTS、进气温度信号 IATS、车速信号 VSS、空调开关信号 A/C 以及爆震传感器 EDS 信号等等，用于修正点火提前角。

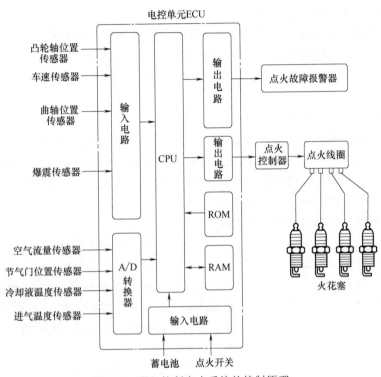

图 3-8　微机控制点火系统的控制原理

发动机工作时，CPU 通过上述传感器把发动机的工况信息采集到随机存储器 RAM 中，并不断检测凸轮轴位置传感器信号，判定是哪一缸即将到达压缩上止点。当接收到信号后，CPU 立即开始对曲轴转角信号进行计算，以便控制点火提前角。与此同时，CPU 根据反映发动机工况的转速信号、负荷信号以及与点火提前角有关的传感器信号，从只读存储器中查询出相应工况下的最佳点火提前角。在此期间，CPU 一直在对曲轴转角信号进行计数，判断点火时刻是否到来。当曲轴转角等于最佳点火提前角时，CPU 立即向点火控制器发出控制指令，使功率三极管截止，点火线圈初级电流切断，次级绕组产生高压，并按发动机点火顺序分配到各缸火花塞跳火点着可燃混合气。

上述控制过程是指发动机在正常状态下点火时刻的控制过程。当发动机启动、怠速或汽车滑行工况时，设有专门的控制程序和控制方式进行控制。

3. 微机控制点火系统点火提前角的确定

汽油发动机的可燃混合气在汽缸内燃烧不是瞬时完成的，需要先经诱导期，然后才能进入猛烈的明显燃烧期。因此，要使发动机发出最大的功率，混合气不应在压缩冲程上止点处点火而应适当地提早一些。通常把发动机发出功率最大和油耗最少的点火提前角称为最佳点火提前角。点火提前角大小直接影响发动机的输出功率、油耗、排放等。发动机工况不同，需要的最佳点火提前角也不相同，怠速时的最佳点火提前角是为了使怠速运转平稳、降低有害气体排放量和减少燃油消耗量；部分负荷时的最佳点火提前角是为了减少燃油消耗量和有害气体排放量，提高经济性和排放性能；大负荷时的最佳点火提前角是为了增大输出转矩，提高动力性能。

微机控制的点火提前角由汽车启动时的初始点火提前角和启动后的基本点火提前角与修正点火提前角三部分组成。

(1) 启动时点火提前角的控制

发动机启动时，由于转速变化大，进气管绝对压力传感器信号或空气流量计信号不稳定，ECU 无法正确计算点火提前角。而是 ECU 根据转速信号和启动开关信号，参照内存储的初始点火提前角（设定值）对点火提前角进行控制，一般设定值为上止点前 10°左右（因发动机型号而异）。

(2) 启动后点火提前角的控制

启动后点火提前角由基本点火提前角和修正角（或修正系数）组成。

① 基本点火提前角。发动机设计的最佳基本点火提前角的数据存储在发动机电脑的存储器中。发动机运行时，发动机电脑根据各种传感器的输入信号，在存储器中查找到这一工况条件下运转时相应的基本点火提前角。

基本点火提前角根据发动机运行工况可分为：

怠速时的基本点火提前角；

正常运行时的基本点火提前角。

怠速工况时基本角确定：ECU 根据节气门位置传感器信号（IDL 信号）、发动机转速传感器信号（Ne 信号）和空调开关信号（A/C 信号）来确定，如图 3-9 所示。

其他工况下基本角：ECU 根据发动机的转速和负荷对照存储器中存储的基本点火提前角控制模型来确定，如图 3-10 所示。

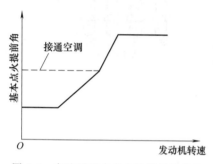

图 3-9 怠速时基本点火提前角的确定

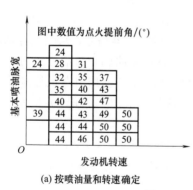

(a) 按喷油量和转速确定图　　(b) 按进气量和转速确定图

图 3-10 基本点火提前角控制模型

② 点火提前角的修正

a. 冷却液温度修正。为了改善发动机的驾驶性能，发动机冷车刚启动后，冷却液温度还比较低，混合气燃烧的速度也比较慢，发生爆燃的可能性比较小，此时应适当地增大点火提前角。暖机过程中，随着冷却液温度的升高，点火提前角应逐渐减小，如图3-11（a）所示，发动机处于部分负荷运行时（如节气门位置传感器的怠速触点断开），如图3-11（c）所示，当冷却液温度过高时，为了避免爆震，可将点火提前角推迟。发动机处于怠速工况（如节气门位置传感器怠速触点闭合），冷却液温度过高时，为避免发动机长时间过热，应将点火提前角增大，以此来提高发动机的怠速转速，从而提高水泵和冷却风扇的转速，增强制冷效果，降低发动机的温度。过热修正曲线如图3-11（b）所示。

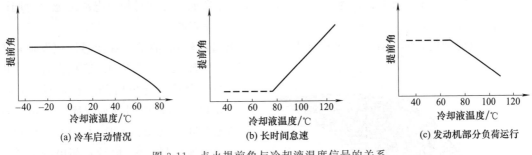

图3-11 点火提前角与冷却液温度信号的关系

b. 怠速稳定性修正。怠速运行期间，发动机负荷变化时发动机转速也会发生改变，为使发动机在规定的怠速运转下稳定运转，需要对点火提前角进行修正。

怠速运转时，发动机电脑不断地计算发动机的平均转速，当平均转速低于或高于规定的怠速转速时，发动机电脑根据与怠速目标转速差值的大小并结合空调的接通与否相应地增大或减小点火提前角，如图3-12所示。

c. 喷油量修正。装有氧传感器和闭环控制程序的电子燃油控制系统中，发动机电脑根据氧传感器的反馈信号对空燃比进行修正。随着修正喷油量的增加和减少，发动机的转速会在一定范围内波动。在喷油量减少时，混合气变稀，发动机转速相应降低，为了提高怠速的稳定性，点火提前角应适当地增加；反之点火提前角应适当地减小，如图3-13所示。

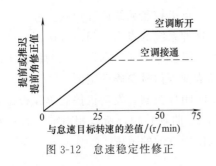

图3-12 怠速稳定性修正

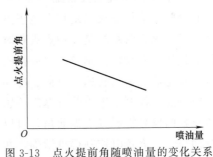

图3-13 点火提前角随喷油量的变化关系

4. 微机控制点火系统的控制过程

微机控制点火系统的控制过程可分为点火提前角控制和点火导通角控制两种。

（1）点火提前角控制的必要性

发动机工作时任何工况都需要一个点火提前角，最佳的点火提前角是保证发动机的动力性、燃油经济性和排放性最佳的前提。当点火提前角过大时，会造成缸内最高压力升高，爆燃倾向大。当点火提前角过小时，燃烧最高压力和温度下降，传热损失增多，排气温度升高。所以，为了保证发动机每一工况下点火角为最佳，即在最高压力出现在上止点后$10°\sim15°$曲轴转角时进行点火，必须通过电控方式来实现。

(2) 导通角控制的必要性

① 通电时间控制的必要性。当点火线圈的初级电路被接通后，其初级电流按指数规律增长，通电时间长短决定初级电流的大小。当初级电流达到饱和时，若初级电路被断开，此瞬间初级电流达到最大值（即断开电流），会感应次级电压达到最大值。次级电压的升高，会使火花塞点火能力增强，所以在发动机工作时，必须保证点火线圈的初级电路有足够的通电时间。但如果通电时间过长，点火线圈又会发热并增大电能消耗。所以，通电时间过长过短，都会给点火系统带来不利，为了保证点火线圈工作性能，必须对初级电路的通电时间进行控制。

② 通电时间的控制。在现代电控点火系统中，通过凸轮轴/曲轴位置传感器把发动机工作信号输入给 ECU，ECU 根据存储在内部的闭合角（通电时间）控制模型，如图 3-14 所示，控制点火线圈初级电路的通电时间。发动机工作时，ECU 根据发动机转速信号（Ne 信号）和电源电压信号确定最佳的闭合角（通电时间），并向点火器输出指令信号（IGt 信号），以控制点火器中晶体管的导通时间，并随发动机转速提高和电源电压下降，闭合角（通电时间）增大。

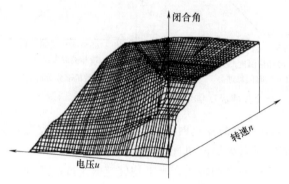

图 3-14 闭合角（通电时间）控制模型

（六）微机控制点火系统高压电的分配方式

微机控制点火系统高压电的分配方式可分为有分电器电控点火系统和无分电器电控点火系统。

1. 有分电器电控点火系统

有分电器电控点火系统具有电子点火正时系统和电子点火控制系统两种形式。

电子点火正时系统是一种点火正时开环控制系统。这种系统的点火时间由分电器内的点火控制模块和发动机控制单元共同控制。点火正时由发动机控制单元根据发动机的特定工况下各个传感器送来的转速、负荷、冷却液温度、混合气浓度等信号精确确定。

电子点火控制系统中装有爆震传感器，属于点火正时闭环控制。发动机控制单元根据爆震传感器的信号控制点火提前角，可以延迟点火提前角20°曲轴转角，所以相对前一种控制系统而言，点火正时控制得更精确，并且扩大了发动机使用汽油的范围。

(1) 组成

有分电器电控点火系统组成如图 3-15 所示。

(2) 配电方式

发动机工作时，ECU 根据各传感器信号确定某缸点火时，向点火器发出指令信号，点火器控制点火线圈内初级电路通电或断电。当点火线圈中的初级电路断电时，次级线圈产生的高压电输送给分电器，分电器按照发动机的点火顺序，依次将高压电输送给各缸火花塞，火花塞跳火，点燃汽缸内的混合气。这种配电方式称分电器配电方式。有分电器电控点火系统的主要特点是：只有1个点火线圈。

(3) 缺点

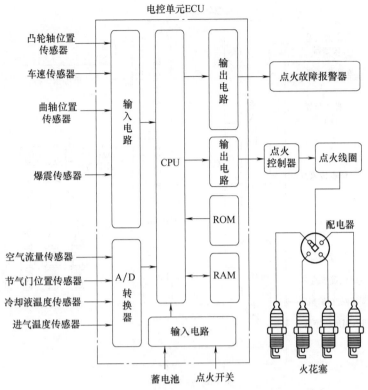

图 3-15 电控点火系统的基本组成

① 分火头与分电器盖旁电极之间必须保留一定间隙才能进行高压电分配，因此，必须损失一部分火花能量，同时也是一个主要的无线电干扰源；

② 为了抑制无线电的干扰信号，高压线采用了高阻抗电缆，也要消耗一部分能量；

③ 分火头、分电器盖或高压导线漏电时，会导致高压电火花减弱、缺火或断火；

④ 曲轴位置传感器转子由分电器轴驱动，旋转机构的机械磨损会影响点火时刻的控制精度；

⑤ 分电器安装的位置和占据的空间，会给发动机的结构布置和汽车的外形设计造成一定的困难。

2. 无分电器电控点火系统

无分电器点火系统完全取消了分电器，它是将点火线圈产生的高压电直接通过高压线传递给火花塞，使其点火。

无分电器电控点火系统及是指在点火控制器控制下，点火线圈的高压电按照一定的点火顺序，直接加到火花塞上的直接点火方式，如图 3-16 所示。

常用无分电器电控点火系可分为双缸同时点火和各缸单独点火两种配电方式。

（1）双缸同时点火的控制

双缸同时点火是指点火线圈每产生一次高压电，都使两个汽缸的火花塞同时跳火。次级绕组产生的高压电将直接加在两个汽缸（四缸发动机的 1、4 缸或 2、3 缸；六缸发动机的 1、6 缸、2、5 缸或 3、4 缸）的火花塞电极上跳火。

双缸同时点火时，一个汽缸处于压缩行程末期，是有效点火，另一个汽缸处于排气行程末期，缸内温度较高而压力很低，火花塞电极间隙的击穿电压很低，对有效点火汽缸火花塞

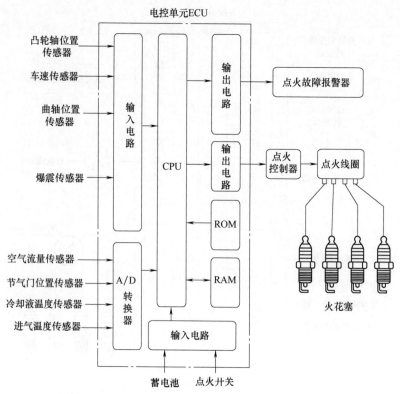

图 3-16 无分电器电控点火系统

的击穿电压和火花放电能量影响很小,是无效点火。曲轴旋转一转后,两缸所处行程恰好相反。双缸同时点火时,高压电的分配方式又分为二极管分配和点火线圈分配两种行程。

① 二极管分配高压电式。利用二极管分配高压电的双缸同时点火电路原理如图 3-17 所示。点火线圈由两个初级绕组和一个次级绕组构成,次级绕组的两端通过 4 只高压二极管与火花塞构成回路。4 只二极管有内装式(安装在点火线圈内部)和外装式两种。对于点火顺序为 1—3—4—2 的发动机,1、4 缸为一组,2、3 缸为另一组。(1 缸、2 缸、3 缸、4 缸所对应的二极管分别是 VD1、VD2、VD3、VD4)。点火控制器中的两只功率三极管分别控制一个初级绕组,两只功率三极管由电控单元 ECU 按点火顺序交替控制其导通与截止。

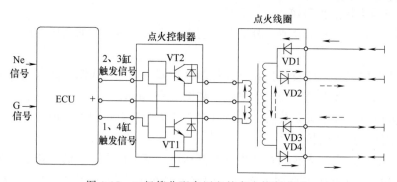

图 3-17 二极管分配高压电的点火控制方式

当电控单元 ECU 将 1、4 缸的点火触发信号输入点火控制器时,功率三极管 VT1 截止,初级绕组(箭头向下)中的电流切断,次级绕组中就会产生高压电动势。在该电动势的作用下,二极管 VD1、VD4 正向导通,1、4 缸火花塞电极上的电压迅速升高直至跳火,高压放电电流经过图中实线箭头所指方向构成回路;VD2、VD3 反向截止,不能构成放电回路,因此 2、3 缸火花塞电极上无高压火花放电电流而不能跳火。

当 ECU 将 2、3 缸点火触发信号输入点火控制器时,三极管 VT2 截止,初级绕组电流(箭头向上)切断,次级绕组产生高压电动势,方向如图 3-17 中虚线箭头方向所示。此时二极管 VD1、VD4 反向截止,VD2、VD3 正向导通,因此 2、3 缸火花塞电极上的电压迅速升高直至跳火,高压放电电流经图中虚线箭头所指方向构成回路。

② 点火线圈分配高压电式。利用点火线圈直接分配高压的同时点火电路原理如图 3-18 所示。

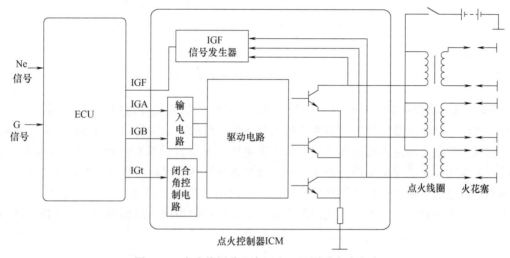

图 3-18 点火线圈分配高压电双缸同时点火方式

点火线圈组件由两个(四缸发动机)或三个(六缸发动机)独立的点火线圈组成,每个点火线圈供给成对的两个火花塞工作(4 缸发动机的 1、4 缸和 2、3 缸分别共用一个点火线圈;6 缸发动机的 1、6 缸、2、5 缸和 3、4 缸分别共用一个点火线圈)。点火控制组件中设有与点火线圈数量相等的功率三极管,分别控制一个点火线圈工作。点火控制器根据电控单元 ECU 输出的点火控制信号,按点火顺序轮流触发功率三极管导通与截止,从而控制每个点火线圈轮流产生高压电,再通过高压线直接输送到成对的两缸火花塞电极间隙上跳火点燃可燃混合气。

(2)单缸独立点火控制

点火系统采用单独点火方式时,每一个汽缸都配有一个点火线圈,并安装在火花塞上方。在点火控制器中,设置有与点火线圈相同数目的大功率三极管,分别控制每个线圈次级绕组电流的接通与切断,其工作原理与同时点火方式相同。单独点火的优点是省去了高压线,点火能量损耗进一步减少;此外,所有高压部件都可以安装在发动机的汽缸盖上的金属屏蔽罩内,点火系统对无线电的干扰可大幅度降低。这种点火方式非常适合在四气门(每缸两个进气门和两个排气门)发动机上使用,在这种结构的点火系统中,火花塞一般安装在两根凸轮轴的中间,每缸火花塞上直接压装一个点火线圈,很容易布置。单独独立点火控制如图 3-19 所示。

综上所述,微机控制无分电器点火系统消除了分电器高压配电的不足。由于点火线圈

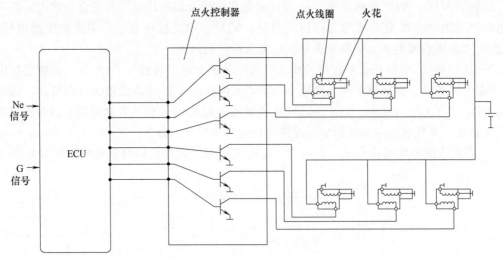

图 3-19 单缸独立点火控制方式

（或初级绕组）数量增加，对每一个点火线圈来说，初级绕组允许通电时间可增加 2~6 倍。因此，即使发动机高速运转时，初级绕组也有足够充裕的通电时间。换句话说，无分电器点火系统具有足够大的点火能量和足够高的次级电压来保证发动机在任何工况都能可靠点火。同时，点火线圈次级输出端即火花塞中心电极均为负极性，因而击穿电压低，且火花塞放电频率小，故电极寿命长；取消了高压线而由点火线圈直接向火花塞供电，因而能量损失小，效率高，电磁干扰少；由于点火线圈能安装在双凸轮轴的中间，因而节省了发动机周围的安装空间。

（七）爆震控制

1. 爆震控制的必要性

发动机工作过程中，燃料燃烧的火焰，在传播的过程中，会使未燃混合气进一步受到压缩和热辐射的作用。如果在火焰前锋尚未到达之前，末端混合气已经自燃，则这部分混合气燃烧速度极快，火焰速度可达每秒百米甚至数百米以上，使燃烧室内的局部压力、温度很高，并伴随有冲击波。压力冲击波反复撞击缸壁，发出尖锐的敲缸声，这种现象称为爆震燃烧，是一种不正常燃烧。轻微时，可使发动机功率上升，油耗下降；严重时，汽缸内发出特别尖锐的金属敲击声，且会导致冷却液过热，功率下降，耗油率上升。所以，应对爆震燃烧加以控制。

2. 发动机爆震的控制作用

汽油发动机获得最大功率和最佳燃油经济性的有效方法之一是增大点火提前角，但是点火提前角过大又会引起发动机爆震。

发动机爆震，是燃烧室内混合气异常燃烧导致汽缸压力骤然上升，而引起发动机缸体产生的震动。在采用闭环控制的发动机电子控制系统中，当发动机产生爆震时，电控系统就能够通过调整点火时刻（点火提前角）来有效地抑制和消除发动机爆震。爆震传感器（Detonation Sensor，DS）是发动机闭环控制系统中的重要部件，其功能是将发动机爆震信号转换为电信号传递给电控单元，电控单元根据爆震信号随时对点火时刻进行修正，使点火提前角保持在最佳状态。

3. 爆震控制过程

火花塞跳火点燃混合气后，如果火焰在传播途中压力异常升高，一些部位的混合气不等火焰传到，自己就会着火燃烧，造成瞬时爆发燃烧，这种现象称为爆震。爆震的危害一是噪声大，二是很可能使发动机损坏，特别在大负荷条件下，这种可能性很大。

要消除爆震，通常可以采用抗爆性能好的燃料、改进燃烧室结构、加强冷却液循环、推迟点火时间等方法。特别是推迟点火时间对消除爆震有明显的作用。

（1）爆震与点火提前角的关系

点火提前角越大，越容易产生爆震。试验证明，发动机发出最大扭矩的点火时刻是在发动机即将产生爆震的点火时刻附近。所以为了使发动机不产生爆震，其点火时刻均设定在爆震边缘的范围以内，使其离开爆震界限并存在较大的余量。但这样会势必降低发动机的功率，使发动机功率输出下降，燃料消耗增加。

（2）爆震控制系统

爆震控制的实质，是发动机控制单元通过爆震传感器检测发动机的爆震界限，控制点火时刻使其保持在爆震边界曲线附近，以提高发动机的功率，降低燃料的消耗。

通常情况下，爆震传感器安装在发动机的缸体上，根据发动机产生的各种不同的振荡频率的振动，而产生不同的电压信号。当发动机发生爆震时，爆震传感器的感应性能最好，产生最大的电压信号，其输出电压特性如图3-20（a）所示。

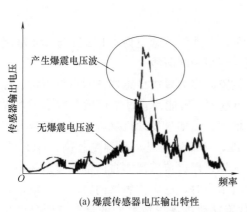

图 3-20 爆震信号的确定

爆震强度以超过基准值的次数计量，次数越多，爆震强度越大；次数越少，爆震强度越小，如图3-20（b）所示。

爆震传感器输入处理回路如图3-21所示，发动机电脑收到爆震传感器的信号后，经过滤波回路滤波，将爆震信号与其他振动信号分离，只允许特定频率范围的爆震信号通过滤波电路，再经峰值检测电路、与基准比较值比较电路使输入信号的最大值与爆震强度基准值进行比较，比较后由爆震判断电路判定是否产生

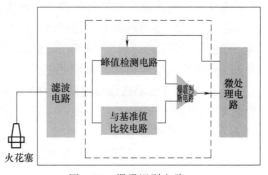

图 3-21 爆震识别电路

爆震，并将判定后的信号传给微处理器，微处理器相应地减小点火提前角来消除爆震。

当发动机的负荷低于一定值时，一般不出现爆震。这时不宜用控制爆震的方法来调整点火提前角，而应该用点火开环控制方案控制点火提前角，即此时发动机控制单元只按存储的信息及有关传感器的输入信号去控制点火提前角，而不再检测和分析爆震传感器的输入信号。发动机控制单元通过对反映负荷的传感器送来的信号进行分析，即可判断在某一时刻点火提前角应采用开环控制还是闭环控制。

当发动机控制单元通过爆震传感器的输入信号和比较电路判别发动机已经产生的爆震时，就减小点火提前角；当爆震现象消失时，发动机控制单元再逐渐恢复正常的点火提前角。控制过程如图 3-22 所示。

图 3-22　爆震控制过程

三、项目实施

（一）实施要求

丰田 5A、AJR 发动机台架；汽车；诊断仪。

（二）实施步骤

1. 爆震传感器的检测

桑塔纳 AJR 发动机有两个爆震传感器，分别安装在进气歧管下面，1/2 缸与 3/4 缸之间，传感器插座上有三根引线，其中两根为信号线，一根为屏蔽线。

爆震传感器本身在实际中很少发生故障，发生故障时多为爆震传感器拧紧力矩不对，标准力矩为 20N·m。如果发动机爆震传感器固定力矩过大，可能使它过于灵敏，减小了点火提前角造成发动机反应迟钝、排气温度过高、油耗增大；而如果发动机爆震传感器固定力矩过小，传感器灵敏度下降，此时发动机容易产生爆震，从而使得发动机温度过高、NO_x 化合物的排放量超标。此外还有插头锈蚀、线束插头损坏、爆震传感器本身内部摔裂损坏等。

爆震传感器是否正常，应该用示波器检测发动机工作时，爆震传感器的输出电压波形来判断。如果有不规则的振动波形出现，并且该波形随发动机爆震情况的变化而有明显的变化，则说明爆震传感器工作正常。如果没有波形输出或者输出波形不随发动机工作情况的变化而变化，说明爆震传感器有故障，应该更换。

在没有示波器的情况下，也可以通过测量电阻的方法对爆震传感器进行粗略的检测。将爆震传感器导线插头拔下，用万用表的欧姆挡测量传感器两个端子与接地之间的电阻，若导通，说明传感器已经损坏，必须更换。

桑塔纳 AJR 发动机爆震传感器的 3 个端子及电路图如图 3-23 所示，在爆震传感器的连接电路中，端子 1 为信号线正极，端子 2 为信号线负极，端子 3 为屏蔽线。

（1）检测传感器电阻

断开点火开关，拔下传感器线束插头，检测结果应与表 3-1 中标准值相符合。

（2）检测线束电阻

断开点火开关，拔下传感器线束插头和 ECU 线束插头，两插头各端子间导线电阻检测结果应与表 3-1 中的标准值相符合。

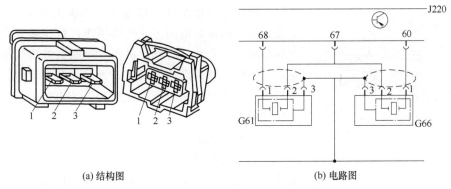

(a) 结构图　　　　　　　　　　　　(b) 电路图

图 3-23　桑塔纳 AJR 发动机爆震传感器

（3）检测输出信号

插上传感器线束插头，启动发动机，测量端子 1 与 2 间的电压，正常值为 0.3～1.4V。爆震传感器的 3 个端子之间不应有短路现象，否则，更换爆震传感器。传感器插头和发动机控制单元线束插头间的线路若有断路或短路应排除故障。

表 3-1　桑塔纳 2000GSi 爆震传感器检修标准

检测项目	检测条件	检测部位	电阻标准值/Ω
爆震传感器的电阻	断开点火开关并拔下传感器插头	传感器插座上端子 1 与 2	>1M
		传感器插座上端子 1 与 3	>1M
		传感器插座上端子 2 与 3	>1M
传感器信号正极线	拔下控制器和传感器插头	控制器 60(11) 端子至传感器插头 1 端子	<0.5
		控制器 68 端子至传感器插头 1 端子	<0.5
传感器信号负极线		控制器 67(30) 端子至传感器插头 2 端子	<0.5
传感器屏蔽线		控制器模块旁边发动机搭铁点至传感器插头 3 端子	<0.5

2. 点火模块的检测

AJR 型发动机点火系统采用无分电器双火花直接点火系统。点火线圈发生故障，发动机立即熄火或不能启动。ECU 不能检测到该故障信息。如果一个火花塞由于开路使这个点火回路断开，那么和它共用一个点火线圈的火花塞也因电气线路故障而不能跳火，如果一个火花塞由于短路而不能跳火，但电气回路没有断开，那么和它共用一个点火线圈的火花塞仍然能够跳火。AJR 型发动机点火系电路接线如图 3-24 所示。

拔下点火线圈 4 针插头，用发光二极管测试灯连接蓄电池正极和插头上端子 4，发光二极管测试灯应亮。如果测试灯不亮，检查端子 4 和接地点的线路是否有断路。

测试点火线圈的供电电压：拔下点火线圈的 4 针插头，用发光二极管测试灯连接在发动机接地点和插头上端子 2 之间，打开点火开关，发光二极管测试灯应亮。如果测试灯不亮，检查中央电器 D 插头 23 端子与 4 针插座端子 2 之间线路是否断路如图 3-25 所示。

测试点火线圈工作：拔下 4 个喷油器的插头和点火线圈的 4 针插头，打开点火开关，用发光

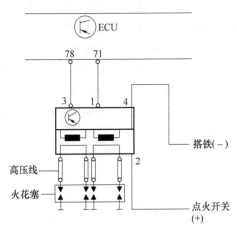

图 3-24　AJR 型发动机点火系电路接线图

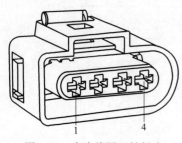

图 3-25 点火线圈 4 针插头

二极管测试灯连接发动机接地点和插头上端子 1，接通起动机数秒，测试灯应闪亮，然后用测试灯连接发动机接地点和端子 3，接通启动电动机数秒，测试灯应闪亮。如果测试灯不闪，检查点火线圈插头上端子和发动机控制单元线束的插头间导线是否开路或短路，如果线路正常，应更换发动机 ECU。

(1) 电阻测试

本项目电阻测试为辅助性测试，主要是检测线束的导通性，以确认线束通畅，无断路短路，插接器牢靠，各信号传递无干扰。测试在汽车微机控制故障检测诊断实验系统的发动机实验台上进行。

① 线束导通性测试：将数字万用表设置在电阻挡，在电路图上找到点火线圈图形下面的针脚号与 ECU 信号测试端口图相应的针脚号，分别测试点火线圈针脚对应至电控单元针脚的电阻，所有电阻都应低于 5Ω，如表 3-2 所示。

表 3-2 点火线圈针脚对应至电控单元针脚的正常阻值

	电脑接脚	点火线圈接脚	导通性
点火线圈(N152)线路电阻的测量	搭铁点	4	<0.5
	点火开关	2	<0.5
	ECU-78	3	<0.5
	ECU-71	1	<0.5

② 线束短路性测试：将数字万用表设置在电阻 200kΩ 挡，测量点火线圈针脚与其不相对应的电控单元针脚之间电阻应为 ∞。

在实际维修中，欲测试各条线束的导通性，应关闭点火开关，拔下传感器插头与电控单元插接器，使用数字万用表分别测量各线束间的电阻，相连导线电阻应当小于 5Ω，不相连导线电阻正常应为 ∞。在实际测量中，由于测量手法、万用表本身的误差以及被测物体表面的氧化与灰尘等因素，发生几欧姆的误差属正常现象，不必拘泥于具体数字。

(2) 电压测试

本项目电压测试有电源电压测试和信号电压测试两部分，其中信号电压测试是确定点火线圈是否失效的主要依据。

① 电源电压测试：在实际维修中，应拔下传感器插头，打开点火开关，测量 2 号端子与接地间电压，接通起动机时应显示 12V。此时电控单元会记录点火线圈的故障码，测试完毕后要使用诊断仪清除故障码。

② 信号电压测试：启动发动机至工作温度，拔下 4 个喷油器的插头和点火线圈的 4 针插头，打开点火开关，用发光二极管测试灯连接发动机接地点和插头上端子 1，接通起动机数秒，测试灯应闪亮，然后用测试灯连接发动机接地点和端子 3，接通启动电动机数秒，测试灯应闪亮。

（三）注意事项

① 爆震传感器要轻拿轻放，避免爆震传感器掉到地上摔坏。

② 点火线圈要轻拿轻放，避免点火线圈掉到地上摔坏。

③ 在实物台架上，测试端口与电控单元直接相连，不要将任何电压加在发动机实验台

的测试端口上，以免损坏电控单元。

四、知识与技能拓展

（一）点火系统波形分析

在不解体情况下，发动机点火系统的检测诊断主要分为点火波形的检测与分析和点火正时检测两个方面。下面向大家介绍一下点火波形的分析知识。

波形分析指把汽车发动机点火系统实际点火波形与标准波形比较以判断点火系统故障的过程。

1. 标准波形

传统触点式一次、二次点火电压波形如图 3-26 所示。

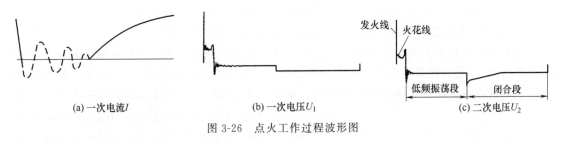

图 3-26　点火工作过程波形图

电子点火系统的二次点火波形与传统点火系统点火波形的主要区别在于，其闭合段后部电压略有上升。有的波形在闭合段中间也有一个微小的电压波动，这反映了点火控制器（电子模块）中限流电路的作用。另外，电子点火波形闭合段的长度随转速变化而变化。电子点火波形如图 3-27 所示。

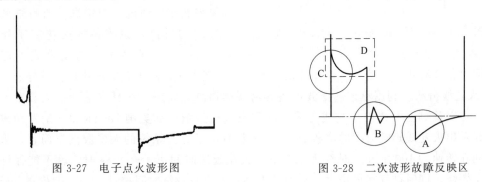

图 3-27　电子点火波形图　　　　图 3-28　二次波形故障反映区

2. 波形分析

（1）波形上的故障反映区

如果用示波器测得的波形与标准波形比较有差异，说明点火系统有故障。传统点火系统故障在波形（以二次波形为例）上有四个主要反映区，如图 3-28 所示。

C 区域为点火区：当一次电路切断时，点火线圈一次绕组内电流迅速降低，所产生的磁场迅速衰减，在二次绕组中产生高压电（15000～20000V），火花塞间隙被击穿。击穿电压一般为 4000～8000V。火花塞电极被击穿放电后，二次点火电压随之下降。

D 区域为燃烧区：当火花塞电极间隙被击穿后，电极间形成电弧使混合气点燃。火花放电过程一般持续 0.6～1.5ms，在二次点火电压波形上形成火花线。

B 区域为振荡区：在火花塞放电终了，点火线圈中的能量不能维持火花放电时，残余能量以阻尼振荡的形式消耗殆尽。此时，点火电压波形上出现具有可视脉冲的低频振荡。

A 区域为闭合区：一次电路再次闭合后，二次电路感应出 1500～2000V 与蓄电池电压相反的感生电压。在点火波形上出现迅速下降的垂直线，然后上升过渡为水平线。

（2）典型故障波形

① 发火线分析。转速稳定时，显示出各缸平列波，若点火电压高于标准值，说明高压电路有高电阻：

a. 若各缸都高，说明高电阻发生在点火线圈插孔及分火头之间，如高压断线、接触不良、分火头脏污等。

b. 个别缸电压高，说明该缸火花塞间隙过大，高压线接触不良或分火头与该缸高压线接触不良。

c. 若全部缸或个别缸电压过低，原因为火花塞脏污、间隙太小或高压短路。

d. 发火线下端出现多余波形，一般为白金触点烧蚀或接触不良。

当显示出各缸平列波，拔下除第一缸以外任一缸的高压线（第一缸高压线上包夹着示波器的传感器），使其距搭铁部位的距离逐渐增大，该缸发火线应明显上升，其电压值应是点火线圈的最高输出电压。对电子点火系统，则应高于 30kV，否则说明点火线圈有故障。若使拔下的高压线搭铁，发火线应明显缩短，其值应低于 5kV，否则说明分火头或分电器盖插孔电极间隙大，或分缸高压线与插孔接触不良，图 3-29 为拔下任一缸高压线后发火线升高的情况。

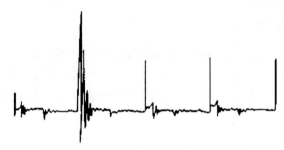

图 3-29 拔下任一缸高压线，发火线升高

当荧光屏上显示二次点火平列波时，如果突然使发动机转速增高，所有缸的发火线均匀升高，说明各缸火花塞工作正常。若一个缸或几个缸的发火线不能升高，说明火花塞有积炭。若某缸高压峰值上升很高，则说明该缸火花塞加速特性不好。

② 火花线分析。利用单缸选择波可较容易观察该缸火花线，在具有毫秒扫描装置的示波器上，可以从刻度上读出火花线延续时间和点火电压值（如美国 BEAR-200 型发动机检测仪可显示出火花线延续时间的毫秒数）。对于装有电子点火系统的大多数汽车而言，火花延续时间在转速为 1000r/min 时约为 1.5ms。火花延续时间小于 0.8ms 时，就不能保证混合气完全燃烧，同时排气污染增大、动力性下降；若火花持续时间超过 2ms，火花塞电极寿命会明显缩短。传统点火系统火花线长度一般为 0.6～0.8ms，燃烧区电压一般为 1～2kV。

若火花线过短，其原因一般为：

a. 火花塞间隙过大。

b. 分火头和分电器盖电极烧蚀或二者间隙过大。

c. 混合气过稀。

若火花线过长，原因一般为：

a. 火花塞脏污。

b. 火花塞间隙过小。

c. 高压线或火花塞短路。

用某些发动机综合检测仪观测点火波形时,尽管不能确定火花线的具体长度,但通过对各缸点火波形的比较,亦可发现火花延续时间较短及电压较低的汽缸。

③ 低频振荡区分析。发动机点火系统技术状况良好时,其低频振荡区应有 5 个以上可见脉冲;高功率线圈所产生的脉冲将多于 8 个。振荡脉冲数少,且振幅也小的原因是:

a. 点火线圈短路。

b. 电容器漏电。

c. 点火线圈一次电路接头或线路连接不良,阻值过大。

若振荡脉冲数过多,则表明电容器容量过大。

对于电子点火系统,低频振荡区异常时,仅表示点火线圈技术状况不正常,而与电容器无关,这是电子点火系统无电容器的缘故。

④ 闭合区分析。对传统点火系统,在触点闭合时,点火波形上产生垂直向下的直线,在此处有杂波说明白金触点烧蚀、接触不良或触点弹簧弹力不足,如图 3-30 所示。同理,在闭合区末端发火线前若有杂波,也说明白金触点技术状况不良。

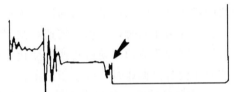

图 3-30 触点烧蚀故障波形

对于电子点火系统而言,闭合区的波形虽与传统点火系统极相似,但反向电压和击穿电压是由于晶体管导通和切断一次电流而产生的。因此,该两处波形异常是由晶体管技术状况不良造成的。电子点火系统闭合区波形的长度、形状与传统点火系统不同,主要表现在:闭合区在高转速时拉长,闭合段内有波纹或凸起;有的电子点火系统在闭合区结束前,先产生一条锯齿状的上升斜线,而后出现点火线。以上均属正常情况。

⑤ 波形倒置。点火线圈正负极接反时,发动机也能启动,但点火消耗的能量增加。这是因为火花塞工作时,中心电极的温度较旁电极高,电子从中心电极向旁电极运动得较容易;反之则稍难。点火线圈正负极接线正确时,发火线向上;极性接反时,则发火线向下,如图 3-31 所示。

图 3-31 点火线圈极性接反的故障波形

⑥ 闭合角检测。汽油机点火过程中,一次电路导通阶段所对应的凸轮轴转角称为闭合角。对于传统点火系统,闭合角为白金触点闭合时期所占的凸轮轴转角;对于电子点火系统,则是三极管导通所占的凸轮轴转角。

利用一次并列波(如图 3-32 所示)可方便地观测各缸的闭合角,闭合角的大小应在以下范围内:

3 缸发动机:60°~66°;

4 缸发动机:50°~54°;

6 缸发动机:38°~42°;

8 缸发动机:29°~32°。

对于传统有触点点火系统而言,测出的闭合角小,说明触点间隙太大,触点闭合时间

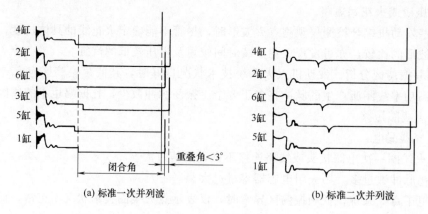

图 3-32 并列波

短,一次电流增长不到需要的数值,会使点火能量不足;若闭合角太大,说明触点间隙小,会使触点间发生电弧放电,反而削弱了点火能量,不利于正常点火。

在闭合角相同时,发动机转速高则闭合时间短,转速低则闭合时间长。因此,为保证点火可靠,闭合角应随发动机转速而变化。电子点火系统中的点火控制器可对闭合角的大小进行控制和调节:低速时,减小闭合角;高速时,增大闭合角。

⑦ 重叠角检测。各缸点火波形首端对齐,最长波形与最短波形长度之差所占的凸轮轴转角称为重叠角(如图3-33所示)。

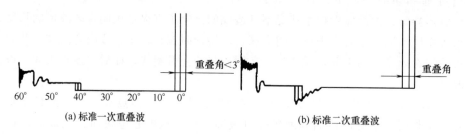

图 3-33 重叠波

重叠角不应大于点火间隔的5%,即:

4缸发动机≤4.5°;

6缸发动机≤3°;

8缸发动机≤2.25°。

重叠角的大小反映多缸发动机点火间隔的一致程度,重叠角愈大,则点火间隔愈不均匀。不仅会影响发动机的动力性、经济性,还影响发动机运转的稳定性。重叠角太大是由分电器凸轮磨损不均或分电器轴磨损松旷、弯曲变形等原因造成的。

(二)故障案例

案例:发动机怠速运转时车身抖动,低速行驶时汽车不稳定,加速时排气管放炮。

1. 故障现象

一辆本田雅阁轿车怠速抖动,驾驶员说该车低速行驶时感觉车身不稳,有顿挫的感觉。加速时发动机有"突突"声,排气管伴有放炮现象,当车速提高后又有好转。

2. 故障原因

火花塞工作不良或个别缸火花塞不工作。

3. 故障诊断与排除

维修人员上路试车后，确实存在驾驶人所描述的故障现象。分析该车故障现象，引起此类故障最有可能的原因是发动机电控燃油喷射或电控点火系统两方面有故障。

① 用故障诊断仪对该车电控系统进行故障自诊断，检查是否有故障码，结果没有任何故障提示。

② 根据以往的维修经验，用试火法检查高压是否有火，结果跳火间隙和火花均正常。

③ 拆下并检查各缸火花塞。当拆下各缸火花塞时，发现火花塞电极均有污物和积炭。

原来是火花塞工作不良或个别缸火花塞不工作，造成部分燃油没有充分燃烧而排出，从而在排气管内燃烧，出现放炮现象。轻度时出现发动机怠速不稳、抖动现象，怠速和加速时发出"突突"声。

更换全部火花塞后，再试车，故障现象消失，故障得以排除。

小 结

本项目详细介绍了微机控制点火系统的结构组成及原理，微机控制点火系统高压电的分配方式，微机控制点火系统的控制过程，爆震传感器在电控点火系统中应用的作用，及电控点火系统的检测知识，爆震传感器的检测方法。

习题及思考

1. 简述曲轴位置传感器和凸轮轴位置传感器的作用和相互关系。
2. 如何进行桑塔纳 2000GSi AJR 发动机磁感应式曲轴位置传感器的检修？
3. 以桑塔纳 2000GSi AJR 发动机为例，说明无分电器点火控制系统的检修方法。
4. 以桑塔纳 2000GSi AJR 发动机为例，说明爆震传感器的检测方法。
5. 点火提前角太大对发动机有哪些影响？
6. 简述共振型压电式爆震传感器的工作原理。

项目四

汽油发动机怠速控制系统检修

一、项目情境引入

一辆轿车发动机怠速时,发动机转速不稳(发动机转速忽高忽低)该如何解决呢?如果要想解决电控发动机怠速不稳的故障,应了解发动机电控系统,空气供给系统的结构和原理,怠速控制系统的组成和功用,燃油供给系统和点火控制系统的结构和原理,能进行相关传感器、执行器的拆装、检测等专业知识。本项目重点学习怠速控制系统,只有具备了上述的汽车专业知识才具备解决发动机怠速不稳故障的能力。

二、项目相关知识

当发动机怠速运转时,由于空调压缩机、动力转向助力泵、发电机等负载的变化会引起怠速转速发生波动,怠速控制阀 ISCV 的功用就是通过调节发动机怠速时的进气量来调节怠速转速,保证发动机在负荷发生变化时发动机运转的稳定性。

(一)怠速控制阀的分类

怠速控制阀安装在发动机节气门体上或节气门体附近。发动机怠速时进气量的控制方式有节气门直接控制式和节气门旁通空气道控制式两种,前者是直接操纵节气门来调节进气量,简称节气门直动式;后者是通过控制节气门旁通空气道的开度来调节进气量,简称旁通空气式,控制原理如图 4-1 所示。桑塔纳 2000GLi、别克世纪型轿车和切诺基吉普车采用旁通空气式,桑塔纳 2000GSi、3000 型和捷达 AT、GTX 型轿车采用节气门直动式。

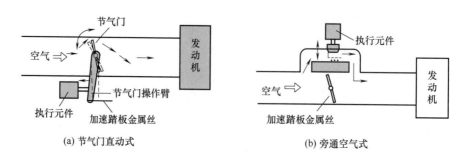

图 4-1 怠速的两种控制方式

（二）怠速控制阀的原理

1. 节气门直动式控制系统

节气门直动式怠速控制系统取消了旁通通道，而是通过控制节气门的开启角度，调节空气通路的截面来控制充气量，实现对怠速的控制。

大众系统轿车多采用节气门直动式怠速控制系统，以下为节气门直动式怠速控制系统的工作原理。

节气门直动式怠速控制系统主要由节气位置传感器、怠速节气门位置传感器、怠速开关和执行器（怠速直流电动机）以及一套齿轮驱动机构组成，图4-2（a）（已拆去节气门体上的塑料盖板）为其结构图，图4-2（b）为其内部线路图。节气门位置传感器和怠速节气门位置传感器都是由一个双轨形碳膜电阻和在其上滑动的触点组成。另外在节气门体上有一个双齿轮，它是由同轴的一个大齿轮和一个小齿轮组成。与怠速直流电动机同轴的小齿轮与双齿轮中的大齿轮啮合，扇形齿轮与节气门同轴并与双齿轮中的大齿轮啮合。当驾驶员踩加速踏板时，怠速开关断开，发动机控制模块根据节气门位置传感器的输入信号判断发动机的运行工况，并进行喷油和点火的控制。当驾驶员不踩加速踏板时，节气门在回位弹簧的作用下关闭，怠速开关闭合。发动机控制模块收到怠速开关闭合的信号，得知发动机处于怠速运行状态，并根据怠速节气门位置传感器的信号和曲轴位置传感器的信号来控制怠速直流电动机的动作，经过小齿轮、双齿轮和扇形齿轮将电动机的转动传递到节气门，使其打开相应的角度，使怠速转速达到最佳值。

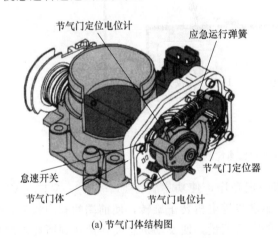

(a) 节气门体结构图

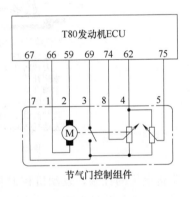

(b) 节气门体电路图

图4-2 节气门体

如图4-3所示为步进电机式怠速空气控制阀（IACV）的结构图，步进电机式怠速空气控制阀安装在发动机进气总管内，发动机控制模块根据各种传感器的信号在怠速空气控制阀接头各端子上加电压（端子见图4-4），从而使电机转子顺转或反转，使阀芯做轴向移动，改变阀芯与阀座之间的间隙，就可调节流过旁通空气道的空气量。间隙小，进气量少，怠速低；间隙大，进气量多，怠速高。

发动机控制模块（ECU）对发动机怠速进行控制时，一般控制程序如图4-5所示。首先，发动机控制模块根据节气门位置传感器（TPS）的信号和车速信号，来判断发动机是否处于怠速运行状态，然后根据发动机冷却液温度传感器（ECT）、空调开关（A/C）、动力转向开关（PS）以及空挡启动开关等信号，按照存储器内存储的参考数据，确定相应的目标转速。一般情况下，怠速控制常采用发动机转速信号作为反馈信号，实现怠速转速的闭环控制，即发动机的实际转速与目标转速进行比较，根据比较得出的差值，确定相应目标转速控制量，去驱动步进电机，使实际转速趋近于目标转速。

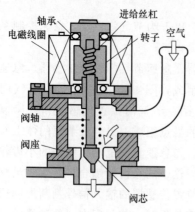

图 4-3 步进电机式怠速空气控制阀的结构

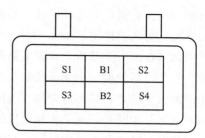

图 4-4 怠速空气控制阀端子分布图

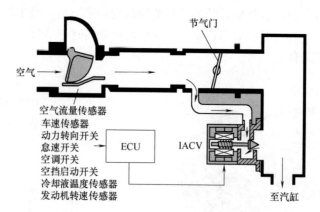

图 4-5 步进电机式怠速控制系统的组成

步进电机的控制，发动机控制模块依一定顺序，使功率管 VT1—VT2—VT3—VT4 适时导通，分别给步进电机定子线圈供电，驱动步进电机转子旋转，使前端的阀门移动，改变阀门与阀座之间的距离，调节旁通空气道的空气流量，使发动机怠速转速达到所要求的目标转速。

2. 旋转滑阀型怠速控制阀

旋转滑阀式怠速控制系统的构造如图 4-6 所示。图 4-7 为广州本田奥德赛的怠速阀实物图。此外，桑塔纳 2000、夏利 2000、富康 1.6A 以及丰田佳美等轿车都用这种怠速控制阀。

旋转滑阀式怠速控制系统主要由永久磁铁、空气旁通道、旋转滑阀和复位弹簧等组成。其中旋转滑阀固装在电枢轴上，与电枢轴一起转动，用以控制通过旁通空气道的空气量；永久磁铁固装在外壳上，形成永磁磁场；复位弹簧的作用是在发动机熄火后使怠速阀旁通道完全打开；电枢铁芯上绕有两组绕向相反的电磁线圈 L1 和 L2（图 4-8），当给线圈通电时，就会产生磁场从而使电枢轴带动旋转滑阀转动，控制通过旁通空气道的空气。电磁线圈 L1 和 L2 由发动机控制模块通过晶体管 V1 和 V2 控制，V1 和 V2 由同一信号进行反向控制，即

V2 导通时，V1 截止；
V2 截止时，V1 导通。

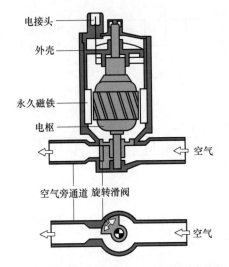

图 4-6 旋转滑阀式怠速空气控制阀结构图　　　图 4-7 广州本田奥德赛的旋转滑阀式怠速阀

由这两组线圈的导通时间的比例关系来决定电枢所受的转矩和偏转角度。电枢受到的转矩有三个：

$T1$——线圈 L1 产生的转矩，逆时针方向，大小与电流有关；

$T2$——线圈 L2 产生的转矩，顺时针方向，大小与电流有关；

$T3$——复位弹簧产生的转矩，逆时针方向，大小与转角有关。

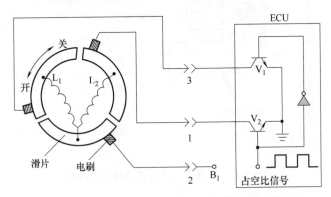

图 4-8 旋转滑阀式怠速空气控制阀的电路连接图

工作时，发动机控制模块根据发动机冷却液温度传感器（ECT）和节气门位置传感器（TPS）等输入的信号，确定发动机所处怠速工况的混合气浓度，并输出占空比信号控制 L1 或 L2 的通电时间。占空比是指发动机控制模块控制信号在一个周期内通电时间与通电周期之比，如图 4-9 所示。若不计复位弹簧的扭矩，则：

当占空比为 50% 时，L1 和 L2 平均通电时间相等，$T1=T2$，电枢停止转动；

当占空比大于 50% 时，线圈 L2 的平均通电时间长，$T2>T1$，电枢带动旋转滑阀顺时针偏转，空气旁通道截面减小，怠速降低；

当占空比小于 50% 时，线圈 L1 的平均通电时间长，$T_1>T_2$，电枢带动旋转滑阀逆时针偏转，空气旁通道截面减小，怠速降低。

旋转滑阀根据控制脉冲信号的占空比偏转，占空比的范围约为18%（旋转滑阀关闭）至82%（旋转滑阀打开）之间。滑阀的偏转角度限定在90°内。

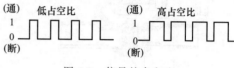

（三）发动机怠速控制过程

怠速控制就是怠速转速的控制。配置怠速控制系统后，发动机的怠速转速在汽车使用期内，不会因发动机老化、汽缸积炭、火花塞间隙和温度等变化而发生变化。

图4-9 信号的占空比

1. 怠速控制系统的组成

设有旁通空气道的怠速控制系统的组成如图4-10所示，由各种传感器、信号控制开关、电子控制单元ECU、怠速控制阀和节气门旁通空气道等组成。

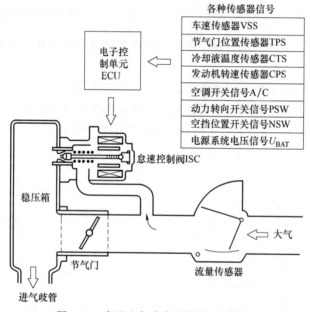

图4-10 旁通空气式怠速控制系统组成

车速传感器提供车速信号，节气门位置传感器提供怠速触点开闭信号，这两个信号用来判定发动机是否处于怠速状态。发动机怠速时，节气门关闭，节气门位置传感器的怠速触点IDL闭合，传感器输出端子IDL输出低电平信号。因此，当IDL端子输出低电平信号时，如果车速为零，就说明发动机处于怠速状态；如果车速不为零，则说明发动机处于减速状态。

冷却液温度信号用于修正怠速转速。在ECU内部，存储有不同水温对应的最佳怠速转速，如图4-11所示。在冷车启动后的暖机过程中，ECU根据发动机温度信号，通过控制怠速控制阀的开度来控制相应的快怠速转速，并随发动机温度升高逐渐降低怠速转速。当冷却液温度达到正常工作温度时，怠速转速恢复正常怠速转速。

空调开关、动力转向开关、空挡启动开关信号和电源电压信号等向 ECU 提供发动机负荷变化的状态信息。在 ECU 内部，存储有不同负荷状况下对应的最佳怠速转速。

各型汽车采用的怠速控制阀不尽相同，切诺基吉普车采用步进电机式怠速控制阀来控制怠速转速，桑塔纳 2000GSi、3000 型和捷达 AT、GXT 型轿车采用节气门控制组件来自动调整怠速转速。

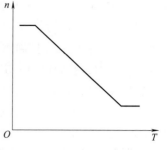

图 4-11　不同温度下的怠速转速

2. 怠速转速控制过程

怠速控制的实质是控制发动机怠速时的进气量。怠速时的喷油量则由 ECU 根据预先试验设定的怠速空燃比和实际进气量计算确定。

怠速控制内容主要是发动机负荷变化控制和电器负荷变化控制。怠速控制系统控制怠速转速的方法如下：

当发动机怠速负荷增大时，ECU 控制怠速控制阀使进气量增大，从而使怠速转速提高，防止发动机运转不稳或熄火，当发动机怠速负荷减小时，ECU 控制怠速控制阀使进气量减少，从而使怠速转速降低，以免怠速转速过高。

在发动机怠速状态下，当空调开关、动力转向开关等接通或空挡启动开关断开时，发动机负荷就会增大，转速就会降低。如果转速降低过多，发动机就可能熄火，会给车辆使用带来不便。因此，在接通空调开关或动力转向开关之前，需要先将怠速转速提高，防止发动机熄火。当空调开关或动力转向开关断开时，发动机负荷又会减小，转速就会升高，不仅油耗会增大，而且会给汽车驾驶带来一定困难（起步前冲，容易导致汽车追尾）。因此在断开空调开关或动力转向开关之后，需要将怠速转速降低，防止怠速转速过高。另外，当电器负荷增大（如夜间行车接通前照灯、按喇叭等）时，电器系统的供电电压就会降低，如果电源电压过低，就会影响电控系统正常工作和用电设备正常用电，因此在电源电压降低时，需要提高怠速转速，以便提高电源电压。

怠速转速控制过程如图 4-12 所示。ECU 首先根据怠速触点 IDL 信号和车速信号，判断发动机是否处于怠速状态。当判定为怠速工况时，再根据发动机冷却液温度传感器信号、空调开关、动力转向开关等信号，从存储器存储的怠速转速数据中查找相应的目标转速，然后将目标转速与曲轴位置传感器检测的发动机实际转速进行比较。

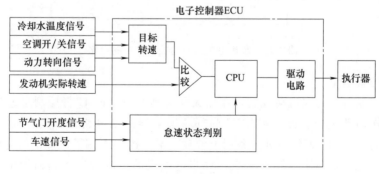

图 4-12　怠速转速控制过程

当发动机负荷增大，需要发动机快怠速运转，目标转速高于实际转速时，ECU 将控制怠速控制阀增大旁通进气量来实现快怠速；反之，当发动机负荷减小，目标转速低于实际转速时，ECU将控制怠速控制阀减小旁通进气量来调节怠速转速。

例如，当接通空调（发动机负荷增大）时，需要发动机快怠速运转（目标转速=快怠速转速），ECU就使怠速控制阀的阀门开大，增大旁通进气量。当旁通进气量增大时，因为怠速空燃比已由试验确定为一定值（一般为12：1），所以ECU将控制喷油器增大喷油量，发动机转速随之增高到快怠速转速运转。国产汽车电控发动机的怠速转速如表4-1所示。当接通空调或动力转向泵时，其快怠速转速约为1000r/min±50r/min。快怠速时，转速升高200r/min左右。同理，当断开空调（发动机负荷减小），需要降低发动机转速，即目标转速低于实际转速时，ECU将使怠速控制阀的阀门关小，减小旁通进气量进行调节。

表4-1 各型汽车燃油喷射式发动机的怠速转速

车型	发动机型号	怠速转速/(r/min)	备注
桑塔纳 2000GLi	AFE	800±50	出厂标准
桑塔纳 2000GSi 桑塔纳 3000	AJR	800±30	出厂标准
捷达 AT、GTX	AHP	840±40	出厂标准
红旗 CA7220E	CA488-3	850±30	出厂标准
奥迪 200	V6型2.6L	750±70	出厂标准

3. 怠速控制系统的控制特性

采用步进电机式怠速控制阀的怠速控制线路如图4-13所示。当发动机怠速负荷变化时，在怠速转速变化之前，ECU将按照一定顺序，控制驱动电路中的三极管VT1、VT2、VT3、VT4适时导通，分别接通步进电机定子绕组电流，使电机转子旋转，带动控制阀的阀芯移动，从而调节进气量，使发动机怠速转速达到目标转速。

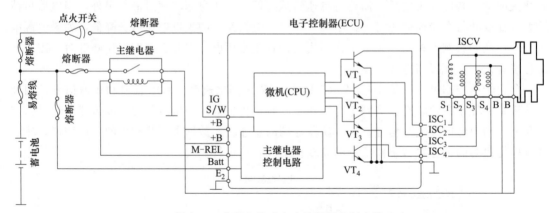

图4-13 步进电机式怠速控制阀控制电路

（1）初始位置确定

为了改善发动机的再次启动性能，在点火开关断开时，ECU将控制怠速控制阀处于全开状态，为再次启动做好准备。当ECU内部主继电器控制电路接收到点火开关拨到OFF（断开）位置的信号时，ECU将利用备用电源输入端（BATT端子）提供的电压控制主继电器（燃油喷射继电器）线圈继续供电2s，使步进电机的控制阀退回到初始位置，以便下次启动时具有较大的进气量。

（2）启动控制特性

启动发动机时，由于怠速控制阀预先设定在全开位置，因此进气量较大，发动机容易启动。一旦发动机被启动，如果阀门保持在全开位置，怠速转速就会升得过高。所以在启动时或启动后，当发动机转速达到规定值（该值由冷却液温度确定）时，ECU 就会控制步进电机步进的步数，使控制阀阀门关小到由冷却液温度确定的阀芯位置，使怠速转速稳定。如发动机冷却液温度在启动时为 20℃，当发动机转速达到 500 r/min 时，ECU 将控制步进电机从全开位置 A 点（125 步）步进到达 B 点（70 步）位置，如图 4-14 所示，使阀门关小，防止转速过高。

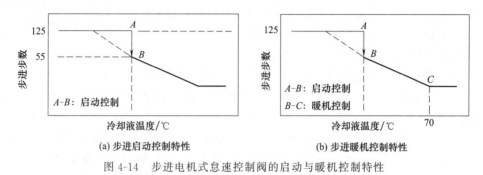

图 4-14　步进电机式怠速控制阀的启动与暖机控制特性

（3）暖机控制特性

在发动机启动后的暖机过程中，ECU 将根据冷却液温度传感器信号确定步进电机步进的位置。随着转速升高和发动机温度升高，控制阀阀门将逐渐关小，步进电机步进的步数逐渐减少，如图 4-14（b）所示。当冷却液温度达到 70℃ 时，暖机控制结束，步进电机及其阀芯位置保持不变。

三、项目实施

（一）实施要求

丰田 5A、AJR 发动机台架；汽车。

（二）实施步骤

1. 怠速控制系统的就车检测

怠速控制系统的就车检测方法有三种，可根据情况选用。

（1）发动机怠速运转状况检测

在冷车状态下启动发动机后，暖机过程开始时，发动机的怠速转速应能达到规定的快怠速转速（通常为 1500r/min）；在发动机达到正常工作温度后，怠速转速应能恢复正常（通常为 750r/min）。如果启车启动后怠速不能按上述规律变化，则怠速控制系统有故障。

发动机达到正常工作温度后，在打开空调开关时，发动机怠速转速应能上升到 900r/min 左右。若打开空调开关后发动机转速下降，则怠速控制系统有故障。

在发动机怠速运转中，若对怠速调节螺钉做微量转动，发动机怠速转速应不会发生变化（转动后应使怠速调节螺钉恢复原来的位置）。若在转动中怠速转速发生变化，说明怠速控制系统不工作。

（2）怠速控制阀的工作状况检查

对于脉冲线性电磁阀式怠速控制阀，可在发动机怠速运转中拔下怠速控制阀线束连接器，观察发动机的转速是否有变化。如此时发动机转速有变化，则怠速控制阀工作正常。对于步进电动机式怠速控制阀，可在发动机熄火后的一瞬间倾听怠速控制阀是否有"嗡嗡"的工作声音（此时步进电动机应工作，直到怠速控制阀完全开启，以利发动机再启动）。如怠速控制阀发出"嗡嗡"声，则怠速控制阀良好。为了检查步进电动机式怠速控制阀的工作状况，也可以在发动机启动前拔下怠速控制阀线束连接器，待发动机启动后再插上，观察发动机转速是否有变化。如果此时发动机转速发生变化，则怠速控制阀工作正常；否则，怠速控制阀或控制电路有故障。

(3) ECU 控制电压的检测

对于脉冲线性电磁阀式怠速控制阀，应拔下怠速控制阀线束连接器，用万用表电压挡测量其端子电压。如果在发动机运转过程中，怠速控制阀线束连接器端子有脉冲电压输出，ECU 和怠速控制系统线路无故障。若无脉冲电压输出，可打开空调开关后再测试。若仍无脉冲电压输出，则怠速控制系统不工作，应检查 ECU 与怠速控制阀之间的线路（是否有接触不良或断路故障）；如怠速系统的线路无故障，则 ECU 有故障，应更换 ECU。

2. 步进电机式怠速控制阀的检测

对于步进电机式怠速控制阀，将点火开关置于"ON"位置，然后测量 ECU 的端子 ICS1、ICS2、ICS3、ICS4 与端子 E1 间的电压值（应为 9～14V），如无电压，则 ECU 有故障。

(1) 怠速控制阀线圈电阻的检测

拆下怠速控制阀，用万用表 Ω 挡测量怠速控制阀线圈的电阻值。脉冲线性电磁阀式怠速控制阀只有一组线圈，其电阻值为 10～15Ω。步进电机式怠速控制阀通常有 2～4 组线圈，各组线圈的电阻值为 10～30Ω。如线圈电阻值不在上述范围内，应更换怠速控制阀。

(2) 步进电动机的动作检查

将蓄电池电源以一定顺序输送给步进电动机各线圈，就可使步进电动机转动，如图 4-15 所示。各种步进电动机的线圈形式和接线端的布置形式都不同。这里以皇冠 3.0 轿车 2JZ-GE 发动机怠速控制阀步进电动机为例说明其检查方法。首先，将步进电动机连接器端子 B1 和 B2 与蓄电池正极相连，然后将端子 S1、S2、S3、S4 依次（S1—S2—S3—S4）与蓄电池负极相接，此时步进电动机应转动，阀芯向外伸出，若将端子 S1、S2、S3、S4 按相反的顺序（S4—S3—S2—S1）与蓄电池负极相接，步进电动机应朝相反方向转动，阀芯向内缩入。

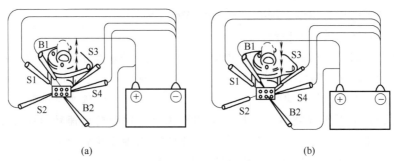

图 4-15　测试怠速空气控制阀

3. 节气门直动式怠速控制阀系统测试

(1) 机械检查

节气门体在长时间使用后,在进气通道和节气门之间有可能形成积炭,而造成节气门卡滞、怠速不稳等现象。此外,节气门体在经受长期剧烈的振动后,有可能出现如怠速直流电动机轴承磨损、塑料齿轮断齿、阀门驱动机构卡滞、驱动机构盖板破裂等,出现这类故障时都无法修复,只能更换新的节气门体总成。所以在对节气门体检查时,可先采用目测有无以上故障发生的方式进行。

(2) 部件测试

① 电阻测试。如节气门直动式(桑塔纳 AJR 发动机)怠速控制阀插头与插座上接线端子的位置如图 4-16 所示。

检修时用万用表电阻挡检测相关端子的电阻。检测时,断开点火开关,拔下传感器线束插头,检测结果应当符合规定。

当用万用表电阻 OHM×200Ω 或 R×1Ω 挡检测线束电阻时,断开点火开关,拔下控制器线束插头和怠速控制阀线束插头,检测两插头上各端子之间导线电阻应当符合规定。如阻值过大或为无穷大,说明线束与端子接触不良或断路,应予修理。

图 4-16 桑塔纳 AJR 发动机
怠速控制阀端子位置

拔下节气门控制组件插头,打开点火开关,测量相关线束端子之间电压至少应符合标准。

② 节气门体供电检测。如图 4-17(a)所示,拔下节气门体接头,有 8 只端子,其中端子 6 是空的(没有接线),端子 1、2、3、4、5、7、8 分别与 ECU 的端子 T80/66、T80/59、T80/69、T80/62、T80/75、T80/67、T80/75 相接。1、2 端子直接接直流电动机,5、8 端子分别接节气门位置传感器和怠速节气门位置传感器的滑动触点,它们的输出信号都不超过 5V,且信号电压与节气门开度成反比。端子 3 输出怠速开关信号,端子 4、7 向节气门体提供 5V 电压,其中端子 7 通过发动机控制模块接地,具体参见表 4-2。

表 4-2 节气门体接头各端子功能

端子号	连接点	功能
1	T80/66(ECU)	怠速提高控制
2	T80/59(ECU)	怠速降低控制
3	T80/69(ECU)	怠速开关
4	T80/62(ECU)	传感器供电(5V)
5	T80/75(ECU)	节气门位置传感器信号
6		空
7	T80/67(ECU)	传感器接地
8	T80/75(ECU)	怠速节气门位置传感器信号

将点火开关置于"ON"(接通而不启动)位置,按如图 4-17 所示方法用万用表进行测量:测量端子 4 与端子 7 之间的电压应为 5.0V±0.5V。若测量值与上述要求不符,将点火开关置于"OFF"挡,拔下 ECU 接头用万用表进行线路检测,节气门体电路图如图 4-2(b)所示。端子 4 与 ECU 接头端子 T80/62、端子 7 与 ECU 接头端子 T80/67 之间的导线阻值小于 1.5Ω,端子 4 与端子 7 间的电阻应为无穷大。若测得结果与上述要求不符,按电

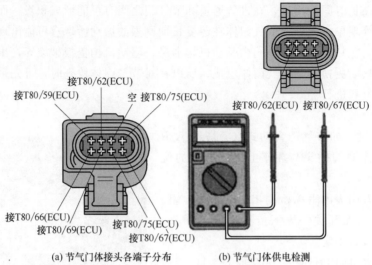

图 4-17 节气门体接头端子的分布和供电检测

路图查找故障并排除。

③ 急速开关检测。将点火开关置于"OFF"挡,拆下节气门体接头。用万用表检测节气门全闭时端子 3 与端子 7 之间的电阻应小于 1Ω。缓慢踩下加速踏板,端子 3 与 7 间阻值应为无穷大,否则更换节气门体。

④ 急速控制装置检测

a. 急速节气门位置传感器性能检测。如图 4-18 所示,将探针插入节气门体接头端子 8 引线内,启动发动机,进入急速运行。在冷却液温度达到 80℃以上时,按图示方法用万用表测量探针检测点与蓄电池负极之间电压应为 2.8~3.6V。

b. 直流电动机检测。把点火开关置于"OFF"位置,拔下节气门体接头,用万用表测量:节气门体接头端子 1 与端子 2 之间的阻值应为 30~200Ω。若不符合要求,更换节气门体总成。

c. 急速节气门位置传感器检测。把点火开关置到"OFF"挡,按照"电机驱动器"操作说明和接线图将其安装在节气门体上,如图 4-19 所示。具体操作如表 4-3 所示。

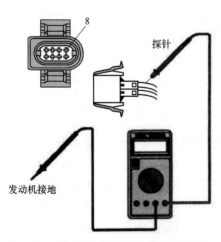

图 4-18 急速节气门开度传感器性能检测

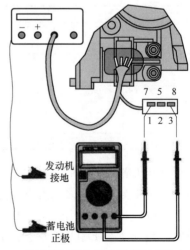

图 4-19 急速节气门位置传感器及直流电机检测

表 4-3 操作步骤

操作步骤	操作
1	打开电机驱动器电源开关,节气门转臂转到初始位置
2	按"-"按钮,节气门转臂从初始位置向怠速最小位置限位块方向移动,每按一次"-"按钮,转臂移动一次,直到该臂靠到怠速最小位置限位块为止
3	按"+"按钮,节气门转臂从当前位置向怠速最大位置限位块移动。同样,每按一次"+",转臂移动一次,直到转臂靠到怠速最大位置限位块为止
4	在上述操作中,用万用表测量节气门体接头端子 8 与端子 7 之间的电压值,电压应不超过 5V
5	关掉电源开关,节气门转臂又自动返回到初始位置

若测得结果与上述要求不符,应更换节气门体总成。图 4-20 为节气门转臂的位置。否则用万用表检测节气门体接头端子与 ECU 端子之间的电阻见表 4-4。

若以上节气门体的各项检查结果全都满足,但怠速控制装置仍不工作,则更换发动机控制模块。

d. 节气门位置传感器检测。打开点火开关,如图 4-21 所示。将万用表表笔插入节气门体插座第 5 端子引线内,缓慢踩下加速踏板从关闭到全开,万用表电压读数应随着节气门开度的增大而缓慢下降。反之,随节气门的逐渐关闭,万用表电压读数应逐渐上升,否则应进行供电和线路检查。

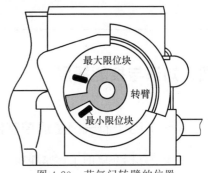

图 4-20 节气门转臂的位置

表 4-4 节气门体接头端子与 ECU 端子之间的电阻

序号	节气门体接头端子	ECU 端子	测量结果
1	8	T80/75	阻值小于 1.5Ω
2	2	T80/59	阻值小于 1.5Ω
3	1	T80/66	阻值小于 1.5Ω
4	7	T80/67	阻值小于 1.5Ω
5	1	T80/59	阻值应为无穷大
6	1	T80/75	阻值应为无穷大
7	1	T80/67	阻值应为无穷大
8	2	T80/66	阻值应为无穷大
9	7	T80/66	阻值应为无穷大

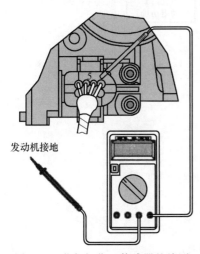

图 4-21 节气门位置传感器的检测

(a) 供电检测。关闭点火开关,拔下节气门体插座,再打开点火开关,检查节气门体接头端子 4 和端子 7 间的电压应为 5.0V±0.5V。

(b) 线路检查见表 4-5。

若供电和线路均无故障则更换节气门体总成。

(三) 注意事项

① 怠速控制阀要轻拿轻放,避免怠速控制阀掉到地上摔坏。

② 上实验台测试电压信号时,注意操作流程和相对应的测试端口。原则上只做本次实验相关的测试。

③ 在实物台架上,测试端口与电控单元直接相连,不要将任何电压加在发动机实验台的测试端口上,以免

损坏电控单元。

④ 严禁未经许可，擅自扳动教具、设备的电器开关、点火开关和启动开关。

表 4-5 线路检查

序号	节气门体接头端子	ECU 端子	测量结果
1	5	T80/75	阻值小于 1.5Ω
2	4	T80/62	阻值小于 1.5Ω
3	7	T80/67	阻值小于 1.5Ω
4	4	T80/75	阻值应为无穷大
5	7	T80/75	阻值应为无穷大
6	4	节气门 7	阻值应为无穷大

四、知识与技能拓展

（一）电子节气门怠速控制执行机构

电子节气门系统的工作原理如下：驾驶员操纵加速踏板，加速踏板位置传感器产生相应的电压信号输入节气门控制单元，控制单元首先对输入的信号进行滤波，以消除环境噪声的影响，然后根据当前的工作模式、踏板移动量和变化率解析驾驶员意图，计算出对发动机扭矩的基本需求，得到相应的节气门转角的基本期望值。然后再经过 CAN 总线和整车控制单元进行通信，获取其他工况信息以及各种传感器信号如发动机转速、挡位、节气门位置、空调能耗等等，由此计算出整车所需求的全部扭矩，通过对节气门转角期望值进行补偿，得到节气门的最佳开度，并把相应的电压信号发送到驱动电路模块，驱动控制电机使节气门达到最佳的开度位置。节气门位置传感器则把节气门的开度信号反馈给节气门控制单元，形成闭环的位置控制。控制原理图如图 4-22 所示。

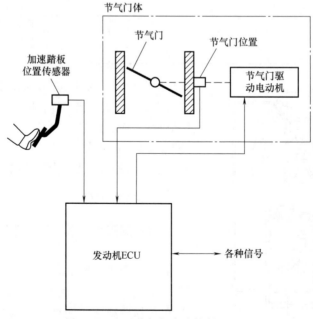

图 4-22 电子节气门怠速控制原理图

（二）直动式节气门的基本设定

对于电喷车的某些系统，在维修后或保养时必须进行基本设定。在基本设定过程中，控制单元中的某些参数（如怠速时的点火正时等）会调整到生产厂家设定的指定值，或者将某些元件（如节气门位置传感器）参数存入控制单元，以便实行精确控制。大众汽车节气门体，无论是半电子式还是电子式的节气门，电脑必须知道电机控制节气门在节气门位置传感器上能达到实际的最小和最大位置。图4-23所示是宝来汽车电子节气门电路图。

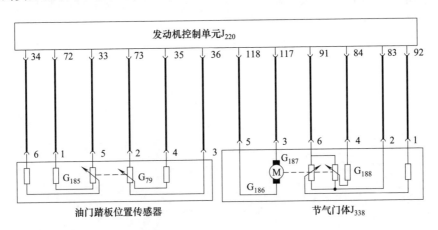

图4-23 宝来汽车电子节气门电路图

电脑通过控制半电子节气门电机把节气门关到尽可能最小的开度，怠速电位计电压传入电脑，电脑就会记忆这个开度（实际上是电脑记忆节气门最小开度电压经模/数转换过来的数字电压），最大位置由怠速开关断开决定，目的主要是重新划定怠速范围。

对于电子节气门最大和最小位置是由电机所能达的位置决定，主要是重新规划怠速范围、规划部分负荷范围、划定全负荷范围，以上在诊断仪读取数据流时可见。

若节气门体过脏，节气门不能完全关闭，电脑的怠速自适应程序自适应后可以使怠速正常，但脏到一定程度超过了电脑内的限值时，即自适应超限后，怠速将变得不稳定。清洗节气门后，此时电脑内记忆的节气门最小值和实际节气门开度能达到的最小值不同，必然造成控制失准，结果发动机怠速居高不下。这种情况会在电脑怠速自适应程序（软件）下，逐渐正常，但时间很长。做基本设定就是让电脑立刻记忆真实的节气门最大、最小位置，让电脑对节气门重新分区。

如果节气门未损坏，电脑损坏，更换新电脑后，由于新电脑记忆的节气门最大、最小位置和实际行驶中的节气门不相同，会导致电机控制节气门时不正常，所以更换电脑后也需要做基本设定。发动机损坏，更换发动机后，发动机的性能提高，如按原来电脑记忆的值进行控制，会有一定误差，所以更换了发动机也需要做基本设定。

小 结

本项目详细介绍了怠速控制阀在电控发动机上的作用，怠速控制阀的结构原理，怠速控制系统的组成，怠速转速的控制过程以及怠速控制系统进行检查的步骤及方法，利用常规方法判断怠速控制阀工作是否正常，怠速控制阀的所有检测项目。

习题及思考

1. 简述怠速控制阀的检测目的。
2. 简述如何进行怠速控制阀检测的准备工作。
3. 简述怠速控制阀检测的步骤。
4. 何为占空比？
5. 发动机怠速控制系统由哪几部分组成？
6. 怠速控制系统检修有哪些注意事项？

项目五

汽油发动机辅助控制系统检修

一、项目情境引入

一辆轿车如果发动机的尾气不合格应如何进行故障排除？想解决电控发动机尾气不合格的故障，应具备排气控制系统、燃油供给系统、空气供给系统、点火控制系统、电控发动机的机械系统、辅助系统等基本知识，本项目重点学习排气辅助控制系统的结构原理与检修知识，能够为排除电控发动机尾气排放不合格的故障提供帮助。

二、项目相关知识

（一）汽车排放对环境影响

随着人们对治理环境越来越重视，对汽车排放污染物的控制也越来越严格，目前汽车排放污染物控制系统，根据污染物来自排气管、曲轴箱和燃油系统的不同，一般分为排气污染物控制系统和非排气污染物控制系统。

排气污染物主要是指从排气管排出的 CO、HC、NO_x 等有害污染物。

CO 是一种无色、无味的有毒气体，它能使血液的输氧能力降低，从而使心脏、头脑等重要器官严重缺氧，引起头晕、头痛、恶心等症状，轻则使中枢神经系统受损，重则会使心血管工作困难，直至死亡。CO 主要是燃油混合气过浓，燃烧时的氧气不足造成的。

HC 包括未燃烧和未完全燃烧的燃油、润滑油及其裂解产物和部分氧化物，其中有些成分会对眼睛和皮肤有强烈的刺激作用，且浓度高时会引起头晕、恶心、贫血甚至急性中毒。HC 是由于混合气过稀、喷油器过脏、点火不良（点火正时不当或火花塞过脏）、排气门泄漏等，导致燃烧不完全而产生。

NO_x 是燃烧过程中形成的多种氮氧化物，主要是 NO，还有 NO_2、N_2O_3、N_2O_5 等，其中 NO 是无色无味的气体，具有轻度刺激性，毒性不大。NO_2 是一种棕红色强刺激性的有毒气体。NO_x 是由于混合气在高温、富氧下燃烧时，含在混合气中的 N_2 和 O_2 发生化学反应而产生的。

（二）排放控制系统的分类

1. 排气污染物的控制系统

① 三元催化系统；

② 废气再循环控制（EGR）系统；
③ 二次空气喷射（AI）系统。

2. 非排气污染物控制系统

（1）非排气污染物途径

非排气污染物是指由排气管以外的其他途径排放到大气中的有害污染物，主要是以下两种方式所产生的 HC 排放：

① 曲轴箱窜气；
② 燃油蒸发。

（2）非排气污染物控制系统

非排气污染物控制系统主要有曲轴箱强制通风（PCV）系统和燃油蒸发控制（EVAP）系统。

（三）各种排放控制系统的原理

1. 曲轴箱强制通风系统

如果发动机燃烧室内的混合气和燃烧后的废气顺着活塞和汽缸体的内壁漏入曲轴箱内，将稀释和污染机油，造成机油的润滑性能下降，因此必须将这些污染物从曲轴箱内排出。此外曲轴箱内的压力随发动机转速升高而增加，如果不通风，会将机油从油封或汽缸垫压出。由于环保的原因，不能将这些混合气直接排入大气，所以为解决此问题，现代汽车一般都采用曲轴箱强制通风（Positive Crankcase Ventilation，PCV）系统，将这些漏入曲轴箱的气体导入进气歧管，使其重新燃烧。

PCV 阀是曲轴箱强制通风系统（PCV）系统中最重要的部件，PCV 阀内有一个锥形阀，如图 5-1 所示，由它控制曲轴箱蒸气流入进气管，同时防止气体或火焰反向流动。当发动机工作时，进气管真空度作用在 PCV 阀上，此真空吸引新鲜空气经空气滤芯、空气软管进入气门室盖，再经过汽缸盖孔、进入曲轴箱，并在曲轴箱中与从燃烧室泄漏的气体混合。这些空气与泄漏气体的混合气由于有进气歧管真空的吸力，所以向上经汽缸盖孔、流经气门室盖及 PCV 阀，进入进气歧管，然后再经进气门进入燃烧室燃烧。

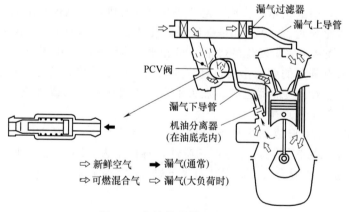

图 5-1 曲轴箱强制通风系统

（1）发动机不工作时

发动机不工作时，弹簧将锥形阀压在阀座上，此时阀内没有真空度，没有蒸气流量，锥形阀压在阀座上,这样可以防止回火。如图5-2所示。

(2) 怠速或减速时

怠速或减速时进气歧管真空度大,它克服弹簧压力,将锥形阀向上吸起。这时在锥形阀与PCV阀壳体之间,存在小缝隙(如图5-3所示)。在怠速或减速工作时,发动机泄漏气体很少,这些气体可以从PCV阀的小缝隙流出曲轴箱。

(3) 在常速行驶发动机负荷增加时

在部分节气门开度下(常速行驶)工作时,进气管的真空度比怠速时小。这时,弹簧向下推压锥形阀,使锥形阀与PCV阀壳体间的缝隙增大(如图5-4所示)。因为在部分节气门开度下,发动机泄漏的气体比较多。锥形阀与PCV阀壳体间的较大缝隙可以使所有泄漏气体被吸入出气管。

(4) 在大负荷或加速下工作时

当发动机在大负荷下工作时,节气门全开,进气管真空度减小,弹簧将锥形阀进一步向下推压(如图5-5所示),从而使锥形阀与PCV阀壳体间的缝隙更大。因为大负荷工作时,产生更多侧漏气体,所以需要更大的缝隙才能使泄漏气体流进进气管。

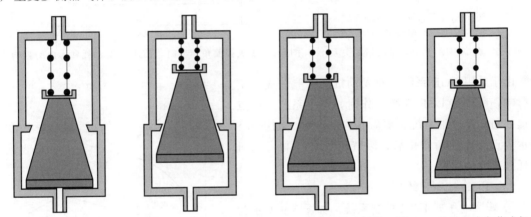

图5-2 发动机不工作　图5-3 怠速或减速时　图5-4 发动机常速行驶　图5-5 发动机大负荷或加速

(5) 当发生回火时

当发动机发生回火时,火焰传播到进气管进入PCV阀体内,火焰的压力压紧PCV阀使其关闭,以防止火焰传到曲轴箱中。如果系统中没有PCV阀,发动机回火时,曲轴箱中的蒸气就有可能发生爆炸。

2. 废气再循环(EGR)控制系统

(1) 废气再循环的作用及NO_x生成机理

废气再循环(Exhaust Gas Recirculation,EGR)系统的作用是把一部分排气引入进气系统中使其和新鲜混合气一起进入汽缸中参与燃烧,其主要目的是减少氮氧化合物(NO_x)的排放。

氮氧化合物(NO_x)是混合气在高温和富氧条件下燃烧时,含在混合气中的N_2和O_2发生化学反应产生的。燃烧温度越高,N_2和O_2越容易反应,排出的NO_x越多,如图5-6所示。所以减少NO_x的最好方法就是降低燃烧室的温度。

EGR系统工作时,将一部分废气引入进气系统,与新鲜的燃油混合气混合,使混合气变稀,从而降低了燃烧速度,燃烧温度随之下降,从而有效地减少NO_x的生成。

由于废气再循环（EGR）会使混合气的着火性能和发动机输出功率下降，因此，应选择 NO_x 排放量比较多的发动机运转工况范围，进行适量的废气再循环。EGR 的控制量用 EGR 率表示，其定义为再循环废气的量占整个进气量的百分比。采用 EGR 系统可降低 NO_x 的排放，但是随着 EGR 率的增加，将导致油耗增加、HC 的排量增加以及由于废气再循环（EGR）造成了缺火率增加，使燃烧变得不稳定，发动机性能下降，如图 5-7 所示，所以必须对 EGR 率进行控制。根据发动机工况不同，进入进气歧管的废气量一般在 6%～23% 之间变化。

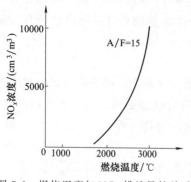

图 5-6　燃烧温度与 NO_x 排放量的关系　　图 5-7　点火提前角不变时，EGR 率对油耗和排放的影响

由于采用 EGR 系统会对发动机的性能造成一定的影响，所以在 EGR 系统工作时，点火系统（即点火提前角）和燃油系统也要做相应的调整。如图 5-8 所示为点火提前角变化后，废气再循环量与发动机油耗和排放的关系。

（2）EGR 控制系统

① 普通电子式 EGR 控制系统。如图 5-9 所示为日产 NISSAN 车 VG30 型发动机所用的 EGR 控制系统示意图。

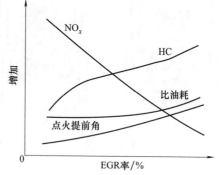

图 5-8　点火提前角改变时，EGR 率对发动机性能的影响

这种系统在早期的 NISSAN 车上曾经采用，它由 EGR 控制电磁阀、节气门位置传感器（TPS）、EGR 阀、曲轴位置传感器（CKP）、发动机控制模块（ECU）、发动机冷却液温度传感器（ECT）等组成。

其工作原理是在发动机工作时，发动机控制模块（ECU）根据各传感器，如曲轴位置传感器（CKP）、发动机冷却液温度传感器（ECT）、节气门位置传感器（TPS）、点火开关等送来的信号，确定发动机目前在哪一种工况下工作，以便发出控制指令，控制 EGR 电磁阀的打开或关闭，使废气再循环进行或停止。

在发动机的某些工况下，发动机控制模块（ECU）控制 EGR 电磁阀通电，从而切断了 EGR 控制阀的真空通道，使 EGR 阀关闭。

在发动机启动时、节气门位置传感器（TPS）的怠速触点接通（即发动机处于怠速运行工况）时、发动机温度低（例如发动机暖机过程中）时、发动机转速低于 900r/min 或高于 3200r/min 时，EGR 控制电磁阀通电（ON），使 EGR 阀处于关闭状态，EGR 系统不起作用；除以上工况外 EGR 控制电磁阀断电（OFF），使 EGR 阀处于打开状态，EGR 系统开始

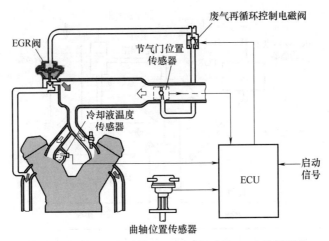

图 5-9 日产 NISSAN 车 VG30 型发动机 EGR 控制系统

起作用。

② 可变 EGR 率废气再循环控制系统。可变 EGR 率废气再循环控制是一种开环控制系统。其工作原理是：将 EGR 率与发动机转速、进气量的对应关系经试验确定后，以数据形式存入发动机控制模块的 ROM 中。发动机工作时，发动机控制模块根据各种传感器送来的信号，并经过与其内部数据对照和计算修正，输出适当的指令，控制电磁阀的开度，以调节废气再循环的 EGR 率。

可变 EGR 率废气再循环系统如图 5-10 所示，当发动机工作时，发动机控制模块（ECU）根据曲轴位置传感器（CKP）、节气门位置传感器（TPS）、发动机冷却液温度传感器（ECT）、点火开关、电源电压等信号，给废气再循环控制电磁阀提供不同占空比的脉冲电压，使其打开、关闭的平均时间不同，从而得到控制 EGR 阀不同开度所需的各种真空度，获得适合发动机工况的不同的 EGR 率。脉冲电压信号的占空比越大，电磁阀打开时间越长，EGR 率越大；反之，脉冲电压信号的占空比越小，EGR 率越小，当小至某一值时，EGR 控制阀关闭，废气再循环系统停止工作。

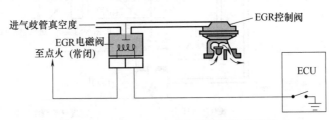

图 5-10 可变 EGR 率废气再循环控制系统

③ 带压力反馈电子（PFE）传感器的废气再循环控制系统。这种系统由废气再循环阀、真空调节阀、计量孔和压力反馈电子传感器等组成。通过检测量孔处的压力，再综合发动机控制模块（ECU）接收的发动机转速、海拔高度、发动机真空度、发动机冷却液温度和节气门位置等输入信号来控制废气再循环的时间和流量，如图 5-11 所示。

压力反馈电子传感器把废气压力信号转换为电压信号传送给发动机控制模块。压力反馈电子传感器有 3 根导线与 ECU 连接。这 3 根导线是接地线、5V 供电压线及信号线。计量孔后的废气压力与再循环的废气流量成正比。压力反馈电子传感器的信号通知 ECU 关于废气

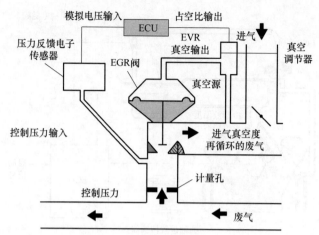

图 5-11 带压力反馈电子传感器的废气再循环控制系统

再循环的流量，ECU 则把此信号与输入信号所要求的废气再循环流量相比较，如果实际的废气再循环流量与所要求的废气再循环流量之间有一些差别的话，那么，ECU 将对输出给真空调节器的占空比信号进行必要的修正。

④ 带压差反馈式电子（DPFE）传感器的废气再循环控制系统。压差反馈式电子废气再循环系统如图 5-12 所示。压差反馈式电子废气再循环控制系统的工作方式和压力反馈式电子废气再循环系统基本一样，只是它还需检测排气系统的废气压力，它的控制更精确。PFE 传感器和 DPFE 传感器都是三线传感器，其中，PFE 传感器有一个压力输入口，DPFE 传感器有两个压力输入口。

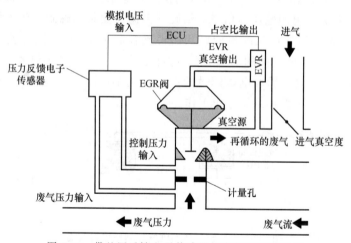

图 5-12 带差压反馈电子传感器的废气再循环系统

⑤ 带 EGR 位置传感器的废气再循环系统。图 5-13 为广州本田雅阁轿车发动机废气再循环（EGR）系统，该系统由 EGR 真空控制阀、EGR 控制电磁阀、EGR 阀以及各种传感器组成。在 EGR 阀上部装有一个可以检测 EGR 阀升程的 EGR 位置传感器，该传感器利用由一个柱塞推动的电位计向发动机 ECM/PCM 传送信号，作为控制废气再循环的参考信号，实现 EGR 系统的闭环控制。发动机 ECM/PCM 中存储有多种工况下 EGR 阀的最佳提升高度信号。如果实际提升高度值与发动机 ECM/PCM 存储的最佳值不同，ECM/PCM 便改变 EGR 控制电磁阀上的电压，从而使 EGR 控制电磁阀通过 EGR 真空控制阀提高或降低 EGR

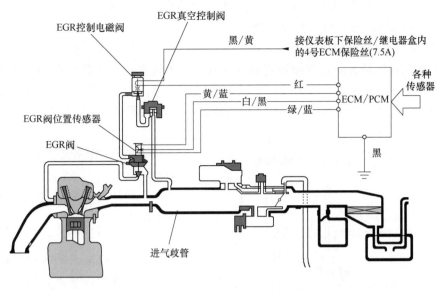

图 5-13 带 EGR 位置传感器的 EGR 控制系统

阀上的真空压力,控制进入燃烧室的废气量。

⑥ 装有背压修正阀的 EGR 系统。如图 5-14 所示为装有背压修正阀的 EGR 控制系统,在 EGR 控制电磁阀和 EGR 阀之间的真空管路中装有一个背压修正阀。其功用是根据排气歧管中的背压,控制废气再循环。

排气歧管的背压通过管路作用在背压修正阀的背压气室下方。当发动机小负荷排气背压低时,在阀门弹簧的作用下气室膜片向下移动,使修正阀门关闭真空通道。此时,EGR 阀在其阀门弹簧作用下保持关闭,因而不进行废气再循环。

当发动机负荷增大、排气歧管背压升高时,修正阀背压气室下方的背压升高,使膜片克服阀门弹簧弹力向上运动而将修正阀门打开。由 EGR 真空电磁阀控制的真空通过背压修正阀而进入 EGR 阀上方的真空气室,将 EGR 阀吸开,废气再循环通道打开,废气进行再循环。

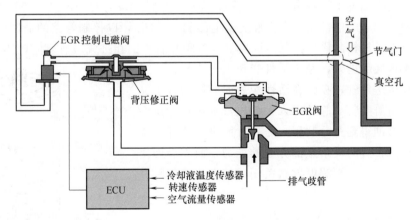

图 5-14 带背压修正阀的 EGR 控制系统

EGR 控制电磁阀受发动机控制模块控制。发动机控制模块根据转速信号、进气压力信号、冷却液温度信号、空气流量信号等,控制 EGR 控制电磁阀的开度,来控制进入 EGR

阀的真空度，从而控制 EGR 阀的开度，改变参与再循环的废气量。

3. 汽油蒸气排放（EVAP）控制系统

（1）EVAP 控制系统的功能

EVAP 控制系统是为防止汽油箱内的汽油蒸气排入大气产生污染而设的，其功能是收集汽油箱和浮子室（化油器式汽油机）内蒸发的汽油蒸气，并将汽油蒸气导入汽缸参加燃烧，从而防止汽油蒸气直接排入大气而造成污染。同时，还必须根据发动机工况，控制导入汽缸参加燃烧的汽油蒸气量。

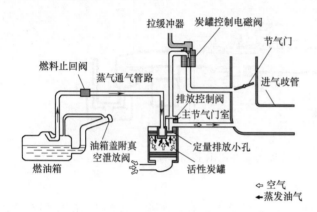

图 5-15 燃油蒸发控制系统示意图

（2）EVAP 控制系统的组成与工作原理

EVAP 控制系统的组成与工作原理如图 5-15 所示。

活性炭罐——充满炭颗粒；真空电磁阀——控制真空气路。该系统能够收集汽油箱内蒸发的汽油蒸气，并将汽油蒸气导入汽缸参加燃烧，防止汽油蒸气直接排入大气而造成污染。

燃油蒸发控制（EVAP）系统的组成和构造，随汽车制造厂和生产年代的不同而不同。早期的燃油蒸发控制（EVAP）系统多是利用真空进行控制，而现在基本上都采用发动机控制模块进行控制。目前常见的比较简单的燃油蒸发控制系统如图 5-15 所示。它主要由燃油箱、活性炭罐（有的叫吸附罐）、炭罐控制电磁阀和发动机控制模块等组成，能够提供比较精确的蒸发流量的控制。

活性炭罐是燃油蒸发系统中贮存蒸气的部件，如图 5-16 所示。活性炭罐的下部与大气相通，上部有接头与油箱和进气歧管相连，用于收集和清除燃油蒸气。中间是活性炭颗粒，它具有极强的吸附燃油分子的作用。燃油箱内的燃油蒸气（HC），经油箱管道进入活性炭罐后，蒸气中的燃油分子被吸附在活性炭颗粒表面。活性炭罐有一个出口，经软管与发动机进气歧管相通。软管的中部设一个活性炭罐电磁阀（常闭），以控制管路的通断。当发动机运转时，如果发动机控制模块控制活性炭罐电磁阀开启，则在进气歧管真空吸力的作用下，空气从活性炭罐底部进入，经过活性炭至上方出口，再经软管进入发动机进气管，吸附在活性炭表面的燃油分子又重新脱附，随新鲜空气一起被吸入发动机汽缸燃烧。这一过程一方面使燃油得到充分利用；另一方面也使活性炭罐内的活性炭保持良好的吸附燃油分子的能力，而不会因使用太久而失效。当活性炭罐电磁阀关闭时，燃油蒸气贮存在活性炭罐中。

（3）燃油蒸发控制（EVAP）系统的控制

为了防止破坏发动机正常工作时的混合气成分，影响发动机正常工作，必须对燃油蒸气进入发动机进气歧管的时机和进入量进行控制。

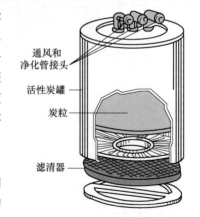

图 5-16 活性炭罐

目前，尽管各汽车生产厂家都采用发动机控制模块控制炭罐控制电磁阀的通断来控制其开启和关闭，线圈通电时，电磁阀开启；线圈断电时，电磁阀关闭，但它们在控制电磁阀开闭的时机和方法上并不完全一样。

一般说来，发动机控制模块（ECU）使炭罐控制电磁阀通电通常考虑以下条件：

① 发动机启动已超过规定的时间；

② 冷却液温度已高于规定值；

③ 急速触点开关处于断开状态；

④ 发动机转速高于规定值。

当满足以上条件时，发动机控制模块（ECU）使电磁阀线圈电路接地通电，电磁阀的阀门开启，储存在活性炭罐内的燃油蒸气经软管被吸入发动机燃烧。此时由于发动机的进气量较大，少量的燃油蒸气进入发动机不会影响混合气的浓度。如果不完全满足上述条件，ECU不会激活炭罐电磁阀，燃油蒸气被储存在炭罐中。

较先进的燃油蒸发控制系统，一般都能根据发动机负荷等情况，适时控制电磁阀的通电占空比，以达到控制电磁阀开启程度的目的。

4. 三元催化转换器（TWC）

（1）TWC 的功能

发动机工作时会产生一些有害的燃烧产物，因此，当今汽车普遍安装三元催化转换器，这个装置串联在排气系统中，目的是在排气气流中一系列化学反应中起催化作用，促使发动机排出的废气中的有害气体转换成无害气体。

三元催化转换器安装在排气管中部，三元催化转换器中主要起作用的是三元催化剂，它是铂（或钯）和铑的混合物，使汽车尾气中有害物质：碳氢化合物（HC）、一氧化碳（CO）、氮氧化物（NO_x），经化学反应转化为无害的二氧化碳（CO_2）、水（H_2O）及氮气（N_2）。但是只有当混合气的空燃比保持稳定时，三元催化转换器的转换效率才能得到精确控制。如图 5-17 所示为三元催化转换器的转换效率与混合气空燃比的关系曲线。从图中可以看出，只有当发动机在标准的理论空燃比 14.7:1 下运转时，三元催化转换器的转换效率才最佳，为此必须对可燃混合气的空燃比进行精确的控

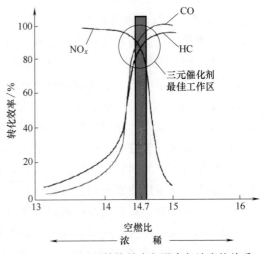

图 5-17 TWC 的转换效率与混合气浓度的关系

制，把空燃比尽量保持在理论空燃比 14.7:1 附近很窄的范围内。

为了将实际空燃比精确地控制在理论空燃比 14.7:1 附近，使三元催化转换器工作在最佳状态，在发动机控制系统中采用氧传感器（O_2S）实现空燃比反馈控制，即闭环控制。

（2）TWC 的构造及工作原理

三元催化转换器一般为整体不可拆卸式，安装在排气消声器的前面，由三元催化转换芯子和外壳等构成，如图 5-18 所示。大多数三元催化转换芯子以蜂窝状陶瓷作为承载催化剂的载体，在陶瓷载体上浸渍铂（或钯）和铑的混合物作为催化剂。当发动机工作不正常时，

排气中的 CO、HC 含量会急剧升高，催化器负担加重，导致温度急剧升高。若高温持续时间过长，将会导致催化性能恶化或损坏（芯子破碎），影响排气不畅，同时由于其安装位置靠近车身底板，容易出危险。所以在有些轿车的三元催化转换器还加有检测排气温度的排气温度传感器。

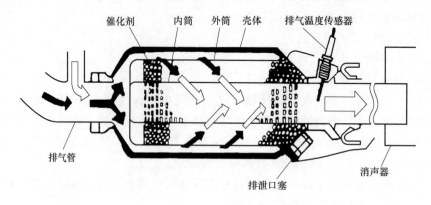

图 5-18　三元催化转换器

5. 进气控制系统

现在最常用的进气控制技术有可变进气技术和涡轮增压技术，它们的目的是增大发动机的扭矩和功率，改善发动机在不同运行状况下的动力性，但两者在实现方式上却有很大的不同，下面对可变进气系统进行介绍。

① 可变进气系统的概念。可变进气系统是利用发动机工作时进气管道的进气动态效应来提高充气效率，以达到在发动机转速范围内增大发动机的扭矩和功率。

为便于分析，常将进气动态效应视为惯性效应和波动效应共同作用的结果。利用进气动态效应工作的进气系统为"谐波控制进气系统"。

a. 进气惯性效应。进气惯性效应一般是指利用进气行程时进气管内高速流动气体的惯性作用来提高充气效率。在发动机进气行程前期，由于活塞下行的吸入作用，汽缸内产生负压。新鲜空气从进气管进入，同时传出负压波，经进气门、气道、沿进气管向外传播。当负压波传到稳压室等空腔的开口端时，又从开口端向汽缸方向反射回正压波。如果进气管的长度和直径适当，从负压波发出到正压波返回到进气门所经历的时间，正好与进气门从开启到关闭所需的时间配合，即正压波返回到进气门时，正值进气门关闭前夕，从而提高了进气门的正压力，起到增压作用，达到提高充气量的效果。

b. 进气波动效应。进气波动效应，一般是指利用进气门关闭后，进气管的气体还在继续来回波动的作用来提高充气效率。在进气门关闭时，气流的波动在进气管中周而复始地来回传播，致使进气门处的压力时高时低。如果进气管的形状、长度和直径较适合，有利于压力波的反射和谐振，使正压波与下循环进气过程重合，就能使进气终了时的压力升高，达到提高充气效率的目的。

② 可变进气系统的结构型式。进气气流在进气管中的变化时非常复杂的。为了有效地利用进气动态效应、提高充气效率，在汽车发动机上采用设置动力腔、谐振腔及各种结构型式的可变进气系统。

一个长度和截面面积固定的进气道，只能在一定的转速范围内有较好动态效应和充气效果。一般在低转速工作时，较细长的进气道充气效果较好，而在高转速工作时，短而粗的进气道充气效果较好。如果采用长度可变的进气道，则可使发动机在较大的转速范围内都有较好的充气效果。

对于采用多点燃油喷射系统的发动机来说，可以按照气体压力波传播的特点设计进气道，使进气道的长度、形状都可以改变，利用进气动态效应来提高充气效率。

在各种车型上采用的可变进气系统并不完全一样。下面简单介绍几种常见的可变进气系统。

a. 奥迪 V6 发动机的可变进气系统。如图 5-19 所示为奥迪 V6 发动机可变进气系统的进气歧管的几何形状。在发动机的进气歧管内设置进气转换阀，受发动机控制模块（ECU）的控制。在发动机转速低于 4100r/min 时，每个汽缸进气道中的转换阀门总是处于关闭位置，形成路径较长而截面较小的进气管道，如图 5-19（a）所示；当转速大于 4100r/min，进气道中的转换阀门开启，构成的路径较短而截面较大的进气管道，如图 5-19（b）所示。

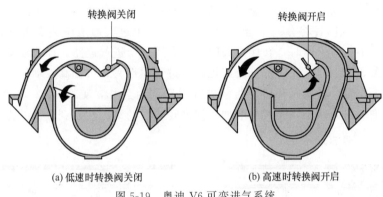

图 5-19 奥迪 V6 可变进气系统

发动机采用这种可变进气系统后，提高了充气效率，其输出扭矩和功率都有提高，如图 5-20 所示为采用可变进气系统后输出特性的比较。

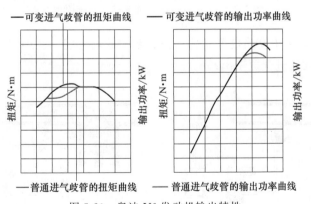

图 5-20 奥迪 V6 发动机输出特性

b. 日产汽车发动机可变进气系统。如图 5-21 所示为日产汽车发动机可变进气系统的示意图。当发动机在低速，中、小负荷工作时，转换阀关闭，进气仅通过细长的进气管流入，可以提高进气流速，由于细长管的动态效应，改善了中低速的扭矩特性，当发动机在高转速大负荷工作时，转换阀开启，空气流经短而粗的进气管道，大大提高了充气量，从而获得较大的功率。

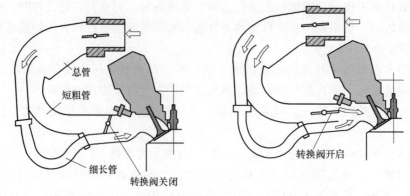

图 5-21　日产汽车发动机可变进气系统的原理图

（a）丰田汽车发动机可变进气系统。如图 5-22 所示为日本丰田汽车公司采用的双进气管分别参加工作的可变进气系统示意图。图中显示每个汽缸配有 4 个气门（2 个进气门和 2 个排气门），2 个进气门各配有一个进气管道，其中一个进气通道中装有进气转换阀。在发动机低速，中、小负荷工作时，转换阀关闭，只利用一个进气通路，即将发动机总的进气通路数减半，见图 5-22（a），此时进气流速提高，进气惯性大，可提高发动机扭矩；当发动机高转速大负荷工作时，转换阀开启，两条进气通路同时工作，见图 5-22（b），此时进气截面大大增加，进气阻力减小，充气量增加，使高转速时的动力性得到很大的提高。

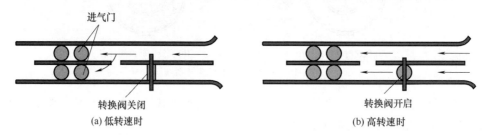

图 5-22　丰田双进气管可变进气系统原理图

如图 5-23 所示为丰田发动机可变进气控制系统的示意图（图中只画带有转换阀的进气道，另一不带转换阀的进气道未画）。

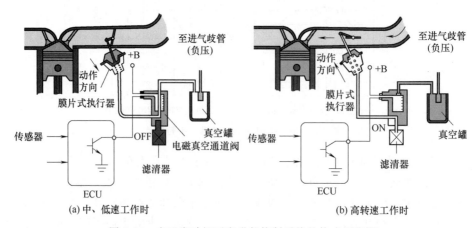

图 5-23　丰田发动机可变进气控制系统的构成原理图

图 5-23 中进气道中进气转换阀的关闭和开启，是由膜片式执行器来完成的。膜片式执行器的工作压力，则由发动机控制模块通过控制电磁真空通道阀来进行控制。进气转换阀（通路）的控制过程如下。

发动机中、低速工作时，在发动机中、低速（低于 5200r/min）工作时，电磁真空通道阀不通电，膜片式执行器与电磁真空通道阀的空气滤清器（通大气）之间的通路被切断（OFF），而与真空罐之间形成通路（ON）。此时储存在真空罐的进气歧管的负压作用在膜片式执行器，吸力作用使执行器带动拉杆，关闭进气转换阀，即关闭了各汽缸中的一个进气通道，如图 5-23（a）所示。

发动机高速工作时，当发动机高速（5200r/min 以上）工作时，发动机控制模块（ECU）输出控制信号，使驱动电路三极管导通，电磁真空通道阀通电工作。膜片式执行器与空气滤清器（大气）之间形成通路（ON），而与真空罐之间的通道则被切断（OFF）。此时大气压作用在执行器膜片室，通过拉杆使进气转换阀打开，结果各汽缸的进气通道扩大为两个，增大了进气通道面积，如图 5-23（b）所示。

(b) 丰田谐波增压进气控制系统（ACIS）。皇冠轿车 2JZ-GE 发动机采用谐波增压进气控制系统。它的进气管长度不能变化，但由于在进气管中加设了一个大容量的空气室和电控真空阀，实现了压力波传播路线长度的改变，从而达到了低速和高速的进气增压效果。

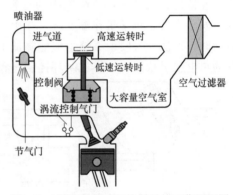

图 5-24 谐波增压进气控制系统工作原理图

谐波增压进气控制系统的工作原理如图 5-24 所示，通过控制进气增压阀就可改变进气管内的脉动压力波传递长度，即：是从空气滤清器到进气门还是空气室出口到进气门。

谐波增压控制系统的控制系统如图 5-25 所示，控制原理如图 5-26 所示。

ECU 根据转速信号控制电磁真空通道阀的开闭。

低速时，电磁真空通道阀电路不通（真空通道阀关闭），真空罐的真空不能进入真空气室，受真空气室控制的进气增压阀处于关闭状态。进气管内的脉动压力波传递长度是空气滤清器到进气门的距离，这一距离较长，适应于发动机中低速时增加气体动力，如图 5-26（a）所示；

高速时，ECU 接通电磁真空通道阀的电路（真空通道阀打开），真空罐的真空进入真空气室，吸动膜片，将进气增压控制阀打开，由于大容量空气室的参与，使进气脉动压力波只

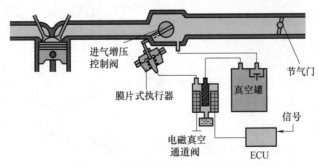

图 5-25 谐波增压进气控制系统图

能从空气室出口到进气门之间传播,缩短了压力波的传播距离,使发动机在高速区也能得到较好的气体动力增压效果,如图 5-26(b)所示。

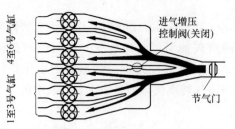 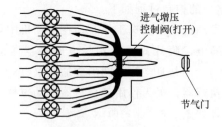

(a) 关闭真空通道阀(进气增压阀关闭)　　　(b) 打开真空通道(进气增压阀打开)

图 5-26　谐波增压进气控制系统控制原理图

6. 二次空气喷射系统

二次空气喷射系统(Air Injection,AI)系统的实质是将一定量的新鲜空气引入排气管或三元催化转换器中,使废气中的有害气体与空气进一步燃烧,以进一步减少有害物的排放。发动机处于正常工作温度时,二次空气喷射系统可降低 HC 和 CO 的排放量。发动机刚启动时,二次空气喷射系统不但能降低 HC 的排放量,而且会缩短氧传感器的加热时间,使发动机电脑尽快进入空燃比闭环控制过程。

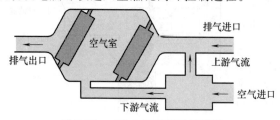

图 5-27　二次空气喷射系统简图

二次空气喷射系统的工作原理:

二次空气又分为上游气流及下游气流,上游气流进入排气歧管,下游气流流进转换器中的空气室中,如图 5-27 所示。空气进入排气歧管及三元催化转换器的时机由发动机电脑进行控制。

① 空气泵系统。许多二次空气喷射系统都是用空气泵将空气泵入排气口或催化转换器。空气泵系统如图 5-28 所示,由真空控制空气旁通阀和空气分流阀组成,它们又控制从空气泵到排气口或催化转换器的空气量。空气分流阀到排气口和催化转换器之间各有一个单向阀,以防止在减速等情况时,排气管中的废气倒流至二次空气喷射系统。发动机电脑控制两个电磁线圈,分别给旁通阀和分流阀供应真空。电磁阀在图中未画出。当点火开关打开,就向电磁阀加了电压,发动机电脑通过控制电磁阀接地而使其通电。

② 脉冲空气系统。同空气泵系统相比,脉冲空气系统不需要动力源注入空气,而是依靠大气压力与废气真空脉冲之间的压力差使空气进入排气歧管,因此减少了成本及功率消耗。其工作原理如图 5-29 所示。空气来自空气滤清器,发动机电脑控制电磁阀的打开及关闭,电磁阀与单向阀相连。由于排气中压力是正负交替的脉冲压力波,当发动机以较低转速运转时,排气压力为负,

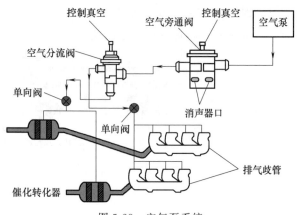

图 5-28　空气泵系统

空气由滤清器通过电磁阀和单向阀进入排气口，与排出的 HC 进一步燃烧，故可降低 HC 的排放量；当排气压力为正时，因有单向阀，所以空气不能反向流动，但此时也没有新鲜空气进入排气口，即不能降低 HC 的排放量。脉冲空气系统的上、下游空气道各有一个电磁阀和一个单向阀。因为排气口的低压脉冲持续时间随发动机转速的提高而缩短，所以脉冲式二次空气喷射系统在发动机转速较低时，降低 HC 排放的效果更好。

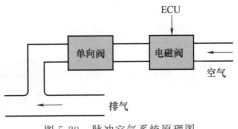

图 5-29　脉冲空气系统原理图

7. 废气涡轮增压系统

（1）废气涡轮增压的概念及组成

涡轮增压技术是常用的进气控制技术，所谓增压是将进入汽缸前的新鲜空气预先进行压缩，然后再以高密度送入汽缸。增压器的结构型式有多种，但目前在轿车上应用最普遍、最有效的是废气涡轮增压系统，它是根据发动机的负荷来控制排气的流动路线，并通过涡轮增压器提高进气压力，增加进气量，从而大大改善发动机的动力性。

如图 5-30 所示为奥迪轿车采用废气涡轮增压的原理图。废气涡轮增压是利用发动机排出具有一定能量（高压、高温）的废气，驱动涡轮增压器中的动力涡轮，再带动与动力涡轮同轴的增压涡轮（工作叶轮）一起转动。增压涡轮一般位于空气流量传感器（MAF）与进气门之间的进气管道中。增压涡轮转动时，对从空气滤清器进入的新鲜空气进行压缩，然后再送入汽缸。

废气涡轮增压系统的主要部件有涡轮增压器、增压压力电磁阀、膜片式控制阀和冷却器。

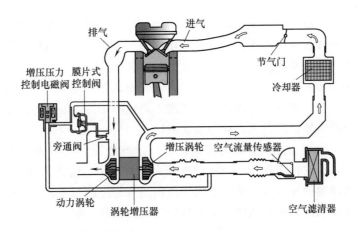

图 5-30　废气涡轮增压原理图

① 涡轮增压器。涡轮增压器内有动力涡轮和增压涡轮，它们安装在同一根轴上，当废气从排气歧管流至动力涡轮机叶轮处，其压力就使动力涡轮叶轮转动，同时增压涡轮也转动，迫使空气进入汽缸。如图 5-31 所示为奥迪 A6 1.8T 的涡轮增压器。

② 增压压力电磁阀和膜片式控制阀。发动机电脑通过控制增压压力电磁阀，进一步控制膜片式控制阀使旁通阀门动作，从而改变实际涡轮增压压力。阀门打开，增压压力下降；

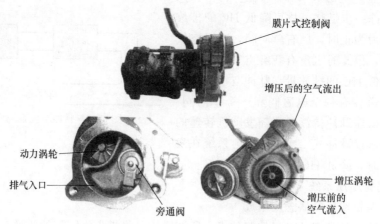

图 5-31 奥迪 A6 1.8T 涡轮增压器

阀门关闭，增压压力上升。

③ 冷却器。在废气涡轮增压系统中，一般都带有冷却器（也称为中冷器），它可降低进气温度、消除发动机爆震、提高进气效率等。

（2）废气涡轮增压的优点

能提高进气密度，增加充气量。能使发动机在各种转速下达到较高的充气效率，增加输出功率，提高扭矩、降低油耗。

能消除大气压力的不同引起的实际充气量的变化对发动机的影响。对一般发动机来说海拔高度升高 1000m，功率约下降 8%～10%，油耗增加 4%～5%。

增压器所消耗的功率是由排出的废气提供，对发动机输出的有效功率影响不大。

（3）增压压力的控制

采用涡轮增压技术后，由于平均有效压力增加，发动机爆震倾向增大，热负荷偏高。为了保证发动机在不同转速及工况下都得到最佳增压值，并防止发动机爆震和限制热负荷，对涡轮增加系统增压压力必须进行控制。

目前多是采用旁通的方法，即调节进入动力涡轮室的废气量从而对增压压力进行控制。当需要增加进气压力时，排气歧管排出的废气进入涡轮增压器，经动力涡轮排出；随着节气门开度的增加和发动机转速的升高，动力涡轮的转速加快，与其同轴的增压涡轮的转速也加快，致使进气增压压力增大。如果此时旁通阀打开，通过动力涡轮的废气量和气压就会减小，动力涡轮和增压涡轮转速降低，进气增压压力就会减小。由此可见，通过控制旁通阀，就可改变通过动力涡轮的废气量，从而实现对增压压力的控制。通常，旁通阀由膜片式控制阀控制，而膜片式控制阀则由发动机电脑通过增压压力控制电磁阀进行控制。

如图 5-32 所示为带有废气涡轮增压的发动机电子控制系统。在发动机电脑的存储器中，存储着发动机增压压力特性图的有关数据，理论增压压力值随发动机转速变化。在发动机工作时，发动机电脑根据增压压力等传感器输入的信息，确定当时的实际进气增压压力，然后将实际进气压力与理论压力值进行比较。若实际增压压力值与理论压力值不相符合，发动机电脑就输出控制信号，通过对增压压力电磁阀进行控制，改变膜片式控制阀上的压力，使旁通阀动作，改变实际增压压力。即当实际进气压力低于理论值时，旁通阀关闭；当进气压力高于理论值时，旁通阀打开。

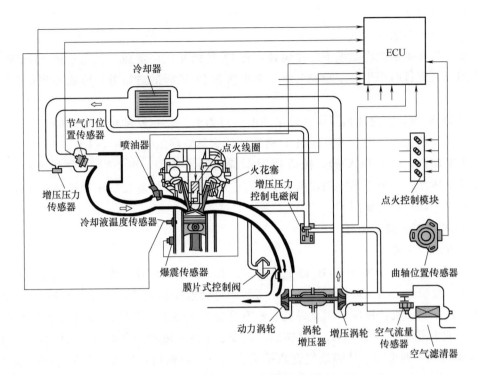

图 5-32 带有涡轮增压的发动机电子控制系统

在实际中，一般都是采用调节点火正时和调节增压压力相结合的办法来获得更好的控制效果。因为单一地通过降低增压压力的办法，会引起发动机运行性能降低；而采用涡轮增压后，发动机排气温度较高，所以也不宜只通过调节点火正时的办法来控制爆震，否则由于温度增高，对高温排气驱动的涡轮有不利影响。因此，两种方法并用是最好的方法。实际应用中，通常是当发动机电脑根据传感器输入的信号鉴别出发动机爆震时，即刻使点火提前角推迟，同时平行地降低增压压力。在这两方面调节生效（爆震消失）时，仍将增压压力慢慢降低，通过点火正时调节装置再将点火提前调节至最佳值，以便可能保持发动机获得最大扭矩。当点火提前角达到最佳值时，再慢慢地增加充气增压压力。

三、项目实施

（一）实施的要求

丰田 5A、AJR 发动机台架；轿车一辆。

（二）实施步骤

1. 曲轴箱强制通风系统的检修

一般测试 PCV 系统工作正常与否，用转速下降法或真空测试法。

（1）转速下降测试法

接上转速表，使发动机达到正常工作温度，在怠速情况下，夹住 PCV 阀与真空源之间的管路，发动机转速应下降 50r/min 或更多。否则，要检查 PCV 阀和管路是否堵塞，必要时进行清洗或更换。

（2）真空测试法

使发动机在正常工作温度下怠速运转，将PCV阀从气门室盖上拔下。拔下PCV阀后，应能听到空气流过时产生的"咝咝"声。手指放在PCV阀的进口处，应能感到很强的真空吸力。

装好PCV阀，将曲轴箱通风孔或机油加油口盖取下。在发动机怠速运转时，将一张轻薄的硬纸轻轻放在开口上，在60s内，应能感觉到真空将纸吸附在开口上。

熄灭发动机，取下PCV阀，摇动PCV阀应听到"喀喀"声。否则，更换该PCV阀。

如果上述测试结果正确，则说明PCV系统工作正常。如果任一项测试结果不正确，则需更换相应元件并重新做测试。

2. EGR控制系统的检修

检查方法及步骤：

① 在冷机启动后，拆下EGR阀上的真空软管，发动机转速应无变化，用手触试真空软管口应无真空吸力；当发动机工作温度正常后，将转速提高到2500r/min左右，从EGR阀上拆下软管，发动机转速应有明显提高。若不符合上述要求，说明EGR系统工作不正常。

② 发动机熄火，拔下EGR电磁阀插头，冷态下测量电磁阀电阻，一般应为33～39Ω。

③ 电磁阀不通电时，从通进气管侧接头吹入空气应畅通，从通大气的滤网处吹入空气应不通。当给电磁阀通电时，从通进气管侧接头吹入空气应不通，从通大气的滤网处吹入空气应畅通，否则应更换电磁阀。

④ 拆下EGR阀，用手动真空泵给EGR阀膜片上方施加约15kPa的真空度时，EGR阀应能开启；不施加真空度时，EGR阀应能完全关闭，否则应更换EGR阀。

3. EVAP控制系统的检修

检查方法及步骤：

① 检查各连接管路有无破损或漏气，必要时更换连接软管；检查活性炭罐壳体有无裂纹、底部进气滤芯是否脏污，必要时更换炭罐或滤芯。

② 将发动机热车至正常工作温度，并使之怠速运转。

③ 拔下蒸气回收罐上的真空软管，检查软管内有无真空吸力。若装置工作正常，在发动机怠速运转中电磁阀应不通，软管内应无真空吸力。如果此时软管内有吸力，应检查电磁阀线束插头内电源电压正常与否。

④ 踩下加速踏板，使发动机转速大于2000r/min，同时检查上述软管内有无真空吸力。若有吸力，说明正常；若无吸力，应检查电磁阀线束插头内电源电压。若电压正常，说明电磁阀有故障；若电压异常或无电压，说明电脑或控制线路有故障。

⑤ 从活性炭罐上拆下真空控制阀，用手动真空泵由真空管接头给真空控制阀施加约5kPa真空度时，从活性炭罐侧孔吹入空气应畅通；不施加真空度时，吹入空气则不通。若不符合上述要求，应更换真空控制阀。

⑥ 发动机不工作时，拆开电磁阀进气管一侧的软管，用手动真空泵由软管接头给控制电磁阀施加一定真空度，电磁阀不通电时应能保持真空度，若给电磁阀接通蓄电池电压，真空度应放；拆开电磁阀线束连接器，测量电磁阀两端子间电阻应为36～44Ω。若不符合上述要求，应更换控制电磁阀。

4. TWC 及氧传感器的检修

① 检查 TWC 是否堵塞。

② 让发动机怠速运转,使用尾气分析仪测量此时的 CO 值。当发动机正常工作时候(空燃比为 14.7∶1),这时的 CO 典型值为 0.5%~1%,当使用二次空气喷射和 TWC 技术可以使怠速时的 CO 值接近于 0,最大不应超过 0.3%,否则说明 TWC 损坏。

③ 测量 TWC 出口管道温度应比进口管道温度至少高出 38℃,在怠速时,其温度也相差 10%。若不符合要求,且检查二次空气喷射泵也完好时,说明 TWC 已经损坏。

④ 对安装两个氧传感器的电喷发动机,可测量两个氧传感器的电压波形,后氧传感器电压波动要比前氧传感器电压波动少得多,如果前、后氧传感器电压波形和波动范围均趋于一致,说明 TWC 损坏。

5. 可变进气系统的检测

下面以丰田皇冠 2JZ-GM 发动机采用的谐波控制进气系统为例,介绍可变进气系统的检测。

(1) 进气增压控制阀和膜片式执行器的检测

用三通接头把真空表接入进气压力增压控制阀的真空管路中。启动发动机,怠速时真空表应无变化。迅速将节气门全开,真空表指针应在 53.3kPa 位置处摆动,并且膜片式执行器的拉杆也应回缩,这说明进气增压控制阀在工作,膜片式执行器也没有问题,如图 5-33 所示。

(2) 电磁真空通道阀的检测

电磁真空通道阀电路图如图 5-34 所示。检测电磁真空通道阀线圈有无断路、短路或搭铁现象;在 20℃时,两端子 1 和 2 的电阻阻值应为 38.5~44.45Ω。

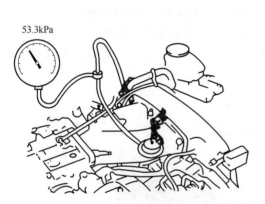

图 5-33 检查进气增压控制阀和膜片式执行器

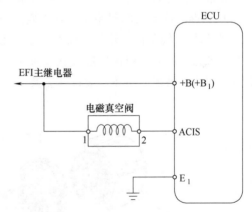

图 5-34 电磁真空通道阀电路图

检查电磁真空通道阀的工作情况,如图 5-35 所示电磁真空通道阀不通电时,空气应从通道 E 进入,只能从滤清器排出;当电磁真空通道阀接通蓄电池电压时,空气应能从通道 E 进入,只能从 F 口出去。

(3) 真空罐的检测

如图 5-36 所示,空气应能从真空罐 A 向 B 流动[如图 5-36(a)所示],但不能从 B 向 A 流动[如图 5-36(b)所示];用手指封住 B 出口,向 A 施加 53.3kPa 的真空,在 1min 内真空应无变化[如图 5-36(c)所示],否则应更换真空罐。

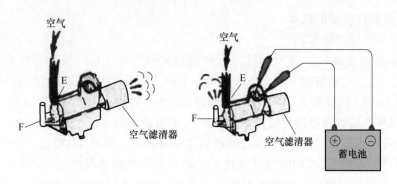

(a) 电磁真空通道阀不通电时　　　　(b) 电磁真空通道阀通电时

图 5-35　检查电磁真空通道阀的工作情况

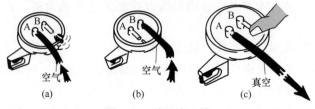

图 5-36　检查真空罐

6. 二次空气喷射系统的诊断

（1）系统测试

如果二次空气喷射系统发生故障，则发动机温度升高时，它不向排气口泵入空气，HC 的排放量也会升高。进行二次空气喷射系统的测试时，应注意以下几点：

① 诊断二次空气喷射系统，首先要检查该系统上所有真空软管和电路连接。

② 此外空气泵在带轮的后面有一个离心式滤清器，空气通过滤清器将灰尘过滤后流入气泵。带轮与滤清器用螺栓连接在泵轴上，可分别检修它们，如图 5-37 所示。如果带轮或滤清器弯曲、磨损或损坏，应将其更换。

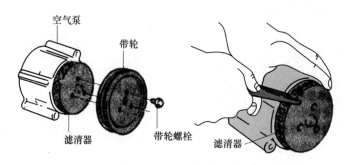

图 5-37　空气泵带轮与离心式滤清器

③ 空气泵的带必须有特定的张力。带轮松动或二次空气喷射系统有故障，会导致二次喷射系统不能正常工作，最终导致废气成分升高或燃油消耗过量。

④ 二次空气喷射系统的泄压阀（其作用是当系统堵塞或阻力过大时，释放压力以防止空气泵压力过高）有的连在旁通阀和分流阀上，也有的连在空气泵上。如果泄压阀卡在开启位置，来自空气泵的空气流将通过该阀连续排出，导致有害气体的排放量增加。

⑤ 如果二次空气喷射系统中的软管有烧坏的迹象,这表明单向阀有泄漏,使排气进入该系统。

⑥ 空气歧管和管道的泄漏会导致废气漏出和产生大量噪声。

⑦ 如果在旁通阀电磁阀或分流阀电磁阀中或相应的导线内有故障,或者是来自空气泵的气流连续逆流(从空气泵流至排气口)或顺流(从空气泵至催化转换器),二次空气喷射系统可能会在发动机控制模块内设置故障码。应使用故障诊断仪检查与二次空气喷射系统有关的所有故障代码。在对系统进行进一步诊断之前,应查明这些代码的原因。

(2) 旁通阀和分流阀的诊断

① 旁通阀的诊断。在启动发动机时,听一听短时间内是否有空气从旁通阀排出。如果没有空气,则从旁通阀拆下真空软管,再启动发动机。如果现在从旁通阀排出了空气,应检查旁通电磁阀和连接导线。当旁通阀仍无排出空气时,应检查从气泵至该阀的空气输送情况,如果有空气输送,需更换旁通阀。

② 分流阀的诊断。在发动机温度升高时,从分流阀处拆下至空气泵排气口的软管,检查是否有来自该软管的气流,如果有气流,表明系统工作正常。如果没有空气流动,应从分流阀上拆下真空软管,再将真空计连接到该软管上。如果真空度高于3.38kPa,则应更换分流阀。如果真空度为零,应检查至分流电磁阀的真空软管、旁通电磁阀和连接导线。

当发动机处于正常工作温度时,将分流阀至催化转换器间的空气软管拆下,检查是否有来自于该软管的气流。如果有气流,表明在顺流模式下系统工作是正常的。如果没有气流,则从分流阀上拆下真空软管,再将真空表连接到该软管上。如果真空表指示真空度为零,应更换分流阀。如果在真空表上指示有一定的真空度,应检查至分流电磁阀的软管管路、旁通电磁阀和连接导线。

7. 废气涡轮增压控制系统故障的诊断

(1) 系统检查

① 在车上进行故障检查。首先检查发动机基本工作条件、压缩和泄漏及点火系和燃油供给系。如果供油量和压力都正常,则再检查点火系的穿透电压是否足以点燃由涡轮增压产生的高度压缩的混合气,点火时刻是否正确。

② 目测软管、垫片和管道。目测全部软管、垫片和管道,看装配是否正确,有无损伤、磨蚀。如破损或变质,将使涡轮装置不能正常工作,导致增压过高或过低。

③ 检查进气负压或空气滤清器。检查进气负压或空气滤清器的真空泄漏情况。检查时可向进气系统注入丙烷,观察发动机转速和真空度,同时检测HC水平。丙烷通过漏气处,真空度和发动机转速会增加,HC水平会下降。

④ 检查涡轮增压器

a. 如果以上各项检查合格,下一步检查涡轮增压器。如果必须从车上拆下涡轮增压器,则在检修时务必保持清洁,任何脏污或污染都会导致严重后果。在拆卸涡轮机前,应将壳体和零件的相对位置加上标志,以保证重新装配时正确无误。拆开涡轮装置,仔细观察增压涡轮和动力涡轮,检查是否存在弯曲、破裂或过度磨损现象。

b. 检查涡轮壳体内部是否存在由轴的摆动范围过量、进入脏污或润滑不当而造成的磨损或冲击损伤。用手旋转涡轮,手感阻力应是均匀的,不应过大,转动应无黏滞感,即应无擦伤或任何接触。

c. 由于对轴承间隙有严格要求,应按生产厂规定的程序检查轴向和径向间隙,以丰田汽车的涡轮增压器为例。可将百分表插入涡轮机壳的孔中,使其接触轴端,沿轴向移动涡轮机轴,测量轴的轴向间隙不应大于 0.13mm,如图 5-38(a)所示。将百分表从机油排出孔插过轴承隔圈的孔,使其接触涡轮机轴的中心,上下移动涡轮机轴,测量轴的径向间隙不应大于 0.18mm,如图 5-38(b)所示。若轴向间隙或径向间隙不符合要求,则更换涡轮增压器。

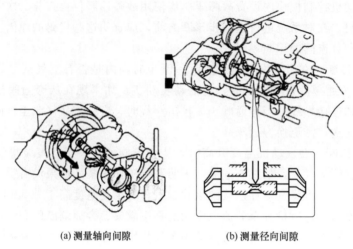

(a) 测量轴向间隙　　(b) 测量径向间隙

图 5-38　涡轮增压器轴向间隙的检查

(2) 增压压力控制电磁阀和膜片式控制阀的测试

① 增压控制电磁阀的检测

下面以一汽大众奥迪 200 1.8T 为例介绍增压控制电磁阀的检测。

a. 连接故障诊断仪 VAG1551,选择读取测量数据块(功能 08)。

b. 从增压控制电磁阀(N75)上拆下软管。接上辅助软管。启动执行元件诊断,并触发增压控制电磁阀(N75)。

c. 显示屏显示如图 5-39 所示。

d. 电磁阀将发出"咔嚓"声响并打开和关闭(通过向辅助软管吹气来检查)。

e. 如果电磁阀无"咔嚓"声,对增压压力控制电磁阀进行电气检查,见"增压控制电磁阀(N75)的电气检测"。

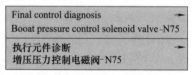

图 5-39　检测增压控制电磁阀
(N75)的显示内容
(图下部为翻译后的内容)

f. 当没有电信号时,电磁阀常闭。

g. 如电磁阀有"咔嚓"声但不正常地打开和关闭,更新增压控制电磁阀(N75)。

② 增压控制电磁阀(N75)的电气检测

a. 拔下电磁阀的供电插头,见图 5-40。用万用表测量其电阻值应该是 25～35Ω。

b. 如果没有达到规定值,更换增压压力控制电磁阀(N75)。

c. 如果达到了规定值,检查增压压力控制电磁阀的供电,见下面所述"增压压力控制电磁阀(N75)的供电"。

③ 增压压力控制电磁阀(N75)的供电检测

a. 使启动机短时工作(允许启动机短时启动),用万用表(电压测量挡)测量端子 1、2

处的电压应该是蓄电池电压，见图 5-41。

b. 如果没有达到规定值，检测增压控制电磁阀的触发情况，见下面所述"检测增压控制电磁阀（N75）的触发情况"。

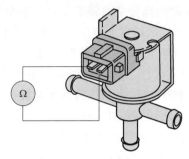 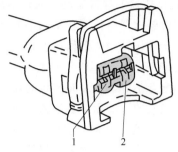

图 5-40　测量触点间的电阻　　　　　图 5-41　电磁阀的供电插头

④ 检查增压控制电磁阀（N75）的触发情况

a. 拔下电磁阀（N75）的供电插头并把二极管检测灯串接在线束侧端子 1 和 2 之间。

b. 启动执行元件诊断并触发增压控制电磁阀，二极管检测灯应闪亮。

c. 如果二极管检测灯不闪亮或常亮，检测线束的插接。

d. 把检测盒 VAG1598/22 接到发动机电控装置的线束上，检测端子 2 与检测盒 VAG1598/22 触点 64 间的导线是否断路或对正极、对负极短路。

（3）涡轮增压器性能下降的故障原因与排除方法

涡轮增压器性能的变化或发动机供油系统及配气系统的故障，会直接影响增压发动机的功率、油耗和排气温度等性能指标。

常见故障现象如下。

① 增压发动机功率下降。涡轮增压器本身及进气管路系统的故障会使增压压力降低，从而导致增压发动机功率下降。其故障原因及排除方法如下：

a. 旁通阀门关闭不严。一般是旁通阀处有积炭，过脏或增压压力控制电磁阀或膜片控制电磁阀损坏造成。

b. 空气进口阻力损失过大。应检查清洁空气滤清器及管道，减少阻力损失。

c. 增压器叶轮、壳体和流道脏污。应拆下增压器进行清洁。

d. 动力涡轮壳流道和叶轮上严重积炭。排除积炭的方法有：更换密封环、排除漏油故障；改变发动机的使用工况，如避免低负荷长时间运转、减少频繁的冷启动等；检查发动机供油系统和机油消耗情况，拆开涡轮增压器，清除动力涡轮端的积炭。

e. 增压涡轮出口管路漏气。产生这一故障的原因大多是软管接头松动脱开、管子焊接处损坏、锁紧机构松动失效等。根据需要采取相应的措施加以排除。

f. 发动机排气管连接处漏气。这种情况比较常见，主要是由于发动机的排气歧管、排气管垫片或排气管与涡轮壳之间连接不紧、螺栓松动或垫片损坏，还可能是涡轮壳产生了裂纹引起的漏气。一般要针对故障原因，采取相应措施。但如若涡轮壳产生裂纹引起漏气，必须更换新的涡轮壳。

② 增压发动机进气压力上升。通常是涡轮增压器及发动机供油系统、配气系统的故障，使增压发动机进气压力上升。但这种故障较前面所述的进气压力下降的故障要少得多。由涡轮增压器直接造成增压压力上升的原因一般是增压压力控制电磁阀或膜片控制电磁阀损坏，

使旁通阀门不能适时打开。

(4) 涡轮增压器机械故障原因与排除方法

涡轮增压器常见机械故障现象是异常振动和异常噪声。

① 涡轮增压器的异常振动。涡轮增压器异常振动大部分是由转子部件不平衡所引起的。虽然转子部件经过严格检测和精确平衡后才允许在涡轮增压器上使用，但在安装和使用中也有各种因素会破坏转子的平衡精度，从而引起增压器异常振动。比较常见的有：

a. 涡轮增压器转子部件不平衡引起的振动。转子部件上的各零件清洗不干净，或零件内孔与轴的配合不好，组装时产生的偏心等都会使转子轴弯曲，导致其平衡被破坏。因此，在转子部件组装前，必须认真地检查清洗转子部件上的所有零件。

b. 涡轮增压器工作时，异物进入涡轮的流道损坏了叶轮，使转子部件失去平衡。在安装涡轮增压器工作时，必须先将涡轮增压器的各进出口用封口罩盖好，待管路调整对好后，再将封口罩取掉，然后，连接好各管路。

c. 增压器叶轮叶片的疲劳断裂。如果出现叶片断裂故障，一律更换新的涡轮增压器。

d. 增压器叶轮叶片被严重沾污后，转子部件的平衡被破坏而产生异常振动。如果发动机长时间使用低质燃油，因其燃烧后的产物中含有五氧化二钒和硫化钠等物质，在一定的温度下，这些物质会粘在涡轮叶片上，形成污垢。排除这种故障时，必须拆开涡轮增压器，取出涡轮叶轮，轻轻地除掉五氧化二钒，但要小心不能碰坏叶片，并用水清除硫化钠和其他污垢。

② 涡轮增压器的异常噪声。增压发动机正常工作时，具有一定的噪声级，有经验的驾驶员很容易就可分辨出来。如果噪声级发生变化或出现异常噪声，则说明有故障发生。

产生异常噪声的原因与排除的方法如下。

a. 涡轮增压器的动力涡轮或增压涡轮的叶片损坏，导致平衡破坏，引起噪声。其原因与排除方法如前所述。

b. 涡轮增压器转子部件和固定件能够碰撞产生噪声。主要原因是安装涡轮壳和压气机壳时，装配不正。可拆开增压器，检查内部是否有损伤、有脏污、转子转动是否平顺、转动时是否有响声等，确认有问题后进行适当的修复或更换。

(5) 涡轮增压器漏油的原因及排除方法

涡轮增压器如有轻微的渗油，虽可继续工作但也应及时到维修站检查或维修，而严重的漏油必须立即加以排除。因为增压涡轮端严重漏油会使机油经增压涡轮进到进气管，最终进入发动机汽缸内，造成发动机性能恶化、机油消耗量增大，并使发动机活塞顶部、喷油器、活塞环等零件严重积炭、胶结。

① 涡轮增压器外部漏油。外部漏油大多是机油进油管和回油管连接不牢固造成的。检查漏油部位之前，先擦干净涡轮增压器外部的油泥，然后再重新启动发动机，认真观察漏油部位。经常出现漏油的原因有：进、回油管接头松动，油管接头外垫片损坏及油管接头出现裂纹或损坏等。

螺纹连接的锥形接头密封不好，可修理接头或更换新的油管；如果垫片损坏，应更换新的垫片。

② 涡轮增压器内部漏油。涡轮增压器内部漏油是比较常见的故障，产生原因主要有以下几种。

a. 涡轮增压器密封装置（密封环）损坏引起漏油；

b. 发动机曲轴箱内的压力过高，使涡轮增压器回油不畅引起漏油；

c. 涡轮增压器回油管截面积小或过多的弯曲，使回油不畅引起漏油；

d. 发动机长时间空载运转，涡轮增压器容易漏油。

排除故障时刻根据漏油部位，进行维修。

（三）注意事项

① 在 EVAP 系统元件附近不要抽烟，也不要让其他火源接近。

② 如果在汽车内或汽车附近有汽油味，应立即检查 EVAP 是否有漏油处。

③ 实验中，传感器要轻拿轻放，以免氧传感器掉到地上摔坏内部电路。

④ 如果发动机已持续运转一段时间，EGR 会很热，在诊断或维修时要戴上防护手套。

⑤ 在诊断 EGR 系统之前，发动机必须处于正常工作温度。

四、知识与技能拓展

（一）可变配气相位与气门升程电子控制系统

为了改善发动机在不同转速范围内的性能，保证发动机的有效功率、转矩尽可能增大，现在可变配气相位控制系统应运而生。目前发动机上应用的可变配气相位控制系统，有些不仅可根据发动机转速和负荷的变化，适时调整配气相位，而且还可以调整气门升程。但由于进气门配气相位和气门升程对发动机性能的影响比排气门大，为简化发动机结构和降低成本，可变配气相位控制系统一般只控制进气门配气相位和升程。可变配气相位控制系统对柴油机和汽油机均可使用，下面以本田公司 VTEC 系统为主介绍该系统的结构和原理。

本田公司 VTEC（可变配气正时及气门升程电子控制机构）可根据发动机运行工况的变化，通过变换驱动进气门工作的凸轮，来实现对进气相位及进气门升程的控制，并完成单进气门工作和双进气门工作的切换。

本田公司 VTEC 的组成如图 5-42 所示。

同一缸的两个进气门有主、次之分，即主进气门和次进气门。每个进气门通过单独的摇臂驱动，驱动主进气门的摇臂称为主摇臂，驱动次进气门的摇臂称为次摇臂，在主摇臂、次摇臂之间装有一个中间摇臂，中间摇臂不与任何气门直接接触，三个摇臂并列在一起组成气门摇臂总成。凸轮轴上相应有三个不同升程的凸轮分别驱动主摇臂、中间摇臂和次摇臂，凸轮轴上的凸轮也相应分为主凸轮、中间凸轮和次凸轮；在凸轮形状设计上，中间凸轮的升程最大，次凸轮的升程最小，主凸轮的形状适合发动机低速时主进气门单独工作时的配气相位要求，中间凸轮的形状适合发动机高速时主、次双进气门工作时的配气相位要求。正时片是在正时活塞处于初始位置和工作位置时，靠复

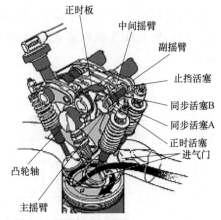

图 5-42 本田公司 VTEC 的组成

位弹簧使其插入正时活塞相应的槽中,使正时活塞定位。

(二) VTEC系统工作原理

VTEC是采用一根凸轮轴上设计两种(高速型和低速型)不同配气定时和气门升程的凸轮利用液压进行切换的装置。高低速的切换是根据发动机的转速、负荷、水温及车速进行检出,由ECU进行计算处理后将信号输出给电磁阀来控制油压进行切换。

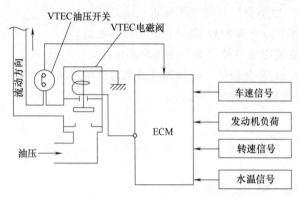

图5-43 VTEC电磁阀控制原理

VTEC不工作时,正时活塞和主同步活塞位于主摇臂缸内,和中间摇臂等宽的中间同步活塞位于中间摇臂油缸内,次同步活塞和弹簧一起则位于次摇臂油缸内。正时活塞的一端和液压油道相同,液压油来自工作油泵,油道的开启由ECU通过VTEC电磁阀控制。如图5-43所示。

在发动机低速运行时,ECU无指令,油道内无油压,活塞位于各自的油缸内,因此各个摇臂均独自上下运动。于是主摇臂紧随主凸轮开闭主进气门,以供给低速运行时发动机所需混合气,次凸轮则迫使次摇臂微微起伏,微微开闭次进气门,中间摇臂虽然随着中间凸轮大幅度运动,但是它对于任何气门不起作用。此时发动机处于单进双排工作状态,吸入的混合气不到高速时的一半。由于仍然是所有汽缸参与工作,所以运转十分平顺均衡。

而当发动机高速运行时,如图5-44所示,即发动机转速在2300~2500r/min、车速在5km/h以上,水温达到一定程度,发动机负荷到达一定程度时,发动机控制电脑ECU就会向VTEC电磁阀供电以开启工作油道,于是工作油道中的压力油就推动活塞移动,压缩弹簧,这样主摇臂、中间摇臂和次摇臂就被主同步活塞、中间同步活塞和次同步活塞串联为一体,成为一个同步活动的组合摇臂。由于中间凸轮的升程大于另两个凸轮,而且凸轮角度提前,故组合摇臂随中间摇臂一起受中间凸轮驱动,主、次气门都大幅度地同步开闭,因此配气相位变化了,吸入的混合气量增多了,满足了发动机全功率时的进气要求。

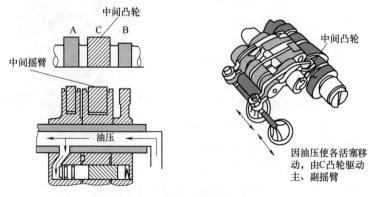

图5-44 液压工作原理

小　结

　　本项目详细介绍了曲轴箱强制通风系统的组成和工作原理及各部件的检查维修；EGR 系统的组成和工作原理及各部件的检查维修；EVAP 系统的组成、控制方式、控制原理及各部件的检查维修；二次空气喷射系统的结构、工作原理及各部件的检查维修；检测排放控制系统零部件性能；使用诊断仪对排放控制系统进行检测等知识。

习题及思考

1. 造成三元催化转换器堵塞的原因有哪些？
2. 如何检查三元催化转换器的性能？
3. 曲轴箱强制通风系统的作用是什么？
4. EVAP 控制系统的组成与工作原理是什么？
5. 可变进气系统如何提高发动机动力性？
6. 二次空气喷射系统的功能是什么？
7. 发动机电脑使炭罐控制电磁阀通电通常考虑哪些条件？

项目六

汽油发动机电控系统典型故障检修

一、项目情境引入

电控发动机的电子控制系统是一个精密而又复杂的系统，其故障的诊断也较为困难。而造成电控发动机不工作或工作不正常的原因可能是电子控制系统，也有可能是电子控制系统外的其他部分的问题。故障检查的难易程度也不一样。如果能遵循故障的一些基本原则，就可能以较为简单的方法准确而迅速地找出故障。

二、项目相关知识

现代轿车的发动机均采用电子控制燃油喷射系统，大量新型电子装置和控制方式在发动机上被广泛应用，使得发动机电子控制系统故障诊断的技术含量越来越高。尽管各种车系的发动机的电子控制系统在外观、形状和安装位置上有不少差异，但其基本控制原理是相似的，故障诊断也有基本规律可循。因此，了解并掌握发动机电子控制系统故障诊断的一些基本原则是十分有益的。

（一）发动机电子控制系统故障诊断原则

1. 先思后行

当发动机出现故障时，根据故障现象先进行故障分析，在清楚可能的故障原因后再选择适当的程序和方法进行故障诊断操作，以防止故障诊断操作的盲目性，尤其是对故障原因比较复杂的故障现象，"先思后行"既可避免对无关部位做无效的检查，又不会漏检有关的故障部位，达到准确迅速排除故障之目的。

2. 先外后内

在选择故障诊断程序和操作次序时，先对发动机电子控制系统以外的故障原因进行检查，然后再对电子控制系统进行诊断操作，以避免费时费力去检查发动机电子控制系统，而不能及时找到真正的故障原因。

3. 故障码优先

当故障自诊断系统监测到电子控制系统故障时，均会以故障码的方式储存故障信息，但并不是所有的故障都通过发动机故障警告灯报警，因此无论仪表板上的发动机故障警告灯是否亮起报警，在对发动机电子控制系统进行检查以前，均应先进行读取故障码操作，以便充分利用故障自诊断系统迅速而准确地排除故障。

4. 先简后繁

能以简单方法检查的可能故障部位优先检查。直观检查最为简单，一些看、摸、听、闻等方法可以确认的故障部位优先检查；需要用仪器、仪表或其它专用工具进行检测的部位，也应将较易检查的安排在前面。这样可使电控发动机的故障诊断变得较为简单。

5. 先熟后生

电控发动机的一些故障现象可能由多个故障原因引起的，不同故障原因出现的概率是不同的，对常见的故障部位先进行检查，往往可迅速确定故障部位，省时省力。

6. 先备后用

电子控制系统元件性能是否良好、电路是否正常，通常以电压或电阻等参数值来判断。没有这些诊断参数，不了解检测的位置，往往会使电子控制系统的故障诊断变得很困难或根本无法进行。所谓先备后用就是在检修前，应准备好有关的诊断参数、检修资料或备件，以保证故障诊断的顺利进行。

（二）电子控制系统的故障诊断的基本方法

电控汽油喷射系统十分复杂，在控制系统中设有故障自诊断功能，我们可以利用仪器通过对发动机控制系统的自诊断程序进行检测从而进行故障诊断。而修理人员的思维能力和工作经验更是保证诊断工作顺利完成最重要的条件。因此，在实际工作中更多的是采用人工直观检查法结合自诊断系统检测的综合诊断法进行诊断。

1. 人工直观诊断法

通过原地检查或道路试验，靠直接观察、感觉或借助简单的工具来确定发动机故障的部位和产生的原因。这种方法较适合于常见和明显的机械性故障，诊断的速度和准确性主要取决于诊断人员的技术水平和工作经验。其基本方法可以归纳为六个字，即："问""看""听""嗅""摸""试"。

① "问"：即询问驾驶员，也叫"问诊"。需要通过问诊掌握维修车辆的基本情况应包括车辆行驶里程、运行条件、以往修理情况、故障的产生时间和症状等。这些信息对诊断分析故障有着非常重要的价值。

② "看"：即察看发动机工作状况，如排气颜色，机油状况，外部附件和线束连接状况，是否漏油、漏水、漏气等。

③ "听"：异响是发生故障和产生事故的前兆，必须认真对待。通过监听发动机各部位工作响声，与正常响声比较判断该部位工作响声是否存在异响。

④ "嗅"：在发动机工作时如有异味产生，如浓烈的汽油味、焦嗅味，必须仔细检查产生味源的部位。

⑤ "摸"：通过手摸感觉有关工作部位的温度和振动来判断该部位工作是否正常。但应注意严格按安全操作规定进行。

⑥ "试"：即通过试车，对发动机整体的技术状况进行测试，从而可以更直观地了解故障发生的条件和症状。

2. 电控自诊断系统检测

电控发动机自诊断系统故障指示灯亮后，如图6-1所示，表明电控系统已侦测到故障并记录下了相应的故障码，这时我们应正确地提取和验证故障码，为故障诊断提供有力的依据。

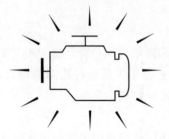

图 6-1 电控发动机故障指示灯点亮

3. 故障征兆的模拟方法

我们必须认识到，故障码实质上仅是对某一控制分支的故障做"有"和"无"的界定，实际修理中，它不可能指出具体的故障原因，甚至有时还会失真，因此我们不能过分地依赖故障码。

如果发动机出现故障，但又没有明显的故障征兆，在这种情况下必须模拟与用户车辆出现故障时相同或相似的条件和环境，然后进行全面的故障分析。例如，一些故障只有在发动机冷态时出现，热车后正常；一些故障是由于车辆行驶时振动引起，时有时无。这些故障决不能仅仅依靠发动机热态和车辆停驶时的故障征兆来进行确诊，故障征兆模拟试验就是解决这种故障的一种有效措施，它可以在停车条件下判断出故障所在。

在试验之前，必须把可能发生故障的电路范围缩小，然后进行故障征兆模拟试验，判断被测试的电路是否正常，同时也验证了故障征兆。

(1) 振动法（当振动可能是主要原因时）

① 连接器：在垂直和水平方向轻轻地摇动连接器。

② 配线：在垂直和水平方向轻轻地摇动配线。连接器的接头、固定支架和穿过开口的连接器体都是应仔细检查的部位。

③ 零件和传感器：用手指轻拍装有传感器的零件，检查是否失灵。注意：不可用力拍打继电器，否则可能会使继电器断路。

(2) 加热法（当怀疑某一部位是受热而引起故障时）

用电吹风机或类似工具加热可能引起故障的零件，检查是否出现故障。

注意：加热温度不得高于 60℃，且不可直接加热 ECU 中的零件。

(3) 水淋法（当故障可能是雨天或高湿度环境引起时）

用水喷淋在车辆上，检查是否发生故障，且应注意：

① 不可将水直接喷在发动机零部件上，而应喷在散热器前面，间接改变温度和湿度。

② 不可将水直接喷在电子器件上。如果车辆漏水，漏入的水可能侵入 ECU，因而此法要慎用。

(4) 电器全接通法（当怀疑故障可能是用电负荷过大而引起时）

接通所有电器负载。包括空调器、鼓风机、前照灯、后窗除雾器等，检查是否发生故障。

4. 部件互换诊断

部件互换诊断是将怀疑有故障的电子部件用正常的电子部件替代，以判断故障原因。如果更换部件后故障消失，则证明判断正确，故障部位确实在该处；反之，若更换部件后故障仍存在，则证明故障不在此处，该部件正常，应查找其他故障原因。若故障有好转但未完全排除，可能除了此故障外，还存在其他故障点，需要进一步查找。这种方法简单易行，效率较高，经常在缺少被修车型技术资料或检测工具的情况下使用。但此方法要求准备较多原车零部件的备件，会使库存增加，加大维修成本。

（三）电子控制系统的故障诊断的流程

发动机电子控制系统故障诊断基本流程如图 6-2 所示。

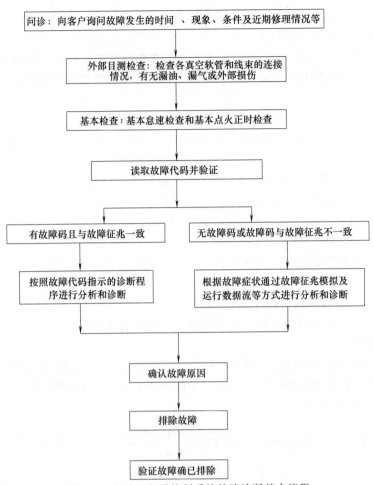

图 6-2 发动机电子控制系统故障诊断基本流程

(1) 问诊

问诊目的：所谓问诊即时通过向顾客询问得到客户对车辆故障的描述，同时还要针对不同的故障现象引导客户补充必要的故障说明以供维修参考。

问诊程序：一般来说可以分为三步：

① 问询故障情况：该故障出现在什么时候（早上、中午或晚上等），出现了多久，出现故障的现象怎样，在什么路面情况下出现（烂路、泥路、水泥路面或沥青路面等），在什么天气或温度下出现（下雨、雪、炎热或寒冷等），何人驾驶（驾驶习惯），何种工况（启动、怠速、加速或减速、巡航等），如果属于周期性故障还要询问以往是否在其他地方修过以及修过什么等等。要注意，不同的故障所询问的参考资料不尽相同。

用户的故障描述只是简单的几种故障类型，需要将之细化到维修人员的故障类型，一般都要有一个通过问诊将之细化的过程。比如发动机无法启动，只有热车不能启动、冷车不能启动、特殊情况下不能启动（如路边停车半小时后不能启动）、无规律性不能启动、所有工况无法启动，每一种不能启动的处理流程和需要的检修项目都不同。

② 核实故障现象：问清楚故障现象后，要根据故障情况进行核实，必要时邀请车间主管或试车员进行试路确认，核实工作有时是非常重要的，因为客户本人并不是专业人士，对于汽车本身的认识处于很粗浅的阶段，有时很难说清楚是哪个系统出了故障或者该故障对于

某种车型来说并不一定是故障，如果照搬车主的叙述直接制定工作单而不进行核实，就有可能使下一步的维修工作陷入误区。

③ 制定专业维修工作单（问诊表）：大部分车主并不是专业人士，而作为专业的接车人员要将车主的口头描述转化为专业文字制定好维修作业单，以便车间的维修人员进行专业化维修作业。

（2）目测检查

检查目的：在进入更为细致的测试和诊断之前，消除一些一般性的故障因素。

检查程序：

① 拆除空气滤清器，检查滤芯及周围是否有脏污或其它污物；

② 检查真空软管是否存在损伤破裂；

③ 检查真空软管是否堵塞，其经过的途径和接头是否恰当；

④ 检查电控系统电路线束的连接情况

a. 传感器及执行器的电连接器是否良好、线束间的连接器是否良好、电线及其绝缘层是否损坏；

b. 检视每个传感器和执行器有无明显损伤；

c. 运转发动机并检视进排气歧管及氧传感器处是否有泄漏等。

（3）基本检查

检查目的：通过检查将故障范围缩小到某一系统。尤其是当故障代码显示正常而发动机存在故障征兆时，在诊断前进行基本检查，有利于更快速、准确地排除故障。

检查程序：如图6-3所示。

图6-3 基本检查程序

（四）电子控制系统的故障诊断的排除程序

汽车故障分析就是根据汽车的故障现象，通过检测、分析和推理判断出故障原因和故障部位之所在。而清晰的检测思路、缜密的综合分析和逻辑推理就是实现快速、准确判断的关键。汽车故障诊断过程中常用故障诊断流程图进行故障分析。

汽车故障诊断流程图。根据汽车故障征兆和技术状况间的逻辑关系，反映汽车故障诊断的综合分析、逻辑推理和判断思路，描述汽车故障诊断操作顺序和具体方法，从原始故障现象到具体故障部位和原因的顺序框图即为汽车故障诊断流程图，它是汽车故障诊断过程中检测思路、综合分析、逻辑推理和判断方法最常用的具体表达方式。

1. 故障码提取和验证的程序

故障码提取和验证的程序如图 6-4 所示。

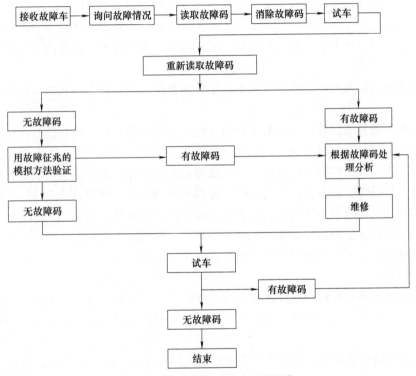

图 6-4 故障码提取和验证的程序

2. 数据流的作用

当系统有故障码存在时，在大多数情况下的确有故障，也会有不同程度的故障症状，而在某些情况下，当故障症状出现时，系统一定有故障，但不一定有故障码（凡不受控制电脑约束的机械、真空部分都没有设置故障点）。此时可以利用自诊断系统的另一功能，通过数据流的读取来查找故障原因所在。

目前所有采用第二代车载电脑自诊断系统的汽车，除了可以用汽车电脑检测仪来读取发动机电控系统的故障码，还可以用电脑检测仪读取汽车发动机电脑通过诊断插座向外输出的、反映发动机电控系统工作状况的数据流。此时维修人员就可以通过对数据流中的各项参数进行数值分析以判断电控系统及其传感器、执行器的工作是否正常，为查找故障原因提供依据。

汽车数据流分析是对数据的数值变化规律和数值变化范围、数值响应的速率、数据与数据之间的关系进行分析，以及相同车种及系统在相同条件下的相同数据组进行比较的分析或与标准数据组进行比较的分析。

数据流变化性质的不同，数据流分析法又可分为：数值分析法、时间分析法、因果分析法、关联分析法、比较分析法。

(1) 数值分析法

是对数据的数值变化规律和数值变化范围的分析，如转速、车速、电脑数值和实际值的差异等的分析。

例如：一辆本田雅阁2.3轿车，发动机启动时间不长冷却风扇即工作，此时用温度计测量散热器只有40～50℃。该车的风扇是由电脑控制的，故接上检测仪，没有故障码存在。但在观察数据时，电脑读取的冷却液温度是115℃。所以，可以判断可能是由于冷却液温度传感器、线束接头或电脑本身有故障。经检查发现传感器的阻值不正确，更换后一切正常。从此例中可以看出，应注意测量值和实际值的关系，对一个确定的物理量，不论是通过诊断仪得到或直接测量得到的值，都应与实际值差异不大，否则就有可能是测量值不准确了。

(2) 时间分析法

在分析某些数据参数时，不仅要考虑传感器的数值，而且要判断其响应的速率，以获得最佳效果。

例如：氧传感器的信号，不仅要求有信号电压和电压的变化，而且信号电压的变化频率在一定时间内要超过一定得次数（如某些车要求大于每秒6～10次）。当小于此值时，就会产生故障码，表示氧传感器响应过慢。有了故障码是比较好解决的，但当次数并未超过限定值，而又反应迟缓时，并不会产生故障码。此时不仔细体会，可能不会感到一丝故障症状。应接上仪器观察氧传感器数据的变化状态以判断传感器的好坏。对采用OBD-Ⅱ系统的催化转换器，前后氧传感器的信号变化频率是不一样的。通常后氧传感器的信号变化频率至少应低于前氧传感器的一半，否则可能催化转换器效率已经降低了。

(3) 因果分析法

是对相互联系的数据间响应情况和相应速度的分析。在各个系统的控制中，许多参数是有因果关系的。例如，电脑得到一个输入，肯定会根据此输入给出一个输出，否则会认为系统有故障。

例如：在自动空调系统中，通常当按下空调选择开关后，该开关并不是直接接通空调压缩信号，而是检查是否满足设定的条件，若满足，就会向压缩机离合器发出控制指令，接通离合器，使压缩机工作。所以当空调不工作时，可观察在按下空调开关后，空调请求（选择）、空调允许、空调继电器等的状态变化，以此来判断故障点。

(4) 关联分析法

电脑对故障的判断是根据几个相关传感器信号的比较，当发现它们之间的关系不合理时，会给出一个或几个故障码，或指出某个信号不合理。此时不要轻易断定是该传感器不良，需根据它们之间的相互关系做进一步的检测，以得到正确结论。

例如：本田雅阁轿车有时会给出节气门位置传感器信号不正确故障信息，但不论用什么方法检查，该传感器和其设定值都无问题。若能认真地观察转速信号（用仪器或示波器），就会发现电脑接收到此时不正确的转速信号后，并不能判断转速信号是否正确（因无比较量），而是比较此时的节气门位置传感器信号，认为其信号与接收到的错误转速信号不相符，故给出节气门位置传感器的故障码。

(5) 比较分析法

是对相同车种及系统在相同条件下的相同数据组进行的分析。因为在很多时候，没有足够的详细技术资料和详细的标准数据，无法正确地断定某个器件的好坏。

汽车电控发动机包括许多传感器、执行器和 ECU，增加了许多电子控制系统，这就使发动机整个电控系统非常复杂。由于系统的复杂化，当系统发生疑难故障时，对于疑难故障的诊断也是非常困难的事情。

（五）电控发动机常见故障诊断的排除程序

1. 不能启动

发动机不能启动故障诊断程序如图 6-5 所示。

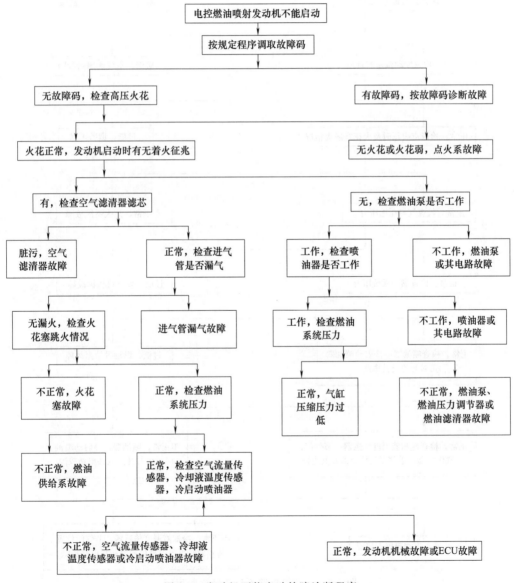

图 6-5　发动机不能启动故障诊断程序

2. 怠速不稳

发动机怠速不稳的故障诊断程序如图 6-6 所示。

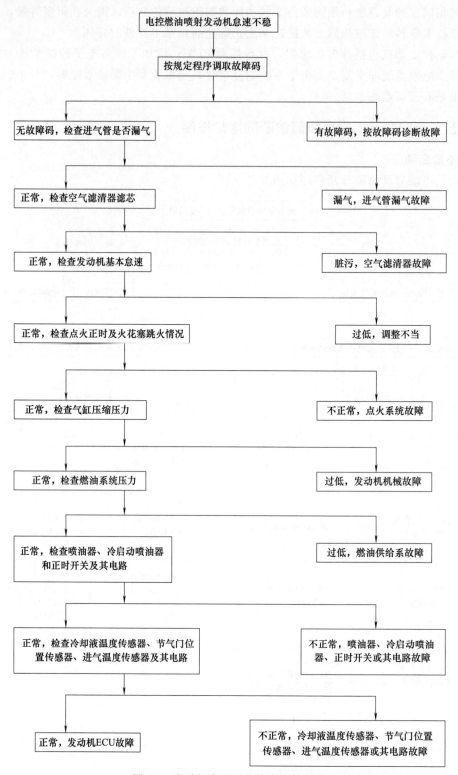

图 6-6　发动机怠速不稳故障诊断程序

3. 动力不足

发动机动力不足的故障诊断程序如图 6-7 所示。

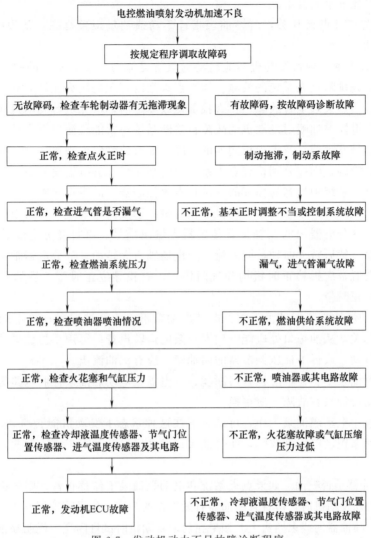

图 6-7 发动机动力不足故障诊断程序

三、项目实施

（一）实施要求

丰田 5A、AJR 发动机台架；轿车一辆。

（二）实施步骤

下面以发动机不能启动且无着车征兆为例，介绍其检修步骤。

电子控制燃油喷射式发动机在设计上具有很好的启动性能，燃油喷射系统的一般故障通常不会导致发动机不能启动。如果出现不能启动且无着车征兆的故障，其原因一定是发动机空气供给系统、燃油供给系统、点火系统或机械系统四者之中的一个或一个以上完全丧失了功能，特别是空气供给系统、燃油供给系统和点火系统。因此，不能启动的故障诊断和排除应重点集中在上述三个系统中。

① 一般应先打开点火开关，若燃油表指针不动或油量报警灯亮，则说明燃油内无油，应加油后再启动。

② 检查点火系统。导致发动机不能启动的最常见原因是点火系统的故障。在做进一步的检查之前，应先排除点火系统的故障。检查点火系统有无高压火花，如果没有高压火花或者火花很弱，说明点火系统有故障。在查找部位故障之前，可先进行发动机故障自诊断，检查有无故障码。电控燃油喷射发动机的故障自诊断系统通常能检测出点火系统中的曲轴位置传感器（点火信号发生器）及点火控制器的故障。如有故障码，则可按显示的故障码查找故障部位；如无故障码，则应分别检查点火系统中的高压线、分电器盖、高压线圈、点火控制器和分电器。点火系统中最容易损坏的零件是点火控制器，应重点检查。

没有高压火花的另一个原因是发动机的正时带断裂或齿轮滑脱，导致由凸轮轴驱动的分电器轴不转动，使分电器内的曲轴位置传感器无输出信号。可打开分电器盖或机油加注口盖、上正时带罩，然后转动曲轴，同时检查分电器轴有无转动。如分电器轴不转动，则说明正时带断裂或滑脱，应拆检正时机构和气门机构，查找导致正时带断裂的原因，排除故障后，再更换新的正时带。

③ 检查电动燃油泵工作是否正常，电动燃油泵不工作是造成发动机不能启动的常见故障。打开点火开关，从油箱口处应能听到燃油泵的运转声音；可用手捏住进油管应能感觉到进油管的油压脉动，或拆下油压调节器的回油管，应有汽油流出。

如果电动燃油泵不工作，应检查熔断丝、继电器及电动燃油泵控制电路等。如果电路正常，则说明电动燃油泵有故障，应更换。

如果在检查中电动燃油泵工作，可试一下在这种状态下发动机能否启动。若可以启动，说明是电动燃油泵控制电路有故障，使燃油泵在发动机启动时不工作。对此，应检查电动燃油泵控制电路。

④ 检查喷油器是否喷油。如果点火系统和电动燃油泵工作都正常，则应进一步检查喷油控制系统。在启动发动机时，检查各喷油器有无工作的声音。如果喷油器不工作；可用一个大阻抗的试灯接在喷油器的线束插头上。如果在启动发动机时试灯闪亮，说明喷油控制系统工作正常，喷油器有故障，应更换；如果试灯不闪亮，则说明喷油控制系统或控制线路有故障。对此，应检查喷油器电源熔断器有无烧断，喷油器降压电阻有无烧断，喷油器与电源之间的接线是否良好，ECU 的电源继电器与 ECU 之间的接线是否良好。如果外部电路均正常，则可能是ECU 内部有故障，可测量 ECU 各接脚电压是否正常来判断 ECU 有无故障，或用一个好的ECU 替换被怀疑有故障的 ECU 看能否启动。如能启动，可确定为 ECU 故障。

⑤ 检查燃油系统压力。燃油系统油压过低会造成喷油量过少，导致不能启动。在电动燃油泵运转时检查燃油系统油压。在发动机未运转的状态下正常燃油压力应达到 300kPa 左右。如果燃油压力过低，可阻断回油通路，若燃油压力迅速上升，说明是油压调节器故障造成油压过低，应更换油压调节器；若燃油压力上升缓慢或不上升，则说明油路堵塞或电动燃油泵有故障，应先拆检燃油滤清器。如果堵塞，应更换；如滤清器良好，则应更换电动燃油泵。

⑥ 检查进气系统有无漏气，检查汽缸压缩压力。若上述检查均正常，则应进一步检查

进气系统有无漏气、检查发动机汽缸压力。若汽缸压力低于标准值，则说明故障在汽缸密封性不好，按汽缸压力不足查找故障。

（三）注意事项

1. 发动机电子控制系统的诊断注意事项

① 在安装蓄电池时，应注意正、负极不可接反。

② 在拆卸电喷系统各导线连接器时，首先要关闭点火开关，并拆下搭铁线。检查发动机电子控制系统时，只关闭点火开关即可。若拆下搭铁线，ECU 中储存的所有故障码和自适应值都会被清除。因此，检测时如果需要拆下搭铁线，应先读取故障码。

带安全气囊的汽车，应在拆下搭铁线 120s 或更长一段时间后，才能开始诊断工作。

③ 拆装时，注意零部件不要弄混，要严防火星。

④ ECU 不能承受下列情况：高于 70℃的温度环境、磁场作用、振动、焊接、水、通信设备干扰、人体静电作用等。

⑤ 充电时，要拆下蓄电池导线，不允许在车上充电。

⑥ 启动时，应按程序启动。当发动机系统蜂鸣器鸣叫时不能启动，汽车过水后不准启动。

⑦ 检测时，不能像检测货车那样用试灯检测，可以用发光二极管串联一个阻值较大的电阻，或者使用高阻抗的万用表。

⑧ 拆卸供油元件和油管时，必须先卸压。

⑨ 没有正确、全面的维修资料时，不要盲目检修车辆。

2. 维修进气系统注意事项

ECU 主要是根据空气流量来控制喷油量，因此进气系统的密封情况对电喷系统有很大的影响。

① 机油尺、机油加油口盖、乙烯塑料软管等脱落会引起发动机失调。

② 当空气流量计与汽缸盖之间的进气系统漏气、管件脱开松动或裂开时，均会导致发动机失调。

3. 维修电子控制系统注意事项

① 因为电子线路比较复杂，存在大量的晶体管电路，有时轻轻接触一下端子，也可能人为地制造故障，所以检查和排除故障时不可大意，不能盲目乱动，否则可能导致新的故障。

② ECU 故障率极低，除人为因素外很少发生故障。如果怀疑 ECU 有故障，尽量不要打开 ECU，因为 ECU 损坏后，通常需专修人员检修。若 ECU 没有故障，打开盖子有可能导致人为损坏。

③ 雨天检修及清洗发动机时，注意电子线路不可溅到水。

④ 拆出导线连接器时，要松开锁紧弹簧或按下锁扣。在装复连接器时，应按到底并锁止。

四、知识与技能拓展

（一）启动困难

启动困难的故障诊断程序如图 6-8 所示。

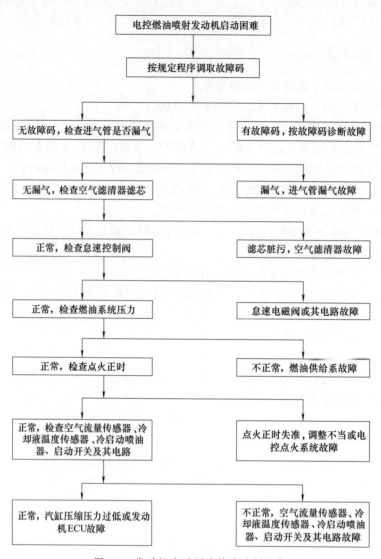

图 6-8　发动机启动困难故障诊断程序

（二）怠速过高

发动机怠速过高故障诊断程序如图 6-9 所示。

（三）混合气过稀

发动机混合气过稀故障诊断程序如图 6-10 所示。

（四）混合气过浓

发动机混合气过浓故障诊断程序如图 6-11 所示。

（五）启动失速

发动机启动失速故障诊断程序如图 6-12 所示。

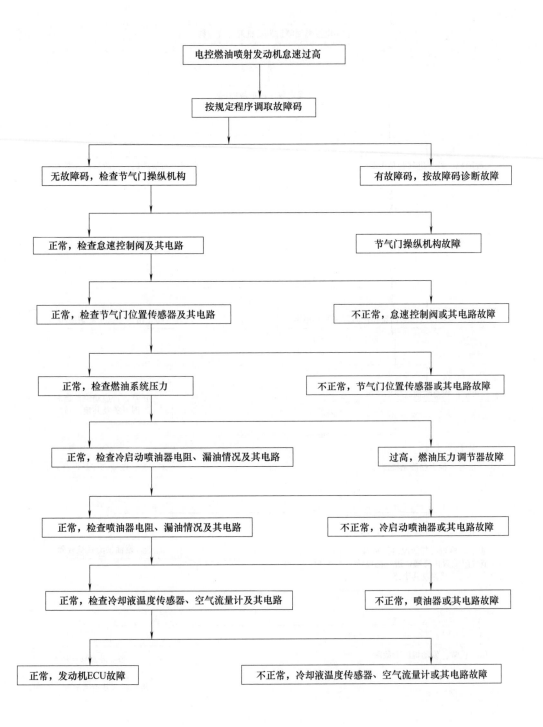

图 6-9 发动机怠速过高故障诊断程序

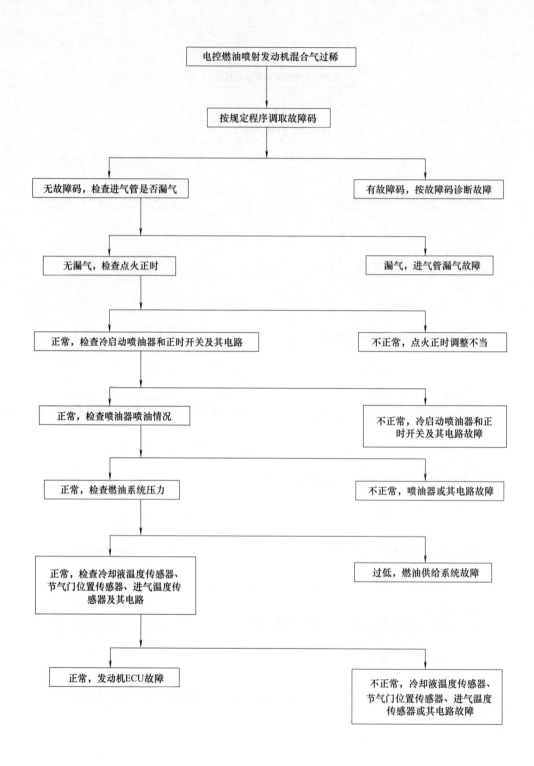

图 6-10 发动机混合气过稀故障诊断程序

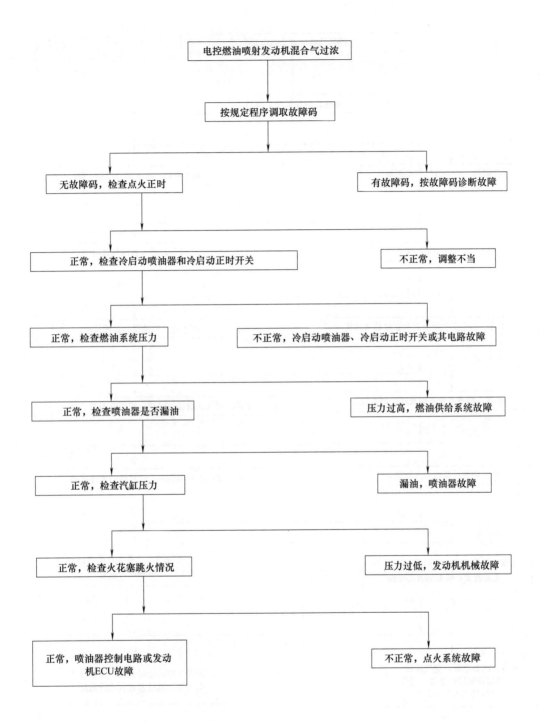

图 6-11 发动机混合气过浓故障诊断程序

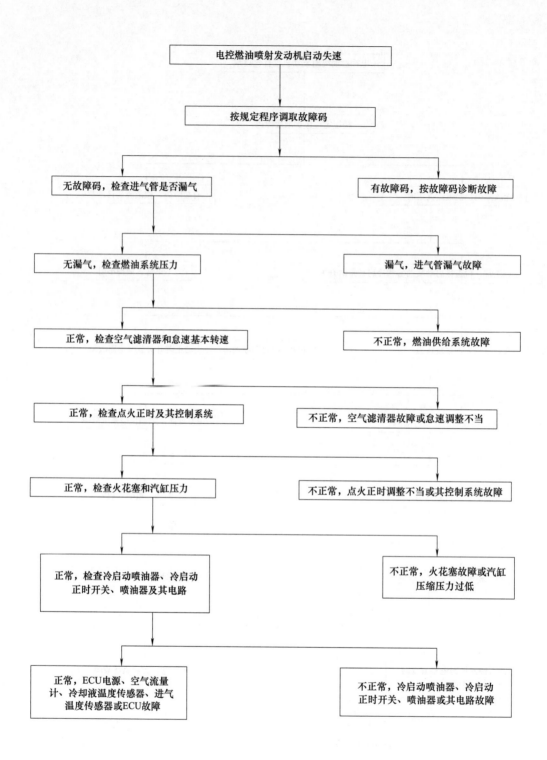

图 6-12 发动机启动失速故障诊断程序

小 结

本项目介绍了故障诊断的方法及发动机电子控制系统故障诊断原则；电子控制系统故障诊断基本流程；故障诊断的一般程序与注意事项；对常见故障进行诊断并能够对故障进行排除。

习题及思考

1. 在进行直观诊断时，如何通过目视对发动机相关部位进行观察？
2. 故障自诊断系统有哪些局限性？
3. 故障码与故障之间是明确的一一对应关系吗？试举例说明。
4. 自诊断系统无故障码显示，电控系统就一定没有故障码？举例说明。
5. 当故障自诊断系统显示有关氧传感器的故障码时，应怎样分析？
6. 发动机电子控制系统故障诊断的原则是什么？
7. 发动机电子控制系统诊断过程中的注意事项有哪些？

参考文献

[1] 杨智勇. 汽车发动机电控技术. 北京：北京人民邮电出版社，2011.
[2] 舒华，姚国平. 汽车电控系统结构与维修. 北京：北京理工大学出版社，2009.
[3] 康国初. 汽车发动机电控系统检修. 北京：北京交通大学出版社，2009.
[4] 张传慧，梁强，张贺隆. 汽车发动机电控系统检修. 北京：北京理工大学出版社，2010.
[5] 曹红兵. 汽车发动机电控技术原理与检修. 北京：机械工业出版社，2008.
[6] 吴宗保. 汽车发动机电控系统维修实训. 北京：机械工业出版社，2009.
[7] 全国汽车维修专项技能认证技术支持中心编写组. 发动机性能. 北京：教育科学出版社，2003.
[8] 齐峰. 汽车电控系统实务. 北京：机械工业出版社，2009.
[9] 赵振宇，李东兵. 电控发动机原理与检修. 2版. 北京：北京理工大学出版社，2012.
[10] 王遂双. 汽车电子控制系统的原理与检修. 北京：北京理工大学出版社，2007.
[11] 宋作军，王玉华. 汽车发动机电控系统检修. 北京：清华大学出版社，2010.

Summary

This item introduces the method of fault diagnosis and the fault diagnosis principle of EEC system, the basic fault diagnosis process of EEC system, the fault diagnosis procedure and notices. Diagnose common faults and be able to troubleshoot them.

Exercises and Thinking

1. In the case of a visual diagnosis, how do you observe the relevant parts of the engine?

2. What are the limitations of the fault self-diagnosis system?

3. Is there a clear one-to-one correspondence between the fault code and the fault? Give examples.

4. The self-diagnosis system has no fault code displayed, and does the electronic control system have no fault? Give examples.

5. When the fault self-diagnosis system displays the fault code for the EGO sensor, how to analyze it?

6. What are the fault diagnosis principles for EEC system?

7. What are the notices in the diagnosis process of EEC system?

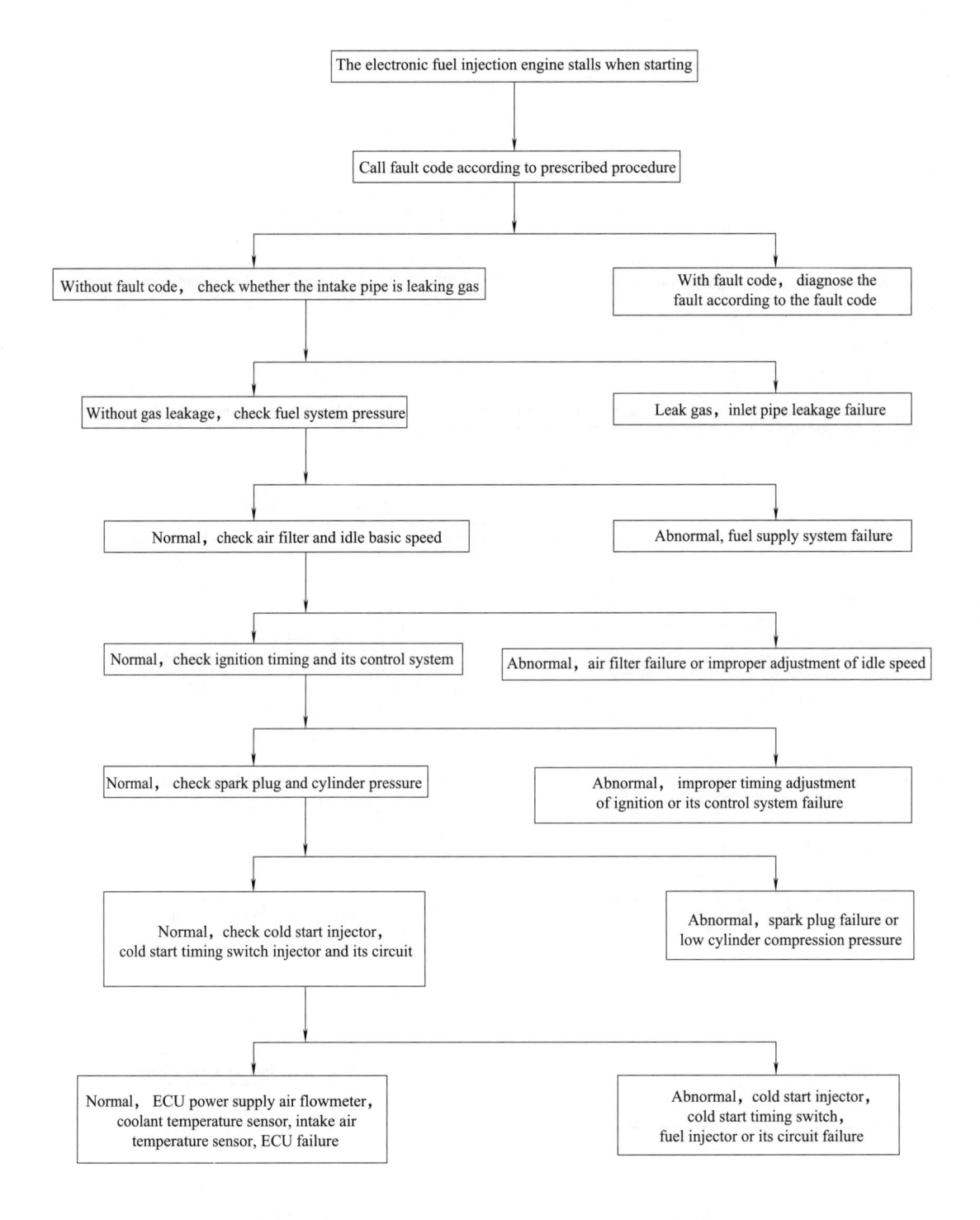

Figure 6-12　Fault Diagnosis Procedure for Engine Starting Stall

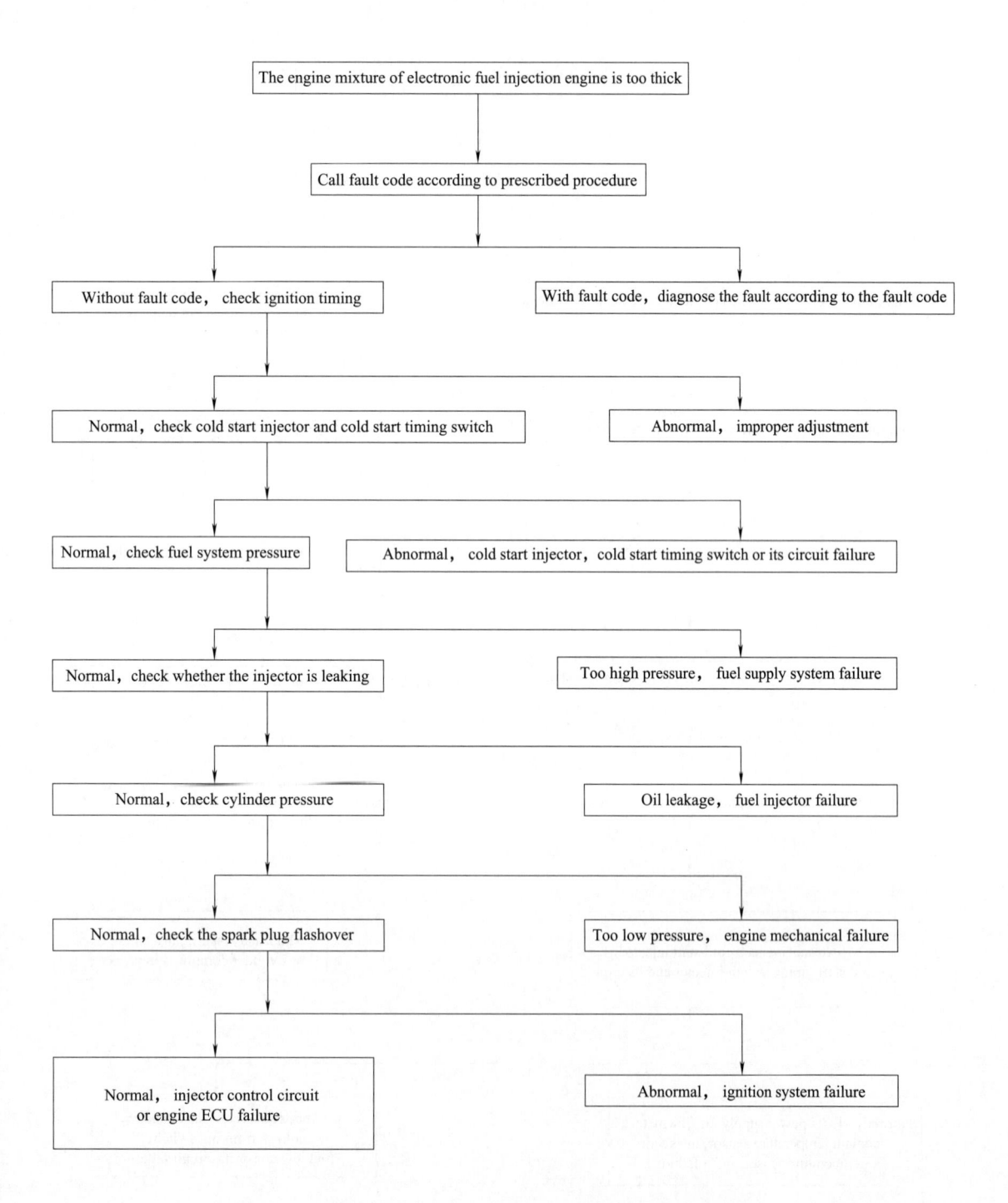

Figure 6-11　Fault Diagnosis Procedure for Too Rich Mixture

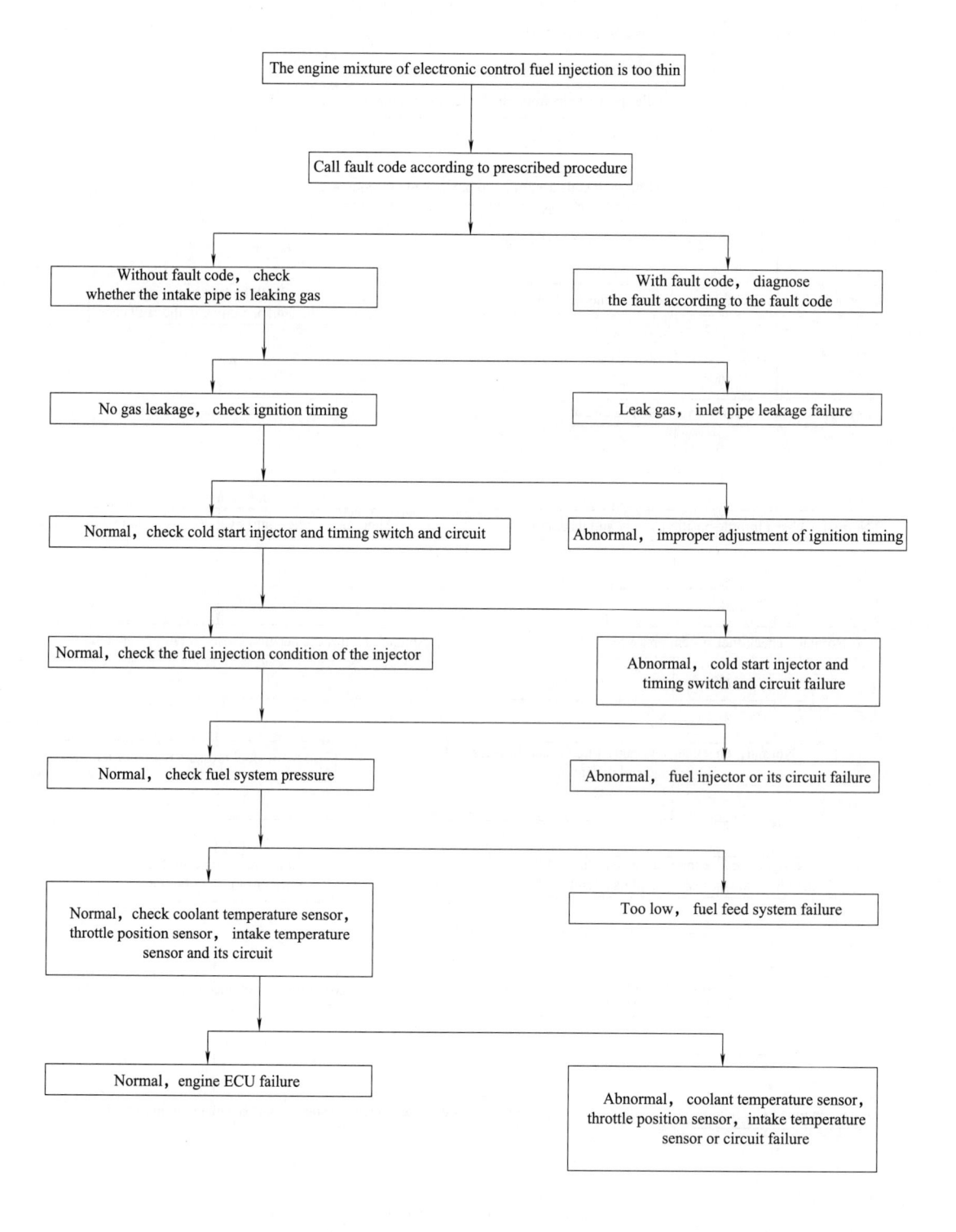

Figure 6-10   Fault Diagnosis Procedure for Too Thin Engine Mixture

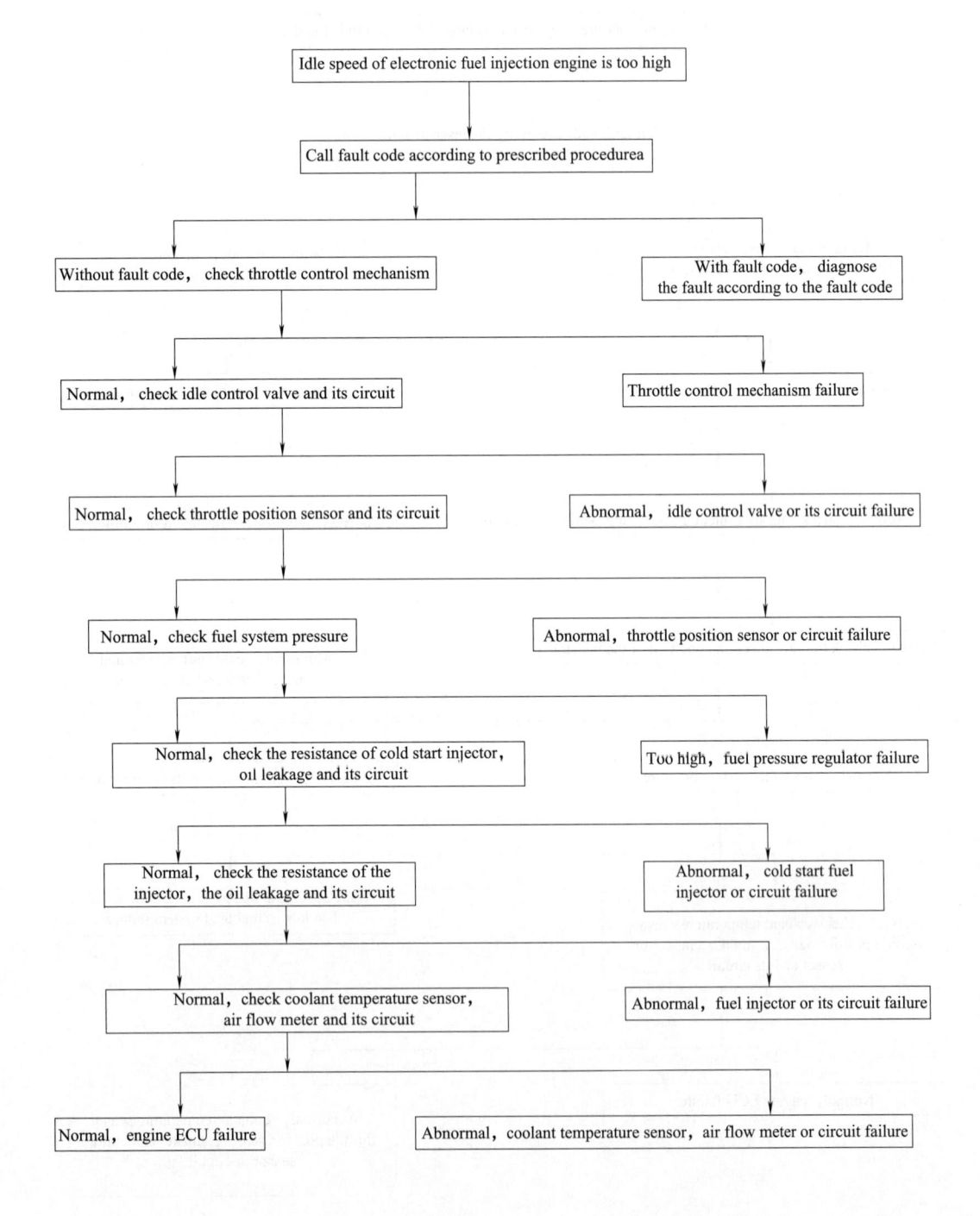

Figure 6-9　Fault Diagnosis Procedure for High Engine Idle Speed

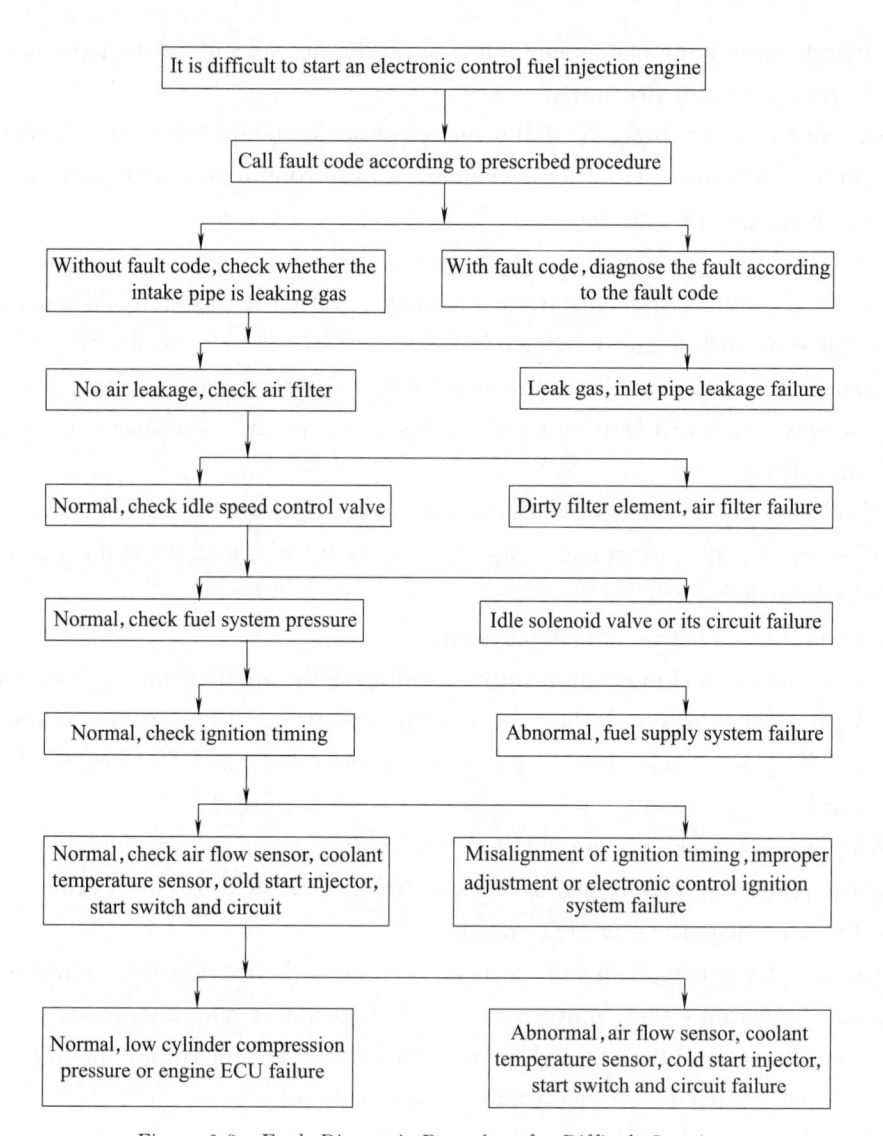

Figure 6-8　Fault Diagnosis Procedure for Difficult Starting.

(Ⅱ) Too high idle speed

Fault diagnosis procedure for high engine idle speed is shown in Figure 6-9.

(Ⅲ) The mixture is too thin

Fault diagnosis procedure for too thin engine mixture is shown in Figure 6-10.

(Ⅳ) Too rich mixture

Fault diagnosis procedure for too rich mixture is shown in Figure 6-11.

(Ⅴ) Starting stall

Fault diagnosis procedure for engine starting stall is shown in Figure 6-12.

③ When disassembling and assembling, be careful not to confuse the parts and components, and strictly prevent fire stars.

④ The ECU cannot bear the following conditions: temperature environment above 70℃, magnetic field action, vibration, welding, water, communication equipment interference, human body electrostatic action.

⑤ When charging, remove the battery wires and do not charge on the vehicle.

⑥ When starting, it should start in accordance with the procedure. When the engine system cannot start with buzzer buzzing, forbid to start the car after contacting with water.

⑦ When testing, it is not allowed to detect with a test lamp, as the detection of a van. It should be detected with a LED in series with a resistor of greater resistance, or a multimeter with high impedance.

⑧ When removing the oil supply element and tubing, the pressure must be released first.

⑨ When there is no correct and comprehensive maintenance information, do not blindly inspect and repair the vehicle.

2. Notice for maintenance of intake system

ECU controls the fuel injection mainly according to the air flow quantity, so the sealing condition of the air intake system has a great influence on the electric injection system.

① The falling off of the dipstick, oil filler lid, and ethylene plastic hose shall cause engine out of order.

② When the air intake system between the air flow meter and the cylinder head is leaking, and the pipefitting is loosened or cracked, the engine shall be out of order.

3. Notice for maintenance of EEC system

① Because of the complexity of electronic circuits, there are a large number of transistor circuits. Sometimes the slightly touch of the terminals may also create a man-made fault. So much more attention should be paid to inspection and troubleshooting, with no blindly movement, otherwise it may lead to a new fault.

② The failure rate of ECU is very low, except for human factors. If you suspect a failure of the ECU, do not open the ECU, because it usually needs to be overhauled by a specialist when it is damaged. If the ECU is not out of order, opening the lid may cause man-made damage.

③ When overhauling and cleaning the engine on rainy days, be careful not to splash water on the electronic circuit.

④ When removing the wire connector, loosen the locking spring or press the latch. When reinstalling the connector, press it to the end and lock it.

Ⅳ. Knowledge and Skills Expansion

(Ⅰ) Difficult in starting

Fault diagnosis procedure for difficult starting is shown in Figure 6-8.

④ Check the fuel injector. If the ignition system and the electric fuel pump are working properly, the fuel injection control system should be checked furthermore. When starting the engine, check whether each injector has a working sound. If the injector does not work, a large impedance test lamp can be attached to the fuel injector's wire harness plug. If the test lamp is flashing when starting the engine, it indicates that the fuel injection control system is working normally, the injector is out of order and it should be replaced; if the test lamp is not flashing, it indicates that the fuel injection control system or control line is out of order. Therefore, it is necessary to check whether the fuel injector power supply fuse has been burnt out, whether the fuel injector voltage drop resistance has been burnt out, whether the connection between the fuel injector and the power supply is good, whether the connection between the power supply relay of ECU and the ECU is good. If the external circuit is normal, it may be that there is a fault inside the ECU, which can be judged by detecting whether the voltage of each pin of the ECU is normal, or replace the ECU with a good one to see if it can start. If it starts, it can be identified as an ECU failure.

⑤ Check fuel system pressure. Too low oil pressure in the fuel system shall result in too little fuel injection, leading to start failure. Check the oil pressure of the fuel system while the electric fuel pump is running. The normal fuel pressure should be about 300 kPa when the engine is not running. If the fuel pressure is too low, it can block the oil return passage. If the fuel pressure rises rapidly, it indicates that the oil pressure is too low due to the failure of the oil pressure regulator, and the oil pressure regulator should be replaced. If the oil pressure rises slowly or does not rise, it indicates that the oil channel is blocked or the electric fuel pump is faulty, and the fuel filter should be removed and checked first. If the oil return passage is clogged, it should be replaced; if the filter is good, replace the electric fuel pump.

⑥ Check the intake system for leakage and check the cylinder compression pressure. If the above inspection is normal, then check the air leakage in the intake system and check the engine cylinder pressure. If the cylinder pressure is lower than the standard value, it indicates that the cylinder seal is not good, find the fault according to the cylinder pressure.

(Ⅲ) Matters needing attention

1. Notice for diagnosis of EEC system

① When installing a storage battery, attention should be paid to the fact that the positive and negative poles are not reachable.

② When disassembling the wire connectors of the electric injection system, the ignition switch should be closed first and the tie-in wire should be removed. When checking EEC system, just turn off the ignition switch. If the ground wire is removed, all fault codes and adaptive values stored in the ECU shall be cleared. Therefore, the fault code should be read first before removing the ground wire during detection.

Vehicles with safety airbags should be removed for 120s or longer before starting the diagnosis.

injection system usually does not cause the engine fail to start. If the engine cannot start and has no start-up signs, it must be that one or more of the four systems (air supply system, fuel supply system, ignition system or mechanical system) completely lose their function, especially the air supply system, fuel supply system and ignition system. Therefore, the fault diagnosis and elimination should focus on the above three systems.

① Turn on the ignition switch first. If the fuel gauge pointer is motionless or the fuel alarm light is on, it indicates that there is no oil in the fuel. It should be refueled before starting.

② Check the ignition system. The most common cause of engine failure is the failure of the ignition system. Therefore, it should be eliminate the failure of the ignition system before making a further inspection Check the ignition system for high-voltage sparks. If there is no high-voltage sparks or sparks are weak, the ignition system is out of order. The engine fault self-diagnosis can be carried out before the fault location is found, and check whether there is the fault code. Fault self-diagnosis system of electronic fuel injection engine can usually detect the fault of CPS (ignition signal generator) and ignition controller in ignition system. If there is a fault code, find the fault location according to the fault code; if there is no fault code, check the high voltage line, distributor cover, high voltage coil, ignition controller and distributor in the ignition system respectively. The most vulnerable part in the ignition system is the ignition controller, which should be checked with more attention.

Another reason for the absence of high-voltage sparks is that the timing belt of the engine is broken or the gears slip off, causing the distributor shaft driven by the camshaft to not rotate, leaving CPS in the distributor with no output signal. Open the distributor cover or the oil filling cap, the upper timing belt cover, turn the crankshaft, at the same time check whether the distributor shaft rotates. If the distributor shaft does not rotate, it indicates that the timing belt is broken or slip off. Remove and detect the timing mechanism and the valve mechanism to find out the cause of the timing belt break, after troubleshooting, a new timing belt should be replaced.

③ Check whether the electric fuel pump is working properly, for it is a common fault that causes the engine to be unable to start. Turn on the ignition switch, you should be able to hear the operation of the fuel pump sound from the oil tank port; hold the intake oil pipe with hand, you should be able to feel the oil pressure pulsation of the oil inlet pipe, or remove the oil return line of the oil pressure regulator, there should be a flow of gasoline.

If the electric fuel pump is not working, check the fuse, relay and electric fuel pump control circuit. If the circuit is normal, it indicates that the electric fuel pump is out of order and it should be replaced.

If the electric fuel pump is working during the inspection, try whether the engine can start in this state. If it can start, it indicates that the electric fuel pump control circuit has the fault, causing the fuel pump not to work when the engine starts. Therefore, you should detect the control circuit of electric fuel pump.

3. Insufficient power

Fault diagnosis procedure for insufficient engine power is shown in Figure 6-7.

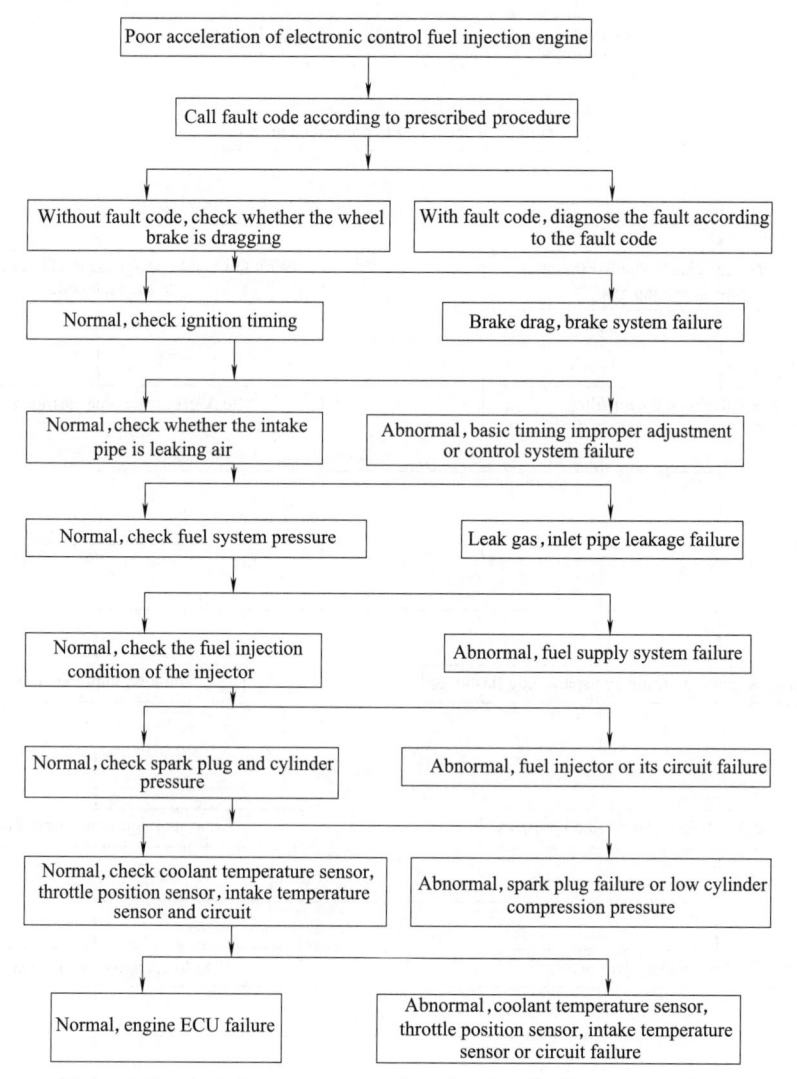

Figure 6-7　Fault Diagnosis Procedure for Insufficient Engine Power

III. Item Implementation

(I) Requirements for Implementation

Toyota 5A, AJR engine bench; Automobile.

(II) Implementation steps

The following takes an engine that can't start and has no start-up signs as an example to introduce its maintenance steps.

Electronic control fuel injection engine has good start-up performance in design. Failure of fuel

2. Unsteady idle

Fault diagnosis procedure for engine unsteady idle is shown in Figure 6-6.

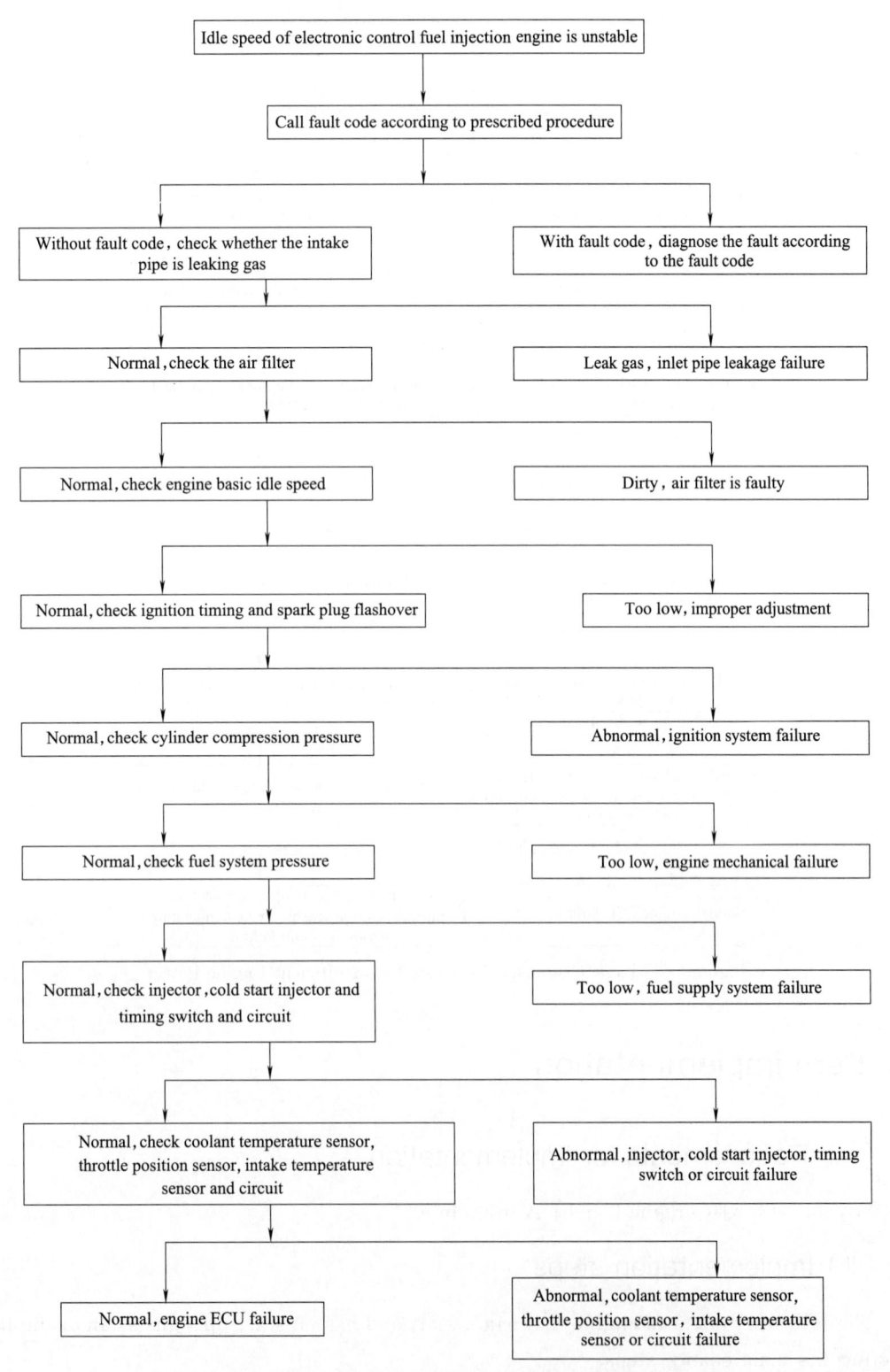

Figure6-6　Fault Diagnosis Procedure for Engine Unsteady Idle

(Ⅴ) Troubleshooting procedure for common fault diagnosis of electronic control engines

1. Unable to start

The fault diagnosis procedure for engine start failure is shown in Figure 6-5.

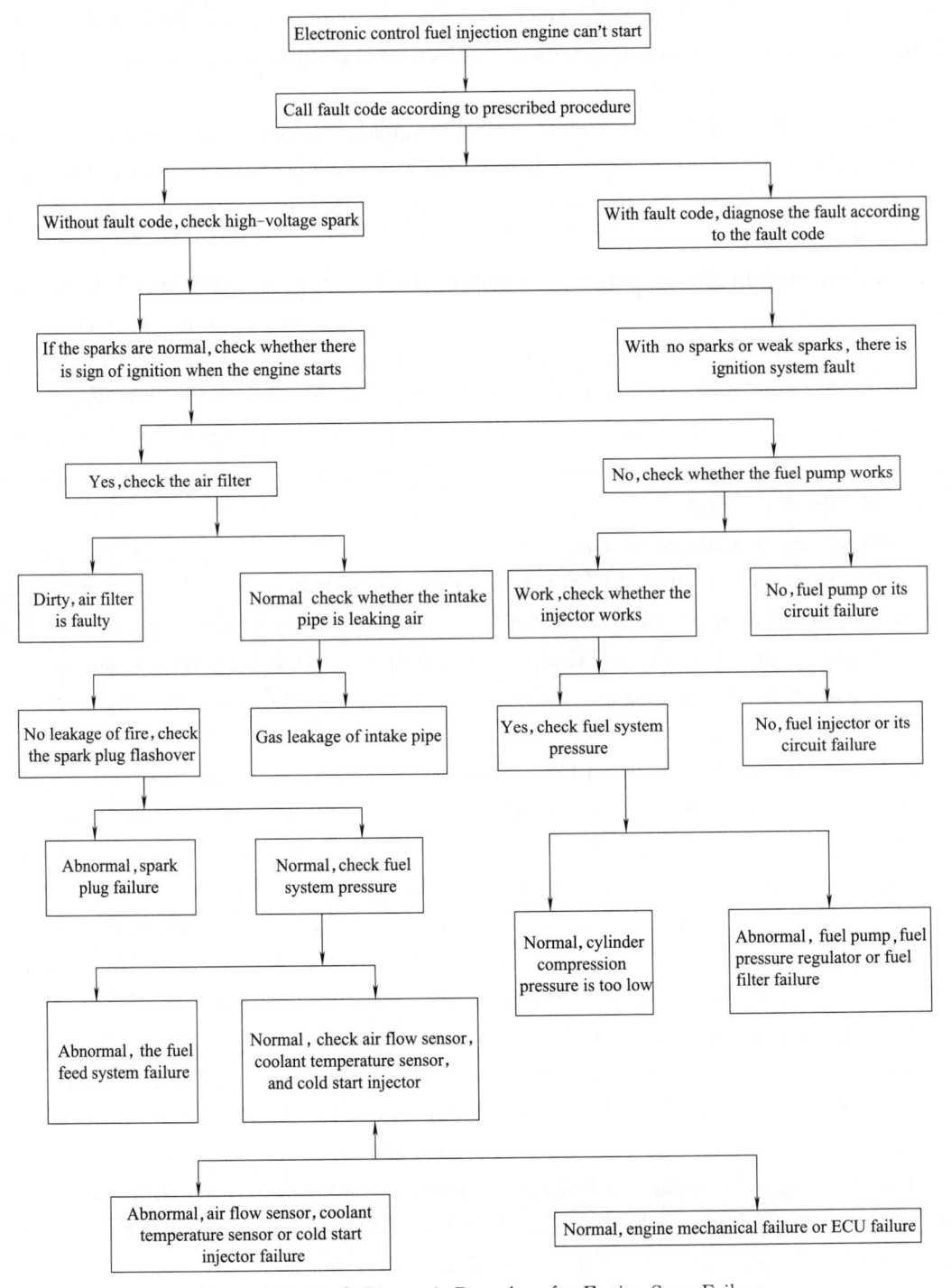

Figure 6-5　Fault Diagnosis Procedure for Engine Start Failure

EGO sensor is responding too slowly. It is helpful to have a fault code, but there is no fault code when the number of times does not exceed the limit and the response is slow. At this time, you may not feel any fault symptom without careful feel. The instrument should be attached to observe the changing state of EGO sensor data to judge whether the sensor is good or bad. For OBD - II system using TWC, the signal frequency of the front and rear EGO sensor is different. Usually the signal frequency of the rear EGO sensor should be less than half of that of the front EGO sensor. Otherwise, the efficiency of the TWC has been reduced.

(3) Causal analysis method

It is the analysis of the response and the corresponding speed of the interrelated data. In each control system, many parameters have casual relationships. For example, if a computer gets an input data, it will definitely output one based on that input, otherwise the system is out of order.

For example: In the automatic air-conditioning system, usually when A/C selection switch, the switch does not directly connect to the air-conditioning compression signal, but checks whether it meets the set conditions. If it meets, it will send instruction to the compressor clutch to connect the clutch, so that the compressor starts working. So when the air-conditioning does not work, observe the state changes after pressing the air-conditioning switch, air-conditioning request (choice), air-conditioning permit, air-conditioning relay, so as to judge the fault point.

(4) Correlation analysis method

The computer determines the fault through the comparison of several related sensor signals. When the relationship between them is unreasonable, it will give one or more fault codes, or point out the unreasonable signal. At this point, do not easily conclude that the sensor is not good, it is necessary to detect furthermore according to the relationship between them to get the correct conclusion.

For example: the Honda Accord sometimes gives incorrect fault information about TPS signal, but no matter what method is used to check the sensor, there is no problem for the sensor and its set value. If carefully observe the rotational speed signal (with the instrument or oscilloscope), you will find that the computer receives the wrong speed signal at this time, and it cannot judge whether the speed signal is correct (there is no comparative quantity). and compares it with TPS signal at this time, determining that the signal is not consistent with the received error rotational speed signal, so it gives the fault code of TPS.

(5) Comparative analysis method

It is an analysis of the same data set of the same vehicle type and system under the same conditions. In many cases, there is not enough detailed technical data and detailed standard data to correctly determine whether a device is good or bad.

The automobile electronic control engine includes many sensors, actuators, ECU, and many EEC systems added, which makes the whole EEC system of the engine very complex. Because of the complexity of the system, it is very difficult to diagnose the problem when the system is out of order.

2. The function of data flow

When the system exists the fault code, in most cases it does have the fault with different degrees. In some cases, when the fault symptom appears, the system must have the fault, but not necessarily fault code (there is no fault code for the mechanical and the vacuum part which are not controlled by ECU). At this time, another function of the self-diagnosis system can be used to detect the fault by reading the data flow.

At present, all vehicles using the second generation of on-board diagnostics ECU detector can be used not only to read the ECU system fault code, but also to read the data flow that ECU outputs through the diagnostic socket, reflecting the working condition of ECU. At this point, the maintenance personnel can make a numerical analysis of the parameter in the data flow to determine whether the electronic control system and its sensors and actuators work normally and provide a basis for detecting the cause of the failure.

The analysis of automobile data flow is to analyze the numerical change law and the change range, the rate of numerical response, the relationship between data and data, and to compare the same data set of the same vehicle and system under the same conditions or with the standard data set.

According to the different change nature, the data flow analysis method can be divided into: Numerical analysis, time analysis, causal analysis, correlation analysis, comparative analysis.

(1) Numerical analysis method

It is the analysis of the numerical change law and the numerical change range of the date, such as the rotational speed, the car speed, the difference between the computer value and the actual value.

For example: A Honda Accord 2. 3 sedan, engine start-up time is not long with cooling fan on, at this time the temperature of the radiator is only 40~50℃ measured with a thermometer. The fan of this car is controlled by computer, so there is no fault code when connected to the detector. But when looking at the data, the computer reads the coolant temperature at 115℃. Therefore, it can be judged that the CTS, the wire harness connector, or the computer itself may be out of order. After checking, it is found that the resistance value of the sensor is not correct, and it is normal after replacement. From this example, we can see that we should pay attention to the relationship between the measured value and the actual value. For a certain physical quantity, whether it is obtained by the diagnostic instrument or by the direct measurement, it should not be little different from the actual value, otherwise the measured value is inaccurate.

(2) Time analysis method

When analyzing parameters of some data, we should not only consider the value of the sensor, but also judge its response rate to get the best result.

For example: the signal of EGO sensor not only requires the change of signal voltage and voltage, but also that the change frequency of signal voltage must exceed a certain number of times in a certain time (for example, some cars require more than 6 ~ 10 times per second). When the result is less than this value, a fault code is generated, indicating that

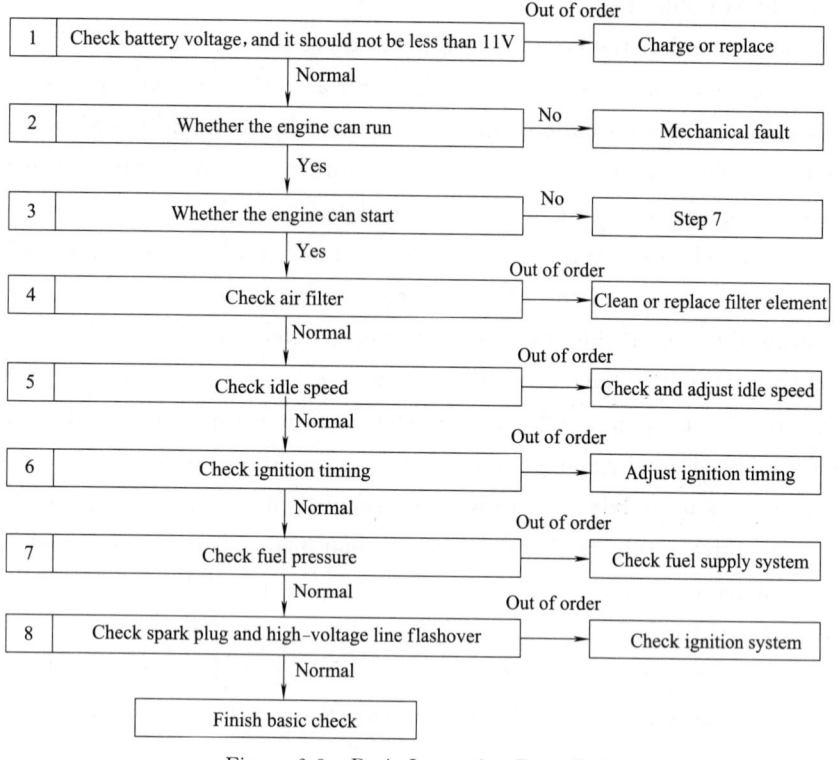

Figure 6-3　Basic Inspection Procedure

1. Procedure for fault code extraction and verification

The procedure for extracting and verifying fault codes is shown in Figure 6-4.

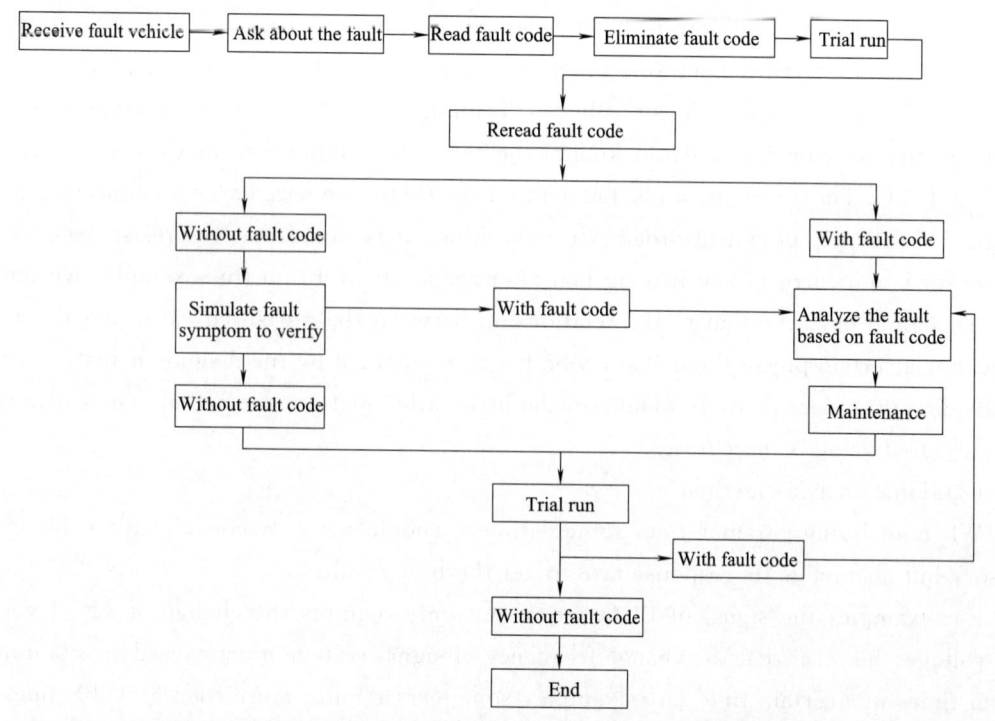

Figure 6-4　Procedure for Fault Code Extraction and Verification

Item Ⅵ　Typical Troubleshooting of Electronic Control System of Gasoline Engine　**175**

say which system is out of order or sometimes the symptoms are not faults for a particular model. Adoption of the owner's description to make a work sheet directly without verification, may mislead maintenance work.

③ Formulate a professional maintenance work sheet (Inquiry Form): Most car owners are not professionals, so a professional car pick-up personnel should turn the owner's oral description into professional text to make a good maintenance work sheet, helping the workshop maintenance personnel to carry out professional maintenance operations.

(2) Visual inspection

Purpose of inspection: eliminate some normal failures before taking more detailed detection and diagnosis.

Inspection procedures:

① Remove the air filter and check whether there is any dirt on or around the filter core;

② Check whether the vacuum hose is damaged or broken;

③ Check whether the vacuum hose is blocked, whether the way it passes through and the connection is proper;

④ Check the connection of the wiring harness of the electronic control system

a. Whether the electrical connector of the sensor and actuator is good, whether the connector between the wire harness is good, and whether the wire and its insulating layer are damaged;

b. Whether each sensor and actuator has obvious damage;

c. Run the engine and check for leaks in the intake and exhaust manifold and EGO sensor.

(3) Basic inspection

Purpose of inspection: Reduce the fault range to a certain system by checking. The basic inspection before diagnosis is helpful for quick and accurate troubleshooting, especially when the fault code shows normal but the engine has fault symptoms .

Inspection procedures: As shown in Figure 6-3.

(Ⅳ) Troubleshooting procedures for fault diagnosis of EEC system

Vehicle fault analysis is to determine the cause and the location of the fault according to the fault symptoms, the detection, analysis and reasoning. And clear detection thought, careful comprehensive analysis and logical reasoning are the key to realize fast and accurate judgment. In the process of automobile fault diagnosis, the fault diagnosis flowchart is often used for fault analysis.

Flowchart of vehicle fault diagnosis. The logic relation between automobile fault symptom and technical condition is used to reflect the comprehensive analysis, logical reasoning and judgment thought of automobile fault diagnosis, and to describe the operation sequence and concrete method of automobile fault diagnosis. The sequence block diagram from the original fault symptoms to the specific fault location and reason is the flow chart of automobile fault diagnosis, which is the most common concrete expression for detection thought, the comprehensive analysis, logical reasoning and judgment in the process of fault diagnosis.

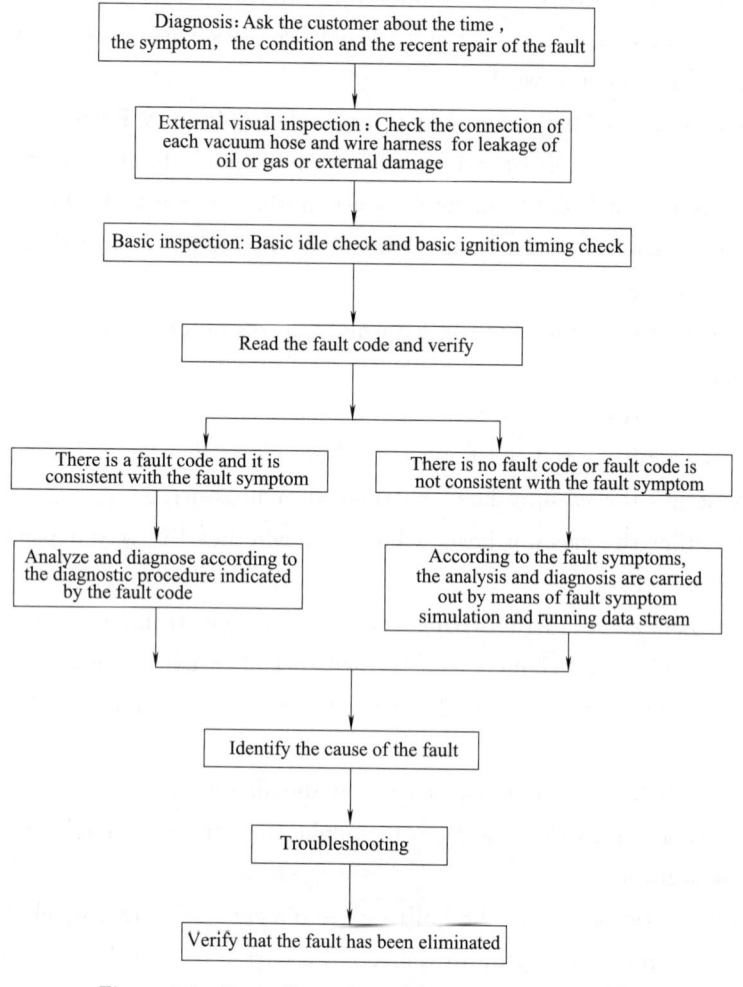

Figure 6-2　Basic flow of EEC System Fault Diagnosis

cold), who was driving (driving habits), what working conditions (starting, idling, accelerating or decelerating, cruising), if it's a periodic fault, ask if it has been repaired in other places in the past and what it has been repaired. Note: the reference materials for different faults are not the same.

The user's fault description is only a few simple fault types. It needs to be refined to the maintenance personnel's fault type, through the inquiry.　For example, the engine can't start, including that the hot cars can't start, cold cars can't start, it can't start in special circumstances (such as it can't start after the roadside stopping for half an hour), it can't start irregularity, and it can't start in all working conditions. The processing flow and the necessary maintenance items for each kind are different.

② Verify failure symptoms: After the inquiry, it is necessary to verify the failure according to the situation. If necessary, the supervisor of the workshop or the tester should be invited to carry out the test confirmation. It is very important for the verification because the customer is not professional, with little understanding of the car, and sometimes it's hard to

③ Parts and sensors: tap the sensors with finger to see if it works. Note: do not hit the relay hard to prevent the relay from being open-circuited.

(2) Heating (when a failure is suspected to be caused by heating)

Heat the parts that may cause failure with an electric hairdryer or similar tool to check if there is a failure.

Note: heating temperature shall not be higher than 60℃, and ECU parts shall not be directly heated.

(3) Water spray method (when the fault may be caused by rain or high humidity environment)

Spray water on the vehicle, check if there is a failure, and pay attention to:

① Do not spray water directly on the engine parts, but spray in front of the radiator, and slowly change increase the temperature and humidity.

② Do not spray water directly on electronics. If the vehicle leaks, the leaking water may invade the ECU, so this method should be used with caution.

(4) Full connection of electrical appliances (when a fault is suspected to be caused by excessive electrical load).

Turn on all electrical loads, including air conditioner, blower, headlight, rear window mist eliminator, to check for failure.

4. Component interchange diagnosis

The component exchange diagnosis is to replace the suspected faulty electronic components with normal electronic components to determine the cause of the failure. If the fault disappears after the replacement of the part, it is proved that the judgment is correct; on the contrary, if the fault still exists after the replacement of the part, it is proved that the fault is not in that location, the part is normal and other fault causes should be found. If the fault is improved but not completely disappears, there may be other fault, which need to be further looked up. This method is simple and efficient, which is often used in the absence of technical data or testing tools for the vehicle being repaired. However, this method requires the preparation of more spare parts for the original car parts, which will increase the inventory and increase the maintenance cost.

(Ⅲ) Process of fault diagnosis for EEC system

The basic flow of EEC system fault diagnosis is shown in Figure 6-2.

(1) Inquiry

Purpose of inquiry: the so-called inquiry is immediately to get the description of the vehicle failure by asking the customer, and to guide the customer to supplement the necessary failure instructions for different failure symptoms as maintenance reference.

Inquiry procedure: it can be divided into three steps:

① Inquiries about failure: when did the failure occur (morning, noon or evening), how long did it occur, how did it happen, what the road conditions (rotten road, mud road, cement road or asphalt pavement), in what weather or temperature (rain, snow, heat or

leakage and air leakage.

③ "Listen": Distortion is a precursor to failure and accidents, so it must be taken seriously. Hear the working noise of all parts of the engine and compare it with the normal noise, we can judge whether there is abnormal working noise of this part.

④ "Sniff": If odor is produced during engine operation, such as the strong smell of gasoline and coke, you must carefully inspect the place where the odor is produced.

⑤ "Touch": Touch and feel the temperature and vibration of the working part by hand to determine whether the part is working properly. However, attention should be paid to strictly in accordance with the safety operation regulations.

⑥ "Try": Test the overall technical status of the engine through the test-run to intuitively understand the conditions and symptoms of the failure.

2. Electronic control self-diagnosis system detection

When the fault indicator lamp of the self-diagnosis system of the electronic control engine is on, as shown in Figure 6-1, it shows that the electronic control system has detected the fault and recorded the corresponding fault code. At this time, we should extract and verify the fault code correctly providing a strong basis for fault diagnosis.

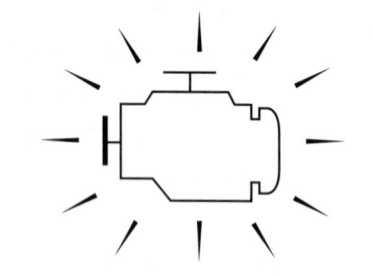

Figure 6-1　Light the Electric Control Engine Fault Indicator Lamp

3. Simulation method of fault symptom

We must know that the fault code is essentially just a "yes" and "no" definition of the fault of a certain control branch. In actual repair, it is impossible to point out the specific cause of the fault, or even sometimes it will be distorted, so we cannot rely too much on the fault code.

If the engine fails, but there are no obvious signs of failure, in this case, it is necessary to simulate the same or similar conditions and environment as when the user's vehicle fails, and then conduct a comprehensive failure analysis. For example, some failure occurs only when the engine is cold while it is normal for the hot car; some failure is caused by the vibration of the vehicle when it is in motion intermittently. These faults can't be diagnosed only by the engine's hot state and the fault symptom when the vehicle stops. The fault symptom simulation test is an effective measure to solve this kind of faults. It can detect the fault when the car is parking.

Before detecting, it is necessary to narrow down the range of circuits that may fail, and then carry out the fault signal simulation test to determine whether the circuit being tested is normal or not, and also to verify the fault signs.

(1) Vibration method (when vibration may be the main cause)

① Connectors: shake the connector gently in both vertical and horizontal directions.

② Wiring: Shake the wiring gently in both vertical and horizontal directions. The connector, the fixing bracket and the connector body through the opening are all parts to be examined carefully.

Item Ⅵ　Typical Troubleshooting of Electronic Control System of Gasoline Engine　**171**

tion shall be stored as fault codes, but not all the faults shall be alerted by the engine fault warning light. So no matter whether the engine fault warning light on the dashboard is on or not, we should read the fault code first before checking EEC system, so as to make full use of the fault automotive fault diagnosis system to remove the fault quickly and accurately.

4. Simplify first and multiply later.

The possible trouble spots that can be checked in a simple way shall be inspected first. Visual inspection is the most simple way: look, touch, listen, and smell, which can confirm the priority fault inspection location; the parts that needs to detect with instruments, meters or other special tools also should be given priority to those that are easy to check. This shall make the fault diagnosis of electronic-controlled engine simple.

5. Familiar fault first and others later.

Some fault symptoms of an electronic control engine may be caused by a number of different fault causes with different probabilities. The common fault site shall be checked first, saving time and effort.

6. Prepare first and use later.

Voltage or resistance value is usually used to determine whether the EEC system element performance is good, and whether the circuit is normal. Without knowing these parameters and the location of the test, it shall be difficult for the fault diagnosis of EEC system or even impossible. The so-called prepare before use means preparing the relevant diagnosis parameters, repair data or spare parts before detecting to ensure the smooth failure diagnosis.

(Ⅱ) Basic methods for fault diagnosis of electronic control systems

Electronic control gasoline injection system is rather complex but with no fault self-diagnosis function. We can carry on the fault diagnosis through the detection of the engine control system self-diagnosis program with the instrument. And the repair personnel's thinking ability and working experience are crucial to ensure the successful diagnosis. Therefore, in the actual work, the artificial visual examination method combined with the self-diagnosis system detection are much more commonly used for the comprehensive diagnosis.

1. Artificial visual diagnosis

It is a kind of method to determine the fault locations and causes through in-situ inspection or road testing, the direct observation, feeling, or by simple means. This method is more suitable for common and obvious mechanical faults. The speed and accuracy of diagnosis mainly depend on the technical level and working experience of the diagnostician. Its basic method can be summed up in 6 words, namely: "Ask", "Look", "Listen", "Sniff", "Touch", "Try".

① "Ask": That is to ask the driver, also known as the "inquiry." Master the basic condition of the maintenance vehicle through inquiry, including the mileage of the vehicle, the running condition, the previous repair, the time and symptom of the failure. This information is of great value in diagnosing and analyzing faults.

② "Look": Observe the engine working conditions, such as exhaust color, oil condition, external accessories and wiring harness connection status, oil leakage, leakage, water

Item VI

Typical Troubleshooting of Electronic Control System of Gasoline Engine

I. Introduction of Item Scene

Electronic control system of EEC is a sophisticated system, so its fault diagnosis is difficult. The reason that the electronic control engine doesn't work or doesn't work properly may be the problem of the EEC system or the other problems. The difficulty of troubleshooting is also different. If follow the basic principles of the failure, it is possible to find the fault accurately and quickly in a simpler way.

II. Item Related Knowledge

The modern car adopts electronic control fuel injection system. A lot of new electronic devices and control methods are widely used in the engine, which improves the technology of fault diagnosis of EEC system. Although there are many differences in the appearance, shape, and installation position of EEC system of various engine systems, the basic control principle is similar, and there are some basic rules for fault diagnosis. Therefore, it is useful to know and master some basic principles of EEC system fault diagnosis.

(I) Fault diagnosis principle of EEC System

1. Think before doing

When the engine is fails, you should analysis the failure symptom first. You should select appropriate procedures and methods after knowing the possible cause of the failure to prevent the blindness of fault diagnosis, especially for the complex fault symptom. "Think before doing" can not only avoid the invalid inspection for irrelevant parts, but also avoid omission of relevant fault parts, so as to achieve accurate and rapid troubleshooting purposes.

2. Start from the outside to the inside

In selecting the fault diagnosis program and operation sequence, the fault causes outside EEC system are checked first, and then EEC system, so as to avoid wasting time and effort to check EEC system.

3. Detect fault code first of all

When the fault self-diagnosis system detects the fault of EEC system, the fault informa-

are opened and closed synchronously. Therefore, the port timing changes, and the mixture increases, which meet the intake requirements of the engine at full power.

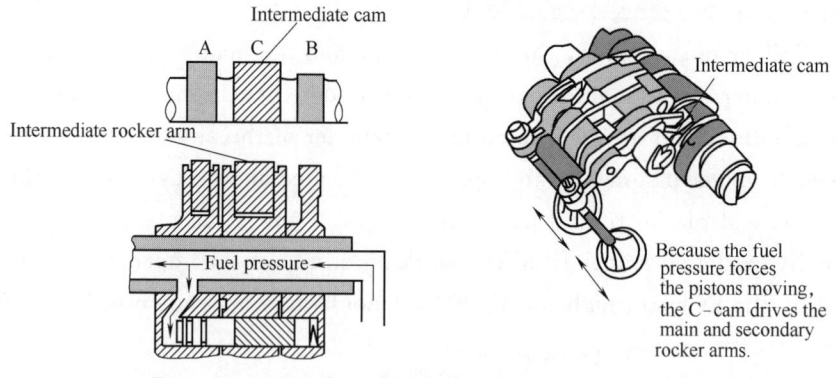

Figure 5-44　Working Principle of Hydraulic Pressure

Summary

This item introduces in detail the composition and working principle and the inspection of the PCV system and the maintenance of each component; the composition and working principle of EGR system and the inspection and maintenance of each component; the composition, control mode, control principle and inspection and maintenance of each component of EVAP system; the structure and working principle of the AI system and the inspection and maintenance of each component. Detection of the performance of parts of the emission control system and diagnosis of the emission control system with diagnostic instrument.

Exercises and Thinking

1. What are the causes of the clogging of the TWC?
2. How to check the performance of a TWC?
3. What is the function of the PCV system?
4. What is the composition and working principle of EVAP control system?
5. How to improve engine power through variable intake system?
6. What is the function of the AI system?
7. What conditions are the usual considered when ECU powers on a carbon canister control electromagnetic solenoid valve?

lic. High and low speed switching is determined by the engine speed, load, water temperature and speed, which shall be output to the solenoid valve to control the oil pressure switch after the calculation and processing of ECU.

When VTEC is not working, the timing piston and the main synchronous piston are located in the cylinder of the main rocker arm, the middle synchronous piston with the same width of the middle rocker arm is located in the cylinder of the middle rocker arm, while the secondary synchronous piston and the spring are located in the cylinder of the secondary rocker arm. One end of the timing piston is located at the same place as the hydraulic oil channel. The hydraulic oil comes from the working oil pump. The opening of the oil channel is controlled by the ECU through the VTEC solenoid valve. As shown in Figure 5-43.

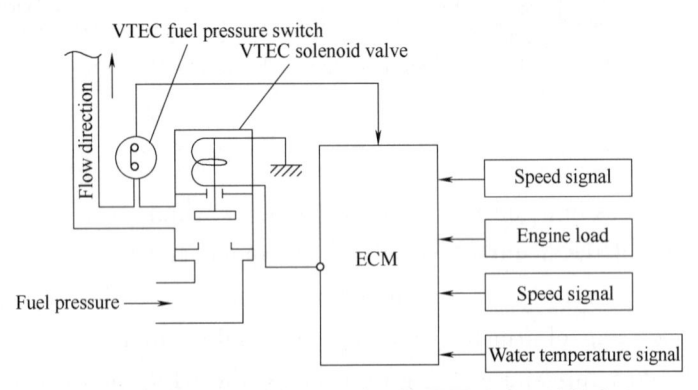

Figure 5-43   Control Principle of VTEC Solenoid Valve

When the engine is running at low speed, the ECU has no instructions, there is no oil pressure in the oil channel, and the pistons are located in their respective cylinders, so each rocker arm moves up and down on its own. Then the main rocker arm follows the main cam to open and close the main intake valve to supply the mixture needed by the engine at low speed. The secondary cam forces the secondary rocker arm to fluctuate, and open and close the secondary intake valve slightly. The middle rocker arm does not work with any valve, although it moves substantially with the middle cam. At this point the engine is in a single-intake double-exhaust working state, the intake of mixture is less than one-half of that at high speed. Since all cylinders are working, the operation is rather smooth and balanced.

When the engine is running at high speed, as shown in Figure 5-44, with the speed of 2300~2500r/min, or above 5 km/h, the water temperature reaches a certain degree, and the engine load reaches a certain degree, ECU shall supply power to the VTEC solenoid valve to open the working oil channel, so the pressure oil in the working oil channel shall push the piston to move and compress the spring. As such, the main rocker arm, the middle rocker arm and the secondary rocker arm shall be connected in series by the main synchronous piston, the middle synchronous piston and the secondary synchronous piston, forming a combined rocker arm with synchronous movement. Since the lift of the middle cam is larger than that of the other two, and the cam angle is ahead of time, the combined rocker arm is driven by the middle cam together with the middle rocker arm, and the main and secondary valves

Item V   Maintenance of Auxiliary Control System of Gasoline Engine   **167**

timing control system can be used for both diesel engine and gasoline engine. The structure and principle of the system are introduced based on Honda VTEC system.

The VTEC (variable port timing and valve lift electronic control system) of Honda can control the inlet port timing and inlet valve lift by changing the cam that drives the inlet valve according to the change of engine operating condition, so as to accomplish the switch of single intake valve and double intake valve.

The composition of Honda VTEC is shown in Figure 5-42.

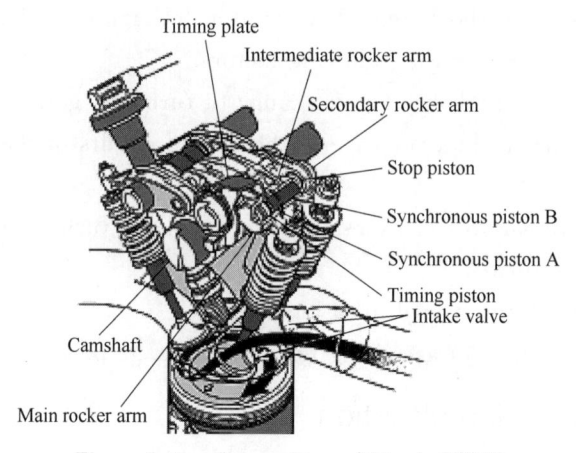

Figure 5-42　Composition of Honda VTEC

The two intake valves of the same cylinder can be divided into the primary one and the secondary one, namely the primary intake valve and the secondary intake valve. Each intake valve is driven by a separate rocker arm. The rocker arm driving the main intake valve is called the main rocker arm and the rocker arm driving the secondary intake valve is called the secondary rocker arm. A middle rocker arm is arranged between the main rocker arm and the secondary rocker arm, which does not directly contact with any valves. The three rocker arms forms the valve rocker arm assembly. There are three cams on the camshaft with different valve lifts to drive the main rocker arm, the middle rocker arm and the secondary rocker arm respectively. The cams on the camshaft are divided into the main cam, the middle cam and the secondary cam correspondingly; In the cam shape design, the middle cam's lift is the largest, the secondary cam's lift is the smallest. The shape of the main cam is suitable for the valve timing requirements of the main intake valve when the engine is at low speed, and the shape of the middle cam is suitable for the valve timing requirements of the main and secondary double intake valves when the engine is at high speed. The timing plate is inserted into the corresponding slot of the timing piston by the return spring when the timing piston is in its initial position and working position, so that the timing piston can be positioned.

(II) Working principle of VTEC system

VTEC is a device designed with two kinds of cams (high speed and low speed) with different port timing and valve lift on one camshaft, which are switched through hydrau-

unstable connection between the oil inlet and oil return line. Before checking the oil leakage part, wipe off the oil sludge outside of the turbocharger, then restart the engine and carefully observe the oil spill. The reasons for the frequent spills are: the joint of inlet and return oil pipe is loose, the outer gasket of oil pipe joint is damaged and the joint of oil pipe is cracked or damaged.

If the conical joint of threaded connection is not well sealed, repair the joint or replace with a new oil pipe; if the gasket is damaged, replace a new gasket.

② Internal leakage of turbocharger. The internal leakage of turbocharger is a common fault, which is mainly caused by the following factors.

a. The damage of sealing device (gasket ring) of turbocharger.

b. The high pressure in the crankcase of the engine results in the uneven turbocharger oil return;

c. Small cross-sectional area or excessive bending of the turbocharger oil return line results in the uneven oil return;

d. The engine runs without load for a long time.

Repair should be carried out according to the oil leakage position.

(Ⅲ) Matters needing attention

① Do not smoke near EVAP system components and do not allow other sources of fire to approach.

② If there is a smell of gasoline in or near the car, check immediately whether there is a leak in the EVAP.

③ In the experiment, the sensor should be lightly placed so that the EGO sensor doesn't fall to the ground and break the internal circuit.

④ If the engine has been running continuously for a period of time, EGR shall be very hot, so wear protective gloves during diagnosis or maintenance.

⑤ The engine must be at normal operating temperature before diagnosing the EGR system.

Ⅳ. Knowledge and Skills Expansion

(Ⅰ) Variable port timing and valve lift electronic control system

In order to improve the performance of the engine in different speed range and increase the effective power and torque of the engine as much as possible, the variable port timing control system has come into being. At present, the variable port timing control system used in the engine can not only adjust the port timing according to the change of engine speed and load, but also adjust the valve lift. However, the influence of intake port timing and valve lift on engine performance is greater than that of exhaust valve, so generally it only controls port timing and lift to simplify the engine structure and reduce the cost. The variable port

ones are:

a. Vibration caused by the unbalance of rotor components of turbocharger. Parts on the rotor components are not cleaned properly, the inner holes are not well matched with the shaft, and the eccentricity produced during assembly shall cause the rotor shaft to bend, destroying its balance. Therefore, before assembling the rotor components, it is necessary to carefully check and clean all parts on the rotor components.

b. When the turbocharger works, foreign matters enter into the flow passage damaging the impeller, causing the rotor components out of balance. In the installation of turbocharger, firstly, all turbocharger inlets and outlets must be covered with the sealing covers, which shall be removed after the adjustment of the pipelines, and then, the pipeline shall be connected.

c. Fatigue fracture of impeller blade of supercharger. If the blade breaks down, replace the new turbocharger with a new one.

d. After the impeller blade of supercharger is seriously contaminated, the balance of rotor components is destroyed with abnormal vibration. If the engine uses low-quality fuel for a long time, some substances contained in its combustion products shall stick to the turbine blades at a certain temperature forming dirt, such as V_2O_5 and Na_2S. To eliminate this problem, the turbocharger must be disassembled, take out the turbine impeller, gently remove V_2O_5, but be careful not to damage the blade, and remove Na_2S and other dirt with water.

② Abnormal noise of turbocharger. A normal working supercharge engine has a certain level of noise, which can be easily distinguished by an experienced driver. If the noise level changes or is abnormal, it indicates that there is a fault.

The reasons for the abnormal noise and the methods to eliminate it are as follows.

a. The blade of the power turbine of the turbocharger or of the supercharge turbine is damaged, which leads to the unbalance and causes noise. The reason and the method of elimination are as mentioned above.

b. The rotor components and fixed parts of turbocharger produce noise by the collision.

The main reason is the incorrect assembly of the turbine shell and compressor shell. Disassembled the supercharger, check whether there is damage inside and dirty, whether the rotor rotation is smooth, and whether there is noise, and repair or replace it after confirming the fault.

(5) Reasons for the leakage of turbocharger and its elimination

If the turbocharger leaks slightly, it should be checked or repaired at the maintenance station in time, although it can continue to work, and the serious oil leakage must be eliminated immediately. Because of the serious oil leakage shall cause the oil flow into the intake pipe through the supercharge turbine and finally into the engine cylinder, causing the deterioration of the engine performance, and the increase of oil consumption, and serious carbon deposition and cementation on the top of the engine piston top, the injector, the piston ring and other parts.

① External leakage of turbocharger. The external oil leakage is mostly caused by the

① The power of the supercharge engine is reduced. The failure of the turbocharger itself and the intake line system shall reduce the supercharge pressure of the turbocharger, resulting in a decrease in the power of the supercharge engine. The causes and troubleshooting methods are as follows:

a. The bypass valve is not closed properly. It is usually caused by carbon deposition at the bypass valve, the valve is too dirty or booat pressure control solenoid valve or diaphragm control solenoid valve is damaged.

b. The air inlet resistance loss is too large. Check and clean air filter and pipe to reduce resistance losses.

c. The impeller, shell and channel of supercharger are dirty. Remove the supercharger for cleaning.

d. Heavy carbon accumulation in the flow passage and impeller of power turbine shell. The methods for removing carbon accumulation are as follows: replace the gasket ring to eliminate the oil leakage fault; change the working condition of the engine, such as avoiding low-load long-time running, reducing frequent cold start; check the engine oil supply system and oil consumption, disassemble the turbocharger and remove the carbon deposition at the power turbine.

e. The supercharge turbine outlet line is leaking gas. The causes of this failure include the loosening of the soft pipe joint, the damage of the pipe welding, the loosening of the locking mechanism. Take corresponding measures to eliminate them as necessary.

f. There is a leak in the connection of the exhaust pipe of the engine. This situation is quite common. It is mainly caused by loose connections, loose bolts or gasket damage between the engine exhaust manifold, the exhaust pipe gasket or the exhaust pipe and the turbine shell , and it may also be caused by the turbine shell cracks. We should take corresponding measures according to the cause of failure. But if a crack in the turbine shell causes a leak, a new turbine shell must be replaced.

② Increase of intake pressure of supercharge engine. Usually, it is the faults of the turbocharger, the engine fuel supply system, and the gas distribution system that cause the supercharge engine intake pressure to rise. However, this failure is much less than those described earlier for the drop of the intake pressure. The reason that the turbocharger directly causes the supercharge pressure to rise is that the booat pressure control solenoid valve or diaphragm control solenoid valve is damaged, so that bypass valve cannot be opened in time.

（4）Causes and troubleshooting of mechanical failure of turbocharger

The common mechanical faults of turbocharger are abnormal vibration and abnormal noise.

① Abnormal vibration of turbocharger. The abnormal vibration of turbocharger is mostly caused by the unbalance of rotor components. Although the rotor components are not allowed to be used on the turbocharger until they are strictly detected and accurately balanced, there are also various factors that can damage the balance accuracy of the rotor, causing abnormal vibration of the turbocharger during installation and use. The more common

a. Unplug the power supply plug of the solenoid valve, see Figure 5-40. The resistance value measured with a multimeter shall be 25~35Ω.

b. Replace the booat pressure control solenoid valve (N75) if it does not reach the specified value.

c. If the specified value is reached, check the power supply of the booat pressure control solenoid valve, see "the power supply of the booat pressure control solenoid valve (N75)" as described below.

③ Power supply detection of booat pressure control solenoid valve (N75)

a. Keep the starter work for a short time (allow the starter to start for a short time), the voltage at terminal 1 and 2 measured with a multimeter (voltage measuring file) shall be the battery voltage, see Figure 5-41.

b. If the specified value is not reached, detect the trigger of the booat pressure control solenoid valve. See "Detection of the trigger of the booat pressure control solenoid valve (N75)" as described below.

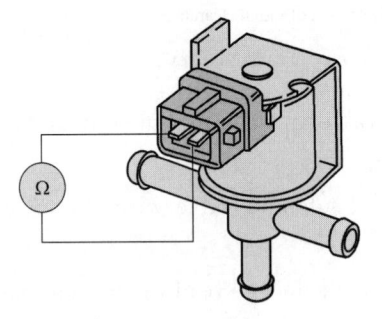

Figure 5-40   Measurement of Resistance
between Contacts

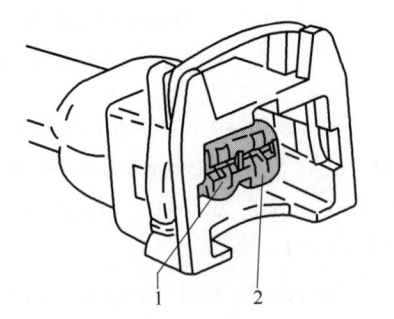

Figure 5-41   Power Supply Plug for
Solenoid Valve

④ Check the trigger of the booat pressure control solenoid valve (N75)

a. Unplug the supply plug of the solenoid valve (N75) and connect the diode detection lamp to the wire harness side terminal 1 and 2.

b. Diagnose the actuating element and the booat pressure control solenoid valve, and the diode detection lamp shall be bright.

c. If the diode detection lamp is not shiny or always bright, check the wiring harness plug.

d. Connect the test box VAG1598/22 to the wire harness of the electronic control device of the engine to detect whether the wire between terminal 2 and the test box VAG1598/22 contact 64 are open-circuited or to the positive pole, and the negative pole is short-circuited.

(3) Fault causes and troubleshooting methods for performance degradation of turbochargers.

Turbocharger performance changes or engine fuel supply system and gas distribution system failure shall directly affect the supercharge engine power, fuel consumption and exhaust temperature.

The common fault symptoms are as follows.

162   Fault Diagnosis and Repair of Automobile Engine Electronic Control System

and down. The radial clearance of the measuring shaft shall not be greater than 0. 18mm, as shown in Figure 5-38 (b). If the axial or radial clearance does not meet the requirements, replace the turbocharger.

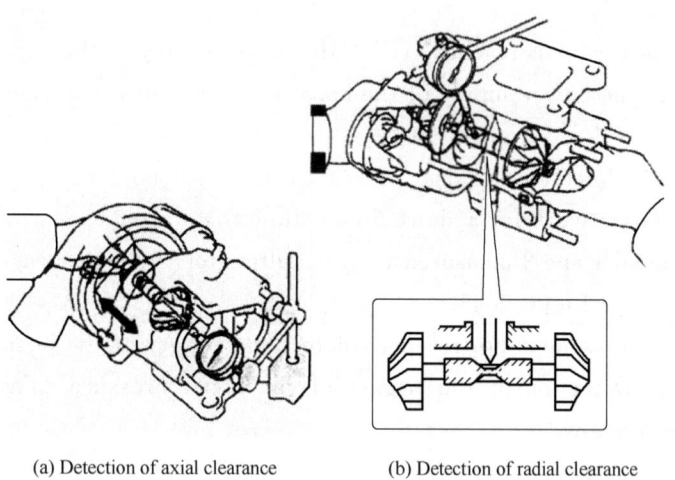

(a) Detection of axial clearance   (b) Detection of radial clearance

Figure 5-38   Inspection of Axial Clearance of Turbocharger

(2) Detection of booat pressure control solenoid valve and diaphragm control valve.

① Booat pressure control solenoid valve detection

In this paper, we will introduce the testing of the solenoid valve with the example of Audi 200 1. 8T.

a. Connect the fault diagnosis instrument VAG1551, select to read the measurement data block (function 08).

b. Remove hose from booat pressure control solenoid valve (N75). Connect the auxiliary hose. Start the actuating element to diagnose and trigger the booat pressure control solenoid valve (N75).

c. The display screen is shown in Figure 5-39 (the lower part of the picture is translated).

> Final control diagnosis   →
> Booat pressure control solenoid valve -N75

Figure 5-39   Display Content of the Detection of the Booat Pressure Control Solenoid Valve (N75)

d. The solenoid valve shall make a "crack" sound and open and close (check by blowing air into the auxiliary hose).

e. If the solenoid valve has no "crack" sound, carry out electrical inspection on the booat pressure control solenoid valve see "electrical detection of booat pressure control solenoid valve (N75)."

f. When there is no electrical signal, the solenoid valve shall be normally closed.

g. If the solenoid valve has a "crack" sound but does not normally open and close, update the booat pressure control solenoid valve (N75).

② Electrical detection of booat pressure control solenoid valve (N75)

When the engine is at normal operating temperature, remove the air hose from the split-flow valve to the TWC to detect if there is any air flow from the hose. If there is an airflow, it indicates that the system is working normally in downstream mode. If there is no air flow, remove the vacuum hose from the split-flow valve and connect the vacuum gauge to the hose. If the vacuum gauge indicates the vacuum of 0, the split-flow valve should be replaced. If there is a certain vacuum on the vacuum gauge, check the hose line to the split-flow solenoid valve, bypass solenoid valve and connecting wire.

7. Fault diagnosis of exhaust turbocharging control system

(1) System inspection

① Perform troubleshooting on the vehicle. First check the engine basic working conditions, compression and leakage, ignition system and fuel supply system. If the fuel supply and pressure are normal, then check if the ignition system's penetration voltage is sufficient to ignite the highly compressed mixture produced by turbocharging and if the ignition time is correct.

② Visual inspection of hose, gasket and pipe. Visually inspect all hoses, gaskets and pipes to see if the assembly is correct, and whether there is damage or abrasion. In the case of breakage or deterioration, the turbine unit shall not work properly, resulting in too high or too low supercharge.

③ Check intake negative pressure or air filter. Check the vacuum leakage of intake negative pressure or air filter. During inspection, inject propane into the intake system, observe the engine speed and the vacuum, and detect HC level. When propane passes through a gas leak, the vacuum and engine speed shall increase and HC levels shall decrease.

④ Check the turbocharger

a. If all the above checks are qualified, the next step is to check the turbocharger. If the turbocharger must be removed from the vehicle, it must be kept clean during overhaul. Any dirt or contamination will cause serious consequences. Before disassembling the turbine, the relative position of the shell and parts shall be marked to ensure correct reassembly. Disassemble the turbine and look closely at the supercharge turbine and power turbines to see if there is any bending, cracking or excessive wear.

b. Examine whether there is wear or impact damage in the turbine shell due to excessive swing of the shaft, dirty or improper lubrication. Rotate the turbine by hand, the resistance should be uniform, not too large, and the rotation should not be sticky, that is, there should be no scratch or any contact.

c. There are strict requirements for bearing clearance, so axial and radial clearance should be checked according to the procedures stipulated by the manufacturer, taking the turbocharger of Toyota automobile as an example. Insert the dial indicator into the hole of the turbine housing so that it contacts the shaft end and move the turbine shaft along the axis. The axial clearance of the measuring shaft shall not be greater than 0.13mm, as shown in Figure 5-38 (a). Insert the dial indicator into the hole of the bearing spacer from the oil discharge hole so that it touches the center of the turbine shaft and move the turbine shaft up

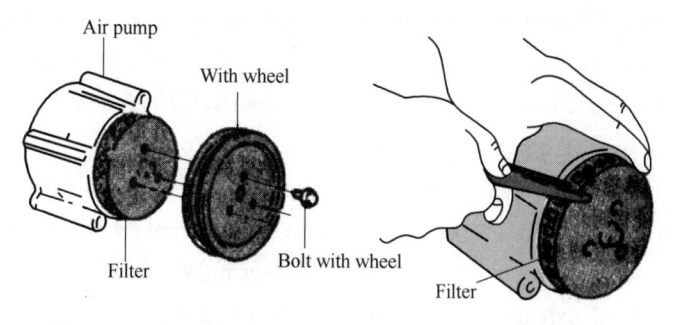

Figure 5-37　Air Pump Belt Pulley and Centrifugal Filter

haust gas or excessive fuel consumption.

④ The decompression valve of the AI system (its function is to release pressure when the system is clogged or the resistance is too large to prevent the pressure of the air pump from being too high) may be connected with the bypass valve and the split-flow valve, or the air pump. If the compression valve is stuck in the open position, the air flow from the air pump shall be continuously discharged through the valve, resulting in the increase of emission of harmful gases.

⑤ If the hose in the AI system shows signs of burning out, this indicates a leakage of the check valve, allowing the exhaust to enter the system.

⑥ The leakage of air manifold and pipeline shall cause the leakage of the exhaust and the production of a lot of noise.

⑦ If there is a fault in the bypass valve solenoid valve or split-flow valve solenoid valve or in the corresponding wire, or if the air flow from the air pump is continuous countercurrent (from the air pump to the exhaust port) or downstream (from the air pump to the TWC), the AI system may set fault codes in ECU. Use diagnostic instrument to check all fault codes associated with the AI system. The cause of the code should be identified before the further diagnosis of the system .

(2) Diagnosis of bypass valve and split-flow valve

① Diagnosis of bypass valve. When starting the engine, listen for a short time to determine if there is any air discharged from the bypass valve. If there is no air, remove the vacuum hose from the bypass valve and restart the engine. If air is discharged from the by-pass valve, check the bypass solenoid valve and the connecting wire. When the bypass valve still does not discharge air, check the air transfer from the air pump to the valve and replace the by-pass valve if there is air delivery.

② Diagnosis of split-flow valve. When the engine temperature rises, remove the hose from the split-flow valve to the air pump outlet, check if there is air flow from the hose, and if there is air flow, it indicates that the system is working properly. If there is no air flow, remove the vacuum hose from the split-flow valve and connect the vacuum gauge to the hose. If the vacuum is higher than 3.38kPa, the split-flow valve should be replaced. If the vacuum is 0, check the vacuum hose to the split-flow solenoid valve, bypass solenoid valve and connecting wire.

Check the working condition of the electromagnetic vacuum passage valve, as shown in Figure 5-35, when the electromagnetic vacuum passage valve is not energized, the air shall enter from the passage E and only be discharged from the filter; when the electromagnetic vacuum passage valve is connected to the battery voltage, the air shall enter from the channel E and only be discharged from F.

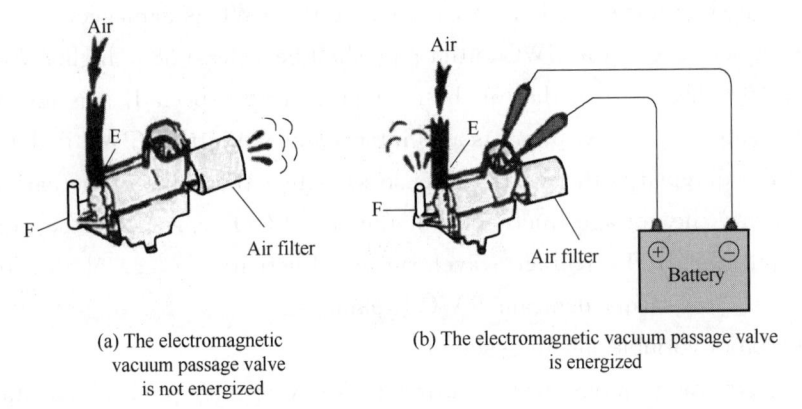

Figure 5-35　Detection of the Operation of the Electromagnetic Vacuum Passage Valve

(3) Detection of vacuum tank

As shown in Figure 5-36, the air shall flow from vacuum tank A to B [Figure 5-36 (a)], not from B to A [Figure 5-36 (b)]; block the outlet B with a finger and apply a 53.3kPa vacuum to A, the vacuum shall not change within 1 minute [Figure 5-36 (c)], otherwise the vacuum tank should be replaced.

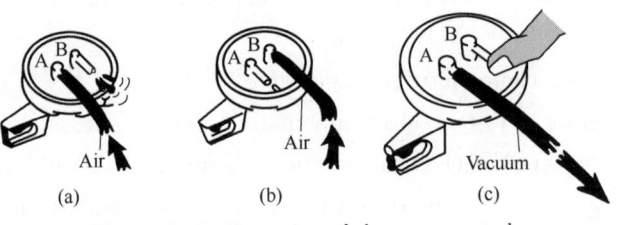

Figure 5-36　Detection of the vacuum tank

6. Diagnosis of AI system

(1) System test

If AI system fails, it shall not pump air into the exhaust port when the engine temperature rises, and HC emissions shall increase too. When testing the AI system for 2 times, you should pay attention to the following points.

① First check all vacuum hoses and circuit connections in the AI system.

② In addition, the air pump has a centrifugal filter at the back of the belt pulley. The air shall flow into the air pump after being filtered. The belt pulley and the filter are bolted to the pump shaft and can be repaired separately, as shown in Figure 5-37. If the belt pulley or filter is bent, worn or damaged, it should be replaced.

③ The belt pulley of the air pump must have a specific tension. A loose belt pulley or a fault AI system can cause AI system to fail to work properly, resulting in an increase of ex-

4. Maintenance of TWC and EGO sensor

① Check whether the TWC is blocked.

② Keep the engine run at idle speed and detect the CO value with the exhaust gas analyzer. When the engine works normally (the air-fuel ratio is 14.7 : 1), the typical CO value is 0.5%~1%. When using AI and TWC technology, the CO value at idle state can be close to 0, the maximum shall not exceed 0.3%, otherwise the TWC is damaged.

③ The temperature of the TWC outlet pipe shall be at least 38℃ higher than that of the inlet pipe and 10% higher than that of the inlet pipe at idle speed. If it is not in accordance with the requirements, and AI pump is also intact, indicating that TWC is damaged.

④ For EFI equipped with two EGO sensors, detect the voltage fluctuation of the two EGO sensors, and the voltage fluctuation of the rear EGO sensor shall be much less than that of the front one. If the voltage waveform and fluctuation range of the front and rear EGO sensors are consistent, it means TWC is damaged.

5. Detection of variable intake system

We shall take the harmonic wave control intake system adopted by Toyota Crown 2JZ-GM engine as an example to introduce the detection of variable intake system.

(1) Inspection of intake plenum control valve and diaphragm actuator

Connect the vacuum gauge to the vacuum tube of the intake pressure booat pressure control valve with tee joint. Start the engine, the vacuum gauge shall not change when idling. Open the throttle quickly, the vacuum gauge pointer shall swing at 53.3kPa position, and the pull rod of the diaphragm actuator shall also be retracted, which means that the intake pressure control valve is working, and the diaphragm actuator is normal, as shown in Figure 5-33.

(2) Detection of electromagnetic passage valve

The circuit diagram of the electromagnetic vacuum passage valve is shown in Figure 5-34. Detect whether the electromagnetic vacuum passage valve coil is broken, short-circuited or overlapped. At 20℃, the resistance values of both ends 1 and 2 should be 38.5~44.45Ω.

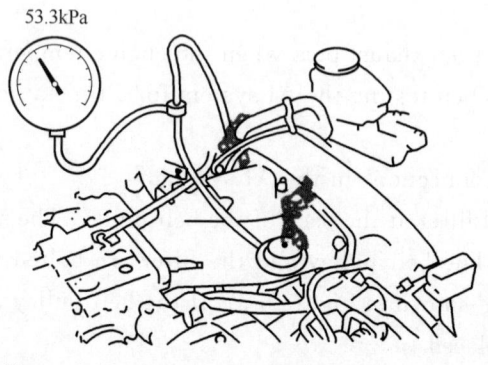

Figure 5-33　Detection of Intake Booat pressure control Valve and Diaphragm Actuator

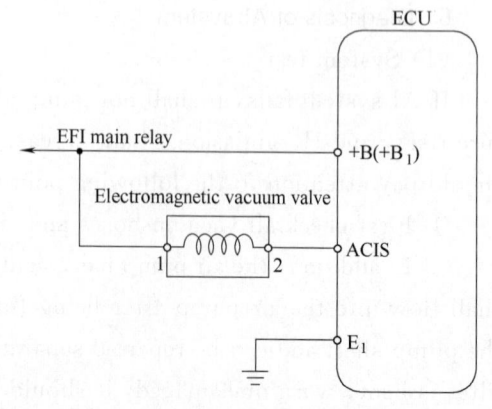

Figure 5-34　Circuit Diagram of Electromagnetic Vacuum Passage Valve

② Turn off the engine, remove EGR solenoid valve plug, the resistance of solenoid valve in cold state shall be $33 \sim 39\Omega$.

③ When the solenoid valve is not energized, the air blowing in from the inlet side connection shall be unobstructed and the air blowing in from the air screen shall be blocked. Energize the solenoid valve, the air from the inlet side connection shall be blocked, and the air from the air filter shall be unobstructed, otherwise the solenoid valve shall be replaced.

④ Remove the EGR valve and a vacuum of about 15kPa is applied to the diaphragm of the EGR valve by means of a manual vacuum pump, the EGR valve shall be capable of being opened; if no vacuum is applied, the EGR valve shall be fully closed, and otherwise the EGR valve shall be replaced.

3. Maintenance of EVAP control system

Inspection methods and procedures:

① Check the connection lines for breakage or leakage, replace the connection hose if necessary, check whether there is crack in the shell of the activated carbon canister, whether the bottom inlet gas filter core is dirty, and replace the carbon canister or filter core if necessary.

② Heat the engine to a normal working temperature and allow it run at an idle speed.

③ Unplug the vacuum hose on the steam recovery tank and check whether there is vacuum suction in the hose. If the device works normally, the solenoid valve shall be closed in the idling operation of the engine, and there shall be no vacuum suction in the hose. If there is suction in the hose at this time, check whether the power supply voltage in the solenoid valve wire harness plug is normal or not.

④ Press the accelerator pedal so that the engine speed is greater than 2000r/min and check whether there is vacuum suction in the hose. If there is suction, it indicates is normal; if there is no suction, check the power supply voltage in the wire harness plug of the solenoid valve. If the voltage is normal, it means that the solenoid valve is out of order; if the voltage is abnormal or there is no voltage, it means that the computer or control line is out of order.

⑤ remove the vacuum control valve from the activated carbon canister and add about 5kPa vacuum to the vacuum control valve through manual vacuum pump, it shall be clear to blow air from the side hole of the activated carbon canister. Otherwise, it shall be blocked without vacuum. If the results cannot meet the above requirements, the vacuum control valve shall be replaced.

⑥ When the engine is not working, disassemble the hose on the first side of the intake pipe of the solenoid valve, apply a certain degree of vacuum to the control solenoid valve with a manual vacuum pump through the soft tube connector, the solenoid valve shall be able to maintain the vacuum when it is not energized, if the solenoid valve is connected to the battery voltage, the vacuum shall be discharged; disconnect the solenoid valve wire harness connector, the resistance between the two ends of the solenoid valve shall be $36 \sim 44\Omega$. If the results cannot meet the above requirements, the control solenoid valve shall be replaced.

be adjusted to the optimal value through the ignition timing adjustment device to maintain the maximum torque. When the ignition advance angle reaches the optimal value, it shall slowly increase the supercharge pressure.

III. Item Implementation

(I) Requirements for implementation

Toyota 5A, AJR engine bench; Automobile.

(II) Implementation steps

1. Maintenance of PCV system

There are two methods to test whether the PCV system is working normally or not, speed descent method and vacuum test method.

(1) Speed descent test method

Connect the tachometer so that the engine can reach the normal operating temperature. In idle state, clamp the pipeline between the PCV valve and the vacuum source, the engine speed shall be reduced by 50r/min or more. Otherwise, check whether the PCV valve and pipeline are clogged, and clean or replace it if necessary.

(2) Vacuum test method

The engine is idle at normal operating temperature, unplug the PCV valve from the valve chamber cover. After removing the PCV valve, you should be able to hear the "sizzling" sound of air flow. Place finger at the inlet of the PCV valve, you should feel a strong vacuum suction.

Install the PCV valve and remove the crankcase air vent or fuel filler lid. When the engine is idle, gently place a thin piece of hard paper on the opening. In 60s, you should feel the vacuum to absorb the paper on the opening.

Turn off the engine, remove the PCV valve, shake the PCV valve, and you shall hear the "click" sound. Otherwise, replace the PCV valve.

If the above test results accord with the requirements, the PCV system works normally. If any of the test results do not accord with the requirements, replace the corresponding component and re-test it.

2. Maintenance of EGR control system

Inspection methods and procedures:

① After starting the cold machine, remove the vacuum hose on the EGR valve, the engine speed shall be unchanged, and the vacuum hose mouth shall be free of vacuum suction by hand; when the engine working temperature is normal, the speed shall be raised to about 2500r/min, and remove the hose from the EGR valve, the engine speed should be improved obviously. If the results fail to comply with the above requirements, it indicates that the EGR system is not working properly.

Item V   Maintenance of Auxiliary Control System of Gasoline Engine   **155**

pressure value changes with the speed of the engine. When the engine works, ECU determines the actual intake supercharge pressure according to the input information of the sensor such as the supercharge pressure sensor, comparing the actual intake supercharge pressure with the theoretical pressure value. If the actual supercharge pressure value does not accord with the theoretical pressure value, the engine computer outputs the control signal to change the pressure on the diaphragm control valve by controlling the supercharge pressure solenoid valve, in ways that drive the by-pass valve to move to change the actual supercharge pressure. That is, when the actual intake pressure is lower than the theoretical value, the by-pass valve shall close; when the intake pressure is higher than the theoretical value, the by-pass valve shall open.

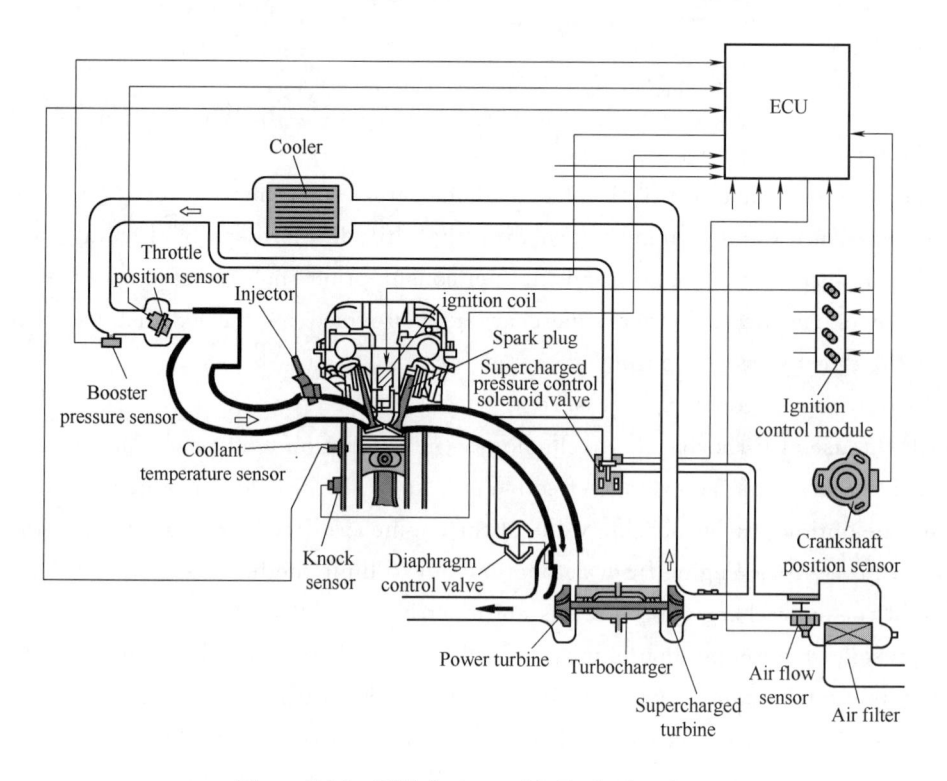

Figure 5-32　EEC System with Turbocharging

In practice, it generally adjusts the ignition timing and supercharge pressure to achieve a better control effect. Because the only use of reducing the supercharge pressure shall reduce the engine performance; while with the only use of turbocharging, the engine exhaust temperature is higher, so it is not appropriate to control the detonation only by adjusting the ignition timing, otherwise, the increase of the temperature has a negative impact on the turbine driven by high temperature exhaust. Therefore, It is better to use both. In practical application, usually when ECU identifies the engine knock according to the input signal of the sensor, it shall delay the ignition advance angle immediately, and reduce the supercharge pressure accordingly. When the two kinds of adjustment take effect (the detonation disappears), the supercharge pressure shall reduce slowly, and the ignition advance angle shall

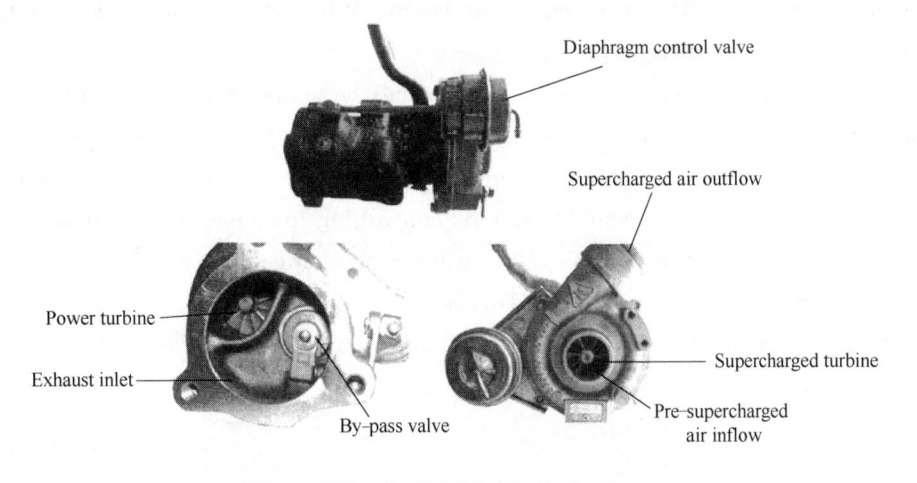

Figure 5-31　Audi A6 1.8T Turbocharger

reduce the fuel consumption.

It can eliminate the effect of the change of the actual aeration rate caused by different atmospheric pressure on the engine. Normally, the altitude increases by 1000m, the engine power shall reduce by $8\% \sim 10\%$, and the fuel consumption shall increase by $4\% \sim 5\%$.

The power consumed by the supercharger is provided by the exhaust gas with little effect on the effective power output of the engine.

(3) Control of supercharge pressure

With the use of turbocharging technology, the detonation tendency of the engine increases with the increase of the average effective pressure. The heat load is a little high. In order to ensure the optimal turbocharging value of the engine at different speeds and operating conditions, to prevent the engine from detonation and to limit the heat load, the turbocharging pressure of the supercharge pressure system must be controlled.

At present, bypass method is mostly used to control the supercharge pressure by regulating the amount of exhaust gas entering into the power turbine chamber. When the intake pressure needs to be increased, the exhaust gas from the exhaust manifold enters the turbocharger and is discharged by the power turbine. With the increase of the throttle opening and the engine speed, the speed of the power turbine and its coaxial supercharge turbine are increased, which leads to the increase of the intake supercharge pressure. If the bypass valve is opened, the amount of exhaust gas and air pressure passing through the power turbine shall be reduced, the speed of the power turbine and the supercharge turbine shall be reduced, and the intake supercharge pressure shall be reduced. It can be seen that by controlling the bypass valve, the amount of exhaust gas passing through the power turbine can be changed and the supercharge pressure can be controlled. Usually, the bypass valve is controlled by the diaphragm control valve, which is controlled by ECU through the booat pressure control solenoid valve.

The EEC system with exhaust turbocharging is shown in Figure 5-32. In the memory of ECU, it stores the data of the pressure characteristic diagram. The theoretical supercharge

the cylinder with high density. There are many types of supercharger, but the most common and effective one is the exhaust turbocharging system, which controls the flow path of the exhaust gas according to the load of the engine, and increases the intake pressure and air intake through the turbocharger, thus greatly improving the engine's dynamic performance.

Figure 5-30 shows the schematic diagram of exhaust turbocharger for an Audi sedan. Exhaust turbocharging is to use the exhaust gas with certain energy (high pressure, high temperature) from the engine to drive the power turbine in the turbocharger, and then drive the supercharge turbine (impeller) which is coaxial with the power turbine to rotate together. The supercharge turbine is usually located in the inlet duct between the air flow sensor (MAF) and the intake valve. As the supercharge turbine rotates, it compresses the fresh air coming from the air filter, and then sends it into the cylinder.

The main components of the exhaust turbocharging system are the turbocharger, the supercharge pressure solenoid valve, the diaphragm control valve and the cooling apparatus.

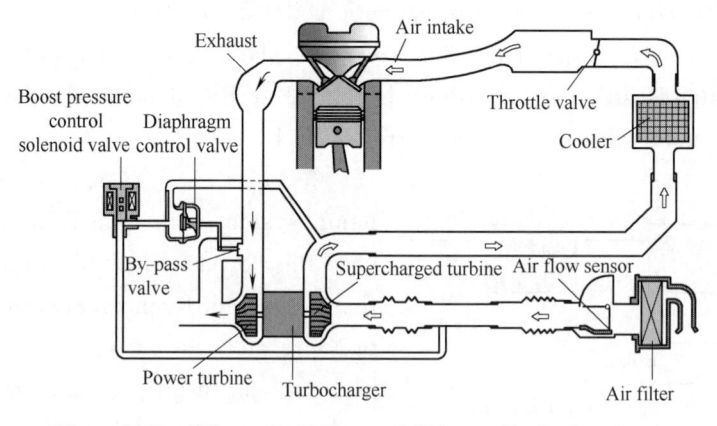

Figure 5-30　Schematic Diagram of Exhaust Turbocharging

① Turbocharger. The turbocharger contains a power turbine and a supercharge turbine, which are mounted on the same shaft. When the exhaust gas flows from the exhaust manifold to the power turbine impeller, the pressure causes the power turbine impeller and the supercharge turbine to rotate, forcing air into the cylinder. Figure 5-31 shows the Audi A6 1.8T turbocharger.

② Supercharge pressure solenoid valve and diaphragm control valve. ECU changes the actual turbocharging pressure by controlling the supercharge pressure solenoid valve and the diaphragm control valve to drive the by-pass valve to move. When the valve is open, the supercharge pressure drops; when the valve is closed, it rises.

③ Cooling apparatus. In the exhaust turbocharging system, there is usually a cooling apparatus (also known as intercooler), which can reduce the intake temperature, eliminate engine knock, and improve the intake efficiency.

(2) Advantages of exhaust turbocharging

It can increase the air intake density and the aeration rate. It enables the engine achieve higher charge efficiency at various speeds, increases the output power, and the torque and

Figure 5-27. ECU controls when the air shall enter the exhaust manifold and TWC.

① Air pump system. Many AI systems use air pumps to pump air into vents or TWC. The air pump system, as shown in Figure 5-28, is controlled by a vacuum air bypass valve and an split-flow valve, which controls the amount of air from the air pump to the exhaust port or the TWC. There is a check valve between the split-flow valve to the exhaust port and the TWC to prevent the exhaust gas from flowing back to AI system in the case of

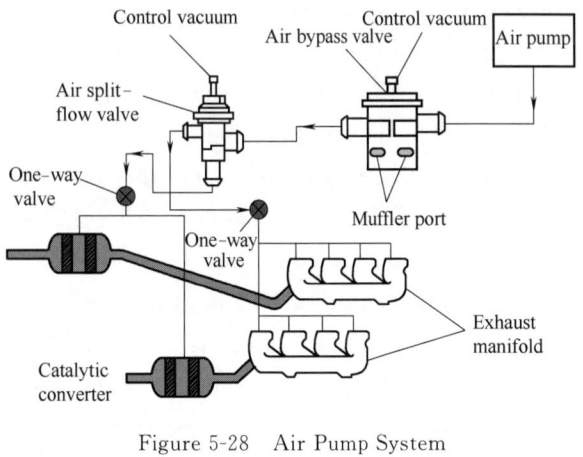

Figure 5-28　Air Pump System

deceleration. ECU controls two electromagnetic coils to supply vacuum to the bypass valve and the split-flow valve respectively. The solenoid valve is not shown in the diagram. When the ignition switch is turned on, a voltage is applied to the solenoid valve, which is energized through the solenoid valve grounding controlled by ECU.

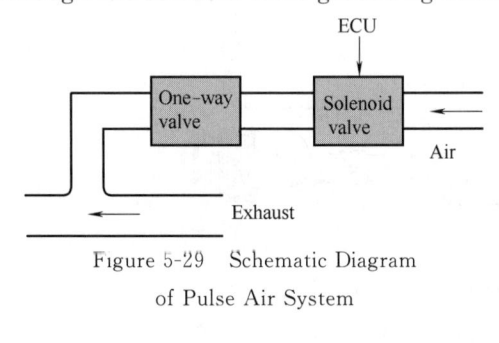

Figure 5-29　Schematic Diagram of Pulse Air System

② Pulse air system. Compared with the air pump system, the pulse air system does not need the power source to inject air. It relies on the pressure difference between the atmospheric pressure and the vacuum pulse of the exhaust gas to get air into the exhaust manifold, thus reducing the cost and power consumption. Its working principle is shown in Figure 5-29. Air is filtered by the air filter. ECU controls the opening and closing of the solenoid valve, which electromagnetic is connected to the check valve. Because the pressure in the exhaust is alternated positive and negative voltage pulses wave, when the engine is running at a lower speed, the exhaust pressure is negative, the air enters into the exhaust port through the filter, the solenoid valve and the check valve, which is further burned with the exhaust HC, thus reducing the HC emissions; when the exhaust pressure is positive, because there is a check valve, the air cannot reverse flow. But, there is no fresh air entering the vent, that is, HC emissions cannot be reduced. There is a solenoid valve and a check valve in the upper and lower air passages of the pulse air system. Because the duration of the low-pressure pulse of the exhaust port is shortened with the increase of the engine speed, the pulse type AI system is more effective in reducing HC emission when the engine is running at lower speed.

7. Exhaustturbocharging system

(1) Concept and composition of exhaust turbocharger

Turbocharging technology is a common intake control techology, the so-called supercharge is to pre-compress the fresh air before entering the cylinder, and then introduce into

At high speed, ECU turns on the circuit of the electromagnetic vacuum passage valve (the vacuum passage valve is opened), the vacuum of the vacuum tank enters the vacuum chamber, sucking diaphragm and opening the intake pressure control valve. With the participation of the large capacity air chamber, the intake pulse pressure wave can only propagate from the air chamber outlet to the intake valve, shortening the transmission distance of the pressure wave, so that the engine in the high speed can also get a better intake plenum, as shown in Figure 5-26 (b).

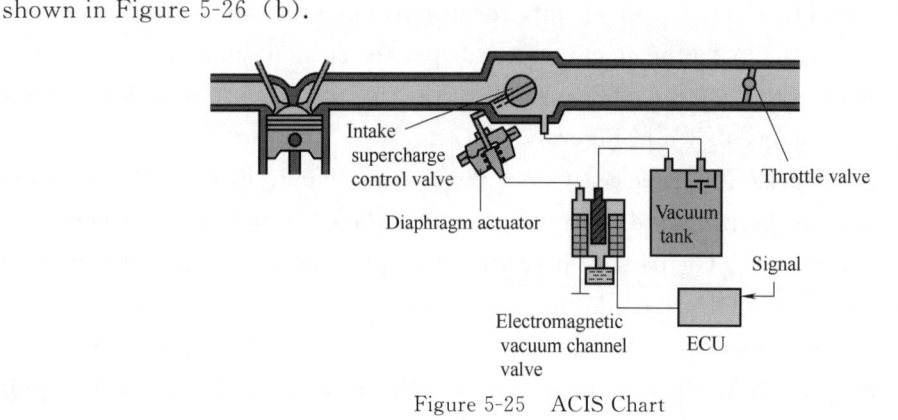

Figure 5-25　ACIS Chart

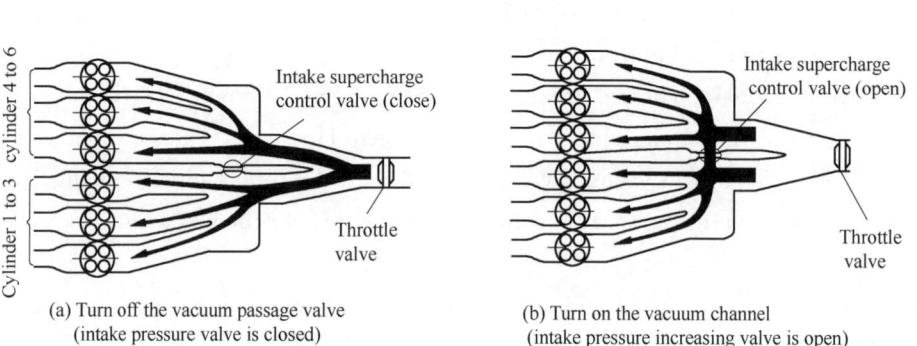

Figure 5-26　Control Principle of ACIS

6. Secondary air injection system

The essence of the Secondary air injection (AI) system is to introduce a certain amount of fresh air into the exhaust pipe or TWC so that the harmful gas and air in the exhaust gas can be burned furthermore to reduce the harmful substances. When the engine is at normal operating temperature, AI system can reduce HC and CO emissions. The AI system can not only reduce HC emission, but also shorten the heating time of EGO sensor, so that the engine computer can enter the closed-loop control process of air-fuel ratio as soon as possible.

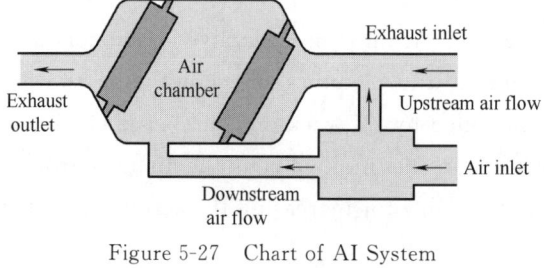

Figure 5-27　Chart of AI System

The working principle of the secondary air injection system:

The secondary air is divided into upstream and downstream airflow, The upstream air flows into the exhaust manifold and the downstream air flows into the air chamber in the converter, as shown in

through the control of the electromagnetic vacuum passage valve. The control process of the inlet switch valve (passage) is as follows.

In the engine, when the engine works at medium or low speed (less than 5200 r/min), the electromagnetic vacuum passage valve shall not be energized, the passage between the diaphragm actuator and air filter (connected with the atmosphere) of the electromagnetic vacuum passage valves cut off (OFF), while the passage between the diaphragm actuator and the vacuum tank is turned on (ON). At this point, the negative pressure of the intake manifold stored in the vacuum tank acts on the diaphragm actuator, the suction action causes the actuator to drive the pull rod to close the intake switch valve, that is, one of the intake passages in each cylinder is closed, as shown in Figure 5-23 (a).

When the engine works at high speed (more than 5200 r/min), ECU shall output the control signal to turn on the BJT on drive circuit, so that the electromagnetic vacuum passage valve shall start working. The passage between the diaphragm actuator and the air filter (atmosphere) is conductive (ON). While the passage between the diaphragm actuator and the vacuum tank is non-conductive (OFF). At this point the atmospheric pressure acts on the actuator diaphragm chamber, and the intake switch valve is opened through a pull rod. As a result, the intake passage of each cylinder is expanded to two, increasing the intake passage area, as shown in Figure 5-23 (b).

(b) Toyota acoustic control intake system (ACIS). Crown 2JZ-GE engine adopts ACIS. The length of the intake pipe cannot be changed. However, a large-capacity air chamber and an electronic control vacuum valve are added to the intake pipe to change the length of the pressure propagation path. As such, intake plenum is achieved at low speed and high speed.

The working principle of ACIS is shown in Figure 5-24. The transmission length of the pulsating pressure wave in the intake pipe can be changed by controlling the intake pressure increasing valve, that is, from the air filter to the inlet valve or the outlet of the air chamber to the inlet valve.

ACIS is shown in Figure 5-25, and the control principle is shown in Figure 5-26.

The ECU controls the opening and closing of the electromagnetic vacuum passage valve according to the speed signal.

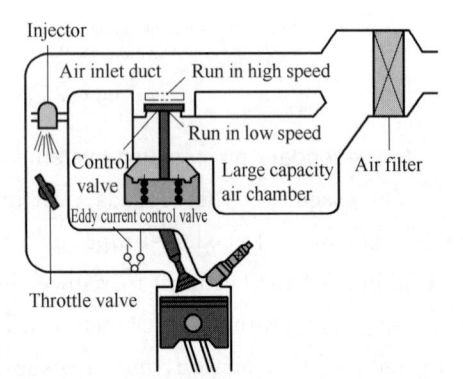

Figure 5-24   Working Principle of ACIS

At low speed, the circuit of the electromagnetic vacuum passage valve is non-conductive (the vacuum passage valve is closed), the vacuum of the vacuum tank cannot enter the vacuum chamber, and the intake pressure valve controlled by the vacuum chamber is closed. The transmission length of the pulsating pressure wave in the intake pipe is the distance from the air filter to the intake valve, which is longer and suitable for increasing the aerodynamic force at medium and low speed, as shown in Figure 5-26 (a).

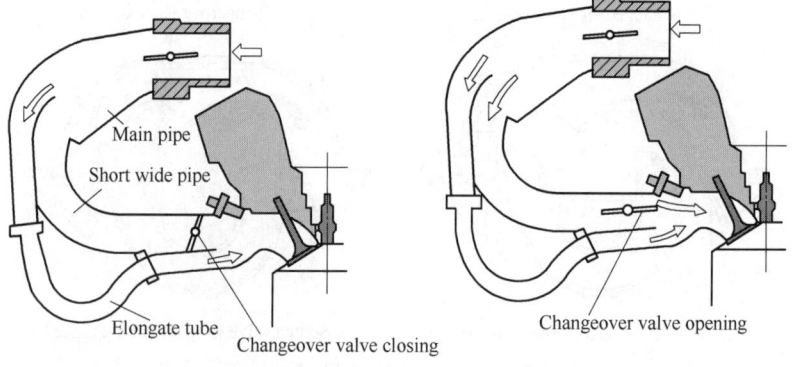

Figure 5-21　the Schematic Diagram of variable Intake System for a Nissan Automobile Engine

torque. When the engine works at high speed with heavy load, the switch valve is opened with two intake channels working at the same time, as shown in Figure 5-22 (b). At this point, the intake cross-section increases greatly, the intake resistance decreases and the aeration rate increases, which greatly improve the dynamic performance.

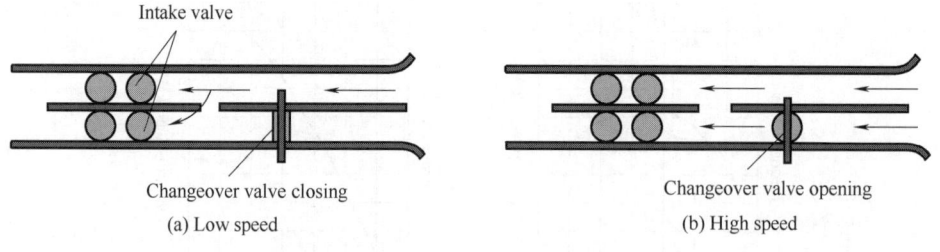

Figure 5-22　Schematic Diagram of the Toyota Variable Intake System with Dual Intake Pipes

Figure 5-23 shows a schematic diagram of a variable intake control system for a Toyota engine (only one inlet with a switch valve is shown, and the other without a switch valve is not shown).

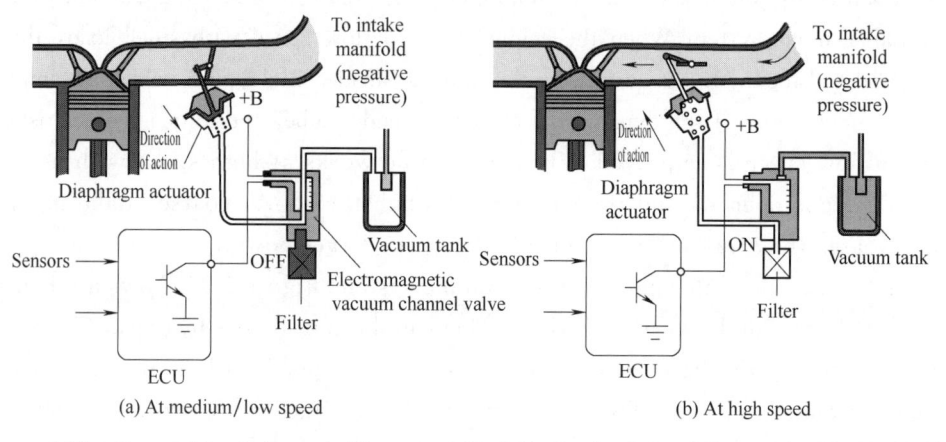

Figure 5-23　Composition Schematic Diagram of Variable Intake Control System for Toyota Engine

The closing and opening of the inlet switch valve in Figure 5-23 is accomplished by a diaphragm actuator. The working pressure of the diaphragm actuator is controlled by the ECU

148　Fault Diagnosis and Repair of Automobile Engine Electronic Control System

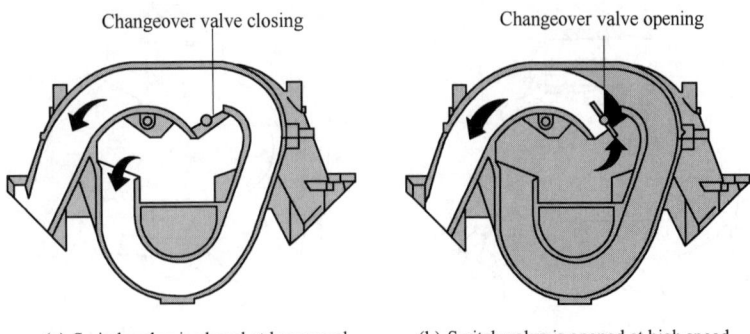

(a) Switch valve is closed at low speed   (b) Switch valve is opened at high speed

Figure 5-19   Audi V6 Variable Intake System

With this variable intake system, the engine improves the charge efficiency, its output torque and power. Figure 5-20 shows the comparison of the output characteristics of the variable intake system.

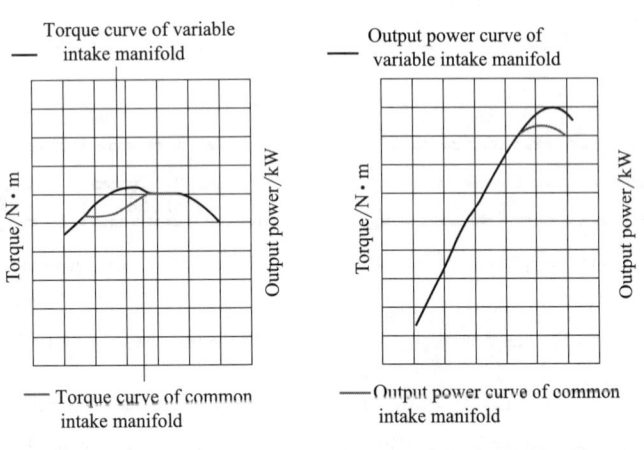

Figure 5-20   Output Characteristics of Audi V6 Engine

b. Nissan motor variable intake system. Figure 5-21 shows a schematic diagram of a Nissan engine variable intake system. When the engine works at low speed with small load, the switch valve is closed and the intake air only flows through the slender intake pipe, which can improve the intake flow rate. Because of the dynamic effect of the slender tube, the torque characteristic of the medium and low speed is improved. When the engine works at high speed with heavy load, the switch valve is opened, and the air flows through the short, coarse intake pipe, which greatly increases the aeration rate, thus obtaining the larger power.

(a) Toyota automobile engine variable intake system. Figure 5-22 shows a schematic diagram of a variable intake system with the dual intake pipes used by Japan Toyota Motor Corporation. The figure shows that each cylinder is equipped with four valves (2 intake valves and 2 exhaust valves). Two intake valves are provided with two inlet ducts, one of which is provided with an intake switch valve. When the engine works at low speed with small load, the switch valve is closed with only one intake channel working, that is, the total intake path of the engine will be halved, as shown in Figure 5-22 (a). At this time, the intake flow rate is increased and the intake inertia is large, which can improve the engine

take pipe, and at the same time, negative pressure wave spreads out along the intake pipe after passing through the intake valve, and the airway. When the negative pressure wave reaches the open end of the cavity such as the pressure stabilizing chamber, the positive pressure wave shall be reflected back from the open end to the cylinder. With appropriate length and diameter of the intake pipe, the time from the spread of negative pressure wave to the positive pressure wave returning to the intake valve is exactly matched with the time required for the inlet valve from opening to closing, that is, when the positive pressure wave returns to the inlet valve, the inlet valve is just closed. Thereby it increases the positive pressure of the intake valve to increase the aeration rate.

b. Intake fluctuation effect. Intake fluctuation effect usually refers to the continuous fluctuation of the gas in the intake pipe after the intake valve is closed to improve the charge efficiency. When the intake valve is closed, the fluctuation of the air flow travels back and forth in the intake pipe, causing the pressure at the inlet valve to be high and low. With appropriate shape, length and diameter of the intake pipe, it is beneficial to the reflection and resonance of the pressure wave, resulting that the positive pressure wave coincides with the lower circulation intake process, and the pressure at the end of the inlet can be raised to improve the charge efficiency.

② Structure of variable intake system. The change of the intake air flow in the intake pipe is very complicated. In order to effectively utilize the intake dynamic effect and improve the charge efficiency, the variable air intake system with power cavity, resonant cavity and various structural types is adopted in the automobile engine.

An inlet with fixed length and cross-section area can only have good dynamic effect and inflating effect within a certain speed range. When working at low speed, the slender inlet has better inflating effect, while the short and thick inlet has better inflating effect when working at high speed. Inlet with variable length can bring a good inflating effect within a large speed range.

For the engine with multi-point fuel injection system, the inlet can be designed according to the spreading characteristics of gas pressure wave, so that the length and shape of the inlet can be changed, and the dynamic effect of the inlet can be used to improve the charge efficiency.

The variable intake system used in different models is not exactly the same. The following is a brief introduction to several common variable intake systems.

a. The variable intake system of Audi v6 engine. Figure 5-19 shows the geometry of the intake manifold for the variable intake system of the Audi V6 engine. The intake valve is arranged in the intake manifold of the engine, which is controlled by ECU. When the engine speed is lower than 4100r/min, the switch valve in each cylinder inlet is always in a closed position, forming an inlet duct with a longer path and a smaller cross-section, as shown in Figure 5-19 (a); when the speed is greater than 4100r/min, the switch valve in the inlet is opened, forming an inlet duct with a shorter path and larger cross-section, as shown in Figure 5-19 (b).

In order to accurately control the actual air-fuel ratio near the theoretical air-fuel ratio of 14.7 : 1 and make the three-way catalyst work in the optimum state, the EGO (O_2S) is used in the engine control system to realize the air-fuel ratio feedback control, a kind of closed-loop control.

(2) Structure and working principle of TWC

TWC is non-removable monolithic and mounted in front of the exhaust muffler. It consists of TWC core and shell, as shown in Figure 5-18. Most TWC cores use honeycomb ceramics as the carrier of the catalyst, and a mixture of platinum (or palladium) and rhodium is impregnated on the ceramic carrier as the catalyst. When the engine works abnormally, the content of CO and HC in the exhaust gas shall increase sharply, and the burden of the catalyst shall increase, which shall cause the temperature to rise sharply. If the high temperature lasts too long, it will lead to deterioration or damage (core broken) of catalyst performance, which will affect the exhaust. At the same time, it is prone to danger because its installation position is close to the bottom of the body. So in some cars, TWC is also equipped with an exhaust temperature sensor to detect the exhaust temperature.

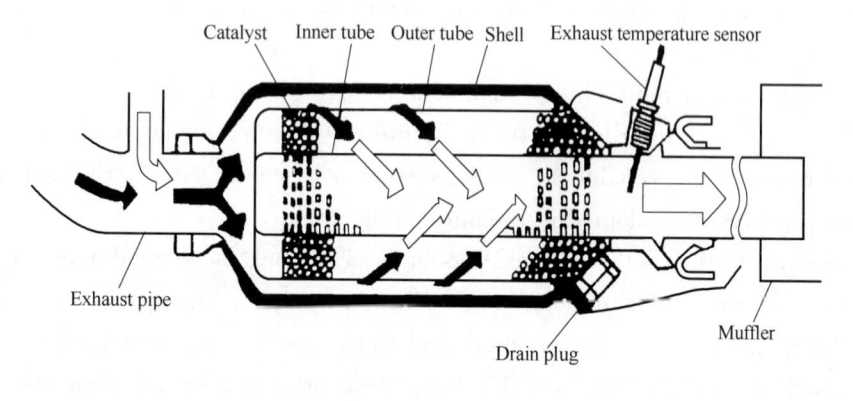

Figure 5-18   TWC

The most commonly used intake control technologies are variable intake technology and turbocharging technology, both of which are designed to increase the torque and power of the engine to improve the power performance of the engine under different operating conditions.

① Concept of variable intake system. The variable intake system makes use of the dynamic effect of the intake duct in the engine to improve the charge efficiency, so as to increase the torque and power of the engine in the range of engine speed.

For analytic purposes, the intake dynamic effect is often regarded as the result of the interaction of inertia effect and fluctuation effect. The intake system using the dynamic effect of the intake air is called "acoustic control intake system".

a. Intake inertia effect. Intake inertial effect usually refers to the use of the inertia of the high-speed flowing gas in the intake pipe during the intake stroke to improve the charge efficiency. In the early stage of the intake stroke of the engine, negative pressure is produced in the cylinder due to the downward suction action of the piston. Fresh air enters from the in-

the timing and method of the opening and closing of the solenoid valve.

As a rule, it usually needs to consider the following conditions when ECU powers on the carbon canister control solenoid valve:

① The engine start-up has exceeded the prescribed time;

② The coolant temperature is higher than the specified value;

③ The IDL switch is turned off;

④ The engine speed is higher than the specified value.

When the above conditions are met, ECU energizes the solenoid coil circuit, the solenoid valve opens, and the fuel vapor stored in the activated carbon canister is inhaled by the engine through the hose. At this point, due to the large air intake quantity of the engine, a small amount of fuel vapor into the engine shall not affect the concentration of the mixture. If the above conditions are not fully met, ECU will not activate the carbon canister solenoid valve, the fuel vapor shall be stored in the carbon canister.

Advanced fuel evaporation control system can control the duty ratio of solenoid valve timely according to the engine load and other conditions, so as to control the opening degree of solenoid valve.

4. Three-way catalyst（TWC）

（1）Function of TWC

The engine produces a number of harmful combustion products when it works, so TWC is commonly installed in today's automobiles, which are connected in series in the exhaust system to catalyze a series of chemical reactions in the exhaust gas flow to convert harmful gases in the exhaust gas from the engine into harmless gases.

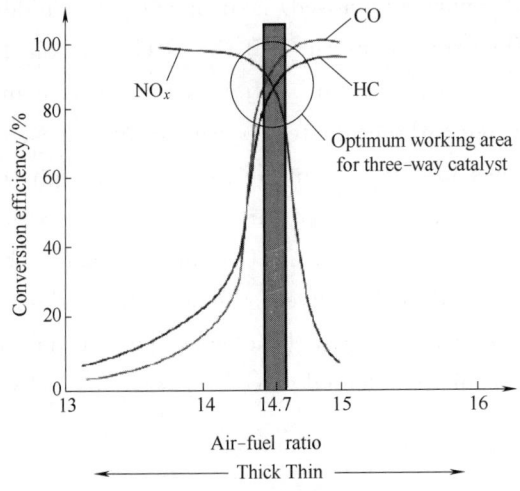

Figure 5-17   Relationship between TWC Conversion Efficiency and Mixture Concentration

TWC is installed in the middle of the exhaust pipe, with the three-way catalyst playing the major role. It is a mixture of platinum（or palladium）and rhodium, and is a harmful substance in the exhaust gas of the automobile: HC, CO, and NO_x are converted into harmless CO_2, H_2O and N_2 by chemical reaction. However, the conversion efficiency of TWC can be controlled accurately only when the air-fuel ratio of the mixture is stable. Figure 5-17 shows the relationship between the conversion efficiency of TWC and the air-fuel ratio of the mixture. It can be seen from the diagram that the conversion efficiency of TWC is best only when the engine is operating at the standard theoretical air-fuel ratio of 14.7 : 1. Therefore, it is necessary to control the air-fuel ratio of the combustible mixture accurately and keep the air-fuel ratio as narrow as possible near the theoretical air-fuel ratio of 14.7 : 1.

trols vacuum air path. The system can collect the vaporized gasoline steam in the gasoline tank and introduce the gasoline steam into cylinder for combustion, preventing the gasoline steam from being discharged directly into the atmosphere to cause pollution.

The composition and construction of EVAP system varies with the automobile manufacturers and the production years. Early EVAP systems were mostly controlled by vacuum, but now they are mostly controlled by ECU. At present, the relatively simple EVAP control system is shown in Figure 5-15. It is mainly composed of fuel tank, activated carbon canister (some called adsorption canister), carbon canister control solenoid valve and ECU, which can provide more accurate evaporation flow control.

Activated carbon canister is the component to store steam in the EVAP system, as shown in Figure 5-16. The lower part of the activated carbon canister is connected with the atmosphere, and the upper part is connected with the fuel tank and the intake manifold to collect and remove the fuel vapor. The middle part is activated carbon particles, which have strong adsorption for fuel molecules. Fuel vapor (HC) in the fuel tank is adsorbed on the surface of the activated carbon particles after it enters the activated carbon canister through the fuel tank pipeline. The activated

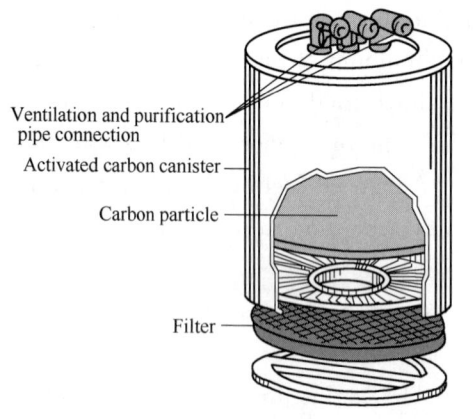

Figure 5-16   Activated Carbon Canister

carbon canister has an outlet which is connected with the engine intake manifold through a hose. An activated carbon canister solenoid valve (normally closed) is arranged in the middle of the hose to control the on-off of the pipe. When the engine runs, if the ECU turns on the activated carbon canister solenoid valve, then under the vacuum suction of the intake manifold, the air enters from the bottom of the activated carbon canister, passes through the activated carbon to the upper outlet, and then flows into the engine intake pipe through the hose. The fuel molecules adsorbed on the surface of the activated carbon are desorbed, and are inhaled into the cylinder for combustion along with fresh air. On the one hand, this process makes full use of the fuel; on the other hand, it also keeps the activated carbon in the activated carbon canister with good adsorption capacity of fuel molecules without failure due to long-term use. When the activated carbon canister solenoid valve is closed, the fuel vapor is stored in the activated carbon canister.

(3) EVAP control system

It is necessary to control the timing and amount of fuel vapor entering the intake manifold of the engine in order to prevent the damage of the mixture components affecting the normal operation of the engine.

At present, many automobile manufacturers use the ECU to control the opening and closing of the solenoid valve, that is, when the coil is energized, the solenoid valve is open, and when the coil is cut off, the solenoid valve is closed, but they are different in controlling

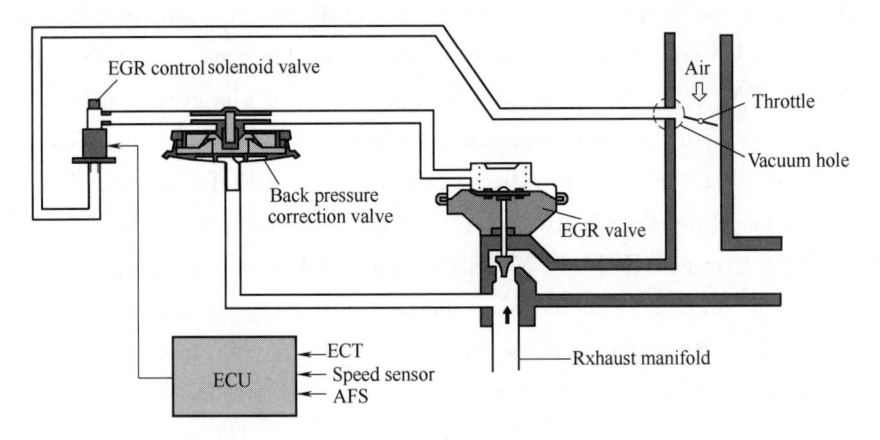

Figure 5-14　EGR Control System with Back Pressure Correction Valve

the EGR channel is opened, and the exhaust gas is recalculated.

　　EGR control solenoid valve is controlled by ECU. According to the speed signal, intake pressure signal, coolant temperature signal, and air flow signal, the ECU controls the opening of EGR control solenoid valve to control the vacuum degree of EGR valve, so as to control the opening of EGR valve to change the amount of exhaust gas involved in recirculation.

3. Fuel evaporation emission (EVAP) control system

（1）Function of EVAP control system

　　The EVAP control system is designed to prevent the exhaust of gasoline vapor in the gasoline tank from polluting the atmosphere. Its function is to collect the vaporized gasoline vapor in the gasoline tank and float chamber (carburetor type gasoline engine), and to introduce the gasoline vapor into cylinder for combustion, so as to prevent the pollution caused by the direct discharge of gasoline vapor into the atmosphere. At the same time, it is necessary to control the amount of gasoline steam in the inlet cylinder for combustion according to the engine condition.

（2）Composition and working principle of EVAP control system

　　The composition and working principle of the EVAP control system are shown in Figure 5-15.

　　Activated carbon canister——full of carbon particles; vacuum solenoid valve——con-

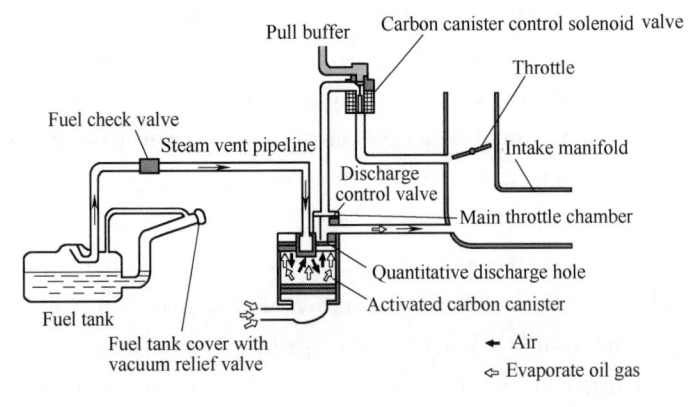

Figure 5-15　Schematic Diagram of EVA Control System

solenoid valve, EGR valve and various sensors. An EGR position sensor is installed on the upper part of the EGR valve to detect the EGR valve lift. The sensor transmits the signal to the engine ECM/PCM by using a potentiometer driven by a plunger, which is used as the reference signal to control the EGR to realize the closed-loop control of the EGR system. The engine ECM/PCM stores the optimum lift height signals for EGR valves under a variety of operating conditions. If the actual lifting height value is different from the optimal value of engine ECM/PCM storage, ECM/PCM will change EGR control voltage on the solenoid valve, so that EGR control solenoid valve increases or decreases the vacuum pressure on EGR valve through EGR vacuum control valve to control the amount of exhaust gas entering into the combustor.

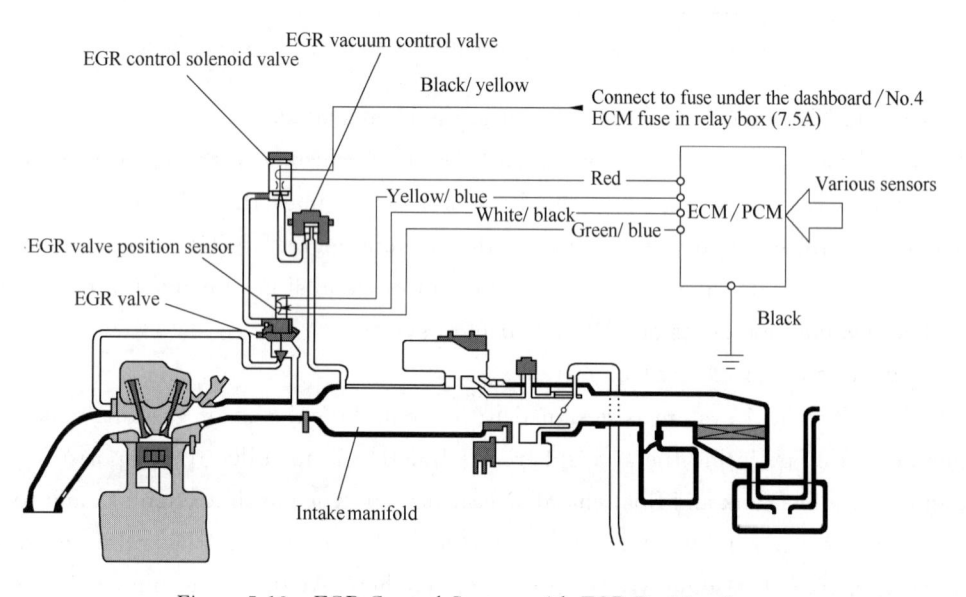

Figure 5-13   EGR Control System with EGR Position Sensor

⑥ EGR system with back pressure correction valve. The EGR control system with back pressure correction valve is shown in Figure 5-14. A back pressure correction valve is arranged in the vacuum line between the EGR control solenoid valve and the EGR valve. Its function is to control the EGR according to the back pressure in the exhaust manifold.

The back pressure of the exhaust manifold acts under the back pressure chamber of the back pressure correction valve through the pipeline. When the exhaust back pressure of the engine is low under small load, the air chamber diaphragm moves downward under the action of the valve spring, so that the modified valve closes the vacuum passage. At this point, the EGR valve remains closed under the action of its valve spring, so no exhaust gas recirculation is carried out.

When the engine load increases and the back pressure of the exhaust manifold increases, the back pressure below the back pressure chamber of the correction valve increases, which enables the diaphragm move upward against the spring's elastic force to open the correction valve. The vacuum controlled by EGR vacuum solenoid valve enters the vacuum chamber above EGR valve through the back pressure correction valve. The EGR valve is sucked open,

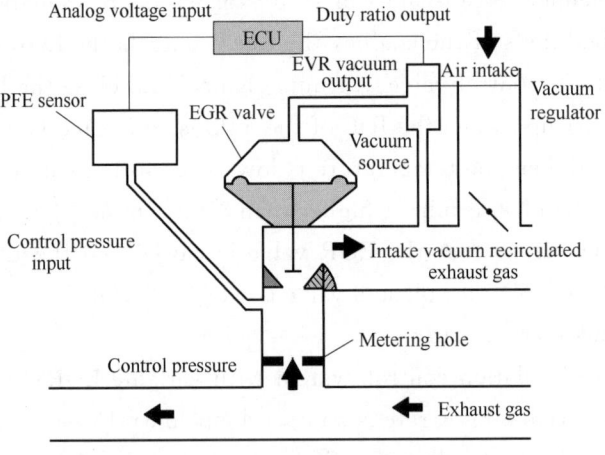

Figure 5-11　EGR System with PFE Sensor

voltage line and one signal line. The exhaust gas pressure behind the metering hole is proportional to the exhaust gas flow rate of the recirculation. The signal of the PFE sensor notifies the ECU of the flow of the exhaust gas recirculation, and the ECU compares this signal with the exhaust gas recirculation flow required by the input signal. If there is a difference between the actual exhaust gas recirculation flow and the required exhaust gas recirculation flow, the ECU shall make necessary corrections to the duty ratio signal output to the vacuum regulator.

④ EGR system with differential pressure feedback electronic (DPFE) sensor. DPFE-type EGR system is shown in Figure 5-12. The working modes of DPFE-type EGR system and PFE-type EGR system are basically the same. But DPEF-type EGR also needs to detect the exhaust gas pressure of the exhaust system, thus its control is more accurate. Both the PFE sensor and the DPFE sensor are 3-wire sensors, in which the PFE sensor has a pressure input port and the DPFE sensor has two pressure input ports.

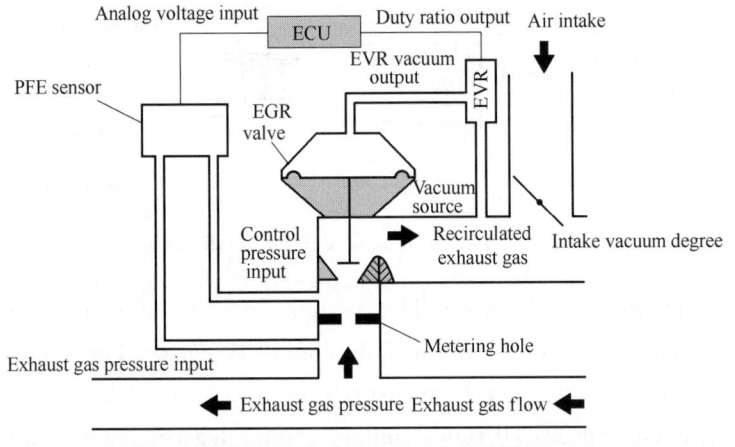

Figure 5-12　EGR System with DPFE Sensor

⑤ EGR system with EGR position sensor. Figure 5-13 is the engine EGR system of Guangzhou Honda Accord sedan, which consists of EGR vacuum control valve, EGR control

140　Fault Diagnosis and Repair of Automobile Engine Electronic Control System

or closing of EGR solenoid valve to start or stop exhaust gas recirculation.

Under certain conditions of the engine, the ECU controls the EGR solenoid valve to energize to cut off the EGR control valve's vacuum channel and close the EGR valve.

During engine start-up, when the IDL of the TPS is connected (i. e. the engine is in idle operating condition), the engine temperature is low (e. g. during engine warm-up), and the engine speed is lower than 900 r/min or higher than 3200 r/min, EGR shall control the solenoid valve energized (ON) so that the EGR valve is closed and the EGR system does not work; besides, EGR controls the solenoid valve power OFF (OFF) so that the EGR valve is open and EGR systems start to work.

② Exhaust gas recirculation control system with variable EGR rate. Exhaust gas recirculation control with variable EGR rate is an open-loop control system. Its working principle is: the corresponding relationship between EGR rate and engine speed and gas intake quantity was determined by experiment, and the data was stored in ROM of ECU. When the engine works, the ECU outputs appropriate commands according to signals from various sensors, compares and corrects with its internal data to control the opening of the solenoid valve, so as to regulate the exhaust gas recirculation EGR rate.

The exhaust gas recirculation system with variable EGR rate is shown in Figure 5-10. When the engine works, the ECU provides pulse voltage with different duty ratio to the EGR control solenoid valve according to signals of the CPS, TPS, CTS, ignition switch, and power supply voltage, so as to make the average time of opening and closing different. As such, it can obtain EGR different vacuum degrees required by different valve openings and different EGR rate suitable for engine condition. The larger the duty ratio of the pulse voltage signal, the longer the open time of the solenoid valve, the larger the EGR rate; on the contrary, the smaller the duty ratio of the pulse voltage signal, the smaller the EGR rate, and when it reaches a certain value, the EGR control valve closes and the exhaust gas recirculation system stops working.

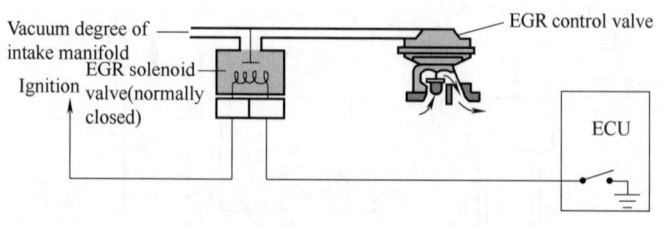

Figure 5-10　EGR with Variable EGR Rate

③ EGR system with PFE sensor. The system consists of exhaust gas recirculation valve, vacuum regulating valve, metering hole and PFE sensor. The time and flow of exhaust gas recirculation are controlled by measuring the pressure at the orifice, integrating input signals for the engine speed, altitude, engine vacuum degree, engine coolant temperature and throttle position by ECU, as shown in Figure 5-11.

The PFE sensor converts the exhaust gas pressure signal into a voltage signal sending to ECU. The PFE sensor has 3 wires connected to ECU, with one ground wire, one 5V supply

controlled. The amount of exhaust gas entering the intake manifold varies from 6% to 23% depending on the engine condition.

As EGR system has influence on engine performance, ignition system (ignition advance angle) and fuel system should be adjusted accordingly when EGR system works. Figure 5-8 shows the relationship between the exhaust gas recirculation volume and engine fuel consumption and emissions after the ignition advance angle changes

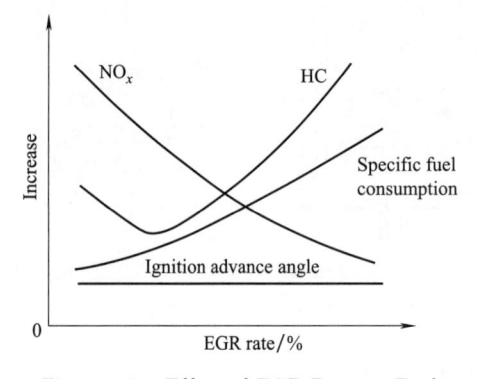 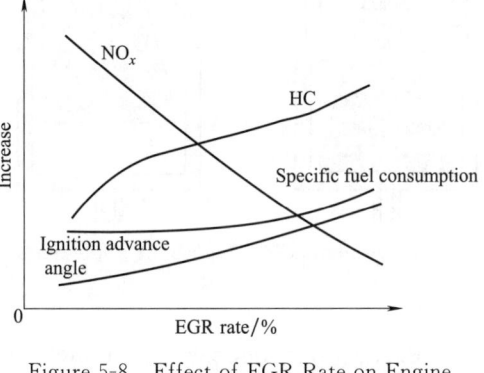

Figure 5-7　Effect of EGR Rate on Fuel Consumption and Emission When Ignition Advance Angle is Constant

Figure 5-8　Effect of EGR Rate on Engine Performance When Ignition Advance Angle Changes

(2) EGR control system

① Common electronic EGR control system. Figure 5-9 shows a schematic diagram of the EGR control system used in NISSAN VG30 engine.

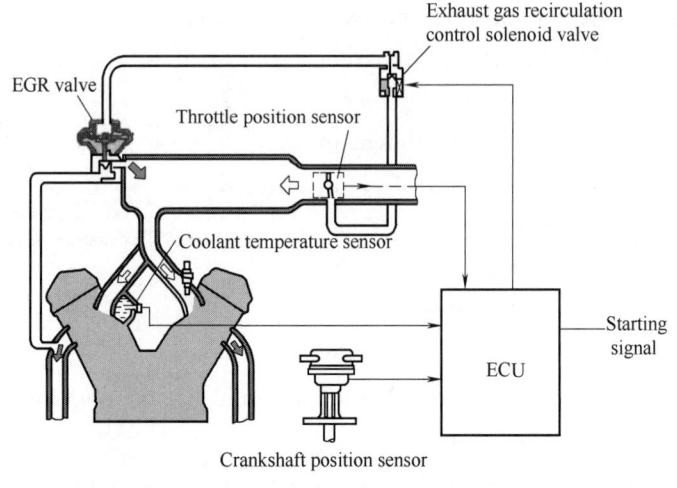

Figure 5-9　Common Electronic EGR Control System

This system was used in early NISSAN cars. It consists of EGR control solenoid valve, TPS, EGR valve, CPS, ECU, ETC and so on.

The working principle is that when the engine works, the ECU determines the engine working condition according to the signals sent by various sensors, such as CPS, ECT, TPS, ignition switch and so on, so as to issue the control instructions to control the opening

flame from reaching the crankcase. If there is no PCV valve in the system, the steam in the crankcase may explode when the engine is tempered.

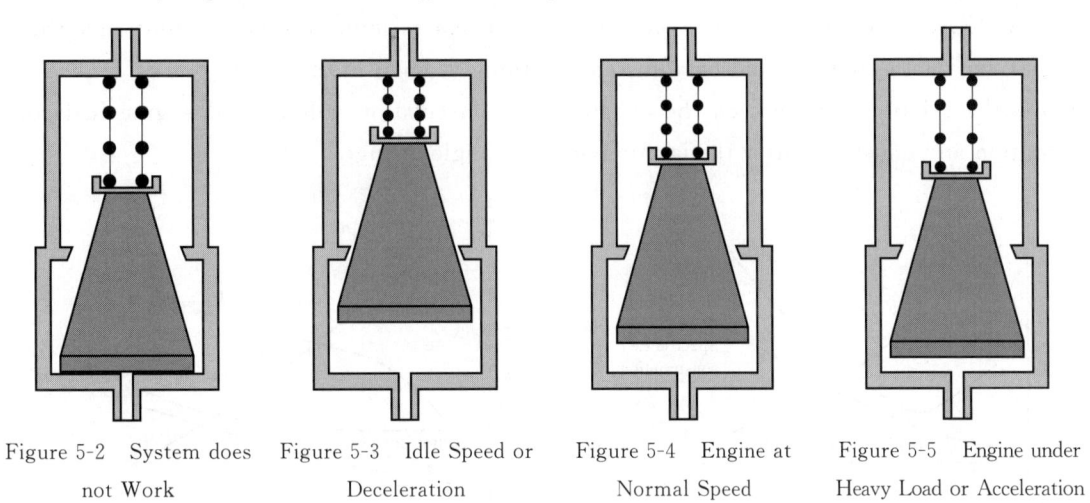

Figure 5-2   System does   Figure 5-3   Idle Speed or   Figure 5-4   Engine at   Figure 5-5   Engine under
         not Work   Deceleration   Normal Speed   Heavy Load or Acceleration

2. Exhaust gas recirculation (EGR) control system

(1) The function of EGR and the mechanism of NO_x

The function of the exhaust gas recirculation (EGR) system is to introduce a part of the exhaust gas into the intake system to burn with fresh mixture in the cylinder. The main purpose is to reduce the emission of nitrogen oxide (NO_x).

NO_x is produced by the chemical reaction of N_2 and O_2 contained in the mixture when the mixture is burned at high temperature and oxygen-rich conditions. The higher the combustion temperature, the more easily N_2 and O_2 react, and the more NO_x is discharged, as shown in Figure 5-6. So the best way to reduce NO_x is to lower the temperature of the combustor.

When the EGR system works, a part of the exhaust gas is introduced into the intake system and mixed with the fresh fuel mixture to make

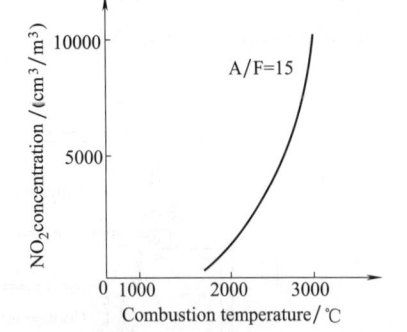

Figure 5-6   Relationship between Combustion
         Temperature and NO_x Emission

the mixture thinner, reducing the combustion speed and the combustion temperature, thus effectively reducing the NO_x generation.

Because EGR will reduce the ignition performance of the mixture and the engine output power, engine operating conditions with more NO_x emission should be selected for proper EGR. The control quantity of EGR is represented by EGR rate, which refers to percentage of recycled exhaust gas to total air intake quantity. The EGR system can reduce NO_x emission, but with the increase of EGR rate, it will lead to the increase of fuel consumption and HC emission. The EGR causes an increase of misfiring rate, which makes the combustion unstable and the poor engine performance decrease, as shown in Figure 5-7, so the EGR rate must be

through the cylinder head hole, the valve chamber cover and the PCV valve, into the intake manifold, and then flows into the combustor through the intake valve for combustion.

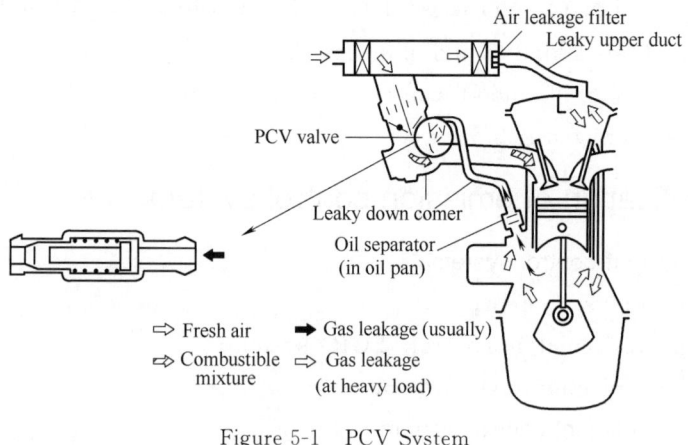

Figure 5-1   PCV System

(1) When the engine doesn't work

When the engine doesn' t work, the spring presses the cone valve on the seat. It is not vacuum in the valve and is no steam flow, and the cone valve is pressed on the seat, so as to prevent tempering, as shown in Figure 5-2.

(2) Idle speed or deceleration

When idling or decelerating, the intake manifold has a large vacuum degree, which o-vercomes the spring pressure and sucks the cone valve upward. There is a small gap between the cone valve and the PCV valve housing (as shown in Figure 5-3) . During idling or decel-eration, the engine leaks very little gas, with the gas flowing out of the crankcase through a small gap in the PCV valve.

(3) When the engine load increases at normal speed

With partial throttle opening (normal speed), the vacuum degree of the intake pipe is smaller than that at idle speed. The spring pushes the cone valve downward, increasing the gap between the cone valve and the PCV valve housing (as shown in Figure 5-4). Because under the partial throttle opening, the engine leaks more gas. A large gap between the cone valve and the PCV valve housing allows all leaking gas to be sucked out of the air outlet pipe.

(4) Working under heavy load or acceleration

When the engine works under heavy load, the throttle valve is fully open, the vacuum degree of the intake pipe is reduced, and the spring pushes the cone valve downward further-more (as shown in Figure 5-5). Thus, the gap between the cone valve and the PCV valve housing is larger. Because more side-leakage gas is produced when working under heavy load, a larger gap is needed to allow the leakage gas to flow into the intake pipe

(5) When tempering occurs

When the engine is tempered, the flame enters into the PCV valve body through the in-take pipe, and the pressure of the flame presses the PCV valve to shut it down to prevent the

ignition (improper ignition or too dirty spark plug), leakage of exhaust valve, etc..

NO_x refers to a variety of nitrogen oxides formed during combustion, mainly including NO, NO_2, N_2O_3, and N_2O_5. NO is a colorless and odorless gas with mild pungent smell and little toxicity. NO_2 is a kind of high pungent, brown-red poisonous gas. NO_x is produced by the chemical reaction of N_2 and O_2 contained in the mixture when the mixture is burned at high temperature and oxygen-rich.

(II) Classification of emission control system

1. Exhaust pollutant control system

① Three-way catalyst system;

② Exhaust gas recirculation control (EGR) system;

③ Secondary air injection (AI) system.

2. Non-exhaust pollutant control system

(1) Pathway of non-exhaust pollutant

Non-exhaust pollutants refer to the harmful pollutants discharged into the atmosphere by other means than the exhaust pipe, with the HC emissions mainly produced by the following two ways:

① Blow-by;

② Fuel evaporation.

(2) Non-exhaust pollutant control system

Non-exhaust pollutant control system mainly includes positive crankcase ventilation (PCV) system and fuel evaporation control (EVAP) system.

(III) Principles of Various Emission Control Systems

1. PCV system

If the mixture in the combustor of the engine and the burned exhaust gas leak into the crankcase along the inner wall of the piston and cylinder body, the oil shall be diluted and contaminated, resulting in a decrease in the lubricity of the oil, so these pollutants must be discharged from the crankcase. In addition, the pressure in the crankcase increases with the increase of the engine speed, and if not ventilated, the oil shall be pressed out of the oil seal or cylinder gasket. For environmental protection, these mixtures cannot be discharged directly into the atmosphere. In order to solve this problem, the modern automobile uses PCV system to lead the gases that leak into the crankcase into the intake manifold for returning.

The PCV valve is the most important part of PCV system. There is a cone valve in the PCV valve, as shown in Figure 5-1, which enable the crankcase steam flow into the intake pipe and prevents the reverse flow of gas or flame. When the engine works, the intake pipe vacuum acts on the PCV valve. This vacuum attracts fresh air to enter the valve chamber cover through the air filter and the air hose, and then to flow into the crankcase through the cylinder cover hole, mixing with the gas leaking from the combustor in the crankcase. With the suction force of the intake manifold vacuum, the air-leakage mixture flows upward

Item V

Maintenance of Auxiliary Control System of Gasoline Engine

I. Introduction of Item Scene

How should a car troubleshoot if the exhaust gas of the engine is not up to standard? In order to solve the problem of unqualified exhaust gas of electronic control engine, we should have the basic knowledge of exhaust control system, fuel supply system, air supply system, ignition control system, mechanical system and auxiliary system of ECU. It is helpful to eliminate the non-conformities of the exhaust emission.

II. Item Related Knowledge

(I) Environmental Impact of Motor Vehicle Emissions

As people pay more and more attention to the treatment of the environment, the control of the vehicle emission pollutants is more and more strict. At present, the vehicle emission pollutants control system is divided into the exhaust pollutant control system and the non-exhaust pollutant control system according to the difference of pollutants from exhaust pipe, crankcase and fuel system.

Exhaust pollutants mainly refer to harmful pollutants such as CO, HC and NO_x discharged from the exhaust pipe.

CO is a kind of colorless, odorless and toxic gas. It can reduce the blood's ability to transfuse oxygen, resulting that the heart, brain and other important organs are seriously hypoxic, with dizziness, headache, nausea and other symptoms. If it is mild, it will damage the central nervous system, and if it is sever, it will make cardiovascular work difficult until death. CO is mainly caused by excessive concentration of fuel mixture and insufficient oxygen during combustion.

HC includes unburned and incompletely burned fuel, lubricants and their splitting products and some oxides, some of which can have a strong irritating effect on the eyes and skin and can cause dizziness, nausea, anemia and even acute poisoning when the concentration is high. HC is caused by incomplete combustion due to too thin mixture, too dirty injector, bad

gine, the performance of the engine is improved. If it is controlled according to the original computer memory value, there will be some error, so the replacement of the engine also needs basic settings.

Summary

This item introduces in detail the function of ISCV on the electronic control engine, the structure principle of ISCV, the composition of idle speed control system, the control process and the detection steps and methods of idle speed control system and detection items of ISCV. Judge whether the ISCV is normal by using the routine methods.

Exercises and Thinking

1. Briefly describe the purpose of ISCV detection.
2. Briefly describe the preparation for ISCV detection.
3. Briefly describe ISCV detection steps.
4. What is the duty ratio?
5. What are the components of the engine idle speed control system?
6. What are the precautions for the maintenance of idle speed control system?

(e. g. ignition timing during idling) are adjusted to the specified value set by the manufacturer, or parameters of some components (e. g. TPS) are stored in the control unit for precise control. For Volkswagen throttle body, whether semi-electronic or electronic throttle, the computer must know the actual minimum and maximum position that can achieved by the motor control throttle in the throttle position sensor. Figure 4-23 shows the electronic throttle circuit diagram of Bora automobile.

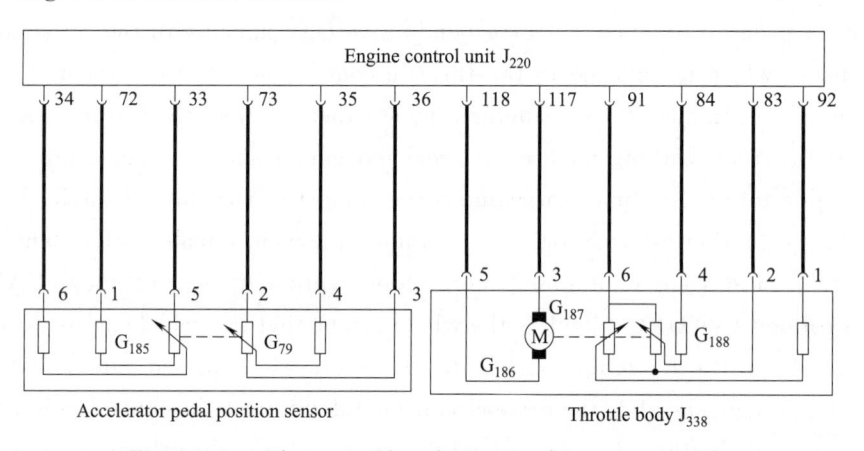

Figure 4-23   Electronic Throttle Circuit of Bora Automobile

The ECU turns the throttle to the smallest possible opening by controlling the semi-electronic throttle motor. The idle potentiometer voltage is transmitted to the ECU, and the ECU shall remember the opening (actually, it is the digital voltage converted from the minimum opening voltage of the throttle through analog/digital conversion). The maximum position is determined by the IVS disconnection, with the purpose of redefining the idle speed range.

The maximum and minimum position of the electronic throttle is determined by the position of the motor to replan the idle range and part load range, and define the full load range, which can be seen when the diagnostic instrument reads the data flow.

If the throttle body is too dirty to close the throttle completely, the idle adaptive program of   can make the idle normal after adaptive. But if the dirty degree exceeds the limits of the ECU, that is, adaptive ability is beyond the limit, idle speed shall become unstable. After cleaning the throttle, at this time the minimum value of ECU memory throttle and the actual minimum value of throttle opening are different, which will inevitably cause inaccurate control, resulting in high engine idle speed. This situation will gradually become normal with function of the computer idle adaptive program (software), but it needs a long time. The basic setting is to let the ECU immediately remember the true throttle maximum and minimum position to repartition the throttle.

The throttle is not damaged, but the ECU is damaged, after a new ECU is replaced, with its memory throttle maximum and the minimum position different from the actual running throttle position. It shall cause the motor to control the throttle abnormally, so the replacement of the ECU also needs the basic setting. After the replacement of the damaged en-

IV. Knowledge and Skills Expansion

(I) Electronic throttle idle control actuator

The working principle of the electronic throttle system is as follows: the driver controls the accelerator pedal to produce the corresponding voltage signal with the acceleration pedal position sensor, which is inputted to the throttle control unit. The control unit first filters the input signal to eliminate the environment noise, then analyzes the driver's intention according to the current working mode, the pedal movement and the change rate to calculate the basic engine torque to obtain the value corresponded to the throttle angle. Then it gets other working condition information and all kinds of sensor signals such as engine speed, gear, throttle position, air conditioning energy consumption and so on through CAN bus and vehicle control unit (VCU) to calculate the whole torque that the vehicle needs. It obtains the best opening of throttle by compensating the throttle angle expected value, and sends the corresponding voltage signal to the drive circuit module to drive the control motor to achieve the best opening of the throttle valve. The TPS feeds back the throttle opening signal to the throttle control unit to form a closed-loop position control. The control schematic diagram is shown in Figure 4-22.

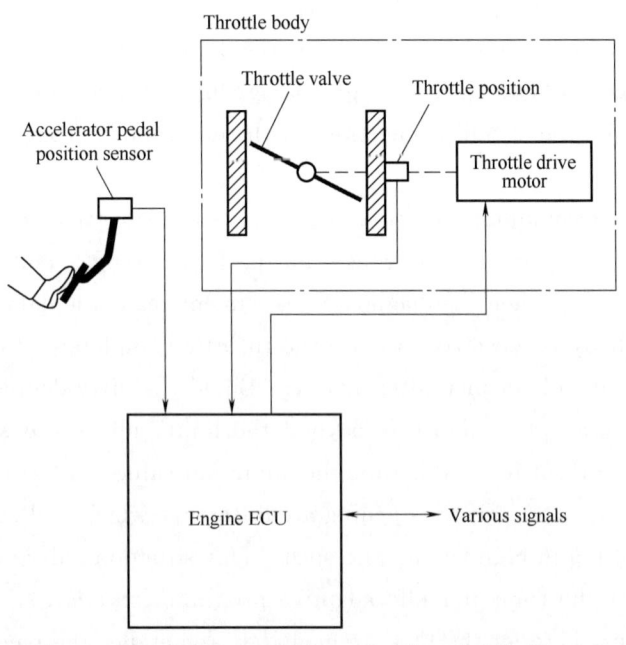

Figure 4-22　Principle of Electronic Throttle Idle Control

(II) Basic setting of direct type throttle valve

For certain systems of EFL vehicle, a basic setting must be made after repair or during maintenance. During the basic setting process, some parameters in the control unit

should decrease slowly with the increase of the throttle opening. Conversely, the multimeter voltage reading should be gradually increased with the gradual closing of the throttle. Otherwise, detect the power supply and lines.

Table 4-4　Resistance between Throttle Body Connector Terminal and ECU Terminal

No.	Throttle Body Connector Terminal	ECU Terminal	Result
1	8	T80/75	The resistance value is less than 1.5Ω
2	2	T80/59	The resistance value is less than 1.5Ω
3	1	T80/66	The resistance value is less than 1.5Ω
4	7	T80/67	The resistance value is less than 1.5Ω
5	1	T80/59	The resistance value should be infinite
6	1	T80/75	The resistance value should be infinite
7	1	T80/67	The resistance value should be infinite
8	2	T80/66	The resistance value should be infinite
9	7	T80/66	The resistance value should be infinite

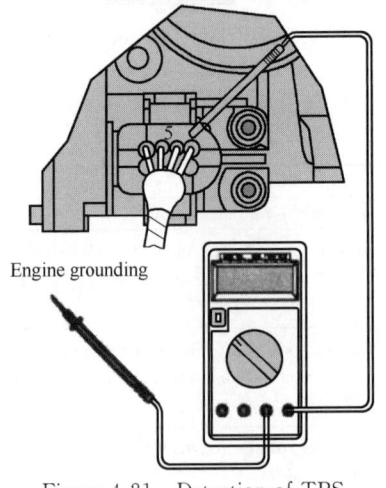

Engine grounding

Figure 4-21　Detection of TPS

（a）Power supply detection. Turn off the ignition switch, unplug the throttle body socket, then turn on the ignition switch, and the voltage between the throttle body connector terminal 4 and the terminal 7 shall be 5.0V ± 0.5V.

（b）Line inspection is shown in table 4-5.

Replace the throttle body assembly if the power supply and the line are fault-free.

(Ⅲ) Matters needing attention

① The ISCV should be lightly held to prevent it from falling to the ground.

② When testing the voltage signal on the test bench, pay attention to the operation flow and the corresponding test port. In principle, only to implement the test related to this experiment.

Table 4-5　Line Inspection

No.	Throttle Body Connector Terminal	ECU Terminal	Result
1	5	T80/75	The resistance value is less than 1.5Ω
2	4	T80/62	The resistance value is less than 1.5Ω
3	7	T80/67	The resistance value is less than 1.5Ω
4	4	T80/75	The resistance value should be infinite
5	7	T80/75	The resistance value should be infinite
6	4	Throttle 7	The resistance value should be infinite

③ On the physical bench, connect the test port directly with the ECU. Do not add any voltage to the test port of the engine test bench to avoid damaging the ECU.

④ It is strictly prohibited to operate teaching aids, the electric switch, ignition switch and starting switch without permission.

wiring diagram, as shown in Figure 4-19. Specific operations are shown in Table 4-3.

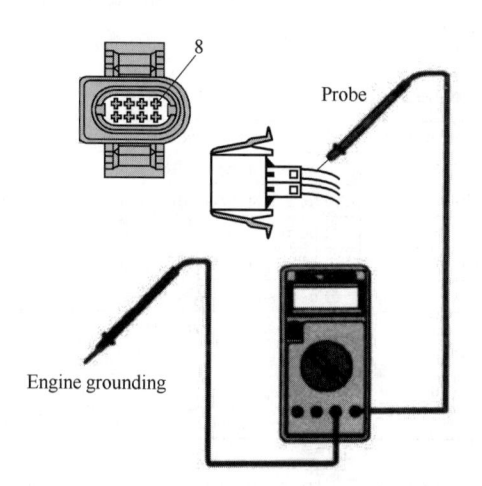

Figure 4-18   Performance Detection of Idle Throttle Opening Sensor

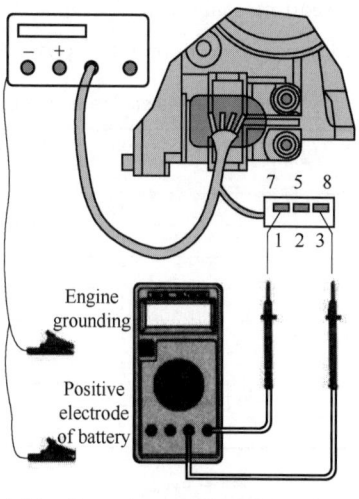

Figure 4-19   Detection of Idle TPS and DC Motor

Table 4-3   Operation Steps

No.	Operation
1	Turn on the motor driver power switch, drive the throttle arm to the initial position
2	Press the "—" button, the throttle arm moves from the initial position to the minimum idle position limit block. The rotary arm moving one time with one press of the "—" button, until the arm reaches the minimum idle position limit block
3	Press the "+" button and the throttle arm moves from its current position to the maximum idle position limit block. Similarly, every time you press "+", the rotary arm moves one time until it reaches the maximum idle position limit block
4	During the above operation, a multimeter is used to measure the voltage between the throttle body connector terminal 8 and the terminal 7. The voltage should not exceed 5V.
5	Turn off the power switch and the throttle arm shall automatically return to its original position

If the measured results are not in conformity with the above requirements, the throttle body assembly shall be replaced. Figure 4-20 shows the position of the throttle arm. Otherwise, detect the resistance between the throttle body connector terminal and the ECU terminal with a multimeter, as shown in Table 4-4.

If all the above inspection results of the throttle body confirm to the standard, but the idle control device is still not working, the ECU shall be replaced.

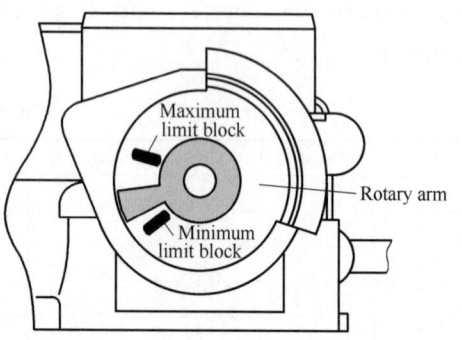

Figure 4-20   Position of Throttle Arm

d. Detection of throttle position sensor. Turn on the ignition switch, as shown in Figure 4-21. Insert the multimeter pen into the terminal 5 lead of the throttle body socket and slowly press the accelerator pedal from close to full open. The multimeter voltage reading

Item IV   Maintenance of Idle Speed Control System for Gasoline Engine   **129**

Place the ignition switch in "ON" (connection without starting) position and measure with a multimeter as shown in Figure 4-17: The voltage between the measuring terminal 4 and the terminal 7 shall be 5. 0V ± 0. 5V. If the value is not in conformity with the above requirements, put the ignition switch in the "OFF" position, pull off the ECU connector, and detect the circuit with a multimeter. The throttle body circuit diagram is shown in Figure 4-2 (b). The resistances between terminal 4 and ECU terminal T80/62 and between terminal 7 and ECU terminal T80/67 are less than 1. 5Ω, terminal 4 and terminal 7 shall be infinite. If the measured results do not conform to the above requirements, find the fault and troubleshoot it according to the circuit diagram.

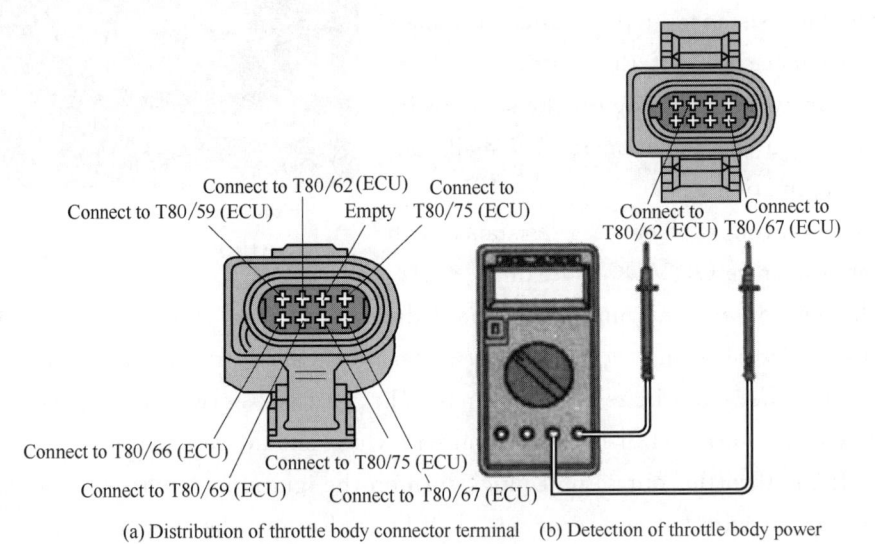

(a) Distribution of throttle body connector terminal   (b) Detection of throttle body power

Figure 4-17   Distribution and Power Supply Detection of Throttle Body Connector Terminal

③ Detection of idle speed switch. Place the ignition switch in "OFF" position and remove the throttle body connector. The resistance between terminal 3 and terminal 7 shall be less than 1Ω. When the throttle is fully closed by a multimeter, and the resistance between terminal 3 and 7 shall be infinite when pressing the accelerator pedal slowly. Otherwise, replace the throttle body.

④ Detection of idle speed control device

a. Performance detection of idle TPS. As shown in Figure 4-18, insert the probe into the lead of the throttle body connector terminal 8, start the engine, and run in idle state. When the coolant temperature is above 80℃, the voltage between the detected point of the probe and the negative pole of the battery should be 2. 8~3. 6V according to the figure.

b. Detection of DC motor. Put the ignition switch in the "OFF" position, unplug the throttle body connector, and measure with a multimeter: The resistance between the throttle body connector terminal 1 and terminal 2 shall be 30~200Ω. Replace the throttle body assembly if it does not meet the requirements.

c. Detection of the idle TPS detection. Place the ignition switch in the "OFF" position and install it on the throttle body according to the "Motor Driver" operating instructions and

128 Fault Diagnosis and Repair of Automobile Engine Electronic Control System

faults such as idle DC motor bearing wear, plastic gear broken teeth, valve drive mechanism stuck, drive mechanism cover plate rupture, and so on. This kind of failure is unrepeatable, so it can only replace the new throttle body assembly. Therefore, in the inspection of the throttle body, we can first visually inspect the above failure.

(2) Component test

① Resistance test. The position of the connector on the plug and socket of the throttle direct type (Santana AJR engine) ISCV is shown in Figure 4-16.

Detect the resistance of the related terminals with the resistance gear of the multimeter. Turn off the ignition switch and plug off the sensor wire harness plug, and the detection results shall conform to the regulations.

When measuring wire harness resistance with multimeter resistance OHM $\times$ 200Ω or $R \times 1\Omega$,

Figure 4-16   Position of Santana AJR Engine ISCV Terminal

turn off the ignition switch, unplug the controller wire harness and the ISCV wire harness plug, and the wire resistance between the two terminals shall conform to the regulations. If the resistance value is too large or infinite, it indicates that the wiring harness is not well-connected with the terminal or is open-circuited, which should be repaired.

Plug off the throttle control unit plug, turn on the ignition switch, and the voltage between the relevant wire harness terminals shall be conform to the standard.

② Throttle body power supply detection. As shown in Figure 4-17 (a), plug off the throttle body connector, there are 8 terminals, of which terminal 6 is empty (without wiring), with terminals 1, 2, 3, 4, 5, 7, and 8 respectively connected with ECU terminals T80/66, T80/59, T80/69, T80/62, T80/75, T80/67, and T80/75. Terminal 1, and 2 are directly connected to the DC motor, and terminal 5 and 8 are respectively connected with the sliding contacts of the TPS and the idle TPS, with all output signals no more than 5V, and the signal voltage is inversely proportional to the throttle opening. Terminal 3 outputs idle validation switch signal, and terminal 4, and 7 supplies 5V voltage to throttle body, of which terminal 7 is grounded through ECU, as shown in Table 4-2.

Table 4-2   Terminal Function of Throttle Body Connector

Terminal Number	Connection Point	Function
1	T80/66 (ECU)	Idle raising control
2	T80/59 (ECU)	Idle decreasing control
3	T80/69 (ECU)	Idle validation switch
4	T80/62 (ECU)	Sensor power supply (5V)
5	T80/75 (ECU)	Throttle position sensor signal
6	Empty	
7	T80/67 (ECU)	Sensor grounding
8	T80/75 (ECU)	Idle throttle position sensor signal

ECU and line of idle speed control system is fault-free. If there is no pulse voltage output, turn on A/C switch to detect again. If there is still no pulse voltage output, it indicates the idle speed control system does not work, and you should detect the line between the ECU and the ISCV (whether there is a bad contact or open fault); if the line of the idle system has no fault, it indicates the ECU has a fault and it should be replaced.

2. Detection of stepping motor ISCV

For stepping motor type ISCV, put the ignition switch in "ON" position, then detect the voltage between ECU terminal ICS1, ICS2, ICS3, ICS4 and terminal E1 (it should be 9~14V), if there is no voltage, the ECU has fault.

(1) Detection of coil resistance of ISCV

Remove the ISCV and measure the resistance of the ISCV coil with omega gear of multimeter. Pulse linear solenoid valve type ISCV has only one group of coils, its resistance value is $10 \sim 15\Omega$. Stepping motor type ISCV usually has $2 \sim 4$ groups of coils, the resistance value of each group of coils is $10 \sim 30\Omega$. If the coil resistance value is not within the above range, the ISCV shall be replaced.

(2) Detection of the action of the stepping motor

The stepping motor can be rotated by transferring the battery power to each coil of the stepping motor in a certain sequence, as shown in Figure 4-15. The coil forms and terminal arrangements of various stepping motors are different. Here it gives an example of the stepping motor for the ISCV of Crown 3. 0 2JZ-GE engine to illustrate its detection. First, connect the stepping motor connector terminal B1 and B2 with the positive pole of the battery, then connect the terminal S1, S2, S3, S4 with the negative pole of the battery in sequence (S1—S2—S3—S4). At this point, the stepping motor should be rotated and the valve core should be extended outward. If the terminal S1, S2, S3, and S4 are connected with the negative pole of the battery in the opposite order (S4—S3—S2—S1), the stepping motor should be rotated in the opposite direction. The valve core retracts inward.

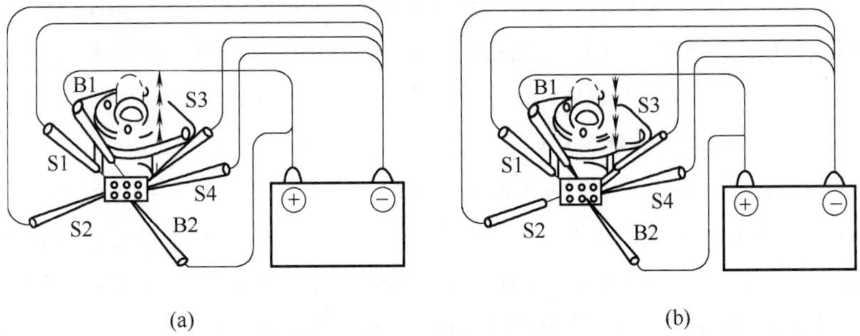

(a)   (b)

Figure 4-15   IACV Detection

3. Detection of throttle direct type ISCV System

(1) Mechanical inspection

After the throttle body is used for a long time, it is possible to form carbon deposition between the intake passage and the throttle, which causes the throttle to be stuck and the idling to be unstable. In addition, after a long period of severe vibration, it may appear some

ping motor and its valve core unchanged.

III. Item Implementation

(I) Requirements for implementation

Toyota 5A, AJR engine bench; automobile.

(II) Implementation steps

1. Vehicle detection of idle speed control system

There are 3 kinds of vehicle detection methods for idle speed control system for selection.

(1) Engine idle condition detection

After starting the engine in cold condition, the idle speed of the engine shall reach the specified fast idle speed (usually 1500 r/min) at the beginning of the warm-up process, and the idle speed shall return to normal (usually 750 r/min) after the engine reaches the normal operating temperature. If the idle speed can't change according to the above rule after the cold start, the idle speed control system is out of order.

When the engine reaches the normal operating temperature, the idle speed of the engine shall rise to about 900r/ min when the A/C switch is turned on. If the engine speed drops after turning on the A/C switch, the idling control system is out of order.

In the idling operation, the idle speed of the engine shall not change when the idle adjusting screw is rotated slightly (the idle adjusting screw should be restored to its original position after turning). If the idle speed changes during rotation, the idle speed control system is inoperative.

(2) Working condition detection of ISCV

For pulse linear solenoid valve type ISCV, the wire harness connector of ISCV can be pulled out during idling operation to observe the change of engine speed. If there is a change in engine speed, it indicates the ISCV is normal. For stepping motor type ISCV, you can listen to the "buzzing" sound of the ISCV after the engine is extinguished (at this point the stepping motor should work until the ISCV is fully opened for the engine to start again). If the ISCV makes a "buzzing" sound, the ISCV is good. In order to check the working condition of the stepping motor type ISCV, the wire harness connector of the ISCV can be pulled out before the engine starts, and then inserted after the engine starts to see if there is any change in the engine speed. If the engine speed changes at this time, the ISCV works normally; otherwise, the ISCV or control circuit fails.

(3) Detection of ECU control voltage

For pulse linear solenoid valve type ISCV, plug off the wire harness connector of ISCV, and measure the terminal voltage with the voltage gear of multimeter. If there is a pulse voltage output at the wire harness connector terminal of the ISCV during engine operation, the

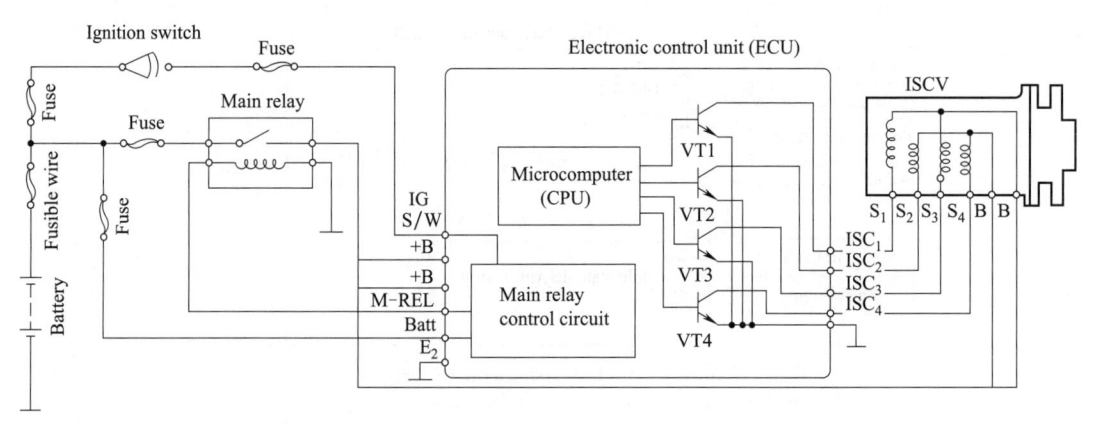

Figure 4-13　Control Circuit of Stepping Motor ISCV

(fuel injection relay) coil for 2 seconds using the voltage provided by the standby power supply input terminal (Batt terminal), so that the control valve of the stepping motor is returned to the initial position for a larger air intake volume of the next start-up.

(2) Start-up control characteristics

When the engine is started, the engine is easy to start because the ISCV is preset in the full open position with large air intake volume. Once the engine is started with the valve in full open position, the idle speed will rise too high. Therefore, when the engine speed reaches the specified value (which is determined by the cooling fluid temperature) at start-up or after start-up, the ECU will control the step number of the stepping motor to turn down the valve to the valve core position determined by the coolant temperature, ensuring the idle speed stable. If the engine coolant temperature is 20℃ at start-up, ECU will control the stepping motor from the full open position A point (125 steps) to the B point (70 steps) position when the engine speed reaches 500 r/min to turn down the valve, as shown in Figure 4-14, to prevent excessive speed.

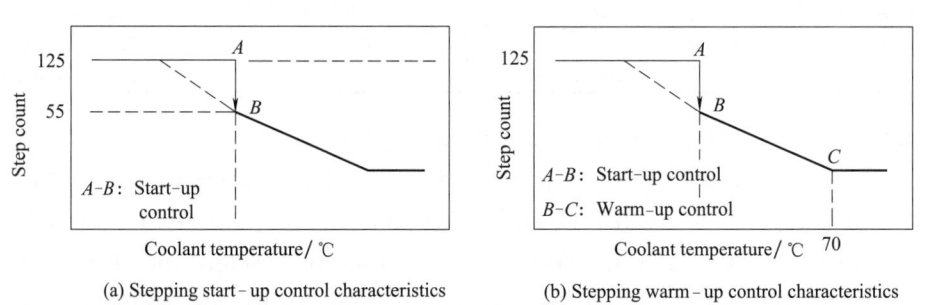

Figure 4-14　Start-up and warm-up control characteristics of stepping motor ISCV

(3) Characteristics of warm-up control

During the warm-up process after engine start-up, ECU will determine the step position of stepping motor according to the CTS signal. As the speed increases and the engine temperature rises, the valve of the control valve will gradually be turned down and the step number of the stepping motor will gradually decrease, as shown in Figure 4-14 (b). When the coolant temperature reaches 70℃, the warm-up control is finished, with the position of the step-

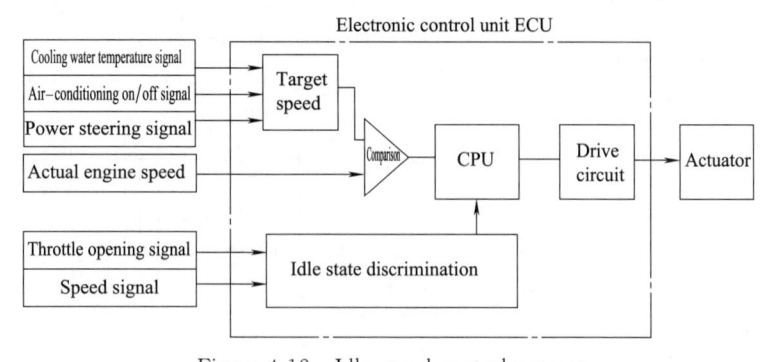

Figure 4-12   Idle speed control process

For example, when switching on the A/C (engine load increases), the engine needs to run at fast idle speed (target speed＝fast idle speed), so the ECU will increase opening of the ISCV and the bypass air intake volume.   When the bypass air intake volume increases, because the idle air-fuel ratio has been determined by the test (normally, 12 ∶ 1), the ECU will control the injector to increase the fuel injection quantity, and the engine speed will increase to the fast idle speed. The idle speed of the electric control engine of domestic automobile is shown in Table 4-1. The fast idle speed is about 1000r/min±50r/min when the A/C or PS pump is switched on, with the speed increased by about 200r/min. Similarly, when turning off the A/C (engine load is reduced), it is necessary to reduce the engine speed, that is, the target speed is lower than the actual speed, the ECU will reduce the opening of the ISCV to reduce the bypass air intake volume.

Table 4-1   Engine Idle Speed of Various Automobile Fuel Injection

Vehicle Type	Engine Type	Idle Speed/(r/min)	Remarks
Santana 2000 GLi	AFE	800 ± 50	Ex-factory standard
Santana 2000 GSi Santana 3000	AJR	800 ± 30	Ex-factory standard
Jetta AT, GTX	AHP	840 ± 40	Ex-factory standard
Hong Qi CA7220E	CA488-3	850 ± 30	Ex-factory standard
Audi 200	V6 type 2. 6 L	750 ± 70	Ex-factory standard

3. Control characteristics of idle speed control system

The idle control circuit of stepping motor ISCV is shown in Figure 4-13. When the engine idle load changes, ECU will turn on bipolar junction transistor VT1, VT2, VT3, and VT4 in the drive circuit timely in accordance with the order before the change of the idle speed, with bipolar junction transistors respectively connected to the stepping motor stator winding current, so that the rotation of motor rotor rotation drive the movement of control valve core to adjust the intake volume to achieve the target idle speed.

(1) Determination of initial position

In order to improve the re-start performance of the engine, when the ignition switch is turned off, the ECU will control the ISCV in a fully open state to be ready for re-start. When the main relay control circuit inside the ECU receives the signal that the ignition switch is at the OFF (turned off) position, the ECU will continue to supply power to the main relay

A/C switch, PS switch, neutral start switch signal and power supply voltage signal provide the engine load changes to ECU. The ECU, stores the optimal idle speed corresponding to different loads.

The ISCVs are different for different types of cars. Cherokee Jeeps use stepping motor ISCV to control idle speed. Santana 2000GSi, 3000, Jetta AT, and GXT sedans use throttle control components to automatically adjust idle speed.

2. Idle speed control process

The essence of idle speed control is to control the air intake volume when the engine is idle. The fuel injection quantity at idle speed is determined by the ECU's calculation of the idle air-fuel ratio and the actual air intake volume according to the pre-test.

Idle speed control mainly includes engine load change control and electrical load change control. The method for controlling idle speed in idle speed control system is as follows:

When the engine idle load increases, the ECU controls ISCV to increase the intake volume, thus increasing the idle speed, preventing the engine from running unstable or flameout. When the engine idle load decreases, the ECU controls ISCV to decrease the intake volume, so as to reduce the idle speed to avoid the idle speed too high.

In the idling state of the engine, the engine load will increase and the speed will decrease when turning on A/C switch, PS switch, or turning off the neutral start switch. If the speed drops too much, the engine may stall, causing inconvenience to the vehicle. Therefore, before switching on the A/C switch or PS switch, it is necessary to increase the idle speed to prevent the engine from flameout. When the A/C switch or PS switch is turned off, the engine load will decrease and the speed will increase, which will not only increase the fuel consumption, but also bring difficulty to the driving. Therefore, after turning off A/C switch or PS switch, the idle speed should be reduced to prevent the idle speed from being too high. In addition, when the electrical load increases (For example, turning on the headlamp at night, honking the horn), the supply voltage of the electrical system will decrease. If the supply voltage is too low, it will affect the normal operation of the ECU and the normal use of electric equipment. So when the supply voltage is low, it is necessary to increase the idle speed to increase the supply voltage.

The idle speed control process is shown in Figure 4-12. The ECU determines whether the engine is idle according to the IDL signal and the speed signal of the IDL firstly. If it is, ECU will search the corresponding target speed is found from the idling speed data stored in the memory according to the engine coolant temperature sensor signal, A/C switch, PS switch and other signals, and then compare the target speed with the actual engine speed measured by CPS.

When the engine load increases and the target speed is higher than the actual speed, the ECU will control the ISCV to increase the bypass air intake volume to achieve fast idle speed; conversely, when the engine load decreases and the target speed is lower than the actual speed, the ECU will control the ISCV to reduce the by-pass air intake volume to adjust the idle speed.

(Ⅲ) Process of engine idle speed control

Idle speed control is the control of idle speed. After the idle speed control system is e-quipped, the idle speed of the engine will not varies with engine aging, cylinder carbon deposition, spark plug clearance and temperature.

1. Composition of idle speed control system

The idle speed control system with bypass air passage is composed of various sensors, signal control switches, ECU, ISCV and throttle bypass air passage, as shown in Figure 4-10.

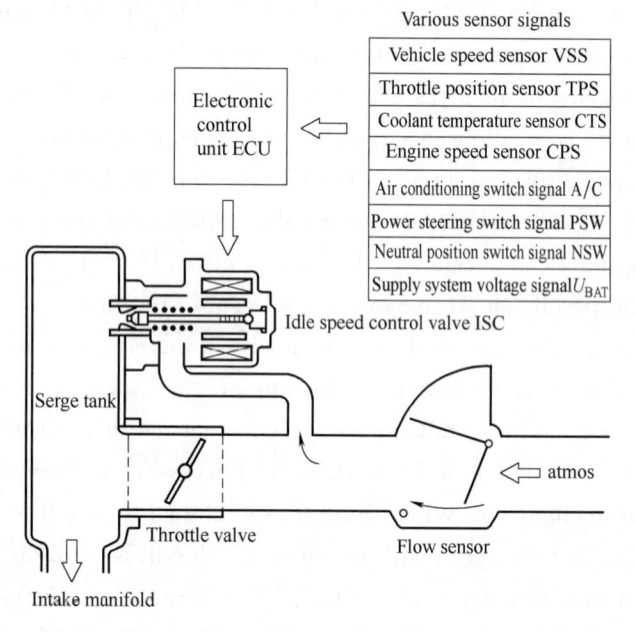

Figure 4-10　Composition of Bypass Air Idle Speed Control System

The speed sensor provides the speed signal, and the TPS provides the IDL on-off signal, both of which are used to determine whether the engine is idle. When the engine is idle, the throttle is closed, the IDL of the TPS is closed, and the sensor output terminal IDL outputs a low-level signal. Therefore, when the IDL terminal outputs a low level signal, if the speed is 0, it indicates that the engine is in idle state; if the speed is not 0, it indicates that the engine is decelerating.

The coolant temperature signal is used to correct idle speed. The ECU stores the optimal idle speed corresponding to different water temperatures, as shown in Figure 4-11. In the warm-up process after cold start, ECU controls the fast idle speed by controlling the opening of the ISCV according to the engine temperature signal, and gradually reduces the idle speed with the increase of engine temperature. When the coolant temperature reaches the normal operating temperature, the idle speed returns to normal idle speed.

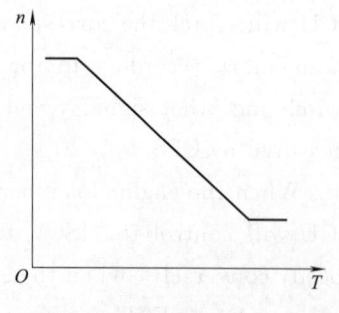

Figure 4-11　Idle Speed at Different Temperature

Item Ⅳ　Maintenance of Idle Speed Control System for Gasoline Engine　**121**

The torque and deflection angle for the armature are determined by the ratio of the conduction time of the two coils. Three torques are applied to the armature:

$T1$——produced by coil L 1, counterclockwise direction, magnitude related with current;

$T2$——produced by coil L 2, clockwise direction, magnitude related with current;

$T3$——produced by the reset spring, counterclockwise direction, magnitude related with angle.

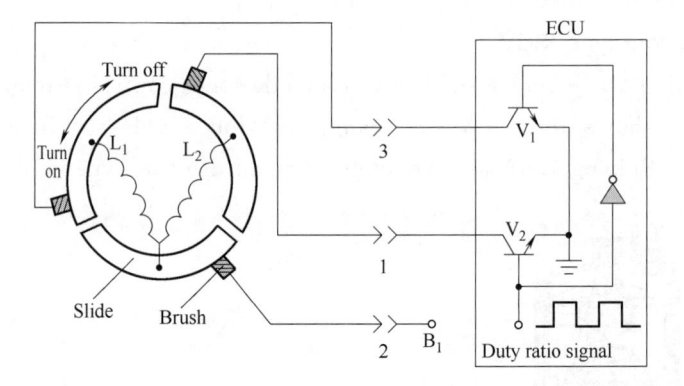

Figure 4-8　Circuit Connection Diagram of Rotary Slide Valve Type IACV

When working, the ECU determines the mixture concentration of the engine in idle condition according to the input signal of the ECT and TPS, and outputs the duty ratio signal to control the power-on time of L1 or L2. The duty ratio is the ratio of the power-on time to the power-on period of the ECU control signal over a period, as shown in Figure 4-9. If the torque of the return spring is not taken into account, then:

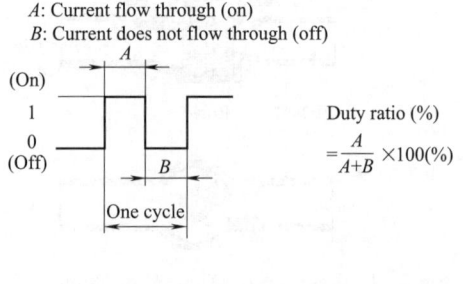

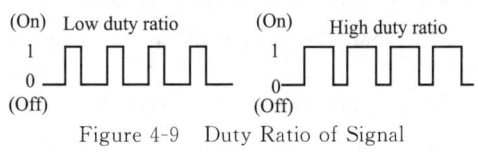

Figure 4-9　Duty Ratio of Signal

When the duty ratio is 50%, the average power-on time of L1 and L2 is equal, $T1 = T2$. The armature shall stop turning;

When the duty ratio is more than 50%, the average power-on time of coil L2 is longer, $T2 > T1$. The armature shall drive the rotary slide valve to deflect clockwise, the cross-section of the bypass air passage shall decrease, and the idle speed shall decrease;

When the duty ratio is less than 50%, the average power-on time of coil L1 is longer, $T1 > T2$. The armature shall drive the rotary slide valve to deflect counterclockwise, the cross section of the bypass air passage shall decrease, and the idle speed shall decrease.

Rotary slide valve defects according to duty ratio of the control pulse signal, with duty ratio range of about 18% (turn off rotary slide valve) to 82% (turn on rotary slide valve). The deflection angle of the slide valve is limited to 90°.

actual speed is compared with the target speed to obtain a difference. According to the difference, it determines the corresponding target speed control quantity, and drives the stepping motor to approach the target speed.

Stepping motor control. ECU conducts power tube VTl-VT2-VT3-VT4 according to a certain order, and supplies power respectively to the stepping motor stator coil to drive the stepping motor rotor to rotate. As such it drives the front-end valve to move, changes the distance between the valve and the seat, and adjusts the bypass air flow quantity, enabling the engine idle speed to achieve the desired target speed.

2. Rotary solenoid type ISCV

The construction of the rotary slide valve type idle speed control system is shown in Figure 4-6. Figure 4-7 shows the ISCV of Guangzhou Honda Odyssey. In addition, Santana 2000, Xia Li 2000, Fukang 1.6A and Toyota Camry all use this type valve.

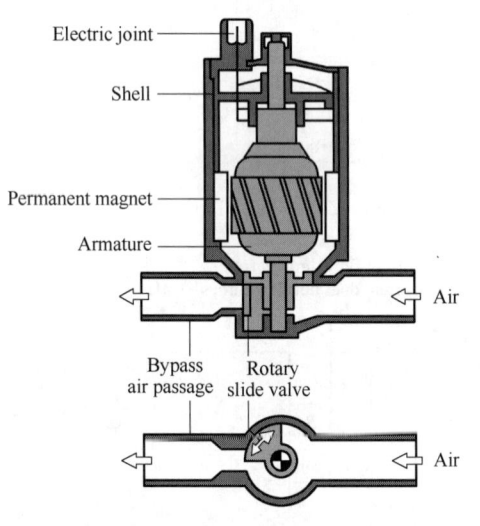

Figure 4-6   Structure Diagram of Rotary
Slide Valve Type IACV

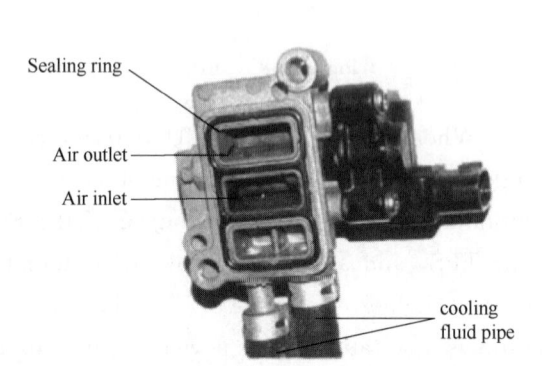

Figure 4-7   Rotary Slide Valve Type ISCV
of Guangzhou Honda Odyssey

The rotary slide valve type idle speed control system is mainly composed of permanent magnet, bypass air passage, rotary slide valve and reset spring. The rotary slide valve is fixed on the armature pivot and rotates with the armature pivot to control the amount of air passing through the bypass air passage; the permanent magnet is fixed on the shell to form a permanent magnetic field; the reset spring is used to turn on the bypass channel of the ISCV completely after the engine is stalled; the armature core is surrounded by two sets of electromagnetic coils L1 and L2 (Figure 4-8), when the coil is energized, a magnetic field will be generated to make the armature pivot drive the rotary slide valve to rotate, so as to control the air passing through the bypass air passage. The electromagnetic coils L1 and L2 are controlled by the ECU through transistors V1 and V2, which are controlled in reverse by the same signal, that is

V2 is on, V1 is off;

V2 is off, V1 is on.

the signals of the idle TPS and the CPS. Through the small gear, double gear and sector gear, the motor's rotation is transmitted to the throttle to open the corresponding angle, so that the idle speed reaches the optimum value.

Figure 4-3 shows the structure diagram of the stepping motor idle air control valve (IACV), which is installed in the main intake manifold of the engine. The ECU adds voltage to each terminal (Figure 4-4) of the IACV joint according to the signals of various sensors to enable the motor to rotor rotate forward or reverse, so that the valve heart moves axially. By changing the gap between the valve center and the valve seat, the amount of air flowing through the by-pass air passage can be adjusted. With mall gap, the air intake volume is small, resulting in low idle speed; with large gap, the air intake volume is large, resulting in high idle speed.

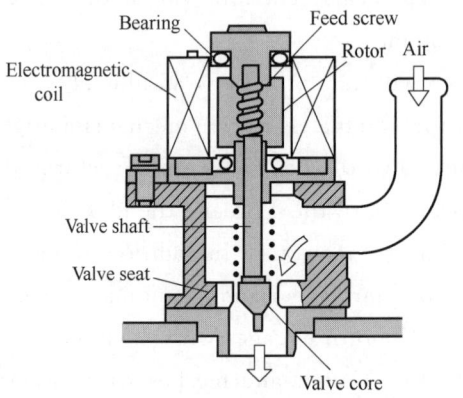
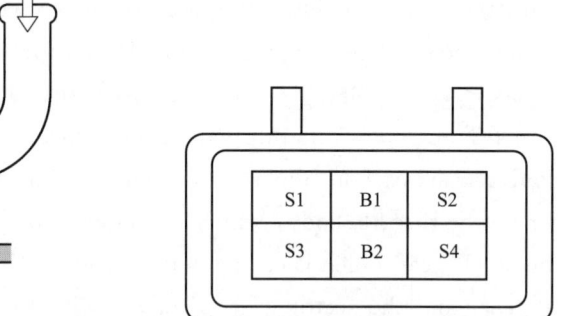

Figure 4-3　Structure of Stepping Motor IACV　　Figure 4-4　Distribution Diagram of IACV Terminal

When the engine control module (ECU) controls the engine idle speed, with the control program shown in Figure 4-5. Firstly, the ECU determines whether the engine is in idle state according to the signal of TPS and speed signal, and then determines the target speed according to the signal of CTS, air conditioning (A/ C) switch, power steering (PS) switch and idle starting switch, and the data stored in the memory. Normally, it uses the engine speed signal as the feedback signal to realize the idle speed closed-loop control, that is, the engine

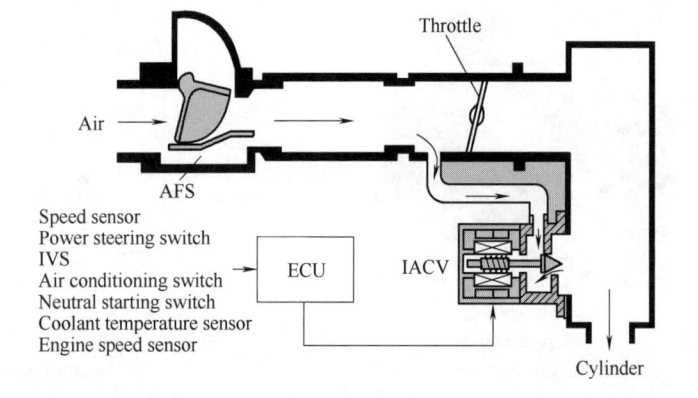

Figure 4-5　Composition of Stepping Motor Idle Control System

118　Fault Diagnosis and Repair of Automobile Engine Electronic Control System

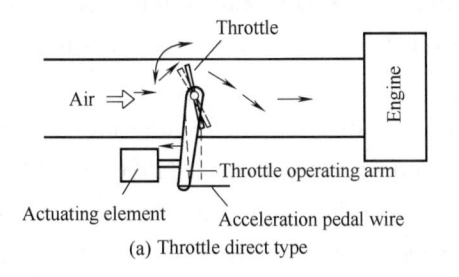 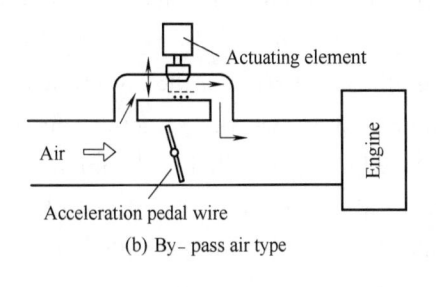

(a) Throttle direct type   (b) By- pass air type

Figure 4-1　Two Control Methods for Idle Speed

the air intake by controlling the opening angle of the throttle valve to adjust the cross section of the air passage to realize the control of the idle speed.

Throttle control system is widely used in Volkswagen cars. The following is the working principle of throttle direct type idle speed control system.

The throttle direct-type idle speed control system consists of a TPS, an idle TPS, an idle validation switch and an actuator (an idle DC motor), and a gear drive mechanism. Figure 4-2 (a) (plastic cover plate is removed from the throttle body) is its structural diagram. Figure 4-2 (b) shows its internal wiring diagram. Both the TPS and the idle TPS consist of a double-track carbon film resistor and a sliding contact on it. In addition, there is a double gear on the throttle body, which is composed of a large gear and a pinion arranged coaxially. The small gear which is coaxial with the idle DC motor engages with the large gear in the double gear, and the sector gear is coaxial with the throttle and meshes with the large gear in the double gear. When the driver steps on the accelerator pedal, the idle validation switch is turned off, and the ECU judges the running condition of the engine according to the input signal of the TPS to control the fuel injection and ignition. When the driver does not step on the accelerator pedal, the throttle is closed by return spring, and the idle validation switch is turned off. The ECU receives the signal that the idle validation switch is turned off to know that the engine is idling. It shall control the action of the idle DC motor according to

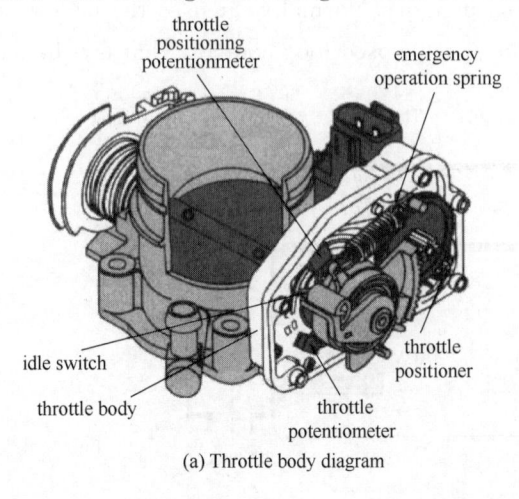 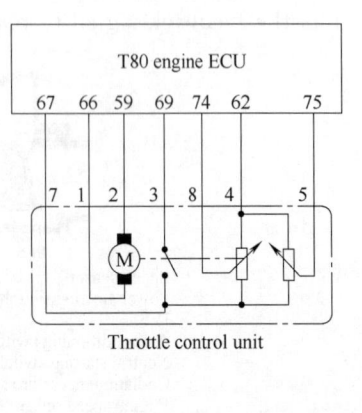

(a) Throttle body diagram   (b) Throttle body circuit diagram

Figure 4-2　Throttle Body

Item IV

Maintenance of Idle Speed Control System for Gasoline Engine

I. Introduction of Item Scene

How to solve the problem that the engine speed is unstable (the engine speed fluctuates up and down) when a automobile engine is idle? If you want to solve the problem of idle instability of electronic control engine, you should know the electronic control system of engine, the structure and principle of air supply system, the composition and function of idle speed control system, the structure and principle of fuel feed system and ignition control system, and be able to disassemble and test relevant sensors and actuators. This item focuses on the idle speed control system, only with the above-mentioned automobile expertise to solve the engine idle instability of the fault ability.

II. Item Related Knowledge

When the engine runs idly, due to the air-conditioning compressor, power steering booster pump, generator and other load changes shall cause idle speed fluctuation. The function of ISCV is to adjust the idle speed by adjusting the engine idling air intake to ensure the stability of the engine operation when the load changes.

(I) Classification of idle speed control valves

Idle speed control valves are installed near the engine throttle body or throttle body. There are two control modes of air intake when engine is idle: throttle direct control and throttle by-pass control. The former is direct control of the throttle to adjust the air intake, which is called throttle direct control; the latter is by controlling the opening of the throttle by-pass air passage to adjust the air intake, which is called by-pass air. The control principle is shown in Figure 4-1. Santana 200GLi, Buick Century sedan and Cherokee jeep adopt by-pass air type, Santana 200GSi, 3000, Jetta AT, GTX automobile adopt throttle direct type.

(II) Principle of ISCV

1. Throttle direct type control system

The throttle direct type idle speed control system cancels the bypass channel. It controls

by the driver. The most likely cause of this kind of fault is the engine electronic fuel injection or electronic ignition system.

① Fault self-diagnosis of the electronic control system is carried out by fault diagnosis instrument, check if there is a fault code, the result is not any fault prompt.

② According to the previous maintenance experience, the spark tester is used to check whether there is fire at high pressure, the result is that the fire gap and sparks are normal.

③ Remove and check each cylinder spark plug. When each cylinder spark plug is removed, it is found that the spark plug electrode had dirt and carbon deposits.

It turns out that the spark plug does not work well or the individual cylinder spark plug does not work, resulting in partial fuel not fully burned and discharged, thus burning in the exhaust pipe, firing. Light engine idling instability, wobble phenomenon, idling and acceleration when the "sudden" sound.

Replacement of all spark plugs, re-test, fault phenomenon disappeared, troubleshooting.

Summary

This item introduces in detail the structure and principle of microcomputer controlled ignition system, the distribution mode of microcomputer controlled ignition system, the control process of microcomputer controlled ignition system, the application of detonation sensor in electronic controlled ignition system, the detection knowledge of electronic controlled ignition system and the detection method of detonation sensor.

Exercises and Thinking

1. Describe the role and relationship of crankshaft position sensor and camshaft position sensor.

2. How to carry out the maintenance of the magnetic induction crankshaft position sensor for Santana 2000 GSi AJR engine?

3. Taking Santana 2000 GSi AJR engine as an example, the maintenance method of non-distributor ignition control system is described.

4. Taking Santana 2000 GSi AJR engine as an example, the detection method of DS is described.

5. What effect does the ignition advance angle have on most engines?

6. Describe the working principle of the resonant piezoelectric detonation sensor.

discharge between the contacts, on the contrary, it shall weaken the ignition energy, which is not conducive to the normal ignition.

When the dwell angle is the same, the engine speed is high, the closing time is short, and the turning speed is low, the closing time is long. Therefore, in order to ensure a reliable ignition, the dwell angle should vary with the engine speed. The ignition control module in the electronic ignition system can control and adjust the size of the dwell angle: At low speed, the dwell angle is reduced; at high speed, the dwell angle is increased.

⑦ Detection of overlap angle. The first end of the ignition waveform of each cylinder is aligned, and the camshaft angle occupied by the difference between the longest waveform and the shortest waveform length is called the overlap angle (Figure 3-33).

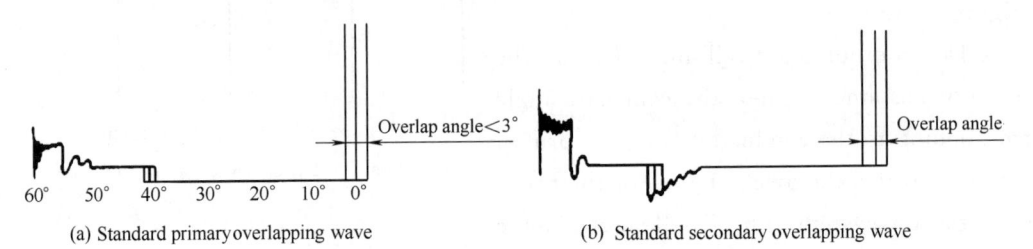

(a) Standard primary overlapping wave   (b) Standard secondary overlapping wave

Figure 3-33   Overlapping wave

The overlap angle should not be greater than 5% of the ignition interval, i. e. :

4-cylinder engine$\leqslant$4.5°;

6 cylinder engine$\leqslant$3°;

8-cylinder engine$\leqslant$2.25°.

The overlap angle reflects the degree of ignition interval of multi-cylinder engine. The greater the overlap angle is, the more uneven the ignition interval is. It shall not only affect the power and economy of the engine, but also affect the stability of the engine. Large overlap angle is caused by uneven wear of distributor cam or loose wear of distributor shaft, bending deformation and so on.

(Ⅱ) Failure cases

Case: "When the engine is idle, the body wobbles, the automobile is unstable at low speeds, and the exhaust pipe fires when it accelerates. "

1. Fault phenomena

When running idly, a Honda Accord automobile wobbles. The driver said the automobile at low speed feel unstable body, there is a sense of frustration. When acceleration, the engine has a "sudden" sound, the exhaust pipe accompanied by the phenomenon of shooting which was improved when the speed are increased.

2. Causes of fault

The spark plug does not work well or the individual cylinder spark plug does not work.

3. Fault diagnosis and elimination

After the maintenance personnel test-run on the road, there is indeed a failure described

tion; some electronic ignition systems produce a zigzag upper oblique line before the closed area ends, and then a spark line appears. All of the above are normal.

⑤ Waveform inversion. When the positive and negative poles of the ignition coil are connected, the engine can also start, but the energy consumed by the ignition is increased. This is because when the spark plug works, the temperature of the center electrode is higher than that of the side electrode, and it is easier for the electrons to move from the center electrode to the side electrode; on the contrary, it is more difficult. When the positive and negative poles of the ignition coil are connected correctly, the firing line goes up; when the polarity is reversed, the firing line goes down, as shown in Figure 3-31.

⑥ Detection of the dwell angle. During the ignition of gasoline engine, the camshaft angle corresponding to the conduction stage in primary circuit is called the dwell angle. For the traditional ignition system, the dwell angle is the camshaft angle occupied by the platinum contact in the closing period; for the electronic ignition system, it is the camshaft angle occupied by the triode conduction.

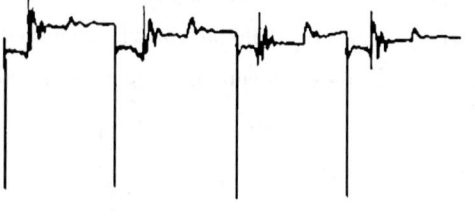

Figure 3-31 Fault Waveform of Positive Reversion of Ignition Coil

The dwell angle of each cylinder can be easily observed by using primary parallel wave (Figure 3-32) . The dwell angle should be in the following range:

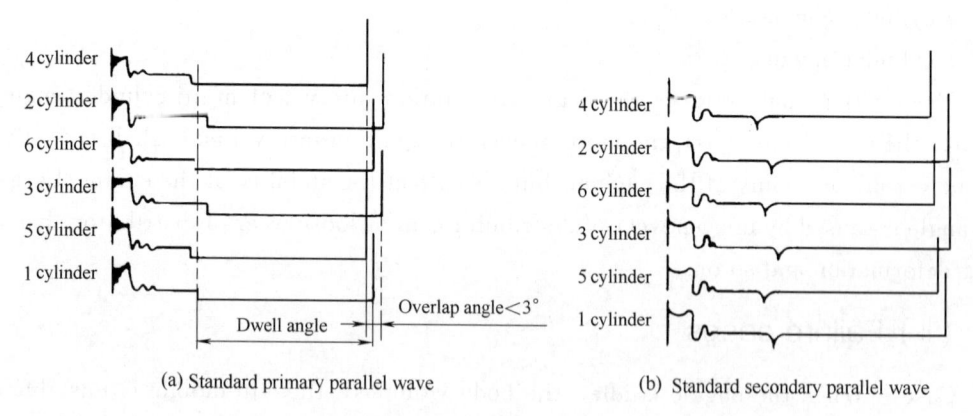

(a) Standard primary parallel wave   (b) Standard secondary parallel wave

Figure 3-32   Parallel Wave

3-cylinder engine: $60°\sim66°$;

4-cylinder engine: $50°\sim54°$;

6-cylinder engine: $38°\sim42°$;

8-cylinder engine: $29°\sim32°$.

For the traditional contact ignition system, the measured dwell angle is small, indicating that the contact gap is too large, the contact closing time is short, the primary current does not increase the required value, which shall make the ignition energy insufficient; if the dwell angle is too large, indicating that the contact gap is small, it shall cause the arc

If the spark line is too short, the reasons are as follows:

a. The spark plug gap is too large.

b. The electrode of rotor and distributor cover is ablative or the gap between rotor and distributor cover is too large.

c. The mixture is too thin.

If the spark line is too long, the reasons are as follows:

a. The spark plug is dirty.

b. The spark plug gap is too small.

c. High-tension wire or spark plug is short-circuited.

Although it is impossible to determine the specific length of the spark line when observing the ignition waveform with some engine integrated detector, it can also be found that the spark duration is shorter and the voltage is lower by comparing the ignition waveform of each cylinder.

③ Low-frequency oscillation area analysis. When the engine ignition system is in good technical condition, the low-frequency oscillation area should have more than 5 visible pulses, and the high-power coil shall generate more than 8 pulses. The reasons for the small number of oscillation pulses and the small amplitude are as follows:

a. The ignition coil is short-circuited.

b. The capacitor leaks electricity.

c. Ignition coil primary circuit connection or line connection is not good, the resistance value is too large.

If the number of oscillation pulses is too large, the capacitor capacity is too large.

For the electronic ignition system, if the low-frequency oscillation area is abnormal, it only means that the ignition coil is not normal and has nothing to do with the capacitor, because the electronic ignition system has no capacitor.

④ Closed area analysis. For the traditional ignition system, when the contact is closed, the ignition waveform produces a vertical downward line, where there is a clutter indicating platinum contact ablation, poor contact or insufficient contact spring elasticity, as shown in Figure 3-30. In the same way, if there is a clutter before the fire line at the end of the closed area, it also indicates that the technical condition of the platinum contact is not good.

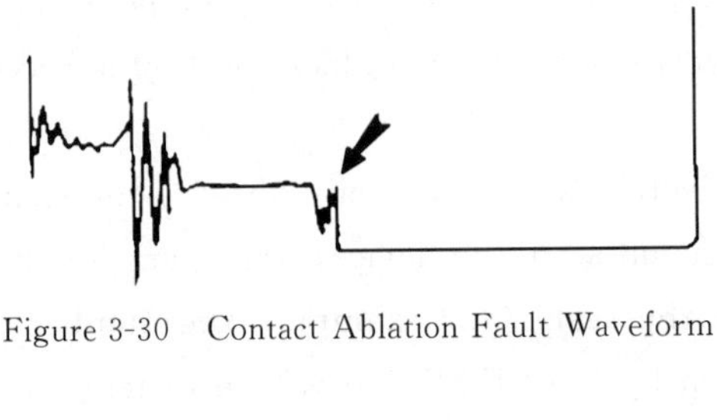

Figure 3-30　Contact Ablation Fault Waveform

For an electronic ignition system, the waveform of the closed area is very similar to that of the traditional ignition system, but the reverse voltage and breakdown voltage are caused by the transistor conduction and cutting off primary current. Therefore, the two waveform anomalies are caused by poor transistor technology. The length and shape of the waveform of the electronic ignition system in the closed area are different from those of the traditional ignition system. The main manifestations are: the closed area is elongated at high speed, and there are ripples or bulges in the closed sec-

rotor, etc.

b. If the voltage is high on individual cylinder, it indicates that the gap of spark plug of the cylinder is too big, the contact of high-voltage line is not good, or the contact with the high-voltage line of the cylinder is not good.

c. If the voltage of all cylinders or individual cylinder is too low, the reason shall be that the spark plug is dirty, the gap is too small or high-voltage is short-circuited.

d. Excess waveforms appear at the lower end of the firing line, which is usually caused by platinum contact ablation or poor contact.

When it displays the parallel wave of each cylinder, plug off the high-voltage line of any cylinder except the fist cylinder (the sensor with an oscilloscope on the high-voltage line of the first cylinder), so that the distance between the cylinder and the ground position is gradually increased. The firing line of the cylinder should rise obviously, and its voltage value should be the highest output voltage of the ignition coil. For the electronic ignition system, it should be higher than 30 kV, otherwise the ignition coil is faulty. If the unplugged high-voltage wire is grounded, the firing line should be obviously shortened, with the value lower than 5kV. Otherwise, it indicates that the electrode gap of the rotor or the distributor

cover jack is large, or the contact between the high-voltage wire of the sub-cylinder and the jack is bad. Figure 3-29 shows that the firing line is rising after the high-voltage wire of the sub-cylinder is plugged off.

When the screen shows secondary ignition parallel wave, if the engine speed suddenly increases, firing lines of all cylinders uniformly increase, indica-

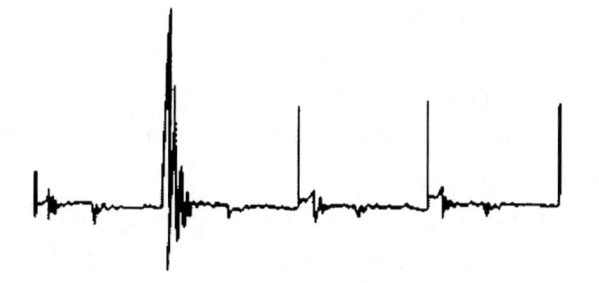

Figure 3-29 Firing Line is Rising after Plugging
off High Voltage Line of any Cylinder

ting that spark plug of each cylinder works normally. If the firing line of one or more cylinders cannot be raised, it indicates that the spark plug has carbon deposits. If the peak value of a cylinder's high pressure rises very high, it indicates that the cylinder's spark plug acceleration characteristic is not good.

② Spark line analysis Using single cylinder selective wave can easily observe the spark line of the cylinder. On the oscilloscope with millisecond scanning device, the spark line duration and ignition voltage value can be read from the scale (for example, the number of milliseconds of the spark line duration can be shown by the BEAR-200 engine tester). For most automobiles equipped with electronic ignition systems, the spark duration is about 1. 5ms at 1000r/min. When the spark duration is less than 0. 8ms, there is no guarantee that the mixture shall burn completely, while the exhaust pollution shall increase and the power shall decrease; if the spark duration is more than 2ms, the spark plug electrode life shall be shortened obviously. The length of spark line of traditional ignition system is 0. 6~0. 8 ms, and the voltage of combustion zone is 1~2 kV.

closed section of the electronic ignition waveform varies with the speed. The electronic ignition waveform is shown in Figure 3-27.

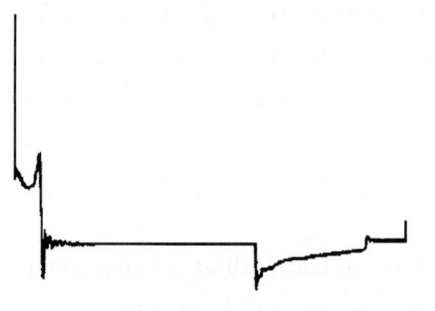

Figure 3-27   Electronic Ignition Oscillograph

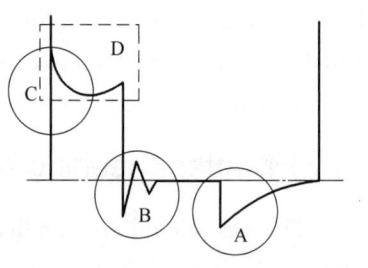

Figure 3-28   Fault Reflection Area
of Secondary Waveform

2. Waveform analysis

（1）Fault reflection area

If there is a difference between the waveform measured by oscilloscope and the standard
waveform, it indicates that the ignition system is out of order. There are four main fault reflection areas in the waveform (taking the secondary waveform as an example) for the traditional ignition system fault, as shown in Figure 3-28. Area C is the ignition area: When the
primary circuit is cut off, the current in the primary winding of the ignition coil is rapidly reduced, the magnetic field is rapidly attenuated, the high voltage (15000～20000V) is produced in the secondary winding, and the spark plug gap is broken down. The breakdown
voltage is generally 4000～8000V. After spark plug electrode is broken down and discharged,
the secondary ignition voltage drops accordingly.

Area D is the combustion area: When the spark plug electrode gap is broken down, an
arc formed between the electrodes ignites the mixture. The spark discharge process lasts
from 0.6 to 1.5 ms, and the spark line is formed in the secondary ignition voltage waveform.

Area B is an oscillation area: At the end of the spark plug discharge, when the energy
in the ignition coil cannot sustain the spark discharge, the residual energy is exhausted in the
form of damped vibration. At this point, a low-frequency vibration with a visible pulse appears on the ignition voltage waveform.

Area A is a closed area: After the primary circuit is closed again, the secondary circuit
generates a induced voltage of 1500～2000V opposite to the battery voltage. A vertical line
that drops rapidly on the ignition waveform and then rises to a horizontal line.

（2）Typical fault waveform

① Analysis of firing line. When the speed is stable, it shows the parallel wave of each
cylinder. If the ignition voltage is higher than the standard value, it indicates that the high
voltage circuit has high resistance:

a. If the voltage is high on each cylinder, it indicates that the high resistance occurs between the rotor and the ignition head, such as high-voltage cut-off, bad contact, and dirty

② Signal voltage test: Start the engine to the working temperature, plug off the plug of 4 injectors and 4-pin plug of ignition coil, turn on the ignition switch, connect the engine ground point and plug head terminal 1 with the LED test lamp, connect the starter for several seconds, and the test lamp should flash. , Then connect the engine ground point and terminal 3 with the test lamp, connect the start motor for several seconds, and the test lamp should flash.

(Ⅲ) Matters needing attention

① The DS should be handled with care to prevent it from falling to the ground and breaking.

② The ignition coil should be lightly placed to prevent the ignition coil from falling to the ground.

③ On the physical bench, the test port is directly connected with the ECU. Do not add any voltage to the test port of the engine test bench to avoid damaging the ECU.

Ⅳ. Knowledge and Skills Expansion

(Ⅰ) Waveform analysis of ignition system

Without breaking, the detection and diagnosis of engine ignition system can be divided into two aspects: detection and analysis of ignition waveform and detection of ignition timing. The following is an introduction to the analysis of ignition waveform.

Waveform analysis refers to the process of judging the ignition system failure by comparing the actual ignition waveform of the ignition system of an automobile engine with the standard waveform.

1. Standard waveform

Traditional contact-type primary and secondary ignition voltage waveform as shown in Figure 3-26.

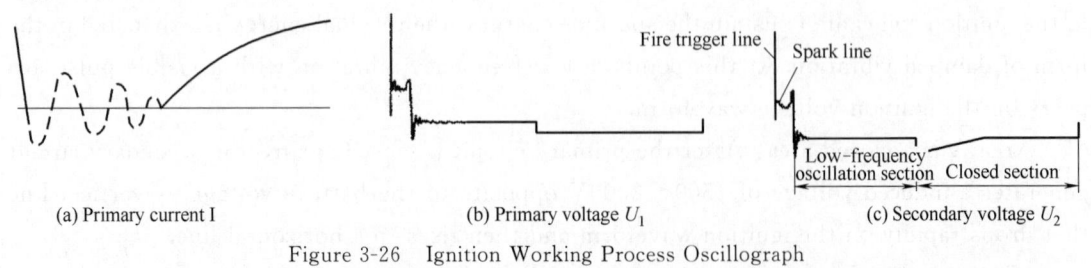

(a) Primary current I　　　　(b) Primary voltage U_1　　　　(c) Secondary voltage U_2

Figure 3-26　Ignition Working Process Oscillograph

The main difference between the secondary ignition waveform of the electronic ignition system and that of the traditional ignition system is that the rear voltage of the closed section of the electronic ignition system rises slightly. Some waveforms also have a small voltage fluctuation in the middle of the closing section, which reflects the role of the current-limited circuit in the ignition control module (electronic module). In addition, the length of the

seconds, the test lamp should flash. Then connect the engine ground point and terminal 3 with the test lamp, connect the starter for a few seconds, the test lamp should flash. If the test lamp doesn't flash, check whether the wire between the plug terminal of the ignition coil and the plug of the ECU wire harness is open-circuited or short-circuited, and if the line is normal, replace the engine ECU.

(1) Resistance test

The resistance test of this project, as an auxiliary test, is mainly to test the conductivity of the wire harness to confirm that the wire harness is unobstructed, with no open circuit and short circuit, reliable connector, and no interference for signal transmission. The test is carried out on the engine test bench of the automobile microcomputer-control fault detection and diagnosis experimental system.

① Conductivity test of wire harness: With the digital multimeter set in resistance gear, find the pin number below the ignition coil figure and the corresponding pin number of the ECU signal test port figure on the circuit diagram, test the resistance of the ignition coil pin corresponding to the pin of the ECU, and all the resistance should be less than 5Ω. As shown in Table 3-2.

Table 3-2 Normal Resistance Value of Ignition Coil Pin Corresponding to Pin of ECU

Measurement of Line Resistance of Ignition Coil (N152)	Computer Pin	Ignition Coil Pin	Conductivity
	Ground point	4	<0.5
	The ignition switch	2 and D23	<0.5
	ECU-78	3	<0.5
	ECU-71	1	<0.5

② Short-circuit test of wire harness: The digital multimeter is set at the resistance of 200kΩ, and the resistance between the ignition coil pin and the non-corresponding ECU pin should be ∞.

In actual maintenance, in order to test the conductivity of each wire harness, turn off the ignition switch, plug off the sensor plug and the ECU connector, and use multimeter to test the resistance between each wire harness. The resistance of the connecting wire should be less than 5Ω, and the resistance of the disconnected wire should be ∞. In the actual measurement, due to the measurement method, the error of the multimeter itself, and the oxidation and dust on the surface of the object being measured, it is normal to have a few ohmic errors, and it is not necessary to stick to the specific figures.

(2) Voltage test

The voltage test of this item includes the power supply voltage test and the signal voltage test, in which the signal voltage test is the main basis to determine whether the ignition coil is invalid or not.

① Power supply voltage test: In actual maintenance, unplug the sensor plug, turn on the ignition switch, test the voltage between terminal 2 and ground. The voltage should be 12V when the starter is hit. At this point, the ECU shall record the fault code of the ignition coil. After the test, the fault code should be cleared with the diagnostic instrument.

(3) Detection of the output signal.

Plug in the sensor wire harness plug, start the engine, detect the voltage between terminal 1 and 2, the normal value is $0.3 \sim 1.4V$. There should be no short circuit between the three terminals of the DS, otherwise, the DS should be replaced. If there is open circuit or short circuit in the circuit between the sensor plug and the ECU wire harness plug, the fault should be eliminated.

2. Detection of ignition module

AJR engine ignition system adopts non-distributor double spark direct ignition system. If the ignition coil is out of order, the engine shall stall immediately or fails to start. The ECU could not detect this fault. If a spark ignition circuit is disconnected due to an open circuit, the spark plug that shares an ignition coil with it shall not spark because of this electrical fault. If a spark ignition circuit cannot spark because of a short circuit, but the electrical circuit is not disconnected, the spark plug that shares an ignition coil with it shall spark. The circuit wiring of the AJR engine ignition system is shown in Figure 3-24.

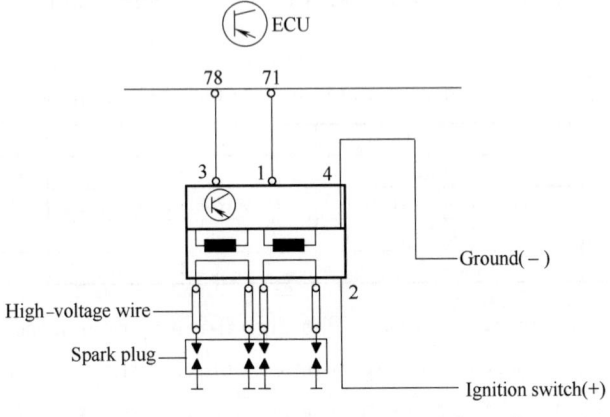

Figure 3-24   AJR Ignition System Circuit Wiring Diagram

Unplug the ignition coil 4-pin plug, connect the battery positive pole and plug terminal 4 with the LED test lamp. The LED test lamp should be on. If the test lamp is not on, check if there is an open circuit between terminal 4 and ground point.

Test the supply voltage of the ignition coil: Unplug the ignition coil 4-pin plug, connect the LED test lamp between the engine ground point and the plug terminal 2, turn on the ignition switch. The LED test lamp should be on. If the test lamp is not on, check whether the line between the central electrical appliance D plug 23 and the 4-pin socket terminal 2 is open-circuited, as shown in Figure 3-25.

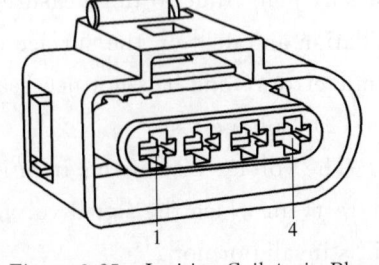

Figure 3-25   Ignition Coil 4-pin Plug

Test ignition coil work: Unplug the plugs of 4 injectors and 4-pin plug of ignition coil, turn on the ignition switch, connect the engine ground point and the plug terminal 1 with the LED test lamp, turn on the starter for a few

The oscillograph should be used to detect the output voltage waveform of the DS when the engine works to detect whether the DS is normal. If there is an irregular vibration waveform, and the waveform changes obviously with the change of the engine detonation, it indicates that the DS works normally. If there is no waveform output or the output waveform does not change with the engine's working conditions, it indicates that the DS is faulty and should be replaced.

In the absence of an oscilloscope, the DS can be roughly detected by measuring the resistance. Unplug the wire of the DS, and measure the resistance between the two terminals of the sensor and the ground with the resistance gear of the multimeter. If it is conductive, it indicates that the sensor has been damaged and must be replaced.

The 3 terminals and circuit diagram of the Santana AJR engine DS are shown in Figure 3-23. In the circuit of the DS, the terminal 1 is the positive pole of the signal line, the terminal 2 is the negative pole of the signal line, and the terminal 3 is the shielding line.

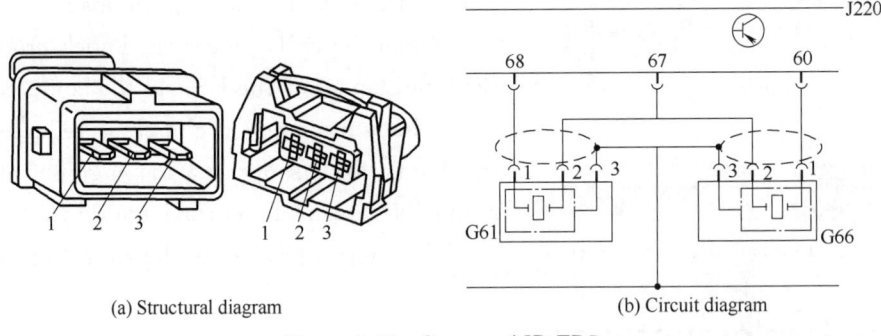

(a) Structural diagram   (b) Circuit diagram

Figure 3-23　Santana AJR EDS

(1) Detection of sensor resistance.

Turnoff the ignition switch and unplug the sensor wire harness plug. The test results should be in accordance with the standard values in Table 3-1.

(2) Detection of the wire harness resistance.

Turn off the ignition switch, unplug the sensor wire harness plug and ECU wire harness plug. The test results of wire resistance between the two plugs should be in accordance with the standard values in Table 3-1.

Table 3-1　Maintenance Standard for DS of Santana 2000GSi

Detection Item	Detection Condition	Detection Part	Resistance Standard Value/Ω
DS resistance	Turn off the ignition switch and unplug the sensor plug	Terminal 1 and 2 of sensor socket	>1M
		Terminal 1 and 3 of sensor socket	>1M
		Terminal 2 and 3 of sensor socket	>1M
Positive line of sensor signal	Unplug the controller and sensor plug	Controller terminal 60 (11) to sensor plug terminal 1	<0.5
		Controller terminal 68 to sensor plug terminal 1	<0.5
Negative line of sensor signal		Controller terminal 67 (30) to sensor plug terminal 2	<0.5
Sensor shielding wire		Engine ground point next to controller module to sensor plug terminals 3	<0.5

106　Fault Diagnosis and Repair of Automobile Engine Electronic Control System

When the engine's load is lower than a certain value, generally there is no detonation. At this point, it is not suitable to adjust the ignition advance angle by controlling the detonation, but to control the ignition advance angle with the ignition open-loop control scheme. That is, the ECU only controls the ignition advance angle according to the stored information and the input signal of the relevant sensor, instead of detecting and analyzing

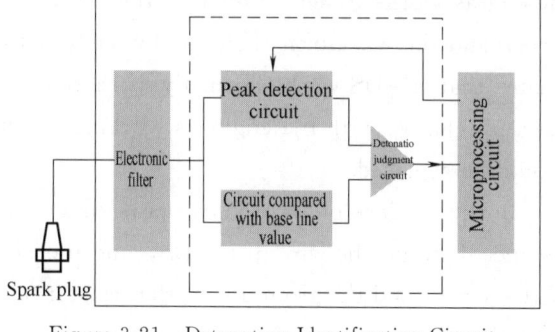

Figure 3-21　Detonation Identification Circuit

the input signal of the DS. The ECU can judge whether open-loop control or closed-loop control should be adopted in the ignition advance angle at a certain time by analyzing the signal sent by the sensor reflecting the load.

When the ECU judges the knock produced by the input signal of the DS and the comparison circuit, the ignition advance angle is reduced; when the detonation disappears, the engine control unit gradually returns to normal ignition advance angle. The control process is shown in Figure 3-22.

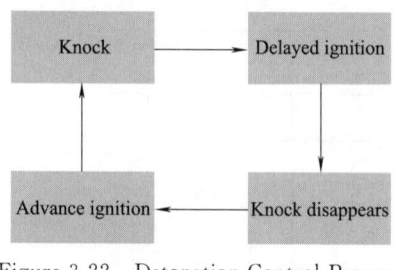

Figure 3-22　Detonation Control Process

III. Item Implementation

(I) Requirements for implementation

Toyota 5A, AJR engine bench; automobile; diagnostic instrument.

(II) Implementation steps

1. Detection of DS

The Santana AJR engine has two DSs installed under the intake manifold and between cylinder 1/2 and cylinder 3/4 respectively. There are three leads on the sensor socket, two of which are signal lines and one is shielding line.

In practice, the DS itself seldom fails. Most of faults are caused by the wrong tightening torque of the DS, and the standard torque is 20N • m. If the engine DS fixed torque is too large, it may make it too sensitive. The decrease of the ignition advance angle shall cause the slow reaction of the engine, the high exhaust temperature, and the increase of fuel consumption, While if the engine DS fixed torque is too small, the sensor sensitivity decreases. At this time, the engine is prone to knock, resulting that the engine temperature is too high, and the NO_x compound emissions exceed the standard. In addition, there are plug corrosion, wire harness plug damage, DS itself internal crack damage and so on.

tion, and the delay of ignition time can be used. In particular, the delay of ignition time has an obvious effect on the elimination of detonation.

(1) Relationship between detonation and ignition advance angle

The larger the ignition advance angle, the more likely it is to produce detonation. The test results shows that the ignition time of the engine with maximum torque is near the ignition time when the engine is about to knock. Therefore, in order to make the engine do not produce detonation, its ignition time is set within the range of detonation edge, so that it leaves the detonation limit with a large surplus. But this will inevitably reduce the engine's power, reduce the engine's power output and increase fuel consumption.

(2) Detonation control system

The essence of the detonation control is that the ECU detects the detonation limit of the engine through the DS, and controls the ignition time to keep it near the detonation boundary curve, so as to increase the power of the engine and reduce the fuel consumption.

Usually, the DS is mounted on the cylinder body of the engine, and generates different voltage signals depending on the vibration of the engine's various oscillatory frequencies. When the engine knock, the DS has the best induction performance and produces the maximum voltage signal. The output voltage characteristic is shown in Figure 3-20 (a).

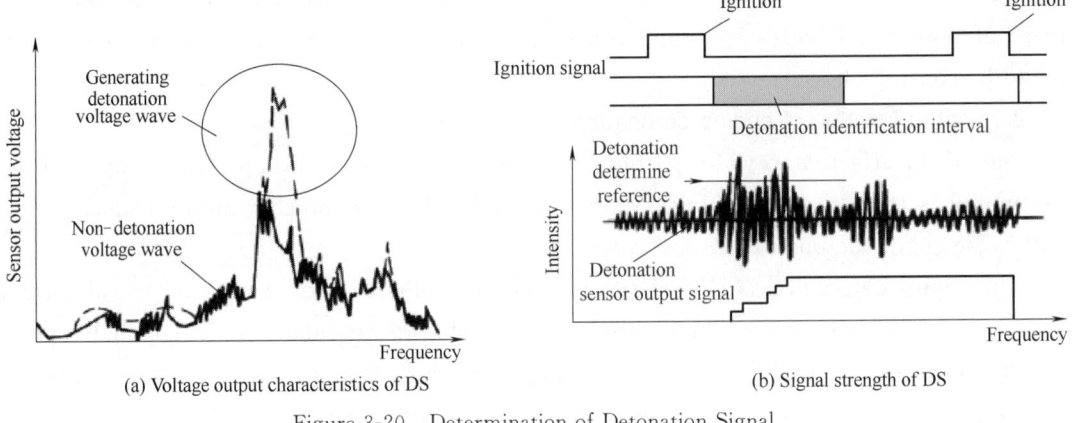

(a) Voltage output characteristics of DS   (b) Signal strength of DS

Figure 3-20   Determination of Detonation Signal

The detonation intensity is measured by the number of times in excess of the base value. The more times, the greater the detonation intensity. The less times, the smaller the detonation intensity, as shown in Figure 3-20 (b).

The input processing circuit of the DS is shown in Figure 3-21. After receiving the signal of the DS, the ECU filters the signal with the filter circuit to separate the detonation signal from other vibration signals, allowing only the detonation signal of a certain frequency range to pass through the filter circuit, then, the maximum value of the input signal is compared with the reference value of knock intensity through the peak detection circuit and the reference value comparison circuit. After comparison, the detonation determination is used to determine whether there is a detonation and the signal is transmitted to the microprocessor. The microprocessor reduces the ignition advance angle accordingly to eliminate the detonation.

tions. At the same time, the secondary output end of the ignition coil, the spark plug center electrode, is negative, resulting that the breakdown voltage is low, and the spark plug discharge frequency is small, so the electrode life is long; the high voltage line is cancelled and the ignition coil supplies power directly to the spark plug, so the energy loss is small, the efficiency is high and the electromagnetic interference is low; because the ignition coil can be installed between the double camshaft, the installation space around the engine is saved.

(VII) Detonation control

1. The necessity of detonation control

During the operation of the engine, the unburned mixture shall be further compressed and radiated by the flame of fuel combustion. If the end mixture has self-ignited before the flame front reaches, the combustion rate of the mixture is extremely fast, and the flame velocity can reach up to 100 meters or more per second, making the local pressure and temperature in the combustor very high accompanied by shock waves. Pressure shock waves repeatedly hit the cylinder wall, making a sharp knock on the cylinder. This is known as detonation combustion. It is a kind of abnormal combustion. When it is slight, it can increase the engine power and reduce the fuel consumption; when it is serious, the cylinder shall emit a particularly sharp metal knocking sound, which will lead to overheating of the coolant, decrease of power and increase of fuel consumption rate. Therefore, detonation combustion should be controlled.

2. Control function of engine detonation

One of the effective ways for gasoline engines to obtain maximum power and optimal fuel economy is to increase the ignition advance angle, but too much ignition advance angle shall cause engine detonation.

The engine detonation is the vibration of engine cylinder body caused by the abnormal combustion of the mixture in the combustor, which leads to sudden rise of cylinder pressure. In the closed-loop EEC, when the engine produces detonation, the electronic control system can effectively suppress and eliminate the engine detonation by adjusting the ignition time (ignition advance angle). Detonation sensor (DS) is an important component of the engine closed-loop control system. Its function is to convert the engine detonation signal into electrical signal and transmit it to the ECU. The ECU can modify the ignition time at any time according to the detonation signal so as to keep the ignition advance angle in the best state.

3. Detonation control process

After the spark plug ignites the mixture, if the flame pressure increases abnormally during the transmission, the mixture in some parts shall ignite and burn before the flame is transmitted, resulting in an instantaneous combustion. This phenomenon is known as detonation. One of the hazard of detonation is noise, and the other is that it may damage the engine, especially under heavy load conditions.

In order to eliminate detonation, methods such as the fuel with good anti-detonation performance, the improvement of combustor structure, the enhancement of coolant circula-

share one ignition coil respectively). The ignition control unit is provided with power triodes equal to the number of ignition coils, which respectively controls the operation of one ignition coil. According to the ignition control signal output by ECU, the ignition control module takes turns to trigger the power triode conduction and cut-off according to the ignition sequence, thus controlling each ignition coil to produce high voltage in turn, which is directly transmitted through the high voltage wire to the spark plug electrode gap to spark fire to ignite the combustible mixture.

(2) Single cylinder independent ignition control

When the ignition system uses independent ignition mode, each cylinder is equipped with an igniter mounted above the spark plug. In the ignition control module, a high-power triode with the same number of ignition coils is arranged to control the turn-on and cut-off of the secondary winding current of each coil, and the working principle is the same as that of simultaneous ignition. The advantage of independent ignition is that the high-voltage wire is eliminated and the ignition energy loss is reduced; in addition, all high-pressure components can be installed in the metal shield on the cylinder head of the engine, greatly reducing the radio interference caused by the ignition system. This type of ignition is very suitable for 4-valve (two intake and two exhaust valves per cylinder) engines. In this type of ignition system, the spark plug is arranged between two camshafts, and a ignition coil is directly pressed on each cylinder spark plug, which is easily arranged. Independent ignition control is shown in Figure 3-19.

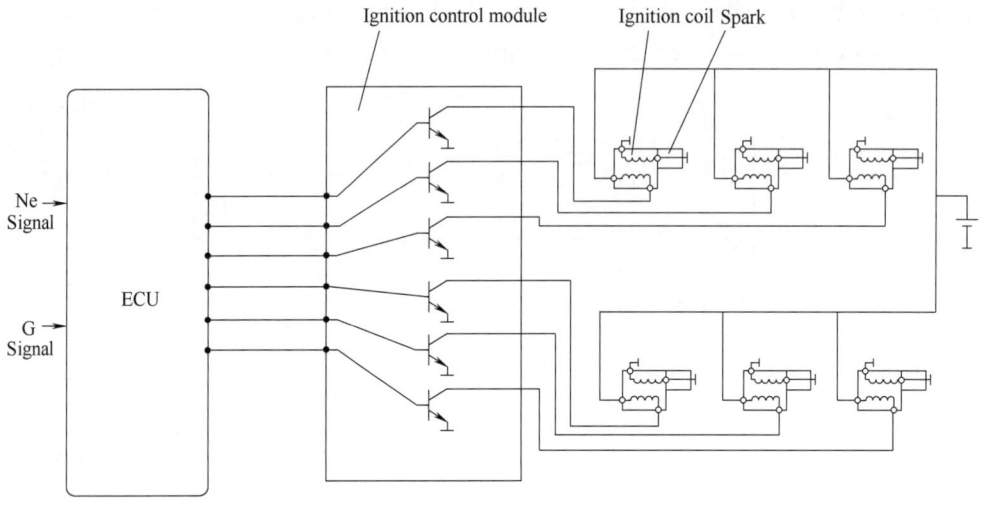

Figure 3-19   Single Cylinder Independent Ignition Control Mode

To sum up, MCI without distributor eliminates the shortcoming of MCI with distributor. As the number of ignition coils (or primary winding) increases, the allowable power-on time of the primary winding can be increased by $2\sim6$ times for each ignition coil. Therefore, even when the engine is running at high speed, the primary winding has sufficient power-on time. In other words, the distributor-less ignition system has enough ignition energy and enough secondary voltage to ensure a reliable ignition of the engine at all operating condi-

group, and cylinder 2 and 3 are another group. (cylinder 1, 2, 3 and 4 correspond to diode VD1, VD2, VD3, and VD4 respectively). The two power triodes in the ignition control module control a primary winding respectively, which are turned on and off alternately by the ECU according to the ignition sequence.

When the ECU inputs the ignition trigger signal of cylinder 1 and 4 into the ignition control module, the power triode VT1 are conductive and the current in the primary winding (arrow down) are cut off, thus producing high voltage electromotive force in the secondary winding. Under the action of the electromotive force, the diode VD1 and VD4 are conductive forwardly, the voltage on the spark plug electrodes of cylinder 1 and 4 rises rapidly until it sparks, and the high-voltage discharge current forms loop through the direction indicated by the solid line arrow in the figure; the diode VD2 and VD3 are reversely cut-off, with no discharge circuit formed, so there is no high-voltage spark discharge current on the sparkplug electrodes of cylinder 2 and 3

When the ECU inputs the ignition trigger signal of cylinder 2, and 3 into the ignition control module, the triode VT2 is cut off, the primary winding current (arrow up) is cut off, and the secondary winding produces a high voltage electromotive force, as shown in the direction of the dotted line arrow in Figure 3-17. At this time diode VD1 and VD4 are reversely cutoff, diode VD2 and VD3 are conductive forwardly, so the voltage on the spark plug electrodes of cylinder 2 and 3 rapidly rises to spark fire, with the high-voltage discharge current forming a circuit through the direction indicated by the dotted arrow in the figure.

② Ignition coil distribution high-voltage. As shown in Figure 3-18, Santana 2000 GSi, 3000, Jetta AT, GTX and Audi 200 car ignition systems use this type of distribution.

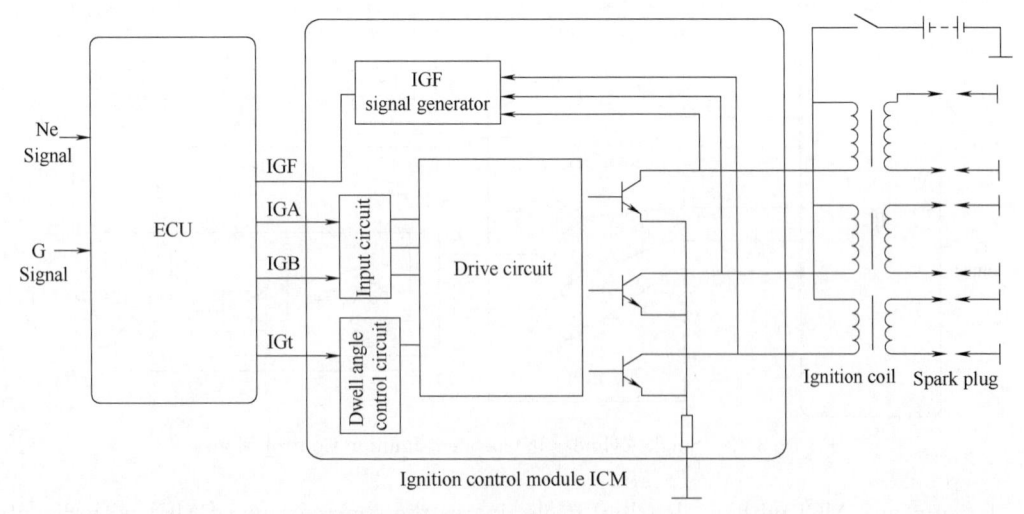

Figure 3-18　Ignition Coil Distribution High Voltage Dual-cylinder Simultaneous Ignition Mode

The ignition coil assembly consists of two (4-cylinder engine) or three (6-cylinder engine) independent ignition coils, each of which is supplied with two spark plugs working in pairs (cylinder 1 and 4 and cylinder 2 and 3 of the 4-cylinder engine share one ignition coil respectively; cylinder 1 and 6, cylinder 2 and 5 and cylinder 3 and 4 of the 6-cylinder engine

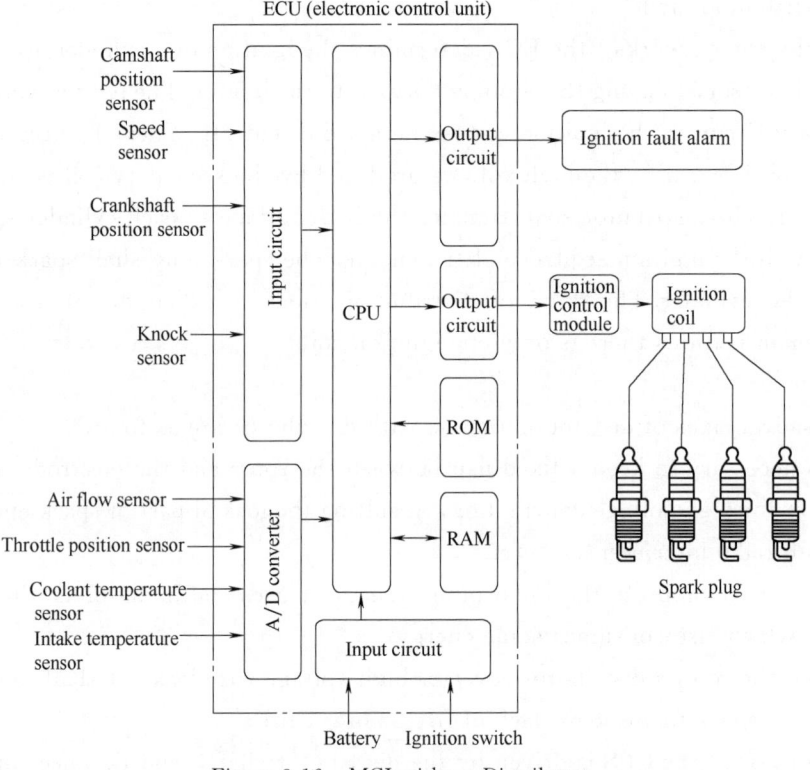

Figure 3-16　MCI without Distributor

is very low, which has little effect on the breakdown voltage and spark discharge energy of the effective ignition cylinder spark plug. When the crankshaft rotates for 1 turn, the two cylinders travel in opposite directions. When the two cylinders are ignited at the same time, the distribution mode of high-voltage is divided into diode distribution and ignition coil distribution.

① Diode distribution high voltage. The circuit principle of a dual-cylinder simultaneous ignition with a high-voltage distribution using the diode is shown in Figure 3-17. The ignition coil is composed of two primary windings and one secondary winding. The two ends of the secondary winding are composed of four high-voltage diodes and spark plugs. The installation modes of the four diodes include: the built-in type (installed inside the ignition coil) and the external type. For engines with ignition sequence of 1—3—4—2, cylinder 1 and 4 are one

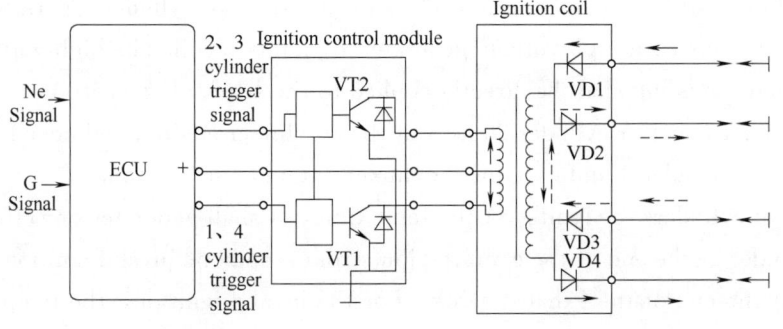

Figure 3-17　Ignition Control Mode of Diode Distribution High Voltage

100　Fault Diagnosis and Repair of Automobile Engine Electronic Control System

(2) Distribution mode

When the engine works, the ECU determines the ignition of a cylinder according to the signal of each sensor, sending the command signal to the igniter. The igniter controls whether the primary circuit in the ignition coil is energized or cut off. When the primary circuit in the ignition coil is cut off, the high voltage produced by the secondary coil is transmitted to the distributor. The distributor shall transfer the high voltage to each cylinder spark plug in accordance with the ignition sequence of the engine. The spark plug shall spark to ignite the mixture in the cylinder. This kind of distribution mode is called distributor distribution mode. The main features there is only one ignition coil.

(3) Defects

The disadvantages of distribution mode with distributor are as follow:

① It is necessary to keep a fixed gap between the rotor and the electrode near the distributor cover for high voltage distribution, resulting the loss of part of spark energy, and it is also a main radio interference source.

② In order to suppress the radio interference, it uses the high-voltage line with high impedance, which also consumes some energy;

③ When the rotor, distributor cover or high-voltage wire leak, it shall cause the high-voltage electric spark to weaken, lack of fire or break fire;

④ The rotor of the CPS is driven by the distributor shaft, and the mechanical wear of the rotating mechanism shall affect the control precision of the ignition timing;

⑤ The location of the distributor and the space occupied shall make it difficult for the structural arrangement of the engine and the shape design of the car.

2. MCI without distributor

It completely cancels the distributor. It transmits the high voltage generated by the ignition coil directly to the spark plug through the high voltage wire to ignite.

It ignites directly by adding the high voltage of ignition coil directly to the spark plug in accordance with the ignition sequence with the control of the ignition control module, as shown in Figure 3-16.

The common ECI without distributor can be divided into two modes: dual-cylinder simultaneous ignition and single-cylinder ignition.

(1) Control of dual-cylinder simultaneous ignition

Dual-cylinder simultaneous ignition refers to that the two cylinders spark plug spark fire at the same time for each high voltage generated by ignition coil. The high voltage generated by the secondary winding shall be directly applied to the spark plug electrodes of the two cylinders (cylinder 1 and 4 or cylinder 2 and 3 of the 4-cylinder engine; cylinder 1 and 6, cylinder 2 and 5, or cylinder 3 and 4 of the 6-cylinder engine) for ignition.

When two cylinders are ignited at the same time, it shall generates one effective ignition with the cylinder at the end of the compression stroke, and one invalid ignition with the other cylinder at the end of the exhaust stroke. For the invalid ignition, the temperature in the cylinder is high and the pressure is low, the breakdown voltage of spark plug electrode gap

crease of the power supply voltage.

(Ⅵ) High voltage distribution mode of MCI

The distribution of high voltage in MCI can be divided into MCI with distributor and MCI without distributor.

1. MCI with distributor

MCI with distributor has two forms: electronic ignition timing system and electronic ignition control system.

Electronic ignition timing system is a kind of open-loop control system. The ignition time of the system is controlled by the ignition control module and the ECU in the distributor. The ignition timing is accurately determined by the ECU according to the speed, load, coolant temperature, mixture concentration and other signals sent by each sensor under the specific condition of the engine.

The electronic ignition control system is equipped with DS, which belongs to the ignition timing closed-loop control. The ECU controls the ignition advance angle according to the signal of the DS, which can delay the ignition advance angle by 20 ° crankshaft angle, so the ignition timing control is more accurate than the previous control system, with the range of gasoline used in the engine enlarged.

(1) Composition

Composition of MCI with distributor is shown in Figure 3-15.

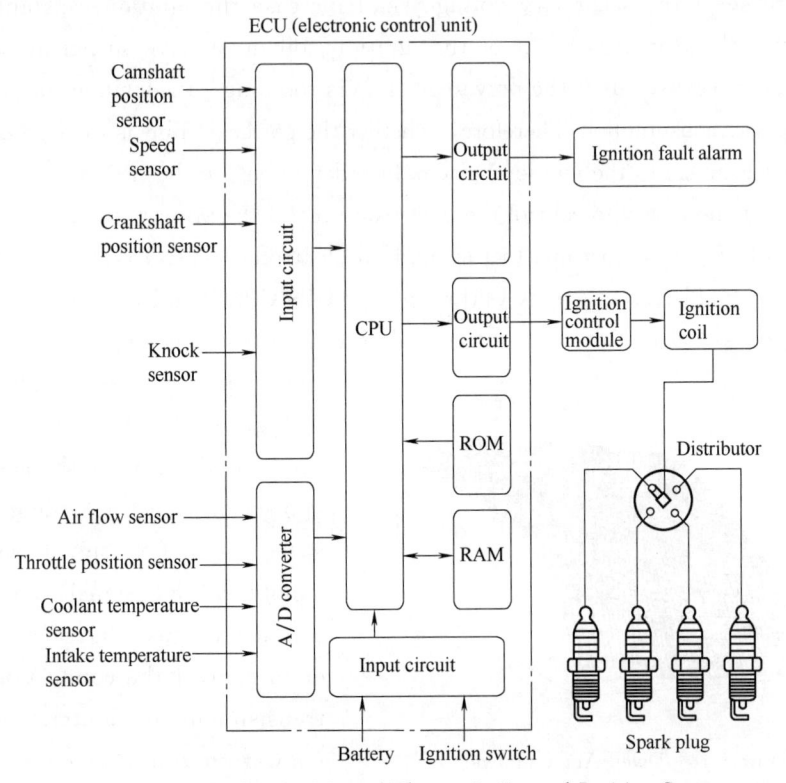

Figure 3-15　Basic Composition of Electronic Control Ignition System

(1) Necessity of ignition advance angle control

An ignition advance angle is required for any working condition of the engine. The best ignition advance angle is the premise to improve the power, fuel economy and emission of the engine. When the ignition advance angle is too large, the maximum pressure in the cylinder shall rise with great tendency of detonation. When the ignition advance angle is small, the maximum combustion pressure and temperature shall decrease, causing the increase of the heat transfer loss and the exhaust temperature. Therefore, in order to ensure the best ignition angle for every working condition of the engine, that is, when the maximum pressure appears at the crankshaft angle of $10°\sim15°$ after the TDC, the ignition must be realized by electronic control.

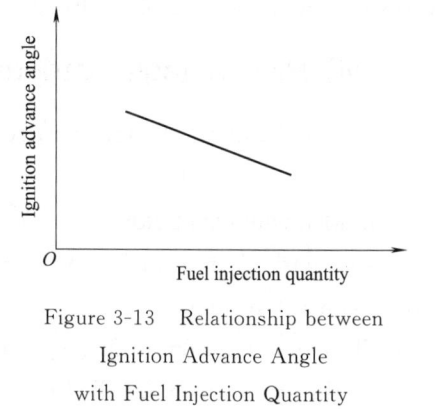

Figure 3-13　Relationship between Ignition Advance Angle with Fuel Injection Quantity

(2) Necessity of conduction angle control

① Necessity of power-on time control. When the primary circuit of the ignition coil is connected, the primary current increases exponentially, with the length of energizing time determining the magnitude of the primary current. When the primary current reaches saturation, the primary current shall reach the maximum (that is, the breaking current) if the primary circuit is disconnected which shall result in the maximum of the secondary voltage. The increase of the secondary voltage shall increase the ignition capability of the low spark plug, so the primary circuit of the ignition coil must have sufficient power-on time when the engine works. But if the power-on time is too long, the ignition coil will heat up and increase the power consumption. Therefore, whether the power-on time is too long or too short, it shall bring disadvantage to the ignition system. In order to ensure the working performance of the ignition coil, it is necessary to control the power-on time of the primary circuit.

② Control of power-on time. In the modern electronic control ignition system, the engine working signal is fed to the ECU through the CIS/CPS. The ECU controls the power-on time of the primary circuit of the ignition coil according to the dwell angle (power-on time) control model stored inside it, as shown in Figure 3-14. When the engine works, the ECU determines the best dwell angle (power-on time) according to the engine speed signal (Ne signal) and the power supply voltage signal, and outputs the command signal (IGt signal) to the igniter to control the conduction time of the transistor in the igniter. The dwell angle (power-on time) increases with the increase of the engine speed and the de-

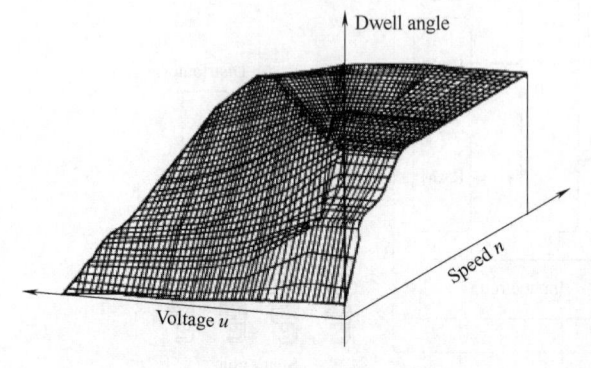

Figure 3-14　Dwell Angle (Power-on Time) Control Model

Item III Maintenance of Electronic Control Ignition System for Gasoline Engine **097**

ture is slow, the possibility of detonation is small. During the heating process, the ignition advance angle should gradually decrease with the increase of coolant temperature, as shown in Figure 3-11 (a) below. When the engine is in partial load operation (such as the IDL of the TPS is disconnected), as shown in Figure 3-11 (c), the coolant temperature is too high. In order to avoid detonation, the ignition advance angle can be delayed. When the engine is in idle condition (such as TPS IDL is connected), the coolant temperature is too high. In order to avoid the engine overheating for a long time, the ignition advance angle should be increased. In this way, it can improve the engine idle speed, and further improve the pump and cooling fan speed, enhance the cooling effect, and reduce the engine temperature. The overheat correction curve is shown in Figure 3-11 (b) .

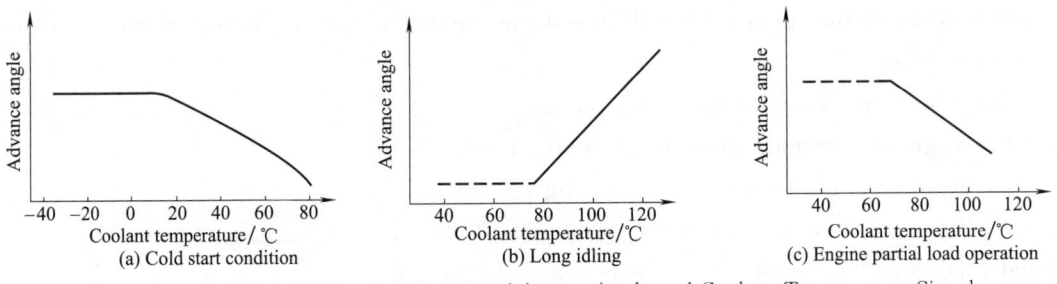

Figure 3-11　Relationship between Ignition Advance Angle and Coolant Temperature Signal

b. Correction of idle speed stability. During idling operation, the engine load varies with the speed. In order to achieve the stable running of the engine at the prescribed idle speed, the ignition advance angle needs to be corrected.

In idling operation, the ECU continuously calculates the average speed of the engine. When the average speed is lower or higher than the specified idle speed, the ECU increases or decreases the ignition advance angle according to the difference between the average speed and the idling target speed and whether the air conditioner is on or off, as shown in Figure 3-12.

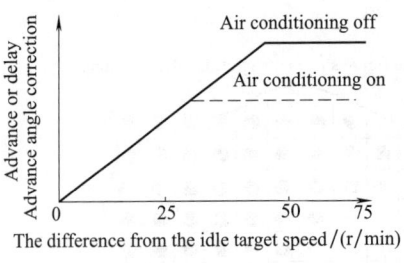

Figure 3-12　Correction of Idling Stability

c. Correction of fuel injection quantity. In an electronic fuel control system equipped with EGO and closed-loop control program, the ECU corrects the air-fuel ratio according to the feedback signal of the EGO. With the increase and decrease of the modified fuel injection quantity, the engine speed shall fluctuate within a fixed range. The mixture becomes thin when the fuel injection quantity decreases, resulting that the engine speed decreases accordingly. In order to improve the stability of idle speed, the ignition advance angle should be increased appropriately, whereas the ignition advance angle should be reduced appropriately, as shown in Figure 3-13.

4. Control process of MCI

The control process of MCI can be divided into two kinds: ignition advance angle control and ignition conduction angle control.

096 Fault Diagnosis and Repair of Automobile Engine Electronic Control System

the ignition advance angle according to the speed signal and the starting switch signal, taking the initial ignition advance angle (set value) stored in memory as reference which is about 10° before the TDC (depending on the engine type).

(2) Control of ignition advance angle after starting

The ignition advance angle after starting is composed of the basic ignition advance angle and the correction angle (or correction coefficient).

① Basic ignition advance angle

The data of the best basic ignition advance angle of the engine is stored in the memory of the ECU. When the engine is running, the ECU checks the corresponding basic ignition advance angle in the memory according to the input signals of various sensors.

According to the operating conditions of the engine, the basic ignition advance angle can be divided into:

Basic ignition advance angle at idle speed;

Basic ignition advance angle during normal operation.

Determination of the basic advance angle at idle speed: It is determined by ECU according to TPS signal (IDL signal), engine speed sensor signal (Ne signal) and air conditioning switch signal (A/C signal), as shown in Figure 3-9.

Basic angle under other working conditions: It is determined by ECU according to the engine speed and load compared with the basic ignition advance angle control model stored in the memory, as shown in Figure 3-10.

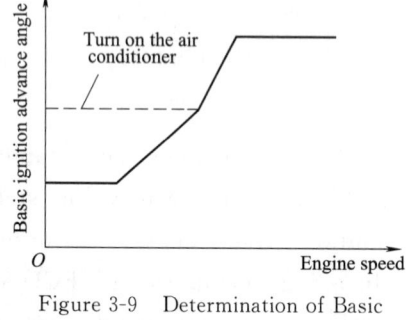

Figure 3-9　Determination of Basic Ignition Advance Angle at Idle Speed

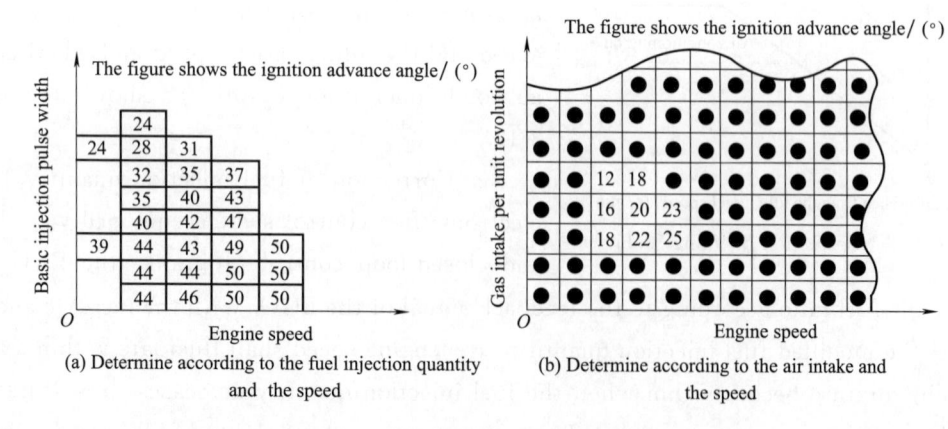

Figure 3-10　Basic Ignition Advance Angle Control Model

② Correction of ignition advance angle

a. Correction of coolant temperature. In order to improve the driving performance of the engine, the ignition advance angle should be increased appropriately after the cold start of the engine, because the temperature of the coolant is low, the combustion speed of the mix-

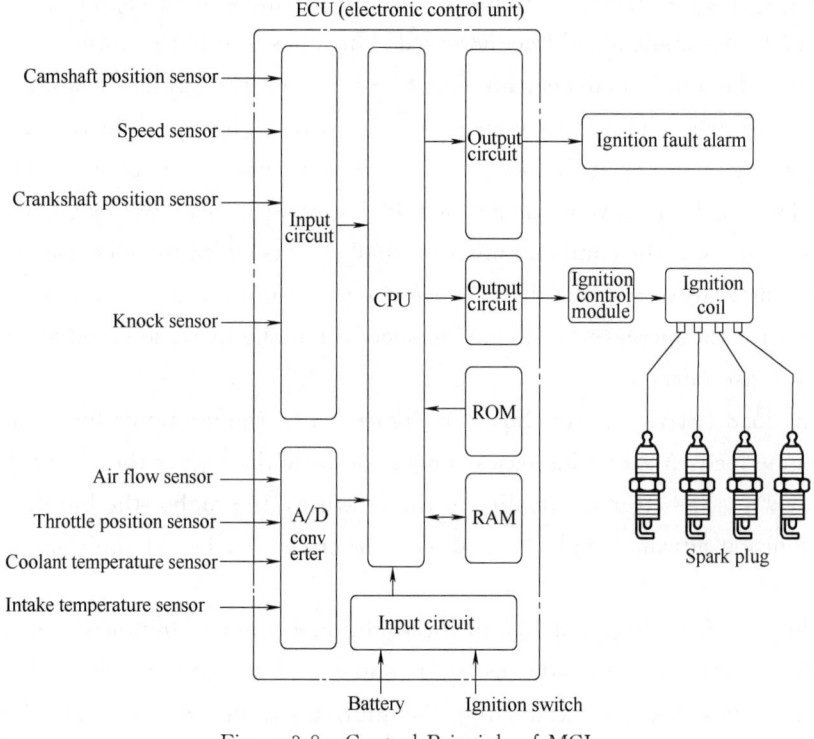

Figure 3-8   Control Principle of MCI

the engine in the normal state. When the engine starts, idles or glides, there are special control program and the control method to control.

3. Determination of ignition advance angle of MCI

Combustion of combustible mixture in the cylinder of gasoline engine is not completed instantaneously. It needs to be induced first, and then it can burn violently and obviously. Therefore, in order for the engine to produce maximum power, the mixture ignition should be appropriately advanced before the TDC of the compression stroke. Generally, the ignition advance angle of the engine with the most power and the least fuel consumption is called the best ignition advance angle. The ignition advance angle directly affects the output power, fuel consumption and emission of the engine. The best ignition advance angle varies with the engine working conditions. The best ignition advance angle at idle speed is to make idle running smoothly, reduce harmful gas emission and fuel consumption; the best ignition advance angle under partial load is to reduce fuel consumption and harmful gas emission, and improve economy and emission performance; the best ignition advance angle under heavy load is to increase the output torque and improve the dynamic performance.

The ignition advance angle controlled by microcomputer consists of three parts: the initial ignition advance angle, the basic ignition advance angle after startup and the modified ignition advance angle.

(1) Control of ignition advance angle at startup

When the engine starts, the ECU can't calculate the ignition advance angle correctly because of the change of the speed, and unstable signals of MAPS or AFS. The ECU controls

① Engine speed. As shown in Figure 3-9, with the increase of engine speed, the optimum ignition advance angle should be increased. The idle speed of the normal car engine is about 800r/min, the ignition advance angle is $6°\sim12°$, and the advance angle can reach 30 ° when the speed is 4000 r/min. This is because when the engine speed increases, the crankshaft turning angle increases at the same time. If the combustion rate of the mixture does not change, the best ignition advance angle should increase linearly. But when the rotational speed continues to rise, the combustion speed shall increase with the increase of the mixture pressure and temperature and the disturbance flow. So the optimum ignition advance angle shall increase with the increase of the engine speed, but the increase speed shall slow down rather than increase linearly.

② Engine load (MAPS). As shown in Figure 3-10, the ignition advance angle decreases as the engine load (MAPS) increases. This is because the higher the MAPS (small vacuum, heavy load), the better the quality of the mixture, the higher the burning speed, the smaller the ignition advance angle is required; otherwise, a bigger ignition advance angle shall be required.

As can be seen from Figure 3-10, in the traditional contact ignition system, the difference between the actual ignition advance angle and the ideal one is much big because of the mechanical centrifugal regulator (adjusting the ignition advance with the speed) and the vacuum advance regulator (adjusting the ignition advance with the load) . In the MCI, the actual ignition advance angle is very close to the ideal one.

2. Principles of MCI

The control principle of the MCI is shown in Figure 3-8. The CPS provides the ECU with engine speed used for the calculation and determination of the ignition advance angle, crankshaft angle signal used for the control of the ignition time (ignition advance angle) . AFS and TPS provide engine load signal to ECU for calculating and determining ignition advance angle. Signals from CTS, IATS, VSS, A/C and EDS are used to correct the ignition advance angle.

When the engine works, the CPU collects the engine's working condition information into the RAM through the above sensors, and continuously detects the CIS signal to determine which cylinder is about to reach the compression TDC. When the signal is received, the CPU immediately begins to calculate the crank angle signal to control the ignition advance angle. At the same time, according to the speed signal, load signal and other sensor signals related to the ignition advance angle, the CPU can get the best ignition advance angle information from the ROM. During this time, CPU keeps counting the crank angle signal to determine whether the ignition time is coming. When the crank angle is equal to the optimum ignition advance angle, the CPU shall immediately send the control instruction to the ignition control module, so that the power triode is cut off, the ignition coil primary current is cut off, and the secondary winding produces high voltage distributed to each cylinder spark plug according to the ignition sequence of the engine to ignite the combustible mixture.

The above-mentioned control process refers to the control process of the ignition time of

4. Ignition control module

The ignition control module, also known as the ignition electronic assembly or igniter, is the power output stage of the MCI, which receives the ignition control signal from the ECU and amplifies the power to drive the ignition coil.

The circuit, function and structure of the ignition control module vary with the models, some made on the same circuit board with ECU, some connected with ECU by wire harness and connector with independent assemble, some equipped with a large area of radiation for cooling with ignition control module and ignition coil installed together.

The structure principle of ignition coil, spark plug and distributor used in MCI is basically the same as that of common electronic ignition system.

(Ⅴ) Control Process of MCI

1. Ignition advance angle and its influencing factors

(1) Definition of ignition advance angle and its influence

Ignition advance angle refers to the angle that the crankshaft turns from the spark plug ignition to the piston to the compression TDC.

Ignition too early (ignition advance angle is too big) will cause detonation, and intake manifold tempering;

Ignition too late (ignition advance angle is too small) will cause the decline performance of the engine performance decline, and the blowout of the exhaust pipe;

The ideal ignition timing should be to control the ignition timing at a time when the detonation is imminent but not yet occurring.

(2) Optimum ignition advance angle

The angle which makes the engine produce the maximum output power is called the optimum ignition advance angle, and the optimum ignition advance angle can greatly improve the engine's power, fuel economy and emission.

Experiments show that: For the burning mixture in the cylinder, when the maximum combustion pressure appears at the crank angle of $4°\sim12°$ after the TDC, the output power of the engine is maximum. The relationship between cylinder pressure and ignition time is shown in Figure 3-8. Figure A is the pressure waveform of the mixture in the cylinder when it is not burning. It is characterized by the bilateral symmetry of the ignition timing with TDC as the center. B, C and D are the combustion pressure waveforms that change the ignition time respectively. Ignition at C: maximum combustion, largest work by pressure and maximum output power (area of shaded part). Ignition at B: maximum combustion and highest pressure, with detonation seen from the diagram. Ignition at D: maximum combustion, minimum pressure and least work.

(3) Factors affecting the ignition advance angle.

The ignition should take place at the optimum ignition advance angle. Factors affecting the optimal ignition advance angle are as follows: engine speed, engine load, and fuel octane number.

（3）Resonant piezoelectric EDS

This type of EDS uses the vibration frequency of the engine when the detonation occurs to match the natural frequency of the sensor itself, producing resonance to detect whether the detonation occurs. The output voltage of the sensor with detonation is much higher than that without detonation, so it is unnecessary to use

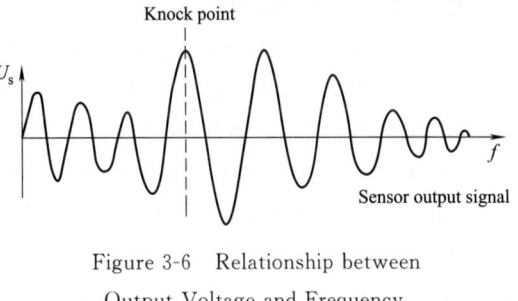

Figure 3-6　Relationship between Output Voltage and Frequency

filter to distinguish whether or not detonation occurs. Figure 3-7shows the structure of a resonant piezoelectric EDS, with the piezoelectric element tightly attached to the oscillating plate. The oscillating plate is fixed on the base of the sensor. The oscillating plate oscillates with the vibration of the engine, which deforms the piezoelectric element to produce a voltage signal. When the vibration frequency of the engine detonation is consistent with the natural frequency of the oscillating plate, the oscillating plate shall resonate, and the piezoelectric element shall produce the maximum voltage signal.

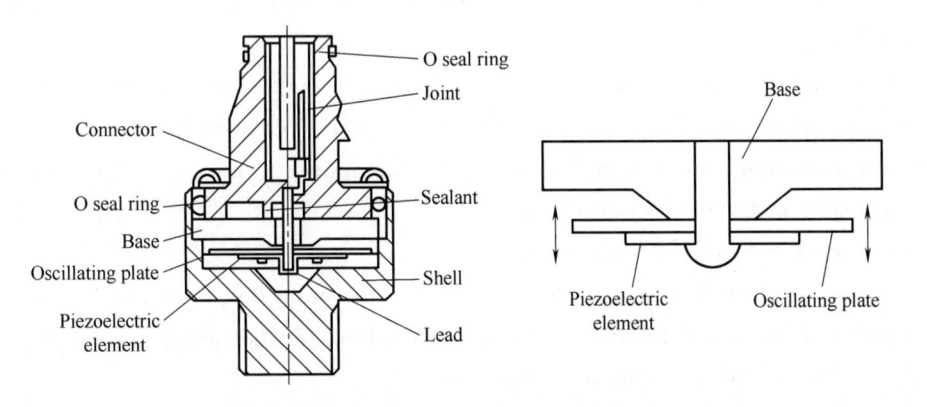

Figure 3-7　Piezoelectric Resonance EDS

3. ECU

Most of modern automobile engine adopt centralized control system, MCI is its subsystem, ECU is not only the control core of fuel injection control system, but also the control core of ignition control system. ECU ROM stores not only the monitoring and self-checking procedures, but also the best ignition advance angle of the engine under various working conditions determined by bench test. RAM is used to store the data that needs to be stored temporarily when the microcomputer works, such as input/output data, the result of single-chip microcomputer operation, fault code, ignition advance angle correction data, etc. These data can be called out at any time or rewritten by new data as needed. The CPU continuously receives the signals from the above-mentioned sensors, calculates and judges them according to the pre-programmed program, and sends the control signal to the ignition control module to switch on and off the primary circuit of the ignition coil.

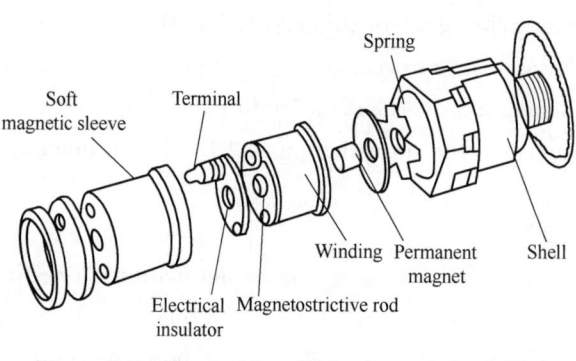

Figure 3-4   Composition of Magnetostrictive EDS

The non-resonant piezoelectric EDS determine whether or not the detonation occurs by receiving acceleration signal. The sensor structure is shown in Figure 3-5.

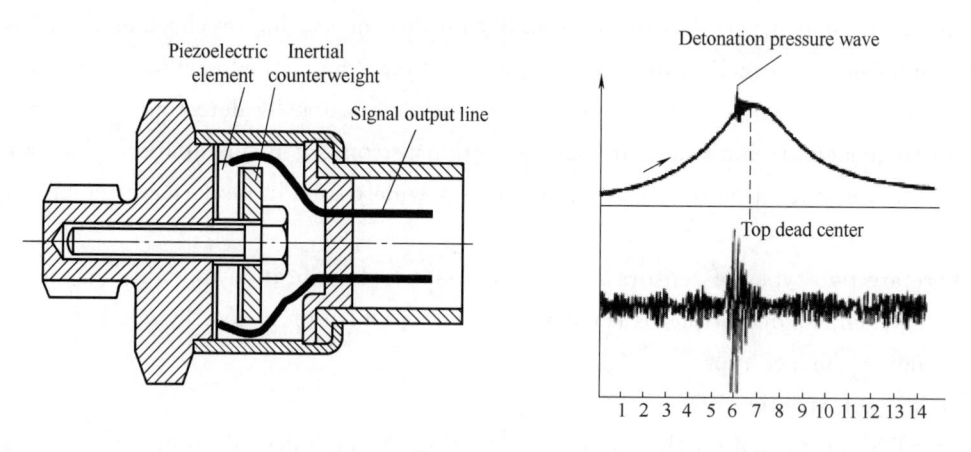

Figure 3-5   Non-resonant Piezoelectric EDS

It is connected by two piezoelectric elements in same polar direction, with the counterweight fixed on the shell with one screw. It converts the acceleration into the pressure acting on the piezoelectric element, and the output voltage comes from the center of the two piezoelectric elements. The sensor is simple in construction and does not need to be adjusted during manufacture.

When the engine vibrates, the internal counterweight of the EDS installed on the engine cylinder shall generate a acceleration due to the affection by the vibration. Therefore, the voltage signal will be produced on the piezoelectric element by the action of the inertial force during the acceleration. Unlike the magnetostrictive EDS, which produces a higher output voltage near the detonation frequency to determine the generation of the detonation, the sensor has a flat output characteristic, which is shown in Figure 3-6 as the relationship between the output voltage and the frequency of the non-resonant piezoelectric EDS. Therefore, it is necessary to send the output voltage signal of the vibration frequency of the reaction engine to the filter which can identify and determine whether there is a detonation signal. The sensor's sensing frequency range is designed from 0 to 10 kilohertz to detect the vibration frequency of an engine with a very wide band.

mission. ECU uses the switch signal to judge whether the engine is in stop state or in the running state, and then makes the necessary correction to the ignition advance angle.

The structure principle and overhaul method of the sensor and switch signal mentioned above have been introduced in the introduction of EFI. The following mainly introduces the knowledge of DS.

2. Application of EDS

There are three methods for detecting engine detonation: The first one is to detect the pressure change of the engine combustor; the second one is to detect the vibration frequency of the engine cylinder; the third one is to detect the noise of the mixture combustion. The detection accuracy is high by directly detecting the pressure change of combustor to measure engine vibration, but the installation of the sensor is complex. The sensor has poor durability and usually used for measuring instrument. The detection mixture combustion noise is contactless. The sensor used has good durability but low measuring precision and sensitivity, and is seldom used in practice. In practical applications, The applied pressure sensor detects the pressure indirectly. The advantages of detecting detonation by detecting engine cylinder vibration frequency are high measurement sensitivity, convenient installation of sensor and large variation of output voltage, so this method is widely used in modern automobile industry.

There are two types of sensors to detect detonation by vibration method: magnetostrictive type and semiconductor piezoelectric type, among which piezoelectric type has resonance type and non-resonance type.

(1) Magnetostrictive EDS

The EDS is mounted on the engine, converting the engine's vibration frequency into a voltage signal, and then sending to the ECU to measure the detonation intensity. When the detonation intensity of the engine is the same as the set value, the EDS shall output the maximum voltage signal to indicate the abnormal vibration frequency of the engine due to the detonation. Figure 3-3 and Figure 3-4 show the shape and structure of an earlier magnetostrictive EDS with a permanent magnet, a strong magnetic core excited by a permanent magnet, and a coil around the core. Its working principle is: When the cylinder body of the engine vibrates,

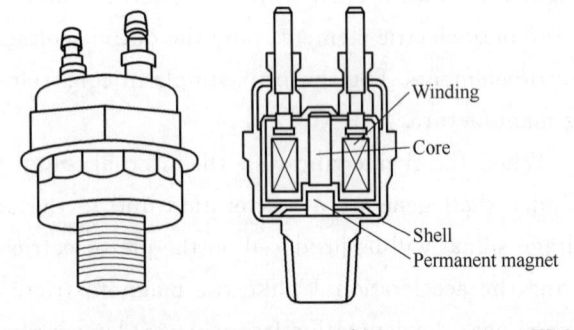

Figure 3-3 Shape and Structure of Magnetostrictive EDS

the sensor resonates with the engine at about 7kHz, and the magnetic conductivity of the core of the strong magnetic material changes. That causes the flux density of the permanent magnet to change, so that the induced electromotive force is generated in the winding around the core, and the electrical signal is fed into the ECU.

(2) Non-resonant piezoelectric EDS

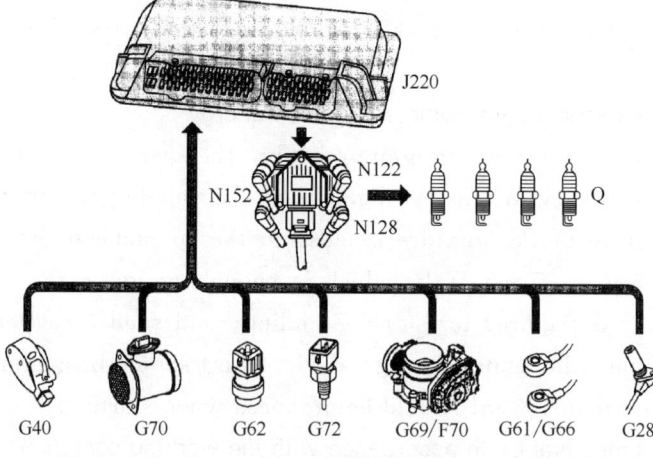

Figure 3-2   Composition of MCI for Santana 2000 GSi

shaft angle signal to calculate the specific position of the crankshaft at any time.

The CPS converts the angle of the engine crankshaft into the electrical signal and inputs ECU. The crankshaft sends out a pulse signal when it rotates a certain angle. The ECU can calculate the angle of the crankshaft by continuously detecting the number of pulses. At the same time, the ECU can calculate the engine speed according to the number of pulses received per unit time. In MCI, the engine crankshaft angle signal is used to calculate the specific ignition time, and the speed signal is used to calculate and read the basic ignition advance angle. Camshaft position and crankshaft position signal are the most basic signals to ensure the normal operation of electronic ignition system controlled by ECU.

AFS is used to determine the quantity of the air intake. In the L-type (flow type) EFI, the flow sensor is used to directly detect the air flow. In the D-type (pressure type) EFI, MAPS is used to indirectly detect the air flow by detecting the negative pressure (vacuum degree) in the rear intake manifold of the throttle. When the air flow signal is input into ECU, it is used to calculate the basic fuel injection time as well as to calculate and determine the basic ignition advance angle as the load signal.

The IATS signal reflects the temperature of the intake air of the engine. In MCI, ECU uses this signal to modify the basic ignition advance angle.

The CTS signal reflects the working temperature of the engine. In MCI, ECU not only uses this signal to correct the basic ignition advance angle, but also to control start-up and the ignition advance angle during the engine is warming up.

TPS converts throttle opening angle to electric signal input ECU. ECU uses this signal and speed sensor signal to synthetically judge engine operating condition (idle speed, medium load, heavy load, deceleration), and to correct ignition advance angle.

Various switching signals are used to correct the ignition advance angle. The start-up switch signal is used to correct the ignition advance angle when start-up; the air-conditioning switch signal is used to correct the ignition advance angle when using the air-conditioning under idle condition; the neutral safety switch is only used in the automobile with auto trans-

gine is running normally, and 19 kV when starting a cold engine. In order to achieve the reliable engine ignition under different working conditions, the spark plug breakdown voltage should be 15～20 kV.

2. Electric sparks should have sufficient ignition energy

In order to ensure the mixture to ignite reliably, the spark produced by the spark plug should have a certain energy. When the engine works normally, the spark energy is small because the temperature of the mixture is close to the spontaneous combustion temperature. The spark energy is 15～50 mJ, which is enough to ignite the mixture. However, higher ignition energy is required for starting, idling, and sudden acceleration. In order to ensure reliable ignition, the ignition energy of 50～80 mJ should be guaranteed, and the ignition energy of more than 100 mJ should be produced when starting.

3. The ignition time shall be in accordance with the working conditions of the engine

First, the ignition time of the engine should meet the requirements of the working cycle of the engine; secondly, it takes a certain time (several thousandths of a second) for the combustible mixture to burn completely in the cylinder after igniting. Therefore, in order to produce the maximum power of the engine, the ignition should not be at the end of the compression stroke (TDC), but should be appropriately advanced by an angle. In this way, by the time the piston reaches the TDC, the mixture is close to full combustion, and the engine can produce maximum power.

4. It should be extremely durable

The ignition system must be very reliable in order to withstand the vibration, high temperature and high voltage of the engine itself.

(Ⅳ) Structure of MCI

The MCI is mainly composed of camshaft position sensor (CIS), crankshaft position sensor (CPS), air flow sensor (AFS), throttle position sensor (TPS), coolant temperature sensor (CTS), intake air temperature sensor (IATS), vehicle speed sensor (VSS), engine detonation sensor (EDS), various control switches, ECU, ignition control module, ignition coil and spark plug. The composition of the MCI for Santana 2000 GSi and 3000 is shown in Figure 3-2.

1. Sensors and switch signals

Sensors are used to detect engine work and status related to ignition and input the test results into ECU as a basis for calculating and controlling ignition time. Although the type, quantity, structure and installation position of the sensors used in each type of vehicle are different, their functions are much the same, and most of these sensors are shared with EFI, idle speed control system and so on.

The CIS is used to determine the crankshaft reference position and ignition reference. The sensor outputs a pulse signal when the crankshaft rotates to a specific position (such as a certain angle before the compression TDC of cylinder 1). The ECU uses the pulse signal as a reference signal to calculate the crankshaft position, and uses the crank-

tions and operating conditions of the engine. For this purpose, the ignition system shall meet the following basic requirements.

1. It can generate enough voltage to breakdown the gap between the two electrodes of a spark plug

The voltage that can breakdown the gap between the two electrodes of a spark plug and produce an electric spark, is called the spark plug breakdown voltage. The breakdown voltage of spark plug is related to the distance between the center electrode and the side electrode (spark plug gap), the pressure and temperature in the cylinder, the temperature of the electrode and the working condition of the engine. The spark plug electrode schematic diagram is shown in Figure 3-1.

The greater the electrode gap, the greater the distance between electrons and ions in the gas around the electrode, the less the effect of electric field force, and the less likely the collision ionization, so a higher breakdown voltage is required to ignite.

The higher the pressure or the lower the temperature in the cylinder, the higher the density of the combustible mixture in the cylinder, the more gas molecules per unit volume, the smaller the free movement distance of the ions, and the less likely the collision ionization will occur. Only by increasing the voltage added to the electrode, increasing the electric field force on the ion, and accelerating the motion of

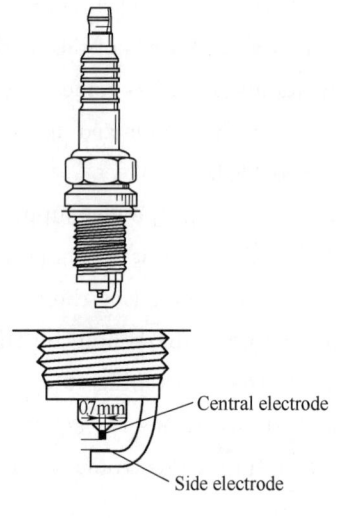

Figure 3-1　Schematic Diagram of Spark Plug Electrode

the ion, can occur collisional ionization between the ions, and the spark plug electrode gap be broke down. Therefore, the greater the pressure or the lower the temperature in the cylinder, the higher the required spark plug breakdown voltage.

The electrode temperature also affects the spark plug breakdown voltage. The higher the temperature of the electrode, the lower the density of the gas surrounding the electrode, the easier the collision ionization, and the lower the spark plug breakdown voltage. It has been proved that the breakdown voltage can be reduced by $30\% \sim 50\%$ when the electrode temperature of spark plug exceeds the temperature of mixture.

The breakdown voltage of spark plug varies with engine speed, load, compression ratio, ignition advance angle and mixture concentration.

The breakdown voltage at start-up is the highest, because the electrode of cylinder wall, piston and spark plug are in cold state, the temperature of inhaled mixture is low, and the atomization is bad. When compressed, the temperature of the mixture does not increase much, and the spark plug electrode may contain gasoline or oil, so the breakdown voltage is the highest, in addition, when the car accelerates, because a large amount of cold mixture is suddenly inhaled into the cylinder, it also needs a higher voltage.

The test results show that the breakdown voltage of spark plug is $7 \sim 8$ kV when the en-

(Ⅱ) Classification of gasoline engine ignition system

The engine ignition system can be divided into traditional ignition system, electronic ignition system, MCI and magneto-motor ignition system according to its composition and different ways of producing high voltage.

The traditional ignition system uses the battery and generator as the power supply. With the help of the ignition coil and the breaker, the low-voltage direct current of 6V, 12V or 24V supplied by the power supply is converted into high-voltage distributed to each cylinder spark plug by the distributor, so as to generate spark between the two electrodes of the spark plug to ignite the combustible gas mixture. The traditional battery ignition system has some disadvantages, such as low voltage, unreliable operation at high speed, frequent inspection and maintenance. At present, it has been replaced by electronic ignition system and MCI.

The electronic ignition system taking a battery and a generator as the power supply, with the help of the ignition coil and the ignition control module composed of semiconductor device (bipolar junction transistor), convert the low-voltage electricity supplied by the power supply into a high-voltage, which shall be distributed to each cylinder spark plug by the distributor to produce electric spark between the two electrodes of the spark plug to ignite the combustible mixture. Compared with the traditional ignition system, it has the advantages of reliable ignition and ease of use. But with the development of engine electronic control technology, it has been replaced by MCI in recent years.

The MCI is the same as the above two ignition systems, taking the battery and generator as the power source. By means of the ignition coil, the low voltage of the power supply is changed into high voltage. Then the distributor distributes the high voltage to each cylinder spark plug. According to the information of the engine working conditions provided by various sensors, the microcomputer control system sends out the ignition control signal to control the ignition time and ignites the combustible mixture. It can also cancel the distributor. The microcomputer control system directly distribute the high-voltage to each cylinder. MCI is the latest type of ignition system, which has been widely used in all kinds of automobiles.

Magnetic motor ignition system produces high voltage directly by the magnetic motor itself, so there is no need to set another low-voltage power supply. It is mainly used for racing engines working at high speed and full load.

The abbreviation for microcomputer control ignition system is MCI. The ignition advance angle can be controlled at the optimum value by MCI, and the temperature and pressure of combustible mixture after combustion can reach the maximum value, so as to improve the engine's power. At the same time, it can improve the fuel economy and reduce the emission of harmful gases.

(Ⅲ) Basic requirements for ignition systems

The ignition system shall ensure reliable and accurate ignition under all working condi-

Item III

Maintenance of Electronic Control Ignition System for Gasoline Engine

I. Introduction of Item Scene

For gasoline engine, the performance of engine not only depends on the control of fuel, but also the ignition. In all gasoline engine systems, the ignition system has the greatest influence on the performance of engine. Statistics show that nearly one-half of the faults are caused by the poor operation of electric system, so the detection of the engine performance often starts from the ignition system. First of all, the ignition system adopts most advanced electronic technology, and the structure and working principle are updated timely. The structure principle of the current ignition system is different from the old one, and the wiring is different when detecting, so it should be treated differently.

II. Item Related Knowledge

(I) Function of ignition system of gasoline engine

The working cycle of automobile engine is composed of intake, compression, work and exhaust. Although at the end of compression, the mixture temperature in the cylinder is very high, it can't burn in the same way as that of diesel engine because of the high ignition point. Therefore, it must be ignited by open fire. The gasoline engine uses high-voltage electric spark to ignite the mixture.

In order to produce a high-voltage electric spark in the cylinder at regular intervals, the gasoline engine is equipped with a special ignition device called engine ignition system. The basic function of the ignition system is to spark the spark plug to ignite the fuel mixture in the cylinder. In order to ignite the compressed fuel mixture, the instantaneous ignition voltage of the spark plug must be above $2000\,V$, but the battery voltage of the automobile is only $12\sim14\,V$. So the ignition system must convert the primary voltage of $12\sim14\,V$ to the secondary high voltage above $2000\,V$ (some new ignition system can even produce a secondary voltage of up to $100,\ 000\ V$), and distribute the high voltage to the spark plug of each cylinder according to the ignition sequence of the cylinder. As such, it can ignite.

tric fuel pump, as well as the testing method of all the components. Students should master the testing method, steps and matters needing attention of all the components, and be able to correctly judge the fault. At the same time, students should master the principle of electronic control system fuel control, and be familiar with the influence of all sensors, actuators on the normal operation of electronic control fuel feed system.

Exercises and Thinking

1. Structure and working principle of automobile ECU.

2. What are the main notices for the maintenance of the power circuit of the automobile ECU?

3. What are the three components of the power supply circuit of the automobile ECU?

4. Describe the control principle of the EFI.

5. What is the function of an electric fuel pump?

6. Electric fuel pump can be divided into several kinds according to the installation position. What are the advantages and disadvantages?

7. How many types of structures that the electric fuel pumps can be divided?

8. How to detect an electric fuel pump?

9. How many types of injector can be divided according to the resistance value? What is the constant resistance value?

10. What is the driving mode of the injector?

11. Are engine start-up difficulty, idling instability or poor acceleration, and poor power performance related to the injector? Why?

12. How to detect the injector?

13. What is an open-loop control system? What is a closed-loop control system?

14. What is the working principle of the hot film AFS?

15. What are the detection contents of the DS?

pump power supply line through the fuel pump relay so as to control the working speed of the fuel pump. Figure 2-75 shows the fuel pump control circuit of the Japanese Toyota Lexus LS400 sedan.

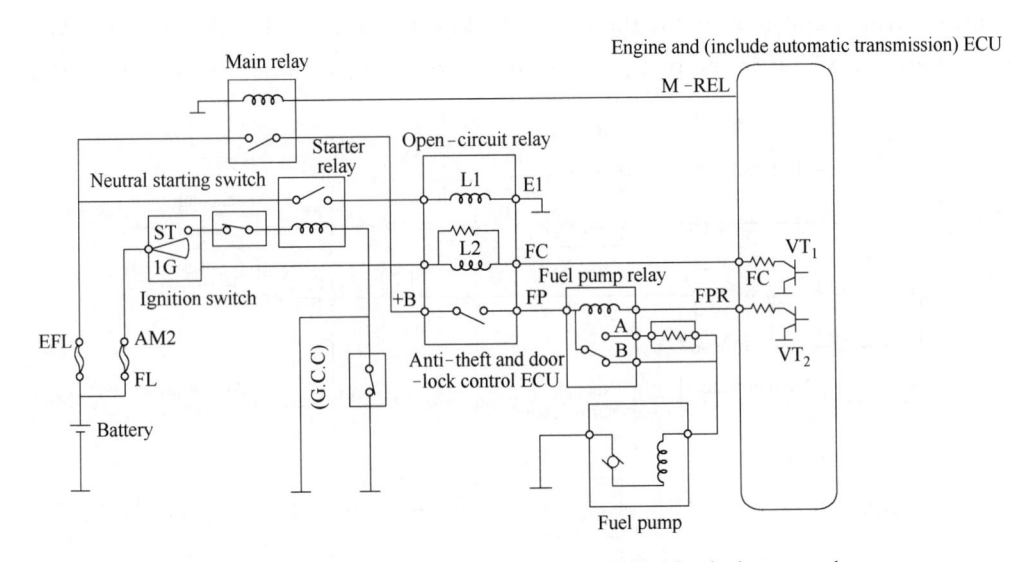

Figure 2-75　Fuel pump control circuit controlled by fuel pump relay

It is basically the same as that of Lexus ES300. After the ignition switch is turned on, the terminal $+B$ of the open-circuit relay is connected with the power supply through the main relay. The coil L1 in the open-circuit relay is energized when starting. When the engine is running normally, the transistor VT1 in the ECU is switched on and the coil L2 in the open-circuit relay is energized. The open-circuit relay contacts are closed. The Terminal FP of the oil pump relay is connected with the power supply. As such, the fuel pump shall work. After the engine is extinguished, the transistor VT1 in the ECU is cut off, and the coil L1 and coil L2 in the open-circuit relay are not energized. The switch disconnects the fuel pump circuit. As such, the fuel pump shall stop working.

Engine ECU controls oil pump relay. When the engine works at low speed and under small load, the transistor VT2 in the ECU is switched on, and the fuel pump relay coil is energized, making contact A closed. The resistance is connected in series to the fuel pump circuit, so the voltage of the fuel pump is lower than the battery voltage. As such, the fuel pump shall run at low speed. When the engine works at high speed and under heavy load, the transistor in the ECU is cut off, the fuel pump relay contact B is closed, the battery voltage is transmitted directly to the fuel pump. As such, the fuel pump shall run at high speed.

Summary

This item mainly introduces the function, classification and working principle of each sensor in the electronic control system, and the structure and working principle of the main actuators in the electronic control system, such as the electromagnetic injector and the elec-

responding terminal on the diagnosis seat for fuel pump inspection.

(Ⅱ) Fuel pump control circuit controlled by fuel pump switch

This control circuit is used for the L-type EFI system equipped with vane-type AFS. As shown in Figure 2-74, it is the fuel pump control circuit of Japanese Toyota Lexus ES300.

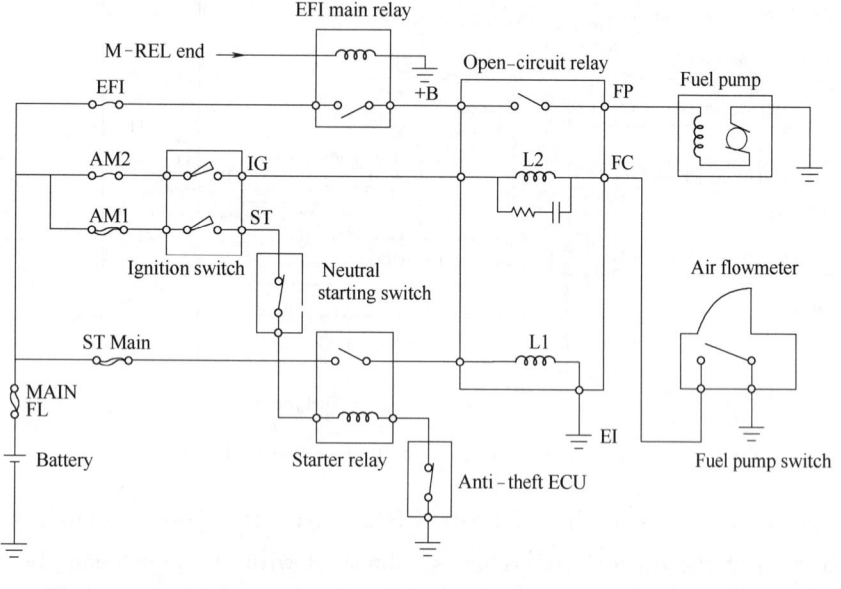

Figure 2-74　Fuel Pump Control Circuit Controlled by Fuel Pump Switch

When the engine starts, the ignition switch terminal ST is connected with the power supply, the starter relay coil is energized to make its contact close. The battery supplies power to the coil L1 in the open-circuit relay through the starter relay to make its contact close, thus supplying power to the fuel pump through the main relay and the open-circuit relay. As such, the fuel pump shall work. When the engine is running normally after starting, the ignition switch is in the ignition position. The terminal IG of the ignition switch is connected with the power supply. At the same time, the measuring board in the AFS rotates so that the fuel pump switch is closed. The coil L2 in the open circuit relay is energized, keeping the open circuit relay contact closed. As such, the fuel pump shall continue to work. During the operation of the engine, the fuel pump keeps working. However when the engine stops, the fuel pump switch in the AFS shall be disconnected, the coil L1 and L2 in the open-circuit relay are not energized, the switch is disconnected with the fuel pump circuit. As such, the fuel pump shall stop working.

The RC circuit in the open-circuit relay can prolong the operation of the electric fuel pump for 2~3s to maintain the a certain residual pressure in the fuel system when the engine is turned off.

(Ⅲ) Fuel pump control circuit controlled by fuel pump relay

According to the change of engine speed and load, the control circuit can change the fuel

outlet valve, fuel pressure regulator return valve or injector are not completely sealed.

⑧ After the detection, the system pressure should be released, the oil pressure gauge should be removed and the fuel system reinstalled. Then, preset the fuel system pressure and start the engine to check for no leakage.

(Ⅲ) Notice

① Sensors are precision electronic devices that need to be held lightly to prevent AFS from falling on the ground and damaging internal circuits and components.

② When testing the sensor with test equipment, pay attention to the operation flow and the corresponding test port.

③ The oil pressure of the system must be released before removing and testing the components of the fuel feed system.

Ⅳ. Knowledge and Skills Expansion

Fuel pump control circuits used in different models are also different, but they are mainly divided into the following three types:

(Ⅰ) Fuel pump control circuit controlled by ECU

This control circuit is mainly used in D-type EFI and D-type EFI equipped with the thermal or Karman vortex AFS. As shown in Figure 2-73, it is the fuel pump control circuit of Japan Toyota Crown 3. 0 sedan.

Battery power enters ECU terminal +B through the main fuse, 20A fuse, the main relay. Fuel pump controls ECU supply power to fuel pump through Terminal FP. Fuel pump controls ECU according to the signal of engine ECU terminal FPC and DI, and controls the connected circuit between terminal + B and terminal FP to change the voltage delivered to fuel pump, so as to control the fuel pump speed. When the engine works at high speed and under heavy load, the FPC terminal of the engine ECU sends instructions to the fuel pump ECU, so that the terminal FP provides 12V battery voltage to the fuel pump, and the fuel pump shall run at high speed. When the engine works at low speed and under small load, the terminal DI of the engine ECU sends instructions to the fuel pump ECU, so that the Terminal FP provides a lower voltage to the fuel pump (normally 9V), and the fuel pump shall run at low speed.

The power supply terminal + B of ECU and fuel pump control terminal FP are respectively connected with the cor-

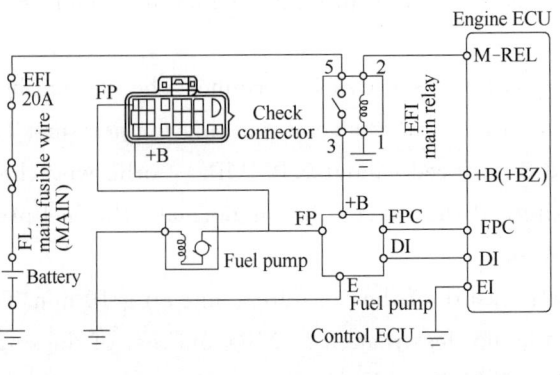

Figure 2-73   Fuel Pump Control
Circuit Controlled by ECU

test results. Special oil pressure gauges and pipe fittings are required for testing. The test methods are as follows:

① Check that the fuel in the tank should be sufficient to release the fuel system pressure.

② Check that the battery voltage should be at 12V (the voltage directly affects the fuel supply pressure of the fuel pump). Remove the negative cable.

③ Connect the special pressure gauge to the fuel feed system, as shown in Figure 2-72.

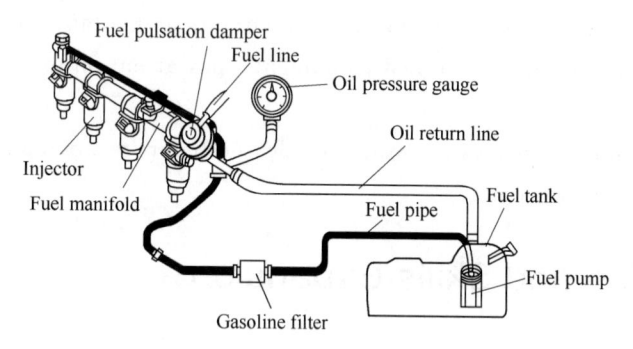

Figure 2-72   Test of Oil Pressure of Fuel feed system

④ Connect the negative cable and start the engine to keep it idly running.

⑤ Remove the vacuum hose on the fuel pressure regulator, block one side of the inlet pipe with hand, check the pressure indicated by the oil pressure gauge. The value of the multi-point injection system should be 0.25~0.35 MPa, and that of the single point injection system should be 0.07~0.10 MPa.

If the fuel system pressure is too low, clip the return oil hose to cut off the return oil line, and then check the oil pressure gauge. If the pressure returns to normal, it indicates that the fuel pressure regulator has a fault and should be replaced; if the pressure is still too low, check whether the fuel system has leakage, whether the fuel pump filter mesh, the fuel filter and oil pipe are blocked; if there is no leakage and blockage, the fuel pump should replaced.

If the oil pressure gauge indicates that the pressure is too high, check if the oil return line is blocked; if the oil return line is normal, the fuel pressure regulator should be replaced.

⑥ If the fuel system pressure is in line with the standard, re-connect the vacuum hose of the fuel pressure regulator after the engine runs to the normal working temperature. The indication of the fuel pressure gauge should be reduced (about 0.05 MPa), otherwise check whether the vacuum line is blocked or leaking; if the vacuum line is normal, the fuel pressure regulator is faulty and should be replaced.

⑦ Turn off the engine and observe the pressure of the pressure gauge after 10 min. The value of multi-point injection system should be not less than 0.20 MPa and that of the single point injection system should be not less than 0.05 MPa. If the pressure is too low, check if there is any leakage in the fuel system. If there is no leakage, it means that the fuel pump

tor should be replaced.

③ Detection of the injector control circuit. Disconnect the injector wire harness connector, turn on the ignition switch, do not start the engine, and use a multimeter to detect the voltage between the power supply terminal and the ground, which should be 12V (that is, the voltage between the plug terminal 1 and the engine ground). Otherwise, check whether the power supply line, ignition switch, relay or fuse is out of order. The resistance between the negative terminal of each injector plug and the engine ECU injector terminal should be less than 1Ω, as shown in Figure 2-70. For example, the resistance between the Santana 2000 injector terminal 2 and the ECU terminal 73, 80, 58, and 65 should be less than 1Ω, otherwise there is open-circuited.

④ Detection of the fuel injection quantity of injector. The fuel injection quantity and atomization effect per unit time of the single cylinder injector and the uniformity of the fuel injection quantity of each cylinder should be checked, as shown in Figure 2-71.

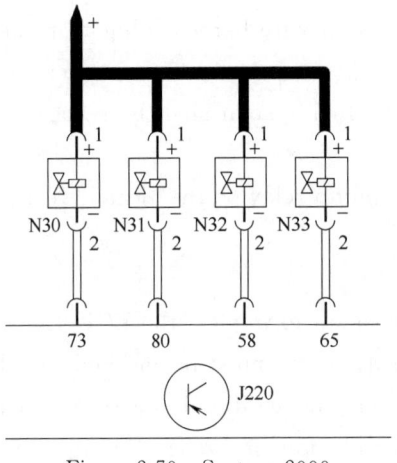

Figure 2-70　Santana 2000
Injector Control Circuit

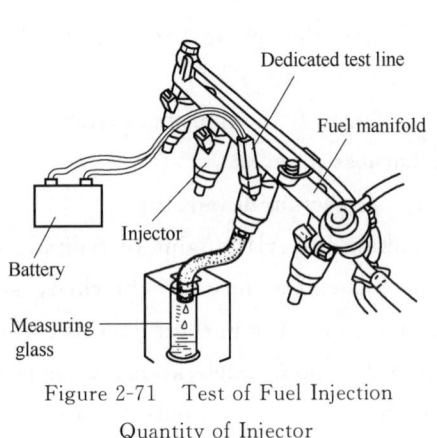

Figure 2-71　Test of Fuel Injection
Quantity of Injector

⑤ Detection of the tightness of the injector. The tightness detection of the injector can be carried out on special equipment. Before testing the fuel injection quantity, power up the fuel pump directly. When the oil pressure reaches the normal value, observe whether the injector drips or not. It can also remove the injector and the oil pipeline from the installation position, and then connect with the fuel system suspended, turn on the ignition switch, power up the fuel pump, and observe whether the injector drips or not. It is required that no more than 1 drop of oil should be dropped from the injector within 2 min, indicating that the injector is well sealed, otherwise the injector should be replaced.

Note: The low-resistance injector cannot be directly connected to the battery but must be connected with an additional resistance of 8~10Ω.

(3) Test the oil pressure of the fuel system

By testing the pressure of the fuel system, it can diagnose whether the fuel system is out of order, and then the nature and location of the fault can be determined according to the

shown in Table 2-2.

Table 2-2 Detection Conditions and Standard Parameters

Water Temperature/℃	Resistance Value/Ω	Water Temperature/℃	Resistance Value/Ω	Water Temperature/℃	Resistance Value/Ω
50	740~900	70	390~480	90	210~270
60	540~650	80	290~360	100	160~200

Although the resistance values of the temperature sensors used in each type of automobile are different, the maintenance methods are basically the same.

2. Maintenance of EFI and actuator

(1) Release the oil pressure of the fuel system

The purpose of releasing the oil pressure of the fuel system is to prevent the hydraulic oil flowing out of the system during disassembly, causing personal injury and fire.

The methods and steps of release are as follows:

① Turn on the ignition switch to make the engine idly run;

② Unplug the oil pump relay or the electric fuel pump wire harness plug to make the engine self-flameout;

③ Start the engine 2~3 times, the pressure of the fuel system shall be released completely;

④ Turn off the ignition switch and plug in the oil pump relay or the electric fuel pump wire harness plug.

(2) Detection of injector

Taking the AJR engine of Santana 2000GSi sedan as an example, the ECU cannot be detected when the injector is blocked, stuck and dripped, and it must be checked and eliminated manually. If a injector does not work, the engine may have difficult start-up, unstable idle speed or poor acceleration, poor power, and other phenomena. When the injector control circuit is open-circuited, the ECU can detect the injector by using the "actuator diagnosis" function of the scan tool to test the fuel injector.

① Diagnosing the operation of the injector in the vehicle. Turn on the ignition switch to make the engine idly run; test the working sound of each cylinder injector with a screwdriver or stethoscope; if the working sound of each cylinder injector is clear and even, it means that all cylinder injector are normal; if you can't hear the working sound of a certain cylinder injector, you should measure the electromagnetic coil resistance of the injector and check the control line of the injector.

② Detection of the resistance of the injector. Remove the injector wire harness plug and measure the resistance between the two terminals of the injector with a multimeter. As shown in Figure 2-69, the low resistance injector should be 2~3Ω, and the high resistance injector should be 13~16Ω. Otherwise, the injec-

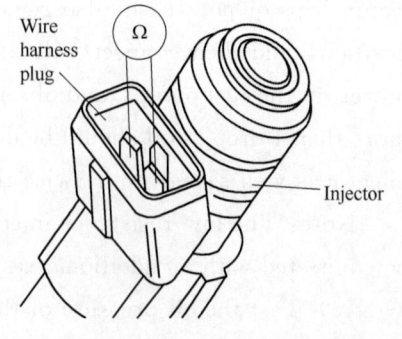

Figure 2-69 Detection of Injector Resistance

② Detection of CTS. CTS signal is used for fuel injection quantity correction, ignition advance angle correction, ACCV control and so on. If the CTS signal is interrupted, it will cause that the engine cold start is difficult, the fuel consumption increases, the Idling Stability reduces, the exhaust gas emission increases and so on. Although the resistance value of the temperature sensor used in each car is different, its maintenance method is basically the same. Figure 2-67 shows the CTS terminal diagram and circuit diagram for the AJR engine of Santana 2000GSi sedan.

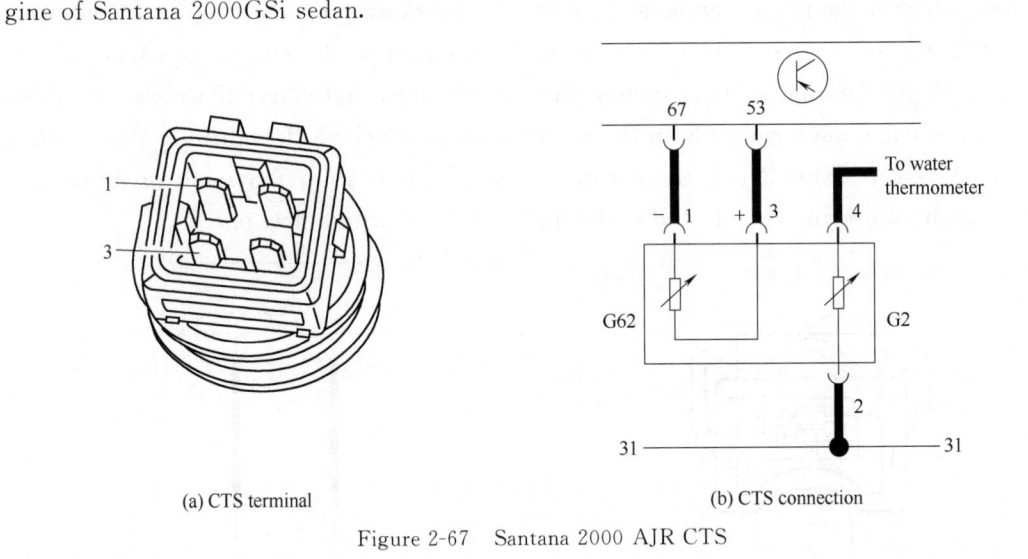

(a) CTS terminal　　　　　　　　　　　　(b) CTS connection

Figure 2-67　Santana 2000 AJR CTS

a. Detection of power supply voltage and signal voltage. When the CTS is overhauled, the power supply voltage and signal voltage of the sensor can be detected by a multimeter. Unplug the CTS plug, turn on the ignition switch, the voltage between the two terminals on the side plug of the sensor ECU should be about 5V. Plug in the sensor plug, turn on the ignition switch, the signal voltage between the two terminals of the sensor plug should be 0.5~3.0V, with the specific resistance value related to the temperature. If the voltage value does not meet the requirements, it means that the sensor is invalid, and it should be replaced.

b. Detection of resistance. The resistance value of the CTS can be detected by the resistance gear of the multimeter. When detecting, turn off the ignition switch, unplug the temperature sensor, remove the temperature sensor, and place the sensor and thermometer in a beaker or a heating container. At different temperatures, the resistance between the two terminals of the sensor shall be in accordance with the regulations. As shown in Figure 2-68, the resistance deviation is too large, too small or infinite, it means that the sensor is invalid and should be replaced. Test conditions and standard values are

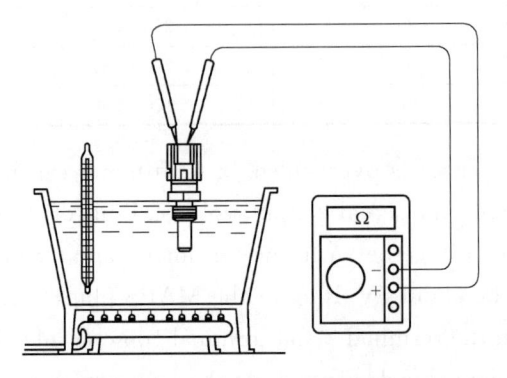

Figure 2-68　Detection of the
Resistance of the CTS

076　Fault Diagnosis and Repair of Automobile Engine Electronic Control System

a. Resistance detection. Figure 2-66 shows the IATS terminal and circuit diagram of the AJR engine of the Santana 2000GSi sedan. The IATS G72 is mounted on the intake manifold. There are two terminals on the sensor socket, with the signal output terminal connected with the terminal 54 on the ECU socket, and the sensor negative pole connected with the ground terminal 67 on the ECU socket. As shown in Figure 2-66 (b), the negative temperature coefficient thermistor can be used to detect the resistance and the voltage of the IATS to determine whether the intake temperature system is working properly. The resistance value of the IATS can be directly tested with the resistance gear of the multimeter. When detecting, turn off the ignition switch, unplug the MAPS plug, and detect the resistance value between terminal 1 and terminal 2 on the sensor socket, which shall confirm to the specified value. As shown in Table 2-1. If the resistance value is too large, too small or infinite, it means that the sensor is invalid, and it should be replaced with a new one.

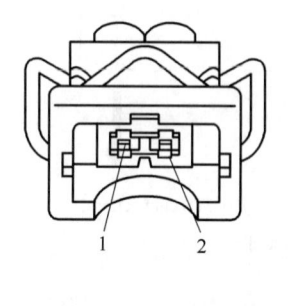

(a) IATS terminal

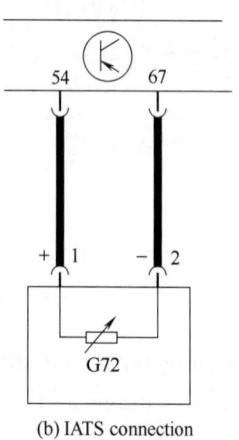

(b) IATS connection

Figure2-66   Santana 2000AJR Engine IATS

Table 2-1   Relationship between Resistance and Temperature of IATS of Santana 2000 GSi

Temperature/℃	Resistance value/Ω	Temperature/℃	Resistance value/Ω
−20	14000~20000	50	720~1000
0	5000~6500	60	530~650
10	3300~4200	70	380~480
20	2200~2700	80	280~350
30	1400~1900	90	210~280
40	1000~1400	100	170~200

b. Voltage detection. When the temperature sensor is overhauled, a multimeter can be used to detect the sensor's power supply voltage and signal output voltage. Plug off the MAPS plug, and turn on the ignition switch, the voltage between the terminal 2 and terminal 1 on the side plug of the sensor ECU should be about 5V. Plug in the MAPS plug, turn on the ignition switch, the signal voltage between the terminal 2 and terminal 1on one side of the sensor ECU should be 0.5~3.0V. If the voltage value does not meet the requirements, it means that the sensor is invalid, and it should be replaced.

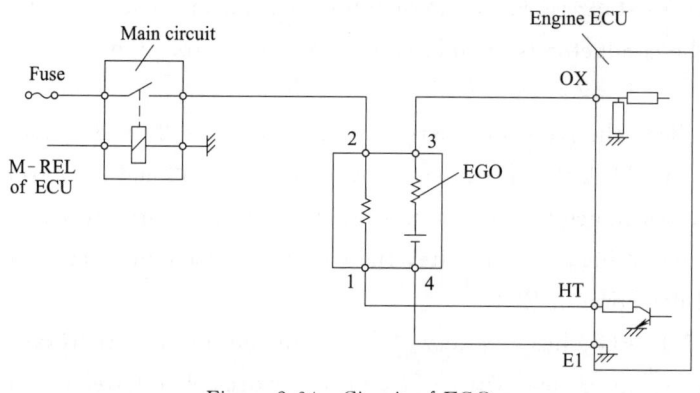

Figure 2-64　Circuit of EGO

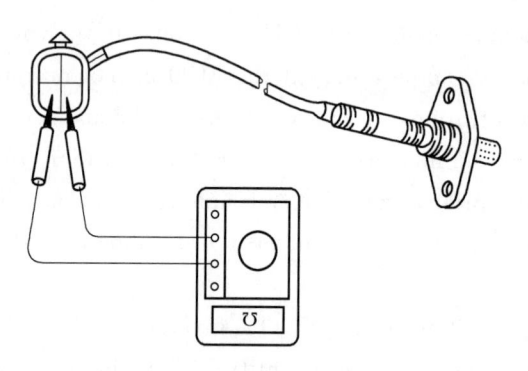

Figure 2-65　Measurement of the
resistance of the EGO heater

EGO, plug off the wire harness connector plug of the EGO first, lead out a thin from the output end of the feedback voltage of the EGO according to the circuit diagram of the model being tested, then plug in the connector, and the feedback voltage should be measured from the outlet line when the engine is running.

For some models, the feedback voltage of the EGO can also be detected from the fault diagnosis socket. For example, a small car made by Toyota Motor Company can detect the feedback voltage of the EGO directly from the OX_1 or OX_2 jack in the fault diagnosis socket. (There is an EGO on both sides of the exhaust pipe of the Toyota V-6 cylinder engine, which is respectively connected with the OX_1 and OX_2 jack in the fault detection socket.)

When detecting the feedback voltage of an EGO, it is best to use a analog voltage meter to visually reflect the change of the feedback voltage. In addition, the voltmeter should be of low range (usually 2V) and high impedance (too low impedance will damage the EGO) .

④ Detection of the appearance color of EGO. Remove the EGO from the exhaust pipe to check whether there is no blockage in the vent hole on the sensor shell and whether the ceramic core is damaged or not. In case of damage, the EGO should be replaced.

By observing the color at the top of the EGO, you can also tell the fault:

Light gray: this is the normal color of the EGO;

White: caused by silicon contamination, EGO must be replaced at this time;

Brown: caused by lead pollution, if it is serious, EGO must be replaced;

Black: caused by carbon deposition, it can be automatically removed after the engine carbon deposition fault is eliminated.

(6) Detection of the temperature sensor

① Detection of IATS

074　Fault Diagnosis and Repair of Automobile Engine Electronic Control System

than 1.5 Ω. If the resistance is too large or infinite, it means that the wire harness is not in good contact or the conductor is open-circuited, and the wire harness should be repaired or replaced.

Continue to check the resistance between terminal 1 and 2, and terminal 1 and 3 of the sensor connector, or check the resistance between terminal 62 and 76, terminal 62 and 67 of the ECU with the resistance gear of the multimeter. The measured resistance should be infinite. If the resistance value is not infinite, the wire is short-circuited and should be replaced.

(5) Use and detection of EGOs

① Use of EGOs. EGO has a variety of forms. In addition to structural differences, there are also different in appearance, with 1, 2, or 3, 4 wires. The latter two are heating EGOs with heating elements. A digital multimeter or oscilloscope is used to detect the variation of the output voltage signal with the mixture concentration and the ECU's response to the voltage signal. When the engine is at normal operating temperature, if the EGO cannot output the corresponding voltage with the mixture concentration, it is proved to be invalid and needs to be replaced. The failure of the EGO will cause the mixture to be too rich or too thin, resulting in idling instability, excessive fuel consumption, excessive emission. At this time the engine on-board diagnostics will light up the engine warning light on the dashboard of the car, prompting for immediate maintenance.

When the mixture gas is rich, and the output voltage of the EGO is greater than 0.45V, the computer receives the signal and reduces the fuel injection quantity; when the mixture gas is thin, and the output voltage is less than 0.45V, the computer receives the signal and increases the fuel injection quantity so as to control the air-fuel ratio. Some high-grade cars are equipped with two sensors, one at front of and one at rear of the three-way catalyst. The rear mounted one is called the secondary EGO, which is used as a supplement to the main EGO mounted at the front of the three-way catalyst. The computer is able to compare the signals provided by the two EGOs to determine whether the three-way catalyst is in good or bad condition. When the computer detects a failure in the three-way catalyst, the fault light of the three-way catalyst shall alerts the driver.

There are two reasons for the failure of the EGO: The first one is that it has already reached its life limit; the second one is that carbon smoke, lead, silica gel, oil and other substances deposited on the EGO, resulting in sensor failure.

The basic circuit of the EGO is shown in Figure 2-64.

② Detection of the resistance of EGO heater. The ignition switch is placed in the "OFF", and the wire connector of the EGO is pulled out. The resistance between the heater terminal and the ground terminal (terminals 1 and 2 as shown in Figure 2-65) of the EGO terminal is measured with the multimeter omega. The resistance value shall conform to the standard value (Generally is 4～40Ω; the specific value is shown in the specification of the specific model). If not up to standard, the EGO should be replaced. After measurement, connect the EGO wire harness connector to make a step-by-step inspection.

③ Detection of the feedback voltage of EGO. When detecting the feedback voltage of the

ance value between terminal 1 and terminal 5, terminal 2 and terminal 13 should not exceed 1.5Ω.

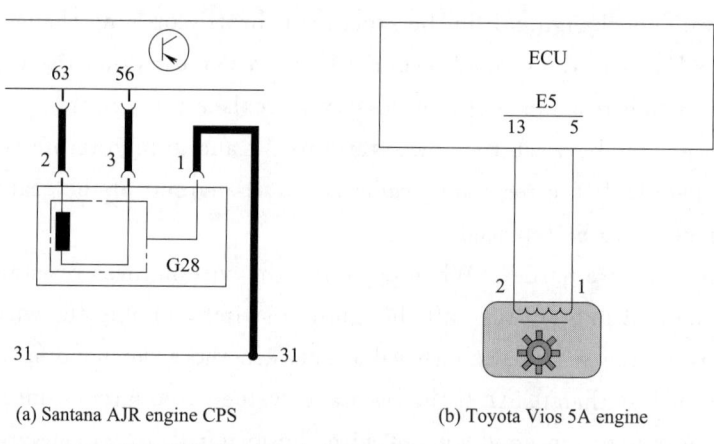

(a) Santana AJR engine CPS   (b) Toyota Vios 5A engine

Figure 2-62   Crankshaft Position Sensor Circuit

b. Detect magnetic circuit air gap of the sensor. The air gap between the signal rotor and the sensing coil head is measured with a non-magnetic thickness gauge. The air gap size should be 0.2~0.4mm, and the sensor assembly should be replaced if the air gap does not meet the requirements.

c. Detect the signal voltage of magnetoelectric crankshaft position sensor. Turn off the ignition switch, disconnect the connection plug between the CPS and the ECU of the automobile, use two probes of the AC voltage gear of the multimeter to connect with the two terminals of the sensor respectively, and at this time start the engine. The multimeter should show the change of the AC voltage, otherwise the sensor is out of order and should be replaced.

② Detection of CIS. The following mainly introduces the detection content of Hall CIS used in the AJR engine of Santana. The CIS used in Toyota Vios 5A engine is magneto-electric, and the detection content is similar to that of the above-mentioned magnetoelectric CPS, which shall be no longer described here.

Figure 2-63 shows the circuit diagram of the Santana Hall CIS.

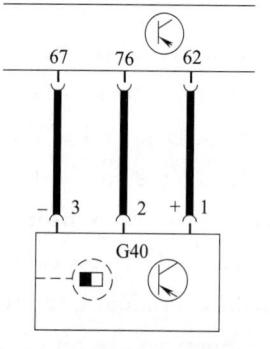

Figure 2-63   Circuit Diagram of the Santana Hall CIS.

Turn on the ignition switch and test the voltage between terminal 1 and terminal 3 with the voltage of multimeter. The voltage should be 5V. If the voltage is too low or 0 V, it means that the wire harness is open-circuit, short-circuited or the ECU is faulty; if the voltage is higher than 5 V, the sensor is damaged.

When turning off the ignition switch, check the resistance between the sensor terminal 1 and the ECU terminal 62, the sensor terminal 2 and the ECU terminal 76, the sensor terminal 3 and the ECU terminal 67 with the resistance gear of the multimeter, the resistance value should not be more

072   Fault Diagnosis and Repair of Automobile Engine Electronic Control System

is used to detect the resistance value between the V_{AT} and the E terminal of the signal output, it should increase with the increase of the resistance value of the throttle opening, with no ∞ when the value is changing. If in the process of throttle opening change, the resistance value between the V_{AT} and the ground terminal E is ∞, it means that the slip back has poor contact with the coating resistance. It is necessary to replace the sensor.

The resistance value between the power terminal V_c and ground terminal E of the sensor shall be $1000 \sim 10000$ Ω. If the resistance value is ∞, the circuit of the coating resistance is open. The sensor needs to be replaced.

Detect the sensor wire harness. When detecting the wire harness resistance with the resistance gear of the multimeter, turn off the ignition switch, unplug the wire harness of the ECU and the sensor, the wire resistance value between the corresponding terminals of the two plugs should be less than $0.5 Ω$. If the resistance value is too large or infinite, it indicates that the wire harness is not in good contact with the terminal or is open-circuited. It should be repaired.

Detect power supply voltage and signal voltage. When detecting, turn on the ignition switch and multimeter. The sensor's power supply voltage should be 5.0 V measured by the multimeter DC voltage. When the throttle is closed, the signal voltage of the sensor should be $0.5 \sim 1.0V$; when the throttle opening is gradually increased, the signal voltage should be increased; when the throttle is fully opened, the signal voltage should be $4.0 \sim 4.8V$. If the test results do not agree with this range, the sensor needs to be replaced.

b. Detect the rheostat TPS without IDL. Toyota 5A engine uses the rheostat TPS without IDL. Compared with the detection of that with IDL, the detection content is the same except for the contact, so it will be no longer described here.

(4) Maintenance of magnetic induction CPS and CIS

① Detection of CPS. The testing method of each type of magnetic induction sensor is basically the same. The magnetic induction CPS used in Santana 2000GSi and Toyota Vios5A engine is introduced as an example.

a. Detect the resistance of the sensing coil. Figure 2-62 shows the circuit diagram of the CPS for the AJR engine of the Santana sedan and the Toyota 5A engine. Plug off the wire harness plug of the sensor, detect the resistance between the terminal 2 and terminal 3 of the sensor of the AJR engine and detect the resistance between the terminal 1 and the terminal 2 of the sensor of the Toyota 5A engine. Under normal circumstances, there should be a certain value, and the value is not 0 or ∞, otherwise it means that the sensing coil of the sensor is short-circuited or open-circuited. However, the resistance value of the coil is different for different models. In the process of measurement, the resistance value of the sensor coil of the same model will be different when the detection state (hot and cold) is different. For Santana AJR engine, the resistance between terminal 1 and terminal 3, terminal 1 and terminal 2 shall be measured, and the value should be ∞. The resistance between terminal 1 and ground should not exceed 1.5 Ω. The resistance between terminal 2 and terminal 63 and between terminal 3 and terminal 56 should not exceed 1.5 Ω. For Toyota 5A engine, the resist-

formance of the sensor and directly affect the engine work. The vacuum hose shall be repaired or replaced according to the situation.

② Detection of the sensor power supply voltage. When the ignition switch is switched on, the voltage on the sensor terminal 1 shall be 4. 5～5. 5 V. If the voltage is 0, then detect the voltage on the terminal 9 of the ECU wire harness plug; if the voltage is 4. 5～5. 5 V, it means that the sensor power cord is broken or the plug is loose.

③ Detection of the sensor signal voltage. The output signal voltage of the sensor can be detected by high impedance digital multimeter DC voltage. There are 3 terminals (terminal 1, terminal 2, and terminal 3) on the sensor socket. When the ignition switch is switched on and the engine is not started, the voltage on the terminal 3 should be 4～5V; when the engine is idle, the voltage on the terminal 3 should be reduced to 1. 5～2. 1V; when the throttle opening is increased, the voltage on the terminal 3 should be increased gradually. If the voltage on terminal 1 of the ECU wire harness plug is detected, the voltage should be the same as that on terminal 3. If the test result is not in conformity with the regulation, it means that the signal line of the sensor is open-circuited, the plug is loose or there is a fault inside the sensor.

④ Detection of the connection of the negative lead of the sensor. The resistance value between the terminal 2 of the sensor and the engine cylinder should be less than 0. 5Ω. If the resistance value is too large, it indicates that the negative lead of the sensor is open-circuited or the ECU plug is not well connected.

(3) Maintenance of TPS

TPS used in electric-controlled vehicle plays the role of "electronic acceleration pump". If the TPS is removed or it fails, the engine will still work, but there will be slow acceleration.

① Detection of the contact TPS. When detecting contact TPS, the output voltage and contact resistance of sensor signal output terminal can be measured by multimeter.

When detecting the output voltage, connect the sensor and turn on the ignition switch, the output voltage should be high level or low level. When the throttle shaft rotates, the output voltage should change alternately (from low level "0" to high level "1" or from high level "1" to low level "0").

When detecting contact state, pull off the sensor wire harness plug, the contact resistance should be less than 0. 5Ω. If the resistance value is too large, it means that the contact is not in good contact due to ablation. The sensor should be repaired or replaced.

② Detection of the rheostat TPS. The multimeter can be used to detect the resistance value and voltage of the rheostat TPS.

a. Detect the rheostat TPS with IDL. As shown in Figure 2-20, detect the resistance of the TPS. First, plug off the wire harness plug of the sensor, then, detect the resistance between the IDL and the terminal E with the multimeter. The resistance value should be less than 0. 5Ω when the throttle valve is fully closed; the resistance value between the IDL and the ground terminal E should be ∞ when the throttle valve is opened; when the multimeter

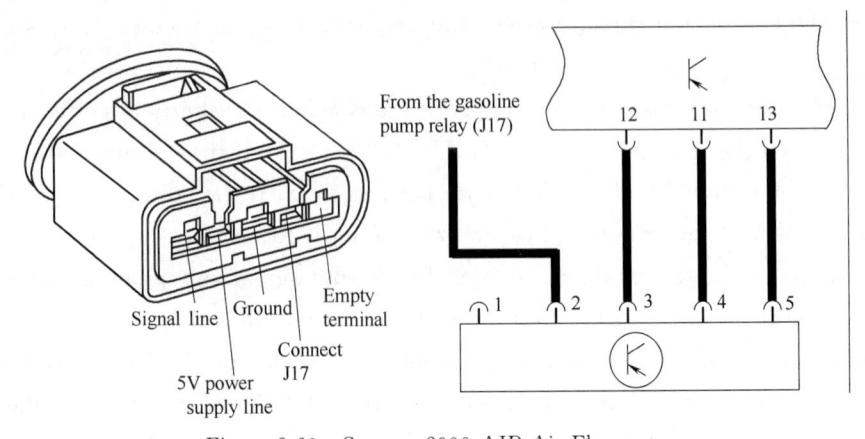

Figure 2-60 Santana 2000 AJR Air Flowmeter

power circuit needs to be overhauled.

② Detection of the signal voltage of the sensor. When checking the signal voltage, un-plug the sensor wire harness plug, connect the positive and negative poles of the battery to the power terminal and the ground terminal on the sensor socket respectively, and measure the output voltage of the signal with the multimeter DC voltage; when blowing air into the sensor air inlet, the signal voltage should rise accordingly.

③ Detection of the self-cleaning function of hot-wire AFS in the car. Plug the wire har-ness of the AFS into the socket first, then start the engine and raise the speed to more than 2500r/min, then run the engine at the idle speed. Remove the intake pipe at the air inlet end of the AFS, turn off the ignition switch, and observe from the sensor air inlet whether the hot wire is red-hot and lasts for 1s after the engine is out of fire for 5s (Editor's Note: hot film AFS and hot wire AFS with temperature higher than 200℃ do not have this function)

(2) Maintenance of MAPS

The maintenance methods of MAPS of various types of automobile are the same. The following examples are given to illustrate the maintenance methods of MAPS used in Vios cars. The installation position and circuit connection of the MAPS are shown in Figure 2-61.

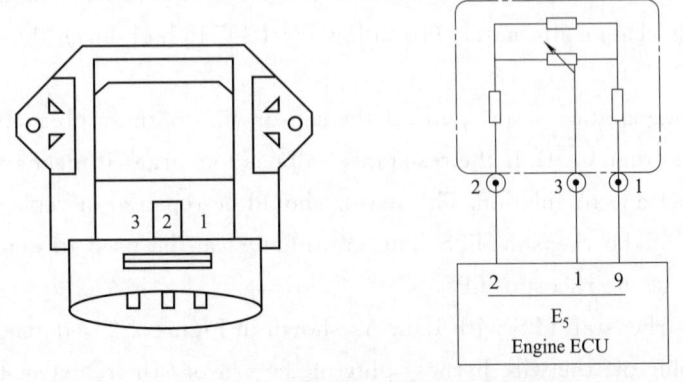

Figure 2-61 Structure and Circuit Diagram of MAPS for Toyota Vios 5A Engine

① Detection of the vacuum hose connection. Carefully check the connection between the MAPS' vacuum hose and the throttle body. Poor connection or air leakage will affect the per-

rate of TPS signal and air intake sensor signal. When the automobile accelerates, the throttle suddenly opens widely, the TPS signal change rate increases, at the same time, the air flow suddenly increases, the manifold pressure suddenly increases, and the AFS signal suddenly rises. When the ECU receives these signals, it will immediately send the control instruction to increase the fuel injection quantity and the mixture intensify. The fuel increment ratio and the enrichment time depend on the temperature of the engine coolant at acceleration, as shown in Figure 2-59. The lower the coolant temperature, the larger the fuel increment ratio and the longer the enrichment duration.

III. Item Implementation

(I) Requirements for implementation

Toyota 5A, AJR engine bench; automobile; automobile multimeter, diagnostic instrument.

(II) Implementation steps

1. Maintenance of EFI sensor

(1) Maintenance of AFS

AFS is not only a kind of precision component, but also the most important part of gas supply system. When it fails, the ECU shall not receive the correct intake signal to control the fuel injection quantity, and the mixture shall become too rich or too thin, causing the engine to run out of order. When overhauling or removing the AFS, it should be carefully operated to avoid collision to damage its parts.

For modern cars, most use hot-wire or hot-film AFS, so here only to introduce the maintenance of this sensor.

The maintenance methods of hot-wire type and hot-film type AFS are basically the same. Now the hot-film AFS used in Santana car is taken as an example to illustrate the methods.

The structure and circuit diagram of the AJR engine of Santana 2000 GSi are shown in Figure 2-60.

① Detection the power supply voltage. When testing the power supply voltage, pull off the sensor wire harness plug, turn on the ignition switch, and use the multimeter DC voltage to detect the voltage between the power supply terminal and the ground terminal.

When detecting the power supply voltage of the AFS of a Santana car, unplug the terminal 5 wire harness plug on the sensor (Editor's Note: the terminal, code 1, is a spare terminal with no connection wires), as shown in Figure 2-60, and then turns on the ignition switch to detect the voltage between the terminal 2 of the harness plug head and the engine cylinder: the specified value shall not be less than 11.5V. If the voltage is 0, it means that the fuel pump relay contact is not closed or the power circuit is open, the fuel pump relay or

state, it is necessary to modify the fuel injection pulse width when the engine is warm-up, that is to increase the fuel injection quantity, which is also a kind of compensation measure for the insufficient fuel supply when the engine is cold. At the same time of fuel increment correction after start-up, the heating engine fuel increment correction is also carried out, until the coolant temperature reaches the specified value.

c. Correction of injection pulse width at high temperature. When a car is running at high speed, the fuel temperature will not be too high, about 50℃, due to the air-cooling effect and the constant flow of fuel. But if the engine shuts down and the fuel stops flowing, the engine will become a heat source, causing the fuel temperature to rise. Once it reaches 80~100℃, the fuel in the fuel tank and the pipe will boil and produce the fuel steam. Thus, the reduction of fuel amount makes the mixture thinner due to the fuel steam. In order to solve the problem of mixture dilution caused by fuel steam, measures should be taken to correct the pulse width of fuel injection during high-temperature start-up. When the coolant temperature rises above the set value (such as 100℃), a high temperature fuel increment correction is carried out.

④ Correction of battery voltage. The electromagnetic coil of the injector is an inductive load, and its current varies exponentially. Therefore, when the injection pulse comes, the opening and closing of the injector valve will be delayed for a certain time. The voltage of the battery has a great influence on the lagging time of the injector opening. The lower the voltage is the longer the lagging time of the opening is. The injection is invalid during the opening and closing process. Therefore, it is necessary to consider the effect of the change of the battery voltage on the ineffective injection time, and modify the injection time, that is, when the battery voltage is reduced, the injection pulse width is increased, and when the battery voltage is increased, the injection pulse width is decreased, As shown in Figure 2-58.

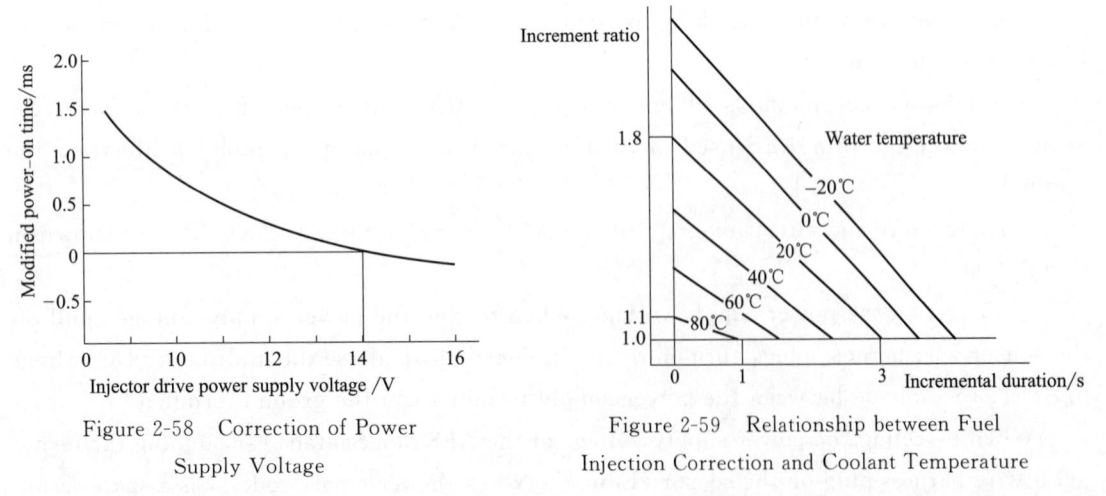

Figure 2-58　Correction of Power
Supply Voltage

Figure 2-59　Relationship between Fuel
Injection Correction and Coolant Temperature

⑤ Correction of fuel injection increment during acceleration. When the automobile accelerates, the fuel injection must be increased in order to ensure that the engine can output enough torque and improve the acceleration performance. In the course of engine operation, ECU will determine whether the engine is in an accelerated condition according to the change

sensor detects the same control flow while driving in the highlands. In order to avoid over-concentration of the mixture and excessive fuel consumption, the basic fuel injection pulse width should be corrected according to the input signal of the atmospheric pressure sensor. The lower the atmospheric pressure detected by the atmospheric pressure sensor using vane-type AFS and Karman vortex AFS and MAPS, the smaller the basic fuel injection pulse width of the injector.

When driving the automobile from the plain to the plateau, if the fuel consumption and exhaust emissions increase or even black smoke, it should be checked whether there is a problem with the atmospheric pressure correction system, resulting in excessive concentration of the mixture causing the above-mentioned fault.

When the hotwire or hot film AFS is used to detect the air intake, there is no need to modify the temperature and atmospheric pressure because the sensor itself is a mass flow sensor. The basic fuel injection pulse width is determined by the ECU according to the signal of the AFS and the engine speed sensor and the set target air-fuel ratio. The larger the air intake measured by the AFS in each working cycle of the engine, the greater the basic fuel injection pulse width of the injector.

③ Correction of fuel injection pulse width related to engine temperature. As shown in Figure 2-57, the engine ECU determines the fuel injection correction according to the signals sent by the corresponding sensors, such as the CTS. As can be seen from the diagram, the fuel injection correction decreases as the increase of the engine temperature. Here are three cases of fuel correction related to engine temperature

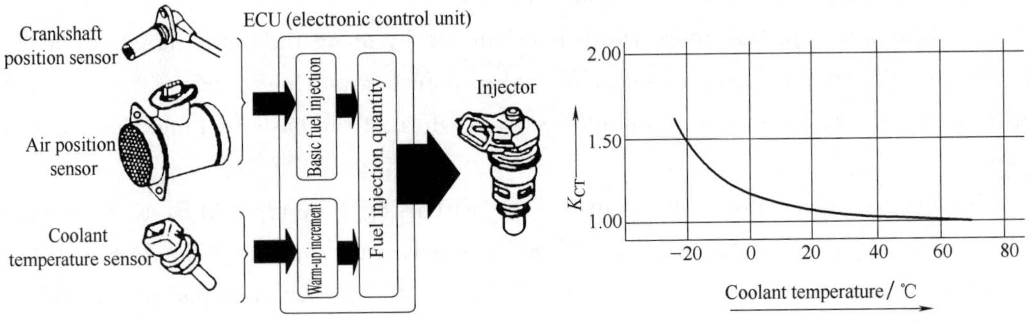

Figure 2-57　ECU Correction Based on Coolant Temperature Signal

a. Correction of injection pulse width after start-up. Within tens of seconds after the cold engine starts, the air flow speed is low, and the engine temperature is low, so the fuel atomization ability is poor. At this time, the fuel injection pulse width should be corrected. The cooler the engine, the greater the fuel increment, and the longer it takes to correct. The incremental correction after the cold start of the engine is actually a compensation measure for the insufficient fuel supply at this time.

b. Correction of injection pulse width in warm-up. After the engine starts, in order to enable the engine, the three-way catalyst and the EGO reach the normal working temperature as soon as possible, and enable the control system enter into the closed-loop working

gine, that is, the fuel injection pulse width is determined according to the ideal target air-fuel ratio stored in the ECU for various working conditions. The relationship between the target air-fuel ratio, intake quality and the amount of fuel required is as follows:

$$\text{Target air-fuel ratio (A/F)} = \frac{\text{Air quantity entering the cylinder in each intake stroke(g)}}{\text{Fuel quantity required for each combustion(g)}}$$

According to the above formula, according to the air quality (g) of the intake cylinder and the target air-fuel ratio (A/F) in each intake stroke, the fuel quality (g) required for each combustion can be calculated, that is,

Fuel quantity required for each combustion (g)

$$= \frac{\text{Air quantity entering the cylinder in each intake stroke(g)}}{\text{Target air-fuel ratio(A/F)}}$$

The fuel injection quantity of the injector is only proportional to the opening time of the injector. Therefore, in the actual control of the engine, the amount of fuel required for each combustion is determined by controlling the opening time of the injector, that is, the width of the fuel injection pulse.

The fuel injection pulse width determined by the target air-fuel ratio can be calculated in the following formula, that is,

Fuel Injection Pulse Width (ms) = Basic Fuel Injection Pulse Width (ms) × Basic Fuel Injection Pulse Width Correction Coefficient + Invalid Fuel Injection Time (ms)

The software design of different combustion injection systems is different, and the calculation method may also be different.

(2) Determination of basic injection pulse width

The basic fuel injection pulse width is calculated by using the input signals of AFS (or MAPS) and the engine speed sensor achieve the air-fuel ratio. Due to different types of AFS (or MAPS), the process of determining the pulse width of the basic fuel injection is also different.

The basic fuel injection pulse width of the EFI using vane-type AFS, Karman vortex-type AFS and MAPS is determined by the ECU based on the signals of the AFS and the engine speed sensor, the target air-fuel ratio (A/F) and the correction signal of the IATS and the atmospheric pressure sensor. The larger the intake gas measured by the sensor in each working cycle of the engine, the greater the injection pulse width of the injector.

(3) Determination of fuel injection correction

① Correction related to intake temperature. Because the density of cold air is higher than that of hot air, the air quality of the inhaled engine decreases with the increase of air temperature when other factors are the same. In order to prevent the mixture from getting rich with the increase of temperature, the ECU will modify the basic fuel injection pulse width according to the intake temperature, that is, the higher the intake temperature, the smaller the basic fuel injection pulse width of the injector.

② Correction related to atmospheric pressure. Because atmospheric pressure and its density decrease with altitude, the actual air flow quantity into the engine decreases when the

Control during normal operation after start-up. It is based on the air quality calculation of the engine to obtain the fuel injection pulse width. This control method is more accurate, and the mixture concentration is more ideal.

1. Control of fuel injection pulse width during start-up

When the engine starts, the ECU determines whether the engine is in the starting condition mainly according to the starting signal or the engine speed (such as under 400r/min) .

When the cold car starts, the injected fuel is not easy to atomize because of the low engine coolant temperature and speed, so the mixture becomes thin. In order to produce sufficient concentration of combustible mixture to start the engine smoothly, the injection pulse width should be extended during start-up, that is, to increase the fuel injection quantity.

The width of the fuel injection pulse is not calculated according to the air quality at start-up, but is determined by the temperature of the engine coolant at that time, the number of revolutions accumulated since start-up and the start-up time. In the case of start-up, the width of the fuel injection pulse can be determined by the following formula, that is

Starting fuel injection pulse width (ms) = starting fuel injection pulse width determined by engine coolant temperature (ms) + ineffective injection time (ms)

The lower the engine coolant temperature is, the harder the fuel is to atomize, and the longer the injection pulse width should be. In the cold start of engine, the following two ways are often used to increase the injection pulse width.

① Injecting some additional fuel into the intake manifold through a cold-start injector.

② Extending its fuel injection pulse width through the control of the injector by the ECU.

At present, many electronic-controlled fuel injection engines do not have cold-start injector; starting fuel increment is direct controlled by ECU. In the start-up condition, in order to enrich the mixture and to form a uniform combustible mixture in the intake pipe and cylinder, it is necessary to avoid the soak of the fuel to the spark plug. As such, the injector is required to conduct multiple injection (asynchronous injection) at each turn of the engine. Because the control of the injector is realized by the control circuit and the function of the software inside the ECU, the control system is more complicated.

The fuel injection system controls the continuous fuel injection time of the injector mainly according to the engine coolant temperature, rotational speed, the number of rotations and time accumulated since start-up.

2. Determination of fuel injection pulse width after starting

(1) Injection pulse width of injector after starting

When the engine is running normally after starting, the fuel injection pulse width of the injector is calculated on the basis of the air quality of the intake cylinder during an intake stroke. The ECU calculates the air quality and the basic injection pulse width of the intake cylinder in an intake stroke according to the input signals from the AFS or the MAPS, the CTS, the IATS, the atmospheric pressure sensor and the engine speed sensor. The basic fuel injection pulse width is modified on the basis of the power, economy and emission of the en-

（3）Sequential injection timing control

Sequential fuel injection is also called independent fuel injection. Every two turns of the crankshaft, the injector of each cylinder injects the fuel at the most suitable crankshaft angle position according to the ignition sequence of the engine. The control circuit of the sequential fuel injection system is shown in Figure 2-56 （a）. Each cylinder injector is controlled by a power amplifier circuit of the ECU. The number of power amplifier circuits is equal to that of injectors.

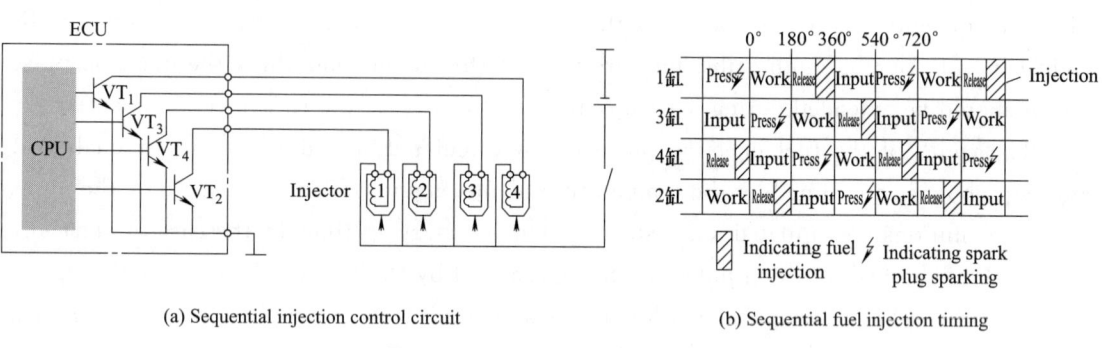

(a) Sequential injection control circuit   (b) Sequential fuel injection timing

Figure 2-56   Sequential Injection

The ECU, which uses sequential fuel injection, needs to "know" which cylinder should be injected at which time. Therefore, it must have a cylinder identification signal, often called cylinder identification signal, which comes mostly from the CPS and the CIS. Sequential fuel injection control have two control functions: timing and cylinder sequence. When the ECU works, the specific position of the piston before the TDC can be known through the input signal of the CPS, and then combined with the cylinder identification signal of the CIS to determine that the TDC is at which cylinder. At the same time, it can determine whether the piston is in the compression stroke or the exhaust stroke. Therefore, when the ECU determines the cylinder stroke and the certain position of the piston in front of the TDC according to the cylinder identification signal and the crankshaft position signal, it will output the fuel injection control instruction, and connect the grounding circuit of the injector solenoid coil. The cylinder injector begins to fuel injection. Figure 2-56 （b）is a sequential fuel injection timing diagram.

（Ⅶ）Control of fuel injection pulse width

The purpose of the fuel injection pulse width control is to control the fuel injection quantity so that the concentration of the mixture in the engine combustion can meet the requirements of the engine operating conditions. The control of the fuel injection pulse width is actually a process that the ECU calculates and outputs fuel injection pulse control signals according to the engine operating conditions and various influencing factors.

It can be broadly divided into two categories:

Control during engine start-up. It is not based on the air quality calculation of the intake engine to get the fuel injection pulse width, but a very extensive control;

the power triode. The electromagnetic coil circuit of each injector can be switched on and off at the same time, so that the injector of each cylinder can be injected at the same time. Usually, the injector of each cylinder injects once every rotation of the crankshaft. The injection timing is shown in Figure 2-54 (b).

		360°		Injection	Ignition	
1cylinder	Input	Press	Work	Release	Input	Press
3cylinder	Release	Input	Press	Work	Release	Input
4cylinder	Work	Release	Input	Press	Work	Release
2cylinder	Press	Work	Release	Input	Press	Work

Indicating fuel injection   Indicating spark plug sparking

(a) Simultaneous injection control circuit   (b) Simultaneous injection timing

Figure 2-54　Simultaneous Injection

Since all injectors of the cylinders injects at the same time, the injection timing has nothing to do with engine intake, compression, work, exhaust. Most of the fuel injection engines produced in the early stage adopt simultaneous injection mode. The disadvantage is that the injection timing of each cylinder is not optimal, which results in the uneven mixture of each cylinder. However, the injection mode does not require cylinder to determine the signal, the fuel injection drive circuit has good versatility, and its circuit structure and software are simple.

(2) Grouping injection timing control

Grouping injection usually divides all cylinder injector into 2～4 groups. The ECU controls each group of injectors to carry out fuel injection alternately. The 4-cylinder engine usually divides the injectors into two groups. The control circuit is shown in Figure 2-55 (a). Each injector ejects once or twice in each working cycle. Figure 2-55 (b) is the timing diagram of group injection.

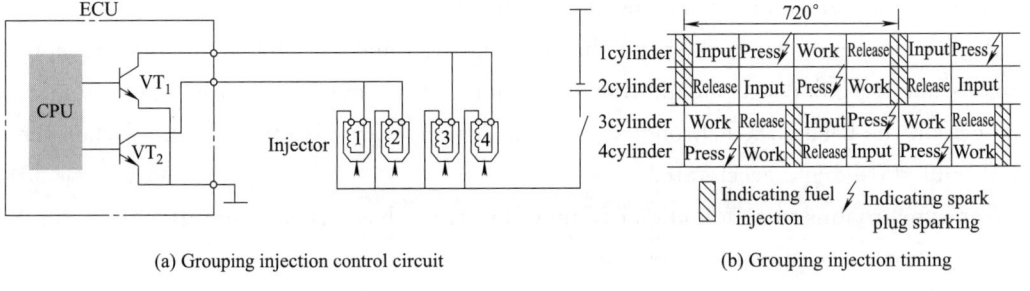

(a) Grouping injection control circuit   (b) Grouping injection timing

Figure 2-55　Grouping Injection

Compared with the simultaneous injection engine, the performance of the group-injection engine is improved. It is mainly reflected in that more cylinders can eject fuel at the right time, and the uniformity of the mixture is improved.

judge engine working state (start state or normal working state) and to run corresponding control program.

For example, when the ignition switch is switched on, the IGN terminal of the ECU will receive a high level signal from the ignition switch. At this point, the ECU will automatically connect the FP circuit to make the oil pump work $1\sim2$s, so that there is enough fuel in the oil circuit when the engine starts. When the ignition switch switches on the starting gear, the STA terminal of the ECU will receive a high level signal from the ignition switch. At this point, the ECU will control the start-up procedure and increase the fuel injection to start the engine.

The battery voltage signal U_{BAT} is the automobile power supply voltage signal. The positive pole of the battery is directly connected with the power supply voltage terminal of the ECU through the wire, which is not controlled by the ignition switch and other switches. When the power supply voltage changes, the ECU will change the fuel injection pulse width and correct the fuel injection duration of the injector; when the engine stops working, the battery will provide $5\sim20$mA current to the ECU and the memory, so that the memory can keep the information such as the fault code without losing; when the ignition switch is disconnected, for the control system using the stepper motor, ECU will also control the fuel injection main relay continue to connect for 2s, so that the stepper motor returns to its initial position. After the signals of various sensors are input into ECU, ECU sends out the pulse signal command to control the injector fuel injection according to the result of mathematical calculation and logic judgment.

2. Injection timing control

Fuel injection timing refers to when the injector (relative to the engine crankshaft angle position) begins to fuel injection.

For a multi-point intermittent fuel injection engine, the relationship between injection timing and crankshaft angle can be divided into two types: synchronous injection and asynchronous injection.

Synchronous injection refers to the working cycle of engine cylinders. The injection is carried out at the given crankshaft position regularly.

Asynchronous injection refers to that the injection and the engine's work are not synchronous and irregular. It is an additional injection that is added to improve the engine's performance on the basis of synchronous injection. A temporary injection, such as when the engine is cold-started and accelerated.

For synchronous injection engines, there are three basic types: simultaneous injection, group injection and sequential injection.

(1) Simultaneous injection timing control

The control circuit and control program of the injector with simultaneous injection mode are simple. The control circuit is shown in Figure 2-54 (a). As can be seen from the diagram, all the injectors are connected in parallel. The ECU, according to the reference signal produced by the CPS, sends out the pulse control signal to control the turnon and turnoff of

tion system uses AFS. Although the number and form of sensors and actuators used in the engine fuel injection system are different, the control process of fuel injection is much the same.

1. Control principle of fuel injection system

The control principle of the L-type fuel injection system is shown in Figure 2-53.

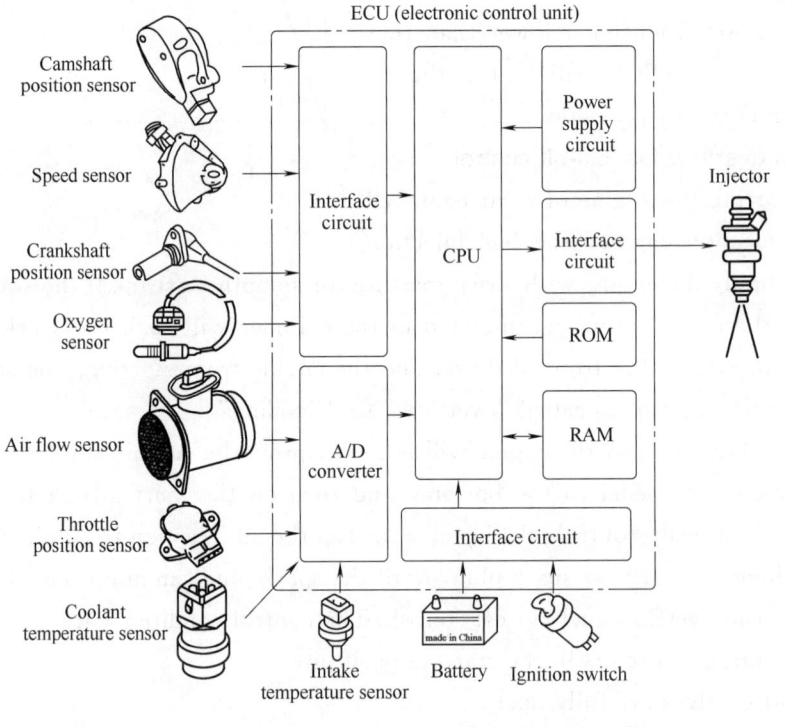

Figure 2-53   L-type Control Principle of Fuel Injection System

During engine operation, the camshaft position sensor (Cylinder Identification Sensor, CIS) provides the ECU with the signal that reflects the position of the piston's TDC in order to calculate and determine the injection advance angle (lead time); the CPS provides the ECU with a signal that reflects the engine's crankshaft speed and rotation angle, and the AFS (or MAPS) provides the ECU with a signal that reflects the amount of air intake. The ECU calculates the fuel injection quantity (fuel injection time) according to these two signals; the TPS provides the ECU with a signal reflecting the size of the engine load, and the ECU determines the increase or decrease of the fuel injection quantity according to the TPS signal; the CTS provides the engine coolant temperature signal to the ECU to calculate the correction value of the fuel injection quantity; and the EGO provides the ECU with a signal reflecting the fuel concentration of the engine in order to increase or decrease the fuel injection quantity, so as to realize air-fuel ratio feedback control and reduce exhaust emissions; VSS provides the ECU with a signal that reflects the automobile's speed to determine whether the engine is running at idle (throttle is closed, and the speed is 0) or at deceleration (throttle is closed, and the speed is not 0), thus determining whether the fuel supply shall be stopped; the start-up switch signal includes IGN and STA, which are used by ECU to

ured by the CPS with the limit speed stored in the memory. When the actual speed reaches or exceeds $80\sim100\mathrm{r/min}$ of the safe speed, the ECU issues a stop fuel injection instruction to control the injector to stop the fuel injection and limit the engine speed to further increase. The control curve is shown in Figure 2-52.

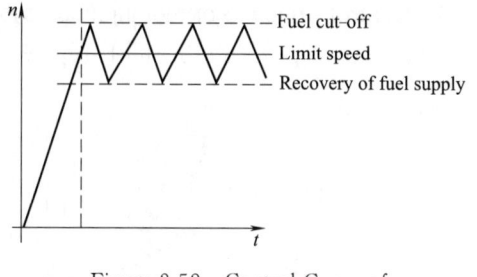

Figure 2-52　Control Curve of Speed Cut-off

After the injector stops the fuel injection, the engine speed will decrease. When the engine speed drops to $80\sim100\mathrm{r/min}$, lower than that of the safe speed, the ECU will control the injector to resume the fuel injection.

3. Clean overflow fuel cut-off control

When starting the engine of a car equipped with a fuel injection engine, the fuel injection system will supply the engine with a rich mixture for smooth start-up. If the start-up fails for many times, the rich mixture accumulated in the cylinder will soak the spark plug, which will prevent the spark plug from flashover and the engine from starting. The spark plug being soaked by the mixture is called "overflow" or "flooding".

When overflow occurs, the engine will not start properly. At this point, you can step on the engine accelerator pedal to the bottom, and turn on the start switch to start the engine. ECU automatically controls the injector to stop the oil injection to eliminate the fuel vapor in the cylinder, to dry the spark plug, until the spark plug can jump. This kind of control is known as clean overflow fuel cut-off control. The control conditions are：

① The ignition switch is in the starting position；

② Throttle valves are fully open；

③ Engine speed is below $500\mathrm{r/min}$.

Only when the three conditions are satisfied at the same time, the fuel cut-off control system can start cleaning the overflow.

It can be seen that when starting the fuel injection engine, you can turn on the start switch directly without pressing the accelerator pedal. Otherwise, the fuel cut-off control system may start cleaning the overflow, causing the engine unable to start.

When the starting switch is turned on while the engine cannot start, the overflow can be cleared first by using the fuel cut-off control system, and then the starting can be carried out.

4. Upshift fuel cut-off control

Automobiles equipped with electric control auto transmission upshift during running, the engine ECU immediately sends a command after receiving the torque sensor signal from the transmission ECU to stop fuel injection of individual cylinders, in order to reduce the engine speed and reduce the shift impact. This control is called upshift fuel cut-off control.

(Ⅵ) Control process of engine fuel injection

As we all know, the D-type fuel injection system uses MAP sensor; L-type fuel injec-

1. Deceleration fuel cut-off control

It refers to that when the engine suddenly decelerates during high speed operation; the ECU automatically controls the injector to interrupt the fuel injection.

When the accelerator pedal of a high-speed automobile is suddenly released, the engine will rotate at high speed under the action of the inertia force of the car. The closed throttle valve makes the air entering the cylinder very little, therefore, if the fuel injection is not stopped, the mixture will be too rich to burn completely, which results in the sharp increase of emissions of harmful gases. The goal of deceleration fuel cut-off is to save fuel and reduce emissions of harmful gases.

The process of deceleration fuel cut-off control is shown in Figure 2-50. According to the sensor signals such as throttle position, engine speed and coolant temperature, the ECU determines whether or not to meet the following three control conditions:

① The IDL of the TPS is closed;

② The coolant temperature has reached the normal temperature;

③ The engine speed is higher than a certain speed.

When all of the three conditions are met, the ECU immediately issues a stop injection order to control the injector to stop the fuel injection. When the fuel injection stops, the engine speed drops to the fuel re-supply speed or the throttle opens (the IDL is disconnected), the ECU then issues an instruction to control the injector to resume the fuel injection, as shown in Figure 2-51.

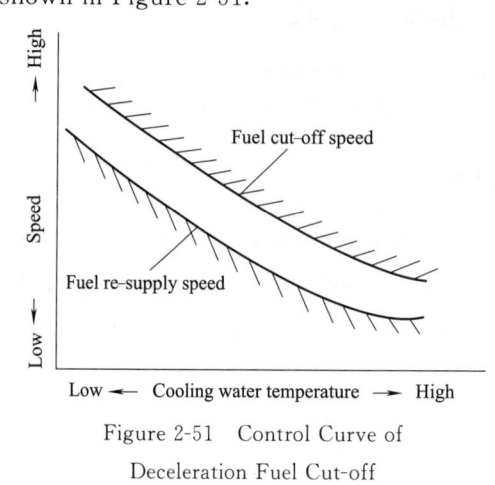

Figure 2-51　Control Curve of Deceleration Fuel Cut-off

Fuel cut-off speed and re-supply speed are related to coolant temperature and engine load, which is determined by ECU according to engine temperature, load and so on. The lower the coolant temperature, and the higher the engine load (such as air conditioning conduction), the higher the fuel shut-off speed and re-supply speed.

2. Speed limit fuel cut-off control

The speed limit fuel cut-off control means that when the engine speed exceeds the allowable speed limit, the ECU immediately controls the injector to interrupt the fuel injection. The purpose is to prevent the engine from overspeed and damage the parts of the engine.

When the engine works, the higher the speed, the greater the centrifugal force of the crank train. When the centrifugal force is too large, the engine is in danger of being damaged by "runaway speed". Therefore, each engine has a limit speed value, and normally it is 6000~7000 r/min. The limit speed of Santana 2000 GLi, 2000 GSi, and 3000 are 6400 r/min, and Jetta AT, GTX are 6800 r/min.

In the process of engine running, ECU always compares the actual engine speed meas-

ple are shown in Figure 2-49. The excess oil pressure of the system is directly discharged back to the fuel tank. Normally, this kind of regulator installs a fuel pulsation damper on the fuel manifold to further adjust the oil pressure of the system.

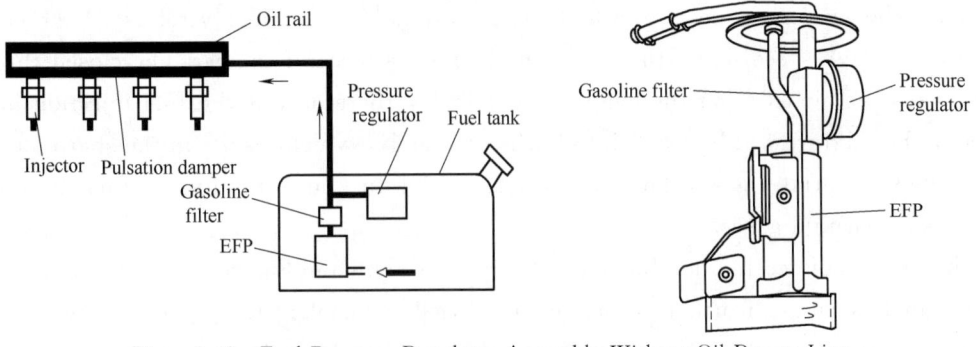

Figure2-48　Fuel Pressure Regulator Assembly Without Oil Return Line

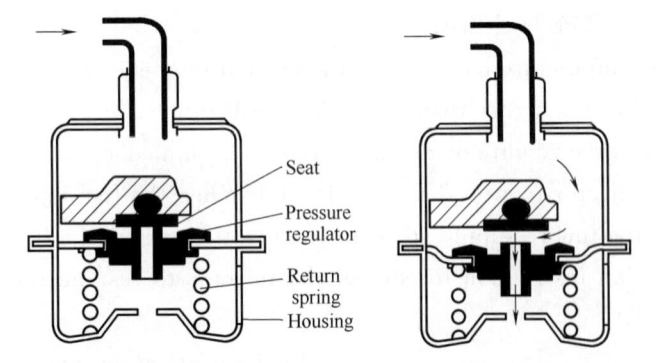

(a) Turn off the pressure regulating valve　(b) Turn on the pressure regulating valve

Figure 2-49　Fuel Pressure Regulator Structure Without Oil Return Line

(V) Engine fuel cut-off control process

Fuel cut-off control means that the fuel injection system temporarily interrupts the fuel injection to meet the special requirements of engine operation under some special conditions. Fuel cut-off control includes engine, deceleration fuel, speed limit fuel cut-off control, clean overflow fuel cut-off control and upshift fuel cut-off control. The control process is shown in Figure 2-50.

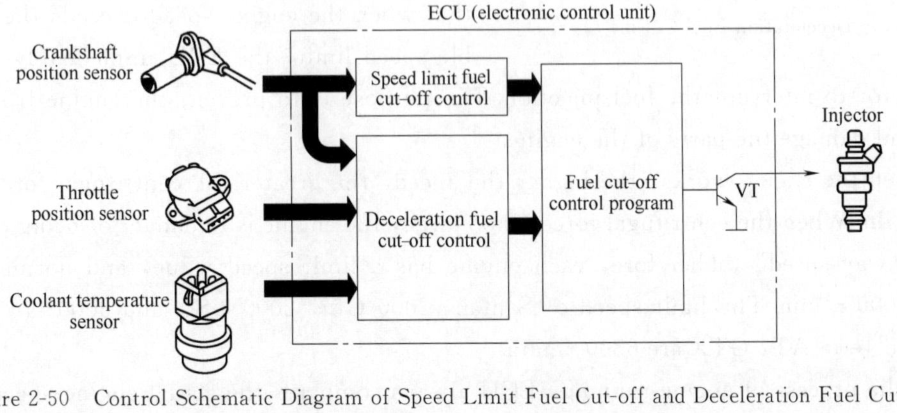

Figure 2-50　Control Schematic Diagram of Speed Limit Fuel Cut-off and Deceleration Fuel Cut-off

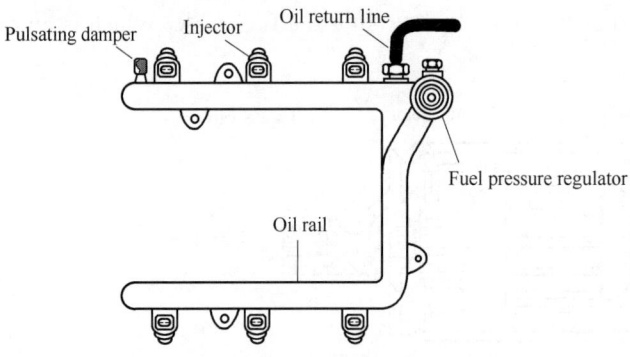

Figure 2-45　General Installation Position of Oil Pressure Regulator for Oil Return Line

pressure regulator, and the fuel pressure acts on the metal diaphragm attached to the valve body. When the oil pressure increases, the pressure acting on the diaphragm and the suction of the vacuum tube acting on the diaphragm exceeds the elastic force of the regulator spring, the oil pressure pushes the diaphragm up the arch, the regulator valve opens, and part of the fuel oil flows back to the tank from the return port tubing, reducing the fuel pressure. As shown in Figure 2-46 (b), when the fuel pressure is reduced to the oil pressure of the system controlled by the regulator, the ball valve is closed so that the oil pressure of the system remains constant. The regulator valve closes and does not return oil when the oil pressure acting on the diaphragm and the suction of the vacuum tube acting on the diaphragm is less than the spring of the regulator. So the role of the fuel pressure regulator

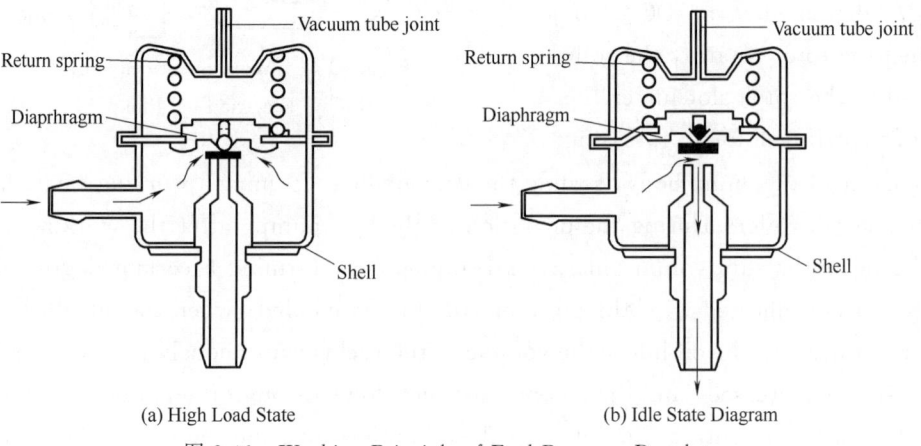

(a) High Load State　　　　　　　(b) Idle State Diagram

图 2-46　Working Principle of Fuel Pressure Regulator

is to keep the system oil pressure and atmospheric pressure difference constant. Figure 2-47 shows the relationship between the pressure in the intake manifold, the pressure in the fuel distribution tube and the throttle opening.

② Fuel pressure regulator without oil return line. The installation position and structural assembly of the fuel pressure regulator without oil return line are shown in Figure 2-48. It is mounted with the oil pump assembly together, as the structure and working princi-

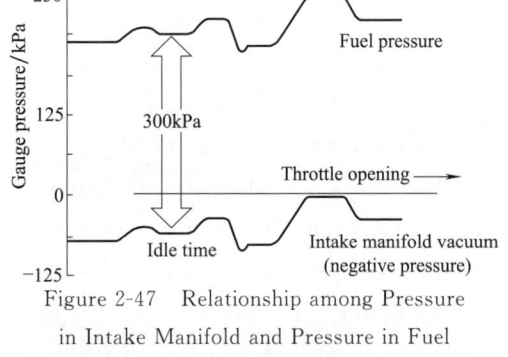

Figure 2-47　Relationship among Pressure in Intake Manifold and Pressure in Fuel Distribution Pipe and Throttle Opening

056　Fault Diagnosis and Repair of Automobile Engine Electronic Control System

ses the volume of the fuel pump, so that it is installed outside the fuel tank, which is an external type.

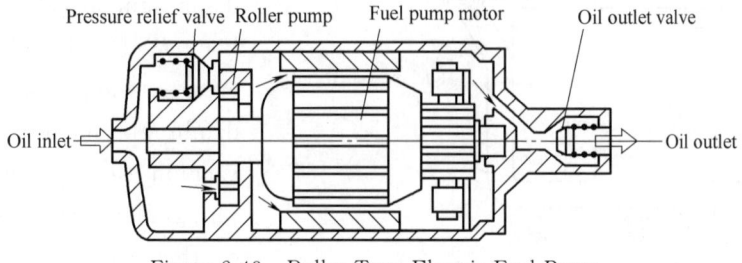

Figure 2-43   Roller Type Electric Fuel Pump

Damping damper is mainly composed of diaphragm and spring, which can absorb the energy of fuel pressure wave and reduce the pressure fluctuation so as to improve the control precision of fuel injection.

The working principle of the roller pump is shown in Figure 2-44. The rotor equipped with a roller is eccentric, placed in the pump housing, driven by a DC motor. When the rotor rotates, the roller located in the rotor slot under the action of centrifugal force, pressing

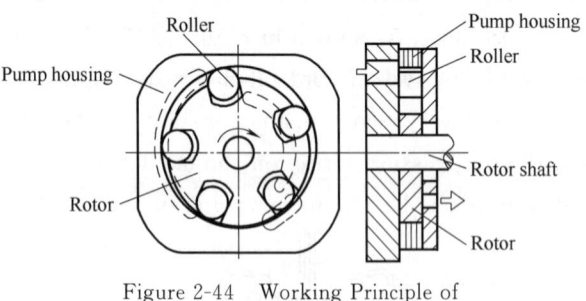

Figure 2-44   Working Principle of Rolling Electric Fuel Pump

on the surface of the pump body, sealing the surrounding, forming a working cavity between the two adjacent rollers. During the operation of the fuel pump, after the working chamber turns the oil outlet, its volume increases continuously, forming a certain degree of vacuum. When it is connected with the oil inlet, the fuel is inhaled; when the oil-filled working chamber is turned to the oil inlet, the volume of the fuel is continuously reduced, so that the fuel pressure is increased, and the compressed fuel flows through the motor, and the fuel is exported from the oil outlet. The action of the oil outlet valve and the relief valve is the same as that of the turbine-type electric fuel pump.

3. Fuel pressure regulator

(1) Function and type of fuel pressure regulator

① Action. The role of the fuel pressure regulator is to keep the difference between the fuel pressure in the pipeline and the gas pressure in the intake pipe constant, i. e. to adjust the fuel pressure according to the change of the pressure in the intake pipe.

② Type. According to the installation position is divided into two kinds, one is connected with the oil rail (also known as the fabricated fuel rail), the characteristic is to bring back the oil pipe; the other is in the fuel tank, the characteristic is no return oil pipe.

(2) Structure and principle of fuel pressure regulator

① The fuel pressure regulator for the oil return line is installed as shown in Figure 2-45.

As shown in Figure 2-46, the fuel for the fuel feed system enters the oil inlet of the oil

the fuel tank into the fuel pump before entering the oil chamber, first through the strainer preliminary filtration.

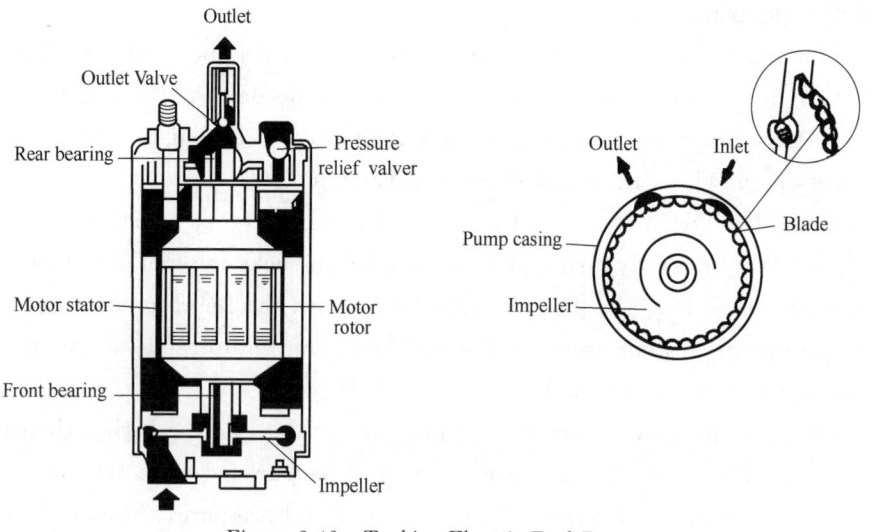

Figure 2-42　Turbine Electric Fuel Pump

　　The turbine pump is mainly composed of impeller, blade, pump shell and pump cover. The impeller is mounted on the rotor shaft of the fuel pump motor. When the oil pump motor is energized, the fuel pump motor drives the turbine pump impeller to rotate, due to centrifugal force, the blades in the small grooves around the impeller are close to the pump housing and carry the fuel from the oil inlet to the oil outlet chamber. Because the fuel intake chamber is constantly taken away, the formation of a certain degree of vacuum, the fuel in the tank through the intake port inhalation; and the outlet chamber fuel increased, the fuel pressure increased, when the oil pressure reached a certain value, the top outlet valve through the outlet output. The oil outlet valve can also prevent the fuel from flowing back to the tank when the fuel pump is not working, thus maintaining the residual pressure in the oil line for the next start.

　　Fuel flows through the inner cavity of the fuel pump to cool and lubricate the motor of the fuel pump. When the fuel pump is not working, the oil outlet valve is closed to maintain constant residual pressure in the tubing to facilitate engine start-up and prevent gas resistance. The pressure relief valve is installed between the oil inlet chamber and the oil outlet chamber. When the output oil pressure of the fuel pump reaches 0.4 MPa, the pressure relief valve is opened to connect the inlet and outlet chambers of the oil pump.

　　Turbine-type electric fuel pump has a large amount of pump oil, pump oil pressure is high (up to 600 kPa), oil supply pressure stability, low operating noise, long service life and other advantages, so the most widely used.

　　② Roller-type electric fuel pump. As shown in Figure 2-43, a roller-type electric fuel pump is mainly composed of fuel pump motor, roller-type fuel pump, oil outlet valve, pressure relief valve and other components. The oil transfer pressure of the roller type electric fuel pump fluctuates greatly. Damping damper must be installed at the oil outlet, which increa-

ance injector driven by voltage is the second, and the injector driven by current is the shortest.

2. Electric fuel pump

Electric fuel pump is the most important component of the fuel feed system of electronic-controlled engine. It is the fuel pressure power source needed for the fuel feed system. It plays an important role in the normal operation of the fuel feed system.

(1) Function and classification of electric fuel pump

① Function of electric fuel pump. Electric fuel pump is the basic part of electronic fuel injection engine. It is driven by a small DC motor, which sucks the fuel out of the fuel tank, pressurizes it and sends it to the pipeline, and works with the fuel pressure regulator to establish the appropriate system pressure. Electric fuel pump motor and fuel pump connected into a body, sealed in the same shell.

The electric fuel pump provides the oil pressure to the injector higher than the intake manifold pressure $250\sim300kPa$, because the fuel oil is pumped from the fuel tank, after compression or momentum conversion shall increase the oil pressure, through the pipeline to the injector, so the maximum oil pressure of the oil pump needs $450\sim600kPa$, its fuel supply is much larger than the maximum fuel consumption of the engine, the excess gasoline shall return to the fuel tank from the return line.

② Classification of electric fuel pump

a. The electric fuel pump can be divided into two types: built-in type and external type according to the installation position.

Built-in electric fuel pump installed in the fuel tank, with low noise, not easy to produce gas resistance, not easy to leak, simple installation pipeline and other advantages, more widely used. Some models also have a small fuel tank in the tank and put the fuel pump in the small tank, which can prevent the fuel around the fuel pump caused by the automobile turning or tilting when the fuel tank is insufficient, so that the fuel pump inhaled air and produced gas resistance.

The external electric fuel pump is connected in series in the pipeline outside the fuel tank. The advantage is that it is easy to arrange and install, but the noise is big, and the fuel feed system is easy to produce gas resistance, so only a few models are used.

b. According to the different structure of electric fuel pump, there are turbine type, roller type, rotor type and side slot type. Most of the built-in electric fuel pumps are turbine type and most of the external electric fuel pumps are roller type.

There are three types of oil pumps: roller type, blade type, and gear type. Santana GLi, 2000 GLi automobile adopts EKP10 double-stage electric fuel pump with low-pressure vane pump and high-pressure gear pump produced by Bosch Company of Germany; Hong Qi CA7200E automobile adopts gear-type electric fuel pump.

(2) Composition and principle of electric fuel pump

① As shown in Figure 2-42, a turbine-type electric fuel pump is mainly composed of a fuel pump motor, a turbine pump, an oil outlet valve, a pressure relief valve, etc. Fuel in

The battery provides direct power to the injector and ECU through the ignition switch and the main relay (or fuse), and the ECU controls the tie-in circuit of the injector and the main relay coil. When the ignition switch is switched on, the relay contacts are closed, and the injector drive circuit in the ECU makes the triode VT_1 turn on, and the current flowing through the injector coil produces voltage drop on the VT_1 emitter resistance; when the voltage at point A reaches the set value, the injector drive circuit makes the VT_1 cut off. When the battery voltage is 14V, the peak current flowing through the injector coil is 8A, and after the injector needle valve reaches the maximum lift, the current in the stationary state is 2A. In this process, VT_1 is switched on or off at a frequency of 20Hz, that is, the voltage change frequency is 20Hz. The function of triode VT_2 is to absorb the opposing electromotive force produced in the injector coil when VT_1 is turned on and off to prevent the current from suddenly decreaseing. The relay is used to prevent excessive current flowing through the injector coil. If the current flowing through the injector coil exceeds the set value, the relay contact is automatically disconnected to cut off the injector power supply.

In the injector current drive circuit, because there is no additional resistance, the impedance of the circuit is small, when the ECU gives orders to the injector, the current flowing through the injector coil increases rapidly, the magnetic force produced by the electromagnetic coil makes the needle valve open fast, the lag time of the injector is shortened, and the response is better. The opening time of the injector needle valve is always later than the time when the ECU gives instructions to the injector. This time is called the injection lag time (or ineffective injection time) of the injector. In addition, the current drive mode is adopted to keep the needle valve open so that the current of the injector is small, the injector coil is not easy to heat up, and the power loss can be reduced.

② Voltage drive mode. The additional resistance must be added when the low resistance injector is driven by voltage. Because the number of turns of the low-resistance injector coil is small, adding additional resistance can reduce the current flowing through the coil at work to prevent the coil from heating and damage. There are three ways of connecting the additional resistance to the injector, as shown in Figure 2-41.

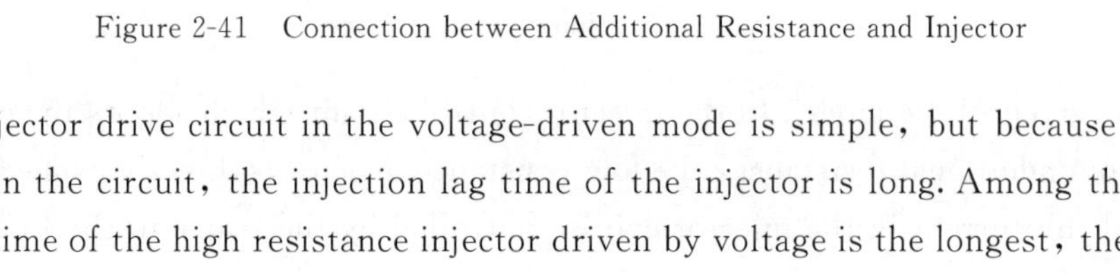

Solenoid resistance Injector

(a) Independent   (b) Grouping(1)   (c) Grouping(2)

Figure 2-41   Connection between Additional Resistance and Injector

The injector drive circuit in the voltage-driven mode is simple, but because of the high impedance in the circuit, the injection lag time of the injector is long. Among them, the injection lag time of the high resistance injector driven by voltage is the longest, the low resist-

The injector is mainly composed of strainer, wire harness connector, electromagnetic coil, return spring, armature and needle valve. The needle valve and armature are made into a whole. The lower part of the needle valve of the pintle injector is provided with a pintle extending into the nozzle.

When the injector does not spray oil, the return spring presses the needle valve against the seat through the armature to prevent drip oil. When the solenoid is energized, electromagnetic suction is generated, the armature is lifted and the needle valve is driven away from the seat, and the return spring is compressed. The valve body compresses the spring and rises, with a small lift stroke of $0.1 \sim 0.2$ mm. The fuel passes through the needle valve and is ejected from the annular gap or orifice between the needle and the nozzle. The shape of the jet fuel is a cone fog of less than $30°$. Because of the high fuel pressure, the injection fuel is fog-like fuel. When the electromagnetic coil is cut off, the electromagnetic suction disappears. The return spring quickly closes the needle valve and the injector stops the injection. When the structure of the injector and the injection pressure is constant, the fuel injection quantity of the injector depends on the opening time of the needle valve, i. e. the energizing time of the electromagnetic coil. The elastic force of the return spring has an effect on the tightness of the needle valve and the fuel cut-off degree of the injector.

The injector of single point fuel injection system adopts the lower feed type, i. e. the inlet is located on the side of the injector, not on the top, mainly to reduce the height of the injector, so as to install in the throttle body. In addition, the injector used in each model can be divided into two types: high resistance (resistance $13 \sim 16\Omega$) and low resistance (resistance $2 \sim 3\Omega$) according to the resistance value of the coil.

(2) Driving mode of injector

The injector can be driven in two ways: current-driven and voltage-driven, as shown in Figure 2-40. The current drive mode is only suitable for low-resistance injector. The voltage drive mode can be used for both high-resistance and low-resistance injector.

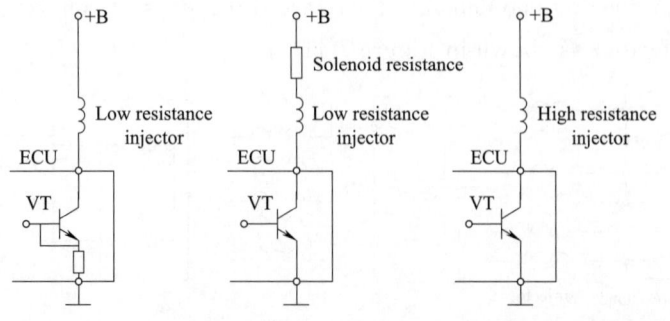

(a) Current drive   (b) Voltage drive(low resistance)   (c) Voltage drive(high resistance)

Figure 2-40   Injector Drive Mode

① The current drive mode . In the injector control circuit which adopts the current drive mode, without additional resistance, the low resistance injector is directly connected with the battery, and the current in the injector coil is controlled by the triode in the ECU.

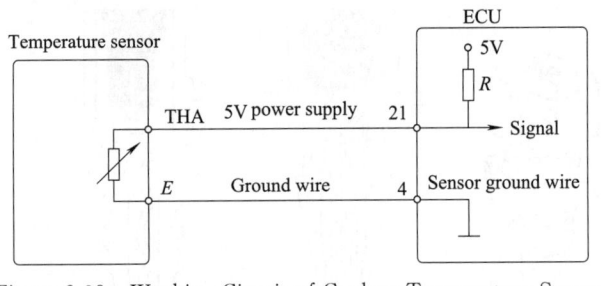

Figure 2-38　Working Circuit of Coolant Temperature Sensor

when the temperature of the tested object decreases, the resistance value of the sensor increases and the partial voltage value on the thermistor increases. According to the received signal voltage value, ECU can calculate the corresponding temperature value, and then carry out real-time control.

(Ⅳ) Structural Principle of Actuator for Engine Fuel Injection System

1. Injectors

The injector is the actuator used in the electronic fuel feed system. The injector is an important actuator in the electronic fuel injection system. It receives the signal from the engine control module and accurately ejects the fuel.

The electronic fuel injection system adopts electromagnetic injector. The injector of single point injection system is installed at the air inlet of the throttle body. The injector of multi-point injection system is installed at the intake ports of each cylinder on the intake manifold or cylinder head.

(1) Structure and working principle of injector

Depending on the structure of the nozzle, the injector can be divided into two types: the pintle type and the hole type, as shown in Figure 2-39.

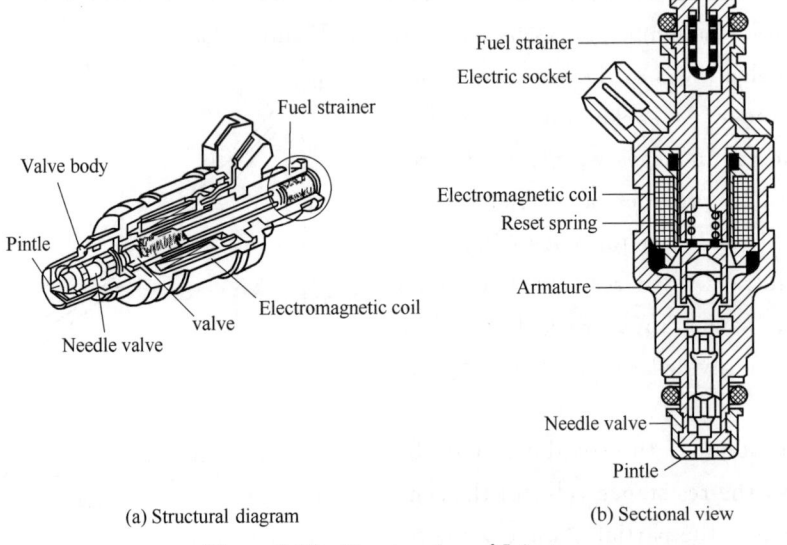

(a) Structural diagram　　　　　　　　(b) Sectional view

Figure 2-39　Construction of Injector

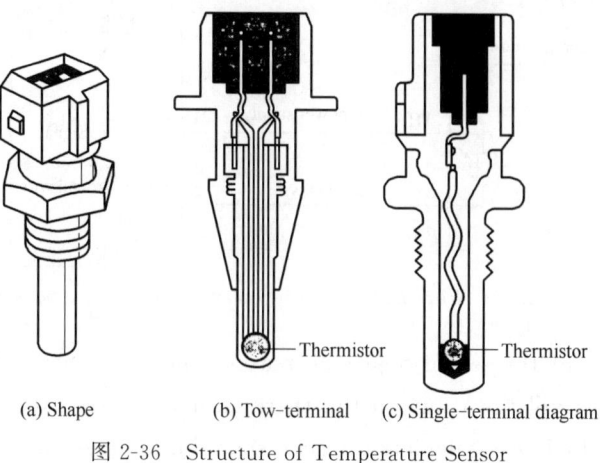

— Thermistor — Thermistor

(a) Shape　　　　(b) Tow-terminal　(c) Single-terminal diagram

图 2-36　Structure of Temperature Sensor

comb-like chip shape, a thick film shape, etc. , and placed in the metal tube shell of the sensor. Each of the two ends of the thermistor leads out an electrode and is connected to the sensor socket.

　　Thread is made on the sensor housing for installation and disassembly. The wiring socket is divided into two types: single terminal type and dual-terminal type. The fuel injection system of middle and high grade passenger automobile uses dual-terminal type temperature sensor, the fuel injection system of low grade passenger automobile and the instrument of automobile uses one terminal type temperature sensor. If there is only one terminal on the sensor socket, the housing is an electrode of the sensor.

　　② Characteristics and circuit of automobile temperature sensor. The negative temperature coefficient NTC thermistor temperature sensor is widely used in automobile electronic control system. The relationship between resistance and temperature is shown in Figure 2-37. The NTC thermistor has the characteristic of decreasing the resistance value when temperature rises and increasing the resistance value when temperature decreases, and it has obvious non-linear relation. The working circuit of the temperature sensor is shown in Figure 2-38.

　　The two electrodes of the sensor are connected with the ECU socket by a wire. The ECU is connected in series with a divided resistor. The ECU provides a stable voltage (5V) to a divided resistor consisting of a thermistor and a divided resistor. The signal voltage of the sensor input ECU is equal to the value of the divided resistor on the thermistor.

　　When the temperature of the tested object increases, the resistance value of the sensor decreases and the partial voltage value on the thermistor decreases; on the contrary,

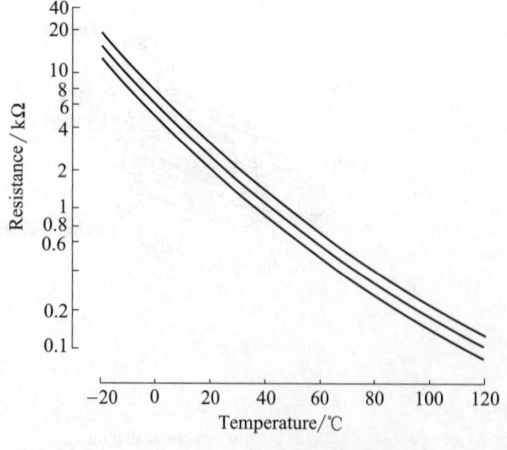

Figure 2-37　Relation Curve between Resistance and Temperature of Temperature Sensor

vance angle correction, activated carbon tank solenoid valve control and so on. Cooling fluid temperature signal is also an important signal of other electronic control system, such as electronic control automatic transmission system, automatic air-conditioning system. In the electronic control automatic transmission system of a few models, if the engine coolant temperature is detected below 60℃, in order to protect the driving device, the automatic transmission control unit shall enter the"safe operation mode", shall not allow the automobile to climb into the overspeed gear, the automobile can only travel at the speed of 90 km/h. If the coolant temperature sensor fails or the signal breaks, the engine electronic control unit shall start the standby mode, set the water temperature to about 80℃, and record the fault code. At this time, although the automobile can run normally, but the engine is cold, hot automobile start difficult, fuel consumption increases, idling stability decreases, exhaust emissions increase and so on.

(2) Classification of temperature sensors

① Classify by test object: Such as the test object is the intake air temperature sensor, the coolant temperature sensor, the exhaust gas temperature sensor and the lubricating oil temperature sensor and so on. This classification method is simple and practical, the user can easily choose the sensor according to the measurement object.

② Classification by structure and physical properties: There are many kinds of temperature sensors, such as thermistor type, metal thermistor type, wire-wound resistor type, semiconductor transistor type and so on. Thermistor-type temperature sensor is widely used in modern automobile.

(3) Thermistor temperature sensor

① Structure characteristics of thermistor type temperature sensor

Thermistor can be divided into positive temperature coefficient (PTC) type thermistor, negative temperature coefficient (NTC) type thermistor, critical temperature type thermistor and linear thermistor. The negative temperature coefficient type thermistor temperature sensor is commonly used in automobile. For example, the thermistor is made by using the characteristic that the resistance of ceramic semiconductor material changes with the temperature. Its outstanding advantages are high sensitivity, prompt response, simple structure, convenient manufacture and low cost. The structure is mainly composed of thermistor, metal or plastic shell, wiring socket and connecting wire. The structure of the temperature sensor is shown in Figure 2-36, divided into single terminal and dual-terminal.

The thermistor is the main component of the temperature sensor. The thermistor for automobile is made by adding a certain amount of metal oxide into the ceramic semiconductor material and sintering it at a high temperature above 1000℃. By controlling the proportion of the oxide and the sintering temperature, different characteristics of the thermistor can be obtained, which can meet the requirements of use. For example, if the engine coolant temperature is measured, the working temperature of the thermistor is −30～+130℃. If the exhaust temperature of the engine is measured, the working temperature of the thermistor is 600～1000℃.

The shape of the thermistor is made into a pearl shape, a disk shape, a washer shape, a

back control must be stopped, that is, using the open-loop control. Feedback control is relieved in the following situations:

① When the engine is started;

② Warm-up process after cold start-up;

③ When the automobile is under heavy load or speeding;

④ When the fuel is out of service;

⑤ When the duration of the air-fuel ratio over-thin signal sent from the EGO is longer than the specified value (if more than 10s);

⑥ When the duration of the air-fuel ratio over-rich signal sent from the EGO is longer than the specified value (if more than 4s);

In addition, since there is no voltage signal when the temperature of the EGO is below 300℃, the feedback control will not work.

6. Temperature sensor

(1) Function of temperature sensor

Temperature is an important parameter reflecting the engine's heat load state. In order to ensure that the electronic control unit can accurately control the engine's normal operation, it is necessary to monitor the engine's intake temperature at any time so as to correct the parameter of control, accurately calculate the mass flow sucked in the cylinder and carry out exhaust purification treatment. Air quality is closely related to inlet temperature (density) and atmospheric pressure. When the inlet temperature is low, the air density increases and the mass of the same volume gas increases, otherwise, when the inlet temperature increases, the mass of the same volume gas decreases. In fuel injection systems using various manifold pressure or air flow sensors, air intake air temperature sensors are required, and in some cases atmospheric pressure sensors are required to monitor changes in ambient temperature and atmospheric pressure at any time and to correct the fuel injection quantity. The electronic control unit automatically adapts to the changes of ambient cold or high temperature and atmospheric pressure at different altitude.

The function of the Intake Air Temperature Sensor (IATS) is to detect the intake temperature and convert the temperature signal into electrical signal and input into the engine electronic control unit. Intake temperature signal is a correction signal of many control functions, including fuel pulse width, ignition timing, idle speed control and exhaust emission. If the intake air temperature sensor signal is interrupted, it shall lead to the difficulty of engine thermal start, increase of fuel pulse width and deterioration of exhaust emission.

The Coolant Temperature Sensor (CTS), also known as the Water Temperature Sensor, is a negative temperature coefficient type thermistor type temperature sensor, which is installed on the outlet pipe of the engine coolant. Its function is to detect the temperature of the engine coolant and transfer the temperature signal to the electronic control unit. The electronic control unit corrects the injection time and ignition time according to the signal. To keep the engine in optimum working condition. Cooling fluid temperature sensor signal is the correction signal of many control functions, such as fuel injection correction, ignition ad-

0. 9V, which is similar to that of ZrO_2 EGO.

(3) Air-fuel ratio feedback control

In order to obtain the air-fuel ratio required by the three-way catalyst, the fuel injection quantity must be accurately controlled. But under the following circumstances, the intake signal measured by the AFS alone cannot reach such high control precision, all of which will cause a wrong mixing ratio of CO, HC and Nox in the exhaust pipe after combustion, low conversion efficiency of three-way catalyst, and serious pollution.

① If the injector leaks or is clogged, it will cause the actual mixture to be too thick or too thin;

② The lack of ignition or spark energy in the ignition system will result in incomplete burned mixture directly entering into the three-way catalyst, decreasing the power, economy and emission;

③ Wrong valve timing will result in the mixture entering directly into the three-way catalyst for combustion;

④ The air leakage of the intake manifold behind the AFS will generate excessive NO_x or the fault AFS will output a curve with deviation;

⑤ There is deviation in the output curve of the water temperature sensor;

⑥ The invalid injection pressure regulating device of the fuel system will result in incorrect system pressure;

⑦ The IATS signal output curve has deviation and so on.

Therefore, the feedback signal from the EGO installed in the exhaust pipe must be used to control the theoretical air-fuel ratio. Controlling the mixture air-fuel ratio according to the input signal of the EGO, is called closed-loop control. It is a simple and practical closed-loop control system. This control system needs some time to respond, that is, from the formation of gas mixture in the intake pipe, to the EGO to detect the oxygen concentration in the exhaust gas. The process includes the response time of the mixed gas intake cylinder, the exhaust gas superoxide sensor and the EGO, etc. Because of the lag time, it is impossible to keep the air-fuel ratio completely in the theoretical air-fuel ratio 14. 7. The actual controlled mixture air-fuel ratio is always in a narrow range near the theoretical air-fuel ratio 14. 7.

(4) Implementation conditions of feedback control

During closed-loop control with GEO for feedback control, the mixture in principle is near the theoretical air-fuel ratio. However, it is not suitable in some conditions. For example, when the engine is started or when it is just started but not warmed up, it needs rich mixture, because the engine cooling water temperature is low. But if the mixture is near the theoretical air-fuel ratio according to the feedback control, the engine may be extinguished. As another example, it also needs rich mixture when the engine is running under the high-load, or high-speed state (actually in the highway, when the speed exceeds more than 130km/h, and the wind resistance is very large, it is necessary to increase the throttle to maintain high engine speed and torque to ensure high speed). But if the mixture is also near the theoretical air-fuel ratio, the engine will not work well. So in some cases the feed-

(2) TiO₂ EGO

TiO$_2$ EGO makes use of the characteristic that the resistance value of TiO$_2$ material varies with the oxygen content in the exhaust gas, so it is also called resistance EGO. The shape of TiO$_2$ EGO is similar to that of ZrO$_2$ EGO. Inside the front shield of the sensor, it is a TiO$_2$ thick film element (as shown in Figure 2-34). The pure TiO$_2$ is a kind of semiconductor with high resistance at normal temperature, but its lattice becomes defective and the resistance decreases when the surface is oxygen-deficient. Since the resistance of TiO$_2$ varies with the temperature, there is also an electric heater inside the TiO$_2$ EGO to keep the temperature of the TiO$_2$ EGO constant during engine operation.

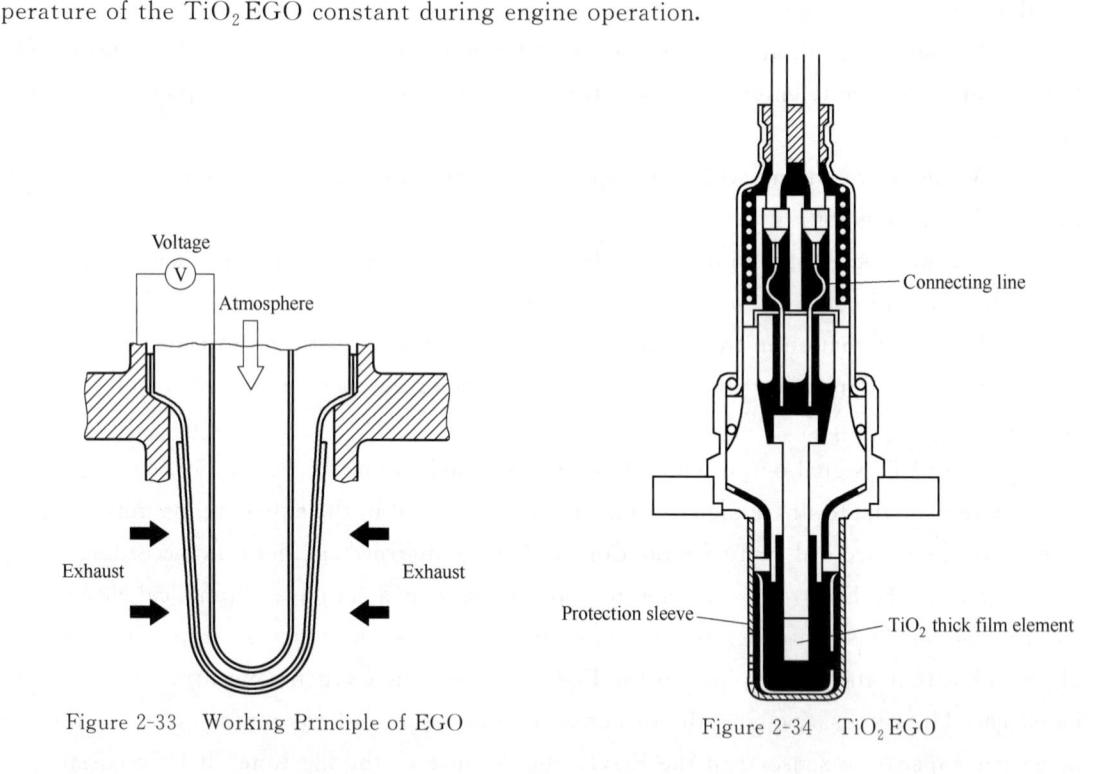

Figure 2-33　Working Principle of EGO

Figure 2-34　TiO$_2$ EGO

As shown in Figure 2-35, the ECU terminal No. 2 adds a constant 1V voltage to one end of the TiO$_2$ EGO, and the other end of the sensor is connected to the ECU terminal No. 4. When the concentration of oxygen in the exhaust gas varies with that in the engine mixture, the resistance of the EGO changes, and the voltage drop on the terminal No. 4 of ECU also changes. When the voltage on the terminal No. 4 is higher than that on the terminal No. 3, the ECU determines that the mixture is too thick. When the voltage on the terminal No. 4 is lower than that on the terminal No. 3, the ECU determines that the mixture is too thin. Through the feedback control of ECU, the concentration of the mixture can be kept near the theoretical air-fuel ratio. In the actual feedback control process, the voltage on terminal No. 4 connected with ECU, varies from 0.1 to

Figure 2-35　Working principle of TiO$_2$ EGO

ZrO_2 can work normally only after the temperature exceeds 300℃. Early EGOs were heated by exhaust, with only one wire connected to the ECU, and it starts to work only after the engine has worked for several minutes [as shown in Figure 2-32 (a)] . Most automobiles now use EGO with a heater [as shown in Figure 2-32 (b)], which contains an electric heating element to heat EGO to the working temperature within 20~30s after the start of the engine. It has three wires, one for ECU, the other two for grounding and power supply.

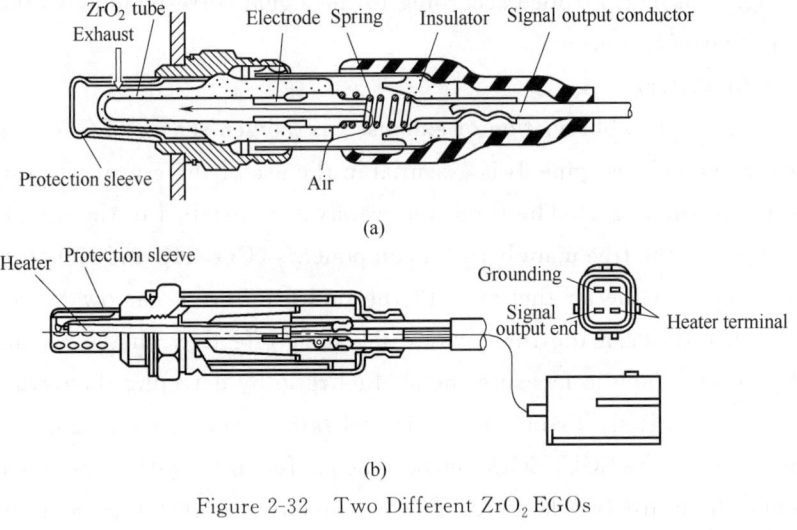

Figure 2-32　Two Different ZrO_2 EGOs

The ceramic body of the ZrO_2 tube is porous. The oxygen in it will be ionized when the temperature is high. As the oxygen content is different between the inner side and outside of the ZrO_2 tube, oxygen ions diffuse from the atmosphere side to the exhaust side. As such, the ZrO_2 tube turns into a micro-cell, with the voltage between the two platinum electrodes (as shown in Figure 2-33) . When the actual air-fuel ratio of the mixture is smaller than that of the theoretical air-fuel ratio, that is, when the engine runs with a dense mixture, there is less oxygen in the exhaust gas, but more CO, HC, H_2 and so on. These gases react with oxygen under platinum catalysis on the outer surface of the ZrO_2 tube, depleting the residual oxygen in the exhaust gas and turning the oxygen concentration on the outer surface of the ZrO_2 tube to 0. It increases the difference of oxygen concentration in the outer and inner side of the ZrO_2 tube, causing a sharp increase of the voltage between the two platinum electrodes. Therefore, the voltage generated by the ZrO_2 EGO will change significantly in the theoretical air-fuel ratio: With the dilute mixture, the output voltage is almost 0; with the dense mixture, the output voltage is close to 1 V.

It is impossible to keep the mixture concentration accurate as the theoretical air-fuel ratio. Actually, the feedback control can only keep the mixture concentration fluctuate in a small range near the theoretical air-fuel ratio, so the output voltage of the EGO varies from 0. 1 to 0. 8 V (usually more than 8 times per 10 s) . If the output voltage of the EGO changes too slowly (less than 8 times per 10s) or the voltage remains constant (whether at high or low level), it indicates that the EGO is faulty and needs to be overhauled.

044　Fault Diagnosis and Repair of Automobile Engine Electronic Control System

When the engine works, the signal voltage generated by the magnetic induction crankshaft position sensor (CPS) and the Hall camshaft position sensor (CIS) is continuously inputted into the ECU. When the ECU simultaneously receives the low level signal corresponding to the large tooth of the crankshaft position sensor and the camshaft position sensor window, it can be determined that the first cylinder piston is in the compression stroke, the fourth cylinder piston is in the exhaust stroke, and the ignition advance angle and the injection advance angle can be controlled according to the signal corresponding to the small tooth of the crankshaft position sensor.

5. O_2S (with heater)

Oxygen sensor is the abbreviation of exhaust gas oxygen sensor (EGO), also known as O_2S, installed in the exhaust pipe. It is essential in the use of three-way catalyst to reduce emission pollution of the engine. The three-way catalyst is installed in the middle part of the exhaust pipe to purify the tree main harmful components (CO, HC and NO_x) in the exhaust gas. However only when the air-fuel ratio of the mixture is in a narrow range close to the theoretical air-fuel ratio, can the three-way catalyst be effective. Therefore, an EGO is inserted into the exhaust pipe to measure the air-fuel ratio by detecting the oxygen concentration in the exhaust gas. It shall convert the air-fuel ratio into a voltage signal or a resistance signal to be fed back to the ECU. ECU controls the air-fuel ratio within the theoretical value.

At present, there are two kinds of EGOs, zirconia (ZrO_2) type and titanium oxide (TiO_2) type, of which ZrO_2 EGO is the most widely used.

(1) ZrO_2 EGO

The basic element of the ZrO_2 EGO is the ZrO_2 ceramic tube (fast ionic conductor), also known as the ZrO_2 tube (Figure 2-31). ZrO_2 tube is fixed in a fixed sleeve with mounting thread, with its inner and outer surfaces covered with porous platinum film. The inner surface is in contact with atmosphere and the outer surface is in contact with exhaust gas. The terminal of the EGO is provided with a metal sheath, on which there is a hole for the connection of the inner cavity of the ZrO_2 tube to the atmosphere; and the wire leads the platinum electrode on the surface of the ZrO_2 tube through the insulating sleeve from the terminal.

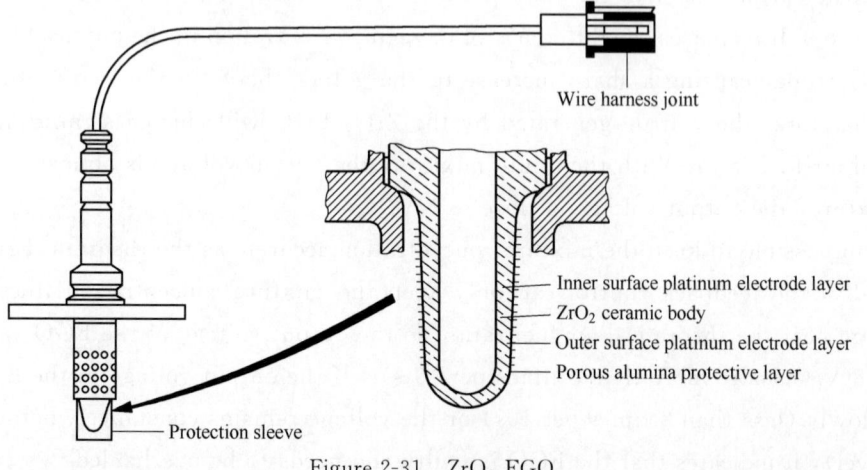

Figure 2-31 ZrO_2 EGO

Item II   Maintenance of Electronic Control Fuel Injection System for Gasoline Engines   **043**

tor.

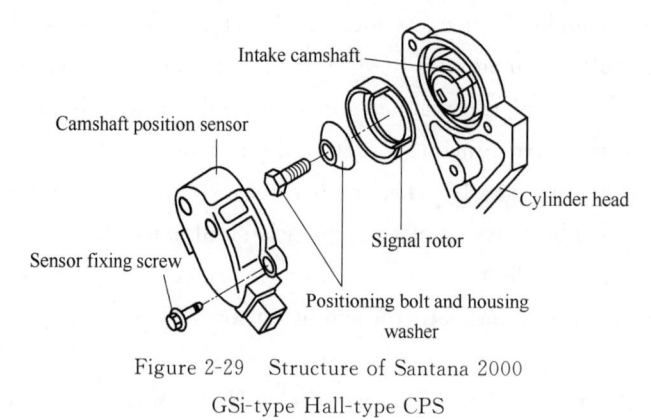

Figure 2-29　Structure of Santana 2000 GSi-type Hall-type CPS

The signal rotor, also known as the trigger impeller, is mounted at one end of the distribution camshaft and fixed by positioning bolts and seat ring. The diaphragm of a signal rotor, also known as a blade, has a window. The window corresponds to low-level signals and the diaphragm (blade) corresponds to high-level signals. Hall signal generator is mainly composed of Hall IC, permanent magnet and conductive steel sheet. Hall IC is composed of Hall component, amplifier circuit, voltage stabilizing circuit, temperature compensation circuit, signal conversion circuit and output circuit. The Hall component is made of silicon semiconductor material, with a gap of 0.2～0.4 mm away from the permanent magnet. When the signal rotor rotates with the distribution camshaft at the same time, the diaphragm and window will turn from the air gap between the Hall IC and the permanent magnet.

(b) The working principle of the sensor. According to the working principle of the Hall sensor, when the diaphragm (blade) enters the air gap (that is, in the air gap), the Hall component does not produce voltage, the sensor outputs a high-level (5V) signal, and when the diaphragm (blade) leaves the air gap (that is, the window enters the air gap), the Hall component produces voltage, and the sensor outputs a low-level signal (0.1V).

The relationship between the output signal of the camshaft position sensor and the output signal of the crankshaft position sensor is shown in Figure 2-30.

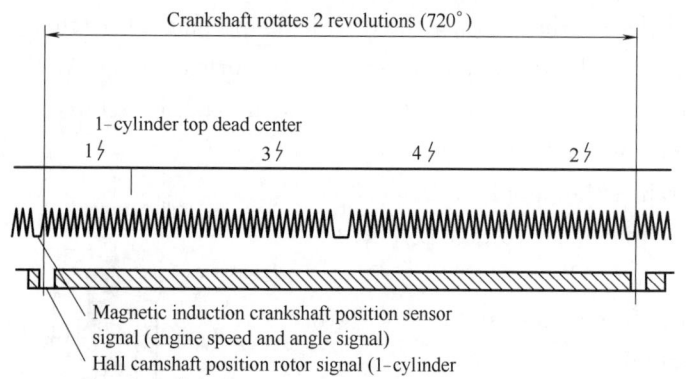

Figure 2-30　Corresponding Relationship between Output Waveform of Santana 2000 GSi Crankshaft/Camshaft Position Sensor

Hall sensor signal rotor turns one turn with every two turns of the engine crankshaft, correspondingly producing a low-level signal and a high-level signal, with the low-level signal corresponding to a certain angle before TDC of 1 cylinder compression.

als, and the Hall coefficient is much larger than that of metal materials. Therefore, semiconductor materials are generally used to make Hall components. The Hall effect not only detects the voltage by switching on and off the magnetic field, but also detects the current flowing through the wire because the intensity of the magnetic field around the wire is proportional to the current flowing through the wire. Since the 1980s, the number of Hall-type sensors used in automobiles has been increasing day by day, mainly because of the two outstanding advantages of Hall-type sensors: The output voltage signal is similar to the square wave signal, and the output voltage is independent of the speed of the object being measured. The Hall effect sensor is different from the magnetic induction sensor in that it requires an additional power supply.

(b) The structure principle of Hall sensor. The basic structure of Hall sensor is shown in Figure 2-28. It is mainly composed of rotor, permanent magnet, Hall transistor and amplifier. The rotor is mounted on the rotor shaft. Hall integrated circuit is composed of Hall component, amplifier circuit, voltage stabilizing circuit, temperature compensation circuit, signal conversion circuit and output circuit.

When the rotor rotates along with the rotor shaft, the blade on the rotor rotates between the Hall integrated circuit and the permanent magnet, the magnetic field in the Hall integrated circuit shall change, and the Hall voltage shall be produced in the Hall component. After the signal processing circuit, the square wave signal can be output.

As the sensor shaft rotates, the blades on the rotor turn from the air gap between the Hall integrated circuit and the permanent magnet. When the blade enters the air gap, the magnetic field in the Hall IC is bypassed by the blade, the Hall voltage U_H is 0, the output level of the IC is triode cut off, and the output signal voltage U_0 of the sensor is high level. (Measured results show that: When the supply voltage $U_{cc}=14.4V$, the signal voltage $U_0=9.8V$; when the supply voltage $U_{cc}=5V$, the signal voltage $U_0=4.8V$.)

When the blade leaves the air gap, the flux of the permanent magnet passes through the Hall integrated circuit and the conductive steel sheet forms a loop. At this point, the Hall component produces a voltage ($U_H=1.9\sim2.0$ V), the Hall integrated circuit outputs a triode conduction, and the sensor outputs a signal voltage of U_0 at a low level. (Measured results show that: When the supply voltage $U_{cc}=14.4V$ or $U_{cc}=5V$, the signal voltage $U_0=0.1\sim0.3V$.)

b. Hall camshaft position sensor for Jetta and Santana automobiles

(a) Structural characteristics of the sensor. Jetta AT, GTX, Santana 2000GSi, 3000-model automobiles adopt Hall camshaft position sensor installed on one end of engine gas distribution camshaft, as shown in Figure 2-29, mainly composed of Hall signal generator and signal ro-

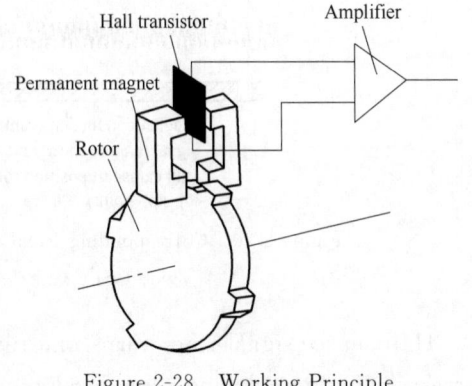

Figure 2-28   Working Principle
of Hall Sensor

fects the magnetic resistance of the magnetic circuit and the output voltage of the sensing coil, the air gap between the rotor convex teeth and the magnetic head can not be changed arbitrarily in use. If the air gap changes, it must be adjusted according to regulations. The air gap size is generally designed to be 0.2~0.4mm.

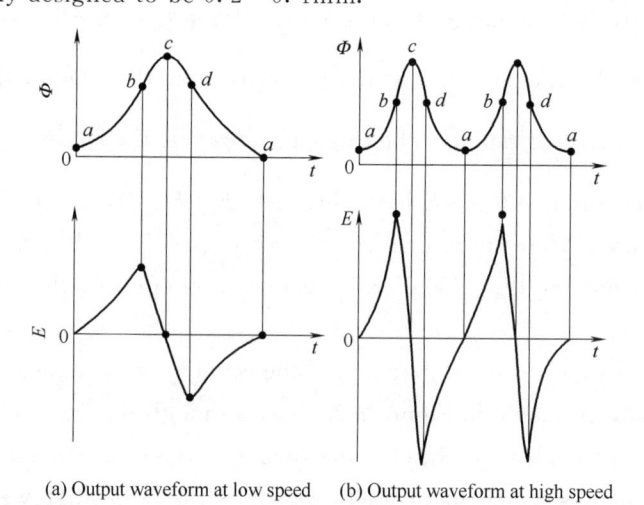

(a) Output waveform at low speed   (b) Output waveform at high speed

Figure 2-26   Magnetic Flux Φ and Electromotive Force E Waveforms in the Sensing Coil

③ Hall type crankshaft and camshaft position sensor

a. The working principle of hall sensor. All types of Hall-type and differential Hall-type sensors are based on the Hall effect. The Hall effect was first discovered by Dr. Hall, a physicist at Johns Hopkins University in the United States.

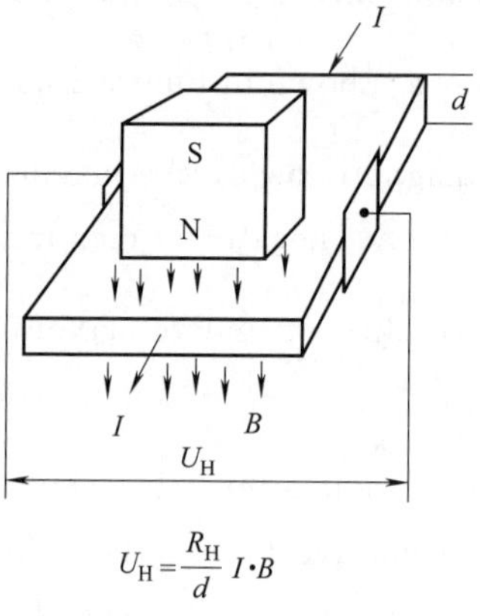

(a) Hall effect. Dr Hall discovered in 1879: When a rectangular platinum conductor with current I is placed perpendicular to the magnetic field with magnetic field intensity B, as shown in Figure 2-27, a voltage U_H perpendicular to the current direction and magnetic field direction is generated on the two transverse sides of the platinum conductor, and the voltage disappears immediately when the magnetic field is removed. The voltage is called Hall voltage, and U_H is proportional to the current I and magnetic induction intensity B passing through the platinum conductor, i. e.

$$U_H = \frac{R_H}{d} I \cdot B \tag{2-1}$$

$$U_H = \frac{R_H}{d} I \cdot B$$

Figure 2-27   Hall Effect Schematic Diagram

The R_H in the formula is the Hall coefficient; d is the thickness of the platinum conductor.

The element that makes use of Hall effect is called Hall component, the sensor that makes use of Hall component is called Hall effect sensor, abbreviation Hall type sensor or Hall sensor. The Hall effect was not applied in the field of automatic control until the discovery of semiconductor devices in 1947, and has been widely used in the field of automotive technology since the 1970s.

The experimental results show that the Hall effect also exists in semiconductor materi-

040 Fault Diagnosis and Repair of Automobile Engine Electronic Control System

When the signal rotor rotates clockwise and the convex teeth of the rotor approach the magnetic head, the air gap between the convex teeth and the magnetic head decreases, the reluctance of the magnetic circuit decreases, the magnetic flux Φ increases, the flux change rate $\dfrac{d\phi}{dT}$ increases >0, and the induced electromotive force E is positive ($E>0$), abc shown in Figure 2-26. When the convex teeth of the rotor are near the edge of the magnetic head, the magnetic flux ϕ increases rapidly, the flux change rate is the largest $\left[\dfrac{d\phi}{dT}=\left(\dfrac{d\phi}{dT}\right)\text{max}\right]$, and the induced electromotive force E is the highest ($E=E_{\text{max}}$), as shown in Figure 2-26 at the point b of the curve. After the rotor turns to b-point position, although the magnetic flux ϕ is still increasing, but the flux change rate decreases, therefore, the induction electromotive force E decreases.

When the rotor rotates to the center line of the convex tooth aligned with the center line of the magnetic head, as shown in Figure 2-25 (b), although the air gap between the salient tooth of the rotor and the magnetic head is the smallest, the magnetic resistance of the magnetic circuit is the smallest, and the magnetic flux ϕ is the largest. However, since the flux cannot continue to increase, the flux change rate is 0, so the induced electromotive force E is 0, as shown in Figure 2-22 at point c.

As the rotor continues to rotate clockwise and the convex tooth leaves the magnetic head, as shown in Figure 2-25 (c), the air gap between the convex tooth and the magnetic head increases, the reluctance of the magnetic circuit increases, and the magnetic flux is reduced $\left(\dfrac{d\phi}{dT}<0\right)$, so the induced electromotive force E is negative, as shown in Figure 2-26 in the curve cda. When the convex tooth turns to the edge of the magnetic head, the magnetic flux is much smaller, the flux change rate reaches a negative maximum $\left[=\dfrac{d\phi}{dT}=-\left(\dfrac{d\phi}{dT}\right)\text{max}\right]$, and the induced electromotive force E reaches a negative maximum ($E=-E_{\text{max}}$), as shown at the d point on the curve in Figure 2-26.

Thus, every time the signal rotor turns a convex tooth, a periodic alternating electromotive force is produced in the sensing coil, that is, the electromotive force appears one maximum and one minimum, and the sensing coil outputs an alternating voltage signal accordingly.

The outstanding advantage of the magnetic induction sensor is that it doesn't need additional power supply. The permanent magnet can change the mechanical energy into electric energy, and its magnetic energy can't be lost. When the engine speed changes, the speed of rotor convex tooth rotation shall change, and the flux change rate in the core shall change accordingly. The higher the speed, the greater the flux change rate, and the higher the induction electromotive force in the sensing coil. The variation of magnetic flux and induced electromotive force at different speeds is shown in Figure 2-26 (b) .

Because the air gap between the rotor convex teeth and the magnetic head directly af-

ger rectangular width corresponds to 70 ° before the top dead center of the first cylinder piston of the engine, so that the ECU can control the injection advance angle and the ignition advance angle. Because Ne signal light hole interval radian is 1° (the light hole part is 0.5°, the shading part is 0.5°), so in each pulse cycle, high and low level each occupy 1° crankshaft rotation angle, 360 signal indicates crankshaft rotation 720°.

From Figure 2-24, when the ECU receives the wide pulse signal from the G signal generator, it can be determined that the piston of cylinder 1 is at a position of 70° before the top dead center of compression; when the ECU receives the next G signal, it is determined that the piston of cylinder 5 is at a position of 70° before the top dead center of compression. After the ECU receives the position signal (G signal) of each top dead center, the control accuracy of the injection advance angle and ignition advance angle can be controlled within 1° (crankshaft angle) according to the crankshaft angle signal (Ne signal).

② Magnetoelectric crankshaft position sensor. Crankshaft position sensors used by Vios Toyota 5A engine camshaft position sensor, engine speed crankshaft position sensor, Santana automobile AJR engine used crankshaft position sensor are this type.

The magnetic induction sensor is mainly composed of signal rotor, sensing coil, permanent magnet and magnetic yoke. The working principle is shown in Figure 2-25. The magnetic force line of permanent magnet forms a closed loop through the rotor, coil and bracket. When the rotor rotates, the magnetic gap between the rotor bump and the bracket changes constantly, and the magnetic flux through the coil also changes constantly. The induction voltage is produced in the coil and outputted in the form of AC. In the practical structure, the engine speed and crankshaft position sensor are usually installed on the distributor, using the compound rotor and coupling coil.

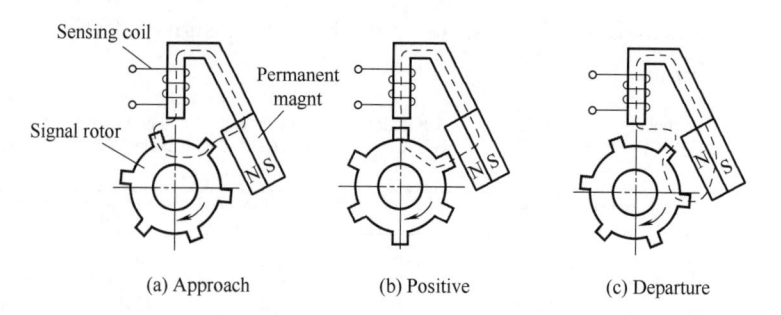

Figure 2-25   Working Principle of Magnetic Induction Sensor

The path the line of magnetic force passes is: The permanent magnet N-pole—gap between stator and rotor—rotor salient tooth—signal rotor—air gap between rotor salient tooth and stator head—head—guide plate (magnetic yoke)—permanent magnet S-pole. When the signal rotor rotates, the air gap in the magnetic circuit changes periodically, and the magnetic resistance of the magnetic circuit and the flux passing through the signal coil head change periodically. According to the principle of electromagnetic induction, alternating electromotive force is induced in the sensing coil.

b. Generating principle of crankshaft speed, angle signal and cylinder identification signal.

The working principle of the photoelectric sensor is shown in Figure 2-23. When the engine drives the sensor shaft to rotate, the light hole on the signal plate turns between the LED of the signal generator and the photosensitive triode, because the bevel gear on the sensor shaft is engaged with the bevel gear on the camshaft of the engine gas distribution mechanism.

When the light holes on the signal plate rotates to the space between the LED and the optical transistor, the optical transistor is turned on with light emitted by the LED shall shine on it, and the collector outputs a low level (0. 1~0. 3V); when the light-shielding part of the signal plate rotates to the space between the LED and the optical transistor, the optical transistor is turned off due to that the light emitted by the LED cannot shine on it, and the collector outputs a high level (4. 8~5. 2V) . If the signal plate rotates continuously, the light holes and the shielding part shall alternately output high levels and low levels.

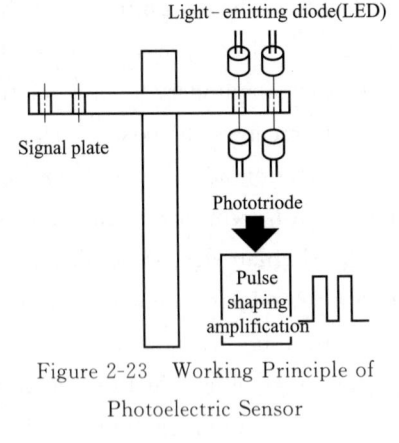

Figure 2-23　Working Principle of Photoelectric Sensor

When the sensor shaft rotates with the crankshaft and the gas distribution camshaft, the light holes and the shielding parts on the signal plate shall pass through the space between the LED and the optical transistor, with the light emitted by the LED alternately shining on the optical transistor of the signal generator producing pulse signals corresponding to the crankshaft position and the camshaft position in the signal sensor. The relationship between the photoelectric crankshaft used by Nissan and the output signal of the camshaft position sensor is shown in Figure 2-24.

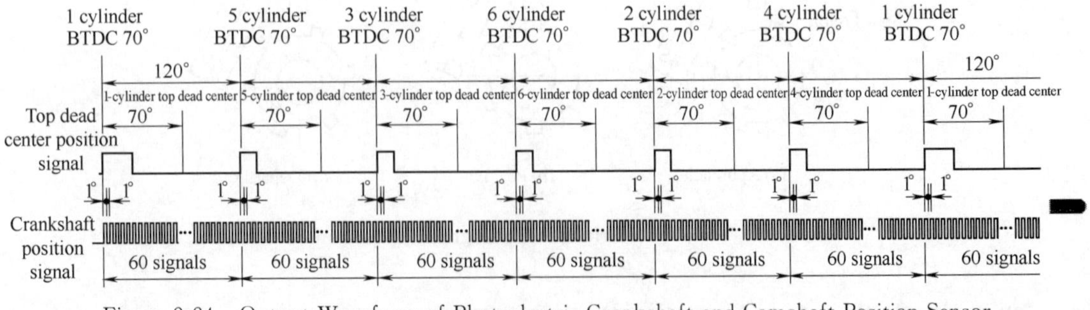

Figure 2-24　Output Waveform of Photoelectric Crankshaft and Camshaft Position Sensor

Because the crankshaft rotates two times, the sensor shaft drives the signal plate to rotate once, so the G signal sensor shall produce 6 pulse signals, and the Ne signal sensor shall produce 360 pulse signals, because the G signal transmits the aperture of 60°, the crankshaft shall produce a pulse signal every 120°, the G signal is usually called 120° signal. The design and installation ensures that the 120° signal is generated at 70° (BTDC70°) before the top dead center, and that the signal produced by the light-transmitting hole with a slightly lon-

tion time when the engine is starting. Therefore, it is also called cylinder identification sensor (CIS).

(2) Classification of crankshaft and camshaft position sensor

Crankshaft position sensor and camshaft position sensor are usually installed together, but in different parts on different models, such as around crankshaft, camshaft, flywheel or distributor. According to the different structure and working principle, it can be divided into three types: electromagnetic type, Hall type and photoelectric type.

① Photoelectric CPS

a. The structural characteristics of the sensor. The photoelectric crankshaft and camshaft position sensors produced by Nissan are developed from the distributor. The structure as shown in Figure 2-22 is mainly composed of signal generator, signal plate (a signal rotor), distributor, sensor shell and wire harness plug.

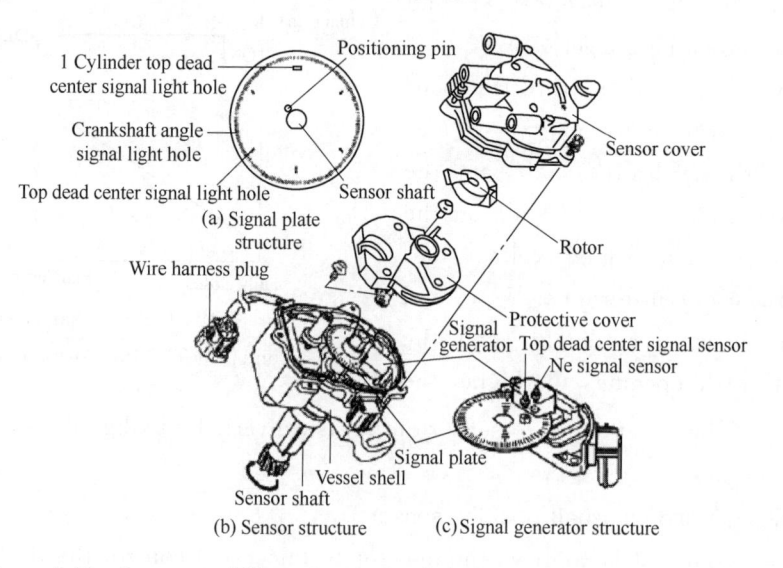

Figure 2-22　Structure of Photoelectric Crankshaft or Camshaft Position Sensor

The signal plate is the signal rotor of the sensor, mounted on the sensor shaft. As the structure is shown in Figure 2-22 (a), there are inner and outer light holes with uniform interval radian near the edge of the signal plate. There are 360 rectangular holes on the outer circle, (gap), with the interval radiant of 1° (transmitting part is 0.5° and shielding part is 0.5°), used to form the crankshaft rotation angle and speed signal; there are 6 holes on the inner circle (rectangular holes), with the interval radiant of 60°, used to form the top dead center position signal for each cylinder, among which there is 1 rectangular hole with a slightly longer width used to generate top dead center position signal for the first cylinder.

The signal generator is fixed on the sensor shell, composed of Ne signal (crankshaft position signal) generator, G signal (camshaft position signal) generator and signal processing circuit. As shown in Figure 2-22 (b), the Ne signal and G signal generator are composed of one light-emitting diode and one optical transistor (triode), with two LEDs facing two photosensitive triodes respectively.

036　Fault Diagnosis and Repair of Automobile Engine Electronic Control System

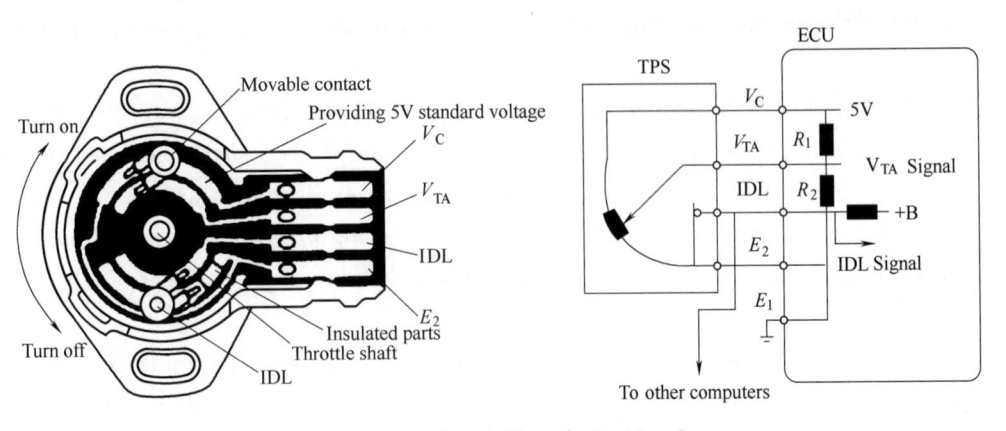

Figure 2-20　Combined Throttle Position Sensor

certain level, the IDL is disconnected, and the "IDL" outputs a high level (5 V) .

With the increase of the throttle opening, the slide arm of variable resistance shall rotate with the throttle shaft, and the contact on the slide arm shall slide on the coated resistance. The signal voltage between the sensor output terminal "V_{TA}" and "E_2" shall change accordingly, and the greater the throttle opening, the higher the output voltage. The linear signal of sensor output is converted into digital signal by A/D converter and then input into ECU.

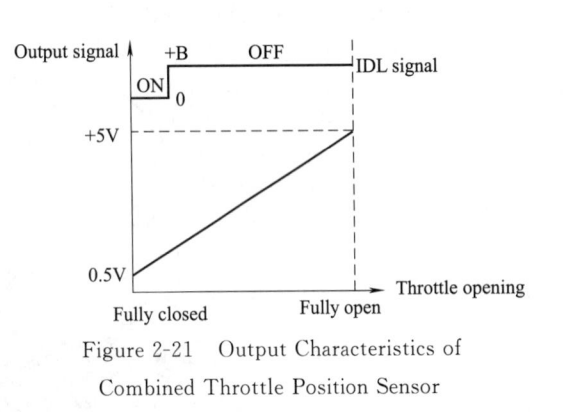

Figure 2-21　Output Characteristics of Combined Throttle Position Sensor

4. Crankshaft and camshaft position sensor

When the engine ECU controls the injector to inject and control the flashover of spark plug, it is necessary to know which cylinder piston is about to reach the top dead center of the exhaust stroke and the compression stroke firstly, and then to control the injection advance angle and the ignition advance angle according to the crankshaft angle signal.

(1) Function of crankshaft and camshaft position sensor

Crankshaft position sensor (CPS), sometimes referred to as engine speed sensor, is used to detect crankshaft angle and engine speed signal to send to ECU to determine fuel injection time and ignition control time. Crankshaft position sensor is one of the most important sensors in engine control system. Its signal is indispensable to confirm crankshaft angle position and engine speed. The engine control module uses this signal to control fuel injection quantity, fuel injection timing, ignition time, closing and opening angle of the charging of the ignition coil, idle speed and operation of electric gasoline pump.

Camshaft position sensor (CPS) is used to detect the camshaft position signal and send it to the ECU so as to determine the compression top dead center of first cylinder for sequential fuel injection control and ignition timing control. It is also used to identify the first igni-

② Output characteristics of contact TPS. The output characteristics of the contact throttle position sensor are shown in Figure 2-19. When the throttle is closed, the IDL (IDL) is closed, and the power contact (PSW) is disconnected, the output signal is low level 0 on the IDL (IDL) output terminal but high level on the PSW. When the ECU receives these two signals from the TPS, if the signal input by the speed sensor indicates that the speed is zero, the ECU shall determine that the engine is in idle state and increase the fuel injection to

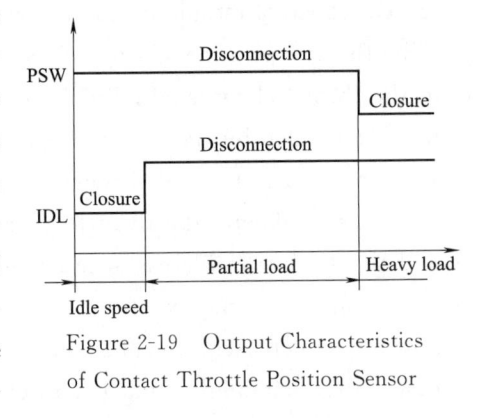

Figure 2-19　Output Characteristics of Contact Throttle Position Sensor

ensure that the engine idle speed is stable with no flameout. If the signal indicates that the speed is not zero, the ECU shall determine that the engine is in a deceleration state and stop the fuel injection in order to reduce emission and improve fuel economy.

When the throttle opening increases, the cam rotates with the throttle shaft and the IDL (IDL) is pushed open. If the PSW remains disconnected, the IDL terminal and the PSW terminal shall output high level 1. When the ECU receives these two high-level signals, it shall determine that the engine is in a partial load state and calculate the fuel injection according to the air flow sensor signal and the crankshaft speed signal to improve the engine's economy and emission performance.

When the throttle is close to full open (more than 80% load), the cam rotation makes the PSW terminal close and outputs low level 0, and IDL terminal keeps open and outputs high level 1. When the ECU receives these two signals, it shall determine that the engine is in a high-load state, increasing the fuel injection to ensure that the engine output sufficient power, so the large-load contact is called power contact. In this state, the control system shall enter the open-loop control mode, and the ECU shall not use the oxygen sensor signal. If the air-conditioning system is still working at this time, ECU shall interrupt the air-conditioning main relay signal about 15s in order to cut off coil current of the air-conditioning electromagnetic clutch. In this way, it stops the air-conditioning compressor, increases the output power of the engine, and improves the power of the automobile.

(2) Combined throttle position sensor

① Structure characteristics of combined TPS. The basic structure and principle circuit of the combined throttle position sensor for Toyota automobiles are shown in Figure 2-20. It is mainly composed of variable resistance, movable contact, throttle shaft, IDL and shell. The variable resistance is coated with a film, located on the base plate of the sensor. The slide arm of the variable resistance connected with the input terminal V_{TA}, rotates with the throttle shaft.

② Output characteristics of combined TPS. The output characteristics of the combined TPS are shown in Figure 2-21. When the throttle is closed or its opening is very small, the IDL is closed, and the input IDL outputs a low level (0 V). When the throttle is open to a

3. Detection of throttle position sensor

The throttle position sensor (TPS), is mounted on the throttle body shaft. Traditionally, the air intake is controlled by the driver's operation of the cable on the accelerator pedal. When the accelerator pedal is pressed down, the throttle opening increases and the air intake increases accordingly too. At the same time, the amount of air controlled by the air flowmeter increases, the fuel injection quantity increases correspondingly, and the total amount of mixed gas increases.

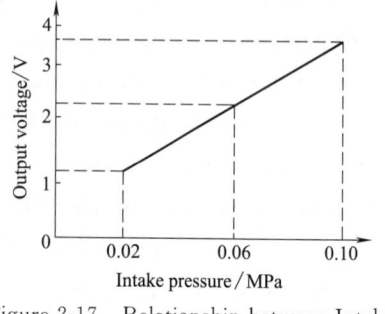

Figure 2-17　Relationship between Intake Pressure and Output Signal Voltage

On the one hand, the throttle position sensor is used to determine the throttle opening position, reflecting the engine operating conditions. On the other hand, it reflects the throttle opening and closing speed. In terms of rapid acceleration or deceleration, the slow reacting of air flowmeter caused by inertia or sensitivity shall affect the automobile's dynamic performance and fuel economy. The defect of air flowmeter can be made up by throttle position sensor, so throttle position sensor is also an important for fuel injection control. In an automatic transmission automobile, the throttle position sensor signal is inputted into the transmission computer simultaneously to control the transmission shift and torque converter lockup. According to the different structure and principle, it can be divided into three types: variable resistance type, contact type and combination type.

(1) Structure and principle of contact TPS

① Structural characteristics of contact throttle position sensor. As shown in Figure 2-18, it is mainly composed of guide cam, throttle shaft, control rod, movable contact, IDL, high power contact, guide slot and terminal. The cam changes with the throttle shaft, while the throttle shaft changes with the throttle opening.

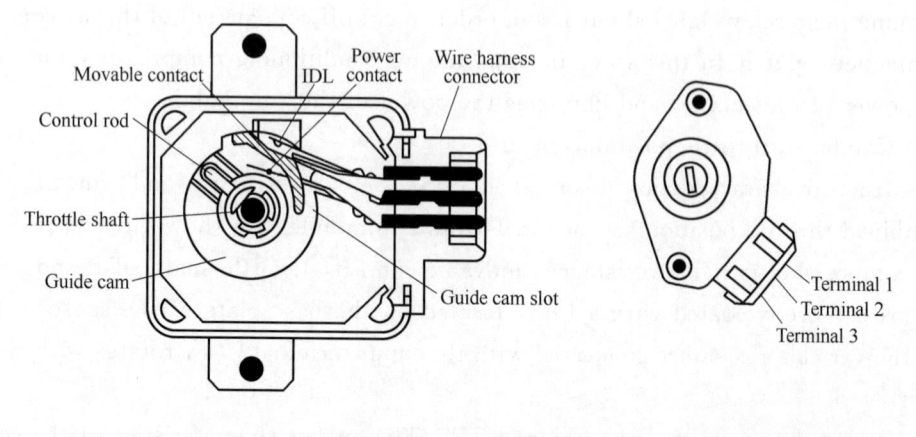

(a) Structure　　　　　　　　　　　(b) Appearance

Figure 2-18　Contact Throttle Position Sensor

Item Ⅱ　Maintenance of Electronic Control Fuel Injection System for Gasoline Engines　**033**

sistance parallel to the diaphragm radius, is called radial resistance R_r (R_1, R_3 in the figure).

The silicon cup normally is made of ferronickel-zirconium alloy (linear expansion coefficient is $47 \times 10^{-7}/\text{℃}$) with linear expansion coefficient close to that of monocrystalline silicon (linear expansion coefficient is $32 \times 10^{-7}/\text{℃}$), which is arranged between the silicon diaphragm and the sensor base to absorb the thermal stress added to the silicon diaphragm caused by the different thermal expansion coefficient between the base material and the silicon diaphragm, thus improving the measuring precision of the sensor. The space between the silicon cup and the shell and the base is made into a vacuum chamber by vacuuming it through the exhaust hole on the bottom of the shell and then sealing with solder. The vacuum chamber is the reference pressure chamber, with pressure of 0. A filter is arranged at the inlet of the pressure-conducting tube to filter the dust or impurities entering the air so as to prevent the corroded and fouled silicon diaphragm from causing the sensor failure.

(2) The working principle of the sensor

The piezoresistive pressure sensor structure is shown in Figure 2-14 (b). One side of the diaphragm is connected to the vacuum chamber and the other to the intake manifold. The silicon diaphragm shall produce stress under manifold pressure. Under the stress, the resistivity of the semiconductor force-sensitive resistance shall be changed, thus changing the resistance and the balance of the resistance value on the Wheatstone bridge. A variable signal voltage or signal current can be obtained at the output end of the bridge when the input end of the bridge inputs a fixed voltage or current. The pressure of the manifold can be detected according to the signal voltage or the signal current.

The principle circuit of the sensor is shown in Figure 2-16.

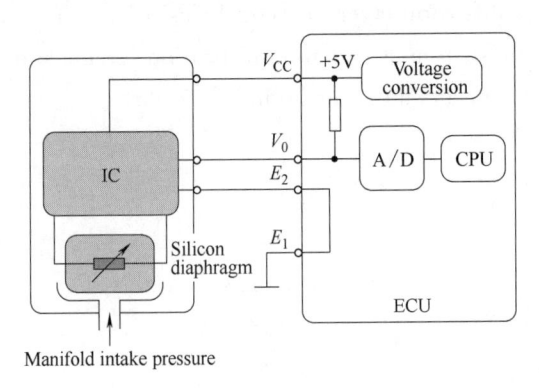

Figure 2-16   Circuit of Sensor Principle

When the engine works, the intake manifold pressure varies with the intake flow. The larger throttle opening (i. e. the intake flow increases) shall increase the air flow cross-section, reduce the airflow velocity, and rise the intake manifold pressure, the diaphragm stress, the resistance of the force-sensitive resistance, the voltage of the bridge output, and the signal voltage of the sensor input by electronic control unit (ECU) after the hybrid integrated circuit is amplified and processed. Conversely, the smaller throttle opening (that is, the intake flow rate decreases), shall decrease the intake flow cross-section, increase the airflow velocity, and reduce the intake manifold pressure, the diaphragm stress, the resistance of the force-sensitive resistance, the output voltage of the bridge, and the signal voltage input by ECU.

The relationship between the pressure variation of the intake pressure sensor and the output voltage is shown in Figure 2-17.

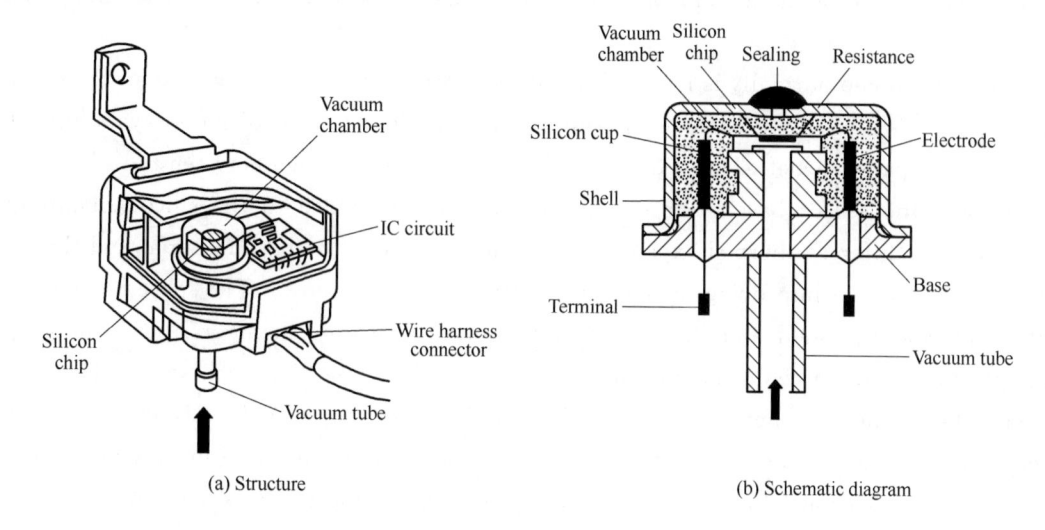

(a) Structure   (b) Schematic diagram

Figure 2-14   Varistor Intake Absolute Pressure Sensor

take air pressure introduction.

The silicon diaphragm is a pressure-converting element made of monocrystalline silicon. The length and width of the silicon diaphragm are about 3 mm and the thickness is about 160 μm. In the middle part of the silicon diaphragm, there is a thin film with a diameter of 2 mm and a thickness of about 50 μm made by corrosion method. On its surface, four semiconductor force-sensitive resistors with the same comb resistance are made by using integrated circuit processing and mesa diffusion technology, usually called solid-state piezoresistive devices or solid-state resistance. As shown in Figure 2-15 (a), four resistors are connected to a Wheatstone bridge circuit using a low resistance diffusion layer (P-type diffusion layer), and then it is connected to a hybrid integrated circuit such as a signal amplification circuit and a temperature compensation circuit inside the sensor, as shown in Figure 2-15 (b).

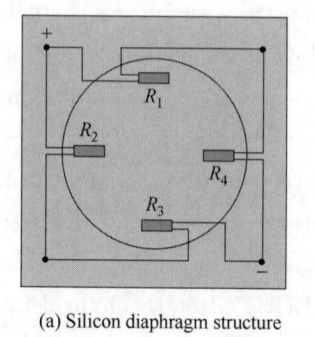
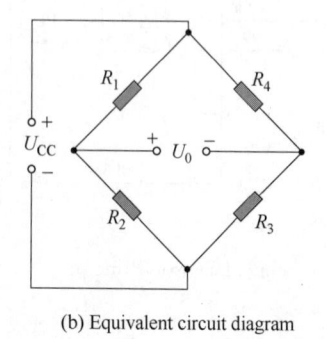

(a) Silicon diaphragm structure   (b) Equivalent circuit diagram

Figure 2-15   Silicon diaphragm and Strain Resistance

The silicon diaphragm is divided into radial resistance and tangential resistance according to the diffusion direction of the force-sensitive resistance. The resistance, with the long edge of the diffusion resistance perpendicular to the diaphragm radius, is called tangential resistance R_t (R_4, R_2 in the figure), and the resistance, with the long edge of the diffusion re-

full closed, or with the same air volume, the higher the air temperature, the smaller the air density. As such, the heating element shall be cooled to a smaller degree, its resistance shall be reduced to a smaller extent, and smaller heating current needs to maintain the bridge balance, all of which result a lower signal voltage on the sampling resistance. The ECU shall calculate the air amount according to the signal voltage. The standard scope of air flow for Jetta AT and GTX automobiles is between 2. 0g/s and 5. 0g/s.

The air flow is bigger when the engine load increases or the air is cold, because it shall increase with the increase of the throttle opening and fast air velocity, or with the increase of cold air density under the same volume, the mass of cold air is heavy. As such the heating element shall become cooler, the resistance shall decrease, and the heating current needed to maintain the balance of the bridge shall increase. Therefore, the signal voltage shall increase with the increase of the engine load.

After being used for some time, the thermal radiation ability of the hot-wire air flow sensor shall decrease due to the dust on the hot wire surface, affecting the measuring precision of the sensor. So the control circuit is designed with "self-cleaning circuit" to clean itself. When the ECU receives the engine's stop signal, it shall connect the self-cleaning circuit to heat the hot wire to 1000℃ and last for about 1s to make the dust burned. Another way to prevent hot wire from tarnishing is to raise the temperature of hot wire, with the temperature higher than 200℃ to burn the tarnishing. The surface area of the platinum metal film of the hot film sensor is much larger than that of the hot wire, with a insulating protective film, so the measurement precision shall not be affect by dust.

2. Intake pressure sensor

In the engine fuel injection system, if the manifold pressure sensor is installed, there is no need to install the air flow sensor; on the contrary, if the air flow pressure sensor is installed, there is no need to install the manifold pressure sensor. The Toyota 5A electronic control engine is equipped with an intake pressure sensor. Manifold pressure sensor is flexible in position, as long as leading its intake pressure to the sensor's vacuum tube. The sensor of the car is installed on the intake serge tank through connecting hose, as shown in Figure 2-13, the installation position of the intake pressure sensor for the Toyota 5A engine.

Figure 2-13　Installation Position
of Intake Pressure Sensor

(1) Structural characteristics of manifold pressure sensor

The structures of manifold pressure sensors for various types of automobiles are similar. As shown in Figure 2-14 (a), it is mainly composed of silicon diaphragm, vacuum chamber, hybrid integrated circuit, vacuum tube connector, wire harness plug.

The sensor shell is separated by a silicon diaphragm into two separate chambers, one for vacuum preset and the other for in-

（2）Working principle of the sensor

The measurement principle of the air flow sensor using hot wire or hot film as heating element is identical with that of the electric blower used in daily life. For the convenience of description, the hot wire and the hot film are collectively referred to as the heating element.

Theory and experiment proof that: under the cooling action of forced air flow, the heat dissipation of the heating element in unit time is proportional to the difference between the temperature of the heating element and the temperature of the air flow. For this reason, the constant temperature difference control circuit shown in Figure 2-11 is used in the hot-wire flow sensor and hot-film flow sensor for flow detection.

In the constant temperature control circuit, the heating element R_H and the temperature compensating resistance (intake air temperature sensor) R_T are respectively connected to the two arms of the Wheatstone bridge circuit. When the temperature of the heating element is higher than the inlet temperature, the bridge voltage can be balanced. The heating current (50 ~ 120mA) is controlled by control circuit A with current amplification, the purpose of which is to keep the difference between the temperature T_H of the heating element and the temperature T_T of the temperature compensating resistance constant, that is, $\Delta T = T_H - T_T = 120℃$.

When the air current flows through the heating element, its temperature and resistance decrease, causing the bridge voltage out of balance. The control circuit shall increase the current supplied to the heating

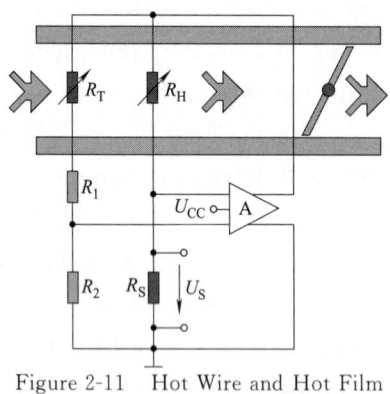

Figure 2-11　Hot Wire and Hot Film Flow Sensors AFS Principle Circuit

R_T—Temperature compensating resistance (inlet temperature sensor)；R_H—heating element resistance (hot wire or hot film)；

R_S—Signal sampling resistance；

R_1，R_2—Precision resistance；

A—control circuit

element so that the temperature is 120℃ higher than that of the temperature compensating resistance. The current increment depends on the cooling degree of the heating element, that is, the amount of air flowing through the sensor.

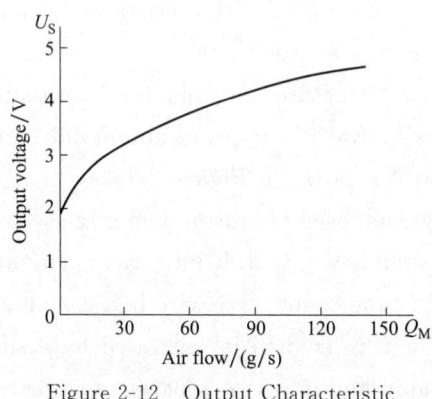

Figure 2-12　Output Characteristic Curve of Hot Wire and Hot Film AFS

When the bridge current increases, the voltage on the sampling resistance R_S rises. The change of the air flow shall be converted into the change of the voltage signal U_S. The output voltage is the root of four of the air flow amount. The characteristic curve is shown in Figure 2-12. After the signal voltage is inputted to ECU, the ECU can calculate the Q_M of air flow according to the signal voltage.

The air amount is smaller when the engine idle speed or the air is hot (such as summer driving), because the throttle is completely closed or almost

ment and the temperature compensating resistance. In this way, the temperature of the temperature compensating Resistance acts as a reference. The current provided by the control circuit shall make the temperature of the temperature compensating resistance 120℃ lower than that of the heating element all the time, so that the change of the inlet temperature shall not affect the accuracy of the heating element (hot wire) measurement.

Early-made flow sensors used platinum wire as temperature compensating resistance, which is close to one inlet side, called cold wire. At present, as the resistance wire is easily broken in use leading to scrapping, printing platinum film resistance on alumina ceramic substrate is widely used to make temperature compensating resistance.

② Structure characteristics of hot-film air flow sensor: it is an improved product of hot-wire sensor. Its heating element adopts planar platinum metal film resistor (thickness is about 200 nm), so it is called hot-film resistance. The manufacturing method of hot film resistance is as follows: first, deposit a platinum metal film on the alumina ceramic substrate through evaporation process; then make a comb pattern resistance through photolithography process, and coat a layer of insulating protective film on the surface after adjusting the resistance to meet the design requirement; and finally connect electrode leads.

A rectangular sheath (equivalent to a sampling tube) is arranged on the intake passage inside the sensor, with the hot-film resistance in the sheath. An air filter layer is equipped on one side of the air inlet of the sheath to filter the dirt in order to prevent it from being deposited on the hot-film resistance. In order to prevent the measurement accuracy from being affected by the change of inlet temperature, a platinum temperature compensating resistance is arranged upstream of the airflow near the hot film resistance, as shown in Figure 2-10. The temperature compensating resistance and the hot-film resistance are connected with the internal control circuit of sensor which is connected with the wire harness connector socket located in the middle of the sensor shell.

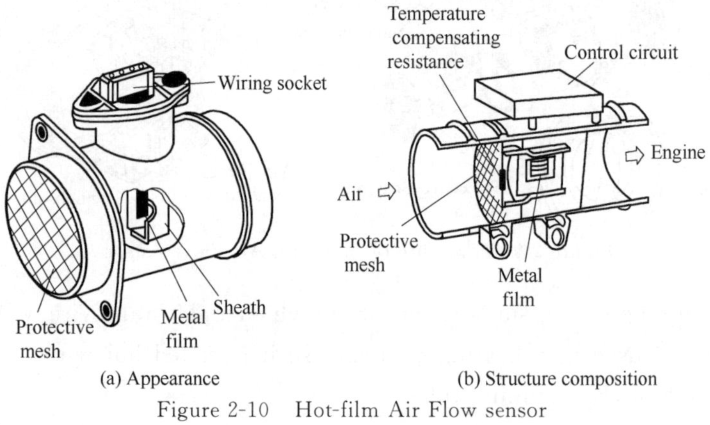

(a) Appearance   (b) Structure composition

Figure 2-10   Hot-film Air Flow sensor

Compared the hot-film type with the hot-wire type, the former consumes less current due to its larger resistance, and has a longer service life. However, as the insulation protective film on its heating element surface can conduct radiation heat, the corresponding characteristics are slightly lower than that of the hot-wire flow sensor.

As vane type and Karman vortex type flow sensor have been eliminated by now, so we only introduce the thermal flow sensor with two types here: the hot-wire type and hot-film type.

Both hot-wire and hot-film air flow sensors directly detect the air volume inhaled by the engine. The detecting principle of the two sensors is totally identical. The detecting element of hot-wire air flow sensor is platinum wire, while the detecting element of hot-film air flow sensor is platinum metal film. The response speed of the platinum element is very fast, reflecting the change of air flow in a few milliseconds, so the measurement accuracy is not affected by the air flow pulsation (the air flow pulsation is most obvious when the engine is running at high load and low speed). In addition, it has the advantages of low air intake resistance, non-wear parts and so on. At present, most high-medium automobiles use this kind of sensor.

(1) Structural characteristics of sensors

The hot-wire and hot-film air flow sensors are mainly composed of heating element (hot-wire or hot-film), temperature compensating resistance (cold-wire or cold-film), signal sampling resistance and control circuit.

① Structure characteristics of hot-wire air flow sensor: the structure of the hot-wire air flow sensor is shown in Figure 2-9. The two ends of the sensor shell are provided with a circular joint connected with the inlet, and the air inlet and outlet are provided with a protective mesh to protect the sensor from mechanical damage. The sensor inlet is connected with the inlet pipe at the one end of the air filter, and the outlet is connected with the inlet pipe at the one end of the throttle body.

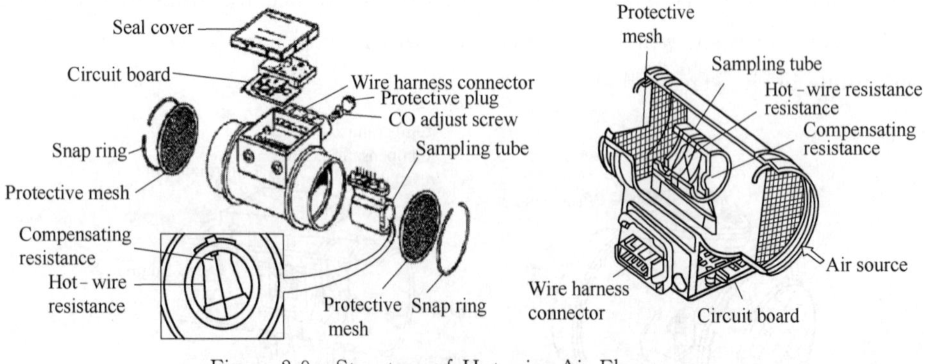

Figure 2-9　Structure of Hot-wire Air Flow sensor

There is a sampling tube inside the sensor, in which a platinum wire with a small diameter (about 70 μm) is used as a heating element, so it is called hot wire and is made into a "Ⅱ" shape mounted in the sampling tube.

A temperature compensating resistance is arranged upstream of the air flow near the hot wire because the temperature changes of the hot wire shall affect the measurement accuracy of the air inlet. The temperature compensating resistance is equivalent to one intake air temperature sensor, with the resistance value varying with the intake temperature. When the drop (or rise) of inlet temperature decreases (or increases) the resistance of the heating ele-

engine condition and the running state of the automobile, into electrical signals (voltage or current) provided to the electronic control unit, so that the electronic control unit can control the engine running or the automobile running correctly.

(2) Electronic control unit: receive signals from the various sensors, and complete the processing of these messages and issue instructions to control the actions of actuators.

(3) Actuators: complete various instructions issued by the electronic control unit, as the executive of the electronic control unit instruction.

(Ⅲ) Structural principle of sensor for engine fuel injection system

1. Air flow sensor

Air flow sensor (AFS), also known as air flowmeter, is the abbreviation of intake manifold air flow sensor. Its function is to detect the intake of the engine, and to convert the air flow signal into electrical signal to input ECU to calculate the injection time (i. e. fuel injection quantity) and ignition time. Air flow signal is the main basis for ECU to calculate fuel injection time and ignition time.

Air flow sensor can be divided into two types: "D" type (pressure type) and "L" type (flow type) according to the way of detecting air intake.

The "D" type flow sensor is used to detect the absolute pressure in the intake manifold through the pressure sensor. The measurement of intake air belongs to indirect measurement method. The injection system equipped with the "D" type flow sensor is called the "D" type fuel injection system. The electronic control unit uses the absolute pressure and engine speed to calculate the air intake inhaled into the cylinder, so it is also called the speed-density type fuel injection control system. Because of the pressure fluctuation caused by the air flowing in the intake manifold, the difference between the intake air when the engine is idle (throttle is closed) and that when the automobile is accelerated (throttle is fully open) is more than 40 times, and the maximum flow velocity of the intake air is up to 80 m/s, the measurement accuracy of the "D" type fuel injection system is not high, but the cost of the control system is low.

The "L" type flow sensor is a kind of sensor which directly measures the air flow inhaled into the intake pipe by the flow sensor. The "L" type flow sensor is mounted on the intake passage between the air filter and the throttle valve. Due to the direct measurement method, the measurement accuracy of intake air is higher. Thus the control effect is better than that of "D" type fuel injection system. The "L" type flow sensor can be divided into two types: volume flow type and mass flow type. The volume flow sensor used in the fuel injection system of automobile engine has three types: vane type, Karman vortex type and thermal type, and the mass flow sensor has two types: hot-wire type and hot-film type.

For "L" type flow sensors, there is no moving part in the mass flow sensor, and the flow resistance is small, so it has advantages of stable working performance and high measuring precision, its manufacture cost is high. For mass flow sensors, the service life of hot-film flow sensor is much longer than that of hot-wire flow sensor.

2. Fuel feed system

The fuel feed system is referred to as FS system, whose function is to provide the engine with the fuel required for the mixture combustion. The structure of fuel injection engine fuel feed system is shown in Figure2-8. It is mainly composed of fuel tank, electric fuel pump, oil pipeline, fuel filter, oil pressure regulator, fabricated fuel pipe, injector and return pipe. Fabricated fuel pipe is also called oil supply main pipe or oil rack.

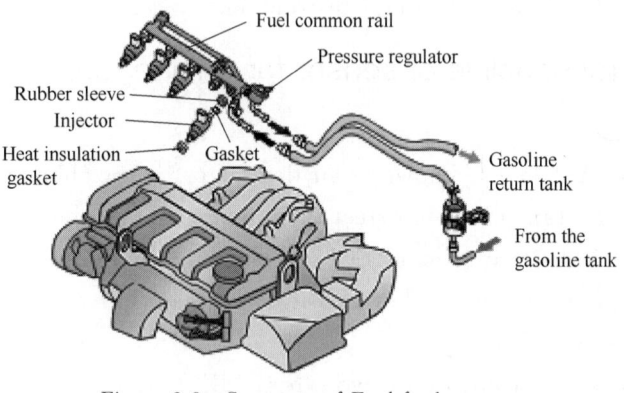

Figure 2-8　Structure of Fuel feed system

When the engine works, the electric fuel pump pumps gasoline out of the tank. The fuel shall be first filtered by the fuel filter, and then its oil pressure shall be adjusted by the oil pressure regulator, ensuring that the oil pressure in the oil pipeline is 300 kPa higher than the pressure in the intake manifold. Finally it shall be distributed to each cylinder injector through the fabricated fuel pipe. When the injector receives the fuel injection instruction issued by the ECU, the gasoline shall be injected around the intake valve, and mixed with the air provided by the air supply system, forming combustible mixture with good atomization. When the intake valve is opened, the mixture is sucked into the cylinder to burn to do work.

The path of the fuel flowing into the engine cylinder is: gasoline tank—gasoline pump—oil pipeline—fuel filter—fabricated fuel pipe—injector. The injector ejects fuel near the intake valve. (for gasoline direct injection system, it shall be ejected directly into the cylinder.)

When more fuel is pumped into the fuel feed system by gasoline pump and the oil pressure in the oil pipeline is raised, the oil pressure regulator shall automatically adjust the fuel pressure to ensure that the oil pressure supplied to the injector is basically unchanged. The excess fuel in the fuel feed system shall flow from the return line back to the tank. The return path is as follows: gasoline tank—gasoline pump—oil pipeline—fuel filter—fabricated fuel pipe—oil pressure regulator—return pipe—fuel tank. However, the pressure regulator of some of the modern new gasoline injection engines is installed on the electric gasoline pump assembly in the gasoline tank, so there is no return pipe.

3. Fuel injection electronic control system

The electronic control system is mainly composed of sensor, ECU and actuator.

(1) Various sensors: transform all kinds of parameters (non-electric), which reflect the

rect air supply system.

(1) By-pass air supply system

The structure of by-pass air supply system is shown in Figure 2-7 (a) . It is mainly composed of air filter, air flow sensor, intake hose, by-pass air passage, idle speed control valve (ISCV), intake manifold, power chamber, throttle position sensor, intake air temperature sensor, etc.

When the engine works properly, the air passage is: air intake—air filter—air flow sensor—intake pipe—throttle—power chamber—intake manifold—engine intake valve—engine cylinder.

When the engine is running in idle state, the air passage is: air intake—air filter—air flow sensor—intake pipe—by-pass air intake in front of the throttle—idle speed control valve—by-pass air outlet behind the throttle—power chamber—intake manifold—engine intake valve—engine cylinder.

(2) Direct gas supply system

The idle speed is controlled by throttle of the engine control system without by-pass air passage. The structure of the air supply system is shown in Figure 2-7 (b) . It is mainly composed of air filter, air flow sensor, intake hose, intake manifold, power chamber, throttle position sensor, intake air temperature sensor and so on.

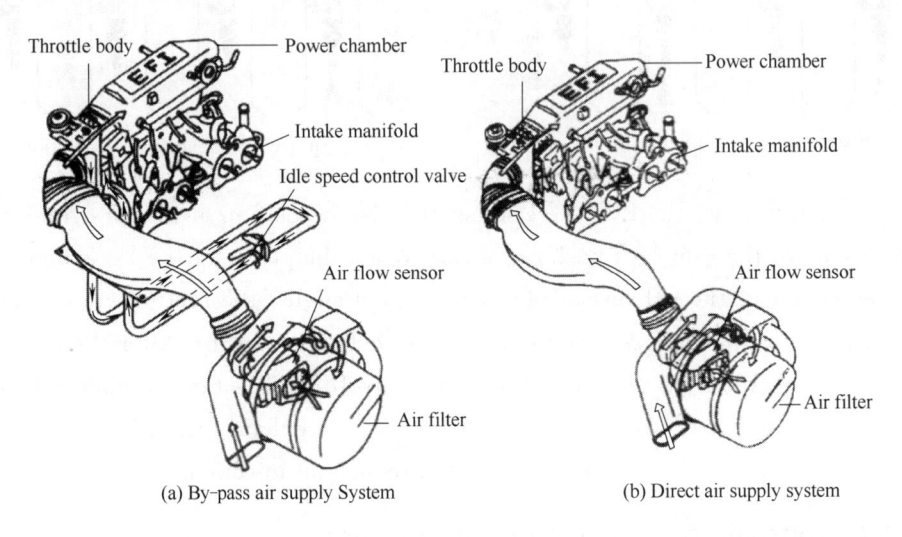

Figure 2-7　Structure of Air Supply System of Fuel Injection Engine

The air passage of the engine in normal operation and idle operation is same. The air passage of the engine is: air inlet—air filter—air flow sensor—intake hose—throttle body—power chamber—intake manifold—engine intake valve—engine cylinder.

After air is filtered through the filter, it flows into the power chamber through the throttle body, then distributed to the intake manifold of each cylinder. The air volume entering the engine cylinder is determined by the electronic control unit (ECU) based on the air intake signal detected by the air flow sensor mounted on the inlet.

2RZ-E simultaneous injection system for the Toyota HIACE minibus. In addition, when the fuel injection system with group injection or sequential injection fails and the control system is in emergency operation, the simultaneous injection mode is usually used to provide sufficient fuel to keep the engine running so that the car can be driven to a repair shop.

(2) Group injection system

Group injection refers to group the injector. The ECU issues injecting order to control each group of injectors, as shown in Figure 2-5, with the same group of injectors injection at the same time. Most medium-and low-grade automobiles use group injection system.

(3) Sequential injection system

Sequential injection refers to that the ECU controls injectors to inject fuel in turn according to the order of the intake stroke during engine operation. Sequential injection is also called order injection, as shown in Figure 2-6.

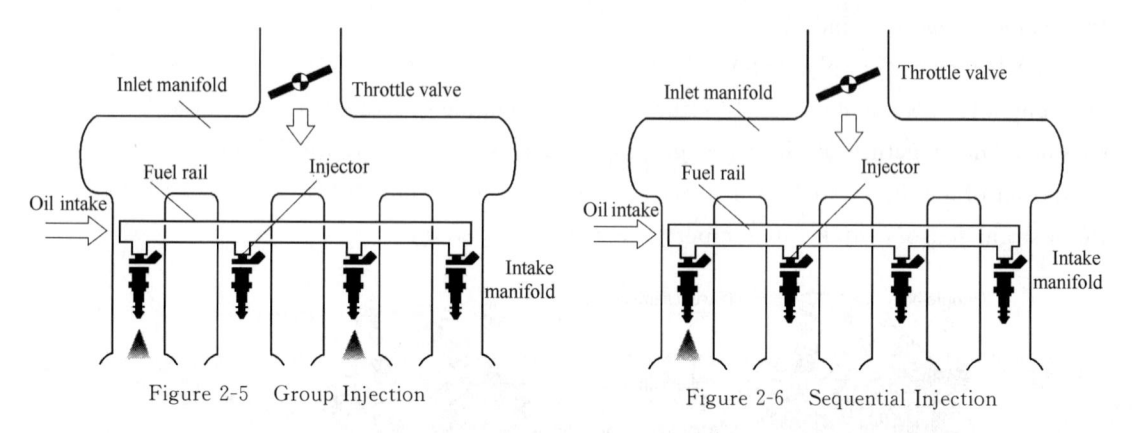

Figure 2-5   Group Injection   Figure 2-6   Sequential Injection

For injection timing, the ECU determines the piston position of the 1st cylinder according to the signal of the camshaft position sensor. When the piston of the 1st cylinder reaches the top dead center of the exhaust stroke with a fixed angle, the fuel injection pulse signal shall be sent out to control fuel injection of the 1st cylinder injector. After the fuel injection of the 1st cylinder, the ECU shall take turns to control fuel injection of other cylinders at a fixed angle before the piston reaches the stop point of the exhaust stroke in accordance with the ignition order of cylinders, thus realizing the sequential injection.

(II) Composition of fuel injection system

The engine fuel injection system is composed of three subsystems: air supply system, fuel feed system and fuel injection electronic control system.

1. Air supply system

Function: provide the necessary air for the formation of the engine combustible mixture, and measure and control the air volume.

According to the different control modes of the idle air intake of the fuel injection engine, the air supply system can be divided into two types: by-pass and direct air supply. The Toyota 5A engine uses a by-pass air supply system, and the Santana AGR engine uses a di-

cylinder port or in each cylinder to ensure the uniformity of the mixture concentration in each cylinder of the engine. And the system injects the fuel on the intake valve or directly into the cylinder, making the mix of fuel and air more fully. There is no need to preheat the intake manifold to help fuel atomization. On the contrary, it can cool the intake air to increase its air inflow, increasing the power and making throttle response faster. After the mixture of fuel and air entering into the cylinder, the oxygen sensor transmits the test results of the oxygen content in the exhaust gas to the engine control module (ECU), and the engine control module shall timely rectify the feedback of the mixture concentration. Furthermore, the fuel is injected around the intake valve or in the cylinder, avoiding the influence on the mixture caused by the shape and surface quality of the intake pipe.

2. Classification according to injection mode of the injector.

(1) Continuous fuel injection system

The continuous fuel injection system is mostly used in mechanical or mechatronic hybrid fuel injection systems, in which an injector is installed at each cylinder port. As long as the system provides a fixed pressure, the injector shall continuously inject fuel. The fuel injection quantity is not dependent on the injector but depends on the opening of the fuel metering slot in the fuel distributor and the pressure difference between the inside and outside of the metering slot.

(2) Intermittent fuel injection system

Intermittent fuel injection system injects fuel intermittently into the intake manifold during engine operation. The fuel injection quantity depends on the opening time of the injector, that is, the injection pulse width of the engine control module (ECU). This fuel injection mode is widely used in modern electronic fuel injection system.

Making a comparison between the two systems, the continuous fuel injection system is poor in the control of mixture accuracy due to its fuel injection amount mostly controlled by mechanical elements, while the intermittent electronic fuel injection system can solve the technical problems effectively.

3. Classification according to control mode of the injector

(1) Simultaneous injection system

Simultaneous injection means that all injectors are turned on or off at the same time by the same command of the ECU during engine operation, as shown in Figure 2-4, such as the

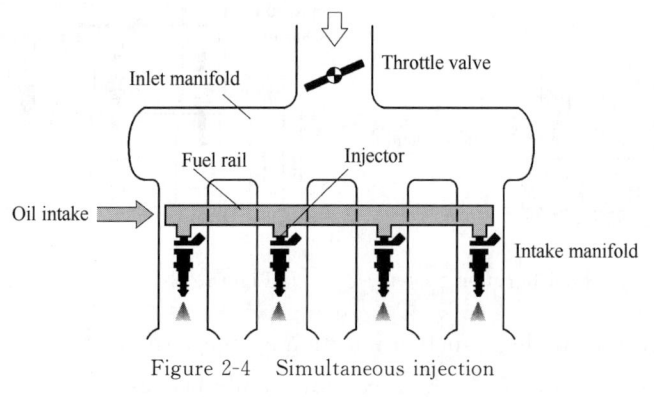

Figure 2-4　Simultaneous injection

for group fuel injection. This injection system controls its air-fuel ratio through the throttle opening angle and engine speed. It omits the air flow sensor, making the structure and control mode simpler. It also improves the engine performance and reduces the cost, with less influence on the engine structure. But it has a low control precision for mixture, with poor uniformity of mixture in each cylinder.

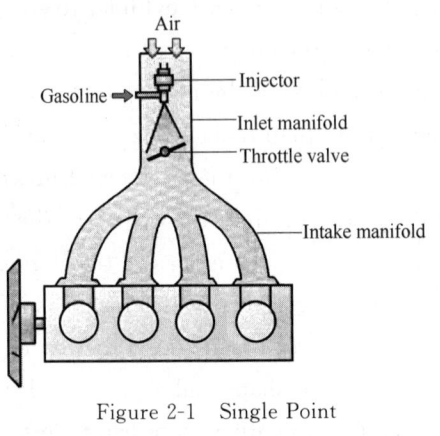

Figure 2-1　Single Point Fuel Injection System

(2) Multi-point fuel injection system

The multi-point fuel injection system can be divided into two types according to the installation position of the injector: port fuel injection and gasoline direct injection.

① Port fuel injection. Port fuel injection refers to installing an injector in front of the intake valve of each cylinder, as shown in Figure 2-2. After the fuel is ejected, the injector mixes with the air near the intake valve to form a combustible mixture, which ensures the uniformity of the total amount and concentration of the mixture in each cylinder. At present, most models use this multi-point fuel injection system.

② Gasoline direct injection. Gasoline direct injection refers to injecting high-pressure fuel directly into the cylinder, as shown in Figure 2-3. It uses a special injector, with sound fuel injecting effect, producing stratified mixture with graded concentration (gradually dilute from the spark plug to the outside) in the cylinder. As a result, ultra-thin mixtures can be used, and the fuel consumption and emissions are much lower than those of conventional gasoline engines. In addition, the injection mode reduces the volume and temperature of the mixture, which reduces the tendency of knock combustion, and the compression ratio of the mixture in the engine is much higher than that in the inlet port.

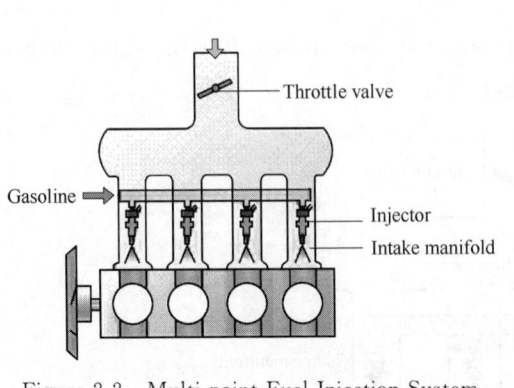

Figure 2-2　Multi-point Fuel Injection System

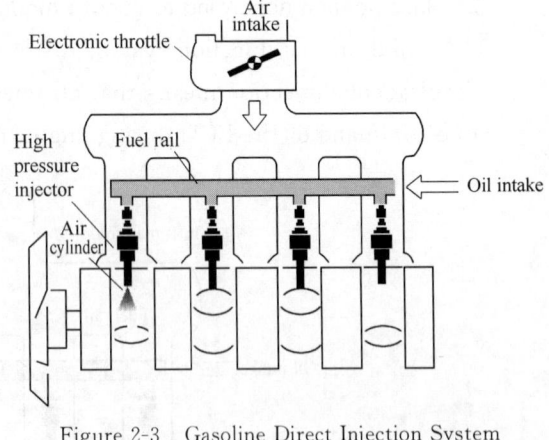

Figure 2-3　Gasoline Direct Injection System

Compared with the single point fuel injection system, the multi-point fuel injection system is more effective in controlling the mixture, mainly because it installs an injector at each

Item II

Maintenance of Electronic Control Fuel Injection System for Gasoline Engines

I. Introduction of Item Scene

The fuel feed system is an important part of the engine electronic control system. On the basis of being familiar with the layout and structure of the main components of the fuel feed system, students shall master the functions and types, structures and principles, maintenance and overhaul methods of the electric fuel pump, fuel pressure regulator, fuel filter and other components and shall master the functions and types, structures and principles, maintenance and overhaul methods of main sensors (such as air flowmeter, intake pressure sensor, throttle position sensor, coolant temperature sensor, crankshaft and camshaft position sensors and so on), electronic control unit, actuator (injector) and other parts of the fuel control system. Only in this way, can students have a more in-depth grasp of principles of electronically controlled fuel control system, and analyze the causes according to faults of the electronic control system.

II. Item Related Knowledge

(I) Classification of fuel injection system

With the development of mechanical control system, mechatronics control system and electronic control technology, the engine electronic control fuel injection system is gradually formed and developed. In order to understand the general situation of engine fuel injection control system, it is necessary to introduce the classification of engine fuel injection system to readers.

1. Classification according to the quantitative relationship between the Injector and the cylinder

(1) Single point fuel injection system

The single point fuel injection system refers to install one or two injectors on the throttle body to form combustible mixture by injecting fuel into the intake manifold. As shown in Figure 2-1, the fuel injection system is also known as the throttle body fuel injection system or the centralized fuel injection system because the injector is mounted on the throttle body

② Pay attention to the operation flow and the corresponding test port, when testing the voltage signal on the test bench.

③ Connect the test port directly with the electronic control unit on the physical bench. Do not apply any voltage to the test port of the engine test bench so as not to damage the electronic control unit.

④ Abide by laboratory rules and regulations. Do not move or disassemble instruments and equipment without permission.

⑤ Pay attention to personal safety and ensure teaching aids in good condition.

⑥ Forbid moving teaching aids, electrical switches, ignition switches and starting switches without permission.

Summary

This item introduces the basic structures and working principles of the automobile electronic control unit. Through the study of this item, students should be able to recognize the advantages of the engine electronic control system, and master the role of each sensor and actuator in the work. At the same time, it also describes the method of using the diagnostic instrument and what preparation shall be done in advance when using the diagnostic instrument. As some faults shall be displayed differently under different working conditions or even not displayed at all, the diagnostic instrument should be used to read the dynamic data stream of the engine. As such, students shall be capable of analyzing the dynamic data of the engine to judge the cause of the fault.

Exercises and Thinking

1. Structures and working principles of automobile electronic control unit.
2. What are the precautions for the overhaul of the power circuit of the automobile electronic control unit?
3. What are the three components of the power supply circuit of the automobile electronic control unit?
4. What are the functions of a diagnostic instrument?
5. What are the precautions for using a diagnostic instrument?
6. What are the benefits of using a diagnostic instrument to read data stream?

new ECU. It shall be reconnected after the ECU is well installed and connected. By this time, the replacing work is not completed. Many ECUs must undergo a "relearning" process after installing or disconnecting the power supply. For some models, it may take a specific procedure to establish a basic idle speed, while some models may require a short drive to allow the ECU to adjust itself.

(3) Notes for power circuit overhaul

Normally ECU power supply circuit provides a voltage between 12V and 14V to the engine control module. If the voltage is too high, it may burn the ECU. If the supply voltage is too low (such as less than 10 V), it shall result in the engine control module working improperly or even stopping working. In addition, if the EFI main relay fails, the engine control module shall not work or not work properly. Therefore, it is necessary to check whether the ECU power supply circuit is normal before suspecting the fault of the engine control module.

In the diagnosis and maintenance of the power supply circuit, it is first to clarify the circuit:

Which lines are connected to the battery positive pole (+BATT);

Which lines are connected to the power supply controlled by the ignition switch (+B, +B);

Which are connected to the power provided by ECU (+5V);

Which line is the ground wire (E1, E2).

Then it shall be detected with the multimeter and other instruments according to the circuit diagram.

(4) Using multimeter to detect automobile electronic control unit

The faults of the electronic control unit and its control circuit can be detected by a special detector or a universal electronic control unit diagnostic instrument. These instruments can pinpoint exactly where the fault is. If these instruments are not available, a multimeter can be used to measure the voltage or working resistance of each pin on the socket on one side of the electronic control unit to determine whether the electronic control unit and its control circuit are faulty. Meanwhile, the detailed maintenance technical information of the automobile subject to inspection must be taken as the basis, including: which devices are connected to each pin on the socket on one side of the electronic control unit respectively, and the standard voltage of each pin in different working state of the engine, etc. If an anomaly is detected at the time of detection, it indicates a fault. An abnormal connection with the actuator indicates a failure of the electronic control unit; an abnormal connection with a sensor may result in a failure of the sensor or circuit. When measuring resistance, the wire harness plug should be removed. By comparing the measured results with standard values, the fault location can be determined.

(Ⅲ) Matters needing attention

① Handle the ECU with care to keep it from dropping to the ground and breaking.

nose the fault according to the procedure stipulated in the maintenance manual, when they failing to solve the engine fault after several attempts, they often blame the fault on the ECU, leading to the inaccuracy of the fault diagnosis, which increases the economic burden of the Owner.

(1) Fault of the ECU and its causes

The main faults of the ECU include: loose solder point, failure capacitor element, damaged integrated circuit, loose anchor bolts for electronic control unit, damaged electronic components and so on. ECU fault shall cause that the engine cannot start or is difficult to start or no high-speed, large fuel consumption and other phenomena. In addition to natural wear and aging due to long time use, faults are normally caused by the following reasons.

① Environmental factors. Water is the main reason. If water flows into the ECU, it shall cause short circuit and irreparable corrosion, joint damage and so on. The second reason is overheating and vibration, which can cause tiny cracks in the circuit board.

② Overload voltage or current. It is usually caused by a short circuit in the solenoid valve or actuator circuit. If the ECU is replaced without detecting or repairing the short-circuited solenoid valve or actuator, the existing overload voltage may still damage the new ECU. Therefore, before replacing the new ECU, it must thoroughly check the reason of the original ECU damage.

③ Non-standard operation. For example, there is no electrostatic protection taken during the disassembly, the battery is connected before the installation of the ECU, and the terminal is measured with low internal resistance meter.

(2) Maintenance of ECU

A normal ECU requires that all sensors input correct signals, the battery voltage is correct, and the grounding is good. Therefore, the above aspects shall be checked and confirmed before checking the ECU.

Normally ECU is not repairable. Thus it must be replaced once a fault is confirmed. Attentions shall be paid to the following points in terms of the replacement of the new engine control module.

① Accurate identification. Accurate identification is the prerequisite for correct replacement, as there are various ECUs. Many ECUs are exactly the same on the surface, but their internal circuits and calibration may not be exactly the same. For the ECU, it must fully meet the needs of the automobile being repaired. It needs to know not only the manufacturing year, the manufacturing factory, the model and the engine displacement of the automobile, but also the OEM part number in the ECU. Most suppliers have these two classifications sheet. So, if you're not sure, you can find the OEM part number on the ECU to look for the required ECU in the supplier's cross-index with this part number.

② Skills for replacement. Changing the ECU is actually changing a box. For some models, the ECU may be not easy to replace, as it is usually fixed under or behind the instrument panel, miscellaneous box, or other parts of the console. No matter where the engine is located, the battery shall be disconnected before dismantling the old ECU and installing the

tion of "ON-BOARD DIAGNOSTICS". OBD-Ⅱ refers to the second generation of on-board diagnostics system. OBD-Ⅱ was proposed by the Society of Automotive Engineers (SAE) and approved by the Environmental Protection Agency (EPA) and the California Air Resources Board (CARB). The main features of OBD-Ⅱ are as follows:

① Automobiles shall be equipped with a standard 16-terminal diagnostic seat as shown in Figure 1-13. The diagnostic seat shall be uniformly installed under the cab instrument panel.

② OBD-Ⅱ can transmit data, with two transmission line standards stipulated: the European unified standard (ISO-Ⅱ) stipulates No. "7" and "15" terminals for data transmission, and the American unified standard (SAE-J1850) stipulates No. "2" and "10" terminals for data transmission.

③ OBD-Ⅱ can record the relevant data of the automobile's driving process; it can memorize and redisplay the fault code, and it can use the diagnostic instrument to read out or clear the fault code conveniently and quickly.

④ Automobile equipped with OBD-Ⅱ shall use the same fault code and the same meaning of the fault code. The fault code consists of 1 English letter and 4 numbers, as shown in Figure 1-14.

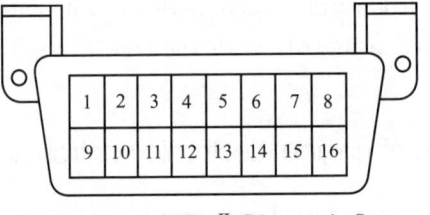

Figure 1-13　OBD-Ⅱ Diagnostic Seat

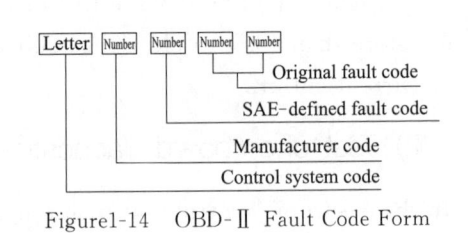

Figure1-14　OBD-Ⅱ Fault Code Form

2. Use of diagnostic instrument

With the function of the on-board diagnostics system of the electronic control system and the function of the automobile diagnostic instrument, it is required that the diagnostic instrument shall be correctly used with its methods and steps of reading the automobile fault code, and the matters needing attention, finding out the fault cause from the fault code, and clearing the fault code with the diagnostic instrument.

Ⅲ. Item Implementation

(Ⅰ) Requirements for implementation

Toyota 5A, AJR engine bench; automobile.

(Ⅱ) Implementation steps

At present, the ECU technology is quite mature, the ECU itself is not prone to failure in normal running. But in the actual maintenance, many maintenance personnel do not diag-

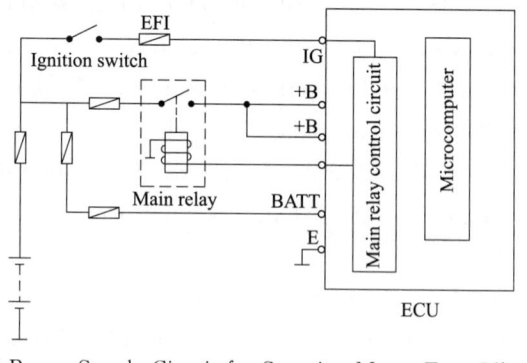

Figure 1-12　ECU Power Supply Circuit for Stepping Motor Type Idle Air Control Valve

position, maximizing the bypass opening and preparing for the next action.

From the circuit diagram, we can see that both of the above two power supply circuits have one wire connected directly from the battery to the "+BATT" terminals of the engine control module through EFI fuse. The function of the circuit is that whether the ignition switch is in "ON" position or "OFF" position, the battery shall continuously supply power to the random access memory (RAM) of the ECU to ensure that the ECU shall store the data such as fault code, air-fuel ratio correction value at any time. That is why some models can use the method of pulling-out the EFI insurance a certain time (such as the Toyota automobile for more than 10s) to clear the fault code stored in RAM, with the continuous power supply current cut off.

(Ⅲ) Test of on-board diagnostics system of engine electronic control system

In the electronic control unit of automobile electronic control system, there is a on-board diagnostics system (OBD) . It can continuously monitor the operation of each part of the electronic control system during operation, detect most of the faults in the electronic control system, and store the faults in the memory of the electronic control unit in the form of code. As long as the battery is not removed, the fault code shall be stored in the electronic control unit permanently. The maintenance personnel can read out the fault code according to the specific method, which provides the basis for detecting and diagnosing the engine electronic control system.

1. OBD-Ⅱ introduction

In the process of the development of automobile technology, the different technical characteristics of the world's major automobile manufacturing companies have different standards, resulting in a variety of forms and locations, and methods of reading and clearing the fault code for on-board diagnostics system fault diagnostic seat, which brings great inconvenience to automobile users and maintenance personnel. Therefore, in the 1970s, the first generation of on-board diagnostics system (OBD-Ⅰ) was adopted in the automobile electronic control system; after 1994, the second generation of on-board diagnostics system (OBD-Ⅱ) was gradually adopted in the electronic control automobiles produced by the major automobile manufacturers in the United States, Japan and Europe. OBD is the abbrevia-

but also the specific terminals of the ECU (such as the "BATT" terminal) are connected to the power supply when the ignition switch is switched off (that is, to the "OFF" position), keeping a constant connection to the power voltage.

When the ignition switch is switched on, the ECU shall obtain the supply voltage through a fuse and adjust the battery voltage (normally $12 \sim 14\text{V}$) to 5V or 12V for internal and external components.

When the ignition switch is turned off, the ECU also needs power to store the corresponding automobile parameters and diagnostic fault code. Therefore, there is another circuit that continuously provides the battery voltage to the ECU through an independent fuse. If that circuit is disconnected, all the information such as idle learning parameters, fuel correction parameters and fault code stored in the ECU shall be lost.

① EFI main relay. The function of the EFI main relay is to connect the ECU to its power supply, preventing the voltage drop of the ECU circuit. When the ignition switch is switched on, the current flows through the relay coil, connecting all contacts. The current flows into the ECU through the fuse.

For the ECU power supply circuit without stepping motor type idle air control valve, the EFI main relay is controlled by ignition switch.

For the ECU power supply circuit with stepping motor type idle air control valve, the EFI main relay is directly controlled by the ECU.

② ECU power supply circuit

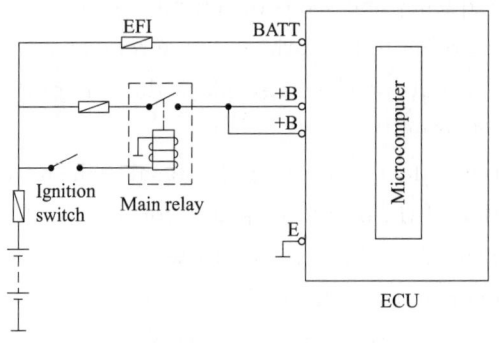

Figure 1-11   ECU power supply circuit without stepping motor type idle air control valve

a. ECU power supply circuit without stepping motor type idle air control valve. The power supply circuit is shown in Figure 1-11, with the EFI main relay controlled by the ignition switch. When the ignition switch is switched on, the main relay shall be pulled-in, with the current flowing through the relay to two "+B" terminals of the computer. When the ignition switch is switched off, the relay is immediately disconnected, with the current flowing to two "+B" terminals of the ECU cut off.

b. ECU power supply circuit with stepping motor type idle air control valve. The ECU power supply circuit with stepping motor type idle air control valve is shown in Figure 1-12. When the ignition switch is switched on, the "BATT" terminal of the ECU shall be power supplied. The ECU shall control the power supply of the circuit and the relay power supply terminal through the internal main relay. The EFI main relay shall be pulled-in and the battery voltage shall be added to two "+B" terminals of the ECU. When the ignition switch is switched off, the ECU shall continue to supply power to the EFI main relay through the main relay control circuit so that the stepping motor shall have time to return to its initial

is used to store information temporarily in a computer. When the power is cut off, all the data stored in RAM shall be completely lost. In the process of engine operation, RAM is connected directly to the battery through the dedicated power backup circuit, so that it's not controlled by the ignition switch, in order to save some data of RAM for a long time, such as fault code, air-fuel ratio learning correction value, etc. , and to prevent the loss of these data when the ignition switch is closed. In this way, it shall not be affected by the ignition switch. However, the data stored in RAM shall also be lost if the dedicated power backup circuit is disconnected or the power cord on the battery is unplugged.

(b) Read only memory (ROM). ROM is used to store fixed data, that is, a variety of permanent programs and permanent, semi-permanent data, such as a series control program software, fuel injection characteristics pulse spectrum, ignition control characteristics pulse spectrum and other characteristics of data in electronic fuel injection systems. All of these data are stored by the manufacturer at the time of manufacturing. The contents cannot be changed in the application, that is, when the computer works, the new data cannot be stored and the original data can be read when needed. When the power is cut off, the information stored in the ROM shall not be lost and can be used immediately after the power is turned on.

(c) I/O interface. Input/output interface is a control circuit for information exchange among CPU and input device (sensor) and output device (actuator) . Input and output device can be connected with computer through I/O interface. At the command of the CPU, the I/O interface receives the input signal at the desired frequency and sends the output signal out (or into intermediate storage) at the optimal speed according to the form and requirements of the output control signal. In addition, the input and output interface also plays the role of data buffering, battery matching, timing matching and so on.

④ Output loop. What the computer outputs is a low-voltage digital signal, which cannot directly drive the actuator to work. The function of the output loop is to convert this low-voltage digital signal into a control signal that can drive the actuator to work. The output loop normally adopts high-power electronic components (such as triode, field-effect transistor, etc.), with the signal output from the microprocessor controlling its turn-on and cut-off, thus controlling the power supply or ground loop of the actuator to control its action.

In addition to the above-mentioned basic equipment, the current ECU is equipped with power supply device, electromagnetic interference protection device, self-checking device, backup system, etc. , which can be assembled in a compact way so as to save space and make its work more reliable.

(2) Power supply circuit of ECU

The ECU must connect an appropriate supply voltage to control the engine management system. ECU power supply circuit is a circuit power supplied by the battery. It is mainly composed of battery, EFI (Electronic Fuel Injection) main relay and ignition switch lamp.

The ECU power supply circuit not only ensures that the ECU gets the power supply voltage immediately when the ignition switch is switched on (that is, to the "ON" position),

Item I Overall Cognition of Electronic Control System for Gasoline Engine **013**

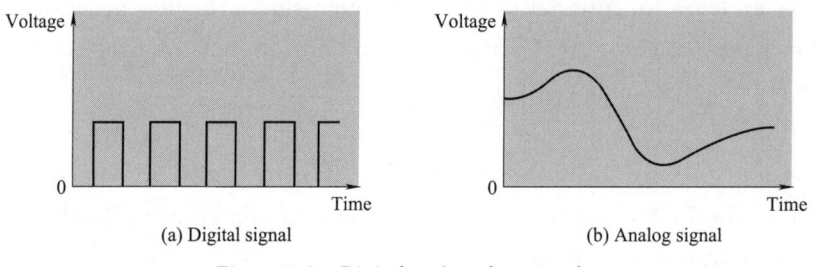

Figure 1-8　Digital and analog signals

b. Analog signal: It includes signals from coolant temperature sensor, potentiometer throttle position sensor and hot-wire air flow sensor. The input characteristic is shown in Figure 1-8 (b). The function of the input loop is to filter out the clutter of the signal waveform and input it into the A/D converter to convert the analog signal into a digital signal, as shown in Figure 1-9.

② A/D (analog/digital) converter. The microprocessor cannot process the analog signal directly. The function of the A/D converter is to convert the analog signal into a digital signal, as shown in Figure 1-10, then input the microprocessor for processing.

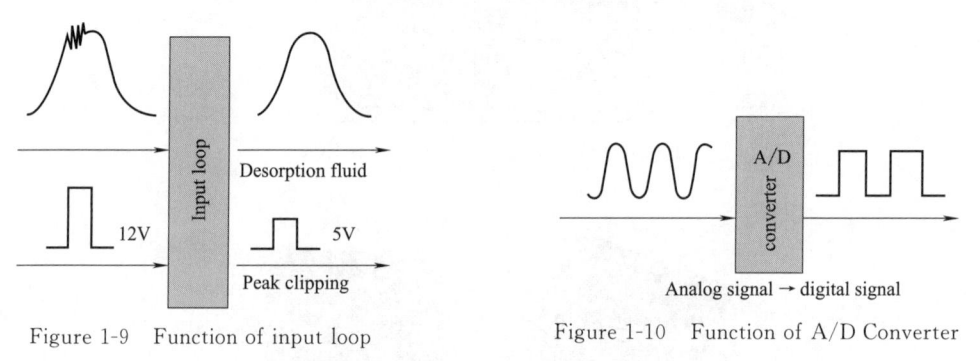

Figure 1-9　Function of input loop

Figure 1-10　Function of A/D Converter

③ Microprocessor. The microprocessor consists of the following three parts: Central process unit (CPU); Memory (RAM, ROM); Input/output (I/O) interface.

a. Central process unit (CPU). The central process unit (CPU) is the core part of the whole control system. All the data should be processed in the CPU. It is composed of an arithmetic unit for arithmetic and logic operation, a register for temporarily storing data, and a controller for signal transmission and task control between devices according to the program. After receiving the signals from each sensor, the CPU performs arithmetic and logic operations according to the pre-designed requirements, and controls fuel injection, ignition, idling, and emission systems.

b. Memory (RAM, ROM). Memory is mainly used to store information. Usually it is divided into two types: one can be written and read, called random access memory (RAM); the other can be read only, called read only memory (ROM).

(a) Random access memory (RAM). RAM is mainly used to store variable data during computer operation, such as input, output data and intermediate data produced during computing. The stored data can be called up or updated at any time according to the need. RAM

ples and its design ideas for internal parameters which shall provide a great help to automobile maintenance personnel in actual work in face of fault diagnosis and automobile detection.

(1) Electronic control unit (ECU)

The electronic control unit is the "brain" of the engine, the sensors are the "eyes and ears", and the actuators are the "hands and feet". After the signal of each sensor is collected and processed by the ECU, the actuator action starts to operate, and finally it enables the engine mechanical system to operate.

Figure 1-6 shows the basic schematic diagram of ECU, consisting mainly of an input loop, an A/D (analog/digital) converter, a microprocessor, and an output loop. Figure 1-7 shows ECU profile.

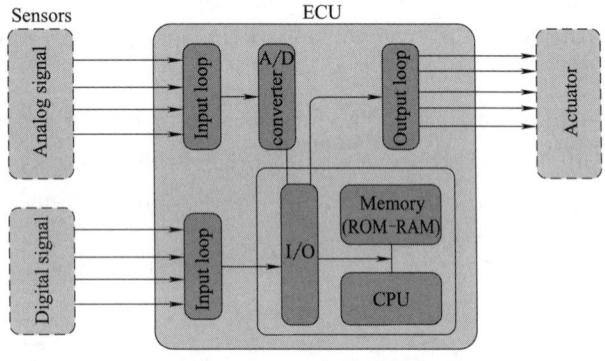

Figure 1-6   Basic Composition of ECU

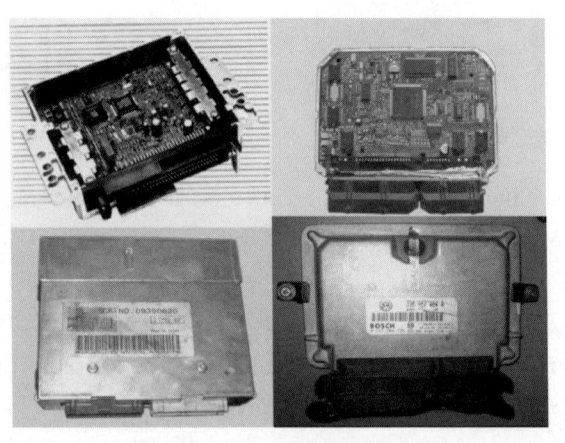

Figure 1-7   ECU Profile

① Input loop. The microprocessor can only recognize the square-wave digital signals from 0 to 5 V. But there are two kinds of signals sent to the ECU by sensors, corresponding to different input signals, with the different function of the input circuit.

a. Digital signal: It includes signals from Hall-type and photoelectric sensors, Karman-type air flow sensors and various switches. The input characteristic is shown in Figure 1-8 (a). The function of the input loop is to peak it and convert it into a square wave digital signal of 0 to 5V, as shown in Figure 1-9.

Automobile engine electronic control system is a comprehensive control system, with a variety of control functions. By combining the sensors and actuators of the engine electronic control system, it shall form the fuel injection system, the microcomputer control ignition system, the air-fuel ratio feedback control system, the engine knock control system, the overspeed fuel cut-off control system, the deceleration fuel cut-off control system, the scavenging overflow control system, the idle speed control system, the fuel vapor recovery system and the fault self-diagnosis system. In addition, certain control system may have multiple control functions at the same time. For example, the electronically controlled fuel injection system can accurately control the fuel injection quantity, with sound atomization and complete combustion. Therefore, it can not only improve the power of the automobile, but also improve the economy and emission of the automobile.

In automobile electronic control system, the engine electronic control system has the most control components and control parameters, the strongest control function, and the most complex control process. Therefore, as long as we are familiar with the structure principle and control process of the engine electronic control system, and master the fault diagnosis and maintenance method, it shall be much easier to learn other electronic control systems.

6. Control mode of electronic control system

The control mode of electronic control system is divided into open-loop control and closed-loop control. Open-loop control means that the ECU controls the actuator according to the signal of the sensor, while the control result has no effect on the control process no matter it reaches the expected target or not. The open-loop control schematic diagram is shown in Figure 1-4. The closed-loop control is also called feedback control. It is based on the open-loop, detecting the control results and feedback to the ECU for the original control correction. The closed-loop schematic diagram is shown in Figure 1-5.

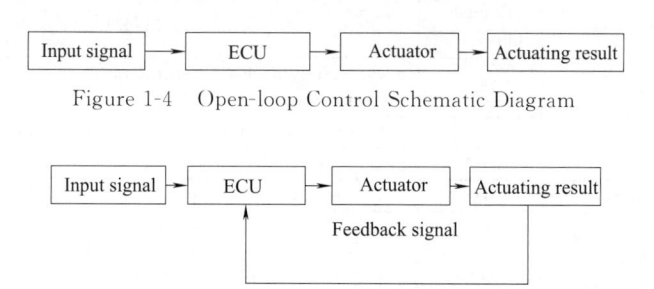

Figure 1-4　Open-loop Control Schematic Diagram

Figure 1-5　Closed-loop Control Schematic Diagram

(II) Composition and function of engine electronic control unit (ECU)

Before learning the various functions of the engine electronic control system, we should know the structure and working principle of the ECU. With the basic knowledge of the ECU, it is easier to learn the complex computer control system. In addition, the electronic control unit (ECU) is the most important part of the automobile, understanding its working princi-

Continued

No.	Type	English abbreviation	Main function
2	Manifold absolute pressure sensor	MAPS	In the D-type electronically controlled fuel injection system, the absolute pressure of the gas in the intake pipe is measured by the manifold absolute pressure sensor, inputting the signal into the ECU as the main control signal of the fuel injection and ignition control
3	Throttle position sensor	TPS	Detect the throttle opening and opening changes, input signals of full shut (idle speed), full open and throttle opening and closing rate (angle of opening and closing per unit time) to ECU, and be used for fuel injection control and other auxiliary control
4	Camshaft position sensor	CPS	Provide the crankshaft angle reference position signal (G signal) to ECU as the main control signal of fuel injection timing control and ignition timing control
5	Crankshaft position sensor (speed Sensor)	CPS	Detect crankshaft angle displacement, provide engine speed signal and crankshaft angle signal to ECU as the main control signal of fuel injection timing control and ignition time control
6	Engine coolant temperature sensor	ECTS	Provide engine coolant temperature signal to ECU as correction signal for fuel injection control and ignition control. The coolant temperature sensor signal is also the control signal of other control systems, such as idle speed control and exhaust gas recirculation control, etc
7	Intake air temperature sensor	IATS	Provide the intake air temperature signal to the ECU as a correction signal for fuel injection control and ignition control
8	Knock sensor	KS	Detect the knock or knock intensity of the engine, transmit the signal to ECU as the correction (feedback) signal of ignition timing control
9	Oxygen sensor	O_2S	Detect the oxygen content in the exhaust gas and transmit the feedback signal of the air-fuel ratio to the ECU for the closed-loop control of the fuel injection
10	Starting switch	ST A	Provide the ECU with a start signal as a correction signal for fuel injection control and ignition control
11	Battery voltage	U_{BAT}	Provide voltage signal to ECU as correction signal for fuel injection control

Table 1-2　Main Function of Actuator for Engine Electronic Control System

No.	Type	English abbreviation	Main function
1	Injector	INJ	Accurately measure the fuel injection quantity according to the injection pulse signal of ECU.
2	Igniter control module	ICM	Control the ignition according to ECU pulse signal
3	Idle speed control valve	ISCV	Control the idle speed of the engine
4	Throttle controller	TC	Control throttle opening according to ECU
5	Fuel pump	FP	Provide fuel with specified pressure to the fuel injection system.
6	Exhaust gas recirculation valve	EGRV	Control the amount of exhaust gas recirculation according to ECU
7	Intake air control valve	IACV	Control intake system operation according to ECU
8	Activated carbon canister valve	ACCV	Recycle the fuel steam inside the engine according to the control command signal of the electronic control unit to reduce pollution
9	Vacuum solenoid valve	VSV	Control vacuum tube on-off according to ECU
10	Secondary air injection valve	SAIV	Control secondary air injection quantity according to ECU pulse signal
11	Cruising control solenoid valve	CCSV	Control cruising system according to ECU
12	Air conditioning control vacuum solenoid	ACU	Control air conditioning according to ECU

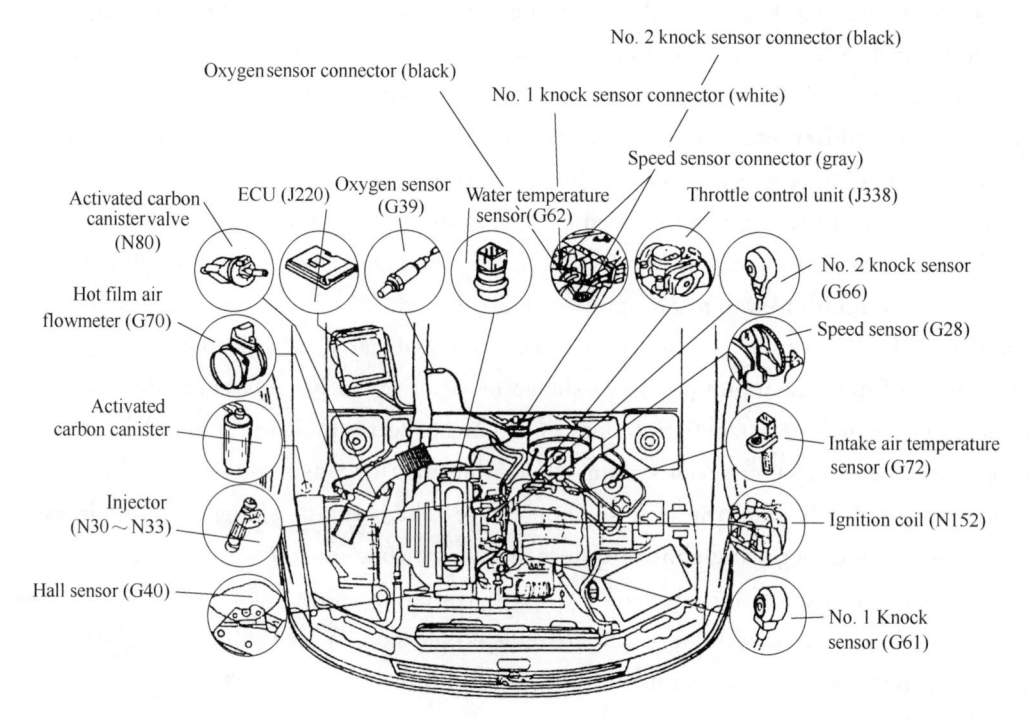

Figure 1-2　Location Layout of Gasoline Injection System and Ignition System

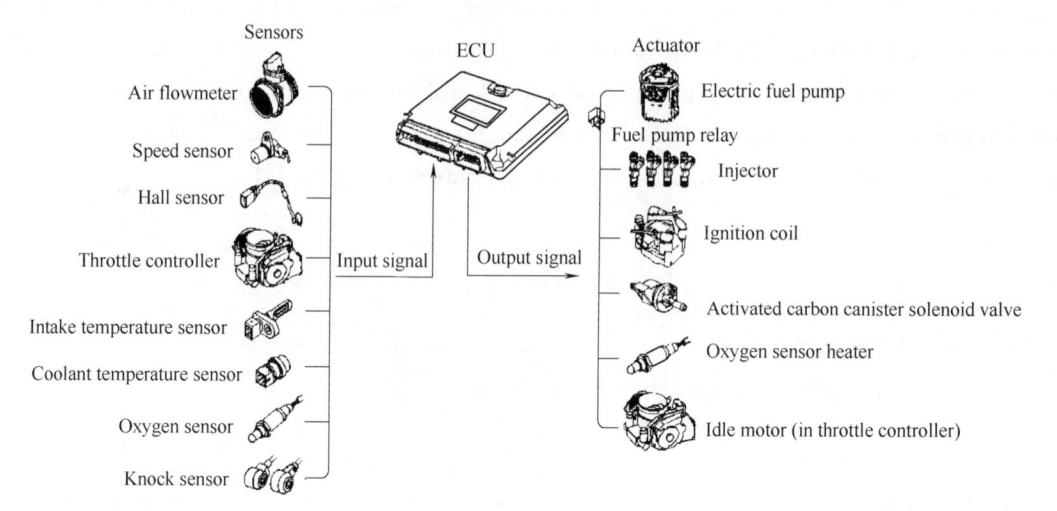

Figure 1-3　Composition of AJR Engine Electronic Control System

The main functions of the electronic control system sensors for automobile engines are shown in Table 1-1 and Table 1-2.

Table 1-1　Functions of Various Sensors and Switch Signals in Engine Electronic Control System

No.	Type	English abbreviation	Main function
1	Mass air flow sensor	MAFS	In the L-type electronically controlled fuel injection system, the mass air flow sensor is used to measure the intake of the engine, inputting the signal to ECU as the main control signal for fuel injection and ignition control

008　Fault Diagnosis and Repair of Automobile Engine Electronic Control System

The actuator, also known as the actuating element, is to actuate the orders from the electronic control system. The function of the actuator is to receive instructions from the electronic control unit (ECU) and perform specific execution actions. The number and type of actuators used in different automobile electronic control systems are also different. The actuators of the engine fuel injection system include electric fuel pump and electromagnetic injector; the actuator of the engine idle speed control system is idle speed control valve; the actuator of the fuel vapor recovery system is Activated carbon canister valve; the actuators of the position control ignition system are ignition control module and ignition coil; the actuator of the anti-lock brake system is 2-position 2-way solenoid valve or 3-position 3-way solenoid valves, brake fluid return pump motor; the actuator of the airbag system is the airbag igniter; the actuator of the seat belt tightening system is the tightened igniter; the actuators of the automatic transmission speed system are the automatic transmission hydraulic oil pump, the shift solenoid valve and the lock solenoid valve; the actuator of the automobile cruising control system is the cruising control motor or the cruising control solenoid valve.

The main function of the electronic control system of automobile engine is to improve the automobile's power, economy and to reduce emission. With the development and progress of automobile electronic control technology, the engine electronic control systems developed by the world's major automobile companies or electronic technology companies are vary widely. With different function, control parameter and control precision of the control system, the types or quantities of the control components (sensors, electronic control units and actuators) are different. A number of sub-control systems can be formed by different combinations of various control components. The structural diagram of the AJR engine electronic control system of the Santana 2000 GSi as shown in Figure 1-1.

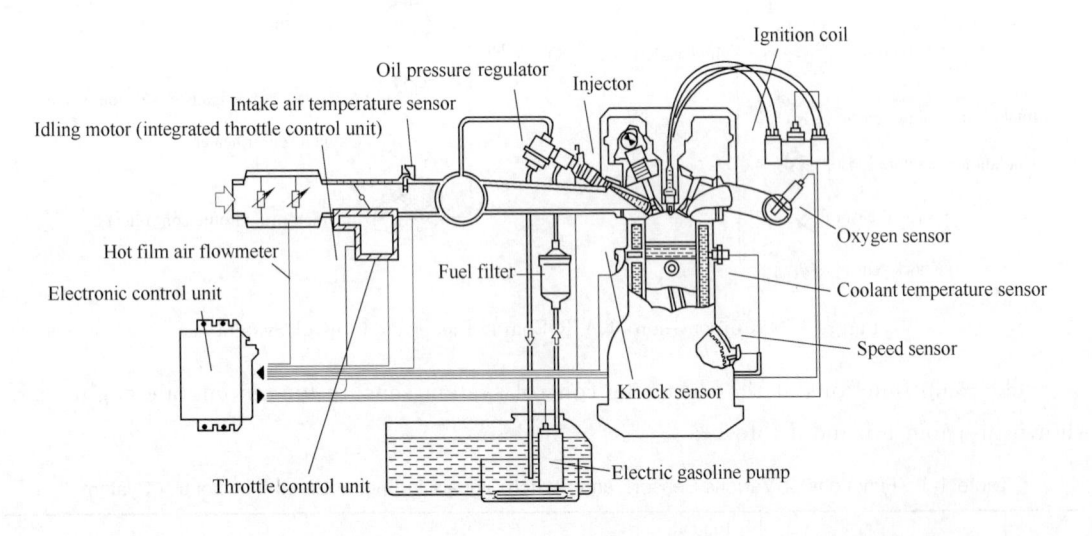

Figure 1-1　Schematic Diagram of Engine Electronic Control System of Volkswagen AJR

The arrangement of its components in the automobile is shown in Figure 1-2, and the composition of the AJR engine electronic control system is shown in Figure 1-3.

sensors varies with the different models and grades of automobiles. Some have only a few sensors (such as the engine control system is only 6～8) and some are equipped with a lot of sensors. Normally, the more sensors an automobile has, the higher the automobile's grade is.

According to the test items, the sensors used in the automobile electronic control system can be divided into the following types.

(1) Flow sensors, such as wing-type, core-type, eddy current type, hot wire type and hot film type air flow sensors adopted by the engine fuel injection system.

(2) Position sensor, such as crankshaft position sensor (also known as engine speed crankshaft position sensor), camshaft position sensor, throttle position sensor used in engine fuel injection system and crisis control ignition system; body position (also known as body height) sensor used in electronic regulation modulated suspension system; various liquid level position (or height) sensor used in information displayed system and liquid level monitoring system; gear selection control handle sensor used in automatic transmission system; throttle position sensor used in cruising control system; steering wheel angle sensor used in electronically controlled power steering system and so on.

(3) Pressure sensors, such as the intake manifold pressure sensor, atmospheric pressure sensor, exhaust pressure sensor, cylinder pressure sensor used in the engine control system; the fuel pressure sensor used in the automatic transmission system; the knock sensor used in the engine detonation control system.

(4) Temperature sensors, such as engine coolant temperature sensor, intake air temperature sensor, exhaust temperature sensor, fuel temperature sensor; the automatic transmission fluid temperature sensor used in automatic transmission system; the temperature sensor inside the automobile used in air conditioning control system.

(5) Concentration sensors, such as the oxygen sensor used in the engine control system, the alcohol concentration sensor used in the safety control system, etc.

(6) Speed sensors, such as wheel speed sensor used in anti-lock brake system, body longitudinal and lateral accelerated (decelerated) speed sensor; the speed sensor used in engine control system; the automobile speed sensor used in engine, automatic transmission and cruising control systems; transmission input shaft speed sensor and output shaft speed sensor.

Electronic control Unit: automobile electronic control unit (ECU) is also called automobile electronic controller or automobile electronic control component, commonly known as "automobile's computer".

Electronic control unit (ECU) is an electronic control device composed of single-chip microcomputer (SCM), which has powerful functions of mathematical calculation, logic judgment, data processing and data management.

Electronic control unit (ECU) is the control center of automobile electronic control system. Its main function is to analyze and process all kinds of information collected by sensors and issue control instructions to the controlled device (i. e. actuator or actuating element).

Emission control system conducts the electronic control to engine emission control device. The main emission control items include exhaust gas recirculation (EGR) control, Activated carbon canister valve control, oxygen sensor and air-fuel ratio closed-loop control, secondary air injection control, crankcase ventilation control and so on.

(5) Intake control system

According to the change of engine working condition, the electronic control system can control the air intake and air flow, improving the aeration efficiency and the atomization condition, so as to upgrade the power of the engine.

(6) Supercharging control system

For an engine equipped with a turbocharger, the electronic control system makes the pressure of the intake pipe to suit the various working conditions of the engine by controlling the supercharging strength.

(7) Cruising control system

In cruising operation mode, the electronic control system automatically adjusts the throttle opening to keep the automobile running at the set speed, thus improving the driving comfort.

(8) Caution and warning system

ECU controls all kinds of caution and warning devices to show the working condition of the control system. It can send out warning signals in time when the control system is out of order, such as oxygen sensor failure, catalyst overheating, too high fuel tank temperature.

(9) Self-diagnosis and alarm system

When the control system fails, the ECU shall light the "Check Engine" lamp on the instrument panel to alert the driver that the engine breaks down, storing the fault information in the ECU. Through the certain program, the fault code can be transferred out as a reference for the repairman.

(10) Failure protection system

In the engine electronic control system, when a sensor fails or the line is disconnected, the electronic control system shall set up a reference signal according to the predetermined procedure to keep the engine and the automobile running. At the same time, the alarm system shall prompt the driver to repair in time.

5. Composition and function of engine electronic control system

The electronic control system is mainly composed of sensor, ECU and actuator.

The sensor, an input part, is a device used to measure physical signals (temperature, pressure, etc.) and to convert them into another physical quantity according to a certain law, which is convenient for transmission and processing.

Sensor is equivalent to the human eye, ear, nose, tongue and so on. In the automobile electronic control system, the function of the sensor is to convert the state parameter of each part of the automobile (all kinds of non-electric signal) into electric signal and transmit it to various electronic control units.

Automobile sensors are installed in different parts of the automobile. The number of

it can guarantee the good comprehensive performance without adjustment.

(6) Improve the performance of high and low temperature start-up and warm-up of gasoline engine

When the engine starts at high temperature or low temperature, the electronic-controlled fuel injection system can supply the fuel injection suitable to the starting condition according to the temperature of the engine cooling water, enabling that the gasoline engine can start smoothly at high temperature and low temperature. After starting at low temperature, the electronic-controlled fuel injection system can automatically adjust the fuel injection and air supply according to the engine cooling water temperature. It can accelerate the gasoline engine warm-up process, so that the engine shall soon be able to enter the normal running state.

4. Electronic control system used in engines

Automobile electronic control technology benefits from the rapid development of electronic technology, computer technology and information technology, and the driving force behind the development of automobile electronic control technology is to improve the performance of automobiles, reduce energy consumption, reduce pollution, improve safety and comfort. In the 21st century, electronic control technology not only penetrates every system and assembly of automobile, but also realizes the coordination and centralized control of each system and assembly through information technology. At present, electronic control systems commonly used in engines include electronic fuel injection system, electronic ignition system, idle speed control system, emission control system, intake control system, supercharging control system, cruising control system, caution and warning system, self-diagnosis and alarm system, failure protection system, etc.

(1) Electronic control fuel injection system

The electronic control unit (ECU) mainly determines the basic fuel injection quantity according to the intake volume, and then modifies the fuel injection quantity according to other sensors (such as coolant temperature sensor, throttle position sensor) signal, so that the engine can get the best concentration of the gas mixture under various operating conditions; at the same time, it also includes injection timing control, oil cut control and fuel pump control.

(2) Electronic control ignition system

The function of electronic control ignition system is the ignition advance angle control. Judge working condition and running conditions, select the optimum ignition advance angle to ignite the mixture in order to improve the combustion process of the engine according to the relevant sensor signals.

(3) Idle speed control system

Under different idle operating conditions, such as the increase of engine operation, air-conditioning compressor work, engine load and so on, by the ECU control idle speed control valve, so that the engine idle speed is always at the best speed.

(4) Emission control system

the application of CAN-BUS bus in automobile is more and more.

3. Advantages of engine electronic control system

The application of electronic control technology of gasoline engine has improved the comprehensive performance of gasoline engine in an all-round way. Its main advantages are as follows:

(1) Improve the uniformity of the gas mixture in each cylinder

It adopts electronically controlled multi-point injection to inject the fuel around the intake valve of each cylinder, so that the concentration of the mixture in each cylinder is basically consistent. This not only improves the economy of the engine, but also reduces the emissions of carbon monoxide (CO) and hydrocarbons (HC).

(2) Improve the power and economy of the engine

There is no pipe in the intake pipe of the electronic fuel injection system, the intake resistance and pressure loss of the intake system are small and the charge efficiency is high, so the engine has better power and economy. In addition, the electronic fuel injection system does not preheat the intake air, which increases the density of the intake air and is beneficial to the improvement of engine power.

(3) Reduce emission pollution

The electronic fuel injection system adopts oxygen sensor feedback control, which can accurately control the air-fuel ratio A/F about 14.7. In this way, the three-way catalyst has the highest conversion efficiency, thus greatly reducing the emissions of harmful gases such as CO, HC and NO_x. In addition, the electronic control system of modern gasoline engine also includes the control functions such as exhaust gas recirculation, secondary air injection systems and the best ignition advance angle, which can further reduce the emission of harmful substances in gasoline engine.

(4) Transit smoothly for working condition

When the engine working condition changes, the electronic fuel injection system can adjust the fuel injection quantity or injection timing quickly according to the input signal of the sensor. It provides the best air-fuel ratio which is suitable for this condition, and improves the response speed of the fuel engine to the acceleration and deceleration condition and the stability of the transition of the working condition. Furthermore, using electronic fuel injection, the atomization quality of gasoline is good, the evaporation speed is fast, and the mixture has good quality under all kinds of working conditions, which is also helpful to improve the performance of gasoline engine under non-stable working conditions.

(5) Improve the adaptability of gasoline engines to geographical and climatic conditions

When the automobile runs in different geographical environment or different climatic conditions, for the electronic-controlled fuel injection system which uses volume flowrate method to measure the intake volume, the electronic control system can modify the air-fuel ratio according to the atmospheric pressure and ambient temperature in time, ensuring that

than 95%. The diesel engine can accurately control the fuel injection quantity and the injection pressure up to 160~200MPa by using the high-pressure common-rail electronic control fuel injection technology, which can not only reduce the fuel consumption but also reduce the emission. The application of anti-lock brake system, electronic brake force distribution system and electronic stability program can greatly improve the stability of automobile braking, especially reduce the accident rate of automobile on wet-slip or ice-snow road by 24%~28% .

Since the 21st century, engine electronic control fuel injection technology, gasoline engine electronic control ignition technology, anti-lock braking technology and airbag technology have been widely used in automobiles at home and abroad.

2. Development of automobile electronic control technology

(1) Automobile electronic control technology is the product of automotive technology and electronic technology.

The fundamental driving forces and reasons for the rapid development of automobile electronic control technology include two aspects: on the one hand, the global energy shortage, environmental protection and traffic safety problems have led to the continuous improvement of automobile fuel consumption regulations, emission regulations and safety regulations; on the other hand, the continuous improvement of electronic technology. The automobile fuel consumption regulations have driven the development of automobile chassis and body electronic control technology. With the improvement of automobile fuel consumption regulation, emission regulation and safety regulation, the electronic control system of automobile engine fuel injection, anti-lock braking and airbag system have become the standard equipment of automobiles at home and abroad.

(2) Development of automobile electronic control technology

The development of automobile electronic technology began in the 1960s, including four stages.

In the first stage, from the mid-1960s to the mid-1970s, it was mainly a technical renovation of automobile products to improve some of their performance, such as the installation of the first electronic device, transistor radio, on an automobile.

In the second stage, from the late 1970s to the mid-1990s, an electronic fuel injection system, an electronic control anti-skid (anti-lock) braking device and an integrated circuit (IC) ignition device were developed, in order to solve the three major problems, that is, safety, pollution and energy saving.

In the third stage, after the mid-1990s, the application of electronic technology in automobiles has been gradually extended to the chassis, body and automobile diesel engines other than gasoline engines.

In the fourth stage, after the late 1990s, CAN-BUS (Controller Area Network) technology has been widely used. CAN-BUS is an open, digital and multi-point control network in bottom layer, which is used in the field and between microcomputerized measuring equipment to realize the digital communication system of two-way serial multi-point. At present,

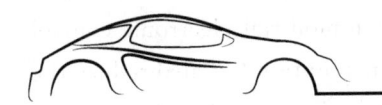

Item I

Overall Cognition of Electronic Control System for Gasoline Engine

I. Introduction of Item Scene

In order to diagnose and troubleshoot the faults of the electronic control system, we must be familiar with the structure and principle of the electronic control system of the automobile engine. Therefore, we must master the application of the sensor, the ECU and the actuator of the electronic control system in the study of this item, understand the control methods and advantages of the electronic control system, and be familiar with the function of the self-diagnosis system at the same time. Through study, we shall make sure students realize the importance of reading data stream of the diagnostic instrument, mastering the correct method of reading data stream of the diagnostic instrument and the matters needing attention in the use of the diagnostic instrument.

II. Item Related Knowledge

(I) Overview

1. Application of automobile electronic control technology

Since 1980s, the improvement of automobile performance, energy saving and environmental protection mainly depend on electronic control technology. Automobile electronic control technology has been widely used in gasoline engine, diesel engine, automobile chassis, automobile body and automobile fault diagnosis and other technical fields.

In today's world, mark to measure the advanced level and grade of automobile is the brand, the appearance and the degree of electronization. Automobile manufacturers generally believe that: increasing the number of automobile electronic devices and promoting electronization is an effective means to seize the future automobile market. Automobile designers generally agree that: the application of electronic technology in automobile has become an important means for automobile design research department to consider the innovation of automobile structure. The gasoline engine can accurately control the air-fuel ratio and realize closed-loop control by using electronic control fuel injection technology. If a three-way catalyst (TWC) is added, the harmful emissions of the gasoline engine can be reduced by more

（Ⅲ）The mixture is too thin 184
（Ⅳ）Too rich mixture 184
（Ⅴ）Starting stall 184
Summary 189
Exercises and Thinking 189

（Ⅱ）Basic setting of direct type throttle valve ································· 131

Summary ··· 133

Exercises and Thinking ··· 133

Item Ⅴ Maintenance of Auxiliary Control System of Gasoline Engine ··· **134**

Ⅰ. Introduction of Item Scene ··· 134

Ⅱ. Item Related Knowledge ··· 134

（Ⅰ）Environmental Impact of Motor Vehicle Emissions ················· 134

（Ⅱ）Classification of emission control system ························· 135

（Ⅲ）Principles of Various Emission Control Systems ················· 135

Ⅲ. Item Implementation ··· 155

（Ⅰ）Requirements for implementation ························· 155

（Ⅱ）Implementation steps ··· 155

（Ⅲ）Matters needing attention ··· 165

Ⅳ. Knowledge and Skills Expansion ··· 165

（Ⅰ）Variable port timing and valve lift electronic control system ········· 165

（Ⅱ）Working principle of VTEC system ························· 166

Summary ··· 168

Exercises and Thinking ··· 168

Item Ⅵ Typical Troubleshooting of Electronic Control System of Gasoline Engine ··· **169**

Ⅰ. Introduction of Item Scene ··· 169

Ⅱ. Item Related Knowledge ··· 169

（Ⅰ）Fault diagnosis principle of EEC System ························· 169

（Ⅱ）Basic methods for fault diagnosis of electronic control systems ··········· 170

（Ⅲ）Process of fault diagnosis for EEC system ························· 172

（Ⅳ）Troubleshooting procedures for fault diagnosis of EEC system ··········· 174

（Ⅴ）Troubleshooting procedure for common fault diagnosis of electronic control engines ··· 178

Ⅲ. Item Implementation ··· 180

（Ⅰ）Requirements for Implementation ························· 180

（Ⅱ）Implementation steps ························· 180

（Ⅲ）Matters needing attention ························· 182

Ⅳ. Knowledge and Skills Expansion ··· 183

（Ⅰ）Difficult in starting ··· 183

（Ⅱ）Too high idle speed ··· 184

(Ⅲ) Fuel pump control circuit controlled by fuel pump relay ·················· 081

Summary ·· 082

Exercises and Thinking ··· 083

Item Ⅲ Maintenance of Electronic Control Ignition System for Gasoline Engine ··· 084

Ⅰ. Introduction of Item Scene ·· 084

Ⅱ. Item Related Knowledge ·· 084

(Ⅰ) Function of ignition system of gasoline engine ····················· 084

(Ⅱ) Classification of gasoline engine ignition system ··················· 085

(Ⅲ) Basic requirements for ignition systems ···························· 085

(Ⅳ) Structure of MCI ·· 087

(Ⅴ) Control Process of MCI ·· 092

(Ⅵ) High voltage distribution mode of MCI ······························ 098

(Ⅶ) Detonation control ··· 103

Ⅲ. Item Implementation ·· 105

(Ⅰ) Requirements for implementation ······································ 105

(Ⅱ) Implementation steps ·· 105

(Ⅲ) Matters needing attention ··· 109

Ⅳ. Knowledge and Skills Expansion ·· 109

(Ⅰ) Waveform analysis of ignition system ································· 109

(Ⅱ) Failure cases ··· 114

Summary ·· 115

Exercises and Thinking ··· 115

Item Ⅳ Maintenance of Idle Speed Control System for Gasoline Engine ··· 116

Ⅰ. Introduction of Item Scene ·· 116

Ⅱ. Item Related Knowledge ·· 116

(Ⅰ) Classification of idle speed control valves ·························· 116

(Ⅱ) Principle of ISCV ··· 116

(Ⅲ) Process of engine idle speed control ·································· 121

Ⅲ. Item Implementation ·· 125

(Ⅰ) Requirements for implementation ······································ 125

(Ⅱ) Implementation steps ·· 125

(Ⅲ) Matters needing attention ··· 130

Ⅳ. Knowledge and Skills Expansion ·· 131

(Ⅰ) Electronic throttle idle control actuator ····························· 131

Contents

Item I Overall Cognition of Electronic Control System for Gasoline Engine ······ 001

I. Introduction of Item Scene ······ 001
II. Item Related Knowledge ······ 001
　（I）Overview ······ 001
　（II）Composition and function of engine electronic control unit（ECU） ······ 010
　（III）Test of on-board diagnostics system of engine electronic control system ··· 015
III. Item Implementation ······ 016
　（I）Requirements for implementation ······ 016
　（II）Implementation steps ······ 016
　（III）Matters needing attention ······ 018
Summary ······ 019
Exercises and Thinking ······ 019

Item II Maintenance of Electronic Control Fuel Injection System for Gasoline Engines ······ 020

I. Introduction of Item Scene ······ 020
II. Item Related Knowledge ······ 020
　（I）Classification of fuel injection system ······ 020
　（II）Composition of fuel injection system ······ 023
　（III）Structural principle of sensor for engine fuel injection system ······ 026
　（IV）Structural Principle of Actuator for Engine Fuel Injection System ······ 050
　（V）Engine fuel cut-off control process ······ 057
　（VI）Control process of engine fuel injection ······ 059
　（VII）Control of fuel injection pulse width ······ 063
III. Item Implementation ······ 068
　（I）Requirements for implementation ······ 068
　（II）Implementation steps ······ 068
　（III）Notice ······ 080
IV. Knowledge and Skills Expansion ······ 080
　（I）Fuel pump control circuit controlled by ECU ······ 080
　（II）Fuel pump control circuit controlled by fuel pump switch ······ 081

Preface
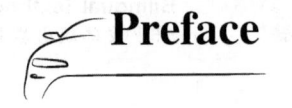

"Fault Diagnosis and Repair of Automobile Engine Electronic Control System" is the core professional course of Automobile Inspection and Maintenance Technology Specialty in higher vocational colleges, which mainly introduces the structure principle and overhaul of modern automobile electronic control engine system. Students studying this course can lay a good foundation for internships and jobs in this industry.

In the process of compiling this book, editors, taking the structure of Volkswagen automobile as the main body, combined with the actual automobile and diagnostic equipment, detailed introduces the modern automobile engine electronic control system structure, working principle and overhaul through six items, as well as the influence of the electronic control engine sensors, actuators on the operation of the electronic control system. In the implementation of items, students can improve their ability of thinking by studying the practice and matters needing attention. In order to enable readers to master the content of the book in a short time, check their learning effect in time, consolidate and deepen their understanding of what they have learned, each item is followed by exercises and questions.

The editors of this book are from the front line, with rich teaching experience and solid professional theoretical knowledge and practical skills. In the process of writing this book, the typical work items are used as teaching materials to clarify the teaching and learning ideas for teachers and students respectively. At the same time, the training of students' practical ability is highlighted to meet the training requirements of vocational education.

This book is edited by Xinyu Liu of Tianjin Transportation technical college, deputy by Xianghong Cao, Jiaze Li, and co-edited by Ruijing Zhang, of which Zhang Ruijing of Tianjin transportation vocational college compiles project 1, Liu Xinyu of Tianjin transportation vocational college compiles project 2, Cao Xianghong of Tianjin transportation vocational college compiles project 3, project 4 and project 5, and Li Jiaze of Tianjin transportation vocational college compiles project 6.

Due to my limited knowledge, it is inevitable that there is something improper in the book. I sincerely hope that the readers shall correct it.

Editor

Bilingual Textbooks of Vocational Education
职业教育双语教材

Fault Diagnosis and Repair of Automobile Engine Electronic Control System

汽车发动机
电控系统故障诊断与修复

英汉
双语教材

Edited by Xinyu Liu

刘新宇 主编

Chemical Industry Press
化学工业出版社

BeiJing
·北京·